Lecture Notes in Computer Science 8956

Commenced Publication in 1973
Founding and Former Series Editors:
Gerhard Goos, Juris Hartmanis, and Jan van Leeuwen

T0213799

Raja Natarajan   Gautam Barua
Manas Ranjan Patra (Eds.)

Distributed Computing and Internet Technology

11th International Conference, ICDCIT 2015
Bhubaneswar, India, February 5-8, 2015
Proceedings

Springer

Volume Editors

Raja Natarajan
Tata Institute of Fundamental Research
School of Technology and Computer Science
Mumbai, India
E-mail: raja@tifr.res.in

Gautam Barua
Indian Institute of Technology Guwahati
Department of Computer Science and Engineering
Guwahati, India
E-mail: gb@iitg.ernet.in

Manas Ranjan Patra
Berhampur University
Department of Computer Science
Berhampur, India
E-mail: mrpatra12@gmail.com

ISSN 0302-9743   e-ISSN 1611-3349
ISBN 978-3-319-14976-9   e-ISBN 978-3-319-14977-6
DOI 10.1007/978-3-319-14977-6
Springer Cham Heidelberg New York Dordrecht London

Library of Congress Control Number: 2014959002

LNCS Sublibrary: SL 3 – Information Systems and Application,
incl. Internet/Web and HCI

Typesetting: Camera-ready by author, data conversion by Scientific Publishing Services, Chennai, India

Printed on acid-free paper

Springer is part of Springer Science+Business Media (www.springer.com)

Preface

The 11th International Conference on Distributed Computing and Internet Technology, ICDCIT-2015, took place in Bhubaneswar, India, during February 5–8, 2015, and was hosted and sponsored by Kalinga Institute of Information Technology (KIIT) University.

The ICDCIT conference series focusses on three broad areas of computer science, viz., distributed computing, Internet technologies, and societal applications. It provides a platform for academicians, researchers, practitioners, and developers to present and publish their research findings and also deliberate on contemporary topics in the area of distributed computing and Internet technology. From the very inception of the ICDCIT series, the conference proceedings are published by Springer as *Lecture Notes in Computer Science* – vol. 3347 (year 2004), 3816 (2005), 4317 (2006), 4882 (2007), 5375 (2008), 5966 (2010), 6536 (2011), 7154 (2012), 7753 (2013), 8337 (2014), and 8956 (2015).

In response to the call for submissions, ICDCIT 2015 received 221 abstracts from authors in different countries. Subsequently, 165 submissions with full versions were reviewed by an international Program Committee (PC) consisting of 35 members from 10 countries. Each submission was peer-reviewed by two to three PC members with the help of external reviewers. After receiving the reviews on the papers, the PC meeting was conducted electronically over a period of ten days in the later part of October 2014 to discuss and finalize the acceptance of submissions under different categories. This year the PC decided to introduce the Poster Paper category in order to encourage larger participation and presentation of ongoing research activities. Based on relevance to the conference theme and quality of technical contents and presentation style, 42 papers (25 %) were accepted for presentation and publication in the LNCS proceedings out of which 12 papers are under the category of regular papers each with a maximum length of 12 pages, 13 short papers of 6 pages each, and 17 poster papers of 4 pages each. We wish to thank all the PC members and external reviewers for their hard work, dedication, and timely submission of the reviews without which it would have been difficult to maintain the publication schedule.

The program also included invited lectures by nine distinguished speakers: Laxmi Parida (IBM T.J. Watson Research Centre, USA), G. Michele Pinna (University of Cagliari, Italy), Catuscia Palamidessi (Inria Saclay, France), Nikolaj Bjorner (Microsoft Research, Redmond, USA), Èric Rutten (Inria Grenoble, France), Krithi Ramamritham (IIT Bombay, India), Sanjiva Prasad (IIT Delhi, India), Manik Lal Das (DA-IICT, Gandhinagar, India), and Bud Mishra (Courant Institute, NYU, USA). We express our sincere thanks to all the invited speakers for accepting our invitation to share their expertise and also submit full papers for inclusion in the proceedings.

Our sincere thanks to Achyuta Samanta (Founder of KIIT University) for his patronage and constant support in the hosting of the ICDCIT conference series. We are grateful to the Vice-Chancellor and administration of the KIIT University for providing us with the infrastructure and logistics to organize this international event. We are indebted to the Advisory Committee members for their constant guidance and support.

We would like to thank and place on record the invaluable service and tireless efforts of the organizing chair, finance chair, publicity chair, registration chair, session management chair, the publications chair, and all members of various committees. We would also like to thank the chair-persons of the satellite events, the Student Symposium and the Industry Symposium. Our special thanks to Hrushikesha Mohanty and D.N. Dwivedy for their valuable advice and whole-hearted involvement in all activities.

We wish to acknowledge and thank all the authors for their scholarly contributions to the conference, which evoked interesting discussions during the technical sessions. Our thanks are also due to the technical session chairs for managing the sessions effectively. We acknowledge the service rendered by EasyChair for efficient and smooth handling of all activities starting from paper submissions to preparation of the proceedings. We sincerely thank Alfred Hofmann and Anna Kramer of Springer for their cooperation and constant support all through the publication process of this LNCS volume.

Last but not the least, we thank all the participants and people who directly or indirectly contributed toward making ICDCIT 2015 a memorable event.

February 2015   Raja Natarajan
                                                            Gautam Barua
                                                        Manas Ranjan Patra

Organization

Program Committee

Gautam Barua	IIT Guwahati, India (Program Co-chair)
Anup Kumar Bhattacharjee	BARC, India
Suman Bhattacharya	Tata Consultancy Services, India
Ajay Kumar Bisoi	KIIT University, India
Nikolaj Bjorner	Microsoft Research, USA
Sung-Bae Cho	Yonsei University, Korea
Hung Dang Van	Vietnam National University, Vietnam
Manik Lal Das	DA-IICT, India
Satchidananda Dehuri	Fakir Mohan University, India
Günter Fahrnberger	University of Hagen, Germany
Manoj Gore	MNNIT, India
Chittaranjan Hota	BITS-Pilani Hyderabad, India
Devesh Jinwala	SVNIT, India
Venkata Swamy Martha	Walmart Labs, USA
Harekrishna Misra	IRMA, India
Krishnendu Mukhopadhyaya	Indian Statistical Institute, India
Vineet Padmanabhan Nair	University of Hyderabad, India
Jukka K. Nurminen	Aalto University, Finland
Adegboyega Ojo	UNU-IIST, China
Bhabhani Sankar Panda	IIT Delhi, India
Bighnaraj Panigrahi	TCS Innovation Labs, India
Manas Ranjan Patra	Berhampur University, India (Program Co-chair)
Dana Petcu	West University of Timisoara, Romania
Kishore Kumar Pusukuri	University of California, Riverside, USA
P. Radha Krishna	Infosys Technologies Limited, India
O.B.V. Ramanaiah	JNTU, India
S. Ramaswamy	ABB Corporate Research, India
R.K. Samanta	University of North Bengal, India
P.G. Sapna	CIT, Coimbatore, India
Hiroshi Sasaki	Kyushu University, Japan
S. Swamynathan	Anna University, India
Hideyuki Takahashi	Tohoku University, Japan
Ranjit Jeba Thangaiah	Karunya University, India
Siba K. Udgata	University of Hyderabad, India
Saravanan Venkataraman	Majmaah University, Saudi Arabia

Additional Reviewers

Ahmadi Zeleti, Fatemeh
Al-Shabi, Waled
Al-Shukri, Shaymaa
Dang, Duc-Hanh
Jetley, Raoul
Lal, Rajendra Prasad
Mandal, Partha Sarathi
Martha, Venkata Swamy
Meenpal, Toshanlal

Mohanty, Hrushikesha
Nayak, Deveeshree
Porwol, Lukasz
Rathinasamy, Lenin
Sarangi, Smruti
Sudarsan, Sithu
Threm, David
Vo, Hieu
Yu, Liguo

Table of Contents

Internet Technologies and Web Services

Secure Computing and Communication

Cloud Computing

Information Retrieval and Recommender Systems

Societal Applications

Models of Circular Causality*

Massimo Bartoletti[1], Tiziana Cimoli[1], G. Michele Pinna[1], and Roberto Zunino[2]

[1] Dipartimento di Matematica e Informatica, Università di Cagliari, Cagliari, Italy
[2] Dipartimento di Matematica, Università degli Studi di Trento, Italy

Abstract. Causality is often interpreted as establishing dependencies between events. The standard view is that an event b causally depends on an event a if, whenever b occurs, then a has already occurred. If the occurrences of a and b mutually depend on each other, i.e. a depends on b and vice versa, then (under the standard notion of causality) neither of them can ever occur. This does not faithfully capture systems where, for instance, an agent promises to do event a provided that b will be *eventually* done, and vice versa. In this case, the circularity between the causal dependencies should allow both a and b to occur, in any order. In this paper we review three models for circular causality, one based on logic (declarative), one based on event structures (semantical), and one based on Petri nets (operational). We will cast them in a coherent picture pointing out their relationships.

1 Motivations

Circular dependencies are a natural aspect of many kinds of interactions. For instance, consider two mutually distrusting participants, Alice and Bob, who want to exchange their resources. Alice wants Bob's resource, and *vice versa*, but only one resource at a time can be transferred. A possible interaction is that where Alice makes the first move, by giving her resource to Bob. At this point, Bob can either give his resource to Alice, or he may even choose not to. Since Alice and Bob do not trust each other, each one is expecting that the other gives their resource first. The two participants are stuck in a situation where no one can move. This is a classical issue, discussed by philosophers at least since Hobbes' Leviathan [14].

The above scenario expresses the basic idea behind *circular causality*: Alice wants to do her action after Bob's action has happened, and *vice versa*. This situation can be represented in many ways in many models.

From a logical point of view, we may say that *"Alice gives her resource to Bob"* and *"Bob gives his resource to Alice"* are two atomic propositions a and b, and we can model the behaviour of Alice and Bob with the formulae:

$$b \to a \qquad\qquad a \to b \qquad\qquad (1)$$

where $\to$ denotes e.g. intuitionistic implication [17].

---

* Work partially supported by Aut. Reg. Sardinia LR 7/07 CRP-17285 (TRICS), PIA 2010 "Social Glue", by MIUR PRIN 2010-11 "Security Horizons", and by EU COST Action IC1201 (BETTY).

R. Natarajan et al. (Eds.): ICDCIT 2015, LNCS 8956, pp. 1–20, 2015.

From a semantical point of view, a and b can be considered *events* of an *event structure* [22], which is one of the classical models of concurrent systems. In event structures, causality among events is represented by *enablings* of the form $X \vdash e$, meaning that the event e can only occur after all the events in the set X have already occurred. Then, our Alice-Bob scenario can be modelled by an event structure with the following enablings:

$$\{b\} \vdash a \qquad\qquad \{a\} \vdash b \qquad\qquad (2)$$

Finally, in a more operational perspective, a and b can be seen as transitions of the following Petri net N [19]:

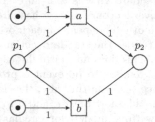

We can now notice that all the above formalisations of the Alice-Bob scenario share some kind of misfeature: neither the atom a nor the atom b can be deduced in the logical theory in (1); neither the events a nor b can ever happen (i.e. they are not *reachable*) in the event structure in (2); and neither transitions a or b can be fired in the net N.

To solve the impasse, one of the participants must do the first move. Alice may decide to give her resource to Bob, without conditions, hoping for his in exchange. This adjustment clearly resolves the circularity issue (since one of the dependencies is removed). From the logical point of view, the modified scenario can be described by the theory:

$$a \qquad\qquad a \to b \qquad\qquad (3)$$

where both a and b are deducible. From the semantic point of view, we obtain an event structure with the following enablings:

$$\emptyset \vdash a \qquad\qquad \{a\} \vdash b \qquad\qquad (4)$$

where both a and b are reachable. Finally, the Petri net is adjusted as follows (we name the resulting net N'):

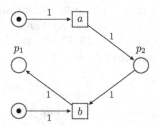

where both transitions a and b can be performed.

However, this new scenario has a flaw: we have lost the information that Alice is willing to trade her resource *only* if she receives what she wants in exchange. Consider for instance that Bob wants to give his resource to Carl, first, and that Carl needs that resource forever. Assume also that this information is not shared with Alice. Since Alice is saying that she will give her resource without conditions, she gives away her resource, but she will receive nothing. If we model this situation in our three settings, in the logic we have a and $a \to c$ (Carl's request), from which we deduce a but not b. In the event structure we have enablings $\emptyset \vdash a$ and $a \vdash c$, and so a is reachable while b is not. In the Petri net, we just replace transition b in N' with a new transition c, and we have that the transition a is fired while b is not. Never has Alice got what she wants, but she always has to do something. We would like to express Alice's constraints in such a way that, if Bob is not promising to give her what she wants, then she is not obliged to do anything.

Our answer to this problem is the introduction of a novel kind of circular dependency of the form "Alice gives her resource to Bob" on the *promise* that "Bob will eventually gives his to Alice". Alice may give away her resource *now*, but only if Bob promises to give her his one. In the logical approach, this is done in [11] by extending Intuitionistic Propositional Logic with a new kind of implication ($\to$); event structures are extended in [7] with a new kind of enabling ($\Vdash$); Petri nets are extended with the possibility of lending tokens [4]. Thus, let us consider again our Alice-Bob example. In the logic, we have:

$$b \to a \qquad\qquad a \to b \qquad\qquad (5)$$

and due to the reduction rules for $\to$, now both a and b are deducible.

In event structures, we have:

$$b \Vdash a \qquad\qquad a \vdash b \qquad\qquad (6)$$

and since $\Vdash$ decouples causality from the order in which events happens, both a and b are reachable.

In Petri nets, we add an arc from p_1 to a labelled in such a way that it means that a token may be lent from p_1:

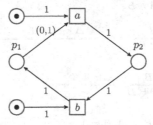

Since transition a can lend a token, the firing sequence $p_1 \xrightarrow{a} p_2 \xrightarrow{b} p_1$ is now possible.

Consider again the situation where Bob and Carl are trying to deceive Alice. Were we to match Alice's condition with Bob's c, we would end with a satisfactory situation: in the logic, $b \rightarrow a$ and c do *not* imply a; in the event structure with enablings $b \Vdash a$ and c, event a is not reachable; in Petri nets, an "honored" marking is not reachable.

This paper is organized as follows: Sections 2 to 4 gently introduce the three models considered in this paper: the logic PCL, *lending* Petri nets, and event structures with circular causality. For each of these models, we will give some examples to stress the flavor of these approaches. Section 5 contains some of the results connecting these three models. Finally, in Section 6 we draw some conclusions.

2   A Logical Approach to Circular Causality

Propositional Contract Logic (PCL [11]) extends intuitionistic propositional logic (IPC) with the connective $\rightarrow$, called *contractual implication*.

Definition 1 (PCL syntax). *The formulae $A, B, \ldots$ of PCL are defined as follows, where we assume that $a, b, \ldots$ range over a given set of atoms.*

$$A, B ::= \perp \mid \top \mid a \mid \neg A \mid A \vee B \mid A \wedge B \mid A \rightarrow B \mid A \rightarrow B$$

The natural deduction system for PCL [3] extends that for IPC with the rules $(\rightarrow I1)$, $(\rightarrow I2)$, and $(\rightarrow E)$ in Figure 1 (wherein, in all the rules, Δ is a set of PCL formulae). Provable formulae are contractually implied, according to rule $(\rightarrow I1)$. Rule $(\rightarrow I2)$ provides $\rightarrow$ with the same weakening properties of intuitionistic implication $\rightarrow$. The paradigmatic rule is $(\rightarrow E)$, which allows for the elimination of contractual implication $\rightarrow$. Compared to the rule $(\rightarrow E)$ for elimination of $\rightarrow$ in IPC, the only difference is that in the context used to deduce the antecedent A, rule $(\rightarrow E)$ also allows for using as hypothesis the consequence B.

$$\frac{}{\Delta, A \vdash A} \text{ (ID)} \qquad \frac{\Delta \vdash A \qquad \Delta \vdash B}{\Delta \vdash A \wedge B} \text{ (}\wedge\text{I)} \qquad \frac{\Delta \vdash A \wedge B}{\Delta \vdash A} \text{ (}\wedge\text{E1)} \qquad \frac{\Delta \vdash A \wedge B}{\Delta \vdash B} \text{ (}\wedge\text{E2)}$$

$$\frac{\Delta \vdash A}{\Delta \vdash A \vee B} \text{ (}\vee\text{I1)} \qquad \frac{\Delta \vdash B}{\Delta \vdash A \vee B} \text{ (}\vee\text{I2)} \qquad \frac{\Delta \vdash A \vee B \qquad \Delta, A \vdash r \qquad \Delta, B \vdash r}{\Delta \vdash r} \text{ (}\vee\text{E)}$$

$$\frac{\Delta, A \vdash B}{\Delta \vdash A \rightarrow B} \text{ (}\rightarrow\text{I)} \qquad \frac{\Delta \vdash A \rightarrow B \qquad \Delta \vdash A}{\Delta \vdash B} \text{ (}\rightarrow\text{E)}$$

$$\frac{\Delta \vdash A \rightarrow B \qquad \Delta, A' \vdash A \qquad \Delta, B \vdash A' \rightarrow B'}{\Delta \vdash A' \rightarrow B'} \text{ (}\rightarrow\text{I2)}$$

$$\frac{\Delta \vdash B}{\Delta \vdash A \rightarrow B} \text{ (}\rightarrow\text{I1)} \qquad \frac{\Delta \vdash A \rightarrow B \qquad \Delta, B \vdash A}{\Delta \vdash B} \text{ (}\rightarrow\text{E)}$$

Fig. 1. Natural deduction system for PCL (rules for $\neg$ and $\perp$ omitted)

Example 1. Let $\Delta = A \to B, B \twoheadrightarrow A$. A proof of $\Delta \vdash A$ in natural deduction is:

$$\cfrac{\Delta \vdash B \twoheadrightarrow A \qquad \cfrac{\Delta, A \vdash A \to B \quad \overline{\Delta, A \vdash A}^{\,(\text{Id})}}{\Delta, A \vdash B}^{\,(\to\text{E})}}{\Delta \vdash A}^{\,(\twoheadrightarrow\text{E})}$$

As in the previous example, we can show that the following is a theorem of PCL:

$$(A \twoheadrightarrow B) \wedge (B \twoheadrightarrow A) \to A \wedge B \qquad\qquad \text{(THEOREM)}$$

whereas the following is *not* a theorem (neither of PCL nor of IPC):

$$(A \to B) \wedge (B \to A) \to A \wedge B \qquad\qquad \text{(NOT A THEOREM)}$$

The above theorem highlights the different nature of contractual and intuitionistic implication: the former allows for a form of *circular* reasoning, while the latter does not. Some other characterizing theorems of PCL are outlined below:

$$\vdash (A \twoheadrightarrow B) \wedge (B \twoheadrightarrow A) \to A \wedge B \tag{7}$$

$$\vdash (A_1 \twoheadrightarrow A_2) \wedge \cdots \wedge (A_{n-1} \twoheadrightarrow A_n) \wedge (A_n \twoheadrightarrow A_1) \to A_1 \wedge \cdots \wedge A_n \tag{8}$$

$$\vdash \bigwedge_{i \in 1..n} \big((A_1 \wedge \cdots \wedge A_{i-1} \wedge A_{i+1} \wedge \cdots \wedge A_n) \twoheadrightarrow A_i\big) \to A_1 \wedge \cdots \wedge A_n \tag{9}$$

$$\vdash (A \twoheadrightarrow B) \to (A \to B) \tag{10}$$

$$\nvdash (A \to B) \to (A \twoheadrightarrow B) \tag{11}$$

$$\vdash (A' \to A) \wedge (A \twoheadrightarrow B) \wedge (B \to B') \to (A' \twoheadrightarrow B') \tag{12}$$

Theorem (7) models a binary *handshaking*; (8) is a generalization to the multiparty case, where the $(i + 1)$-th party, in order to do A_{i+1}, relies on an action A_i made by the i-th party; (9) is a sort of "greedy" handshaking, because now a party does A_i only provided that *all* the other parties do their actions, i.e. $A_1, \ldots, A_{i-1}, A_{i+1}, \ldots, A_n$. Theorem (10) states that contractual implication is *stronger* than intuitionistic implication, while (11) says that the converse does not hold. The consequence in a contractual implication can be arbitrarily weakened, while the precondition can be arbitrarily strengthened (12).

The main results about PCL, among which consistency (under the full set of rules, which also deal with negation and $\perp$) and decidability, are established in [11]. The proof of decidability follows the lines of the one for IPC given by Kleene in [15]. The result relies on a formulation of the PCL sequent calculus with implicit structural rules (to limit the proof search space of a given sequent, as in Kleene's G3 calculus) and the subformula property, obtained as consequence of the cut-elimination theorem.

While PCL is clearly a conservative extension of IPC, there cannot be sound and complete homomorphic encodings of PCL into IPC: that is, $\twoheadrightarrow$ cannot be regarded as syntactic sugar for some IPC context.

Definition 2 (Homomorphic encoding). *A homomorphic encoding m is a function from PCL formulae to IPC formulae such that: m is the identity on* *prime formulas,* $\top$, *and* $\bot$; *it acts homomorphically on* $\wedge, \vee, \rightarrow, \neg$; *it satisfies* $m(A \twoheadrightarrow B) = \mathbb{C}[m(A), m(B)]$ *for some fixed IPC context* $\mathbb{C}(\bullet, \bullet)$.

Of course, each homomorphic encoding is uniquely determined by the context $\mathbb{C}$. Several *complete* encodings, (i.e. satisfying $\vdash p \implies \vdash_{IPC} m_i(p)$) exist: for instance, $m_0(A \twoheadrightarrow B) = m_0(B)$ and $m_1(A \twoheadrightarrow B) = (m_1(B) \rightarrow m_1(A)) \rightarrow m_1(B)$ are both complete encodings. However, there can be no *sound* encodings. Indeed, a sound encoding would allow us to derive Peirce's axiom in PCL, violating the fact that PCL conservatively extends IPC [10].

Theorem 1. *If m is a homomorphic encoding of PCL into IPC, then m is not sound, i.e. there exists a PCL formula A such that $\vdash_{IPC} m(A)$ and $\not\vdash A$.*

3 An Operational Approach to Circular Causality

In Petri nets [19] dependencies among transitions are encoded by stipulating that tokens produced by a transition are consumed by others, and it may well be that two or more transitions may share places in such a way that tokens produced by one are used by the others and vice versa. Thus, on an abstract level, the issue of circularity is already present in the general Petri nets setting, and circularity is not considered a relevant issue. This is not longer true when considering nets where transitions represent events and the requirement that a transition is executed just once is enforced, *e.g.* occurrence nets (adopting the terminology of van Glabbeek and Plotkin in [21]). In this case to establish a circular dependency a transition should use a token produced by another transition which in turn expects (one of) the token produced by the former. According to the ordinary interpretation of firing in Petri nets these transitions cannot fire.

To overcome this problem *debit* arcs have been introduced in [20]. In a net with debit arcs transitions may be executed even if some tokens are not available. The motivations behind this approach rely on language theoretic considerations (Petri nets are indeed a kind of automata able to recognise a class of languages [23]): nets with debit arcs are inspired by the so called *blind-one way multicounter machines* described by Greibach in [13].

We are more interested in characterising in an operational way the capability of a place to *lend* tokens allowing in this way the execution of a transition otherwise *blocked*. To this aim we present *Lending Petri nets*, defined in [4] and further studied in [5], which are basically debit nets with some additional constraints. A Petri net is a tuple $\langle S, T, F, m_0 \rangle$, where S is a set of *places*, T is a set of *transitions* (such that that $S \cap T = \emptyset$), $F \colon (S \times T) \cup (T \times S) \rightarrow \mathbb{N}$ is a *weight function*, and $m_0 \colon S \rightarrow \mathbb{N}$ is a function from places to natural numbers, called *marking*, which models the initial state of the net. $F(s,t) = n$ means that the transition t can be fired whenever n tokens are available at place s, while $F(t, s') = m$ means that firing the transition t will result in m tokens added to place s'. Lending Petri nets extend standard nets by allowing transitions to fire even in the absence of the required number of tokens. However, this is done in a controlled manner: only a fixed number of tokens can be obtained "on credit", and credits must be eventually honored. We introduce a *lending function* $L : S \times T \to \mathbb{N}$, which specifies how many tokens a transition may borrow from a place. Thus if $F(s,t) = n$ and $L(s,t) = l$, then firing the transition t costs $n + l$ tokens, of which only l can be taken on credit. We equip Lending Petri nets with a labelling ℓ of places and transitions, where labels are drawn from a set $\mathcal{L}$. These labels have a role similar to the one played by input/output interfaces in the open nets as defined in [1], and play a major role when defining operations on these nets.

Definition 3. *A lending Petri net (LPN) is a tuple $N = \langle S, T, F, L, \ell, m_0 \rangle$ where: (a) $\langle S, T, F, m_0 \rangle$ is a Petri net, (b) $L: S \times T \to \mathbb{N}$ is the lending function, and (c) $\ell : S \cup T \rightharpoonup \mathcal{L}$ is a partial labeling of places and transitions, Further, we require that for each $t \in T$, there exists some $s \in S$ such that $F(s,t) + L(s,t) > 0$.*

The last requirement says simply that no transition can happen *spontaneously* but must consume or *lend* some tokens.

This model is clearly a conservative extension of the classical one: indeed, an ordinary Petri net is an LPN where the lending function is constant and equal to 0, which means that no token can be borrowed from any place. The drawing conventions we adopt are mostly standard, the unique difference is for arcs connecting places to transitions we have a pair of natural numbers, the first representing the weight of the *standard* arcs (possibly 0) and the second the weight of the lending ones (in red, only written when nonzero). We omit the arc between a place and a transition if standard and lending arcs have null weights.

We define the *pre-set* and the *post-set* of a transition/place as usual: $^\bullet x = \{y \in T \cup S \mid F(y,x) > 0\}$ and $x^\bullet = \{y \in T \cup S \mid F(x,y) > 0\}$, respectively. These are lifted to sets of transitions/places in the obvious way. The current state of a net is described by a *marking*, which in the case of LPNs is no longer constrained to be a function from places to natural numbers, but it is a function $m : S \to \mathbb{Z}$ from places to *integers* (with the exception of the initial marking m_0 that must be non-negative). We shall adopt the following drawing convention for markings. First, we associate each place p with a *co-place* $\bar{p}$, which represents a negative token in p. Then, a marking m is represented as a multiset of places and co-places, containing $m(p)$ occurrences of p if $m(p)$ is positive, and $-m(p)$ occurrences of $\bar{p}$ is $m(p)$ is negative. For instance, we represent the marking $m = \{p_1 \mapsto 2, p_2 \mapsto -1\}$ as $p_1, p_1, \bar{p_2}$. We denote with $\emptyset$ the empty multiset.

The behavior of a net is described by a labeled relation between markings, where labels are transitions in T. Intuitively, a transition t can be fired at a certain marking whenever each place in the pre-set of t contains enough tokens: more precisely, each place $s \in {}^\bullet t$ must contain at least $F(s,t)$ tokens. If a transition t is enabled at a marking m then it can be *fired*, leading to a new marking where the number of tokens in the places of the net is accordingly updated. To do that, each place s in the pre-set of t gives away $F(s,t) + L(s,t)$ tokens (of which, only $F(s,t)$ need to be already available at s, while the others can be taken on credit), and it receives $F(t,s)$ tokens.

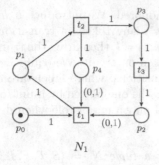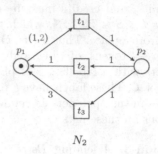

N_1 N_2

Fig. 2. Two Lending Petri nets

Definition 4. *Let* $N = \langle S, T, F, L, \ell, m_0 \rangle$ *be an LPN. We say that* $t \in T$ *is enabled at* m *iff* $m(s) \geq F(s,t)$ *for all* $s \in {}^\bullet t$. *We have a step* t *from* m *to* m' *(in symbols,* $m \xrightarrow{t} m'$*) whenever* t *is enabled at* m, *and, for all* $s \in S$: $m'(s) = m(s) - \big(F(s,t) + L(s,t)\big) + F(t,s)$

A consequence of this notion is that the number of tokens in a place can become negative, if the weight of the lending arc is not zero.

A *firing sequence* is a finite sequence of steps. The *trace* of a firing sequence is the string of labels associated to its transitions, *i.e.* the trace of $m_0 \xrightarrow{t_1} m_1 \cdots m_{n-1} \xrightarrow{t_n} m_n$ is the string $\ell(t_1) \cdots \ell(t_n)$, which is the empty string ε when $n = 0$, and it is undefined when $\ell(t_i)$ is undefined for some i. The set of all traces of a net N is denoted with $Tr(N)$. As usual, we denote with $\rightarrow^*$ the reflexive and transitive closure of $\rightarrow$. Hereafter, we denote with $Mk(N)$ the set of *reachable markings* of a net N, *i.e.* those markings m for which there exists a firing sequence starting at m_0 and leading to m.

Not all reachable markings represent good states of a system: a marking where some places have a negative number of tokens models a state where some resources have been taken on credit, but the credit has not been honored yet. *Honored markings* are those markings which model states where all credits have been honored. Thus in honoured markings the possible circular dependencies among transitions have been *solved*.

Definition 5. *A marking* m *of* N *is honored iff* $m(s) \geq 0$ *for all places* s *of* N.

If the net has no lending arcs, all the reachable markings are honored. An honored firing sequence is a firing sequence where the final marking is honored.

Example 2. Consider the LPN N_1 in Figure 2. The initial marking is the multiset p_0. The transition t_1 is enabled at p_0 as it may borrow tokens from places p_2 and p_4. The other two transitions (t_2 and t_3) are not enabled. We have exactly one maximal firing sequence: $p_0 \xrightarrow{t_1} p_1, \overline{p_2}, \overline{p_4} \xrightarrow{t_2} \overline{p_2}, p_3 \xrightarrow{t_3} \emptyset$. Note that the marking reached after firing all the three transitions is a non-negative one, hence it is honored.

Consider now the LPN N_2 in Figure 2. The transition t_1 is enabled, as it may borrow two tokens from place p_1. Firing t_1 leads to the marking $\overline{p_1}, \overline{p_1}, p_2$. Then, if the transition t_2 is fired, one token is given back to place p_1, and we reach a deadlock, *i.e.* a not honored state where no transitions are enabled. Instead, if the transition t_3 is fired then we return to the initial state, with one token at place p_1.

LPNs are intended to represent systems, hence a notion of composition should be introduced. The idea is that labelled places are the *interface* of the LPN. Those without outgoing transitions play the role of *outputs*, whereas those incoming transitions play the role of *inputs*. If a net N has an input place, and N' has an output place with the same label, then in their composition $N \oplus N'$ these places will be plugged together. This models an asynchronous communication channel between nets, which does not preserve the order of messages (as usual in nets, see e.g. [1]). A transition with a certain label of a component is supposed to produce tokens in all the interface places of the other component, that have the same label.

The composition of LPNs we introduce is subject to some conditions, which altogether take the name of *correct labeling*, and are collected in Definition 6. The transitions of each components are labeled with actions, and the tokens produced by these transitions may carry this information. When these tokens are produced in labeled places, we require that this information is preserved (this is the requirement (a) of Definition 6). Accordingly to the same intuition, all the labeled places in the post-set of a transition should carry the same label (requirement (b) of Definition 6). Finally, input/output places are not initially marked (requirement (c)). This is because we want have input/output places as the *communication* medium among the components.

Definition 6. *A LPN $\langle S, T, F, L, \ell, m_0 \rangle$ is correctly labeled iff for all $s \in S$ such that $\ell(s) \neq \bot$: (a) $\forall t, t' \in {}^{\bullet}s.\ \ell(t) = \ell(s) = \ell(t')$ (b) $\forall t \in {}^{\bullet}s.\ |\{\ell(s')\ |\ s' \in t^{\bullet} \wedge \ell(s') \neq \bot\}| = 1$, and (c) $m_0(s) = 0$.*

The underlying idea of LPN composition is rather simple: input and output places with the same label are merged together and the flow relation is defined accordingly. Formally, the output places s in N with a label occurring in N' are removed, and the ingoing transitions of s are connected to the input places in N' with label $\ell(s)$. Furthermore, if a component has a transition t with the same label of a place s of the other component, then a flow arc is created from the transition to the place. We require that arcs connecting a labeled transition to a labeled place have always weight 1. All the other ingredients of the composed net are inherited from the components.

Definition 7. *Let $N = \langle S, T, F, L, \ell, m_0 \rangle$ and $N' = \langle S', T', F', L', \ell', m_0' \rangle$ be two correctly labeled LPNs. We say that N, N' are composable whenever (a) $S \cap S' = \emptyset = T \cap T'$, and (b) $\forall t \in T,\ \forall s \in S.\ \ell(s) \neq \bot \implies F(t, s) \leq 1$ and $\forall t \in T',\ \forall s \in S'.\ \ell'(s) \neq \bot \implies F'(t, s) \leq 1$ and in such case their composition $N \oplus N'$ is the LPN $\langle \hat{S}, T \cup T', \hat{F}, \hat{L}, \hat{\ell}, \hat{m}_0 \rangle$ in Figure 3.*

$$\hat{S} = (S \setminus \mathbb{S}) \cup (S' \setminus \mathbb{S}')$$

$$\text{where } \mathbb{S} = \{s \in S \mid \ell(s) \in \ell'(S') \text{ and } s^\bullet = \emptyset\}$$
$$\text{and } \mathbb{S}' = \{s' \in S' \mid \ell'(s') \in \ell(S) \text{ and } s'^\bullet = \emptyset\}$$

$$\hat{F}(s,t) = \begin{cases} F(s,t) & \text{if } s \in S \text{ and } t \in T \\ F'(s,t) & \text{if } s \in S' \text{ and } t \in T' \end{cases}$$

$$\hat{F}(t,s) = \begin{cases} F(t,s) & \text{if } s \in S \text{ and } t \in T \\ F'(t,s) & \text{if } s \in S' \text{ and } t \in T' \\ F(t,s') & \text{if } s \in S' \text{ and } s' \in \mathbb{S} \text{ and } t \in T \text{ and } \ell(t) = \ell'(s) \\ F'(t,s') & \text{if } s \in S' \text{ and } s' \in \mathbb{S}' \text{ and } t \in T' \text{ and } \ell'(t) = \ell(s) \\ 1 & \text{if } t \in T \text{ and } s \in S' \text{ and } \ell(t) = \ell'(s) \\ 1 & \text{if } t \in T' \text{ and } s \in S \text{ and } \ell'(t) = \ell(s) \end{cases}$$

$$\hat{L}(s,t) = \begin{cases} L(s,t) & \text{if } s \in S \text{ and } t \in T \\ L'(s,t) & \text{if } s \in S' \text{ and } t \in T' \end{cases}$$

$$\hat{\ell}(x) = \begin{cases} \ell(x) & \text{if } x \in S \cup T \\ \ell'(x) & \text{otherwise} \end{cases}$$

$$\hat{m}_0(\hat{s}) = \begin{cases} 1 & \text{if } s \in S \text{ and } m_0(s) = 1, \text{ or } s \in S' \text{ and } m'_0(s) = 1 \\ 0 & \text{otherwise} \end{cases}$$

Fig. 3. Composition of two LPNs

Observe that composing two nets N and N' such that $\ell(S) \cap \ell'(S') = \emptyset$ results in the disjoint union of the two nets. Further, if the common label $a \in \ell(S) \cap \ell'(S')$ is associated in N to a place s with empty post-set and in N' to a place s' with empty pre-set (or *vice versa*) and the labelings are injective, we obtain precisely the composition between open nets defined in [1].

Example 3. Consider the nets in Figure 4. In the LPN N the transition t_a can be executed only if a token is present in the interface place p_1 labeled a, which has no ingoing to any transition. In the LPN N' the transition t_b is enabled as it may lend a token from the interface place p'_1 labeled b. The result of composition of these two nets is the LPN $N \oplus N'$, where now the execution of the transition t_a puts a token in the interface place p_1 (the resulting marking is $p_1, p_b^*, \overline{p'_1}$) and at this marking firing t_b leads to the empty marking.

Proposition 1. *Let N_i, $i \in \{1, 2, 3\}$ be pairwise composable LPNs. Then $N_1 \oplus N_2 = N_2 \oplus N_1$, and $N_1 \oplus (N_2 \oplus N_3) = (N_1 \oplus N_2) \oplus N_3$.*

The composition $\oplus$ does not have the property that, in general, restricting to the transitions of one of the components, we obtain the LPN we started with.

A *subnet* is a net obtained by restricting places and transitions of a net, and correspondingly the flow function, the lending function and the initial marking.

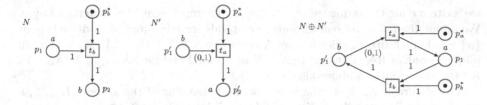

Fig. 4. Two LPNs and their pairwise composition

Definition 8. *Let $N = \langle S, T, F, L, \ell, m_0 \rangle$ be an LPN, and let $T' \subseteq T$. We define the subnet $N|_{T'} = \langle S', T', F', L', \ell, m_0' \rangle$, where: (a) $S' = \{s \in S \mid F(t,s) > 0 \text{ or } F(s,t) > 0 \text{ for } t \in T'\} \cup \{s \in S \mid m_0(s) > 0\}$, (b) $F' = F|_{(S' \times T') \cup (T' \times S')}$, (c) $L' = L|_{S' \times T'}$, (d) $\ell' = \ell|_{S' \cup T'}$, and (e) $m_0' = m_0|_{S'}$.*

Definition 9. *Let N and N' be two LPNs. We say that N is trace equivalent to N' (in symbols, $N \sim N'$) whenever $Tr(N) = Tr(N')$.*

Proposition 2. *For two composable LPNs N_1, N_2, we have that $N_i \sim (N_1 \oplus N_2)|_{T_i}$, for $i = 1, 2$.*

4   A Semantic Approach to Circular Causality

We review now a semantic approach to circularity based on the notion of *event structure with circular causality*, which have been introduced in [6] and further studied in [12] and [7]. Since [18,22], event structures (ES) are one of the classical model for concurrency, and they are at least equipped with a relation (written $\vdash$ in [22]) modelling *causality*, and another one modeling non-determinism (usually rendered in terms of conflicts or consistency). Extensions to ES often use other relations to model other kind of dependencies, *e.g.* or-causality [2]. ES can provide a basic semantic model for concurrent systems, by interpreting the enabling $\{a\} \vdash b$ as: "event b can be done *after* a has been done". We use a relation to model circular causality. Given a set of events E and an irreflexive and symmetric relation representing conflicts (denoted with $\#$), we say that a set $X \subseteq E$ is *conflict-free* ($CF(X)$ in symbols) whenever $\forall e, e' \in X.\neg(e \# e')$. We denote with Con the set $\{X \subseteq_{fin} E \mid CF(X)\}$.

Definition 10. *An event structure with circular causality (CES) is a quadruple $\mathcal{E} = (E, \#, \vdash, \Vdash)$ where: (a) E is a set of events, (b) $\# \subseteq E \times E$ is an irreflexive and symmetric relation, called conflict relation, (c) $\vdash \subseteq Con \times E$ is the enabling relation, and (d) $\Vdash \subseteq Con \times E$ is the circular enabling relation, The relations $\vdash$ and $\Vdash$ are saturated, i.e. for all $X, Y \in Con$ and for $\circ \in \{\vdash, \Vdash\}$: $X \circ e \wedge X \subseteq Y \implies Y \circ e$. We say that $\mathcal{E}$ is finite when E is finite; we say that $\mathcal{E}$ is conflict-free when the conflict relation is empty.*

For a sequence $\sigma = \langle e_0\, e_1 \ldots \rangle$ (possibly infinite), we write $\overline{\sigma}$ for the set of events in σ. We write σ_i for the subsequence $\langle e_0 \ldots e_{i-1} \rangle$. If $\sigma = \langle e_0 \ldots e_n \rangle$ is finite, we write $\sigma\, e$ for the sequence $\langle e_0 \ldots e_n\, e \rangle$. The empty sequence is denoted by ε. We adopt the following conventions: $\vdash e$ stands for $\emptyset \vdash e$ and we write $a \vdash b$ for $\{a\} \vdash b$. For a finite, conflict-free set X, we write $X \vdash Y$ for $\forall e \in Y.\ X \vdash e$. For an infinite, conflict-free X, we write $X \vdash Y$ as a shorthand for $\exists X_0 \subseteq_{fin} X.\ X_0 \vdash Y$. All the abbreviations above also apply to $\Vdash$.

A configuration C is a "snapshot" of the behaviour of the system. In [22], a set of events C is a configuration if and only if for each event $e \in C$ it is possible to find a *trace for e in C*, *i.e.* a finite sequence of events containing e, which is closed under the enabling relation:

$$\forall e \in C.\ \exists \sigma = \langle e_0 \ldots e_n \rangle.\ e \in \bar{\sigma} \subseteq C \,\wedge\, \forall i \leq n.\ \{e_0, \ldots, e_{i-1}\} \vdash e_i$$

We refine the notion in [22] to deal with circular causality. Intuitively, for all events e_i in the sequence $\langle e_0 \ldots e_n \rangle$, e_i can either be $\vdash$-enabled by its predecessors, or $\Vdash$-enabled by the *whole* sequence, i.e.:

$$\forall e \in C.\ \exists \sigma = \langle e_0 \ldots e_n \rangle.\ e \in \bar{\sigma} \subseteq C \,\wedge\, \forall i \leq n.\ (\{e_0, \ldots, e_{i-1}\} \vdash e_i \,\vee\, \bar{\sigma} \Vdash e_i)$$

Clearly, the configurations of a CES without $\Vdash$-enablings are also configurations in the sense of [22], hence CES are a conservative extension of Winskel's general ES. Differently from ES, if C is a finite configuration of a CES, and σe is a trace for all the events in C, not necessarily σ is a trace for $C \setminus \{e\}$ (see *e.g.*, $\mathcal{E}_2$ in Figure 5).

To allow for reasoning about sets of events which are not configurations, we introduce the auxiliary notion of *X-configuration* in Definition 11 below. In an *X-configuration* C, the set C can contain an event e even in the absence of a justification through a standard/circular enabling — provided that e belongs to the set X. This allows, given an X-configuration, to add/remove any event and obtain a Y-configuration, possibly with $Y \neq X$. We shall say that the events in X have been taken "on credit", to remark the fact that they may have been performed in the absence of a causal justification. With this new concept in mind, we can say that standards configurations are just $\emptyset$-configurations: they represent sets of events where all the credits have been "honoured".

Definition 11. *Let $\mathcal{E} = (E, \#, \vdash, \Vdash)$ be a CES, and let $X \subseteq E$. A conflict-free sequence $\sigma = \langle e_0 \ldots e_n \rangle \in E^*$ without repetitions is an X-trace of $\mathcal{E}$ iff:*

$$\forall i \leq n.\ (e_i \in X \,\vee\, \bar{\sigma_i} \vdash e_i \,\vee\, \bar{\sigma} \Vdash e_i) \tag{13}$$

For all $C, X \subseteq E$ we say that C is an X-configuration of $\mathcal{E}$ iff $CF(C)$ and:

$$\forall e \in C.\ \exists \sigma\ X\text{-trace.}\ e \in \bar{\sigma} \subseteq C \tag{14}$$

The set of all X-traces of $\mathcal{E}$ is denoted by $\mathcal{T}_{\mathcal{E}}(X)$, abbreviated as $\mathcal{T}_{\mathcal{E}}$ when $X = \emptyset$. The set of all X-configurations of $\mathcal{E}$ is denoted by $\mathcal{F}_{\mathcal{E}}(X)$, or just $\mathcal{F}_{\mathcal{E}}$ when $X = \emptyset$.

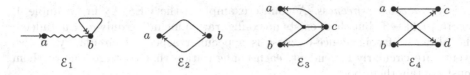

Fig. 5. Four CES . We adopt the following graphical notation for depicting CES : they are denoted as directed hypergraphs, where nodes stand for events. An hyperedge from a set of nodes X to node e denotes an enabling $X \circ e$, where $\circ\, =\, \vdash$ if the edge has a single arrow, and $\circ\, =\, \Vdash$ if the edge has a double arrow. A conflict $a\#b$ is represented by a waved line between a and b.

Example 4. Consider the CES in Figure 5. $\mathcal{E}_1$ has enablings $\vdash a$, $b \Vdash b$, and conflict $a\#b$. By Definition 11, $\emptyset, \{a\}, \{b\} \in \mathcal{F}_{\mathcal{E}_1}$, but $\{a,b\} \notin \mathcal{F}_{\mathcal{E}_1}$. $\mathcal{E}_2$ has enablings $a \vdash b$ and $b \Vdash a$. Here $\emptyset, \{a,b\} \in \mathcal{F}_{\mathcal{E}_2}$, while neither $\{a\}$ nor $\{b\}$ belong to $\mathcal{F}_{\mathcal{E}_2}$. Also, $\mathcal{F}_{\mathcal{E}_2}(\{b\}) = \{\emptyset, \{b\}, \{a,b\}\}$, and $\mathcal{F}_{\mathcal{E}_2}(\{a\}) = \{\emptyset, \{a\}, \{a,b\}\}$. $\mathcal{E}_3$ has enablings $\{a,b\} \vdash c$, $c \Vdash a$, and $c \Vdash b$. The only non-empty configuration of $\mathcal{E}_3$ is $\{a,b,c\}$. $\mathcal{E}_4$ has enablings $\{a,b\} \Vdash c$, $\{a,b\} \Vdash d$, $c \vdash a$, and $d \vdash b$. We have that $\{a,b,c,d\} \in \mathcal{F}_{\mathcal{E}_4}$. Note that, were one (or both) of the $\Vdash$ turned into a $\vdash$, then the only configuration would have been $\emptyset$.

Following [22], we assume the *axiom of finite causes*, that is, we always require an event to be enabled by a *finite* chain of events. For instance, consider the event structure: $\cdots e_n \to \cdots e_3 \to e_2 \to e_1 \to e_0$ For e_0 to happen, an infinite number of events must have happened *before* it. As in [22], we do not consider the set $\{e_i \mid i \geq 0\}$ as a configuration, because a justification of e_0 would require an infinite chain. Similarly, in the CES : $a_0 \leftarrow a_1 \leftarrow a_2 \leftarrow a_3 \cdots \leftarrow a_n \cdots$ where, for a_0 to happen, an infinity of events must happen either *before* or *after* it, the set $\{a_i \mid i \geq 0\}$ is *not* a configuration according to Definition 11, because a justification of a_0 would require an infinite chain.

We relate Winskel's ES with CES in Theorem 3 below. First, we introduce the needed definitions.

Let $\mathcal{F}$ be a family of sets. We say a subset $\mathcal{A}$ of $\mathcal{F}$ is *pairwise compatible* if and only if $\forall e, e' \in \bigcup \mathcal{A}.\ \exists C \in \mathcal{F}.\ e, e' \in C$.

For a set of sets $\mathcal{F}$ we define the following three properties:

Coherence: If $\mathcal{A}$ is a pairwise compatible subset of $\mathcal{F}$, then $\bigcup \mathcal{A} \in \mathcal{F}$.
Finiteness: $\forall C \in \mathcal{F}.\ \forall e \in C.\ \exists C_0 \in \mathcal{F}.\ e \in C_0 \subseteq_{fin} C$
Coincidence-freeness:

$$\forall C \in \mathcal{F}.\ \forall e, e' \in C.\ (e \neq e' \implies (\exists C' \in \mathcal{F}.\ C' \subseteq C \wedge (e \in C' \iff e' \notin C')))$$

We say that $\mathcal{F}$ is a *quasi-family of configurations* iff it satisfies coherence and finiteness; if $\mathcal{F}$ also satisfies coincidence-freeness, then we call $\mathcal{F}$ a *family of configurations*. In that case, we say that $\mathcal{F}$ is a family of configurations of E when $\bigcup \mathcal{F} = E$.

A basic result of [22] is that the set of configurations of an ES forms a family of configurations. On the contrary, the set of configurations of a CES does not satisfy *coincidence-freeness*. A counterexample is the CES $\mathcal{E}_2$ in Example 4, where $\{a, b\} \in \mathcal{F}$, but there exists no configuration including only a or b. Indeed, the absence of coincidence-freeness is a peculiar aspect of circularity: if two events are circularly dependent, each configuration that contains one of them must contain them both.

Theorem 2. *For all CES $\mathcal{E}$, and for all $X \subseteq E$, the set $\mathcal{F}_{\mathcal{E}}(X)$ is a quasi-family of configurations.*

Despite faithfully representing the legitimate states of a system where all the credits are honoured, sets of configurations are not a precise semantic model for CES. Indeed, they are not able to discriminate among substantially different CES, e.g. like the following: $\mathcal{E}$: $a \Vdash b$, $b \Vdash a$, $\mathcal{E}'$: $a \vdash b$, $b \Vdash a$, and $\mathcal{E}''$: $a \Vdash b$, $b \vdash a$. It is easy to check that the sets of X-configurations of $\mathcal{E}, \mathcal{E}', \mathcal{E}''$ coincide, for all X. This contrasts with the different intuitive meaning of $\vdash$ and $\Vdash$, which is revealed instead by observing the traces: $\mathcal{T}_{\mathcal{E}} = \{\langle ab \rangle, \langle ba \rangle\}$, $\mathcal{T}_{\mathcal{E}'} = \{\langle ab \rangle\}$, and $\mathcal{T}_{\mathcal{E}''} = \{\langle ba \rangle\}$. To substantiate our feeling that configurations alone are not sufficiently discriminating for CES, in Theorem 3 we show that for all CES $\mathcal{E}$ there exists a CES $\mathcal{E}'$ *without $\vdash$-enablings* which has exactly the same configurations of $\mathcal{E}$. Therefore, the meaning of $\vdash$, that is the partial ordering of events, is completely lost by just observing configurations.

Definition 12. *Let $\mathcal{F}$ be a quasi-family of configurations of a set E. We define the CES $\hat{\mathcal{E}}(\mathcal{F}) = (E, \#, \emptyset, \Vdash)$ as follows:*

(a) $e \# e' \iff \forall C \in \mathcal{F}. e \notin C \vee e' \notin C$
(b) $X \Vdash e \iff CF(X) \wedge X$ is finite $\wedge \exists C \in \mathcal{F}. e \in C \subseteq X \cup \{e\}$

Theorem 3. *For all quasi-families of configurations $\mathcal{F}$, we have $\mathcal{F}_{\hat{\mathcal{E}}(\mathcal{F})} = \mathcal{F}$.*

The consequence of this theorem, formalized by the corollary below, is that the $\Vdash$-enabling is the only (circular) causality relation needed, as the standard one can be encoded into this one.

Corollary 1. *For all ES $\mathcal{E}$, there exists a CES $\mathcal{E}'$ without $\vdash$-enablings such that $\mathcal{F}_{\mathcal{E}} = \mathcal{F}_{\mathcal{E}'}$.*

The theorem below yields a polynomial-time algorithm for computing the set $\mathcal{R}_{\mathcal{E}}$ of *reachable* events, i.e. those events which belong to some configuration of $\mathcal{E}$. The algorithm exploits Kleene's fixed point theorem, by defining the set $\mathcal{R}_{\mathcal{E}}$ as the greatest fixed point of a monotonic (increasing) function F.

Theorem 4. *For all $X, Y, Z \subseteq E$, let:*

$$G_Y(Z) = Y \cup \{e \mid Z \vdash e\} \qquad F(X) = \mathit{lfp}\, G_{\{e \mid X \Vdash e\}}$$

Then, for all finite conflict-free CES $\mathcal{E}$, we have $\mathcal{R}_{\mathcal{E}} = \mathit{gfp}\, F$

Following the characterization provided by Theorem 4, an algorithm for constructing $\mathcal{R}_\mathcal{E}$ can be devised as follows. Let X_0 be the set of all events in $\mathcal{E}$. At step 0, we compute $X_1 = F(X_0)$. This can be done by interpreting the (minimal) $\vdash$-enablings of $\mathcal{E}$ as a set of propositional Horn clauses, and then by applying the forward chaining algorithm with input $\{e \mid X_0 \Vdash e\}$. The forward chaining can be computed in polynomial-time in the number of $\vdash$-enablings. If $X_1 = X_0$, then we have finished, i.e. $X_1 = \mathcal{R}_\mathcal{E}$. Otherwise, we compute $X_2 = F(X_1)$ and so on, until reaching a fixed point. In the worst case, this requires $|E|$ steps, hence we have a polynomial-time algorithm for computing $\mathcal{R}_\mathcal{E}$.

5   Relating Models

We now cast the three formalisms illustrated in the previous sections in a more coherent picture, by pointing out some relations among them. In particular, we show that:

- each conflict-free CES $\mathcal{E}$ can be associated to a Horn PCL theory Δ such that the atoms provable in Δ are exactly the events reachable in $\mathcal{E}$.
- each Horn PCL theory Δ can be associated to a LPN N such that the places marked in some honoured marking of N are exactly the atoms provable in Δ.

Taken together, these results state that finite conflict-free CES have the same expressivity of Horn PCL, and that PCL is no more expressive than LPNs; further, CES and LPNs provide two different models of Horn PCL.

5.1   CES *vs.* PCL

In Definition 13 we show a translation from CES into PCL formulae. In particular, our mapping is a bijection of finite, conflict-free CES into the Horn fragment of PCL , which comprises atoms, conjunctions and non-nested (standard/contractual) implications. When writing $X \vdash e$ we shall mean that X is a minimal set of events such that $(X, e) \in \vdash$ (similarly for $\Vdash$).

The encoding $[\cdot]$ maps an enabling $\vdash$ into an $\rightarrow$-clause, and a circular enabling $\Vdash$ into an $\twoheadrightarrow$-clause.

Definition 13. *Let* $\mathcal{E} = \langle E, \#, \vdash, \Vdash \rangle$ *be a conflict-free CES. The encoding* $[\mathcal{E}]$ *of* $\mathcal{E}$ *into a Horn PCL theory is defined as follows:*

$$[(X_i \circ e_i)_{i \in I}] = \{[X_i \circ e_i] \mid i \in I\} \qquad where\ [\circ] = \begin{cases} \rightarrow & if \circ\ =\ \vdash \\ \twoheadrightarrow & if \circ\ =\ \Vdash \end{cases}$$
$$[X \circ e] = \left(\bigwedge X \right) [\circ]\ e$$

Notice that the encoding above can be inverted, i.e. one can also translate a Horn PCL theory into a conflict-free CES . The following theorem the correctness and completeness of the encoding.

Theorem 5. *Let* $\mathcal{E}$ *be a finite, conflict-free CES . An event* c *is reachable in* $\mathcal{E}$ *iff* $[\mathcal{E}] \vdash_{\text{PCL}} e$.

$$T \quad = \{(X, a, \rightarrow) \mid X \rightarrow a \in \Delta\} \cup \{(X, a, \twoheadrightarrow) \mid X \twoheadrightarrow a \in \Delta\}$$

$$S \quad = \mathcal{L}(\Delta) \times (T \cup \{*\})$$

$$F(s, t) = \begin{cases} 1 & \text{if } \big(s = (a, *) \wedge t = (X, a, -)\big) \ \bigvee \ \big(s = (a, t) \wedge t = (\{a\} \cup X, c, \rightarrow)\big) \\ 0 & \text{otherwise} \end{cases}$$

$$F(t, s) = \begin{cases} 1 & \text{if } s = (a, t') \wedge t = (X, a, -) \wedge t' \neq * \\ 0 & \text{otherwise} \end{cases}$$

$$L(s, t) = \begin{cases} 1 & \text{if } s = (a, t) \wedge t = (\{a\} \cup X, c, \twoheadrightarrow) \\ 0 & \text{otherwise} \end{cases}$$

$$\ell(x) \quad = \begin{cases} a & \text{if } x = (a, t) \in S \text{ or } x = (X, a, -) \in T \\ \bot & \text{otherwise} \end{cases}$$

$$m_0(s) = \text{if } s = (a, *) \text{ then } 1 \text{ else } 0$$

Fig. 6. Mapping from Horn PCL theories to Lending Petri Nets

A consequence of Theorem 5 is that we can exploit properties of PCL to derive properties of conflict-free CES. For instance, from the tautology $(a \rightarrow b) \wedge (b \rightarrow c) \rightarrow (a \twoheadrightarrow c)$ of PCL we deduce that any conflict-free CES with enablings $a \vdash b$ and $b \Vdash c$ can be enriched with the enabling $a \Vdash c$, without affecting the reachable events.

5.2 LPNs *vs.* PCL

The result in Theorem 7 below gives a correspondence between LPNs and Horn PCL theories. Technically, we associate Horn PCL theories with LPNs which preserve the provability relation, in the sense that $\Delta \vdash X$ if and only if the LPN associated to Δ reaches a suitable configuration where all the atoms in X have been fired. The idea of our construction is to translate each Horn clause into a transition of an LPN, labeled with the action in the conclusion of the clause.

Definition 14. *For a Horn PCL theory Δ, we define $\mathcal{P}(\Delta)$ as the lending Petri net $\langle S, T, F, L, \ell, m_0 \rangle$ in Figure 6.*

We briefly comment below the construction in Figure 6. For each clause $X \circ a$ in Δ (with $\circ \in \{\rightarrow, \twoheadrightarrow\}$), we introduce a transition of the form $(X, a, \circ)$, and we label it with a (the component X keeps track of the premises of the implication). Places can have two forms: (a, t) for some label a and transition t, or $(a, *)$. Intuitively, a place $(a, *)$ is used to ensure that a transition labeled a can only be fired once, while a place (a, t) (labeled a) is used to collect the tokens produced by transitions labeled a, and to be consumed by transition t. Indeed, the definition of $F(t, s)$ ensures that each transition labeled a puts a token in each place labeled

$F(t,s)$	s_a^a	s_a^b	s_a^*	s_b^a	s_b^b	s_b^*
t_a	1	1				
t_b				1	1	

$F(s,t)$	s_a^a	s_a^b	s_a^*	s_b^a	s_b^b	s_b^*
t_a			1			
t_b		1				1

$L(s,t)$	s_a^a	s_a^b	s_a^*	s_b^a	s_b^b	s_b^*
t_a			1			
t_b						

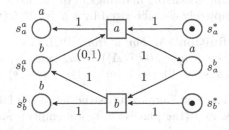

Fig. 7. LPN obtained from the PCL theory Δ of Example 5

a, while that of $F(s,t)$ (resp. $L(s,t)$) yields a non-lending (resp. lending) arc from each place (a,t) to t whenever t has a in its premises. Observe that a transition $t = (X, a, \circ)$ puts a token in each place (a, t') with $t' \neq *$, and all the transitions bearing the same labels, say a, are mutually excluding each other, as they share the unique input place $(a, *)$. The initial marking will contain all the places in $\mathcal{L}(\Delta) \times \{*\}$; if a token is consumed from one of these places, then the place will be never marked again. Finally we observe that each transition has a non empty pre-set: for a transition $t = (X, a, \circ)$ we have at least $(a, *)$ in the pre-set, and in particular if $\circ = \twoheadrightarrow$ then the pre-set $^\bullet t$ contains exactly $(a, *)$, as $^\bullet t$ does not include places connected through lending arcs.

Example 5. Let $\Delta = a \to b, \; b \twoheadrightarrow a$. According to Definition 14, $\mathcal{P}(\Delta)$ has the following places and transitions:

$$T = \{t_a, t_b\}, \text{ where } t_a = (b, a, \twoheadrightarrow), t_b = (a, b, \to)$$
$$S = \{s_a^a, s_a^b, s_a^*, s_b^a, s_b^b, s_b^*\}, \text{ where}$$
$$s_a^a = (a, t_a), s_a^b = (a, t_b), s_a^* = (a, *), s_b^a = (b, t_a), s_b^b = (b, t_b), s_b^* = (b, *)$$

The arcs and the labels of $\mathcal{P}(\Delta)$ are depicted in Figure 7. Observe that the LPN $\mathcal{P}(\Delta)$ has exactly one maximal firing sequence, i.e.:

$$s_a^*, s_b^* \xrightarrow{t_a} s_b^*, s_a^a, s_b^b, \overline{s_b^a} \xrightarrow{t_b} s_a^b, s_b^b$$

All the transitions in $\mathcal{P}(\Delta)$ labeled with a consume the token from the place $(a, *)$ in its pre-set, and this place cannot be marked again as it does not belong to the post-set of any transition, hence among them only one can fire. As each transition may be fired at most once, the net associated to a Horn PCL theory is an *occurrence net*, in the sense of van Glabbeek and Plotkin in [21].

A relevant property of $\mathcal{P}$ is that it is an homomorphism with respect to composition of theories. Thus, since both $\oplus$ is associative and commutative, we can construct an LPN from a Horn PCL theory $\Delta_1 \cdots \Delta_n$ componentwise, i.e. by composing the LPNs $\mathcal{P}(\Delta_1) \cdots \mathcal{P}(\Delta_n)$.

Theorem 6. *For all Δ_1, Δ_2, we have that $\mathcal{P}(\Delta_1, \Delta_2) \sim \mathcal{P}(\Delta_1) \oplus \mathcal{P}(\Delta_2)$.*

The reachable markings m of the LPN associated to a Horn PCL theory are completely characterized by a pair $(\overline{m}, \Omega(m))$, called *configuration* of the LPN.

Definition 15. *For a Horn PCL theory Δ, the configuration associated to a marking $m \in Mk(\mathcal{P}(\Delta))$ is the pair $(\overline{m}, \Omega(m))$, defined as: (i) $\overline{m} = \{a \in \mathcal{L} \mid m((a, *)) = 0\}$ (ii) $\Omega(m) = \{\ell(s) \mid m(s) < 0\}$.*

The first component is the set of the labels of the transitions that have been executed (the places $(a, *)$ are empty), and the second one is the set of labels of places with a negative marking, which means that the corresponding transitions have not been executed yet (as the LPN is correctly labeled). Clearly, the marking m is honored whenever $\Omega(m)$ is empty.

The following proposition establishes that configurations characterize markings of the LPNs associated to Horn PCL theories.

Proposition 3. *Let m and m' be markings of $\mathcal{P}(\Delta)$, for some Horn PCL theory Δ. If $\overline{m} = \overline{m'}$ and $\Omega(m) = \Omega(m')$, then $m = m'$.*

In Theorem 7 below we state the core correspondence between lending Petri nets and PCL: our construction maps the provability relation of PCL into the reachability of certain configurations in the associated LPN.

Theorem 7. *For all Horn PCL theories Δ, and for all conjunctions of atoms X:*

$$\Delta \vdash X \iff \exists m \in Mk(\mathcal{P}(\Delta)).\ X \subseteq \overline{m} \wedge \Omega(m) = \emptyset$$

6   Conclusions

We have presented three formalisms which can model circular causal dependencies, and we have established some relations among them. We conclude by pointing out some differences, as these may open new research directions.

PCL and CES do not have a way to control the usage of resources, whereas LPNs have this feature: once a resource is used, it is not any longer available. For instance, consider the following lending Petri net:

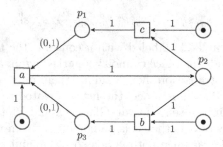

Here the unique resource produced by a can be used either by b or by c, but never by both. Note that in no one of the maximal firing sequencess, i.e. $\emptyset \xrightarrow{a} p_2, \overline{p_1}, \overline{p_3} \xrightarrow{b} \overline{p_1}$ and $\emptyset \xrightarrow{a} p_2, \overline{p_1}, \overline{p_3} \xrightarrow{c} \overline{p_3}$, the reached marking is not honored.

Instead, by modelling the above situation as the PCL theory $a \to b$, $a \to c$ and $(b \wedge c) \twoheadrightarrow a$, we can deduce both $a \wedge b \wedge c$, as the atom a contractually implied by $b \wedge c$ can be "consumed" by *both* implications $a \to b$ and $a \to c$. The logical approach may be possibly accommodated when moving to resource-oriented logics like linear logic (indeed, the idea of connecting Petri nets and linear logic is not new, see [16]); this appears more difficult to obtain when semantic models (like event structures) are considered.

Lending Petri nets, unlike CES and PCL, can express situations where executing a transition depends on the availability of two resources, one of which may possibly be lent. Consider, for instance, the following LPN:

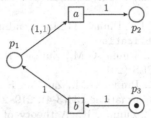

Transition a can be fired after b, because it needs at least one token in place p_1, whiel the other required token can be lent. Hence, we have the following firing sequence: $p_3 \xrightarrow{b} p_1 \xrightarrow{a} p_2, \overline{p_1}$. Were b allowed to fire twice (e.g. with p_3, p_3 as the initial marking), then an honored final marking would be reached.

We finally point out that these models have found a common ground in the framework of *contract-oriented computing* [11,9]. There, participants advertise their contracts to a contract broker. The broker composes contracts which admit some kind of agreement, and then establishes a session among the participants involved in them. In such scenario, the broker guarantees that — even in the presence of malicious participants — no interaction driven by the contract will ever go wrong. At worst, if some participant does not reach her objectives, then some other participant will be culpable of a contract infringement. In this workflow, it is crucial that contract brokers are honest, that is they never establish a session in the absence of an agreement among all the participants. Recall the scenario outlined in Section 1, where Alice and Bob are willing to exchange their resources. In her contract, Alice could promise to give a (unconditionally), declaring that her objective is to obtain b. A malicious contract broker could construct an attack by establishing a session between Alice and Mallory, whose contract just says to take a and give nothing in exchange. Mallory does not violate her contract, because it declares no obligations, and so Alice loses.

Models of circular causality like those presented here can be used by Alice to protect herself against untrusted contract brokers. By advertising the contract $b \twoheadrightarrow a$, Alice is saying that she promises to do a, but only under the guarantee that b will be done. Then, if the broker puts Alice in a session with Mallory (whose contract is *not* guaranteeing b), then Alice will not be culpable if she refuses to do a. Of course, also the contract $b \to a$ would have protected Alice, but this would have limited the interactions to those contexts where some other participants are not protected [8].

References

1. van der Aalst, W.M.P., Lohmann, N., Massuthe, P., Stahl, C., Wolf, K.: Multiparty contracts: Agreeing and implementing interorganizational processes. Comput. J. 53(1) (2010)
2. Baldan, P., Corradini, A., Montanari, U.: Contextual Petri nets, asymmetric event structures, and processes. Inf. Comput. 171(1), 1–49 (2001)
3. Bartoletti, M., Cimoli, T., Giamberardino, P.D., Zunino, R.: Contract agreements via logic. In: Proc. ICE (2013)
4. Bartoletti, M., Cimoli, T., Pinna, G.M.: Lending petri nets and contracts. In: Arbab, F., Sirjani, M. (eds.) FSEN 2013. LNCS, vol. 8161, pp. 66–82. Springer, Heidelberg (2013)
5. Bartoletti, M., Cimoli, T., Pinna, G.M.: Lending petri nets (submitted), http://tcs.unica.it/publications
6. Bartoletti, M., Cimoli, T., Pinna, G.M., Zunino, R.: An event-based model for contracts. In: Proc. PLACES (2012)
7. Bartoletti, M., Cimoli, T., Pinna, G.M., Zunino, R.: Circular causality in event structures. Fundamenta Informaticae 134(3-4), 219–259 (2014)
8. Bartoletti, M., Cimoli, T., Zunino, R.: A theory of agreements and protection. In: Basin, D., Mitchell, J.C. (eds.) POST 2013 (ETAPS 2013). LNCS, vol. 7796, pp. 186–205. Springer, Heidelberg (2013)
9. Bartoletti, M., Tuosto, E., Zunino, R.: Contract-oriented computing in CO_2. Scientific Annals in Computer Science 22(1), 5–60 (2012)
10. Bartoletti, M., Zunino, R.: A logic for contracts. Tech. Rep. DISI-09-034, DISI - Univ. Trento (2009)
11. Bartoletti, M., Zunino, R.: A calculus of contracting processes. In: LICS (2010)
12. Cimoli, T.: A theory of Agreement and Protection. Ph.D. thesis, University of Cagliari (May 2013)
13. Greibach, S.A.: Remarks on blind and partially blind one-way multicounter machines. Theoretical Computer Science 7, 311–324 (1978)
14. Hobbes, T.: The Leviathan (1651), chapter XIV
15. Kleene, S.: Introduction to metamathematics. North-Holland Publishing Company (1952)
16. Martí-Oliet, N., Meseguer, J.: From Petri nets to linear logic. Mathematical Structures in Computer Science 1(1), 69–101 (1991)
17. Moschovakis, J.: Intuitionistic logic. In: Zalta, E.N. (ed.) The Stanford Encyclopedia of Philosophy (2008)
18. Nielsen, M., Plotkin, G.D., Winskel, G.: Petri nets, event structures and domains, part i. Theor. Comput. Sci. 13, 85–108 (1981)
19. Reisig, W.: Petri Nets: An Introduction, Monographs in Theoretical Computer Science. An EATCS Series. Springer (1985)
20. Stotts, P.D., Godfrey, P.: Place/transition nets with debit arcs. Inf. Proc. Lett. 41(1) (1992)
21. van Glabbeek, R.J., Plotkin, G.D.: Configuration structures. In: LICS (1995)
22. Winskel, G.: Event structures. In: Brauer, W., Reisig, W., Rozenberg, G. (eds.) APN 1986. LNCS, vol. 254, pp. 325–392. Springer, Heidelberg (1987)
23. Zielonka, W.: Notes on finite asynchronous automata. Theoretical Informatics and Applications 21(2), 99–135 (1987)

Checking Cloud Contracts in Microsoft Azure

Nikolaj Bjørner[1] and Karthick Jayaraman[2]

[1] Microsoft Research
nbjorner@microsoft.com
[2] Microsoft Azure
karjay@microsoft.com

Abstract. *Cloud Contracts* capture architectural requirements in data-centers. They can be expressed as logical constraints over configurations. Contract violation is indicative of miss-configuration that may only be noticed when networks are attacked or correctly configured devices go off-line. In the context of Microsoft Azure's data-center we develop contracts for (1) network access restrictions, (2) forwarding tables, and (3) BGP policies. They are checked using the SecGuru tool that continuously monitors configurations in Azure. SecGuru is based on the Satisfiability Modulo Theories solver Z3, and uses logical formulas over bit-vectors to model network configurations. SecGuru is an instance of applying technologies, so far developed for program analysis, towards networks. We claim that *Network Verification* is an important and exciting new opportunity for formal methods and modern theorem proving technologies. Networking is currently undergoing a revolution thanks to the advent of highly programmable commodity devices for network control, the build out of large scale cloud data-centers and a paradigm shift from network infrastructure as embedded systems into software controlled and defined networking. Tools, programming languages, foundations, and methodologies from software engineering disciplines have a grand opportunity to fuel this transformation.

1 Introduction

Modern large-scale cloud infrastructures are inherently complex to configure and deploy: Network access restrictions are enforced at multiple points, forwarding and filtering policies are programmed or configured in various formats targeting devices that span different vendors and generations. Access restrictions evolve with organizational changes and operators come and leave. The general problem of analyzing networks is daunting, inhumane, and can really only be solved using rigorous tools.

As part of an arsenal of tools to take on this challenge we show in very recent work [11] how policies can be checked through a set of *beliefs*. Beliefs are confirmed, refuted or refined by posing queries about the network. Checking beliefs in packet switched networks without having any architectural knowledge of the network requires solving Boolean combinations of reachability properties. To make general belief checking practical we developed a general purpose Network

R. Natarajan et al. (Eds.): ICDCIT 2015, LNCS 8956, pp. 21–32, 2015.

Optimized Datalog engine that scales to data-center sized networks and used in many different contexts: Datalog over bit-vectors is very general and not confined to reasoning about IPv4, IPv6 networks, but applies also to Multi-protocol Label Switching (MPLS) networks, other arbitrary packet formats and is adaptable to many scenarios. The Network Optimized Datalog engine is also available with Z3.

This paper takes a narrower perspective to a specialized but very important deployment scenario. We describe a system currently used in production, based on technologies that have been matured for some time. Our starting point is a carefully designed infrastructure, Microsoft Azure, where relevant properties are articulated already in well-motivated design goals. These principles can be captured using a set of high-level *contracts* that are enforced throughout the life-cycle of a deployment. This scenario allows us to take advantage of the properties we know of the data-center architecture to pose queries that are solved using specialized logics and efficient, well-established, reasoning engines. The flip-side is that the contracts we present in this paper do not translate to arbitrary scenarios. The scale and economic significance of Microsoft Azure, however, motivates our specialized solution, and we postulate that many of the techniques we describe here are of general interest. The three sources of cloud contracts for Azure's data-center networks are: (1) network access restrictions, (2) forwarding tables, and (3) Border Gateway Protocol (BGP) policies.

Many contracts can be captured in fragments of first-order logic. In this context, we describe the SecGuru tool that checks cloud contracts in the Microsoft Azure public cloud infrastructure. The tool is based on the Satisfiability Modulo Theories solver Z3 [6]. SecGuru models network configurations using quantifier-free logical formulas over bit-vectors. SecGuru's checking of network access restrictions is a subject of a separate paper. It is described in detail in [8]. We will here recall the highlights of network access restriction checking, and then develop our newer extensions for checking forwarding tables and BGP policies.

Network Verification is an exciting new area for both modern networking and verification technologies. In the broader context, networking is undergoing a revolution thanks to new highly programmable commodity devices for network control, the build out of large scale cloud data-centers and a paradigm shift from network infrastructure as embedded systems into software controlled and defined networking. The latter begs for the attention of techniques developed hitherto for software engineering and CAD disciplines. Many techniques can be adapted in a straight-forward way to modern packet switched networking, but many more problems require new techniques and new ideas. It is also useful to appreciate the differences of the correctness, business and deployment models for networking, hardware and software. Bugs that ship in silicone are in the best case fixed by firmware updates, and worst case by a costly recall; software bugs can be addressed by periodic updates, but is vulnerable to the update distribution process and adaption; cloud networking, in our context, is run as a (web) service and bugs lead to outages and missed service level agreements (SLAs). The dynamics are different: hardware designs are driven by advances in circuitry that enables more complex designs; large software systems have to deal with features, legacy and interoperability; cloud services are constrained by capacity, energy requirements and current complexities are in part due to a heavy churn in new technologies and the challenges of deploying large scale distributed monitoring services. Lessons from the last two decades of static software analysis also include the often referenced obstacles of the *false positives*, or even for *true positives*, the practical obstacles and business impacts of fixing bugs[1]. The class of bugs we address in networking seems to have a somewhat different flavor: each alert that SecGuru raises is directly actionable. The cost of ignoring alerts translates to opening a network to attacks, missed revenue (by breaking SLAs), decreased performance, increased costs, and missing out of a competitive advantage. The advantages of SecGuru are on the other hand, reduced time for building out new data-centers, allowing more sophisticated and hence complex policies, making the service auditable and even using a successful report to save precious time by ruling out miss-configuration as a culprit during live site incidents.

Sections 2, 3 and 4 describe cloud contracts for access control lists, routing tables and BGP policies, respectively. The material in Section 2 is described in more detail in [8]. Section 3 extends the summary from [3] to discuss the impact of checking routing configurations. Section 4 describes select BGP contracts for configurations that we check statically. Contracts for the three configuration sources are now checked on a continuous basis in Microsoft Azure by the SecGuru tool. Section 5 provides background on the SMT solver Z3, reflects on broader opportunities around Network Verification.

2   Access Control Lists

The SecGuru [8] tool has been actively used in our production cloud in the past years for continuous monitoring and validation of Azure. It has also been used for maintaining legacy edge ACLs. In continuous validation, SecGuru checks policies over ACLs on every router update as well as once a day. This is more than 40,000 checks per month, where each check takes 150-600 ms. It uses a database of predefined contracts. For example, there is a policy that says that SSH ports on fabric devices should not be open to guest virtual machines. While these policies themselves rarely change, IP addresses do change frequently, which makes using SecGuru as a regression test useful. SecGuru had a measurable positive impact in prohibiting policy misconfigurations during build-out, raising in average of one alert per day; each identifies 3-5 buggy address ranges in the /20 range, e.g., ~16K faulty addresses. We also used SecGuru to reduce our legacy corporate ACL from roughly 3000 rules to 1000 without any derived outages or business impact.

In more detail, the Azure architecture enforces network access restrictions using ACLs. These are placed on multiple routers and firewalls in data-centers and on the edge between internal networks and the internet. Miss-configurations, such

---

[1] A classical issue in the in context of static tools, such as Prefix and Coverity, e.g., see http://popl.mpi-sws.org/2014/andy.pdf for an insightful discussion.

as miss-configured ACLs, are a dominant source of network outages. SecGuru translates the ACLs into a logical predicate over packet headers that are represented as bit-vectors. These predicates are checked for containment and equivalence with contracts that are represented as other bit-vector formulas. For illustration, representative contracts are of the form:

Cloud Contract 1. *DNS ports on DNS servers are accessible from tenant devices over both TCP and UDP.*

Cloud Contract 2. *The SSH ports on management devices are inaccessible from tenant devices.*

The routers that are dedicated to connect internal networks to the Internet backbone are called Edge routers and they enforce restrictions using ACLs. Figure 1 provides a canonical example of an Edge ACL. The ACL in this example is authored in the Cisco IOS language. It is basically a set of rules that filter IP packets. They inspect header information of the packets and the rules determine whether the packets may pass through the device.

```
1    remark Isolating private addresses
2    deny ip 10.0.0.0/8 any
3    deny ip 172.16.0.0/12 any
4    deny ip 192.0.2.0/24 any
5    ...
6    remark Anti spoofing ACLs
7    deny ip 128.30.0.0/15 any
8    deny ip 171.64.0.0/15 any
9    ...
10   remark permits for IPs without
11          port and protocol blocks
12   permit ip any 171.64.64.0/20
13   ....
14   remark standard port and protocol
15          blocks
16   deny    tcp any any eq 445
17   deny    udp any any eq 445
18   deny    tcp any any eq 593
19   deny    udp any any eq 593
20   ...
21   deny    53 any any
22   deny    55 any any
23   ...
24   remark permits for IPs with
25          port and protocol blocks
26   permit ip any 128.30.0.0/15
27   permit ip any 171.64.0.0/15
28   ...
```

Fig. 1. An Edge Network ACL configuration

Each rule of a policy contains a packet filter, and typically comprises two portions, namely a traffic expression and an action. The traffic expression specifies a range of source and destination IP addresses, ports, and a protocol specifier. The expression 10.0.0.0/8 specifies an address range 10.0.0.0 to 10.255.255.255. That is, the first 8 bits are fixed and the remaining 24 (= 32-8) are varying. A wild card is indicated by *Any*. For ports, *Any* encodes the range from 0 to $2^{16} - 1$. The action is either *Permit* or *Deny*. They indicate whether packets matching the range should be allowed through the firewall. This language has the first-applicable rule semantics, where the device processes an incoming packet per the first rule that matches its description. If no rules match, then the incoming packet is denied by default.

The meaning of network ACLs can be captured in logic as a predicate ACL over variables src, a source address and port, dst, a destination address and port, and other parameters, such as protocol and TCP flags. For our example from Figure 1, we can capture the meaning as the predicate:

$$ACL \equiv$$
$$\textbf{if } src = 10.0.0.0/8 \wedge proto = 6 \textbf{ then } \textit{false } \textbf{else}$$
$$\textbf{if } src = 172.16.0.0/12 \wedge proto = 6 \textbf{ then } \textit{false } \textbf{else}$$
$$\textbf{if } src = 192.0.2.0/24 \wedge proto = 6 \textbf{ then } \textit{false } \textbf{else}$$
$$\cdots$$
$$\textbf{if } dst = 171.64.64.0/20 \wedge proto = 6 \textbf{ then } \textit{true } \textbf{else}$$
$$\cdots$$
$$\textbf{if } proto = 4 \wedge dstport = 445 \textbf{ then } \textit{false } \textbf{else}$$
$$\cdots$$

For ease of readability, we re-use the notation for writing address ranges. In bit-vector logic we would write the constraint $src = 10.0.0.0/8$ as $src[31 : 24] = 10$, e.g., a predicate that specifies the 8 most significant bits should be equal to the numeral 10 (the bit-vector 00000110).

Traffic is permitted by an ACL if the predicate ACL is true. Traffic permitted by one ACL and denied by another is given by $ACL_1 \oplus ACL_2$ (the exclusive or of ACL_1 and ACL_2). The SecGuru tool uses the encoding of ACLs into bit-vector logic and poses differential queries between ACLs to find differences between configurations. It also checks contracts of ACLs by posing queries of the form $ACL \Rightarrow Property$, where an example property is that UDP ports to DNS servers are allowed. The main technological novelty in SecGuru is an enumeration algorithm for compactly representing these differences. Compact representation of differences help network operators understand the full effect of a miss-configuration.

3 Routing Tables

We recently added new capabilities to SecGuru. Most notably, using lessons from our work on the more powerful Network Optimized Datalog engine, we developed techniques for checking reachability properties for routing tables in Azure. Routers in Azure are configured to follow a specific layered data-center architecture that we describe in more detail below. Figure 2 shows a schematic overview of Azure's data-centers are configured. It is a variant of the VL2 architecture [7]. In this architecture, each rack (at the bottom) is a top-of-rack switch that relays packets from the rack to a hierarchy of routers above. The hierarchy provides redundant routes to other racks within the a group called a *cluster* and to other racks belonging to other clusters, and external traffic is routed to and from the internet.

While the architecture is fixed, each data-center is deployed using a different number of machines and clusters. Data-centers grow and shrink when tenants are migrated between machines and assumptions on the topologies change when new technologies are deployed. Thus, there are ample of opportunities for miss-configuring routers in spite of the overall fixed design. It may be entirely possible to miss-configure all but one router in a redundancy group and only observing the mistake when the correctly configured router goes off-line. Our tool checks routers from Azure networks. It catches any such miss-configurations and at the same time provides a certificate when routers are configured correctly. The latter is indispensable for operators when trouble-shooting live site incidents - knowing which parts are healthy saves precious time and resources. SecGuru retrieves a very significant amount of data from routers: Each router has a few thousand rules and each data-center can have between dozen and a few hundred routers. Some 500GB of routing tables are retrieved and checked for contracts on a daily basis.

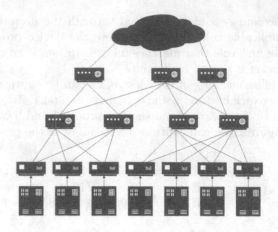

Fig. 2. Schematic overview of data-center routes

Figure 3 shows an excerpt of a routing table from an Arista network switch Similarly to ACLs we can model routing tables as relations *Router* over destination addresses and next-hop ports that can be represented as atomic Boolean predicates. Each rule in the routing table is either provisioned based on static configurations specified in the device, or derived based on BGP network announcements that the device receives.

```
 1    B E    0.0.0.0/0 [200/0] via 100.91.176.0, n1
 2                            via 100.91.176.2, n2
 3
 4    B E    10.91.114.0/25 [200/0] via 100.91.176.125, n3
 5                                 via 100.91.176.127, n4
 6                                 via 100.91.176.129, n5
 7                                 via 100.91.176.131, n6
 8    B E    10.91.114.128/25 [200/0] via 100.91.176.125, n3
 9                                   via 100.91.176.131, n6
10                                   via 100.91.176.133, n7
11    ...
```

Fig. 3. A BGP routing table

We here choose an encoding of *Router*, such that for each destination address dst and next-hop address n:

$$Router[dst \mapsto \text{dst}, \text{n} \mapsto true] \text{ is true}$$
$$\text{iff}$$
$$\text{n is a possible next hop for address dst}$$

The routing tables have an ordered interpretation, wherein rules whose destination prefixes are the longest applies first. The default rule with mask 0.0.0.0/0, listed first, applies if no other rule applies. For our example, our chosen encoding of the predicate *Router* is of the form:

$$Router \equiv$$
$$\textbf{if } \dots$$
$$\textbf{if } dst = 10.91.114.128/25 \textbf{ then } n_3 \vee n_6 \vee n_7 \textbf{ else}$$
$$\textbf{if } dst = 10.91.114.0/25 \textbf{ then } n_3 \vee n_4 \vee n_5 \vee n_6 \textbf{ else}$$
$$n_1 \vee n_2$$

Each Azure data-center is built up around a hierarchy of routers that facilitate high-bandwidth traffic in and out as well as within the data-center. Traffic that leaves and enters the data-center traverses four layers of routers, while traffic within the data-center may traverse only one, two or at most three layers depending on whether the traffic is within a rack, a physical partition called a *cluster*, or be-

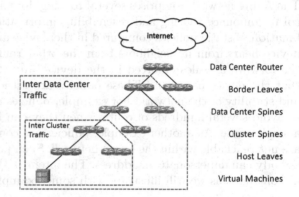

Fig. 4. Hierarchies in Azure.

tween clusters. Figure 4 illustrates the hierarchies employed in Azure. Routers close to the host machines belong to one of the clusters. Traffic in a correctly configured data-center is routed without loops and along the shortest path for cluster-local traffic. Sample (slightly simplified from the ones checked for Azure) contracts are:

Cloud Contract 3. *Traffic from a host leaf directed to a different cluster from the leaf is forwarded to a router in a layer above. In other words, suppose that Router belongs to a cluster given as a predicate Cluster, and that RouterAbove is the set of routers above Router, then*

$$\neg Cluster(dst) \wedge Router(dst) \Rightarrow \bigvee_n RouterAbove(n)$$

On the other hand,

Cloud Contract 4. *Traffic from a host leaf directed to the same cluster is directed to the local VLAN or a router in the layer above that belongs to the same cluster as the host leaf router:*

$$Cluster(dst) \wedge Router(dst) \Rightarrow VLAN(dst) \ \vee \ \bigvee_{n} RouterAbove(n) \wedge Cluster(n)$$

The routing behavior of routers at the same level from the same cluster should also act uniformly for addresses within the cluster (they can behave differently for addresses outside of a cluster range).

Cloud Contract 5. *Let $Router_1, Router_2$ be two routers at the same layer within the cluster Cluster, then*

$$Cluster(dst) \Rightarrow Router_1(dst) \equiv Router_2(dst)$$

4   BGP: Border Gateway Protocol Policies

The Azure network comprises several routing domains, and uses the BGP protocol to announce routing and reachability information between them. The combination of static policies configured in the device and the route information the device hears from its neighbors from the other routing domains determines (1) the forwarding rules enforced in the device, and (2) the BGP announcements that the device can make. These policies are critical to assure the availability and stability of the network. For example, policies are configured in the devices to avoid several hundreds of routes when they can be succinctly summarized as a single route. As another example, policies are configured to reject routes that are not reachable within the origin network. Such policies critical to enforce that nobody can impersonate an address. The intent of these policies can be captured as contracts, as we will illustrate with some examples.

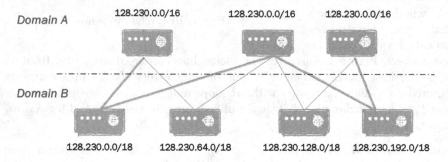

Fig. 5. BGP Aggregate Addresses

Aggregate network statements (ANS) are used to specify a coarse aggregate of address ranges Given a device, aggregate network statements (ANS) are used to specify a that are accessible from the device. Figure 5 provides an example scenario. In this figure, domain A comprises 3 routers, and domain B comprises 4 routers. Each router The addresses reachable from the routers in domain A are a union of all the addresses reachable in domain B. All the four address ranges reachable in domain B, namely 128.230.0.0/18, 128.230.64.0/18, 128.230.128.0/16, and 128.230.192.0/18, can be merged into a single address range, namely 128.230.0.0/16. Thus, we could configure an aggregate network statement in the routers in domain A to announce the combined aggregate 128.230.0.0/16 instead of announcing each of the four address ranges. Other routers receiving the announcements from the routers in domain A thus have to store only one route instead of four, thus saving memory consumption in the device. In real large IP networks such as Azure, the savings from these statements are in the order of several hundreds of rules. The contract for the ANS is that the set of configured tenant addresses that are handled by a given router

Given a device, aggregate network statements (ANS) are used to specify a coarse aggregate of address ranges that are accessible from the device. Figure 5 provides an example scenario. Domain A comprises 3 routers, and domain B comprises 4 routers. The addresses reachable from the routers in domain A are a union of all the addresses reachable in domain B. All the four address ranges reachable in domain B, namely 128.230.0.0/18, 128.230.64.0/18, 128.230.128.0/16, and 128.230.192.0/18, can be merged into a single address range, namely 128.230.0.0/16. Thus, we could configure an aggregate network statement in the routers in domain A to announce the combined aggregate 128.230.0.0/16 instead of announcing each of the four address ranges received from the routers in domain B. Routers receiving the announcements from the routers in domain A thus have to store only one route instead of four, thus saving memory consumption in the device. In large IP networks such as Azure, the savings from these statements are in the order of several hundreds of rules. The contract for the ANS is that the set of configured tenant addresses that are handled by a given router coincides with the configured ANS address ranges. In other words:

Cloud Contract 6. *The set of designated tenant addresses reachable from a router coincides with the address ranges summarized in the BGP aggregate network statements.*

Safety contracts for route announcements are enforced using a construct called route maps. Route maps specify policies for filtering or transforming route annoucements before either redistributing them or incorporating them as forwarding rules. For example, a safety contract for this configuration is that the devices in domain A reject any route announcements for an address range that is not contained in 128.230.0.0/16. In other words:

Cloud Contract 7. *The device rejects any BGP route announcement with an address range that is contained in the complement of tenant addresses reachable from the router.*

5   Z3, SMT, Model Checking and Network Verification

The Satisfiability Modulo Theories [2,5] (SMT) solver Z3 [6], from Microsoft Research, is a core of several advanced program analysis, testing and model-based development tools. Figure 6 highlights the functionality and use of Z3. Z3 determines *satisfiability* of logical formulas. Furthermore, Z3 can provide witnesses for satisfiable formulas. This is useful for analysis tools that rely on components using logic for describing states and transformations between system states[2]. Consequently, they require a logic inference engine for reasoning about the

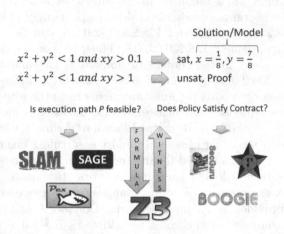

Fig. 6. Symbolic analysis with Z3

state transformations. Z3 is particularly appealing because it combines specialized solvers for domains that are of relevance for computation and it integrates crucial innovations in automated deduction. It is tempting to build custom ad-hoc solvers for each application, but extending and scaling these require a high investment and will inevitably miss advances from automated deduction. New applications introduce new challenges for Z3 and provide inspiration for improving automated deduction techniques. It is not uncommon that when improvements to Z3 are made based on one application, other applications benefit as well.

The source code, as well as nightly builds of Z3 is available online from `http://z3.codeplex.com`. There are several online resources around Z3. An interactive tutorial on using Z3 is available from `http://rise4fun.com/z3/tutorial`.

Z3 has recently been applied in a number of contexts related to *Network Verification*. These contexts require quite different capabilities. The use we described in this paper only relies on the quantifier-free theory of bit-vectors. On the other hand, the Network Optimized Datalog engine that we use in other work [11] requires optimized data-structures to maintain sets of reachable states. Checking firewall configurations is central to securing networks. Several other tools address checking firewall configurations. These include Margrave [14], which provides a convenient formalism for expressing rich properties of networks and firewalls (but

---

[2] Online demonstrations of the tools mentioned in the bottom of Figure 6 are available from `http://rise4fun.com`

counter-examples are only available for one address at a time), and the firewall testing tool in [4], which builds upon Isabelle/HOL and Z3 for generating test-cases. Z3 is also used in a very different twist for verifying compilers for software defined networks [15,1].

More broadly, SAT, QBF (Quantified Boolean Formula) and other SMT solvers are actively purused for network data plane verification [18,12]. It is beneficial to use specialized data-structures for analyzing IP networks, and this is explored in [10,9,17]. Model checkers are also currently being developed for verifying controller code for software defined networks [16,13].

6   Conclusion

We developed *Cloud Contracts* to capture main architectural constraints in Microsoft Azure. The SecGuru tool is used to check these contracts on a continuous basis. By handling ACLs, routing tables and BGP policies, we covered the main sources of how IP networking is managed in Azure. It provides indispesible value for both more rapidly building out correctly configured data-centers, during the life-cycle of data-centers, as part of certifying isolation boundaries in data-centers and for analyzing live site incidents. SecGuru leverages the SMT solver Z3 for checking cloud contracts. Many software analysis, testing and verification tools already rely on Z3 and other SMT solvers to handle logical queries. The experience with SecGuru illustrates that the domain of engineering modern networks is a fresh new area where many problems can be reduced to logical queries and solved using advanced software engineering tools.

Acknowledgment. We would like to express our gratitude to George Varghese and Charlie Kaufman for numerous interactions that have shaped this work. Our perspective on directions in current networking is influenced by conversations with Nick McKeown. Our experiences with network verification is based on joint work with several collaborators, including: Mooly Sagiv, Geoff Outhred, Nuno Lopes, Mingchen Zhao, Jeff Jensen, Monika Machado, Garvit Juniwal, Ratul Mahajan, Ari Fogel, Jim Larus, Thomas Ball, Aaron Gember, Shachar Itzhaky, Aleksandr Karbyshev, Michael Schapira and Asaf Valadarsky.

References

1. Ball, T., Bjørner, N., Gember, A., Itzhaky, S., Karbyshev, A., Sagiv, M., Schapira, M., Valadarsky, A.: VeriCon: towards verifying controller programs in software-defined networks. In: O'Boyle, M.F.P., Pingali, K. (eds.) PLDI, p. 31. ACM (2014)
2. Barrett, C.W., Sebastiani, R., Seshia, S.A., Tinelli, C.: Satisfiability Modulo Theories. In: Biere, A., Heule, M., van Maaren, H., Walsh, T. (eds.) Handbook of Satisfiability. Frontiers in Artificial Intelligence and Applications, vol. 185, pp. 825–885. IOS Press (2009)
3. Bjørner, N., Jayaraman, K.: Network Verification: Calculus and Solvers. In: SDN and FSI: The Next Generation Networking Infrastructure (2014)

4. Brucker, A.D., Brügger, L., Wolff, B.: HOL-TESTGEN/FW. In: Liu, Z., Woodcock, J., Zhu, H. (eds.) ICTAC 2013. LNCS, vol. 8049, pp. 112–121. Springer, Heidelberg (2013)
5. de Moura, L., Bjørner, N.: Satisfiability Modulo Theories: Introduction & Applications. Comm. ACM (2011)
6. de Moura, L., Bjørner, N.S.: Z3: An Efficient SMT Solver. In: Ramakrishnan, C.R., Rehof, J. (eds.) TACAS 2008. LNCS, vol. 4963, pp. 337–340. Springer, Heidelberg (2008)
7. Greenberg, A.G., Hamilton, J.R., Jain, N., Kandula, S., Kim, C., Lahiri, P., Maltz, D.A., Patel, P., Sengupta, S.: VL2: a scalable and flexible data center network. Commun. ACM 54(3), 95–104 (2011)
8. Jayaraman, K., Bjørner, N., Outhred, G., Kaufman, C.: Automated analysis and debugging of network connectivity policies. Technical Report MSR-TR-2014-102, Microsoft Research (July 2014)
9. Kazemian, P., Varghese, G., McKeown, N.: Header space analysis: static checking for networks. In: NSDI (2012)
10. Khurshid, A., Zhou, W., Caesar, M., Brighten Godfrey, P.: Veriflow: Verifying Network-wide Invariants in Real Time. SIGCOMM Comput. Commun. Rev., 467–472 (September 2012)
11. Lopes, N., Bjørner, N., Godefroid, P., Jayaraman, K., Varghese, G.: Dna pairing: Using differential network analysis to find reachability bugs. Technical Report MSR-TR-2014-58, Microsoft Research (April 2014)
12. Mai, H., Khurshid, A., Agarwal, R., Caesar, M., Godfrey, P.B., King, S.T.: Debugging the Data Plane with Anteater. In: Proceedings of the ACM SIGCOMM 2011 Conference, SIGCOMM 2011. ACM, New York (2011)
13. Majumdar, R., Tetali, S.D., Wang, Z.: Kuai: A model checker for software-defined networks. In: FMCAD (2014)
14. Nelson, T., Barratt, C., Dougherty, D.J., Fisler, K., Krishnamurthi, S.: The Margrave tool for firewall analysis. In: LISA, pp. 1–8. USENIX Association, Berkeley (2010)
15. Roy, S., Kot, L., Foster, N., Gehrke, J., Hojjat, H., Koch, C.: Writes that fall in the forest and make no sound: Semantics-based adaptive data consistency. CoRR, abs/1403.2307 (2014)
16. Sethi, D., Narayana, S., Malik, S.: Abstractions for model checking SDN controllers. In: Formal Methods in Computer-Aided Design, FMCAD 2013, Portland, OR, USA, October 20-23, pp. 145–148. IEEE (2013)
17. Yang, H., Lam, S.S.: Real-time verification of network properties using atomic predicates. In: 2013 21st IEEE International Conference on Network Protocols, ICNP 2013, Göttingen, Germany, October 7-10, pp. 1–11. IEEE (2013)
18. Zhang, S., Malik, S.: SAT Based Verification of Network Data Planes. In: Van Hung, D., Ogawa, M. (eds.) ATVA 2013. LNCS, vol. 8172, pp. 496–505. Springer, Heidelberg (2013)

Privacy and Security Challenges in Internet of Things

Manik Lal Das

DA-IICT, Gandhinagar, India
maniklal_das@daiict.ac.in

Abstract. Internet of Things (IoT) envisions as a global network, connecting any objects around us, ranging from home appliances, wearable things to military applications. With IoT infrastructure, physical objects such as wearable objects, television, refrigerator, smart phones, supply-chain items and any objects across the globe would get connected using the Internet. Sensing, radio waves, mobile technology, embedded systems and Internet technology are promising actors which play significant roles in IoT infrastructure. Security and privacy issues in IoT scenarios would be much more challenging than what is been used in the conventional wireless scenarios. In particular, the constrained environments require lightweight primitives, secure design and effective integration into other environments in order to see IoT in its desired shape. In this paper, we discuss security and privacy challenges in IoT scenarios and applications with special emphasis on resource-constrained environments' security objectives and privacy requirement. We provide different perspectives of IoT, discuss about important driving forces of IoT, and propose a generic construction of secure protocol suitable for constrained environments with respect to IoT scenarios and applications.

Keywords: Internet of Things, Sensor networks, RFID system, Mobile communications, Security, Privacy.

1 Introduction

The term *Internet of Things* was introduce by the Auto-ID Center in 1999 [1]. After a decade, in 2009, European Commission action plan envisioned "Internet of Things" as a general evolution of the Internet *from a network of interconnected entities (e.g., PC-based LAN, Personal Digital Assistance) to a network of interconnected objects (e.g., household items, consumer electronics)* [2]. With Internet of Things (IoT) infrastructure it is aimed that the Web of world would get connected to all physical objects across the globe, ranging from home appliances, consumer electronics to chemical reactors, military equipments and so on. While connecting these objects (a.k.a. *things*) the Internet would act as the main communication backbone, supported by Bluetooth, Radio waves, Near Field Communication (NFC) as other communication mediums to connect each and every object around us [3]. Embedding technologies such as RFID

R. Natarajan et al. (Eds.): ICDCIT 2015, LNCS 8956, pp. 33–48, 2015.

(Radio Frequency Identification) tags, sensing devices, smart phones are de-facto driving forces in IoT infrastructure along with the conventional PC-based computing environments. Roughly, IoT is an integration of several complementary technological advancements aiming at bridging the gap between the Web of world and the physical world. For example, assume that smart refrigerator is sensor (and reader) enabled, where items inside the refrigerator are RFID tag-enabled. The refrigerator (or items inside it) can be monitored from office or from a shopping complex with the help of a handheld devices (e.g. smart phone). One could also monitor (and control) the status of air conditioning machines at home, door safety, vehicles, and so on, remotely through these resource-constrained systems. Smart energy, intelligent communications, machine-to-machine collaboration, smart home, all these can be realized through IoT infrastructure. Naturally, sensor networks, RFID systems and mobile communications found huge applications in IoT infrastructure. A typical view of IoT scenarios and applications is shown in Figure 1.

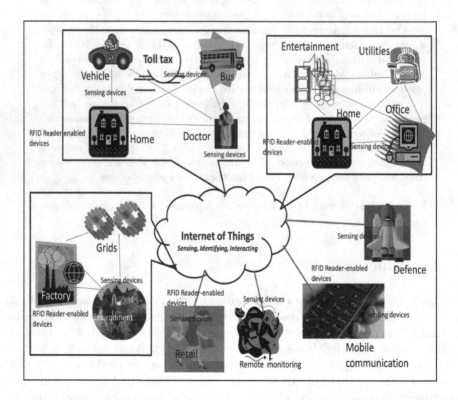

Fig. 1. *Internet of Things* Scenarios and Applications [4]

Wireless Sensor Networks (WSN) [5] has found enormous applications due to its ubiquitous nature, easy deployment and the range of applications they enable.

Networks of thousands tiny sensing devices which have low processing power, limited memory and energy, provide an economical solution to some challenging problems such as military surveillance, real-time traffic monitoring, building safety, wildlife monitoring, measurement of seismic activity and healthcare applications. In the context of IoT, WSN should not be limited with a single or homogeneous application, instead, WSN will act as clusters to manage heterogeneous applications.

RFID system seems to occupy significant places in IoT infrastructure. With RFID tags millions of tiny objects (e.g., books, consumable items, supply chains) would get connected to readers, and then through reader it can connect to Web of world. Typically, an RFID system consists of a set of tags, readers and a back-end server. In IoT scenarios, RFID-enabled things require to talk to other things such as sensors, mobile devices and embedded systems through RFID reader-enabled capability (assume that other devices are also RFID reader-enabled).

The advances of mobile technology (e.g. 4G, 5G) with apps world have made Web of world smart enough to extend its reach to more and more physical objects. Nowadays, mobile technology is used not only for voice communications or text messaging but also mobile phone equipped with available resources acts as a resourceful computing-communicating device for secure billing, trading, content up/downloading and so on. Furthermore, mobile technology helps in connecting sensing/tags-enabled things much easier than the conventional Internet based client-server model.

Other embedding systems, systems-on-chip, and Robotics technology can also contribute enormously in IoT applications. Constrained Application Protocol (CoAP) [6] is a timely designed web transfer protocol for use of these constrained environments. CoAP is an application layer protocol that translates to HTTP for integration with the existing Web while meeting specialized requirements such as multicast support, very low overhead and simplicity for constrained networks (e.g., 6LoWPAN [7]). It is prudent that these constrained environments require need-based security and privacy services to resist potential attackers from controlling their applications. We note that the security requirement varies from application to application. The security primitives used in constrained environment should not consume expensive computational and communication cost. In addition, the integration of these constrained devices along with conventional computing model requires strong security and privacy support in IoT scenarios and applications.

Our Contributions. In this paper, we discuss the security and privacy issues of IoT scenarios and applications. The discussion takes us through the different perspectives of IoT, security and privacy requirements, and important actors of constrained environments in IoT infrastructure. We present a generic construction of secure protocol suitable for constrained environments in the context of IoT. The security goals of the protocol are mutual authentication, key establishment, data confidentiality under the shared key and identity protection. We show how the proposed construction can preserve privacy of the sender and intended security services under an adaptive adversarial model.

Organization of the Paper. The remainder of the paper is organized as follows. Section 2 provides some preliminaries. Section 3 discusses about important actors of IoT. Section 4 presents our generic construction of protocol suitable for constrained environment with respect to IoT scenarios and applications. Section 5 gives the adversarial model. We conclude the paper in Section 6.

2   Preliminaries

2.1   Perspectives of Internet of Things

Technological perspectives. In all terms such as hardware, software, middleware and communication channels, IoT requires context-based technological advancement, keeping consumers' convenience as the primary concern. This leads to a number of issues such as upgrading, migrating, compliance and/or deleting existing technology appropriately and integrating new technology wherever needed, without affecting much impact on service provider and service consumer, based on application requirement. Security, privacy, trust relationship, ownership of data as well as service for Cloud computing, machine-to-machine computing, all these are important concerns that open up significant challenges and opportunities to manufacturers, developers, service providers and service consumers. Embedded devices, handheld devices, RFID tags-readers, smart tokens, sensors, robotics, service-on-chip, nanotechnology and near filed connectivity technologies are to have rapid change in technological advancement. As a result, realization of IoT can be seen as a paradigm shift in all sectors of technological front, which makes significant changes in organizational and societal progress.

Business perspectives. IoT has a wider spectrum of business goal than what Internet-based applications can support these days while writing the paper. Tremendous potential for electronic business has already been arrived, and that is going to scaled up in multiple folds in IoT scenarios. Different countries' strategic drivers require to discuss with standardized forums (e.g., IEEE, ISO/IEC, IETF, SWIFT, ITU) in order to formulate an acceptable business policy that would be applicable to IoT infrastructure. The factors that could work for adopting IoT in industry are Standards, specification, compliance, interoperability, integration, security, privacy, trusts, and ownership. Roughly, the maximum beneficiary of IoT infrastructure is industry itself. Therefore, consumers' privacy, application providers' data protection, service providers' business interest, countries' Information Technology Act compliance, export-import laws are some crucial concerns that need to be addressed globally by research and scientific communities in consultation with Governments and industries.

Economic perspectives. The economic perspectives of IoT offer two kinds of incentives - one to consumers and other to suppliers. On one hand, consumers will directly benefit from IoT infrastructure in terms of optimal time management (e.g. connecting home appliances to office premises), greater flexibility (e.g. anytime-anywhere service), effective security (e.g. door/vehicle-lock/unlock alarm to mobile handset carrying by a person), and increasing revenue (e.g. smart energy, smart transport, smart shopping). On the other hand, suppliers will benefit by generating revenues in terms of smart services, smart devices and smart technology to assess vulnerabilities and solving them for consumers satisfaction. Small scale service providers can use third party infrastructure for resource sharing/pooling, and large scale providers can make best use of small industries' services.

Human perspectives. Intellectual property, technologies, and information on core processes reside in human minds can be used in IoT in a controlled way depending upon consumers and suppliers requirement. With IoT, things around us could distribute risks far more widely than conventional Internet-based computing environment. Security and privacy of objects could pose a serious threat to some application, and manufacturers could act a single source and/or a single point of failure for mission-critical application. Trust deficiency, inter-dependency and (in)competitive advantage among stake holders of business processes will consume more than expected efforts for IoT to take its desired shape in our modern society. Perhaps, to the best of author's knowledge, this is one of the main reasons why till date individuals, organizations, and Governments are unprepared (or under prepared) for adopting IoT as a global network connecting each and every object across the globe.

In order to provide intended supports towards these perspectives, IoT infrastructure requires to address some of the major challenges [8], [4] as follows.

- Standards: Standards and specifications by international forums are the foremost requirements in order to see IoT in its desired shape. Although European communities have been investing significant efforts for making IoT mission successful, a collective effort by IEEE, NIST, ITU, ISO/IEC, IETF, SWIFT and other standardized body could probably make this mission faster, effective, and implementable
- Identity management: In order to integrate trillions objects in IoT infrastructure, managing identities of objects is a major task in IoT. Both addressing and uniqueness issues have to be addressed suitably. Some existing technologies, such as smart cards, RFID tags [9], IPv6 are going to play important roles for identifying (and addressing) objects in IoT infrastructure.
- Privacy: One of the major challenges in global acceptance of IoT is the privacy of objects, where the privacy issue involves object privacy, location privacy, and human privacy.
- Security: In IoT, the primary means of communication channel is the Internet. Therefore, IoT applications must be safeguarded from both passive and active attackers. In addition to Internet security, IoT infrastructure should provide Intranet security, data security, software security, hardware security, and physical security.
- Trust and Ownership: IoT infrastructure enables communication among various hosts, intermediate systems and end-entity devices. Therefore, trust at device level as well as at protocol level is a key factor in IoT. At the same time, data ownership is an important concern when one system relies on other in order to serve some designated task.

- Integration: One of the main hurdles of IoT infrastructure is the integration of heterogeneous technologies and devices that linked to the Web of world and the physical world. The factors that need to be resolved at integration stage are computation, bandwidth, storage, interoperability and security.
- Scalability: IoT has a wider spectrum than the conventional Internet of computers. Therefore, basic functionalities such as communication and service discovery along with upgrading/migrating/revoking services to function efficiently in both small scale and large scale environments.
- Regulation: In order to have IoT a reality, regulatory issues are key implementation issues for application and software that use public and/or proprietary technology. Every country has its own Information Technology Act and one can enforce certain regulatory norms before allowing a party to implement some application that has larger interest to its citizens. Roughly speaking, this is perhaps the most crucial concern in many countries in order to agree or disagree on IoT's adoption for future Internet applications.

2.2   Security and Privacy Challenges in Constrained System

Embedded devices are increasingly integrated into personal and commercial infrastructures, ranging from home applications to spacecraft applications. When these embedded devices communicate over-the-air, security and privacy issues of entities as well as data are challenging tasks for protecting application from malicious intention. Furthermore, the design criteria of security for embedded systems differs from traditional security design, because these systems are resource-constrained in their capacities and easily accessible to adversaries. When two entities send or receive information using public channels, attackers can eavesdrop/replay/alter messages between communicating entities. Based on application requirement security services such as data confidentiality, integrity, authentication and availability can be enabled in it, but, we note that, the requirement varies from application to application. Data confidentiality protects sensitive information from unauthorized entities. Data integrity ensures that the information has not been altered illegitimately. Entity authentication assures that the information is sent and received by legitimate entities. Another important security property is the availability of intended services. Applications' unresponsive behaviour for just few seconds could be a potential threat to a patient's life in medical application, a disaster to mission critical applications, and also not customer centric for conventional applications. In order to resist potential attacker to deny legitimate customer from applications' services, application must be enabled with appropriate intrusion detection and prevention mechanism.

Embedded devices are small and thus, can be attached to consumer goods, library books, home appliances for identification and tracking purposes. In case of any misuse (e.g. stolen device-enabled items), the terminal can trigger an appropriate message to seller/vendor/owner of the item. The privacy issue could link to object or location. In addition, human privacy may be a concern in embedded system. On one hand, person who carries embedded device could be tracked, on the other hand, devices' could allow tracing device-enabled objects or person in a controlled way, which could save money, national assets and human lives. We note that the constrained systems should consider suitable primitives (preferably, lightweight primitive), clear design criteria of protocol and implementation aspects with reasonable adversarial assumptions.

2.3 Elliptic Curves Arithmetic

An elliptic curve E over a field F is a cubic curve [10] with no repeated roots. The set $E(F)$ contains all points $P(x, y)$ on the curve, such that x, y are elements of F along with an additional point called the *point at infinity*($\mathcal{O}$). The set $E(F)$ forms an Abelian group under elliptic curve point addition operation with $\mathcal{O}$ as the additive identity. For all $P, Q \in E(F)$, let F_q be a finite field with order prime q. The number of points in the elliptic curve group $E(F_q)$, represented by $\#E(F_q)$, is called the *order of the curve* E over F_q. The order of a point $P \in E(F_q)$ is the smallest positive integer r, such that $rP = \mathcal{O}$. Without loss of generality, the elliptic curve equation can be simplified as $y^2 = x^3 + ax + b$ (mod q), where $a, b \in F_q$ satisfy $4a^3 + 27b^2 \neq 0$, if the characteristic of F_q is neither 2 nor 3. There are two main operations on elliptic curves, point addition and scalar multiplication of point.

Point Addition. The line joining of points P, Q intersects the curve at another point R. This is an interesting feature of elliptic curve and one has to choose a suitable elliptic curve to obtain an elliptic curve group of order sufficiently large to accommodate cryptographic keys.

Scalar Multiplication of a Point. For a scalar n, multiplication of a curve point P by n is defined as n-fold addition of P, i.e., $nP = P + P + \cdots + P$ (n-times). There are fast algorithms [10] for computation of scalar multiplication of point on elliptic curves.

Complexity Assumptions. *Elliptic Curve Discrete Logarithm Problem (ECDLP).* Elliptic Curve Discrete Logarithm Problem (ECDLP) is a standard assumption in which elliptic curve based cryptographic algorithm can rely upon. The ECDLP is stated as: given two elliptic curves points P and $Q(= xP)$, finding scalar x is an intractable problem with best known algorithms and available computational resources.

Decisional Diffie-Hellman (DDH) assumption: Let P be a generator of $E(F_q)$. Let $x, y, z \in_R Z_q$ and $A = xP$, $B = yP$. The DDH assumption states that: the distribution $< A, B, C(= xyP) >$ and $< A, B, C(= zP) >$ is computationally indistinguishable.

Computational Diffie-Hellman (CDH) assumption: Let P be a generator of $E(F_q)$. Let $x, y \in_R Z_q$ and $A = xP$, $B = yP$. The CDH assumption states that: given $< P, A, B >$, it is computationally intractable to compute the value xyP.

3   Driving Forces of Internet of Things

IoT infrastructure requires to facilitate seamless data collection/update between objects with the help of Internet. Sensor networks, RFID system, Smart phone domain, and other embedded systems would have a strong hold in IoT infrastructure, where conventional PC-based LAN/WLAN paradigm remains pivotal functional body that may control other environments suitably.

3.1   Wireless Sensor Networks

In IoT infrastructure, wireless sensor networks (WSN) require interaction with RFID system, handheld devices, and other constrained devices including conventional PC-based LAN setup to reaching out both static and movable objects. WSN consists of several tiny sensing devices and one or more base stations who collect data from sensors as per application's goal. Furthermore, depending on applications' goals, the network adopt cluster-based architecture, where each cluster head is equipped with more resources than sensor nodes deployed in it. Irrespective of cluster-based or non-cluster based architecture, most of the WSN applications require authentication and integrity of data exchanged between sensor nodes and base station. Moreover, some applications (e.g. healthcare) require data confidentiality, privacy preserving, and availability of data in addition to authentication and integrity.

3.2   RFID System

RFID system has found enormous applications in retail, supply-chain, health care, transport, and home appliances. An RFID system consists of a set of tags, readers and a back-end server. A tag is basically a microchip with limited memory along with a transponder. Every tag has a unique identity, which is used for its identification purpose. A reader is a device used to interrogate RFID tags. The reader also consists of one or more transceivers which emit radio waves by which passive tags respond back to the reader. The back-end server is assumed to be a trusted server that maintains tags and readers information in its database. In the context of IoT, RFID-enabled things require to talk to other things such as sensors, mobile devices and embedded systems through RFID reader-enabled capability.

3.3   Mobile System

Mobile technologies (e.g. 3G, 4G) have revolutionized the computing and communicating world. Mobile phones along with Internet have virtually substituted the need of desktop PC in wired or wireless environment. Smart phones equipped with multi-core processors support services such as emailing, trading, video conferencing, social networking and so on. Mobile communication system consists of Mobile station, Base station subsystem and Network subsystem. The network subsystem is governed by other entities like AuC (authentication centre), EIR (equipment identification register), HLR (home location register) and VLR (visiting location register). The security part of mobile communication is primarily controlled by the network subsystem with the help of these entities. Furthermore, it has been seen that the security algorithm used mobile communication in some cases are proprietary, not available for public scrutiny. In the context of IoT, mobile technology is going to act as an important contact point to other resource-constrained systems (e.g., RFID system, WSN). Therefore, standard and uniform security specification and interoperable standards among heterogenous technologies/devices are an imperative demand in industry for protecting applications from potential adversaries.

3.4 Connectivity Technology

The success factor of IoT primarily relies on the power of Internet technology. Internet technology supports unique addressing for computers on a network. The addressing field is of 128-bit length while using IPv6. In other words, Internet technology has enough space to connect trillions objects by uniquely assigned IP addresses. Internet along with near filed communication (NFC) such as bluetooth, radio waves, infrared can reach out each and every object around us. In addition,low-power wireless mesh networking standard like ZigBee [11] along with IEEE 802.15.4 MAC can connect tiny sensors embedded in low-cost devices. The 6LoWPAN (IPv6 over Low-power Wireless Personal Area Networks) [7] can also run on physical layers and allows for seamless integration with other IP-based systems. Importantly, 6LoWPAN offers interoperability with other wireless 802.15.4 devices as well as with devices on any other IP network link (e.g., Ethernet, WiFi). In summary, these connectivity technologies are adequate in communication strength to connect all objects across the globe. The Figure 2 tries to capture the important actors of IoT infrastructure.

3.5 CoAP-Constrained Application Protocol

Constrained Application Protocol (CoAP) [6] is a recently devised web transfer protocol for use of constrained nodes (e.g., low-power sensors, switches, or valves) in constrained (e.g., low-power, lossy) networks. CoAP translates to HTTP for integration with the existing Web while meeting specialized requirements such as multicast support, very low overhead and simplicity for constrained environments, and machine-to-machine applications. Using CoAP, entities can provide services over any IP network using UDP. Any HTTP client or server can interoperate with CoAP enabled entities by installing a translation proxy between the communicating devices. As a result, CoAP with tiny embedded device has huge potential to integrate other constrained environments with IoT by using Internet. In the context of security, the CoAP supports flexible security services such as no key, symmetric key and public key based DTLS [12], which could provide need-based security layers based on application requirement.

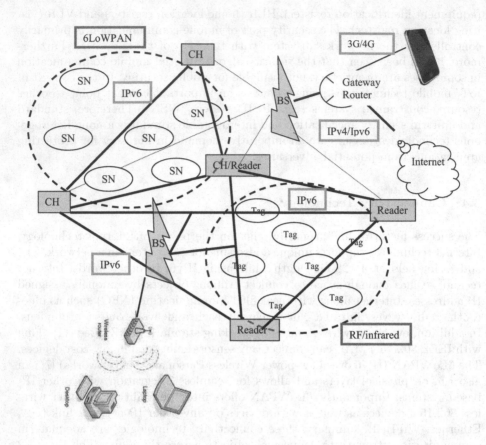

Fig. 2. Constrained environments for IoT Infrastructure

4   Secure Protocol for IoT Applications

A protocol should have precise goal, assumption and clear design principle. The construction that we consider for modelling the proposed protocol has following objectives.

Goals. The protocol aims to provide entity authentication, authenticated key establishment and data confidentiality with a shared key established during the current run of the protocol. The protocol can also support effective privacy of protocol initiator (sender of the proposed protocol).

Assumptions. We consider an adaptive adversary who can gather any number of message exchange between sender and receiver, and add/delete message components. The adversary can also compromise any sender to impersonate a target sender or receiver. We assume that the secret(s) stored in the sending/receiving devices is not know to the adversary. The protocol resists replay, impersonation, and linkability under standard complexity assumption.

Design Choice. The protocol requires to use public key primitives for strong authentication, key exchange and privacy preserving properties. Based on application requirement, the other properties like anonymity, unlinkability, non-repudiation can be required services. However, we consider primarily the former set of security properties. We use elliptic curve cryptography [10] because of its small key size and other interesting features. Furthermore, standard symmetric key cryptography and pseudo-random function are to be used for data confidentiality and authentication codes generation.

We consider the architecture depicted in Figure 3 for modelling our protocol. The protocol provides a generic sender-receiver communication structure that can be implemented between two communicating entities such as tag–reader in RFID system, sensor node–base station in WSN, mobile phone–base station in mobile scenario and so on. The communication between receiver and proxy server (or between proxy to proxy server) could rely on some standard protocol (e.g. TLS [13]) where certificate-based proxy delegation, revocation and other required security services be enabled in the protocol based on application requirement.

4.1   Generic Construction

The protocol consists of two principal participants - *sender* and *receiver*. The sender could be sensor, mobile station, or tag; and receiver could be cluster head, base station, or reader. The protocol has four phases - system initialization, pre-deployment, authenticated key establishment, and data confidentiality.

System Initialization. The system may consist of many senders and receivers. For the sake of simplicity, we consider the system with many senders and one receiver. The receiver acts as the server's agent (e.g., proxy server) or the server itself.

The setup server chooses a suitable elliptic curve $E(F_q)$ over a finite field F_q where q is a prime number sufficiently large enough to accommodate cryptographic keys. Let $P \in E(F_q)$ be the generator of $E(F_q)$. The parameters $E(F_q)$, q and P are made public. We refer interested readers to [10] for more on elliptic curves arithmetic and properties.

Pre-deployment Phase. All senders and the receiver of the system require to register into the system before deployment. The registration process follows a a secure mechanism by which sending and receiving devices are being personalized with intended security parameters. We assume that a trusted setup server does the personalization process of sender and receiver during their registration.

Sender personalization: The setup server personalizes the sender with a private key $x \in_R Z_q^*$. The corresponding public key X $(=xP)$ is stored in the sender's memory. In addition, the public parameters $E(F_q)$, q and P are also stored in the sender's memory.

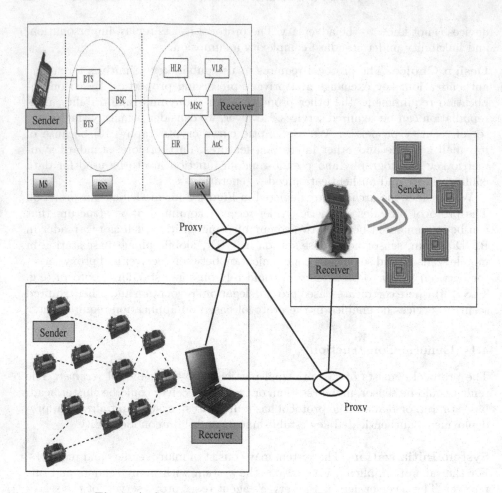

Fig. 3. Architecture considered for modelling the protocol

Receiver personalization: Like sender personalization the setup server personalizes a receiver with a private key $y \in_R Z_q^*$. The corresponding public key Y ($=yP$) is stored in receiver's memory. The receiver's memory has to be personalized with the public parameters $E(F_q)$, q and P.

We note that X and Y provide identity information of the sender and the receiver, respectively. Furthermore, a sender is also personalized with receiver's public key Y and the receiver is personalized with all senders public keys Xs. It is also noted that the personalization phase is executed for sender/receiver only once before its deployment into the system.

Authentication, Key Establishment, and Data Confidentiality. This phase is invoked as and when sender wants to communicate with receiver. By successful execution of this phase both sender and receiver mutually authenticate each other. They also establish a shared secret key followed by traffic confidentiality under the shared key. The phase works as follows:

1. Sender selects a random number $n_s \in_R Z_q$, and computes $N_s = n_s P$, $chl = \mathcal{F}(X, n_s, Y)$. The sender sends $< N_s, chl >$ to the receiver.
2. Upon receiving $< N_s, chl >$, the receiver first retrieves X from chl [1]. Then, the receiver checks whether X is a registered entity. If not, the receiver terminates the operation; else, the receiver selects a random $n_r \in_R Z_q$ and computes

$$N_r = n_r P$$
$$res = \mathcal{F}(Y, n_r, X)$$
$$k_r = \mathcal{G}(N_s, y, n_r, X)$$
$$c_r = \mathcal{H}(X\|Y\|k_r\|N_s\|N_r)$$

The receiver sends $< N_r, res, c_r >$ to the sender as a response to sender's challenge chl. Here, $\mathcal{F}$, $\mathcal{G}$, and $\mathcal{H}$ are suitable operations/functions (e.g., elliptic curve arithmetic, pseudo-random function).

3. Upon receiving $< N_r, res, c_r >$, the sender retrieves Y from res. If Y is not found in sender's memory, the sender discards the message. If Y is found, the sender computes

$$k_s = \mathcal{G}(N_r, x, n_s, Y)$$
$$c'_r = \mathcal{H}(X\|Y\|k_s\|N_s\|N_r)$$

then checks whether $c'_r = c_r$. If it holds, then the receiver's authentication is confirmed. Now, the sender computes $confirm = \mathcal{H}(k_s\|$ all previous messages$)$ and sends $confirm$ to the receiver.

4. Receiver checks whether $confirm = \mathcal{H}(k_r\|$ all previous messages except the last one$)$. If it holds, then the sender's authentication is confirmed.

4.2 Security and Privacy Claim

We show how the above construction achieves intended security and privacy goals.

Mutual Authentication. In step 2, the receiver confirms the sender's participation by checking X's presence in its memory, and sender's authentication is confirmed with step 4. In step 3, the sender confirms the receiver's authentication. In step 4, the key confirmation is achieved. It is noted that the authentication of sender and receiver is achieved with a standard message authentication code (i.e., with the pseudo-random function $\mathcal{H}$ and secret parameters).

Key Establishment. After successful run of the protocol, both sender and receiver have established a transient key k_s (resp. k_r). Using this transient key they can derive a shared key $SK = \mathcal{H}(X\|k_{s/r}\|Y)$. The shared key SK has input

---

[1] This requires some additional parameter be communicated along with chl; however, one can use any alternative ways to do this part. We refer readers to [4] for a ready reference.

of the private key, the public key and the transient secrets. Once the session is expired, the transient secrets n_s and n_r get erased from the respective local state of the sender and receiver. This would also enable the protocol in achieving *forward secrecy*, a useful security property required for many applications.

Data Confidentiality. Depending on the nature of applications where resource-constrained devices are being deployed, the sender-receiver communication may require protection from unauthorized access. The sender and receiver can generate their write key $E_s = \mathcal{H}(X\|SK\|SID\|'sender')$ and $E_r = \mathcal{H}(Y\|SK\|SID\|'receiver')$, respectively. Note that the parameter SID is the session identifier. Now, the sender (*resp.*, receiver) can use E_s (*resp.*, E_r) for encrypting data, and thereby, communicating over a secure channel.

Identity Protection. In the proposed construction, the messages exchange between sender and receiver do not leak any identification of sender and receiver. This guarantees the protection of the identities of the communicating parties. This would help in preserving privacy of sender (and also receiver), which is an important feature of many emerging applications.

5   Security Analysis

Adversarial model. An adaptive adversary is considered who can intercept messages between sender and receiver, and can replay, manipulate the message by adding or deleting data in it. The adversary is allowed to run following queries:

- `initialize virtual sender`. on input a sender identity, this oracle personalizes a virtual sender with x^v, X^v, Y as secret parameters and stores other public parameters in its memory. Then, it returns the personalized device to the adversary. Note that the adversary can know the reader's public key with this query, so reader's privacy is not aimed in this case; otherwise, the adversary should not have reader's public key Y. The system may also consider the sending device is tamper resistant, so the stored parameters can not be extracted from its memory. But, this costs more to the applications like RFID and WSN, where number of tags and sensors are large, and therefore, having device tamper-proof is not a practical solution. We assume that by running the `initialize virtual sender` query, the adversary has knowledge of Y. In other words, the privacy of the receiver is not aimed at this adversarial model.
- `response query`. on input $< N_s^v, chl^v >$ with respect to the adversary's controlled device, this oracle returns the tuple $< N_r^v, res_r^v, c_r^v >$ to the adversary if X^v is in receiver's database. If X^v is not found in the receiver's database, it returns $\perp$.
- `auth query`. on input $< confirm^v >$, this oracle returns a bit indicating whether or not the receiver accepts the session of the protocol run that resulted in successful authentication of the sender. If the bit value is 1 then

the receiver has established a session with the sender, whereas, bit value 0 indicates unauthorized attempt and no session has been established with the sender.

- **corrupt query**. on input target device, this query returns x_{target} and Y to the adversary.

5.1 Security experiment

In this experiment, the adversary's goal is to convince the receiver to accept an unauthorized sender. In order to convince the receiver, the adversary requires to compute a valid chl and $confirm$ on a target sender, where the target sender has not participated in above queries.

Claim 1. *The proposed construction of the protocol is secure as no polynomial time adversary can establish a session with the receiver with non-negligible advantage in the security parameter used in the initialization phase under standard complexity assumptions.*

The above claim can be proved by the security proof sketch used in [4], [14].

5.2 Privacy experiment

The goal of the adversary in this experiment is to distinguish between two different participating senders. Let us assume that the experiment consists of a challenger C and an adversary A. The experiment is defined as follows.

$\mathrm{Exp}^b_{S,A}(k)$:

1. $b \in_R \{0, 1\}$
2. Setup Receiver(1^k), where k is the security parameter
3. $g \leftarrow A^{\mathtt{Queries}}(adversarial\ capability)$
4. Check whether $g = b$

The challenger C presents to A the system where either S_i (if $b = 0$) or S_j (if $b = 1$) is selected when returning a **response** query.

The adversary A is allowed to query the above mentioned oracles any number of times and then outputs a guess bit g. We say that A breaks the privacy of the protocol if and only if $g = b$, that is, if it correctly identifies which of the sender was in participation. The advantage of the adversary is defined as $\mathrm{Adv}_A(k) = \mathrm{Pr} [\ \mathrm{Exp}^0_{S,A}(k) = 1\ ] + \mathrm{Pr} [\ \mathrm{Exp}^1_{S,A}(k) = 1] - 1$

Claim 2. *The proposed construction of the protocol preserves privacy of senders as any polynomial time adversary can have advantage in guessing a sender participation negligible (not more than a random guessing) in security parameter k under standard assumptions.*

The above claim can be proved by the security proof sketch provided in [4], [14].

6 Conclusions

Internet of Things (IoT) envisions as a global network, which would connect any objects across the globe through Internet. In addition to conventional PC-based Internet computing, WSN, RFID system, mobile computing are essential components that would contribute significantly to IoT infrastructure. In IoT infrastructure, these complimentary technologies require to interact each other in order to connect objects around us. As a result, security and privacy of these constrained environments are important concerns in IoT scenarios and applications. We discussed various security and privacy issues pertaining to IoT infrastructure. We have highlighted different perspectives of IoT, discussed about important driving forces of IoT. We then proposed a generic construction of secure protocol for resource-constrained environment in the context of IoT infrastructure. The proposed construction can support authentication, key establishment and data confidentiality security properties. Furthermore, the construction allows to to achieve effective privacy of the communication parties by protecting their identities in message exchange.

References

1. Sarma, S., Brock, D.L., Ashton, K.: The Networked Physical World. MIT Auto-ID Center (2000)
2. European Commission: Internet of Things - An action plan for Europe, http://europa.eu/legislation_summaries/information_society/internet/si0009_en.htm (accessed January 2014)
3. Yan, L., Zhang, Y., Yang, L.T., Ning, H.: The Internet Of Things. Auerbach Publications, Taylor and Francis Group, New York (2008)
4. Das, M.L.: Strong Security and Privacy of RFID System for *Internet of Things* Infrastructure. In: Gierlichs, B., Guilley, S., Mukhopadhyay, D. (eds.) SPACE 2013. LNCS, vol. 8204, pp. 56–69. Springer, Heidelberg (2013)
5. Callaway Jr., E.H.: Wireless Sensor Networks. Architectures and Protocols. Auerbach Publications (2003)
6. Shelby, Z., Hartke, K., Bormann, C.: The Constrained Application Protocol (CoAP). RFC 7252 (June 2014), https://tools.ietf.org/html/rfc7252 (accessed July 2014)
7. Kushalnagar, N., Montenegro, G., Schumacher, C.: IPv6 over Low-Power Wireless Personal Area Networks (6LoWPANs). RFC 4919 (August 2007), http://www.ietf.org/rfc/rfc4919.txt (accessed December 2013)
8. Roman, R., Najera, P., Lopez, J.: Securing the Internet of Things. IEEE Computer 44(9), 51–58 (2011)
9. ISO/IEC 14443-2:2001. Identification cards – Contactless integrated circuit(s) cards – Proximity cards – Part 2: Radio frequency power and signal interface
10. Hankerson, D., Menezes, A., Vanstone, S.: Guide to Elliptic Curve Cryptography. Springer (2004)
11. ZigBee Specification, http://www.zigbee.org/Specifications.aspx (accessed December 2013)
12. Rescorla, E., Modadugu, N.: Datagram Transport Layer Security. RFC 4347 (April 2006), https://tools.ietf.org/html/rfc4347 (accessed December 2013)
13. Dierks, T., Rescorla, E.: The Transport Layer Security (TLS) Protocol. RFC 5246 (August 2008), http://www.rfc-base.org/txt/rfc-5246.txt (accessed December 2013)
14. Songhela, R., Das, M.L.: Yet Another Strong Privacy-Preserving RFID Mutual Authentication Protocol. In: Chakraborty, R.S., Matyas, V., Schaumont, P. (eds.) SPACE 2014. LNCS, vol. 8804, pp. 171–182. Springer, Heidelberg (2014)

Geo-indistinguishability: A Principled Approach to Location Privacy

Konstantinos Chatzikokolakis[1,2], Catuscia Palamidessi[2,3], and Marco Stronati[2]

[1] CNRS, France
[2] LIX, École Polytechnique, France
[3] INRIA, France

Abstract. In this paper we report on our ongoing project aimed at protecting the privacy of the user when dealing with location-based services. The starting point of our approach is the principle of geo-indistinguishability, a formal notion of privacy that protects the user's exact location, while allowing approximate information – typically needed to obtain a certain desired service – to be released. We then present two mechanisms for achieving geo-indistinguishability, one generic to sanitize locations in any setting with reasonable utility, the other custom-built for a limited set of locations but providing optimal utility. Finally we extend our mechanisms to the case of location traces, where the user releases his location repeatedly along the day and we provide a method to limit the degradation of the privacy guarantees due to the correlation between the points. All the mechanisms were tested on real datasets and compared both among themselves and with respect to the state of the art in the field.

1 Introduction

The widespread use of Location-Based Services (LBS) in today's world has created new risks to user privacy that users are increasingly becoming aware of. In large part, the worries are caused by the shocking episodes of violations and leaks that keep appearing on the news. Just to mention a couple of them, on April 20th, 2011 it was discovered that the iPhones were storing and collecting location data from their users, syncing them with iTunes and transmitting them to Apple, all without the users' knowledge. More recently, the Guardian has revealed, on the basis of the documents provided by Edward Snowden, that the NSA and the GCHQ have been using certain smartphone apps, such as the wildly popular Angry Birds game, to collect users' private information such as age, gender and location [1].

To some extent, also the research and the experimentation on privacy contribute to raise the awareness about the practical risks. For instance, the "Please Rob Me" website [2] aggregates location check-ins and presents them as "robbery opportunities", pointing out the fact that publically announcing one's location effectively reveals to the world that they are not home.

A survey among 180 smartphone users, described in [3], reported that 78% of the participants believe that apps accessing their location can pose privacy threats. Furthermore, 85% of them declared that they care about who accesses their location information. All these worries about location privacy may seem exaggerated at first, but one

R. Natarajan et al. (Eds.): ICDCIT 2015, LNCS 8956, pp. 49–72, 2015.

can see that they are fully justified when thinking to the possible malicious uses of location information, such as robbing and stalking. For instance, the application "Girls Around Me", combines social media and location information to find nearby women (who hadn't necessarily agreed to be found), and, with one click the user can access the Facebook profiles of targeted girls [4]. Particularly worrisome is the perspective of potential combination with the users' most sensitive information, such as sexual orientation. Again, according to the Guardian [1], there have been cases of smartphone applications from which such information was collected without the user's knowledge.

Furthermore, location information can be easily used to obtain a variety of other information that an individual usually wishes to protect: by collecting and processing accurate location data on a regular basis, it is possible to infer an individual's home or work location, sexual preferences, political views, religious inclinations, etc.

There are numerous programs that collect location data from mobile devices. In this paper, we focus our attention to those applications which collect such data to provide an agreed-upon service, i.e., the LBSs. Obviously there exist methods for preventing the collection of location data entirely, however they would completely nullify the benefits of applications which provide location services. Our primary goal is to develop methods that hinder the undesired tracking capacities of LBSs, while preserving as much as possible the quality of the desired services.

Several notions of privacy for location-based systems have been proposed in the literature. In Section 2 we give an overview of such notions, and we discuss their shortcomings in relation to our motivating LBS applications. Aiming at addressing these shortcomings, we propose a formal privacy definition, called *geo-indistinguishability*, that allows a user to disclose *enough location information* to obtain the desired service, while satisfying the aforementioned privacy notion. Our proposal is based on a generalization of *differential privacy* [5] developed in [6]. Similarly to differential privacy, our notion and technique abstract from the side information of the adversary, such as any prior probabilistic knowledge about the user's actual location.

To explain the principle of geo-indistinguishability, consider a user located in Paris who wishes to query an LBS provider for nearby restaurants in a private way. To achieve this the user employs *obfuscation*, i.e. he discloses some approximate location z instead of his exact one x. Interestingly, 52% of the surveyed individuals in [3] stated no problem in supplying apps with imprecise location information to protect their privacy; only 18% objected to providing imprecise location information. Note that, in contrast to various works in the literature, we assume that the user is interested in hiding his *location*, not his *identity*; in fact, the user might be authenticated to the service provider in order to obtain personalized recommendations.

We say that the user enjoys ℓ-*privacy within* r if, any two locations at distance at most r produce observations with "similar" distributions, where the "level of similarity" depends on ℓ. The idea is that ℓ represents the user's *level* of privacy for that radius: the smaller ℓ is, the higher is the privacy.

The definition of geo-indistinguishability abstracts from r by requiring that the (inverse of the) level of privacy ℓ depend on the radius r. Formally: A mechanism satisfies geo-indistinguishability iff for any radius $r > 0$, the user enjoys ϵr-privacy within r.

This definition implies that the user is protected within any radius r, but with a level $\ell = \epsilon r$ that increases with the distance. Within a short radius, for instance $r = 1$ km, ℓ is small, guaranteeing that the provider cannot infer the user's location within, say, the 7th arrondissement of Paris. Farther away from the user, for instance for $r = 1000$ km, ℓ becomes large, allowing the LBS provider to infer that with high probability the user is located in Paris instead of, say, London.

We propose a mechanism that achieves geo-indistinguishability by perturbating the user's location x. The inspiration for our mechanism comes from one of the most popular approaches for differential privacy, namely the Laplace noise. We adopt a specific planar version of the Laplace distribution, allowing to draw points in a *geo-indistinguishable* way; moreover, we are able to do so efficiently, by using polar coordinates. Another advantage of the resulting mechanism is that it is independent from the particular user or the area it is used in, the only parameter is the desired level of privacy or conversely the desired level of accuracy of the service.

Clearly, the perturbation of the information sent to the LBS provider leads to a degradation of the quality of service, and consequently there is a trade-off between the level of privacy that the user wishes to guarantee and the service quality loss (QL) that he has to accept. The study of this trade-off, and the design of mechanisms which optimize it, is an important research direction started with the seminal paper of Shokri et al. [7]. In [8] we have compared our mechanism with other ones in the literature, using the privacy metric proposed in [9]. It turns our that our mechanism offers the best privacy guarantees, for the same utility, among those which do not depend on the user.

The advantages of the independence from the user are obvious: first, the mechanism is designed once and for all, we do not need different mechanisms for different users. Second, even the same user may have different behaviors, for instance during different parts of the day, and it would not be practical to change the mechanism all the time. Finally, computing the prior of the user can be an expensive operation, and in some cases even unfeasible.

However, if we are interested in protecting a particular user, then in general there are mechanisms, specific for that user, that do better than the generic Laplace mechanism. Thus, we are also interested in defining specialized mechanisms that optimize the trade-off between geo-indistinguishability and quality of service for a particular user. More precisely, given a certain threshold on the degree of geo-indistinguishability, and a prior, we aim at obtaining the mechanism K which minimizes the QL. Based on the fact that the geo-indistinguishability threshold can be expressed by linear constraints, we can reduce the problem of producing such an optimal K to a linear optimization problem, which can then be solved by using standard techniques of linear programming.

The two mechanisms discussed above correspond to a *sporadic* use of the service in which a single location needs to be sanitized. In practice, however, a user might performs *repeated* location-based queries from several locations, forming a *location trace* that he wishes to protect. For each query, a new obfuscated location needs to be reported to the service provider, which can be easily obtained by independently adding noise at the moment when each query is executed. We refer to independently applying noise to each location as the *independent mechanism*.

However, it is easy to see that privacy is degraded as the number of queries increases, due to the *correlation* between the locations. Intuitively, in the extreme case when the user never moves (i.e. there is perfect correlation), the reported locations are centered around the real one, thus revealing it more and more precisely as the number of queries increases. Technically, the independent mechanism applying ϵ-geo-indistinguishable noise (where ϵ is a privacy parameter) to n locations can be shown to satisfy $n\epsilon$-geo-indistinguishability. This is typical in the area of differential privacy, in which ϵ is thought as a privacy *budget*, consumed by each query; this linear increase makes the mechanism applicable only when the number of queries remains small. In order to deal with multiple queries we propose a *trace obfuscation* mechanism with a smaller *budget consumption rate* than applying independent noise [10]. The main idea is to actually use the correlation from previous locations to try to *predict* a point close to the user's actual location. Predicted points are safe to report directly and thus have a smaller footprint on the privacy budget.

We experimentally compare the above mechanisms on two large real-life data sets, Geolife and Tdrive. The results show the utility improvements of the optimal constructed mechanism wrt the Laplace one, as well as the improvements of the predictive mechanism wrt the independently applied noise.

This paper presents a systematic overview of the approach to location privacy developed by our INRIA team Comète. Some of the results presented here have appeared in previous papers of ours specialized in particular aspects of the project [8,10,11].

Road Map. In Section 2 we discuss notions of location privacy from the literature and point out their weaknesses and strengths. In Section 3 we formalize the notion of geo-indistinguishability in three equivalent ways. We then proceed to describe two mechanisms that provide geo-indistinguishability in Section 4: one general, the other with optimal utility. In Section 5 we propose a predictive mechanism that exploits correlations on the input by means of a prediction function to improve the privacy guarantee. In Section 6 we give an overview of the experimental analysis and comparison of the mechanisms and Section 7 concludes.

2   Existing Notions of Privacy

In this section, we examine various notions of location privacy from the literature, as well as techniques to achieve them. We consider the motivating example from the introduction, of a user in Paris wishing to find nearby restaurants with good reviews. To achieve this goal, he uses a handheld device (e.g.. a smartphone) to query a public LBS provider. However, the user expects his location to be kept private: informally speaking, the information sent to the provider should not allow him to accurately infer the user's location. Our goal is to provide a *formal* notion of privacy that adequately captures the user's expected privacy. From the point of view of the employed mechanism, we require a technique that can be performed in real-time by a handheld device, without the need of any trusted anonymization party.

Expected Adversary Error. The expected error of an optimal Bayesian adversary [7,9,12] is a natural way to quantify the privacy offered by a location-obfuscation mechanism.

Intuitively, it reflects the degree of accuracy by which an adversary can guess the real location of the user by observing the obfuscated location, and using any side-information available to him.

There are several works relying on this notion. In [12], a perturbation mechanism is used to confuse the attacker by crossing paths of individual users, rendering the task of tracking individual paths challenging. In [9], an optimal location-obfuscation mechanism (i.e., achieving maximum level of privacy for the user) is obtained by solving a linear program in which the constraints are determined by the quality of service and by the user's profile. In [13] bandwidth constraints are also taken into account, while [14] considers the case of repeated location reporting, as opposed to a sporadic use of the mechanism. Furthermore, [15] analyzes the case where the attacker can also exploit co-location information, such as geo-located pictures, shared on a social network, in which several friends are tagged together.

It is worth noting that this privacy notion and the obfuscation mechanisms based on it are explicitly defined in terms of the adversary's side information. In contrast, our notion of geo-indistinguishability abstracts from the attacker's prior knowledge, and is therefore suitable for scenarios where the prior is unknown, or the same mechanism must be used for multiple users.

k-anonymity. The notion of k-anonymity is the most widely used definition of privacy for location-based systems in the literature. Many systems in this category [16,17,18] aim at protecting the user's *identity*, requiring that the attacker cannot infer which user is executing the query, among a set of k different users. Such systems are outside the scope of our problem, since we are interested in protecting the user's *location*.

On the other hand, k-anonymity has also been used to protect the user's location (sometimes called l-diversity in this context), requiring that it is indistinguishable among a set of k points (often required to share some semantic property). One way to achieve this is through the use of *dummy locations* [19,20]. This technique involves generating $k-1$ properly selected dummy points, and performing k queries to the service provider, using the real and dummy locations. Another method for achieving k-anonymity is through *cloaking* [21,22,23]. This involves creating a cloaking region that includes k points sharing some property of interest, and then querying the service provider for this cloaking region.

Even when side knowledge does not explicitly appear in the definition of k-anonymity, a system cannot be proven to satisfy this notion unless assumptions are made about the attacker's side information. For example, dummy locations are only useful if they look equally likely to be the real location from the point of view of the attacker. Any side information that allows to rule out any of those points, as having low probability of being the real location, would immediately violate the definition.

Counter-measures are often employed to avoid this issue: for instance, [19] takes into account concepts such as ubiquity, congestion and uniformity for generating dummy points, in an effort to make them look realistic. Similarly, [23] takes into account the user's side information to construct a cloaking region. Such counter-measures have their own drawbacks: first, they complicate the employed techniques, also requiring additional data to be taken into account (for instance, precise information about the environment or the location of nearby users), making their application in real-time by a handheld device challenging. Moreover, the attacker's actual side information might simply be inconsistent with the assumptions being made.

As a result, notions that abstract from the attacker's side information, such as differential privacy, have been growing in popularity in recent years, compared to k-anonymity-based approaches.

Differential Privacy. Differential Privacy [5] is a notion of privacy from the area of statistical databases. Its goal is to protect an individual's data while publishing aggregate information about the database. Differential privacy requires that modifying a single user's data should have a negligible effect on the query outcome. More precisely, it requires that the probability that a query returns a value v when applied to a database D, compared to the probability to report the same value when applied to an *adjacent* database D' – meaning that D, D' differ in the value of a single individual – should be within a bound of e^ϵ. A typical way to achieve this notion is to add controlled random noise to the query output, for example drawn from a Laplace distribution. An advantage of this notion is that a mechanism can be shown to be differentially private independently from any side information that the attacker might possess.

Differential privacy has also been used in the context of location privacy. In [24], it is shown that a synthetic data generation technique can be used to publish statistical information about commuting patterns in a differentially private way. In [25], a quadtree spatial decomposition technique is used to ensure differential privacy in a database with location pattern mining capabilities, while [26] uses variable-length n-grams to disclose sequential data, such as mobility traces, in a differentially private way.

As shown in the aforementioned works, differential privacy can be successfully applied in cases where *aggregate* information about several users is published. On the other hand, the nature of this notion makes it poorly suitable for applications in which only a single individual is involved, such as our motivating scenario. The secret in this case is the location of a single user. Thus, differential privacy would require that any change in that location should have negligible effect on the published output, making it impossible to communicate any useful information to the service provider.

To overcome this issue, Dewri [27] proposes a mix of differential privacy and k-anonymity, by fixing an anonymity set of k locations and requiring that the probability to report the same obfuscated location z from any of these k locations should be similar (up to e^ϵ). This property is achieved by adding Laplace noise to each Cartesian coordinate independently. There are however two problems with this definition: first, the choice of the anonymity set crucially affects the resulting privacy; outside this set no privacy is guaranteed at all. Second, the property itself is rather weak; reporting the geometric median (or any deterministic function) of the k locations would satisfy the same definition, although the privacy guarantee would be substantially lower than using Laplace noise.

Nevertheless, Dewri's intuition of using Laplace noise[1] for location privacy is valid, and [27] provides extensive experimental analysis supporting this claim. Our notion

---

[1] The planar Laplace distribution that we use in our work, however, is different from the distribution obtained by adding Laplace noise to each Cartesian coordinate, and has better differential privacy properties (c.f. Section 4.1).

of geo-indistinguishability provides the formal background for justifying the use of Laplace noise, while avoiding the need to fix an anonymity set by using the generalized variant of differential privacy from [6].

Other location-privacy metrics. [28] proposes a location cloaking mechanism, and focuses on the evaluation of Location-based Range Queries. The degree of privacy is measured by the size of the cloak (also called *uncertainty region*), and by the coverage of sensitive regions, which is the ratio between the area of the cloak and the area of the regions inside the cloak that the user considers to be sensitive. In order to deal with the side-information that the attacker may have, ad-hoc solutions are proposed, like patching cloaks to enlarge the uncertainty region or delaying requests. Both solutions may cause a degradation in the quality of service.

In [29], the real location of the user is assumed to have some level of inaccuracy, due to the specific sensing technology or to the environmental conditions. Different obfuscation techniques are then used to increase this inaccuracy in order to achieve a certain level of privacy. This level of privacy is defined as the ratio between the accuracy before and after the application of the obfuscation techniques.

Similar to the case of k-anonymity, both privacy metrics mentioned above make implicit assumptions about the adversary's side information. This may imply a violation of the privacy definition in a scenario where the adversary has some knowledge about the user's real location.

Transformation-based approaches. A number of approaches for location privacy are radically different from the ones mentioned so far. Instead of cloaking the user's location, they aim at making it completely invisible to the service provider. This is achieved by transforming all data to a different space, usually employing cryptographic techniques, so that they can be mapped back to spatial information only by the user [30,31]. The data stored in the provider, as well as the location send by the user are encrypted. Then, using techniques from *private information retrieval*, the provider can return information about the encrypted location, without ever discovering which actual location it corresponds to.

A drawback of these techniques is that they are computationally demanding, making it difficult to implement them in a handheld device. Moreover, they require the provider's data to be encrypted, making it impossible to use existing providers, such as Google Maps, which have access to the real data.

Effectiveness of attacks. An indirect way of assessing the privacy guarantees of a mechanism is to measure the effectiveness of various location inference attacks. Several works present attacks and practical challenges for location privacy. In [32] the authors develop and test a toolkit for inference attacks on the reported locations of users to discover points of interests, future locations and co-location of two individuals. The same technique was employed in [33] focusing on de-anonymization attacks with the goal of evaluating the effectiveness of sanitization mechanisms. In [34] the authors tested the resilience of Geo Indistinguishability to identification of Points of Interests of users over two real GPS traces datasets, with varying level of privacy (and therefore noise).

3   Geo-indistinguishability

In this section we formalize our notion of geo-indistinguishability. As already discussed in the introduction, the main idea behind this notion is that, for any radius $r > 0$, the user enjoys ϵr-privacy within r, i.e. the level of privacy is proportional to the radius. Note that the parameter ϵ corresponds to the level of privacy at one unit of distance. For the user, a simple way to specify his privacy requirements is by a tuple (ℓ, r), where r is the radius he is mostly concerned with and ℓ is the privacy level he wishes *for that radius*. In this case, it is sufficient to require ϵ-geo-indistinguishability for $\epsilon = \ell/r$; this will ensure a level of privacy ℓ within r, and a proportionally selected level for all other radii.

So far we kept the discussion on an informal level by avoiding to explicitly define what ℓ-privacy within r means. In the remaining of this section we give a formal definition, as well as two characterizations which clarify the privacy guarantees provided by geo-indistinguishability.

Probabilistic Model. We first introduce a simple model used in the rest of the paper. We start with a set $\mathcal{X}$ of *points of interest*, typically the user's possible locations. Moreover, let $\mathcal{Z}$ be a set of possible *reported values*, which in general can be arbitrary, allowing to report obfuscated locations, cloaking regions, sets of locations, etc. However, to simplify the discussion, we sometimes consider $\mathcal{Z}$ to also contain spatial points, assuming an operational scenario of a user located at $x \in \mathcal{X}$ and communicating to the attacker a randomly selected location $z \in \mathcal{Z}$ (e.g. an obfuscated point).

Probabilities come into place in two ways. First, the attacker might have side information about the user's location, knowing, for example, that he is likely to be visiting the Eiffel Tower, while unlikely to be swimming in the Seine river. The attacker's side information can be modeled by a *prior* distribution π on $\mathcal{X}$, where $\pi(x)$ is the probability assigned to the location x.

Second, the selection of a reported value in $\mathcal{Z}$ is itself probabilistic; for instance, z can be obtained by adding random noise to the actual location x (a technique used in Section 4). A *mechanism* K is a probabilistic function for selecting a reported value; i.e. K is a function assigning to each location $x \in \mathcal{X}$ a probability distribution on $\mathcal{Z}$, where $K(x)(Z)$ is the probability that the reported point belongs to the set $Z \subseteq \mathcal{Z}$, when the user's location is x.[2] Starting from π and using Bayes' rule, each observation $Z \subseteq \mathcal{Z}$ of a mechanism K induces a *posterior* distribution $\sigma = \mathbf{Bayes}(\pi, K, Z)$ on $\mathcal{X}$, defined as $\sigma(x) = \frac{K(x)(Z)\pi(x)}{\sum_{x'} K(x')(Z)\pi(x')}$.

We define the *multiplicative distance* between two distributions σ_1, σ_2 on some set S as $d_\mathcal{P}(\sigma_1, \sigma_2) = \sup_{S \subseteq \mathcal{S}} |\ln \frac{\sigma_1(S)}{\sigma_2(S)}|$, with the convention that $|\ln \frac{\sigma_1(S)}{\sigma_2(S)}| = 0$ if both $\sigma_1(S), \sigma_2(S)$ are zero and ∞ if only one of them is zero.

---

[2] For simplicity we assume distributions on $\mathcal{X}$ to be discrete, but allow those on $\mathcal{Z}$ to be continuous (c.f. Section 4). All sets to which probability is assigned are implicitly assumed to be measurable.

3.1 Definition

We are now ready to state our definition of geo-indistinguishability. Intuitively, a privacy requirement is a constraint on the distributions $K(x)$, $K(x')$ produced by two different points x, x'. Let $d_2(\cdot, \cdot)$ denote the Euclidean metric. Enjoying ℓ-privacy within r means that for any x, x' s.t. $d_2(x, x') \leq r$, the distance $d_{\mathcal{P}}(K(x), K(x'))$ between the corresponding distributions should be at most ℓ. Then, requiring ϵr-privacy for all radii r, forces the two distributions to be similar for locations close to each other, while relaxing the constraint for those far away from each other, allowing a service provider to distinguish points in Paris from those in London.

Definition 1 (geo-indistinguishability). *A mechanism K satisfies ϵ-geo-indistinguishability iff for all x, x':*

$$d_{\mathcal{P}}(K(x), K(x')) \leq \epsilon d_2(x, x')$$

Equivalently, the definition can be formulated as $K(x)(Z) \leq e^{\epsilon d_2(x,x')} K(x')(Z)$ for all $x, x' \in \mathcal{X}, Z \subseteq \mathcal{Z}$. Note that for all points x' within a radius r from x, the definition forces the corresponding distributions to be at most ϵr distant.

The quantity $\epsilon d_2(x, x')$ can be viewed as the *distinguishability level* between the secrets x and x'. The use of the Euclidean metric d_2 is natural for location privacy: the *closer* (geographically) two points are, the *less distinguishable* we would like them to be. Note, however, that other metrics could be used instead of d_2, such as the Manhattan metric or driving distance, depending on the application. The definition that we obtain by using an arbitrary distinguishability metric $d_{\mathcal{X}}$, i.e. requiring that $d_{\mathcal{P}}(K(x), K(x')) \leq d_{\mathcal{X}}(x, x')$, is referred to as $d_{\mathcal{X}}$-privacy[3], and is studied on its own right in [6]. Some of the results of this paper do not depend on the actual metric, so they are given in the general framework of $d_{\mathcal{X}}$-privacy.

Note also that standard differential privacy simply corresponds to $\epsilon d_h(x, x')$-privacy, where d_h is the Hamming distance between databases x, x', i.e. the number of individuals in which they differ. However, in our scenario, using the Hamming metric of standard differential privacy – which aims at completely protecting the value of an individual – would be too strong, since the only information is the location of a single individual. Nevertheless, we are not interested in completely hiding the user's location, since some approximate information needs to be revealed in order to obtain the required service. Hence, using a privacy level that depends on the Euclidean distance between locations is a natural choice.

Protecting Location Traces. So far, we have assumed a *sporadic* use of an LBS, meaning that the service is used infrequently enough that we can assume no correlation between different uses and treat each one of them independently. In this case, the user's secret is a single location. In the case of *repeated* use, however, the user forms a *location trace* which should be protected; the provider is allowed to obtain only approximate information about the locations, their exact value should be kept private.

---

[3] Note that we can generally consider the scaling factor ϵ to be part of the metric, although sometimes we emphasize it by talking of $\epsilon d_{\mathcal{X}}$-privacy.

In this case, the secret is the trace, i.e. a tuple of points denoted by $\mathbf{x} = [x_1, \ldots, x_n]$, while $\mathbf{x}[i]$ denotes the i-th element of the trace. The notion of ϵ-geo-indistinguishability extends naturally by defining the distance between two tuples $\mathbf{x}, \mathbf{x}'$ as:

$$d_\infty(\mathbf{x}, \mathbf{x}') = \max_i d_2(\mathbf{x}[i], \mathbf{x}'[i])$$

and using ϵd_∞-privacy as our privacy definition. Following the idea of reasoning within a radius r, this definition requires that two traces at most r away from each other (i.e. such that $\mathbf{x}[i], \mathbf{x}'[i]$ are all within distance r from each other) should produce distributions at most ϵr apart.

3.2 Characterizations

In this section we state two characterizations of geo-indistinguishability, obtained from the corresponding results of [6] (for general metrics), which provide intuitive interpretations of the privacy guarantees offered by this notion.

Adversary's Conclusions under Hiding. The first characterization uses the concept of a *hiding function* $\phi : \mathcal{X} \to \mathcal{X}$. The idea is that ϕ can be applied to the user's actual location before the mechanism K, so that the latter has only access to a hidden version $\phi(x)$, instead of the real location x. A mechanism K with hiding applied is simply the composition $K \circ \phi$. Intuitively, a location remains private if, regardless of his side knowledge (captured by his prior distribution), an adversary draws the same conclusions (captured by his posterior distribution), regardless of whether hiding has been applied or not. However, if ϕ replaces locations in Paris with those in London, then clearly the adversary's conclusions will be greatly affected. Hence, we require that the effect on the conclusions depends on the maximum distance $d_2(\phi) = \sup_{x \in \mathcal{X}} d_2(x, \phi(x))$ between the real and hidden location.

Theorem 1. *A mechanism K satisfies ϵ-geo-indistinguishability iff for all $\phi : \mathcal{X} \to \mathcal{X}$, all priors π on $\mathcal{X}$, and all $Z \subseteq \mathcal{Z}$:*

$$d_{\mathcal{P}}(\sigma_1, \sigma_2) \leq 2\epsilon d_2(\phi) \qquad where \qquad \begin{aligned} \sigma_1 &= \mathbf{Bayes}(\pi, K, Z) \\ \sigma_2 &= \mathbf{Bayes}(\pi, K \circ \phi, Z) \end{aligned}$$

Note that this is a natural adaptation of a well-known interpretation of standard differential privacy, stating that the attacker's conclusions are similar, regardless of his side knowledge, and regardless of whether an individual's real value has been used in the query or not. This corresponds to a hiding function ϕ removing the value of an individual.

Note also that the above characterization compares two *posterior* distributions. Both σ_1, σ_2 can be substantially different than the initial knowledge π, which means that an adversary does learn some information about the user's location.

Knowledge of an Informed Attacker. A different approach is to measure how much the adversary learns about the user's location, by comparing his prior and posterior distributions. However, since some information is allowed to be revealed by design, these distributions can be far apart. Still, we can consider an *informed* adversary who already knows that the user is located within a set $N \subseteq \mathcal{X}$. Let $d_2(N) = \sup_{x,x' \in N} d_2(x, x')$ be the maximum distance between points in x. Intuitively, the user's location remains private if, regardless of his prior knowledge within N, the knowledge obtained by such an informed adversary should be limited by a factor depending on $d_2(N)$. This means that if $d_2(N)$ is small, i.e. the adversary already knows the location with some accuracy, then the information that he obtains is also small, meaning that he cannot improve his accuracy. Denoting by $\pi_{|N}$ the distribution obtained from π by restricting to N (i.e. $\pi_{|N}(x) = \pi(x|N)$), we obtain the following characterization:

Theorem 2. *A mechanism K satisfies ϵ-geo-indistinguishability iff for all $N \subseteq \mathcal{X}$, all priors π on $\mathcal{X}$, and all $Z \subseteq \mathcal{Z}$:*

$$d_{\mathcal{P}}(\pi_{|N}, \sigma_{|N}) \leq \epsilon d_2(N) \qquad where \qquad \sigma = \mathbf{Bayes}(\pi, K, Z)$$

Note that this is a natural adaptation of a well-known interpretation of standard differential privacy, stating that an informed adversary who already knows all values except individual's i, gains no extra knowledge from the reported answer, regardless of side knowledge about i's value [35].

Abstracting from Side Information. A major difference of geo-indistinguishability, compared to similar approaches from the literature, is that it abstracts from the side information available to the adversary, i.e. from the prior distribution. This is a subtle issue, and often a source of confusion, thus we would like to clarify what "abstracting from the prior" means. The goal of a privacy definition is to restrict the information *leakage* caused by the observation. Note that the lack of leakage does not mean that the user's location cannot be inferred (it could be inferred by the prior alone), but instead that the adversary's knowledge does not increase *due to the observation*.

However, in the context of LBSs, no privacy definition can ensure a small leakage under any prior, and at the same time allow reasonable utility. Consider, for instance, an attacker who knows that the user is located at some airport, but not which one. The attacker's prior knowledge is very limited, still any useful LBS query should reveal at least the user's city, from which the exact location (i.e. the city's airport) can be inferred. Clearly, due to the side information, the leakage caused by the observation is high.

So, since we cannot eliminate leakage under any prior, how can we give a reasonable privacy definition without restricting to a particular one? First, we give a formulation (Definition 1) which does not involve the prior at all, allowing to verify it without knowing the prior. At the same time, we give two characterizations which explicitly quantify over all priors, shedding light on how the prior affects the privacy guarantees.

4   Mechanisms for the Sporadic Case

In this section we present two mechanisms for applying noise to a single location while satisfying geo-indistinguishability. The first one, the *planar Laplace mechanism*, is a simple and efficient mechanism that scales to any number of possible locations while being generic and independent from the user's behaviour. The second is adapted to a specific user and guarantees *optimal utility* (or minimum quality loss) for that user, however it is only applicable when the number of possible locations is limited.

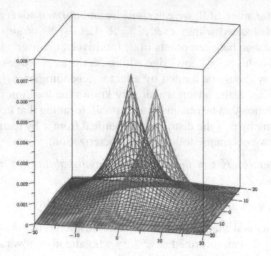

Fig. 1. The pdf of two planar Laplace distributions, centered at $(-2, -4)$ and at $(5, 3)$ respectively, with $\epsilon = 1/5$

4.1 The Planar Laplace Mechanism

We start by defining a mechanism for geo-indistinguishability on the continuous plane. The idea is that whenever the actual location is $x \in \mathbb{R}^2$, we report, instead, a point $z \in \mathbb{R}^2$ generated randomly according to a distribution with probability density function:

$$D_\epsilon(z) = \frac{\epsilon^2}{2\pi} e^{-\epsilon d_2(x,z)} \tag{1}$$

This function is called the *planar Laplace centered at x* and is is illustrated in Figure 1. The resulting mechanism can be shown to satisfy ϵ-geo-indistinguishability [8].

Note that this definition of the two-dimensional Laplace distribution follows [36] and is different than generating the two coordinates independently from a standard (one dimensional) Laplace distribution. Such an approach would not, in fact, satisfy geo-indistinguishability.

Drawing a Random Point. We illustrate now how to draw a random point from the pdf defined in (1). First of all, we note that the pdf of the planar Laplace distribution depends only on the distance from x. It will be convenient, therefore, to switch to a system of polar coordinates with origin x. A point z will be represented as a point (r, θ), where r is the distance of z from x, and θ is the angle that the line $x\,z$ forms with respect to the horizontal axis of the Cartesian system. After the transformation, the pdf of the *polar Laplace* centered at the origin x is:

$$D_\epsilon(r, \theta) = \frac{\epsilon^2}{2\pi} r\, e^{-\epsilon r} \tag{2}$$

Let R, Θ be the random variables representing the radius and the angle; the property that allows to efficiently draw from the polar Laplace is that the two variables are *independent*, that is $D_\epsilon(r, \theta)$ is the product of the two marginals:

$$D_{\epsilon,R}(r) = \int_0^{2\pi} D_\epsilon(r, \theta)\, d\theta = \epsilon^2 r\, e^{-\epsilon r}$$

$$D_{\epsilon,\Theta}(\theta) = \int_0^\infty D_\epsilon(r, \theta)\, dr = \frac{1}{2\pi}$$

Note that $D_{\epsilon,R}(r)$ corresponds to the *gamma distribution* with shape 2 and scale $1/\epsilon$.

Hence, in order to draw a point (r, θ) it is sufficient to draw separately r and θ from $D_{\epsilon,R}(r)$ and $D_{\epsilon,\Theta}(\theta)$ respectively. Since $D_{\epsilon,\Theta}(\theta)$ is constant, θ can be drawn from a uniform distribution on the interval $[0, 2\pi)$.

We now show how to draw r. Following standard lines, we consider the cumulative distribution function (cdf) $C_\epsilon(r)$:

$$C_\epsilon(r) = \int_0^r D_{\epsilon,R}(\rho)d\rho = 1 - (1 + \epsilon r)\, e^{-\epsilon r}$$

Intuitively, $C_\epsilon(r)$ represents the probability that the radius of the random point falls between 0 and r. Finally, we generate a random number p with uniform probability in the interval $[0, 1)$, and we set $r = C_\epsilon^{-1}(p)$. Note that

$$C_\epsilon^{-1}(p) = -\frac{1}{\epsilon}\left(W_{-1}\left(\frac{p-1}{e}\right) + 1\right)$$

where W_{-1} is the Lambert W function (the -1 branch), which can be computed efficiently and is implemented in several numerical libraries.

Note that in practice only a discretized version of the continuous mechanism can be implemented; the discretized variant can be shown to also satisfy geo-indistinguishability, for a slightly bigger ϵ, although the difference is negligible on a double precision machine. A detailed discussion of discretization issues can be found in [8].

The planar Laplace mechanism has two main advantages: first, it is simple and efficient to compute without restricting the number of possible locations. Second, it can be applied to a generic user without prior information on his behaviour. The usefulness of the mechanism for generic applications is showcased in *Location Guard* [37], a browser extension for Chrome and Firefox, which provides location privacy for websites accessing the user's location through the HTML5 geolocation API, by adding noise to the reported location using the planar Laplace mechanism.

On the other hand, being generic, the planar Laplace mechanism offers no optimality guarantees for the quality loss of the reported location. In the following section, we show how to improve utility by construct mechanisms adapted to the behaviour of a particular user.

4.2 Geo-indistinguishable Mechanisms of Optimal Utility

The goal of a privacy mechanism is not to hide completely the secret but to disclose enough information to be useful for some service while hiding the rest to protect the user's privacy. Typically these two requirements go in opposite directions: a stronger privacy level requires more noise which results in a lower utility.

From the user's point of view, we want to quantify the service *quality loss (QL)* produced by the mechanism K. Given a *quality metric* d_Q on locations, such that $d_Q(x, z)$ measures how much the quality decreases by reporting z when the real location is x (the Euclidean metric d_2 being a typical choice), we can naturally define the quality loss as the expected distance between the real and the reported location, that is

$$\mathrm{QL}(K, \pi, d_Q) = \sum_{x,z} \pi(x)K(x)(z)d_Q(x, z)$$

where π is a prior on $\mathcal{X}$ modeling the user's behaviour.

Despite the generality of the planar Laplace mechanism, in some cases we want to be able to build a mechanism that optimizes the trade-off between privacy (in terms of geo-indistinguishability) and quality loss (in terms of QL) for a specific *user*. Our main goal is, given a set of locations $\mathcal{X}$ with a privacy metric $d_{\mathcal{X}}$, a privacy level ϵ, a user profile π and a quality metric d_Q, to find an $\epsilon d_{\mathcal{X}}$-private mechanism such that its QL is as small as possible. We start by describing a set of linear constraints that enforce $\epsilon d_{\mathcal{X}}$-privacy, which allows to obtain an optimal mechanism as a linear optimization problem. However, the number of constraints can be large, making the approach computationally demanding as the number of locations increases. As a consequence, we then propose an approximate solution that replaces $d_{\mathcal{X}}$ with the metric induced by a spanning graph.

Constructing an optimal mechanism. The constructed mechanism is assumed to have as both input and output a predetermined finite set of locations $\mathcal{X}$. For instance, $\mathcal{X}$ can be constructed by dividing the map in a finite number of regions (of arbitrary size and shape), and selecting in $\mathcal{X}$ a representative location for each region. We also assume a prior π over $\mathcal{X}$, representing the probability of the user being at each location at any given time. Since $\mathcal{X}$ is finite, a mechanism K can be represented by a stochastic matrix, where k_{xz} is the probability to report z from location x.

Given a privacy metric $d_{\mathcal{X}}$ and a privacy parameter ϵ, the goal is to construct a $\epsilon d_{\mathcal{X}}$-private mechanism K such that the *service quality loss* with respect to a quality metric d_Q is minimum. This property is formally defined below:

Definition 2. *Given a prior π, a privacy metric $d_{\mathcal{X}}$, a privacy parameter ϵ and a quality metric d_Q, a mechanism K is $\epsilon d_{\mathcal{X}}$-OPTQL(π, d_Q) iff:*

1. *K is $\epsilon d_{\mathcal{X}}$-private, and*
2. *for all mechanisms K', if K' is $\epsilon d_{\mathcal{X}}$-private then*
   $\mathrm{QL}(K, \pi, d_Q) \leq \mathrm{QL}(K', \pi, d_Q)$

In order for K to be $\epsilon d_{\mathcal{X}}$-private it should satisfy the following constraints:

$$k_{xz} \leq e^{\epsilon d_{\mathcal{X}}(x,x')}k_{x'z} \qquad x, x', z \in \mathcal{X}$$

Hence, we can construct an optimal mechanism by solving a linear optimization problem, minimizing $QL(K, \pi, d_Q)$ while satisfying $\epsilon d_{\mathcal{X}}$-privacy:

Minimize: $\quad \sum_{x,z \in \mathcal{X}} \pi_x k_{xz} d_Q(x, z)$

Subject to: $\quad k_{xz} \leq e^{\epsilon d_{\mathcal{X}}(x,x')} k_{x'z} \qquad\qquad x, x', z \in \mathcal{X}$

$$\sum_{z \in \mathcal{X}} k_{xz} = 1 \qquad\qquad\qquad x \in \mathcal{X}$$

$$k_{xz} \geq 0 \qquad\qquad\qquad\qquad x, z \in \mathcal{X}$$

It is easy to see that the mechanism K generated by the previous optimization problem is $\epsilon d_{\mathcal{X}}$-OPTQL(π, d_Q).

A more efficient method using spanners. In the optimization problem of the previous section, the $\epsilon d_{\mathcal{X}}$-privacy definition introduces $|\mathcal{X}|^3$ constraints in the linear program. However, in order to be able to manage a large number of locations, we would like to reduce this amount to a number in the order of $O(|\mathcal{X}|^2)$.

So far we are not making any assumption about $d_{\mathcal{X}}$, and therefore we need to specify $|\mathcal{X}|$ constraints for each pair of locations x and x'. However, it is worth noting that if the distance $d_{\mathcal{X}}$ is induced by a weighted graph (i.e. the distance between each pair of locations is the weight of a minimum path in a graph), then we only need to consider $|\mathcal{X}|$ constraints for each pair of locations that are *adjacent in the graph*.

It might be the case, though, that the metric $d_{\mathcal{X}}$ is not induced by any graph (other than the complete graph), and consequently the amount of constraints remains the same. In fact, this is generally the case for the Euclidean metric. Therefore, we consider the case in which $d_{\mathcal{X}}$ can be *approximated* by some graph-induced metric.

If G is an undirected weighted graph, we denote with d_G the distance function induced by G, i.e. $d_G(x, x')$ denotes the weight of a minimum path between the nodes x and x' in G. Then, if the set of nodes of G is $\mathcal{X}$ and the weight of its edges is given by the metric $d_{\mathcal{X}}$, we can approximate $d_{\mathcal{X}}$ with d_G. In this case, we say that G is a spanning graph, or a spanner [38,39], of $\mathcal{X}$.

Definition 3 (Spanner). *A weighted graph $G = (\mathcal{X}, E)$, with $E \subseteq \mathcal{X} \times \mathcal{X}$ and weight function $w : E \to \mathbb{R}$ is a spanner of $\mathcal{X}$ if*

$$w(x, x') = d_{\mathcal{X}}(x, x') \quad \forall (x, x') \in E$$

Note that if G is a spanner of $\mathcal{X}$, then

$$d_G(x, x') \geq d_{\mathcal{X}}(x, x') \quad \forall x, x' \in \mathcal{X}$$

A main concept in the theory of spanners is that of dilation, also known as stretch factor:

Definition 4 (Dilation). *Let $G = (\mathcal{X}, E)$ be a spanner of $\mathcal{X}$. The dilation of G is calculated as:*

$$\delta = \max_{r \neq r' \in \mathcal{X}} \frac{d_G(x, x')}{d_{\mathcal{X}}(r, r')}$$

A spanner of $\mathcal{X}$ with dilation δ is called a δ-spanner of $\mathcal{X}$.

Informally, a δ-spanner of $\mathcal{X}$ can be considered an approximation of the metric $d_{\mathcal{X}}$ in which distances between nodes are "stretched" by a factor of at most δ.

If G is a δ-spanner of $\mathcal{X}$, then it holds that

$$d_G(x, x') \leq \delta d_{\mathcal{X}}(x, x') \quad \forall x, x' \in \mathcal{X}$$

which leads to the following proposition:

Proposition 1. *Let $\mathcal{X}$ be a set of locations with metric $d_{\mathcal{X}}$, and let G be a δ-spanner of $\mathcal{X}$. If a mechanism K for $\mathcal{X}$ is $\frac{\epsilon}{\delta} d_G$-private, then K is $\epsilon d_{\mathcal{X}}$-private.*

We can then propose a new optimization problem to obtain a $\epsilon d_{\mathcal{X}}$-private mechanism. If $G = (\mathcal{X}, E)$ is a δ-spanner of $\mathcal{X}$, we require not the constraints corresponding to $\epsilon d_{\mathcal{X}}$-privacy, but those corresponding to $\frac{\epsilon}{\delta} d_G$-privacy instead, that is, $|\mathcal{X}|$ constraints for each edge of G:

$$
\begin{aligned}
\textbf{Minimize:} \quad & \sum_{x, z \in \mathcal{X}} \pi_x k_{xz} d_Q(x, z) \\
\textbf{Subject to:} \quad & k_{xz} \leq e^{\frac{\epsilon}{\delta} d_G(x, x')} k_{x'z} & z \in \mathcal{X}, (x, x') \in E \\
& \sum_{x \in \mathcal{X}} k_{xz} = 1 & x \in \mathcal{X} \\
& k_{xz} \geq 0 & x, z \in \mathcal{X}
\end{aligned}
$$

Since the resulting mechanism is $\frac{\epsilon}{\delta} d_G$-private, by Proposition 1 it must also be $\epsilon d_{\mathcal{X}}$-private. However, the number of constraints induced by $\frac{\epsilon}{\delta} d_G$-privacy is now $|E||\mathcal{X}|$. Moreover, as discussed in the next section, for any $\delta > 1$ there is an algorithm that generates a δ-spanner with $O(\frac{|\mathcal{X}|}{\delta - 1})$ edges, which means that, fixing δ, the total number of constraints of the linear program is $O(|\mathcal{X}|^2)$.

It is worth noting that although $\epsilon d_{\mathcal{X}}$-privacy is guaranteed, optimality is lost: the obtained mechanism is $\frac{\epsilon}{\delta} d_G$-OPTQL$(\pi, d_Q)$ but not necessarily $\epsilon d_{\mathcal{X}}$-OPTQL(π, d_Q), since the set of $\frac{\epsilon}{\delta} d_G$-private mechanisms is a subset of the set of $\epsilon d_{\mathcal{X}}$-private mechanisms. The QL of the obtained mechanism will now depend on the dilation δ of the spanner: the smaller δ is, the closer the QL of the mechanism will be from the optimal one. In consequence, there is a trade-off between the accuracy of the approximation and the number of constraints in linear program.

5   Mechanisms for the Repeated Case

In the previous section we considered a sporadic use of a service, in which case only a single location needs to be obfuscated. We now turn our attention to the repeated case, in which the user's location *trace* (sometimes called *trajectory* in the literature) needs to be protected. We denote by $\mathbf{x} = [x_1, \dots, x_n]$ a trace, by $\mathbf{x}[i]$ the i-th element of $\mathbf{x}$, by $[\,]$ the empty trace and by $x :: \mathbf{x}$ the trace obtained by adding x to the head of $\mathbf{x}$. We also define $\texttt{tail}(x :: \mathbf{x}) = \mathbf{x}$. As already discussed in Section 3.1, geo-indistinguishability can be naturally extended to the case of location traces by using d_∞ as the underlying distinguishability metric.

5.1 Independent Mechanism

mechanism IM(**x**)
  z := []
  for $i := 1$ **to** $|\mathbf{x}|$
    $z := N(\epsilon_N)(\mathbf{x}[i])$
    $\mathbf{z} := z :: \mathbf{z}$
  return z

Fig. 2. Independent Mechanism

In order to sanitize **x** we can simply apply a *noise mechanism* independently to each secret x_i. We assume that a family of noise mechanisms $N(\epsilon_N) : \mathcal{X} \to \mathcal{P}(\mathcal{Z})$ are available, parametrized by ϵ_N, where each mechanism $N(\epsilon_N)$ satisfies ϵ_N-privacy. Both mechanisms of Section 4 can be used for this purpose. The resulting mechanism, called the *independent mechanism* IM : $\mathcal{X}^n \to \mathcal{P}(\mathcal{Z}^n)$, is shown in Figure 2. As explained in the introduction, the main issue with IM is that it is $n\epsilon d_\infty$-private, i.e. the budget consumed increases linearly with n.

5.2 A Predictive $d_\mathcal{X}$-Private Mechanism

We introduce now our prediction-based approach. The fundamental intuition is that the correlation of the points in the trace can be exploited to the advantage of the mechanism. A simple way of doing this is to try to predict new points from past information; if the point can be predicted with enough accuracy it is called *easy*; in this case the prediction can be reported without adding new noise. One the other hand, *hard* points, that is those that cannot be predicted, are sanitized with new noise. However testing if a point is easy or hard reveals some information about the real location and violates $d_\mathcal{X}$-privacy as for different locations we might have different answers. In order to respect the definition we will need to make the test $d_\mathcal{X}$-private itself, reducing its precision and adding a new cost to our global budget. We will show that with enough correlation in the input the gain in predicted points is worth the cost of the test.

Let $\mathcal{B} = \{0, 1\}$. A boolean $b \in \mathcal{B}$ denotes whether a point is easy (0) or hard (1). A sequence $\mathbf{r} = [z_1, b_1, \ldots, z_n, b_n]$ of reported values and booleans is called a *run*; the set of all runs is denoted by $\mathcal{R} = (\mathcal{Z} \times \mathcal{B})^*$. A run will be the output of our predictive mechanism; note that the booleans b_i are considered public and will be reported by the mechanism.

Main Components. The predictive mechanism has three main components: first, the *prediction* is a deterministic function $\Omega : \mathcal{R} \to \mathcal{Z}$, taking as input the run reported up to this moment and trying to predict the next *reported point*, which should be at an acceptable distance from the actual one. The output of the prediction function is denoted by $\tilde{z} = \Omega(\mathbf{r})$. Note that the possibility of a successful prediction should not be viewed as a privacy violation because Ω predicts the reported location, not the actual one.

Second, a *test* is a family of mechanisms $\Theta(\epsilon_\theta, l, \tilde{z}) : \mathcal{X} \to \mathcal{P}(\mathcal{B})$, parametrized by $\epsilon_\theta, l, \tilde{z}$. The test takes as input the point x and reports whether the prediction $\tilde{z}$ is acceptable or not for this point. If the test is successful then the prediction will be used instead of generating new noise. The purpose of the test is to guarantee a certain level of utility: predictions that are farther than the threshold l should be rejected. Since the test is accessing the actual location, it should be private itself, where ϵ_θ is the allowed budget for testing.

mechanism PM(**x**)
  r := []
  for $i := 1$ **to** $|\mathbf{x}|$
    $(z, b) := \text{Step}(\mathbf{r})(\mathbf{x}[i])$
    r := $(z, b) :: \mathbf{r}$
  return r

mechanism Step(**r**)(x)
  $(\epsilon_\theta, \epsilon_N, l) := \beta(\mathbf{r})$
  $\tilde{z} := \Omega(\mathbf{r})$
  $b := \Theta(\epsilon_\theta, l, \tilde{z})(x)$
  if $b == 0$ **then** $z := \tilde{z}$
  else $z := N(\epsilon_N)(x)$
  return (z, b)

(a) Predictive Mechanism   (b) Single step of the Predictive Mechanism

Fig. 3. Pseudo code of Predictive mechanism

The test mechanism that will be used throughout the paper is the one below, which is based on adding Laplace noise to the threshold l:

$$\Theta(\epsilon_\theta, l, \tilde{z})(x) = \begin{cases} 0 \text{ if } d_x(x, \tilde{z}) \leq l + Lap(\epsilon_\theta) \\ 1 \text{ ow.} \end{cases} \tag{3}$$

The test is defined for all $\epsilon_\theta > 0, l \in [0, +\infty), \tilde{z} \in \mathcal{Z}$, and can be used for any metric d_x, as long as the domain of reported locations is the same as the one of the actual locations, so that $d_x(x, \tilde{z})$ is well defined.

Finally, a *noise mechanism* is a family of mechanisms $N(\epsilon_N) : \mathcal{X} \to \mathcal{P}(\mathcal{Z})$, parametrized by the available budget ϵ_N. The noise mechanism is used for hard secrets that cannot be predicted and can be any of the sporadic mechanisms presented in Section 4, although in the following we will assume the use of the planar Laplace for simplicity.

Budget management. The parameters of the mechanism's components need to be configured at each step. This can be done in a dynamic way using the concept of a *budget manager*. A budget manager β is a function that takes as input the run produced so far and returns the budget and the threshold to be used for the test at this step as well as the budget for the noise mechanism: $\beta(\mathbf{r}) = (\epsilon_\theta, \epsilon_N, l)$.

Of course the amount of budget used for the test should always be less than the amount devoted to the noise, otherwise it would be more convenient to just use the independent noise mechanism. Still, there is great flexibility in configuring the various parameters and several strategies can be implemented in terms of a budget manager.

The Mechanism. We are now ready to fully describe our mechanism. A single step of the predictive mechanism, displayed in Figure 3b, is a family of mechanisms $\text{Step}(\mathbf{r})$: $\mathcal{X} \to \mathcal{P}(\mathcal{Z} \times \mathcal{B})$, parametrized by the run **r** reported up to this point. The mechanism takes a location x and returns a reported location z, as well as a boolean b denoting whether the secret was easy or hard. First, the mechanism obtains the various configuration parameters from the budget manager as well as a prediction $\tilde{z}$. Then the prediction is tested using the test mechanism. If the test is successful the prediction is returned, otherwise a new reported location is generated using the noise mechanism.

Finally, the predictive mechanism, displayed in Figure 3a, is a mechanism PM : $\mathcal{X}^n \to \mathcal{P}(\mathcal{R})$. It takes as input a trace **x**, and applies $\text{Step}(\mathbf{r})$ to each point, while extending at each step the run **r** with the new reported values (z, b).

Note that an important advantage of the mechanism is that it is *online*, that is the sanitization of each location does not depend on future ones. This means that the user can query at any time during the life of the system, as opposed to *offline* mechanisms were all the requests need to be generated before the sanitization.

The main innovation of this mechanism if the use of the prediction function, which allows to decouple the privacy mechanism from the correlation analysis, creating a family of modular mechanisms where by *plugging* in different predictions we are able to work in new domains.

Privacy. It can be shown that the predictive mechanism, given a family of test functions and noise functions respectively ϵ_θ and ϵ_N d_x-private, is itself d_x-private. The global budget $\epsilon_\beta(\mathbf{r})$ is actually dependent on the budget manager and on the specific run, which is incompatible with d_x-privacy that is always independent from the prior. The reason is that a hard step is more expensive than an easy step because of the cost of the noise mechanism. Therefore there is a difference between the budget spent on a "good" run, where the input has a considerable correlation, the prediction performs well and the majority of steps are easy, and a run with uncorrelated secrets, where any prediction is useless and all the steps are hard. In the latter case it is clear that our mechanism wastes part of its budget on tests that always fail, performing worse than an independent mechanism.

However we can still enforce the definition with the use of a ϵ-bounded budget manager. Such a budget manager provides a fixed privacy guarantee by sacrificing utility: in the case of a bad run it either needs to lower the budget spend per secret, leading to more noise, or to stop early, handling a smaller number of requests. In this case the budget manager moves the impact of the runs away from the privacy budget and to utility. Two such managers were developed, both with fixed global privacy, one improving QL for a fixed number of requests, the other increasing the number of requests for a certain fixed QL.

6 Evaluation

We experimentally verify the effectiveness of our mechanisms on the motivating example of a user performing various activities in a city, using two large data sets of GPS trajectories in the Beijing urban area ([40,41]). Geolife [40] collects the movements of several users, using a variety of transportation means, including walking, while in Tdrive [41] we find exclusively taxi drivers trajectories. Due to space restrictions, only a small part of the results are given here; a detailed evaluation is available in [8,10,11].

Optimal Mechanism. To show the benefits of using a mechanism with optimal utility, we compare now the QL of the optimal mechanism (OPTQL) and of the planar Laplace (PL) when both are generated with the same privacy level ϵ. We can see the results in Figure 4a. The OPTQL mechanism clearly offers a better utility to the user, while guaranteeing the same level of geo-indistinguishability.

Regarding the spanner approximation of the optimal mechanism, the relation between the dilation and the number of constraints is shown in Figure 4b. It is clear that

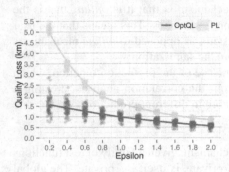
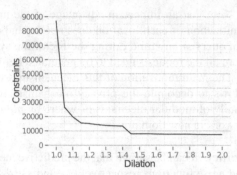

(a) Left: Quality loss of the OPTQL and PL mechanisms for different values of ϵ. The mechanisms were calculated for all users. Here, points represent the utility for every user, while the two lines join the medians for each mechanism and each value of ϵ.

(b) Right: Relation between the approximation ratio and the number of constraints in the linear program. This number is independent from the user and from the value of ϵ.

Fig. 4. Optimal mechanism evaluation

the number of constraints decreases exponentially with respect to the dilation, and therefore even for small dilations (which in turn mean good approximations) the number of constraints is significantly reduced with the proposed approximation technique. For instance, we have 87250 constraints for $\delta = 1$ (the optimal case), and 25551 constraints for $\delta = 1.05$. This represents a decrease of 71% with respect to the optimal case, with only 1.05 approximation ratio.

Predictive Mechanism. In order to model both frequent (easier to predict) as well as seldom users, the GPS traces were sampled with a different probability of *jumping*, i.e. performing a query with a long delay (one hour) after the previous one. The test included two budget managers, one optimizing QL for a fixed number of queries (fixed-rate), the other reducing budget consumption to prolong the use of the system at a fixed QL (fixed-ql). The results, shown in Figure 5, show considerable improvements with respect to independently applied noise, for both managers: we are able to decrease the average error up to 40% and the budget consumption rate up to 64%. The improvements are significant enough to broaden the applicability of geo-indistinguishability to cases impossible before: in our experiments we cover 30 queries with reasonable error which is enough for a full day of usage; alternatively we can drive the error down from 5 km to 3 km, which make it acceptable for a variety of applications.

7   Related Work

Several related works have been already presented in Section 2, a few more are discussed in this section.

On the side of the optimal mechanism construction, the work closest to ours is [42], which independently proposes a linear programming technique to construct an optimal

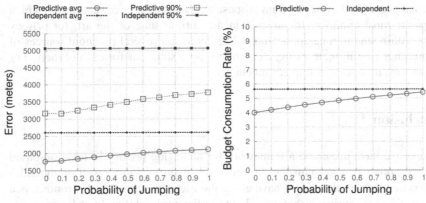

(a) Average and 90th percentile error for fixed-rate

(b) Budget consumption rate for fixed-ql

Fig. 5. Predictive mechanism evaluation with two budget managers

obfuscation mechanism wrt either the expected adversary error or geo-indistinguishability. Although there is an overlap in the main construction (the optimization problem of Section 4.2), most of the results are substantially different. The approximation technique of [42] consists of discarding some of the geo-indistinguishability constraints when the distance involved is larger than a certain lower bound. This affects the geo-indistinguishability guarantees of the mechanism, although the effect can be tuned by properly selecting the bound for discarding constraints. On the other hand, our approximation technique, based on spanning graphs, can be used to reduce the number of constraints from cubic to quadratic without jeopardizing the privacy guarantees, by accepting a small decrease on the utility.

On the side of the predictive mechanism, our work was mainly inspired by the median mechanism [43], a work on differential privacy for databases based on the idea of exploiting the correlation on the queries to improve the budget usage. The mechanism uses a concept similar to our *prediction* to determine the answer to the next query using only past answers. An analogous work is the multiplicative weights mechanism [44], again in the context of statistical databases. The mechanism keeps a parallel version of the database which is used to predict the next answer and in case of failure it is updated with a multiplicative weights technique.

A key difference from our context is that in the above works, several queries are performed against the *same database*. In our setting, however, the secret (the position of the user) is always changing, which requires to exploit correlations in the data. This scenario is explored also in [45] were the authors consider the case of an evolving secret and develop a differentially private counter.

Another work very close in spirit to ours is [46]. The authors of this paper also consider the problem of location privacy for location based services, and use random noise to conceal the actual location. However their work is mainly focused on exploiting the features of existing technology, and does not attempt to give a rigorous definition of privacy guarantees.

In a recent paper [3], Fawaz and Shin propose the *Location Privacy Guardian*, which is perhaps the most complete framework, in the current state of the art, for privacy protection within smartphone applications. They consider several potential sources of privacy breaches (profiling, tracking, etc.) and propose solutions for each of them. For location privacy, they use our Laplace mechanism.

8   Conclusion

In this paper we have presented a framework for achieving privacy in location-based applications, taking into account the desired level of protection as well as the side-information that the attacker might have about the user. The core of our proposal is a new notion of location privacy, that we call geo-indistinguishability. In order to ensure this kind of privacy protection in location-based services, we have proposed mechanisms that achieve geo-indistinguishability by perturbating the actual location with random noise. We have considered two kinds of mechanisms: the first one is universal, i.e., it does not depend on the user, and uses a bivariate version of the Laplace function as the density function of the noise. The second one is designed assuming a particular user, and for that user it achieves the optimal trade off between privacy and utility. This is done by formulating the optimal trade off as a linear programming problem, whose solution are the conditional probabilities that compose the noise matrix. Finally, we have considered the problem of traces, namely the repeated use of the mechanism to generate a sequence of points (a situation that may arise, for instance, when the user makes several requests to the service during a walk), and we have addressed the problem of the degradation of the level of privacy due to the correlation of the actual locations. We have proposed a method that limits the degradation by applying a prediction mechanism, which allows to generate new reported locations without applying the mechanism at each step. Finally, we have evaluated our methods and showed that they are a considerable improvement w.r.t. the state of the art, and that our proposal to limit the negative effects of the correlation in traces is effective in practice.

Acknowledgments. This work was partially supported by the MSR-INRIA joint lab, by the European Union 7th FP project MEALS, by the project ANR-12-IS02-001 PACE, and by the INRIA Large Scale Initiative CAPPRIS.

References

1. Ball, J.: Angry birds and 'leaky' phone apps targeted by nsa and gchq for user data. The Guardian (2014),
   http://www.theguardian.com/world/2014/jan/27/
   nsa-gchq-smartphone-app-angry-birds-personal-data
2. Please Rob Me, http://pleaserobme.com/
3. Fawaz, K., Shin, K.G.: Location privacy protection for smartphone users. In: Proc. of CCS, pp. 239–250. ACM Press (2014)

4. Brownlee, J.: This creepy app isn't just stalking women without their knowledge, it's a wake-up call about facebook privacy [update]. Cult of Mac (2012), http://www.cultofmac.com/157641/this-creepy-app-isnt-just-stalking-women-without-their-knowledge-its-a-wake-up-call-about-facebook-privacy/
5. Dwork, C.: Differential privacy. In: Bugliesi, M., Preneel, B., Sassone, V., Wegener, I. (eds.) ICALP 2006. LNCS, vol. 4052, pp. 1–12. Springer, Heidelberg (2006)
6. Chatzikokolakis, K., Andrés, M.E., Bordenabe, N.E., Palamidessi, C.: Broadening the scope of Differential Privacy using metrics. In: De Cristofaro, E., Wright, M. (eds.) PETS 2013. LNCS, vol. 7981, pp. 82–102. Springer, Heidelberg (2013)
7. Shokri, R., Theodorakopoulos, G., Boudec, J.Y.L., Hubaux, J.P.: Quantifying location privacy. In: Proc. of S&P, pp. 247–262. IEEE (2011)
8. Andrés, M.E., Bordenabe, N.E., Chatzikokolakis, K., Palamidessi, C.: Geo-indistinguishability: differential privacy for location-based systems. In: Proc. of CCS, pp. 901–914. ACM (2013)
9. Shokri, R., Theodorakopoulos, G., Troncoso, C., Hubaux, J.P., Boudec, J.Y.L.: Protecting location privacy: optimal strategy against localization attacks. In: Proc. of CCS, pp. 617–627. ACM (2012)
10. Chatzikokolakis, K., Palamidessi, C., Stronati, M.: A predictive differentially-private mechanism for mobility traces. In: De Cristofaro, E., Murdoch, S.J. (eds.) PETS 2014. LNCS, vol. 8555, pp. 21–41. Springer, Heidelberg (2014)
11. Bordenabe, N.E., Chatzikokolakis, K., Palamidessi, C.: Optimal geo-indistinguishable mechanisms for location privacy. In: Proc. of CCS (2014)
12. Hoh, B., Gruteser, M.: Protecting location privacy through path confusion. In: Proc. of SecureComm, pp. 194–205. IEEE (2005)
13. Herrmann, M., Troncoso, C., Diaz, C., Preneel, B.: Optimal sporadic location privacy preserving systems in presence of bandwidth constraints. In: Proc. of WPES (2013)
14. Theodorakopoulos, G., Shokri, R., Troncoso, C., Hubaux, J., Boudec, J.L.: Prolonging the hide-and-seek game: Optimal trajectory privacy for location-based services. CoRR abs/1409.1716 (2014)
15. Olteanu, A.-M., Huguenin, K., Shokri, R., Hubaux, J.-P.: Quantifying the effect of co-location information on location privacy. In: De Cristofaro, E., Murdoch, S.J. (eds.) PETS 2014. LNCS, vol. 8555, pp. 184–203. Springer, Heidelberg (2014)
16. Gruteser, M., Grunwald, D.: Anonymous usage of location-based services through spatial and temporal cloaking. In: Proc. of MobiSys. USENIX (2003)
17. Gedik, B., Liu, L.: Location privacy in mobile systems: A personalized anonymization model. In: Proc. of ICDCS, pp. 620–629. IEEE (2005)
18. Mokbel, M.F., Chow, C.Y., Aref, W.G.: The new casper: Query processing for location services without compromising privacy. In: Proc. of VLDB, pp. 763–774. ACM (2006)
19. Kido, H., Yanagisawa, Y., Satoh, T.: Protection of location privacy using dummies for location-based services. In: Proc. of ICDE Workshops, p. 1248 (2005)
20. Shankar, P., Ganapathy, V., Iftode, L.: Privately querying location-based services with SybilQuery. In: Proc. of UbiComp, pp. 31–40. ACM (2009)
21. Bamba, B., Liu, L., Pesti, P., Wang, T.: Supporting anonymous location queries in mobile environments with privacygrid. In: Proc. of WWW, pp. 237–246. ACM (2008)
22. Duckham, M., Kulik, L.: A formal model of obfuscation and negotiation for location privacy. In: Gellersen, H.-W., Want, R., Schmidt, A. (eds.) PERVASIVE 2005. LNCS, vol. 3468, pp. 152–170. Springer, Heidelberg (2005)
23. Xue, M., Kalnis, P., Pung, H.: Location diversity: Enhanced privacy protection in location based services. In: Choudhury, T., Quigley, A., Strang, T., Suginuma, K. (eds.) LoCA 2009. LNCS, vol. 5561, pp. 70–87. Springer, Heidelberg (2009)

24. Machanavajjhala, A., Kifer, D., Abowd, J.M., Gehrke, J., Vilhuber, L.: Privacy: Theory meets practice on the map. In: Proc. of ICDE, pp. 277–286. IEEE (2008)
25. Ho, S.-S., Ruan, S.: Differential privacy for location pattern mining. In: Proc. of SPRINGL, pp. 17–24. ACM (2011)
26. Chen, R., Ács, G., Castelluccia, C.: Differentially private sequential data publication via variable-length n-grams. In: Proc. of CCS, pp. 638–649. ACM (2012)
27. Dewri, R.: Local differential perturbations: Location privacy under approximate knowledge attackers. IEEE Trans. on Mobile Computing 99(PrePrints), 1 (2012)
28. Cheng, R., Zhang, Y., Bertino, E., Prabhakar, S.: Preserving user location privacy in mobile data management infrastructures. In: Danezis, G., Golle, P. (eds.) PET 2006. LNCS, vol. 4258, pp. 393–412. Springer, Heidelberg (2006)
29. Ardagna, C.A., Cremonini, M., Damiani, E., De Capitani di Vimercati, S., Samarati, P.: Location privacy protection through obfuscation-based techniques. In: Barker, S., Ahn, G.-J. (eds.) Data and Applications Security 2007. LNCS, vol. 4602, pp. 47–60. Springer, Heidelberg (2007)
30. Khoshgozaran, A., Shahabi, C.: Blind evaluation of nearest neighbor queries using space transformation to preserve location privacy. In: Papadias, D., Zhang, D., Kollios, G. (eds.) SSTD 2007. LNCS, vol. 4605, pp. 239–257. Springer, Heidelberg (2007)
31. Ghinita, G., Kalnis, P., Khoshgozaran, A., Shahabi, C., Tan, K.L.: Private queries in location based services: anonymizers are not necessary. In: Proc. of SIGMOD, pp. 121–132. ACM (2008)
32. Gambs, S., Killijian, M.O., del Prado Cortez, M.N.: Show me how you move and i will tell you who you are. Trans. on Data Privacy 4(2), 103–126 (2011)
33. Gambs, S., Killijian, M., del Prado Cortez, M.N.: De-anonymization attack on geolocated data. In: Proc. of TrustCom 2013, pp. 789–797. IEEE (2013)
34. Primault, V., Mokhtar, S.B., Lauradoux, C., Brunie, L.: Differentially private location privacy in practice. In: Proc. of MoST 2014. IEEE (2014)
35. Dwork, C., Mcsherry, F., Nissim, K., Smith, A.: Calibrating noise to sensitivity in private data analysis. In: Halevi, S., Rabin, T. (eds.) TCC 2006. LNCS, vol. 3876, pp. 265–284. Springer, Heidelberg (2006)
36. Lange, K., Sinsheimer, J.S.: Normal/independent distributions and their applications in robust regression. J. of Comp. and Graphical Statistics 2(2), 175–198 (1993)
37. Location Guard, https://github.com/chatziko/location-guard
38. Narasimhan, G., Smid, M.: Geometric spanner networks. CUP (2007)
39. Sack, J., Urrutia, J.: Handbook of Computational Geometry. Elsevier (1999)
40. Zheng, Y., Xie, X., Ma, W.Y.: Geolife: A collaborative social networking service among user, location and trajectory. IEEE Data Eng. Bull. 33(2), 32–39 (2010)
41. Yuan, J., Zheng, Y., Zhang, C., Xie, W., Xie, X., Sun, G., Huang, Y.: T-drive: driving directions based on taxi trajectories. In: GIS, pp. 99–108 (2010)
42. Shokri, R.: Optimal user-centric data obfuscation. Technical report, ETH Zurich (2014), http://arxiv.org/abs/1402.3426
43. Roth, A., Roughgarden, T.: Interactive privacy via the median mechanism. In: Proc. of STOC, pp. 765–774 (2010)
44. Hardt, M., Rothblum, G.N.: A multiplicative weights mechanism for privacy-preserving data analysis. In: FOCS, pp. 61–70. IEEE (2010)
45. Dwork, C., Naor, M., Pitassi, T., Rothblum, G.N.: Differential privacy under continual observation. In: STOC, pp. 715–724. ACM (2010)
46. Merrill, S., Basalp, N., Biskup, J., Buchmann, E., Clifton, C., Kuijpers, B., Othman, W., Savas, E.: Privacy through uncertainty in location-based services. In: IEEE 14th Int. Conf. on Mobile Data Management, pp. 67–72. IEEE Computer Society (2013)

Fusing Sensors for Occupancy Sensing
in Smart Buildings*

Nabeel Nasir, Kartik Palani, Amandeep Chugh, Vivek Chil Prakash,
Uddhav Arote, Anand P. Krishnan, and Krithi Ramamritham**

Department of Computer Science
Indian Institute of Technology Bombay,
Mumbai, India
{nabeel12,kartik,amandeepchugh12,
vivekcp,uddhava,anandkp,krithi}@cse.iitb.ac.in
http://www.cse.iitb.ac.in

Abstract. Understanding occupant-building interactions helps in personalized energy and comfort management. However, occupant identification using affordable infrastructure, remains unresolved. Our analysis of existing solutions revealed that for a building to have real-time view of occupancy state and use it intelligently, there needs to be a smart fusion of affordable, not-necessarily-smart, yet accurate enough sensors. Such a sensor fusion should aim for minimalistic user intervention while providing accurate building occupancy data. We describe an occupant detection system that accurately monitors the occupants' count and identities in a shared office space, which can be scaled up for a building. Incorporating aspects from data analytics and sensor fusion with intuition, we have built a *Smart-Door* using inexpensive sensors to tackle this problem. It is a scalable, plug-and-play software architecture for flexibly realizing smart-doors using different sensors to monitor buildings with varied occupancy profiles. Further, we show various smart-energy applications of this occupancy information: detecting anomalous device behaviour and load forecasting of plug-level loads.

Keywords: Smart Door, Smart Building, Energy Saving, User Comfort, Electrical Energy.

1 Introduction

Designing new "green" buildings and retrofitting existing buildings with green technologies pose numerous research challenges but essential for society. Two of the main motivations for this transition towards a smarter and greener electricity grid have been capping total usage or flattening the peak and reducing the carbon footprint and costs. This has sparked new interest in developing smarter

---

* The authors would like to thank DeitY, Govt. of India and TCS for their generous support of this work.
** Corresponding author.

R. Natarajan et al. (Eds.): ICDCIT 2015, LNCS 8956, pp. 73–92, 2015.

Table 1. Approaches to tracking occupancy using various sensors and their fusion

Sensor	Advantages	Disadvantages	Occupancy Information
Passive Infra Red	Cheap; Scalable; RT Response; No User Intervention	When users become stationary (eg., working on PC) room occupancy detected as NIL	Presence of occupants in room
CO_2 [3]	Cheap; User intervention is not required; Scalable	Response is not real-time; Accuracy reduces when there is proper air circulation	Presence of occupants in room
Radio Frequency Identification	Accurate when proper measures taken;Real Time response; No user intervention req.	User should carry RFID tag; Tags must not be kept near metallic objects; Accuracy depends on speed of walking[5]	Count and identity
Face Recognition [9]	No user Intervention required	Computationally challenging; Expensive; Accuracy is less for moving objects; Not easily scalable; Requires 2 cameras to detect Entry and Exit	Count and identity
Sound Detection [10]	Cheap; Real-Time Response; Scalable	Not suitable for environments like labs and libraries	Presence of occupant in room
PIR+Reed[1]	Cheap; Scalable	The sensor fails to detect occupancy in a multi user environment	Presence of occupant in room
WiFi+Lan+ IM+Calender +Access Badge[6]	Cheap;Scalable	Accuracy reduces when users don't comply to the rules of the system, WiFi can't distinguish a person who is right outside the room, will be detected as inside the room	Count and identity

buildings, which can sense instances of undesired energy usage and intelligently take decisions towards curbing such occurrences. For instance, smart buildings may use sensors to track occupants and opportunistically disconnect loads in empty rooms; we use the term "load" to refer to any appliance or device that draws electricity.

Smart buildings inherently possess knowledge about their energy consumption at any given instant. Considering that smart meters that record aggregate power at fine granularity with high accuracies are ubiquitous in modern residential and commercial environments, it can be assumed that most new buildings will possess this level of smartness. What can accentuate the smartness, is the ability to calculate how much energy should optimally be consumed, given the various parameters (like temperature, relative humidity, etc.) that influence energy usage. One such parameter is the occupancy state of the building: the electricity demand of a building is driven by its occupants. Having real-time knowledge about the occupants adds to the building's intelligence significantly. This information can be put to use not only for energy savings but also for other important applications ranging from knowing the health of appliances to priority evacuation of children and the elderly in times of emergencies.

A review of existing occupancy monitoring systems shows that even the most accurate of them have certain bottle-necks. For example, with biometric identification systems, which score well on accuracy, people have to stop at a place to record their entry. This might be acceptable for a one-time check-in into a building. However, for room-level occupancy monitoring, the system becomes inconvenient due to the the fact that occupants need to register their identity every time they enter/exit the room. Another familiar occupant monitoring system is the Active RFID based system. RFID systems are generally used for access control in buildings, but it also logs the occupant identity which can be used to monitor occupancy. Active RFID systems, unlike passive RFID systems, do not require a stop and swipe mechanism. They are also known to have high accuracies. But in order to obtain high accuracy users need to carry the tag at all times, they also have to be careful not to keep the tag next to metallic objects and be wary of the speed with which they walk across the RFID reader. Moreover, RFID readers are expensive and can't be deployed in each and every doorway of the building. In addition, these systems are deactivated during evacuation of buildings so that the access control of the building doesn't hinder the free flow of occupants. If these systems are disabled during evacuation then finding who and how many are still inside the building becomes troublesome. In general, sensors need to be examined against characteristics such as, accuracy, cost, reliability, interruption/inconvenience caused, computational complexity and the occupancy data they help infer (how many, who and where). Table 1 summarizes the pros and cons of existing occupancy tracking systems along with the occupancy questions they answer. Given this, it is clear that for a building to have a real-time view of occupancy state, and use it intelligently, there needs to be a smart fusion of cost-effective, not-necessarily-smart, yet accurate-enough sensors. Such a sensor-fusion system should aim to respect the users' natural behavior by allowing for minimalistic user intervention while providing accurate occupancy data about the building. [7] talks about a probabilistic approach of identifying occupants in a home environment, focuses on using height sensors with the main goal as tracking the occupants. Our work, although has used few similar sensors, focuses more on the energy saving application of the occupant data and has been implemented using Machine Learning techniques in a lab environment where the number of users are much larger than a home environment. These considerations prompted the work reported in this paper which lead to the following contributions:

Firstly, we propose and report on the experiences with a set of novel solutions to the occupancy tracking problem:

- Incorporating aspects from data analytics and sensor fusion, combined with intuition, we have developed a *smart door* to tackle the occupancy detection problem.
- The experience with the building of multiple versions of the smart door lead to the design and creation of a plug-and-play architecture to flexibly address the door's controller's design and construction.
- We have installed the whole system in our lab's premises and have gathered extensive experiential data. We report on the occupancy prediction accuracy results, offer a comparative analysis of the operation and usefulness of different combinations of sensors and draw inferences that will be useful for researchers and practitioners alike.

It is important to point out that the smart door design along with embellishments such as a personalized appliance control system can help with matters related to occupancy, such as "how many are in a given space" and "who is in a given space".

Secondly, with occupancy-related data in hand, in conjunction with smart meter data, we show how some interesting energy-related practical questions can be answered:

- How can smart meter data be used to detect the occurrence of "unusual", "abnormal" or "unexpected" energy usage profiles?
- How can knowing occupant identities help forecast plug-level load better?
- Can knowing "who" help give personalized actionable energy savings advice?

These experiences clearly demonstrate that occupancy matters!

2   The Smart Door

In this section, we describe the *Smart Door*, a system capable of providing occupant identities and count, in a room. The smart door achieves occupancy identification and counting without any user interaction, supports easy sensor integration and at the same time is cost effective. The design philosophy of smart door is to enable its user to add sensors easily based on the accuracy required for the occupant detection/identification; thanks to the plug and play architecture described in Section 4. The base version of smart door has two LDR-laser pairs for occupancy counting and detecting direction of movement. The sequence of lasers being cut determine if an occupant is entering or exitting a room. Hence the base version of the Smart Door was capable of only keeping the real-time occupant count and not the user identification. Further versions have both paraphernalia and capability to infer identity of the occupants too. The plug and play architecture helped to experiment with multiple occupant identification sensors used to measure height, weight and skeletal parameters and are detailed in Section 2.1.1, 2.1.2 and 2.1.3 respectively. Their accuracies with various learning algorithms are also detailed in the section. We believe that the smart door can be implemented under $100 when manufactured in large quantities, making it a cheap system for building wide implementation.

2.1   Occupant Identification

We believed that sensing signatures from the human body, when people walked through the smart door, could be used to uniquely identify people. To achieve cost effectiveness, only signatures which could be sensed during both entry and exit, using a single sensor, were considered.

When a person passes through the smart door, his/her signature is obtained by the controller board, using the sensor. A Raspberry Pi board running Linux is used as the controller board. A tablet is deployed at the entrance using which people can manually tag their identity as they enter. The measured signature along with the tagged identity information is used as training data for a supervised learning algorithm. The algorithm, after sufficient training, would then be able to predict occupants' identities based on their body signature. The entire system, when used with a height sensor is designed as shown in Figure 1. Other versions maintain the same design except for the sensor, which is switched on depending on what body signature is being sensed.

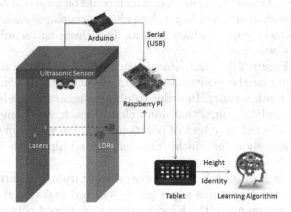

Fig. 1. Occupant Identification: Height

The learning algorithm used for our implementation was Support Vector Machines (SVM). The prediction results for each individual signature (height, skeletal parameters and weight) and a comparison of SVM with Naive Bayes classifier is presented in Section 2.3.

2.1.1   Occupant Identification: Height.
Height was chosen as the first signature that was sensed, since it could be easily sensed and does not vary significantly over time, in adults.

An ultrasonic sensor is mounted on the smart door, which gives the distance to any object placed under it. The distance values are recorded between two subsequent laser obstructions. We take the minimum of all the recorded values, since the minimum distance from the ultrasonic sensor is when the beam hits the topmost point of the head of a person and reflects back. From this obtained minimum distance and the height of the smart door frame, the height of the person is estimated.

2.1.2   Occupant Identification: Weight.
A weight mat can be used to measure weight even when a person is walking, and moreover only a single sensor is required for measurement during entry and exit. Although it can be argued that the weight measured for a moving object will be less when compared to a static measurement, it is important to note that the goal is to obtain a unique signature. This goal is still achieved considering that the difference in weight propagates through the data.

A weight mat was designed by attaching strain gauges underneath a wooden board - four gauges fixed near the corners of the board. The strain on a strain gauge produces a change in resistance and a Wheatstone bridge circuit can be used to measure this. Proper calibration of all four gauges can thus give the weight of a person standing or walking on the board. This board is placed between the legs of the walk-through frame of the Smart Door to obtain weights of people as they enter/exit the room.

2.1.3   Occupant Identification: Skeletal Parameters.
Adhering to the design philosophy of choosing signatures which could be sensed in both directions using a single sensor, we decided to get data about occupants' skeletal structures. The Microsoft Kinect sensor, which uses its depth sensing technique to obtain these parameters, was used.

As shown in Figure 2 [8], the Kinect can deduce the skeletal structure for a person by obtaining the positions of about twenty joints of the body, using its infrared and depth sensors. In order to obtain signatures useful to uniquely identify humans, skeletal points that don't change much, across multiple sensing runs, were to be selected. A subset of points in the torso were identified as being the most consistent: shoulder width, torso length and hip width were picked as the signatures.

The Kinect was kept at a height, few feet away from the entrance into the room, to capture the signatures when people entered and exited the room. As with the height measurement, the Kinect values were record between subsequent laser cuts of the smart door.

2.2   Results

The data acquired comprised of around 5000 records - signatures along with the tagged identity information collected during entry and exit. The data set for all

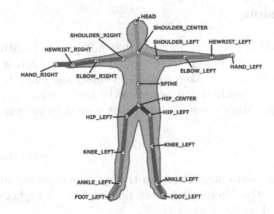

Fig. 2. Skeletal structure obtained from Kinect [8]

the five signatures taken individually - height, weight, shoulder width, hip width and torso length were put through an 10-fold cross validation using an SVM classifier as well as a Naive Bayes classifier and the accuracy was measured. The results are shown in Figure 3.

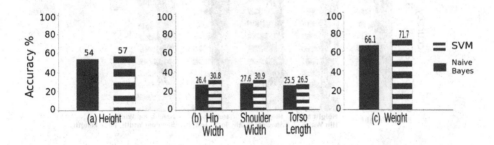

Fig. 3. Prediction Accuracy: (a) Height (b) Skeletal Parameters (c) Weight

Kinect parameters taken individually fared poorly (30%). Height individually achieved double the accuracy of the Kinect (60%) and weight fared even better than height with an accuracy around 70%. One worthwhile observation is that the low-cost height and weight sensors fared better in comparison to the costlier Kinect sensor (it can, although, be argued that the Kinect sensor can be put to a variety of other uses like face recognition, voice recognition, etc. but these do not adhere to our design philosophy of a single sensor sensing for both entry and exit). It was also observed that for the data set we had, SVM had a clear edge over Naive Bayes in terms of prediction accuracy.

3 Sensor Fusion

The results obtained in Section 2 indicate that individual signatures taken from users were not necessarily unique to the individuals. However, we hypothesized that multiple such signatures taken from individuals and fused together had the potential to increase identification accuracy. In this section we show how this accuracy significantly went up when intelligent sensor fusion was performed.

3.1 Results

The fusion of height data acquired from the ultrasonic sensor and the skeletal data obtained from the Microsoft Kinect provided much higher accuracy than they provided individually (Figure 4).

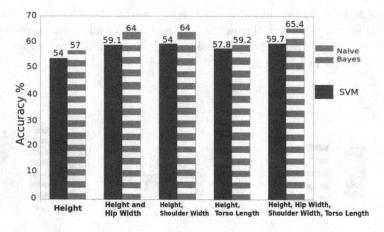

Fig. 4. Prediction Accuracy: Height and Kinect features

When multiple combinations of height and skeletal features are examined, an interesting trend was noticed: any combination of intuitively correlated features leads only to a small increase in accuracy. In order to mathematically examine this hypothesis, Pearson correlation was applied to combinations of two features. Pearson correlation is used to show how strong the association is between two variables. It ranges from +1 (indicating direct proportionality between variables) to -1 (indicating inverse proportionality). A correlation of 0 indicates that the two variables are independent of each other.The results are shown in Table 2.

Table 2 indicates that the highest correlation is between the hip-width and the shoulder-width (0.733). Table 3 shows how their combination performs in terms of occupant identification accuracy.

The result indicates that as a virtue of the high correlation, no additional information is added to the model for it to improve. In order to test if less correlation meant higher accuracy, we calculated the correlation between height

Table 2. Correlation between features

Feature 1	Feature 2	Pearson Correlation
height	weight	0.599
height	hip-width	-0.008
height	shoulder-width	0.034
height	torso-length	0.173
weight	hip-width	0.066
weight	shoulder-width	0.088
weight	torso-length	0.385
hip-width	shoulder-width	0.733
hip-width	torso-length	-0.207
shoulder-width	torso-length	-0.152

Table 3. Prediction Accuracy: hip-width, shoulder-width

Features	Accuracy%
hip-width	30.8
shoulder-width	30.9
hip-width, shoulder-width	31.0

and hip-width which are almost uncorrelated (-0.008). As can be seen from
Figure 4 the combination accounts for an accuracy of 64%.

In order to validate our original claim that adding sensors to the occupancy
detection system makes it more intelligent, we tested how weight performs when
combined with height. Figure 5 shows that a fusion of these two human parameters increases prediction accuracy to 87.1%. What makes this result even
more exciting is the fact that a simple combination of two low-cost and readily-
available sensors produces such high accuracy.

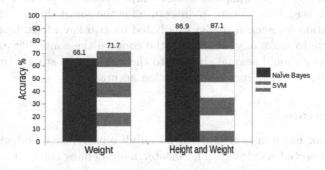

Fig. 5. Prediction Accuracy: Height and Weight

This performed extremely well considering that the two parameters have a
relatively high correlation (0.59). Analyzing this led to multiple plots like the one

shown in Figure 6. The first plot shows the probabilities with which an individual is identified among a certain subset of people with similar heights by the smart door described in Section 2. It becomes evident that it is hard to distinguish the individual uniquely. However, as shown in the second plot, for the same subset of people, by using weight as a metric for identification the system can identify them uniquely. Thus, along with correlation, it becomes important for the sensors fused to be able to understand the distribution of features among the occupants. This led to the formulation of a software architecture that seamlessly incorporates these learnings in order to monitor occupants for a room of any occupancy profile.

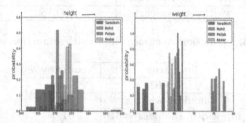

Fig. 6. Distribution of heights and weights for a subset of people

4   The Plug and Play Architecture

While installing various sensors to the smart door, we learnt a few key lessons. First, the accuracy of the smart door's prediction improved when an additional sensor was added, which meant that there needed to be support for adding multiple sensors to the setup. Second, the task of adding a new sensor can be very tedious and user-unfriendly. In order to create a system which, from the users' perspective, was a plug and play model where they could just plug in a sensor to the controller and hope to achieve improvement in prediction accuracy, we developed a scalable software architecture for the smart-door.

The foundation for such a model was based on two key ideas; first, the user should not have to make any changes in the code on the controller and second, any added sensor should seamlessly fit into the system and start improving the learning model and hence increase prediction accuracy.

4.1   Architecture

The Smart-Door has a master node to which all sensors(slave nodes) are wired directly or connected wirelessly. The master node defines the actions that the associated sensors must perform by exchanging messages with them. The master is responsible for detecting entry/exit events, framing meaningful messages for the slave nodes and reporting failures in the nodes to the administrator. The master also collects data from all the local nodes and sending it to a common database.

A slave node consists of a sensor that is attached to a micro controller board capable of storing sensed readings and performs local node aggregation. There are two kinds of slave nodes associated with the master: local nodes, which receive commands and sends data to master through wired connections and remote nodes, which performs message and data exchange with the master over a Wi-Fi network. Figure 7(a) gives a schematic detailing of these connections.

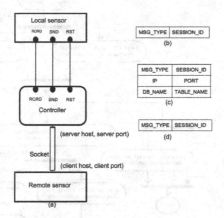

Fig. 7. (a) shows the schematic for sensor connections to controller. (b), (c), (d) illustrate formats of RCRD, RST and SND messages respectively, exchanged between network sensor and the controller.

A configuration file exists on the master which contains a list of the local and remote nodes and their locations (IP address in case of remote nodes and pin numbers in case of local nodes). Whenever a new sensor is added to the system, the administrator adds a new entry to the configuration file stating the type of sensor and its location. Thus, no change is made to any code. Internally, the master reconfigures and automatically incorporates the new sensor into the mix.

4.2 Messaging Protocol

A unique messaging protocol is designed in order for the master to communicate with the slave nodes. The messaging protocol is different for the local nodes and remote nodes. The activity diagram for the master and the state diagram for the slaves are shown in Figures 8 and 9.

4.2.1 Local Node Messaging
- Upon detecting a possible entry/exit event (recorded by emitting sensor 1 (Section 2.1)), the master sets the RCRD pin HIGH on the local nodes. This causes an interrupt in the nodes, which then starts data sensing.
- A possible entry/exit event may either be successful (recorded by emitting sensor 2) in which case, the RCRD pin is set LOW and the SND pin is set HIGH, which is an instruction to the node to calculate an average of recorded values and send the data to the local node manager via the serial interface.

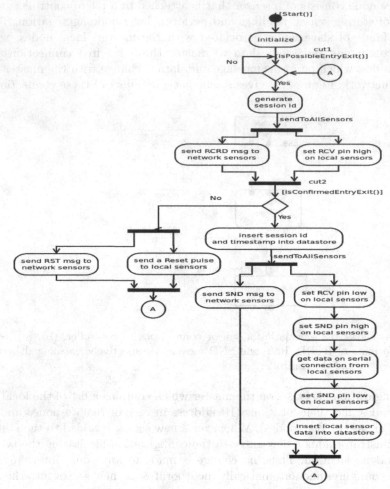

Fig. 8. Activity diagram for controller

- If the possible entry is not successful, i.e., it times out, the RCRD pin is set LOW and a RST pulse is sent which clears the data structures on the local nodes.
- In case of a successful entry/exit event, the host inserts an entry into the database table with the unique session_id and the timestamp. The data received by the local node manager is then updated in the the table.

4.2.2 Remote Node Messaging

- A possible entry/exit event triggers the master to frame a RCRD message (Figure 7 (b)) which is transmitted to the client ports on all the remote nodes. This prompts the remote sensors to begin storing sensed data.
- If the entry/exit event is successful, the master frames a SND message (Figure 7 (c)) which contains details about the common database where the

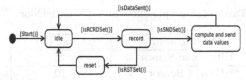

Fig. 9. State diagram for local and network sensors

sensor values are stored. The remote node then calculates the average and updates the entry in the database table.

– In case of a timeout event, a RST message is sent (Figure 7 (d)) which clears all the sensed data stored in the remote node.

All remote node messages are sent over Wi-Fi, thereby using existing infrastructure.

Since most low cost processing boards do not have a real time clock on them, a unique session_id is used for synchronization instead of the conventional timestamp synchronization. The time of the event is marked by the host which is Network Time Protocol synchronized. Thus, exact times of entry/exit events are recorded with high precision (to the second).

4.3 Database Design

Considering the goal of the smart door is to achieve maximum scalability while allowing minimal user intervention, another design choice that has been made is the use of a NoSQL database [12] instead of a traditional relational database model. With the addition of sensors, we wanted horizontal scalability and high write operation performance, both of which were achieved very well by the open source NoSQL database, MongoDB. This made it the database of choice for the software architecture.

4.4 Cost Considerations

From the results presented, the smart door is able to predict identities of people at fairly high accuracy and is scalable owing to the plug and play architecture, enabling fusion of additional sensors with ease. It is interesting to analyze the deployment cost of such a system including only the most essential sensors which were identified from the experiments. Such a minimalistic Smart Door comprises of a height sensor, a weight sensor, two Laser-LDR pairs, an Arduino board, and two low-cost Android Tablets. From Table 4 we can see that these components amount to around $150 and this cost can be further cut down upon mass production. At this cost, the system can be deployed at all doors in a building without incurring much. The applications that arise from deploying in such a scale are appealing and described in the following section.

5 Applications Enabled by Occupancy Information

The fusion of occupancy data and electricity consumption data can enable a rich set of applications necessary for smart buildings to become smarter and

Table 4. ComponentCost for Smart Door

Component	Cost ($)
Ultrasonic Sensor	3
Weight Sensor	10
2 Laser-LDR Pairs	10
Arduino Board	25
2 Android Tablets	100

greener. In this section we explore some applications which use this fused data, focusing on cases other than the conventional ones like load forecasting of HVAC loads [2] [4] and room automation – in order to provide insights into other important energy saving applications. The applications described here stem from our experiences with buildings at IIT Bombay.

5.1 Auxiliary Sensing and Actuation for Energy Applications

5.1.1 Smart Meter Setup. The smart meter's ability to provide high accuracy consumption data at fine frequencies makes it an important sensor. We use three EM6400 smart meters (named LSM-A, LSM-P, and LSM-F respectively) in order to understand the consumption profile of our lab. Table 5 shows what appliances' usage the respective smart meters monitor.

Table 5. SEIL smart meter connection and device profile

	Phase 1	AC 1 & AC 4
LSM-A	Phase 2	AC 2
	Phase 3	AC 3
LSM-P	Phase 1, 2, 3	Computers and Wall Sockets
LSM-F	Phase 1	Light Arrays and Fans
	Phase 2, 3	Null

5.1.2 Relay Control. The fans, lights and air conditioners in the lab are controlled using a relay system. Occupants turn ON/OFF their devices after logging into a web portal, which sends actuation messages to the relays. The resulting knowledge of who uses what devices allows for the appliance preferences of the occupants to be learnt.

5.2 Anomaly Detection

The plot in figure 10 compares the electricity consumption profile of our academic building on a day in which one of the 185 air conditioners in the building was malfunctioning, to the day on which the anomalous device was rectified. The exact details the anomaly are discussed later in this section. When we examine the peak power and total energy consumption, shown in Table 6, on these days, we notice that on the day of the AC anomaly, the peak was higher by 31 kW and the energy consumed was higher by almost 222 kWh. Considering that our electricity usage is charged at $0.10/unit, we could have saved $22.2/ day had the anomaly been identified earlier. This is admittedly very small compared to the average electricity bill for the academic building, which is around $13300/month.

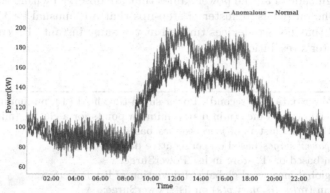

Fig. 10. Comparison of an anomalous day to a normal day

Considering the relatively negligible saving, identifying the anomaly might not seem like an issue worth addressing. However, the seriousness can be realized when we understand that in a building with a large number of such AC units (185 in our case), with each room fitted with about 3-4 of them, these anomalies go easily undetected. The primary cause for this is the fact that the non-anomalous ACs in the room compensate for the lack of cooling by the malfunctioning one. Now, when we look back at the problem and realize that an excess usage like this might go unnoticed for months, as it has been in our case before we installed smart meters, we realize that a single malfunctioning AC accounts for almost 5% ($666) of the monthly electricity bill for the building.

Table 6. Load profile – on an anomalous day (Jul 10) compared to the day it was rectified (Jul 11)

Date	Peak Power (kW)	Energy Consumed (kWh)
July 10	204.98	2975.87
July 11	173.93	2753.02

Smart-meters have been put to use, beyond their conventional usage [11] of monitoring electricity consumption, to detect such anomalous behavioral patterns. If the plot for the anomalous device is examined, we notice periodic spikes in the power drawn. It has been found that these spikes are due to a commonly occurring fault in ACs: the compressor overload trip, which is caused by compressor malfunction or non-function. In this section we provide an algorithm that successfully detects such an occurrence, using the smart meter data for the building, and isolates the fault to a small set of devices.

In order to first identify the anomaly in real time, a Density-Based Spatial Clustering of Applications with Noise (DBSCAN) algorithm is run over a 15 minute window of data. DBSCAN is a scalable and almost linear algorithm which identifies clusters in large spatial data sets using only one input parameter and gives out information about outliers in the same. As an input, the algorithm takes the magnitude of all the power values that are observed within the interval of interest. The output is a cluster of step-ups that are unusual for the profile. It is assumed that no two devices turn on at the same instant (1 second as per our smart-meter's resolution).

---

input : Power data (per second), Power-surge threshold (T), minimum
                neighbor distance (min_dis), minimum points for a cluster (min_pts)
output: Unusual clusters of *power-surges* based on magnitude
Calculate *power-surges* based on consecutive data points;
Filter them based on T, store in list_PowerSurge;
Calculate global_mean and global_std_deviation of list_PowerSurge;
Run DbScan (min_dis, min_pts) on list_PowerSurge;
for *cluster with mean > (global_mean +global_std_deviation)* **do**
| Mark the cluster as **Unusual**;
end

Algorithm 1. Clustering *Power-Surges* with unusual magnitudes

Once the spikes are identified, the anomaly is isolated to a small set of devices. The flowchart in Figure 11 succinctly describes the fault localization algorithm. If a spike is detected by the peak detection algorithm, the spike is evaluated to find its phase information. This information is passed to a process that uses the occupancy of the building in the relevant 15-minute interval and the set of devices that those occupants are known to have used in the past (learnt over a period of time using the system discussed in Section 4.1.2) to decipher which given appliances on that phase are active.

In our experience, the output list generally contains only a set of 3-4 devices. Thus, adding occupancy information leads to quick, almost real-time, identification of anomalous devices. This algorithm has been put to use in the academic building and has helped identify five major anomalies in the two months that it has run.

5.3   Load Forecasting: Plug-Level Loads

In most offices and academic buildings, most of the loads are at the plug-level. These loads, like desktop computers, laptops, printers and copiers are considered to consume significantly lesser energy than HVAC loads. But our experiences in the lab, which closely parallels an office space, taught us that this was not completely true. Figure 12 shows the plot of the energy consumed by various devices

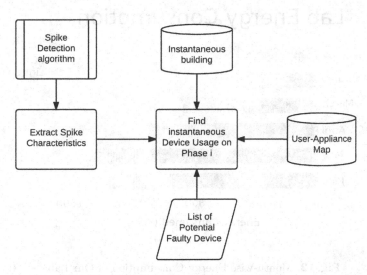

Fig. 11. Algorithm for detecting faulty devices

in this environment. Although the expected behavior of air conditioners consuming significantly higher power than the other loads is noticed in the summer months (April, May, June), during the winter months, the plug-level usage becomes comparable to the cooling load, with plug-level consumption being higher in the month of January. With this trend we expect that for at least half the year, plug-level energy consumption is of prime importance. It is also worth noting that in developing countries like ours, the majority of office spaces lack air conditioning in which case their primary usage comes from plug loads.

These findings motivated us to research how the accuracy of predicting plug-level load is affected by occupancy information.

5.3.1   Methodology. Since we had accurate occupancy and electrical consumption data only for 25 days at the time of experimentation, the time intervals for learning/prediction was chosen as 15 minutes so as to have more records for the experiment. The features considered for learning and their representation is as follows:

- Time of Day - A feature vector representing every 15th minute of the day
- Week End/Week Day - Binary feature representing if its a weekend or weekday
- Who - A feature vector of size k is maintained for each time interval. k denotes the total number of unique persons present in the occupancy records. Each cell indicates the amount of time a person was present in the room, for that interval, normalized to unity. For example, for the 15 minute interval of 21:00 -21:15, if $Person_1$ was inside the lab for half the interval time, then his feature value would be 0.5. Similarly, if $Person_2$ was present for 75% of the time, his feature value would be 0.75.

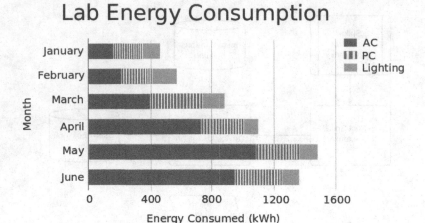

Fig. 12. Month-wise Energy Consumption of Our Lab

– Occupancy Count - Since, a room's occupancy count can change within a
time interval, average occupancy count of the room is taken as a feature.
This is computed using occupancy count numbers and corresponding time.

In order to forecast the load requirement, we experimented with two well
known models: Support Vector Regression (SVR) and Decision Tree Regression
(DTR). The performance of the model was judged using the CV-RMSE (Coefficient of Variation of Root Mean Square Error) which measures the difference in
values predicted by the model to the observed values.

5.3.2   Results. Different combinations of the features described in the previous section were supplied to the forecasting models. The performance is detailed
in Table 7.

Table 7. Plug-level load forecasting results

Interval	Weekday/Weekend Time of Day	Who	Occupancy count	DTR CV(RMSE) %	SVR CV(RMSE) %
15	✓	✓		21.94	18.40
15	✓		✓	25.08	28.1
15	✓			30.36	29.12

One behavior observable from the table is that greater the occupancy information (count, identity) the building has, the better it is able to forecast its energy
requirements. The model performs best, with only a 18.4% error, when the identities of the occupants are available. This indicates that a building which knows
its occupants' identities performs load forecasting of plug-level loads 36.8% more

accurately than a building that just uses calendar information to do the same, thus making it smarter.

6   Conclusions

We have reported on a repertoire of techniques contributing to occupancy detection and using the detected/inferred information for better energy management. Our design and implementation choices were driven by the following considerations:

- *Cost effectiveness*: For example, using occupant signatures which could be sensed using the same sensor during both entry and exit.
- *Minimal User Intervention*: The occupants should be allowed to freely walk in and out of a room and the system should still be able to monitor the occupancy.
- *Resilient to Errors Thereby giving High Accuracy Prediction*: Given the nature of office environments, errors like electromagnetic interference were resolved and accuracies as high as 87.1% were achieved.
- *Extensible Architecture*: Allow seamless addition of sensors, in a plug-and-play fashion, into the mix of existing sensors to improve the functionality/accuracy of the system.

It is clear that a single solution will not fit all occupancy detection scenarios. For example, since many of the actions triggered following occupancy detection are themselves prone to further validation, (for examples see Section 5), depending on the applications at hand, some amount of inaccuracy can be tolerated in occupancy detection and that can be exploited in trading-off between design choices. It is in this context that the flexible architecture described in this paper has a significant role to play.

Incorporating the lessons learnt in sensor fusion from Section 3.1, we are currently building a *sensor-recommender-tool* that aids users in selecting the best set of sensors for their room profile and intended purpose of deployment. Sensor recommendations are made to the user based on how the features of the room's occupants are distributed, existing sensors on the smart door, the desired accuracy and the required cost.

In our future work we also plan to look at further applications, including some that are unrelated to energy management, but are related to smarter building management, such as those that are necessary for emergency management and disaster recovery.

References

1. Agarwal, Y., Balaji, B., Gupta, R., Lyles, J., Wei, M., Weng, T.: Occupancy-driven energy management for smart building automation. In: Proceedings of the 2Nd ACM Workshop on Embedded Sensing Systems for Energy-Efficiency in Building, BuildSys 2010, pp. 1–6. ACM, New York (2010), http://doi.acm.org/10.1145/1878431.1878433

2. Balaji, B., Xu, J., Nwokafor, A., Gupta, R., Agarwal, Y.: Sentinel: Occupancy based hvac actuation using existing wifi infrastructure within commercial buildings. In: Proceedings of the 11th ACM Conference on Embedded Networked Sensor Systems, SenSys 2013, pp. 17:1–17:14. ACM, New York (2013), http://doi.acm.org/10.1145/2517351.2517370
3. Emmerich, S., Persily, A.: State-Of-The-Art Review of Co2 Demand Controlled Ventilation Technology and Application. Diane Publishing Company (2001), http://books.google.co.in/books?id=1hrONzju3IYC
4. Erickson, V.L., Carreira-Perpiñán, M.A., Cerpa, A.E.: Occupancy modeling and prediction for building energy management. ACM Trans. Sen. 10(3), 42:1–42:28 (2014), http://doi.acm.org/10.1145/2594771
5. Floerkemeier, C., Lampe, M.: Issues with rfid usage in ubiquitous computing applications. In: Ferscha, A., Mattern, F. (eds.) PERVASIVE 2004. LNCS, vol. 3001, pp. 188–193. Springer, Heidelberg (2004), http://dx.doi.org/10.1007/978-3-540-24646-6_13
6. Ghai, S., Thanayankizil, L., Seetharam, D., Chakraborty, D.: Occupancy detection in commercial buildings using opportunistic context sources. In: 2012 IEEE International Conference on Pervasive Computing and Communications Workshops (PERCOM Workshops), pp. 463–466 (March 2012)
7. Hnat, T.W., Griffiths, E., Dawson, R., Whitehouse, K.: Doorjamb: unobtrusive room-level tracking of people in homes using doorway sensors. In: Proceedings of the 10th ACM Conference on Embedded Network Sensor Systems, pp. 309–322. ACM (2012)
8. Labs, K.: Kinect sdk xna [Programming Guide] (2011), http://www.kosaka-lab.com/tips/2011/06/kinect-sdk-xna.php
9. Lee, K.C., Ho, J., Yang, M.H., Kriegman, D.: Video-based face recognition using probabilistic appearance manifolds. In: Proceedings of 2003 IEEE Computer Society Conference on Computer Vision and Pattern Recognition, vol. 1, pp. I–313–I–320 (June 2003)
10. Padmanabh, K., Malikarjuna V, A., Sen, S., Katru, S.P., Kumar, A., Vuppala, S.K., Paul, S.: isense: A wireless sensor network based conference room management system. In: Proceedings of the First ACM Workshop on Embedded Sensing Systems for Energy-Efficiency in Buildings, BuildSys 2009, pp. 37–42. ACM, New York (2009), http://doi.acm.org/10.1145/1810279.1810288
11. Palani, K., Nasir, N., Prakash, V.C., Chugh, A., Gupta, R., Ramamritham, K.: Putting smart meters to work: Beyond the usual. In: Proceedings of the 5th International Conference on Future Energy Systems, e-Energy 2014, pp. 237–238. ACM, New York (2014), http://doi.acm.org/10.1145/2602044.2602084
12. van der Veen, J., van der Waaij, B., Meijer, R.: Sensor data storage performance: Sql or nosql, physical or virtual. In: 2012 IEEE 5th International Conference on Cloud Computing (CLOUD), pp. 431–438 (June 2012)

Discrete Control-Based Design
of Adaptive and Autonomic Computing Systems*

Xin An[1], Gwenaël Delaval[2], Jean-Philippe Diguet[3], Abdoulaye Gamatié[4],
Soguy Gueye[2], Hervé Marchand[5], Noël de Palma[2], and Eric Rutten[6]

[1] Hefei University of Technology, Hefei, China
xin.an@hfut.edu.cn
[2] LIG, Grenoble, France
{gwenael.delaval,Soguy-Mak-Kare.Gueye,noel.depalma}@imag.fr
[3] Lab-STICC, Lorient, France
jean-philippe.diguet@univ-ubs.fr
[4] LIRMM, Montpellier, France
abdoulaye.gamatie@lirmm.fr
[5] INRIA, Rennes, France
herve.marchand@inria.fr
[6] INRIA, Grenoble, France
eric.rutten@inria.fr
https://team.inria.fr/ctrl-a/members/eric-rutten

Abstract. This invited paper makes an overview of our works addressing discrete control-based design of adaptive and reconfigurable computing systems, also called autonomic computing. They are characterized
by their ability to switch between different execution modes w.r.t. application and functionality, mapping and deployment, or execution architecture. The control of such reconfigurations or adaptations is a new
application domain for control theory, called feedback computing. We approach the problem with a programming language supported approach,
based on synchronous languages and discrete control synthesis. We con-
cretely use this approach in FPGA-based reconfigurable architectures,
and in the coordination of administration loops.

Keywords: Autonomic computing, adaptive systems, reconfigurable
architectures, reactive systems, synchronous languages, discrete control.

1 Adaptive Computing Systems, and their Control

Computing systems are present in ever more aspects of society, and they have
to comply with two complementary, and sometimes contradictory, requirements:
adaptability to continuous changes in their environment or functionality, and
dependability w.r.t. the goal they fulfill and the persons in their contact.

---

* This presentation is an overview of work done with support from several projects: Mi-
nalogic MIND, ANR Famous, CNRS PEPS API, ANR Ctrl-Green, Labex Persyval-
Lab Projet Exploratoire Staars, Inria Action Exploratoire Ctrl-A.

R. Natarajan et al. (Eds.): ICDCIT 2015, LNCS 8956, pp. 93–113, 2015.
© Springer International Publishing Switzerland 2015

1.1   Administration Loops in Computing Systems

Motivations for being dynamically reconfigurable or adaptive are manifold: on the one hand, systems should dynamically react to changes in application objectives, in environment of operation, and also in their implementation platform or infrastructure, especially in open systems like the Cloud. On the other hand, systems are too large or complex to be administrated manually and must be automated, in order to avoid error-prone or slow decisions and manipulations.

This trend can be observed at very diverse levels of services and application software, middleware and virtual machines, operating systems, and hardware reconfigurable architectures. The automation of such dynamical adaptation manages various aspects such as computing and communication resources, quality of service, fault tolerance. It can concern small embedded systems like sensors networks, up to large-scale systems such as data-centers and the Cloud. For example, data-centers infrastructures have administration loops managing their computing resources, typically with energy-aware objectives in mind, and possibly involving management of the cooling system. At a lower level, FPGA-based architectures (Field-Programmable Gate Arrays) are hardware circuits that can be configured at run-time with the logics they should implement: they can be reconfigured dynamically and partially (i.e. on part of the reconfigurable surface) in response to environment or application events; such reconfiguration decisions are taken based on monitoring the system's and its environment's features.

Autonomic computing [21,20] is an approach for the design of systems evolving in a self-managed way while continuing to run and deliver the service. It is based on an engineering of the administration of systems in the form of a feedback loop, automating the decisions and actions to be taken according to observations on the state and events of the system.

1.2   The Need for Control

The other vital requirement for these systems is dependability, be it w.r.t. damage in the finality of the system (information, business, ...) or w.r.t. safety (goods, persons, ...) [6]. The need for guarantees and assurances on the behavior of these automated systems can benefit from generally meaningful and classical formal methods in Computer Science like Model Checking for logical or temporized aspects, or can make use of models from performance evaluation, or concerning probabilistic aspects (e.g. Markov chains).

A specificity of autonomic systems is that they are based on a feedback loop, the behavior of which calls for a corpus of design theories and techniques stemming from Control Theory, where they have been studied for many decades. This control oriented approach to autonomic computing [18] is a new interaction between control and computer science, along with classically established ones:

- computer science for control systems, widely considered in embedded and real-time systems for the digital implementation of control;

- theoretical computer science and control theory, designing hybrid systems as mathematical models to combine discrete and continuous dynamics;
- control theory for computing systems, considered here, for designing well-behaved automated computer management loops.

The autonomic loop is also naturally reactive, hence a new potential domain for reactive languages and models, like synchronous languages [3], different from hard real-time safety critical embedded systems, and bringing different perspectives for their validation and verification tools.

1.3 Approach and Outline

We address the problem of combining adaptivity and dependability, requiring run-time abilities to detect or even predict changes requiring an adaptation, decide upon the appropriate adaptation, with possible anticipation, and give guarantees on this appropriateness as a notion of correction of the control.

We propose an approach which is language-based and tool-supported, and which we validated early on by confronting the method and its supporting language and tools to concrete real-life systems from different domains, in order to insure relevance and generality. This paper makes an overview of the approach, as well as mentioning different facets of the work, that have been developed in more specialized and detailed presentations elsewhere.

In the remainder, first Section 2 recalls basic notions in relevant domains: Autonomic Computing in Section 2.1 ; reactive systems and their control in Section 2.2. Then Section 3 presents the BZR language on which the approach is based. Subsequently, Section 4 shows how the approach is validated in a range of domains : software components and coordination of multiple autonomic loops in Section 4.3 ; reconfigurable FPGA architectures in Section 4.2. Lastly, Section 5 concludes, discusses results and draws perspectives.

2 Background

2.1 Autonomic Computing

The aim of Autonomic Computing is to have networked computing systems able to manage themselves, trough decisions made automatically, without direct human intervention. The Autonomic Computing Initiative (ACI) initiated by IBM aims at providing the foundation for autonomic systems [21]. It is inspired by the autonomic nervous system of the human body. This nervous system controls important bodily functions (e.g. respiration, heart rate, and blood pressure) without any conscious intervention. In the past dozen years Autonomic Computing has gained momentum, both academically and industrially [20].

Autonomic objectives have been defined for self-management aspects, often called self-*, covering essential features:

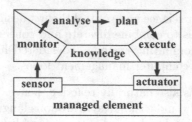

Fig. 1. MAPE-K autonomic manager for administration loop

- Self-configuration: automatic configuration of the system components at deployment time, or also later during runtime, typically without stopping;
- Self-healing: automatic discovery, and correction of faults;
- Self-optimization: automatic monitoring and control of resources to ensure the optimal functioning with respect to the defined requirements;
- Self-protection: identification and protection from arbitrary attacks: this security aspect can be addressed on external or internal aspects [9].

Interestingly, these objectives can interact, and their interferences can require coordination, typically between self-protection and self-optimization.

The autonomic loop is a general feedback loop structure to take this into account [21]. In this closed loop, systems are instrumented with monitors or sensors, and with reconfiguration actions or actuators; these two kinds of interfaces with the managed element (ME) have to be related by a control and decision component, the autonomic manager (AM), which implements the dynamic adaptation policy or strategy. It can be defined as shown in Figure 1 with the MAPE-K approach, with sub-components for:

- Monitoring: extracting relevant information from sensors, probes or monitors instrumenting the managed element, and available at its API;
- Analysis: using the monitored information as well as other knowledge e.g., on past history, to decide on reactions to take;
- Planning: transforming the decisions into actions
- Execution: implementing the action according to the managed element control interfaces or actuators;
- Knowledge: storing and maintaing relevant information of the managed element, used in the other sub-components, and updated by them.

Such autonomic loops can be designed and developed in many different ways, relying on techniques from e.g. Artificial Intelligence, but an important issue remains in providing guarantees on the behavior of such automated closed-looped systems as the are generally difficult to master. A typical example is the so-called "state-flapping" problem [20, p. 7:21], where reconfigurations altern back and forth between two states because transition conditions are too close.

Control for feedback computing is therefore a particularly interesting approach where this feedback loop is considered as a case of a control loop, where techniques stemming from control theory can be used to design efficient, safe, and predictable controllers [18]. Control theory provides designers with a framework of methods and techniques to build automated systems with well-mastered behavior. It involves sensors and actuators that are connected to the process or "plant" i.e., the system to be controlled. A model of the dynamic behavior of the process is built, and a specification is given for the control objective, and on these bases the control is derived, following a formal computation. Although there are approaches to the formal derivation of software from specifications, this methodology is not usual in Computer Science, where often a solution is designed directly, and only then it is analyzed and verified formally, and the distinction between the process and its controller is not made systematically. This approach, sometimes called Feedback Computing [18,29], although well identified, is still only emerging. Works are scattered in very separate and dispersed efforts, in different communities. Some surveys exist [5,8,10], offering a classification [25], or concentrating on Real-Time computing systems [2].

The control approach advantages [29] come from its rigorous methodology for modeling, designing, and analyzing feedback loops. It supports the design of controllers that effectively manage uncertainties in computing systems, without needing accurate models. They bring interesting properties of stability or robustness, which, in the context of computer systems improves predictability. On the other hand, there are of course difficulties and limitations. Making the mapping from high-level management objectives to actual system-level sensors and actuators, and to appropriate control models can be hard. Modeling computing systems does not easily fit classical control methodologies: difference in cultures shows for example in that many classical control problems are formulated as regulation or tracking problems, rather than optimization, and deal only with continuous metrics. On the side of the objects of control, most computing systems were not designed to be controllable in the first place, and it is a real architectural research problem to build and instrument them appropriately.

2.2   Reactive Systems, their Programming, and Discrete Control

The AM shown above is intrinsically a reactive component, therefore some design approaches originally intended for embedded systems and general feedback loops can be of interested for autonomic managers, for which they can be adapted.

Reactive systems and synchronous languages are characterized by their continuous interaction with their environment, reacting to flows of inputs by producing flows of outputs. They are classically modeled as transition systems or automata, with classically famous languages like StateCharts [17]. We adopt the approach of synchronous languages [3], because we then have access to the control tools used further. Well known languages feature the imperative Esterel, the equational declarative Lustre and Signal. The synchronous paradigm refers

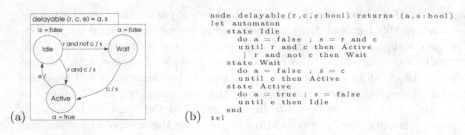

Fig. 2. Heptagon/BZR example: : (a) graphical / (b) textual syntax

to the automata parallel composition that we use in these languages, allowing for clear formal semantics, while supporting modelling asynchronous computations [15]: actions can be asynchronously started, and their completion is waited for, without blocking activity continuing in parallel.

The Heptagon/BZR language [13] supports programming of mixed synchronous data-flow equations and automata, called Mode Automata, with parallel and hierarchical composition. The basic behavior is that at each reaction step, values in the input flows are used, as well as local and memory values, in order to compute the next state and the values of the output flows for that step. Inside the nodes, this is expressed as a set of equations defining, for each output and local, the value of the flow, in terms of an expression on other flows, possibly using local flows and state values from past steps. This can already be seen as a programmatic solutions for reconfiguring the data flow between in- and outputs, providing for control and coordination of data-flow tasks.

Figure 2 shows a small Heptagon/BZR program. The node **delayable** programs the control of a task, which can either be idle, waiting or active. When it is in the initial Idle state, the occurrence of the **true** value on input **r** *requests* the starting of the task. Another input **c** can either allow the activation, or temporarily block the request and make the automaton go to a waiting state. Input **e** notifies termination. The outputs represent, resp., a: activity of the task, and s: triggering the concrete task start in the system's API.

Such automata and data-flow reactive nodes can be reused by instantiation, and composed in parallel (noted "**;**") and in a hierarchical way, as illustrated in the body of the node in Figure 3, with two instances of the **delayable** node. Particularly, in the second instance, input c is fed with the constant flow **true**: hence, the behavior of this instance is specialized in that the requests are always immediately starting the task. They run in parallel, in a synchronous way: one global step corresponds to one local step for every node. In particular, when r_1, r_2, c_1 are received **true** at the same step from the initial state, the resulting state is such that $a_1 \wedge a_2$.

Synchronous languages are tool-supported, and compilers automatically generate executable code, e.g., in C or Java, typically structured as a **reset** function to initialize variables, and a **step** function, implementing the global transition function. The code calling this function is application-dependent, and can be an infinite loop, a periodical call, or an event-based or interruption mechanism.

Verification and discrete control are the available when using a reactive language, which gives all the support of the the classical formal framework of Labelled Transition Systems (LTS): they involve two main features. On the one hand there is a memorization of a *state*, the current value $x(k)$ resulting from the previous transition at $k - 1$ (with an initial value $x(0)$). On the other hand is a *transition function* T computing the next value of the state in function of the current observed input value $y(k)$ and current state. It also computes output values $o(k)$, to send commands to the controlled system:

$$(\mathbf{x}(k + 1), \mathbf{o}(k)) = T(\mathbf{y}(k), \mathbf{x}(k)), x(0) = x_0$$

Particularly, we benefit from state-space exploration techniques, like Model-Checking, in order to check whether or not a temporal logic formula is satisfied by all the possible executions of the program.

More originally, the LTS of a program can be applied the operation of Discrete Controller Synthesis (DCS). Initially defined as supervisory control of discrete event systems in the framework of language theory [26], DCS has been adapted to symbolic LTS and implemented in synchronous tools [23]. The LTS variables $\mathbf{y}$ are partitioned into controllable ones $\mathbf{c}$ and uncontrollable ones $\mathbf{uc}$. For a given control objective (e.g., staying invariantly inside a given subset of states, considered "good", or keeping some states reachable), the DCS algorithm automatically computes, by exploration of the state space, the constraint on controllable variables, depending on the current state, for any value of the uncontrollables, so that remaining behaviors satisfy the objective. This constraint is inhibiting the minimum possible behaviors, therefore it is called *maximally permissive*. The resulting synthesized controller C gives values to controllable variables c, which are part of the parameters of the transition function T. In brief:

$$\begin{aligned} \mathbf{x}(k + 1) &= T(\mathbf{uc}(k), \mathbf{c}(k), \mathbf{x}(k)), x(0) = x_0 \\ \mathbf{c}(k) &= C(\mathbf{uc}(k), \mathbf{x}(k)) \end{aligned}$$

Algorithms are related to model checking techniques for state space exploration. If no solution is found, because the problem is over constrained, then DCS plays the role of a verification. Discrete control objectives can be logical : ensuring, for a given subset of states characterized by a predicate, its invariance (by control, it will not be left), reachability (from all visitable states), attractivity (no cyclic sequence of transitions can avoid it). They can involve weights associated

```
twotasks(r1, c1, e1, r2, e2) = a1, s1, a2, s2

(a1, s1) = delayable(r1, c1, e1) ;
(a2, s2) = delayable(r2, true, e2)
```

Fig. 3. Heptagon/BZR example: nodes composition

with states for quantitative aspects : bounding capacity, optimizing performance. Multiple criteria optimization can also be supported. In the framework of the synchronous languages and technology, the tool Sigali [23] is integrated in the programming environments, and in the compiler of the BZR language [19].

Discrete feedback computing i.e., applying discrete control theory to computing systems, is more recent than using classical control theory [18], as was noted by other authors, essentially because it is less well-known than classical control and less developed than classical verification and model-checking. Earliest works deal with controlling workflow scheduling [27] or application-specific task schedulers [24,22]. A whole line of work focuses on the computing systems problem of deadlock avoidance in shared-memory multi-threaded programs [28]. Another kind of software problem concerns run-time exceptions raised by programs and not handled by the code [14].

Some related work can be found in computer science, in the notions of program synthesis. It consists in translating a property on inputs and outputs of a system, expressed in temporal logics, into a lower-level model, typically in terms of transition systems. For example, it is proposed in a UML-related framework, with the synthesis of StateChart from Live Sequence Charts [16]. These program synthesis approaches do not seem to have been aware of Discrete Control Theory, or reciprocally: however there seems to be a relationship between them, as well as with game theory, but it is out of the scope of this paper. Also, interface synthesis [7] is related to Discrete Controller Synthesis. It consists in the generation of interfacing wrappers for components, to adapt them for the composition into given component assemblies w.r.t. the communication protocols between them.

3   The BZR Language for Tool-Supported Design

Given our goal of combining adaptivity and dependability in adaptive and reconfigurable computing systems, we will combine reactive languages and models with the autonomic computing structures and objectives. A central aspect in our tool-supported approach is the specification and programming language Heptagon/BZR, which provides for high-level design of controllers, and encapsulates discrete control as a compilation operation.

Contracts on nodes are defined in the Heptagon/BZR language [19] using a behavioral contract syntax [13]. It allows for the declaration, using the **with** statement, of *controllable variables*, the value of which are not defined by the programmer. These free variables can be used in the program to describe choices between several transitions. They are defined, in the final executable program, by the controller computed off-line by DCS, according to the Boolean expression given in the **enforce** statement. Knowledge about the environment such as, for instance event occurrence order can be declared in an **assume** statement. This is taken into account during the computation of the controller with DCS. Heptagon/BZR compilation invokes a DCS tool, and inserts the synthesized controller in the generated executable code, which has the same structure as above:

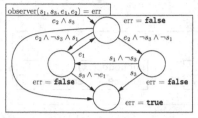
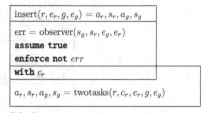

(a) Observer: always 1 between 2 and 3   (b) Contract node for task insertion

Fig. 4. Observer and contract node

reset and *step* functions. Figure 4(b) shows an example of contract coordinating two instances of the **delayable** node of Figure 2(a), as assembled together in the **twotasks** node of Figure 3. The **insert** node has a **with** part declaring controllable variable c_r, and the **enforce** part asserts the property to be enforced by DCS: **not** *err*. The **assume** part is set to **true**, meaning that there is no assumption on the environment. The contract can itself feature a program, typically automata observing traces and defining states, to express a variety of safety properties. For example, an error state can be defined where the intended property is false, with the intention to keep it outside an invariant subspace. Such an observer is illustrated in Figure 4(a) : given input flows for the starting and stopping events of three tasks, it outputs value true on flow *err* when a sequence is observed such that task 3 is started (upon s_3) after task 2 (upon its end event e_2), without a complete execution of task 1, from s_1 to e_1, having taken place in between : this sequence violates the property that we have always 1 between 2 and 3. The contract in Figure 4(b) uses this observer for having always an execution of the simple task between two executions of the delayable task; this amounts to make invariant the state space where *err* is false. To enforce this, cr will be used by the synthesized controller to delay the starting of the delayable task until a full execution of the other one ends. The constraint produced by DCS can have several solutions: the Heptagon/BZR compiler generates deterministic executable code by favoring, for each controllable variable, value **true** over **false**, in the order of declaration.

The need for modularity comes when designs become complex. Advantages of our DCS-based approach, more constructive than classical verification, are:

- (i) high-level language support for controller design (tedious and error-prone to code manually at lower C or Java level) with declarative objectives ;
- (ii) correctness of the controller, w.r.t. the objectives, by definition of the algorithms (hard to guarantee manually) ;
- (iii) maximal permissiveness of controllers : they are minimally constraining, and in that sense optimally flexibile (even harder to obtain manually);
- (iv) automated formal synthesis of these controllers (rather than tedious hand-writing followed by verification);
- (v) automated executable code generation in C or Java.

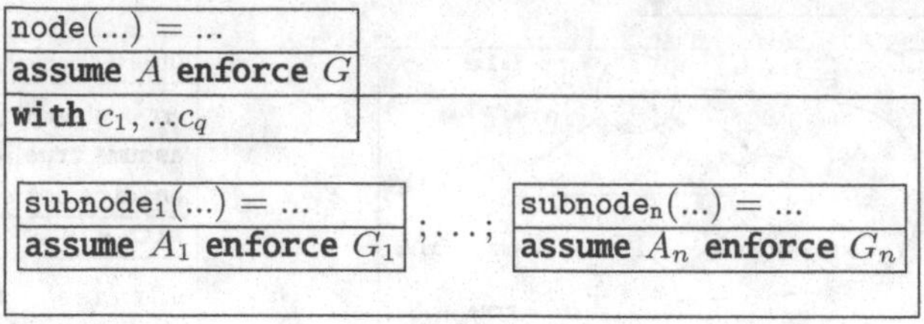

```
node(...) = ...
assume A enforce G
with c_1, ...c_q

  subnode_1(...) = ...         subnode_n(...) = ...
  assume A_1 enforce G_1  ;...; assume A_n enforce G_n
```

Fig. 5. Modular contracts in Heptagon/BZR

However, when considering a large number of managers, this monolithic approach might not succeed, because exploring the large state space is very time consuming, and can fail due to computing resource limits, which limits the scalability of the approach. Furthermore, a modification, even partial, leads to a recompilation of the overall coordinated composition invalidating previous generated codes which limits the re-usability of management components.

To address this issue, we exploit modular DCS, where the control objectives can be decomposed in several parts, each part managed by a controller. Each controller manages a limited number of components. This decreases the state space to explore for the synthesis of each controller. The recompilation of a controller that has no impact on other controllers does not require the recompilation of the latter. This makes possible the re-use of controllers generated codes.

Modular contracts in Heptagon/BZR are based on the modular compilation of the nodes: each node is compiled towards one sequential function, regardless of its calling context, the inside called nodes being abstracted. Thus, modular DCS is performed by using the contracts as abstraction of the sub-nodes. One controller is synthesized for each node supplied with local controllable variables. The contracts of the sub-nodes are used as environment model, as abstraction of the contents of these nodes, to synthesize the local controller. As shown in Figure 5, the objective is to control the body and coordinate sub-nodes, using controllable variables $c_1, ..., c_q$, given as inputs to the sub-nodes, so that G is true, assuming that A is true. Here, we have information on sub-nodes, so that we can assume not only A, but also that the n sub-nodes each do enforce their contract : $\bigwedge_{i=1}^{n}(A_i \implies G_i)$. Accordingly, the problem becomes that: assuming the above, we want to enforce G as well as $\bigwedge_{i=1}^{n} A_i$. Control at composite level takes care of enforcing assumptions of the sub-nodes. This synthesis considers the outputs of local abstracted nodes as uncontrollable variables, constrained by the nodes' contracts. A formal description, out of our scope here, is available [13].

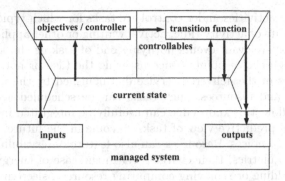

Fig. 6. Autonomic loop based on discrete control

4   Discrete Control-Based Autonomic Managers

The specification and programming language presented before, independently of AM design, can now be integrated in a method first exposed generally in Section 4.1, and then illustrated by brief summaries of works concerning reconfiguration control in DPR FPGA-based architectures in Section 4.2, and the coordination of administration loops in Section 4.3.

4.1   General Design Method

An interpretation of the MAPE-K loop of Figure 1 in terms of the discrete control framework of Section 2.2 is illustrated in Figure 6. For simplification, the Monitoring and Execution parts are considered as simply forwarding sensor inputs and action outputs to the ME. The Knowledge part is assimilated to the current state of the reactive system. The Analysis part is in charge of making decisions w.r.t. choices in reconfiguration, according to the adaption strategy or policy : we assimilate it to the specification of the control objectives, at design time, which is then transformed by DCS and compilation into a controller taking the same place at execution time. The decisions are encoded as values on choice points corresponding to the controllable variables, which are internal to the AM. The Planning part in assimilated to the transition function, computing, from the previous choice and current state (as well as inputs, here shown through the controller for simplification), which are the actions to be executed to implement them. Our discrete control-based approach is an effective tool-supported method for the design of AMs, which at the same time provides the designer with guarantees on the behaviour of the controller, through the use of DCS.

Typical modeled features appearing in the design of AM are related to computing systems and their common aspects in different fields. Of course the management of data-centers supporting the Cloud is not identical to the reconfiguration controllers of embedded FPGA architectures. However there are similarities in the manipulated objects, all resorting to computing.

The computing activities under control are tasks for which typical observability involves the state of activity (idle, active, waiting or other application specific aspects), as well as relevant events notifying end of task or check points ; controllability through choice points concerns firing the task or not, and choosing variants or modes of the delivered service distinguished by the use of different implementations and resources. Such tasks can be scheduled according to an application workflow: this knowledge can usefully be integrated in the model, in that it provides a predictive view of tasks to come in the future, which can influence the present choices. Resources can also feature observability (their usage level according to metrics, their charge level in the case of energy supply) and controllability (adding or removing computing resources, sleep modes).

The adaptation policies or strategies have to be explicited and formulated formally themselves, in the form of control objectives. The typically concern resource access control (exclusivity or bounded capacity), application termination (reaching a target state), fault tolerance (maintaining activity on other resources upon failures), or more elaborate sequencing patterns. These commonalities observed in case studies suggest a level of generality of the problem and the proposed solutions.

Granularity levels can be quite diverse, both in time or pace (the period of the loop can be in minutes or even hours) and detail (the managed computations can be whole systems). At the **lowest level of MEs**, computations should, just as usual, of course be as fast as possible and the possible overhead of monitoring and sensing should not interfere with system performance. Especially in parallel and distributed systems the feedback loop should not impose costly synchronizations.

At the **level of an AM**, it is indeed the case however that the MAPE-K loop is not supposed to run at that pace, and is mostly much slower or even sporadic when event-based. This depends completely on the level of the decision to be made, and on the duration of the execution of actions implementing it. As such, it is similar to the period of control systems begin determined by the dynamics of the process that has to be controlled. This dictates the maximal allowable period between two significants events to be observed, and not to be missed ; in turn, the latter gives an upper bound to the decision technique used, which should not cost more time (hence limiting e.g., optimization techniques).

At the **level of AMs coordination** the pace can be naturally considered even slower, and the feedback loop makes a step sufficiently rarely (compared to e.g., processor frequency) for enabling the use of synchronizations such as in distributed algorithms (e.g., leader election) when needed.

In our case, the most costly part in our method is DCS, but it is performed off-line and therefore is not limited by the ME dynamics, but rather by the design-time computing resources. The run-time cost is only that of the execution of a decision diagram function i.e., very low. However an important aspect is the size of the state space, in which DCS algorithms are exponential: therefore it is vital to determine the highest possible level of the model, abstracting away from fine-grain computations and from detailed fine-grain state-spaces.

4.2   Reconfiguration Control in DPR FPGA-Based Architectures

Dynamically reconfigurable hardware has been identified as a promising solution for the design of energy efficient embedded systems. However, its adoption is limited by the costly design effort including verification and validation, which is even more complex than for non dynamically reconfigurable systems. Therefore, we appley our tool-supported formal method to automatically design a correct control of the reconfiguration [1]. We design generic modeling patterns for a class of reconfigurable architectures, taking into account both hardware architecture and applications, as well as relevant control objectives. We validate our approach on case studies implemented on Dynamic Partial Reconfigurable (DPR) FPGA.

The considered class of architectures is presented informally through an example. Three levels are modeled separately, for which we will control the interactions according to global objectives:

- **architecture** is multiprocessor on n reconfigurable tiles $A1-An$, plus a general purpose processor $A0$ (e.g., ARM core). A tile Ai can be configured by uploading a bitstream encoding the function to be executed, and put to sleep mode with a *clock gated mechanism* to consume a minimum static power. A battery supplies energy, with a sensor for charge going up or down.
- **tasks** are defined with choices, upon request, between starting immediately or delaying ; between different bitstreams characterized each by : tiles used, WCET (Worst Case Execution Time), reconfiguration time, power peak.
- **application** is specified as a dependency graph between tasks: upon end notification of a task, requests are emitted for its following task(s);

The control problem is to use choices in order to satisfy global constraints according to resource state and activities in parallel or further in the application. The desired reconfiguration policy informally involves :

1. resource usage constraint: e.g., exclusive use of reconfigurable tiles $A1-A4$;
2. energy constraint: switch tiles to active mode if and only if needed;
3. power peak constraint: bounded by a maximum w.r.t battery level;
4. reachability: application graph execution can always finish once started;
5. optimizing e.g., global power peak is also possible [1].

A typical example of decision to be made is that, upon progress in the task graph, new tasks must be started by choosing the mode or bitstream compatible with available resources constraints, taking into account possible futures in the application, which can require to keep resources for a later task. Figure 7 summarizes, in the framework of Figure 6, what we need to formalize, and identifies controllable and uncontrollable variables, as well as the relevant state information, which determine the model abstraction level.

Generic models are shown in Figure 8, with patterns for modelling relevant states and controllable or uncontrollable events. Architecture is modeled in (a)

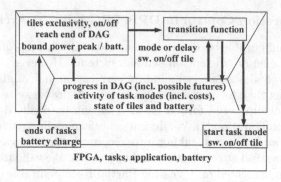

Fig. 7. Autonomic loop for DPR FPGA

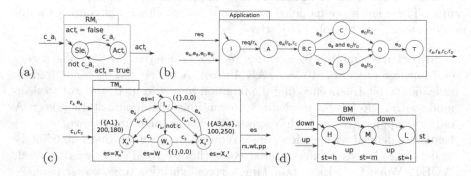

Fig. 8. Generic models: (a) tile i, (b) task graph, (c) two modes task, (d) battery

for each tile (with state act_i, controlled by c_a_i), and (d) battery observer (giving its state st, high, medium or low, according to received sensor values). In (c) a task example with two modes has uncontrollable requests r_i and end notifications e_i, and controllables c_1, c_2 to choose between modes, emitting state es and values characterizing them. In (b) an application example with 4 tasks $(A; (B||C); D)$ shows states recording progress in the graph, giving predictive model on which tasks can be fired in the future, in reaction to end notifications e_i, emitting requests r_i towards tasks, with terminal state T. In order to model possible behaviors of the system, these patterns are instantiated for all components, and composed in parallel: $(RM_1||...||RM_4||BM||TM_A||...||TM_D||Application)$ with values from modes of the active tasks being also composed, defining global values for the different resources metrics (e.g., sum of local pp_i into PP, union of rs).

Invariance and optimal control objectives are defined in contracts upon this global behavior model. Controllable variables are declared in the **with** statement, other inputs being uncontrollable inputs. The policy above can be formulated in a generic way [1] in terms of properties mentioned in Section 2.2: Objective 1 to 3 are *invariance* objectives on state variables and associated metrics constant values, e.g., for 3 : $PP < (v_1$ if $st = h$ else v_2 if $st = m$ else v_3 if $st = l)$. Objective 4 concerns *reachability* of terminal state T.

Two experimental case studies have been implemented to demonstrate the previous control models on real FPGAs [1]. After compilation towards executable code, the controller is running on a Microblaze soft core (i.e. $A0$) on the FPGA.

4.3   Coordination of Administration Loops

Real autonomic systems require multiple management loops, each complex to design, and possibly of different kinds (quantitative, synchronization, involving learning, ...). However their uncoordinated co-existence leads to inconsistency or redundancy of action. Therefore we apply our method to the discrete control of the interactions of managers [11]. We follow a component-based approach and explore modular discrete control, allowing to break down the combinatorial complexity inherent to the state-space exploration technique. It also allows re-using complex managers in different contexts without modifying their control specifications. We validate our method on a multiple-loop multi-tier system.

The administration loops and their need for coordination are considered in the context of JEE multi-tier applications which consist of: an apache web server receiving incoming requests, and distributing them with load balancing to a tier of replicated tomcat servers. The latter access to a database through a mysql-proxy server which distributes the SQL queries, with load balancing, to a tier of replicated mysql servers The global system running in the data-center consists of a set of such applications in parallel.

A set of autonomic managers are used to administrate the system: **Self-sizing** decides on the degree of replication of servers depending of the system over- or under-load measured through the CPU usage. It aims at lowering the resources usage while preserving the performance. It can add new replicas (which takes time), or remove some (considered immediate); each of these two actions can be inhibited. **Self-repair** targets a load balancer as well as replicated servers. It manages fail-stop failure detected through heartbeat. It aims at preserving the availability of the service. It triggers repair actions (taking time), which can be inhibited. **Consolidation** targets the global virtualized data-center. It adapts the computing capacity made available in a virtualized data-center, to either decrease or increase it. It can be controlled by delaying the actions.

Coordination problems can occur when e.g., several loops react to the same overload whereas one would have sufficed, or a failed load balancer leads to down-sizing followed by upsizing again right after repair. Also, consolidation requires to operate on a stable system in order to be consistent. The desired coordination policy informally involves the following constraints:

1. In a replicated tier, avoid size-up when repairing.
2. In a load-balanced tier, avoid size-down when repairing the load-balancer.
3. In general, avoid size-down in a successor tier when repairing a predecessor.
4. At global data-center level, when consolidating, avoid self-sizing or repairing.
5. Wait until repairs or add finish before consolidation decreasing, and until removals finish before increasing.

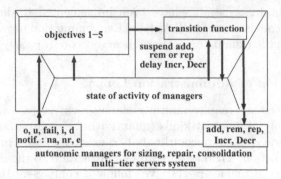

Fig. 9. Autonomic loop for Coordination

Figure 9 summarizes, in the framework of Figure 6, what we need to formalize. It shows that the relevant information here is the state of activeity of AMs, abstracting away from the way the individual controllers are working: we do not consider how they perform, but observability on their activity and controllability on their actions. The pace at which the coordination loop must work is defined by the input events, much slower than the underlying data-center computations.

Their coordination by modular control is based on generic models for each of them. **Self-sizing** control is an instance of node `ctrl-mgr` in Figure 10(a), with outputs `la` for long action `add`, `sa` for short action `rem` and `s` for busy state `adding` ; and with inputs for control: `ca` and `crm` for the actions, and for monitoring: `ml` for overload `o`, `ms` for underload `u`, and notification `nl` for adding `na`. This defines `(add, rem, adding) = self-sizing(ca, crm, o, u, na)`. **Self-repair** control is a simpler case, with only a long action of repairing, also an instance of `ctrl-mgr` with outputs: long action `rep`, and busy state `repairing` ; and inputs: control `ca`, failure `fail`, and notification of repair done `nr`. Unused parameters can be, for inputs, given the constant value `false`, and for outputs be left unused. This defines: `(rep, repairing) = self-repair(cr, fail, nr)`. **Consolidation** control in Figure 10(b) presents essentially the waiting mechanism of the delayable action of Figure 2(a), for each of its two long actions, the activity of which is given by `Incr` and `Decr`. In the initial `Idle` state, when `i` is **true** (increase is required), if `ci` is **true** it goes to `I` and emits `si` to start the increase plan, otherwise it goes to `WaitI` and awaits `ci` to go to `Incr` and emit `si`. When in `Incr`, it awaits until the notification of end `e` then returns back to `Idle`. The case for decrease is similar.

Coordination Objectives. The models are instantiated for each AM in the system, and their composition gives the global behavior before control. The control is specified on this composed behavior. We formalize the strategy above:

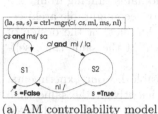

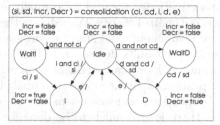

(a) AM controllability model   (b) Consolidation control behavior model

Fig. 10. Modelling managers control

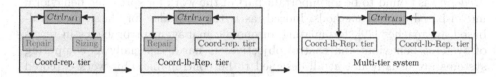

Fig. 11. Bottom-up re-use of nodes

1. **not** (repairing **and** add).
2. **not** (repairingL **and** rem) with repairingL from load-balancer self-repair.
3. between predecessor and successor tiers: **not** (repairing$_{pred}$ **and** rem$_{succ}$).
4. **not** ((Incr **or** Decr) **and** (repairing* **or** adding* **or** rem*))   where   * stands for conjunction of all corresponding states.
5. **not** ((repairing* **or** or adding*) **and** sd) and **not** (rem* **and** si).

These properties can be grouped into a global contract to synthesize an invariance controller, but in order to have scalability and reusability, the system can be built up bottom-up as shown in Figure 11. A first node Coord-rep. tier cares for coordination within a replicated tier, with Objective 1. In order to be re-usable, the node has to have a contract that exposes to upper nodes that when a long action is started it is actually executed [11]. It is re-used in Coord-lb-Rep. tier, composed with the load-balancer self-repair, with Objective 2. For complete application, this node can be re-used twice, to form node Multi-tier system, with Objective 3. At data-center level, this last node is instantiated for each application, and composed with the consolidation model, with Objectives 4 and 5. This decomposition of DCS operations improves synthesis time dramatically, and the modular code generation enables distributing the controller. These controllers have been validated on an experimental data-center [11].

5   Discussion and Perspectives

Results. This invited paper makes an overview of our works addressing discrete control-based design of adaptive and reconfigurable computing systems, also called autonomic computing. We propose a tool-supported method, involving a reactive language and its compiler encapsulating techniques stemming from discrete control theory. We validate the approach in domains ranging from software components and smart environments to hardware reconfigurable architectures. Our results demonstrate that control-based techniques for the design of autonomic loops can augment computing systems with, at the same time, self-adaptation capabilities and also predictability.

Limitations and extensions are of course made visible by our experiments, and there is still much to be done for supporting efficiently at the same time predictable and adaptive computing systems through behavioral model-based methods. Some perspectives are as follows.

Modeling is bound to be an important part of the work for spreading behavioral model-based control methods. Indeed, as is the case also for classical control-based approaches [29], formulating autonomic management problems in terms of systems behaviors and control objectives is hard, especially as computing systems are usually not at all designed to be controllable. Our work explored aspects related to computing resources like servers or cores on a multiprocessor architecture, but other aspects of computing systems should be considered, such as memory management issues (migration for proximity with a cache ; Software Transactional Memory contention management), communications (choice of media between e.g., wire, WiFi, Bluetooth, ..., w.r.t. throughput, energy cost, ...) or also security aspects. There often are favorable situations where the choices to be made at run-time are between predefined sets of configurations: the control is to enable efficient and appropriate use of these resources following dynamical changes in the environment and system. Changes anticipated at design time can be reified as variation points and exploited by the controller.

Expressivity and scalability of the modeling formalism need to be extended in order to improve the applicability of discrete control to realistic systems. Expressivity can be extended in order to account for more aspects of the systems, and incorporate logico-numeric properties [4], or have a combined control where, amongst the possibly several solutions satisfying the objective, determined by discrete control, a choice can be specified according to other criteria e.g., probabilistic or related to the continuous dynamics of the system.

Scalability requires efficiency in the DCS tools, which can benefit from progress made in Model Checking: algorithms have similar cost, intrinsically exponential in the worst case. This limits dramatically the above requirements of expressivity, as timed or hybrid formalisms have even higher costs. However, there is a way to attack this problem in the modeling phase, by identifying carefully chosen levels of abstraction, for acceptable overhead / cost, at least in small to medium systems. With modular and hierarchical decomposition of the problems, controllers can be built for the different levels of decision, with different paces, as mentioned in Section 4.1.

High-level languages and Domain Specific Languages (DSLs) are a useful help for usability of these methods: their aim is to allow of designers to describe their systems in terms of the entities and components they manipulate, rather than in terms of the formalisms. we are building upon the experience of Nemo [12] in order to define a component-based systems language, extending known Archtecture Description Languages (ADLs), where not only assemblies of components are structurally defined, but also the different configurations and the reconfiguration behavior between them are described explicitly. As for other languages built on top of underlying tools, this poses problems for diagnostic, when there are several layers of translation between DSL and verification or synthesis tool. Also, the specifity of DCS is that it works like a constraints solving tool, making diagnostic in case of failure difficult to isolate and locate in the program.

Adaptive control is a desirable feature for autonomic computing, especially in open systems, typically the Cloud, where new components can enter, and others can leave the system to be managed. Another source of change is that new policies or strategies must be enforced, which translates into a change of control objective. Adaptive discrete control has hardly been studied in research on Discrete Event Systems, and can be seen as a new challenge motivated from applications such as Autonomic Computing. Directions to address it can be seen amongst having an upper controller switching between previously prepared controllers, or, for slow-paced systems, having a DCS phase at run-time (for reasonably sized subsystems) producing a new controller.

References

1. An, X., Rutten, E., Diguet, J.-P., le Griguer, N., Gamatié, A.: Autonomic management of dynamically partially reconfigurable fpga architectures using discrete control. In: In Proc. of the 10th International Conference on Autonomic Computing (ICAC 2013) (June 2013)
2. Årzén, K.-E.: al. Conclusions of the ARTIST2 roadmap on control of computing systems. ACM SIGBED (Special Interest Group on Embedded Systems) Review 3(3) (July 2006)
3. Benveniste, A., Caspi, P., Edwards, S., Halbwachs, N., Guernic, P.L., de Simone, R.: The synchronous languages twelve years later. Proc. of the IEEE, Special issue on Embedded Systems 91(1), 64–83 (2003)
4. Berthier, N., Marchand, H.: Discrete Controller Synthesis for Infinite State Systems with ReaX. In: IEEE International Workshop on Discrete Event Systems, Cachan, France, pp. 420–427 (2014)
5. Brun, Y., et al.: Engineering self-adaptive systems through feedback loops. In: Cheng, B.H.C., de Lemos, R., Giese, H., Inverardi, P., Magee, J. (eds.) Software Engineering for Self-Adaptive Systems. LNCS, vol. 5525, pp. 48–70. Springer, Heidelberg (2009)
6. Calinescu, R., Ghezzi, C., Kwiatkowska, M., Mirandola, R.: Self-adaptive software needs quantitative verification at runtime. Communications of the ACM 55(9), 69–77 (2012)
7. Chakrabarti, A., de Alfaro, L., Henzinger, T.A., Mang, F.Y.C.: Synchronous and bidirectional component interfaces. In: Brinksma, E., Larsen, K.G. (eds.) CAV 2002. LNCS, vol. 2404, pp. 414–427. Springer, Heidelberg (2002)

8. Cheng, B.H.C., et al.: Software engineering for self-adaptive systems: A research roadmap. In: Cheng, B.H.C., de Lemos, R., Giese, H., Inverardi, P., Magee, J. (eds.) Software Engineering for Self-Adaptive Systems. LNCS, vol. 5525, pp. 1–26. Springer, Heidelberg (2009)

9. Chess, D.M., Palmer, C., White, S.R.: Security in an autonomic computing environment. IBM Syst. J. 42(1), 107–118 (2003)

10. de Lemos, R., et al.: Software engineering for self-adaptive systems: A second research roadmap. In: de Lemos, R., Giese, H., Müller, H.A., Shaw, M. (eds.) Software Engineering for Self-Adaptive Systems. LNCS, vol. 7475, pp. 1–32. Springer, Heidelberg (2013)

11. Delaval, G., Gueye, S.M.-K., Rutten, E., De Palma, N.: Modular coordination of multiple autonomic managers. In: Proceedings of the 17th International ACM Sigsoft Symposium on Component-based Software Engineering, CBSE 2014, pp. 3–12. ACM, New York (2014)

12. Delaval, G., Rutten, É.: A domain-specific language for multitask systems, applying discrete controller synthesis. EURASIP Journal on Embedded Systems 2007, 084192 (2007)

13. Delaval, G., Rutten, E., Marchand, H.: Integrating discrete controller synthesis into a reactive programming language compiler. Discrete Event Dynamic Systems 23(4), 385–418 (2013)

14. Gaudin, B., Vassev, E.I., Nixon, P., Hinchey, M.: A control theory based approach for self-healing of un-handled runtime exceptions. In: Proceedings of the 8th ACM International Conference on Autonomic Computing, ICAC 2011, pp. 217–220. ACM, New York (2011)

15. Halbwachs, N., Baghdadi, S.: Synchronous modeling of asynchronous systems. In: Sangiovanni-Vincentelli, A.L., Sifakis, J. (eds.) EMSOFT 2002. LNCS, vol. 2491, pp. 240–251. Springer, Heidelberg (2002)

16. Harel, D., Kugler, H., Pnueli, A.: Synthesis revisited: Generating statechart models from scenario-based requirements. In: Kreowski, H.-J., Montanari, U., Orejas, F., Rozenberg, G., Taentzer, G. (eds.) Formal Methods in Software and Systems Modeling. LNCS, vol. 3393, pp. 309–324. Springer, Heidelberg (2005)

17. Harel, D., Naamad, A.: The statemate semantics of statecharts. ACM Trans. Softw. Eng. Methodol. 5(4), 293–333 (1996)

18. Hellerstein, J., Diao, Y., Parekh, S., Tilbury, D.: Feedback Control of Computing Systems. Wiley-IEEE (2004)

19. Heptagon/BZR language, http://bzr.inria.fr

20. Huebscher, M.C., McCann, J.A.: A survey of autonomic computing: degrees, models, and applications. ACM Comput. Surv. 40(3), 7:1–7:28 (2008)

21. Kephart, J.O., Chess, D.M.: The vision of autonomic computing. IEEE Computer 36(1), 41–50 (2003)

22. Kloukinas, C., Yovine, S.: Synthesis of safe, qos extendible, application specific schedulers for heterogeneous real-time systems. In: Proceedings of 15th Euromicro Conference on Real-Time Systems, pp. 287–294 (July 2003)

23. Marchand, H., Bournai, P., Le Borgne, M., Le Guernic, P.: Synthesis of discrete-event controllers based on the signal environment. Discrete Event Dynamic Systems: Theory and Applications 10(4), 325–346 (2000)

24. Marchand, H., Rutten, É.: Managing multi-mode tasks with time cost and quality levels using optimal discrete control synthesis. In: 14th Euromicro Conference on Real-Time Systems (2002)

25. Patikirikorala, T., Colman, A., Han, J., Wang, L.: A systematic survey on the design of self-adaptive software systems using control engineering approaches. In: ICSE Workshop on Software Engineering for Adaptive and Self-Managing Systems (SEAMS), Zurich, Switzerland (2012)

26. Ramadge, P.J., Wonham, W.M.: Supervisory control of a class of discrete event processes. SIAM J. Control Optim. 25(1), 206–230 (1987)

27. Wallace, C., Jensen, P., Soparkar, N.: Supervisory control of workflow scheduling. In: Advanced Transaction Models and Architectures Workshop (ATMA), Goa, India (1996)

28. Wang, Y., Lafortune, S., Kelly, T., Kudlur, M., Mahlke, S.: The theory of deadlock avoidance via discrete control. In: Principles of Programming Languages, POPL, Savannah, USA, pp. 252–263 (2009)

29. Zhu, X.: Application of control theory in management of virtualized data centres. In: Fifth International Workshop on Feedback Control Implementation and Design in Computing Systems and Networks (FeBID), Paris, France (2010), http://controlofsystems.org/febid2010/program.html

Designing for Scalability and Trustworthiness in mHealth Systems

Sanjiva Prasad

Indian Institute of Technology Delhi, New Delhi, India

Abstract. Mobile Healthcare (mHealth) systems use mobile smart-phones and portable sensor kits to provide improved and affordable healthcare solutions to underserved communities or to individuals with reduced mobility who need regular monitoring. The architectural constraints of such systems provide a variety of computing challenges: the distributed nature of the system; mobility of the persons and devices involved; asynchrony in communication; security, integrity and authenticity of the data collected; and a plethora of administrative domains and the legacy of installed electronic health/medical systems.

The volume of data collected can be very large; together with the data, there is a large amount of metadata as well. We argue that certain metadata are essential for interpreting the data and assessing their quality. There is great variety in the kinds of medical data and metadata, the methods by which they are collected and administrative constraints on where they may be stored, which suggest the need for flexible distributed data repositories. There also are concerns about the veracity of the data, as well as interesting questions about who owns the data and who may access them.

We argue that traditional notions of relational databases, and security techniques such as access control and encryption of communications are inadequate. Instead, end-to-end systematic (from sensor to cloud) information flow techniques need to be applied for integrity and secrecy. These need to be adapted to work with the volume and diversity of data collected, and in a federated collection of administrative domains where data from different domains are subject to different information flow policies.

Keywords: mHeath, smart phones, system design, scalability, privacy, metadata, contextual evidence, hyper-graphs, CAP theorem, eventual consistency, convergent replicated data types, distributed hash tables, trustworthiness, decentralised information flow control, structure-preserving hash functions.

1 Introduction

The term *mHealth* refers to the use of mobile phone technologies in the delivery of health care in a variety of settings [WHO11]. mHealth has become an attractive approach for providing better health care outcomes at lower cost and greater convenience to both the patients as well as to health care providers [GMS05].

R. Natarajan et al. (Eds.): ICDCIT 2015, LNCS 8956, pp. 114–133, 2015.

Such solutions have become viable due to significant technological developments, which include:

1. Cheaper, relatively reliable and more portable sensors of various kinds;
2. The wide adoption of increasingly inexpensive but computationally more powerful smart phones;
3. Almost ubiquitous cellphone and wireless coverage at low costs to consumers;
4. Cloud storage and computing technologies.

mHealth is of interest to both the developed world and the developing world since the same set of technologies involved can be adapted to work in quite different socio-economic environments. For instance, senior citizens or patients who need regular monitoring can be provided individual care at their residences by equipping them with a set of sensors, the readings of which are aggregated by a smart phone and transmitted at regular intervals or at times of emergency to a doctor, nurse or other caregiver in a remote hospital. Their condition can be monitored, reviewed and care advised or provided as and when required without their having to make periodic inconvenient and expensive visits to a hospital facility [WHO12]. (Such visits which take place in the current healthcare arrangements are often unnecessary and sometimes disrupt the equanimity and routine of such patients.)

At the other end of the spectrum, in developing countries with severe resource constraints, rural health workers equipped with a smart phone or tablet and a kit of sensors can periodically visit different settlements under their purview and take readings of various parameters such as height, weight, temperature, blood pressure, haemoglobin, pulse rates and even ECGs of say a couple of hundred villagers. They can also make *in situ* reports on the prevalent environmental conditions, documenting these with environment sensor readings and visual evidence taken with the camera on the phone. The health worker can report these public health data and medical data back to a primary health care centre, at which location this information can be analysed and eventually relayed back to a district hospital or public health research agency. While it may take some time for such a model to become reality [MBN+10], kits such as the Swasthya Slate – an Android tablet and kit of medical sensors – have been built and deployed to provide effective low-cost health care to underserved communities [Swa12].

In the first setting, the purpose is primarily monitoring, with the sensors dedicated to collecting medical and environmental data of a single patient. Often the sensors are medical grade (and so compliant to the appropriate medical standards) and a high level of assurance about the quality of data is necessary. If the patient requires continuous monitoring of her condition, then constant real-time communication is required with the nearest treatment facility. Emergency situations also require immediate and real-time communication. The data collected need to be communicated and stored in the patient's electronic medical health record, with integrity and privacy [ABK12] being major concerns. In the rural health care setting, the focus is more on using the technology for screening and public health. One may probably not require extremely high fidelity and accuracy on the sensors if they are only being used for preliminary screening (thus providing an opportunity for low-cost innovations); however, they need to be rugged enough to work in challenging physical settings. In addition, the health care providers may not be highly trained or literate, and therefore the entire kit should be portable, easy to use and "fool-proof". If patients are not being continuously monitored, one may be able to accommodate some slack in the communication infrastructure, such as lower bandwidth or the ability to *tolerate delays*.

1.1   Scalability and Trustworthiness

In order to be widely adopted and effective, two critical issues that mHealth systems need to address are *scalability* and *trustworthiness*. Effective health care can be provided to a large populace only if the system conserves the valuable time of highly-skilled doctors at multi-speciality hospitals, by screening out those patients who with a high degree of assurance do not require urgent or immediate treatment. Regular screening and monitoring of community health can identify potential problems in individual patients (as well as communities) well before their condition develops to a point where treatment is both more expensive and possibly less efficacious. Low-cost medical sensors reduce the cost of deployment though usually by sacrificing accuracy of the medical readings. However, if these were to be used only for screening, then they can potentially improve healthcare. Coupled with a reliable communication system that links the patient readings taken in the field to data bases of electronic medical records, the entire model of health care delivery may be radically improved. Scalability means that the system can deal with a huge *volume* of data collected over a wide geographical area over a sustained period of time. The data collected may display a wide *variety* in the kinds of medical parameters monitored, as well as in formats in which they are presented. Finally there is a need to *validate* the data being collected, and to ascertain their *veracity*. Otherwise, we would be saddled with large amounts of data of dubious quality, on the basis of which no sensible or effective medical decisions may be possible [OKOG12].

This paper presents some of our early learning experiences in trying to develop parts of an mHealth system such as developing low-cost sensors, collecting information from the sensors in a systematic manner, and transmitting it using technologies available on stock mobile phone to standard repositories currently being used in hospitals and regional health centres. As stated above, our primary interest has been to ensure that the solution is scalable, and that there is a modicum of quality assurance in the data that have been collected. We do not present here any new technical results in the theory of distributed computing, but suggest that certain ideas that have been proposed appear to be promising in engineering a workable solution for mHealth, under a collection of "legacy" constraints.

The rest of this paper is structured as follows. In the remainder of this introduction, we discuss some of the requirements of an mHealth system that we envisage, focussing only on some aspects related to scalability and trustworthiness. We do not address here several other aspects of the system which are addressed using standard techniques well established in the distributed computing literature. In particular, we do not delve into network design and communication protocols. Nor do we discuss a variety of distributed data base issues such as fault-tolerance and efficient information retrieval. In the domain of security, we do not concern ourselves here with the algorithms used for encryption and hashing, or about access control mechanisms. We believe that many of these issues have been addressed by existing software systems; moreover, one of the design constraints under which we operate is that it would be too ambitious and also infeasible to redesign the entire healthcare information system. Instead we concentrate on what security- and storage-related ideas will allow the design of a decentralised, interoperating federated collection of extant systems that have been deployed, with minimal modifications and as modest a trusted computing base as necessary to achieve a reasonable (but by no means absolute) degree of trustworthiness. We indicate how the architecture of the system must avoid common fallacies encountered in the design of distributed computing systems. We do not attempt in this paper to survey the field of mHealth systems since there already are good surveys of the area [WHO11].

In §2, we present the notion of a *medical encounter* as the basic unit of gathering medical information, and indicate why it is important to include metadata concerning the context in which those data were collected. We present a few examples of how such metadata may be used to answer questions in the medical domain, as well as in domains related to the administration of health care and to research in public health. Following that, in §3 we address the question of how data and metadata should be stored, suggesting hyper-graphs as a suitable model for representing the data and their interrelationships. We mention how data repositories may be distributed across different places and administrative domains and possibly be of very different character. Furthermore, different fragments of a single data record may be spread across these distributed repositories. We indicate that graph-oriented distributed hash tables offer an efficient solution for accessing values from such distributed data repositories. We end the section by suggesting that *eventual consistency* provides reasonable semantics, and that *conflict-free convergent data types* can be implemented in mHealth settings without incurring prohibitive overheads in achieving this weaker degree of consistency between replicated copies of distributed fragments of a medical record.

In §4, we address the other major issue on which we have focussed, namely privacy and integrity of medical data (and metadata) [ABK12]. We argue that merely securing communication using encryption and storage using access control is inadequate when different principals exchange information sensitive to them, especially across different administrative domains. We identify the possibilities of security being compromised due to information flow between different applications in different components of the system, and examine techniques from information flow control [Den76] that have been extended to decentralised settings [ML98, KYB+07] for end-to-end information flow control. We mention how mechanisms for information flow control can be systematically incorporated into the "stack" developed for collecting data and contextual metadata, and mention some of the issues in building suitable security infrastructure into the mHealth system. We conclude in §5.

1.2 Requirements

We identify some common requirements which should be satisfied by a large-scale distributed mHealth system involving people, devices and communication and storage infrastructure:

- **Sensors:** These need to be robust, efficient, reliable and easy to use by lay persons (e.g., the patient or her family, a not-very-literate health worker). There already are several low-cost sensors that can be used for screening. However, these "stock" sensors often have no built-in communication facilities (Bluetooth LE), and may not be of medical grade; nor do they have any security features.
- **Configuration:** Configuration for collection of the data should be simple and not have many device dependencies. The sensor kits should easily connect with a smart phone, exploiting the computing power there for all the necessary analysis of the readings, collation of related readings, etc. Upstream communication can then be from the smart phone using a variety of options (3G, 4G, WiFi,...), and preferably opportunistically, using the most appropriate medium based on cost, time-criticality, importance and availability.
- **Communication:** The choice of communication media and protocols should not be hard-wired into the solution. The system should be neutral about the particular media used, especially since such a system is expected to operate for several years, if not decades, in the face of ever-changing technologies.
- **Data Representation Formats:** The data (and metadata) collected display great variety. Readings can be
  - discrete symbolic readings such as "clear", "bloody", "murky", etc.;
  - discrete numerical values such as temperature or blood pressure;
  - sampled readings taken over an interval;
  - waveforms such as ECGs;
  - graphical images such as X-rays;
  - audio or video recordings, MRIs, etc.

  A versatile system should be able to represent all these various types of data, from the collection phase to their storage in a data repository. Moreover, since these data are intended to be long-lived (the lifetime of patients, if not longer), the encodings for interpreting their bit representation should perhaps be encapsulated within the representational formats. Encryption for privacy, and hashing for anonymity add further complexity to the endurability of any data representation solution.
- **Interoperability and Seamless Integration with Medical Records Systems:** Medical data collected must be converted into a standard electronic medical record (EMR), health record (EHR) or patient health record

(PHR). Since different hospitals may have invested in data bases and hospital information systems (whether proprietary or open source), and are unlikely to convert to yet another system, the design of the system must be agnostic with respect to the data repositories.

– **Security:** If an mHealth solution is to be acceptable to the public, it must provide a degree of data security expected by patients and users of the system. Moreover, health care providers require a high degree of integrity and trustworthiness of the data collected using mobile sensors, since the collection of health data is removed in time and space from the usual hospital setting where doctors may trust their staff, equipment and facilities (laboratories, information systems) to comply with standard procedures.

– **Interactive Queries:** The data collected using such a widespread and diverse system must support interactive querying. This also requires appropriate decentralised organisation of data respecting administrative boundaries and ownership policies and access control, with suitable semantics regarding consistency of data.

– **Fault Tolerance:** The system is expected to work in an operating environment where there can be a variety of faults. An appropriate adversary model needs to be defined, that can capture the various kinds of failures with respect to with the system is resilient.

– **Legacy issues and compatibility with existing systems:** In addition to network and data bases, as well as security policies, there may be a host of other legacy issues which any mHealth solution must respect.

1.3 Avoiding Common Fallacies in System Design

The architecture of the mHealth system should perforce avoid common fallacies about distributed systems:

– *We do not assume that network at any layer is reliable.* In particular, our experience with protocols such as Bluetooth used in collecting sensor readings is that users often do not configure the connections securely, and that connections may break due to mobility of devices (sensors, phones), or electromagnetic interference. We also note that sensors may slip from their ideal position while taking a reading, or that a particular protocol for taking readings may not have been properly followed (e.g., ensuring that the patient should be seated, at rest and readings are not taken immediately after vigorous activity, and that the cuff is at heart level when taking a blood pressure reading). The challenge there is met by designing a network protocol stack that sets up a secure, reliable connection between the sensor kit and the Android device over protocols such as Bluetooth, with different layers of the stack dealing with elicitation, validation, provenance or contextual information and security [KGPP14].

– *We do not assume that communication latencies are zero or even negligible. Nor do we assume that there is unlimited bandwidth, or that transport costs are zero.* In fact, the system is based on the premise that it must work properly in the face of being often disconnected, and most portions of the system are configured to be delay-tolerant, when permitted by the application. The communication protocols are designed to avoid wasted bandwidth and dropped packets.

- *The network is not assumed to be secure.* Security is an important concern in any healthcare system, particularly the privacy of sensitive information, and more importantly the integrity of the data (and metadata) collected. A major part of our ongoing research lies in defining appropriate models of security by identifying attacker models and mechanisms that can ensure end-to-end secure flow of information permitted by reasonable sets of policies. We do not assume that there can be a centralized solution to security when a variety of different principals are involved.

- *The topology of the system is not assumed to be static.* In fact, mobility – of sensors, devices and principals – is a defining characteristic of an mHealth system. Accordingly, we do not try to embed rigid routing policies into the communication protocols and structures. Mobility also has important consequences on scalability, especially in dealing with namespaces and routing tables, as well as with security and trustworthiness.

- The most important realisation we reached in the design of a healthcare system is that the system is decentralised not merely in space but also in that *there is no single administrator either of namespaces or of security policies. There is great diversity and autonomy* in the different health care organisations (hospitals, research organisations, etc.), each with their own data security policies, different data base access control mechanisms and information disclosure and privacy policies.

- *The network is not assumed to have a uniform or homogeneous structure.* The communication media, bandwidths, protocols, etc. exhibit great variety. Clearly at the peripheries, especially in the developing world, the network is slow, "flaky" and often inaccessible; communication may be over mobile phone carriers. On the other hand, within a hospital or a research organisation it may be over reliable wired high-speed optical fibre networks.

- We realise that it will be prohibitively expensive as well as infeasible to attempt to design a uniform solution that can be adopted by all principals and organisations involved, so the focus has to be on developing a system that *works with the pre-existing infrastructural arrangements* chosen by the different healthcare organisations involved (network, operating systems, data bases,...), supplementing them with components that can ensure a degree of trustworthiness and value-addition while ensuring scalability.

2   Healthcare Encounters

Consider a developing world scenario where health worker Heena, equipped with a kit of sensors and a smart phone, visits a patient Puja in a village, and takes her readings for body temperature, pulse, blood pressure, weight, haemoglobin, and an ECG. All of these readings are annotated with Puja's ID, Heena's employee code, the time and place where the readings were taken. In addition, a few environmental parameters such as the ambient temperature, pollution levels, humidity, etc. may be captured by sensors. Also consider a personal healthcare scenario, where a set of sensors worn by the patient constantly collect and send to a medical facility or doctor via a smart phone readings of the patient's heart rate, temperature etc., together with readings from an accelerometer worn by the patient. The capturing of all this information taken together constitutes a *healthcare encounter*, the outcome of which is a single record consisting of the various medical data readings bundled together with critical metadata (who, whose, when, where, with what, etc.) regarding the context in which the readings were taken. An encounter is the basic unit around which the mHealth system records may be built. A patient's medical history may then be viewed as a collection of records produced by such encounters.

However, a more useful metaphor is that of a "conversation", where the encounter records are utterances but following which connections and correlations may be made between this encounter record and those of, say, the patient's earlier encounters, or of encounters of the patient's family members, or others in the same locality, or those taken by the same health worker Heena, etc. In other words, if the encounter results in a record in a data base, various "meta" records are created by various analyses that are performed either on the smart phone or in the hospital or at a regional level in a public health researcher's data base. Such meta-level observations are similar to commentary about previous utterances, or "asides" between a subset of listeners that may or may not be accessible to all the participants of a conversation. By making such meta-records first-class in the data repositories, we obtain a rich information system which may be queried in different ways for greater effectiveness.

The richness of this system may be successfully exploited by representing the data as a federated decentralised data repository. There have been various proposal's (e.g., by the NHS of the UK) to build centralised data repositories of all patients, which can be accessed by various health care providers. However, these proposals have assumed that the system would be highly centralized, and operating within a single administrative domain. While there are obvious benefits (to the patients, to the nation, to caregivers, to insurance companies, ...) of building such a system that exceed the costs involved, they have met with resistance from both caregivers, who may possibly be wary of the disruptions involved in migrating from their existing systems, as well as privacy advocate groups who worry about the compromising and exploitation of sensitive personal information of patients. Moreover the complexity of designing such a system and having it adopted uniformly is perhaps its greatest drawback.

2.1 Metadata Matters!

The metadata collected by various sensors including those on a smart phone play an extremely important role in effective decision making, both medical and administrative. An ultrasound image is of little value to a doctor unless she know whose it is and when and where it was taken. There are also other uses of the metadata, some of which may include:

- If Heena is paid by the number of patients she visits, she may have an incentive for defrauding the system by uploading readings from a small set of locations passing them off as readings from far-flung villages. Or she may be passing off old readings as new ones. If the metadata associated with an encounter were bundled in a secure, nontamperable manner with the readings, such fraud may easily be detected.
- The readings coming from a particular device may be observed to be consistently lower that an expected range. This may be for a variety of reasons: the health worker or patient has not placed the sensors properly; or there is a fault in that particular device; or a design and/or manufacturing problem with a particular batch of devices of particular brand; etc. Having metadata related to the context of the encounter can help detect problems with the data collected, and appropriate corrective actions can then be initiated;
- Researchers may be able to query anonymised data, correlating them across time or space or other demographic information. This requires being able to perform statistical analysis "underneath" the anonymising transformations on the data.
- A device manufacturer may be able to keep track of the deployment, use and performance of various devices that they have manufactured and sold to the health care providers.

Many of these metadata are implicit in traditional hospital-based care, where the trustworthiness of the data derives from it being collected in controlled contexts that provide the medical practitioner or administrator a high degree of quality assurance. This assurance of quality is what is lost when the encounter is removed in time and space from the consumer of the information. An important design consideration is therefore to record sufficient *contextual evidence* for the data to enable informed decision-making [PPM+13].

2.2 Data Collection

Most sensors do not come equipped with facilities to collect the contextual evidence metadata. We have proposed and prototyped systems [KGPP14, KG14] where a set of sensors are connected via a micro controller board (Arduino currently, but Raspberry Pi or Intel's Galileo may be used) to take readings from the sensors in a coordinated fashion and communicate these to an Android smart phone over Bluetooth, Wifi or even physically via USB. An Android app running on the smart phone initiates the process of taking readings during the encounter, and establishes connection with the micro controller board, which then elicits readings from the sensors, and bundles them into a communication packet that is sent to the smart phone. The readings are examined for validity and some corrective actions are initiated locally. Various parameters are set by the Android app using the phone sensors (e.g., GPS, time, the camera parameters).

The protocol has been organised as a "Sensor Stack" with layers for connection establishment and management, elicitation, validation, and adding contextual metadata. Security layers for secure information flow are currently being incorporated. The Android app finally compiles the data and metadata collected during an encounter into a commonly interpretable format (XML in our case) suitable for communication to a variety of EMR/EHR systems.

3   Data Base Design Issues

Due to the great variety in the kind of information being collected, a uniform template-based representation is probably *not* the best approach to representing medical data records. New kinds of information are likely to be added. Of particular interest to us are the metadata that constitute "contextual evidence". These may not be of interest to the hospital (and thus no provision may be made for such information in their health care records). The data generated in an encounter seem to be semi-structured. There also are temporal and causal links between records. Yet various electronic medical records systems are built over relational data bases such as SQL and MySQL. As noted earlier, it is unlikely that a hospital will migrate to a new kind of data base even if the benefits are apparent. Moreover, the system needs to accommodate several hospitals, each of which may have their own preferred EMR system. Therefore, one needs a flexible, EMR-agnostic way of incorporating the extra (meta) data into existing installed data bases. A solution is to build a separate data repository for the metadata and then placing references to and from it in the various hospital EMR systems. This has the advantages of:

- permitting more flexibility in the representation of contextual metadata, which may even be represented as key-value stores;
- decentralised management of the information, with each hospital as well as even patients controlling certain information according to their policies, and managing these policies locally;
- flexibility in expansion of the system, incorporating new kinds of data bases, more hospitals and a variety of healthcare/medical record formats;
- more efficient query-processing by exploiting locality of storage.

However, to realise such these advantages, one needs a model that is general enough to capture and anticipate the various usages. We have already alluded to the kinds of correlations between different medical records that a doctor, patient, researcher or administrator may make. Such questions translate into queries on data and metadata, and even on information derived from analyses done on them. It is our position that *hyper-graphs* provide the correct abstraction for the representing the information. Hyper-graphs are graphs where an edge can connect more than one node. Moreover, they can easily accommodate higher-order hyper-edges, that connect hyper-edges. Currently there are a few hyper-graph data bases, e.g., [Ior10]. Some of the advantages of hyper-graph-based data bases are that they:

- provide a powerful medium for data modelling and knowledge representation;
- can express n-ary and higher order relationships between graph nodes;
- provide for graph-oriented storage, and so can support graph traversals and path-queries as well as relational-style queries;
- can support customisable indexing and storage management; and
- can accommodate extensible, dynamic data base schema through appropriate typing.

The typing frameworks and query language design issues here provide interesting problems for programming language researchers.

3.1   Distributed Data Base Issues

Apart from representational issues, this being a heterogeneous distributed system, with a high degree of mobility, asynchrony, concurrent operation and possibility of a variety of failures, there are significant problems related to concurrency and fault-tolerance that need to be addressed in the design. Any centralised solution is not an option. The system comprises numerous smart phones connected to one another and to health care centres and their data repositories "in the cloud", all working asynchronously; so any approaches based on synchronisation are precluded.

The first issue is that of atomicity, which immediately raises the question about what constitute transactions in such a system. A candidate answer is "the collection of information during an encounter". *It is reasonable to view an encounter as the basic unit for updates.* However, what is the span of an encounter? Does it complete with the collection of readings by the micro controller board, or when the information is transferred to the Android app, which makes an XML (or similar) record for upstream transmission? Or does it conclude when the information is uploaded to the cloud or to a hospital repository? We have already noted that the data and metadata within even one record may be distributed spatially (due to ownership and administrative constraints). Thus it is not entirely trivial how such a distributed write should be atomically executed across the different sites involved. Thus the atomicity of transactions is not an easy question, and the possible answers have an immediate bearing on notions such as consistency.

Indeed we confront the issues of consistency, availability and operation under network partition, as in Brewer's so-called CAP theorem [Bre01]. Network partitioning should be assumed to be the normal mode of operation, and availability of the system is essential for its functioning. Therefore, we have to relax the requirements of strict consistency. Indeed, it seems that working with a notion of *eventual consistency* yields workable solutions which do not require a significant overhead, and support autonomous functioning of entities in the mHealth system. Fortunately, in the case of medical records, we can exploit the fact that *no records should be deleted*. Readings that have become irrelevant, e.g., a normal body temperature reading from last year, or even readings known to be erroneous are preserved in the store; they may be *deprecated* and *discarded* during medical decision making by a doctor, but are still maintained for historical reasons, or to answer meta-queries unrelated to the patient's health care (e.g., did the thermometer work correctly, or was the reading taken as prescribed in a healthcare protocol?). Thus we can operate under the assumption that information in the system grows monotonically. (In practice, there may be a hierarchy of storage, with old, irrelevant, wrong and other such data that are unlikely to be useful banished to lower, slower rungs of the hierarchy).

Recall that the contents of a logical record may be distributed across many repositories. In distributed records, some information needs to be replicated across different repositories, both for efficiency, and to be able to link information in different parts of a hyper-edge which are stored on separate repositories. This replicated and cross-referencing information must necessarily be maintained in a consistent manner. Writing of semantically unrelated parts of a single record into distinct repositories allows a degree of flexibility (e.g., commutation) in the order in which writes may happen in a single distributed write transaction.

The monotonicity assumption makes it possible to design the system to exhibit local coherence and eventual consistency. Causal linkages must of course be preserved (these are recorded perhaps as "why-provenance" information [BKT01] in some hyper-edge) but not all temporal precedences are relevant for justifying treatment decisions made on information available at a particular time and place. Thus if we can ensure that updates to hyper-edges can commute, and all of its replicas execute all updates in causal order, then the replicas can (eventually) converge without invoking any elaborate coordination mechanisms. Monotonicity of information and adopting weaker notions of consistency thus make it possible to organise the health records as a (bunch of) Commutative Replicated Data Types (CRDTs) [SPBZ11]. CRDTs have the excellent property that they eventually converge without any complex concurrency control mechanism. They are ideally suited for extremely large information systems; the principal difficulty in designing CRDTs lies in efficient representation of the data type to have good local coherence and convergence properties across replicas, with respect to the series of operations performed on them. Write-monotonicity and read-only operations in the hyper-graph data type greatly facilitate building a large, scalable distributed data repository with good fault-tolerant properties. We have previously experimented with a prototype implementation of hyper-graphs as a CRDT [Pri11], with promising results, and intend to incorporate these ideas into our prototype mHealth data repository implementation.

3.2 Accessing Records

Even with migration of data to the cloud, there is a need to have fast and reliable protocols for accessing records. We assume that, in general, the minimal organisation of data in any repository will be some variant of a *(key, value)*-store; any additional structure will be built on this basis. As we assumed that the basic records in the system will be encounters, each encounter will be given a unique key, perhaps derived from the personal IDs of the participants and the time and place of the encounter. Using suitable hashing functions, a key may be derived, which can be used for locating the record using Distributed Hash

Tables. We envisage using a DHT based on ideas from systems such as Chord [SMK+01] or Koorde [KK03] which have a high degree of scalability and which exploit graph-theoretic properties to make retrieval more efficient and robust. In particular, given that many queries will involve some commonality of information between the records sought to be retrieved (the same patient, or the same health worker, or spatial location, or time period), we plan to use *locality preserving hashing* techniques, which map closely related records to the same or nearby repositories, thus making retrieval more efficient.

3.3   Presentation of Information

The more interesting challenges lie in how information is to be presented to various consumers of information. It must, of course, conform to the access privileges and privacy policy pertinent to that information. Moreover, the consumer of the information (doctor, administrator, patient, ...) must not get overwhelmed by the entire record, with data and metadata, and should also not be presented with a complete medical history of a patient *as recorded, replete with loads of dated, irrelevant, deprecated information.* This comprises a whole set of interesting research problems in data science, information retrieval, security and query processing.

A further issue that needs greater conceptualisation concerns the long-term preservation of the data. The interpretation of bits (that represent records) lies embedded in the software used to create and read the records. One has to design for preservation of backward compatibility whenever the software is upgraded or when any component of the system is upgraded or replaced. Alternatively, all data should come with a generalised self-strapping protocol using which the interpretation of bits is never mutilated.

4   Ensuring Trustworthiness

In any large distributed system dealing with such voluminous data, it is necessary to ensure data integrity (that it not be tampered with) and also that the sensitive information of each principal in the system is not divulged to any unauthorised party. Data stored in the data repositories (data bases, file systems, key-value stores, etc.) are said to be "at rest". Such data are secured by using access control mechanisms, which are supported by the operating systems and/or data bases. When data are "in motion", i.e., when that information is being communicated between systems, security protocols based on modern encryption techniques are used so that an attacker (active or passive) cannot compromise the integrity of the data, or learn secrets etc. However, just these two sets of techniques are inadequate to ensure that sensitive information is not improperly divulged, nor that information that is trusted is derived from untrusted information sources and untrusted data. The leakage, as they say, happens "at the joints", namely from the applications that access the data stores, process the information, and then put the results onto communication channels, transferring information from one administrative and security domain to another. Very often the information is leaked implicitly (i.e., the secret is not explicitly divulged, but can be inferred by the adversary from information accessed by it that is derived from the secret information).

It is our contention that ensuring trustworthiness of an mHealth system requires addressing security not just of data at rest and data in motion but also of data during computations. In other words, ensuring secrecy and privacy are end-to-end design issues [SRC84]. Security cannot be ensured piecemeal even if one were to use the best techniques and implementations for individual components; the users of the mHealth system should be able to specify and rely on the system to correctly deal with privacy and integrity of their data.

4.1 Information Flow Control

The problem of programs leaking information or computing results from untrusted sources is addressed by the techniques of *Information Flow Control* (IFC) [Den76] . Programs are analysed to check whether during their execution information can flow from data sources (input variables, files, etc.) considered secret to public or insecure sinks (output variables, output files,...). Dually, for integrity, the analyses check whether output values that are trusted are dependent from data that are considered untrusted. The analyses can be at run-time (dynamic), prohibiting accidental disclosure for instance. Alternatively, the analyses can be performed statically (at compile time) and programs certified as secure or (conservatively) labelled as insecure [DD77]. The analyses assume that security classes form a lattice, and permitted information flows are those conforming to the lattice structure. Each programming language primitive is abstractly interpreted in terms of meet and join operations over this lattice.

IFC analysis at the programming language level is a fine-grained analysis technique to ensure security (whether privacy or integrity). It assumes that the source code of the entire program is available, and that the entire program executes within one security administration domain. For large-scale distributed systems with thousands of principals each with their own labelling of particular pieces of information as private, such an analysis is not viable. IFC techniques were modified by Myers and Liskov to work in a *decentralised* label management framework to protect data for different users, each with their individual policy [ML97]. These DIFC techniques, which work by each principal labelling its information (without there being any single security authority) [ML98], have been implemented at the operating system level in systems such as Asbestos [EKV+05], HiStar [ZBWKM06], Aeolus [CPS+12], and Flume [KYB+07], the last of which introduces the concept of an *endpoint*. DIFC techniques have also been adapted for data bases [SL13].

4.2   Security Model

Before we describe how DIFC techniques need to be further adapted for mHealth applications, we briefly describe the security model. Characterising the *adversary* is one way of understanding the operating environment in which the system needs to be able to function. (The notion of an *adversary* is not merely one that we encounter in security literature; it is perhaps a fundamental idea for understanding the limitations of a computational system, whether in complexity theory or in failure models, etc.)

The environment includes typical adversarial behaviour for any communication protocol (not merely a cryptographic one). Messages between components of the system can get lost, duplicated, corrupted and an eavesdropper may attempt to analyse (by decryption using available keys, or even brute force attempts to learn the inputs from the output of a function) a message to learn its component contents. The adversary can also fabricate messages using any keys, nonces, hash functions and any other available data. We may consider a variety of adversarial behaviours, from the Dolev-Yao model that assumes perfect encryption to computationally-bounded and resource-bounded adversaries. We have not considered *denial-of-service attacks* though these are a real possibility in mHealth systems. (At the very least, we should ensure that components of the system do not flood others with unboundedly many messages.)

We require that the system function properly even if some components fail, though perhaps at a reduced capacity and functionality. For example, a smart phone should continue to be available for recording encounters even if the communication link to the nearest hospital or the cloud fails temporarily. More importantly, data that have been understood to have been committed to permanent storage should not be lost if a smart phone or micro controller board in a health kit malfunctions. We believe that standard replication and transaction management techniques in distributed data bases can handle the vast majority of such faults. We do not assume that components within the trusted computing base of the system will behave in Byzantine ways. However, the system should be able to work in conjunction with a large number of devices and with software outside the trusted computing base. (Ensuring that the trusted computing base is free of bugs will however be no easy task.)

At the storage level, the adversary can attempt to read stored data with whatever access control privileges and rights are at its disposal. It can also forge information and store it in the repositories, in the hope of making principles act as oracles to learn some critical information. Again, we do not consider an adversary being able to fill up the repositories with "junk" thus preventing genuine mHealth data from being saved on it.

At the computational level, we assume that the adversary may corrupt the integrity of *bona fide* medical data or metadata by tampering with them during processing or by linking to malicious libraries at runtime or forging information; it may also compromise confidentiality by gaining access to sensitive information by requesting permission at installation time or by uploading the information to a public server without informing the concerned user.

At the policy level and deployment level, we assume that principals and organisations involved have reasonable security policies, and that the hardware and software components employed can correctly implement these policies. Moreover, we assume that they will employ strong cryptographic techniques and reliable access control mechanisms. The challenge is to support interoperation of different organisations by ensuring information exchange amongst them while respecting the privacy/integrity policies of one another.

The security mechanisms that we explore in our design cannot address threats that arise due to the faulty working of sensors. To some extent, such problems are dealt with in the validation layer of the "sensor stack".

4.3 Tags, Labels, Authority

The DIFC framework of Myers and Liskov [ML97, ML98] allow principals to express their privacy/integrity concerns about their data by *tagging* program and data components. The tags indicate ownership of the components as well as who may legally read the data according to a desired policy. Labels are sets of tags. DIFC mechanisms track data as they flow through the system and restrict the release of information. In systems such as IFDB [SL13], data objects are immutably labelled, whereas processes reading the data get "tainted" by the labels of the data read. Very roughly, information is permitted to flow from a source s to a destination d if the label of s is contained in the label of d. Thus information may be released to the public only by processes having the lowest possible label. In Flume [KYB+07], which uses DIFC framework at the level of standard OS abstractions, the focus is information declassification/endorsement as data flow through interprocess communication *endpoints*.

Declassification allows particular tags to be removed from labels, and is useful in releasing information to authorised principals or to declassify summary information that may not reveal individual sensitive data. Since it removes constraints on permitted information flow, declassification is permitted only for processes having the requisite authority on the corresponding tags. Ownership of data determines having the capability to declassify and to delegate this authority to others (and to perhaps revoke this authority later).

DIFC frameworks presented in the literature rely on principals providing tags appropriately for the various components. We believe that while this may be possible in a small system, especially one involving security-aware users, it is unrealistic for the general populace, particularly uneducated or uninformed individuals, to provide tags or to even comprehend the consequences of a security policy. Since users cannot be expected to tag their data, *we propose that data be tagged automatically and systematically*, by which we mean that tags are provided for different data fields of an encounter record by a layer within the "sensor stack". The granularity at which data are labelled in data bases may be at the level of relations (tables), records (tuples) or fields. While in [SL13], an excellent case is made for labelling data at the level of tuples, in mHealth systems we suggest that labelling may have to be at the level of fields (or more precisely, collections of fields), even though per-field labelling may involve a significant overhead. The reason for this is the following: it is not obvious who the owner of an encounter record should be. The common belief that the *patient* should be the owner of her data is not appropriate, since the encounter record may have several fields, particularly metadata fields, of which she was totally unaware and probably unconcerned. These metadata were collected as contextual evidence, and may include the unique device number of a sensor, that may be of interest to the hospital administrator or the device manufacturer, but have no relevance for the patient. Were the patient the owner of these metadata, explicit declassification would become necessary for queries related to this information. Moreover, as discussed earlier, different portions of the encounter record may be distributed across different data stores, each operating under a different privacy/integrity policy. Therefore labelling at the granularity of records is not appropriate. Preventing a blow-up in the size of tagging information is a crucial problem that we are studying.

4.4 Non-invertible, Structure-Preserving Functions

It is a mistaken belief that anonymity and privacy can be achieved by eliding identifying information from records. It is also often believed that by renaming identifiers (obfuscation), one can achieve anonymity. There have been numerous instances of data compromise due to such unjustified assumptions. It is therefore necessary to transform the data by applying functions that are difficult to invert (e.g., hash functions, one-way functions etc.). However, any query on the data, such as range queries, need to be performed on the data "going below" the transformations. Very roughly, if h is a transformation and $\oplus$ an operation on data $x_1, \ldots, x_n$, we would like to compute $\oplus(x_1, \ldots, x_n)$. However, we are not given $x_1, \ldots x_n$ but instead are presented $h(x_1) \ldots h(x_n)$. h is said to be *homomorphic* with respect to $\oplus$ if $h(\oplus(x_1, \ldots, x_n)) = \oplus'(h(x_1), \ldots, h(x_n))$ for some $\oplus'$. In the kind of operations we have examined, it may not be necessary to require that the transformations be fully homomorphic. Finding weaker structure-preserving properties and transformations that allow us to perform the desired operations is a topic for future study.

The requirement of non-invertible functions also applies to the labels that we generate systematically. The tags are usually opaque strings that should not themselves reveal information. However, if they are being systematically generated, they may be created based on the kind of data with which they are associated (the field name) as well as other metadata that can be used to identify an encounter. It is therefore necessary to use one-way functions or hash functions that do not reveal much information about the inputs. The operation that one performs on tags are checking subset inclusion, which may only require weak structure preservation.

Finally, the mHealth system that we envisage involves data being shared between different administrative domains. Of course, this should be permitted when the domains agree that they will respect each other's security policies, without necessarily having to take an union of the two sets of policies. This requires checking tags that were generated in another domain, with the interpretation of the tags being understood only in that domain. We believe that the right approach to truly decentralised information flow control lies in being able to transform tags generated in one namespace to those in another namespace through a difficult-to-invert transformation, and to perform the information flow control checks in the transformed domain.

5   Conclusion

In trying to address scalability and trustworthiness issues in developing an mHealth system, we encountered the full variety of issues that distributed systems have to address:

- Communication protocols at different levels of the stack, especially within the application layer;
- Data base representation and efficient data retrieval issues;
- Consistency semantics in distributed data repositories;
- Security issues beyond encryption and authentication;
- Making systems work with legacy applications and taking into account future changes in software used.

The major system design issues involved are understanding the requirements, picking a good model and set of associated techniques, optimising them with respect to the constraints placed on the system, and finally understanding whether these design choices allow the system to operate efficiently at scale.

Among various ideas in distributed computing, some concepts stand out as pearls, using which dependable and reliable systems can be built: sequential consistency, serialisability, linearisability, atomicity, idempotent operations; store-and-forward communication, pipes for interprocess communication; public-key encryption; failure detectors, and several others. Real-world problems help us identify such key concepts from a gamut of proposals. Our still-early study of mHealth systems suggests that to this list one may add: (i) Hyper-graph data bases; (ii) graph-oriented distributed hash tables; (iii) CRDTs; and (iv) Decentralised Information Flow Control techniques.

Acknowledgements. This work has been supported by DeitY, Government of India, for the project "Foundations of Trusted and Scalable "Last-Mile' Healthcare". I wish to acknowledge fruitful discussions with Kolin Paul, David Kotz, and Aarathi Prasad, and the work of Ashwani Priyedarshi, Chandrika Bhardwaj, Aruna Bansal, Avval and Anju Kansal.

References

[ABK12]   Avancha, S., Baxi, A., Kotz, D.: Privacy in mobile technology for personal healthcare. ACM Computing Surveys 45(1), 3 (2012)

[BKT01]   Buneman, P., Khanna, S., Tan, W.-C.: Why and where: A characterization of data provenance. In: Van den Bussche, J., Vianu, V. (eds.) ICDT 2001. LNCS, vol. 1973, pp. 316–330. Springer, Heidelberg (2000)

[Bre01]   Brewer, E.A.: Lessons from Giant-Scale Services. IEEE Internet Computing 5(4), 46–55 (2001)

[CPS⁺12]   Cheng, W., Ports, D.R.K., Schultz, D.A., Popic, V., Blankstein, A., Cowling, J.A., Curtis, D., Shrira, L., Liskov, B.: Abstractions for Usable Information Flow Control in Aeolus. In: USENIX Annual Tech. Conf., pp. 139–151 (2012)

[DD77]   Denning, D.E., Denning, P.J.: Certification of Programs for Secure Information Flow. Commun. ACM 20(7), 504–513 (1977)

[Den76]   Denning, D.E.: A Lattice Model of Secure Information Flow. Commun. ACM 19(5), 236–243 (1976)

[EKV⁺05]   Efstathopoulos, P., Krohn, M.N., Vandebogart, S., Frey, C., Ziegler, D., Kohler, E., Mazières, D., Kaashoek, M.F., Morris, R.: Labels and event processes in the Asbestos operating system. In: ACM Symp. on Operating Systems Principles, pp. 17–30 (2005)

[GMS05]   Germanakos, P., Mourlas, C., Samaras, G.: A Mobile Agent Approach for Ubiquitous and Personalized eHealth Information Systems. In: Proc. of the Workshop on Personalization for e-Health of the 10th International Conf. on User Modeling, pp. 67–70 (2005)

[Ior10]   Iordanov, B.: HyperGraphDB: A generalized graph database. In: Shen, H.T., Pei, J., Özsu, M.T., Zou, L., Lu, J., Ling, T.-W., Yu, G., Zhuang, Y., Shao, J. (eds.) WAIM 2010. LNCS, vol. 6185, pp. 25–36. Springer, Heidelberg (2010)

[KG14]   Kansal, A., Gupta, A.: Sensor Stack on Android for mHealth Applications. Master's thesis, Department of Computer Science & Engineering, IIT Delhi (2014)

[KGPP14]   Kansal, A., Gupta, A., Paul, K., Prasad, S.: mDROID - An Affordable Android based mHealth System. In: International Conf. on Health Informatics. SciTePress - Science and Technology Publications (2014)

[KK03]   Kaashoek, F., Karger, D.R.: Koorde: A simple degree-optimal hash table. In: Kaashoek, M.F., Stoica, I. (eds.) IPTPS 2003. LNCS, vol. 2735, pp. 98–107. Springer, Heidelberg (2003)

[KYB⁺07]   Krohn, M.N., Yip, A., Brodsky, M.Z., Cliffer, N., Kaashoek, M.F., Kohler, E., Morris, R.: Information flow control for standard OS abstractions. In: ACM Symp. on Operating Systems Principles, pp. 321–334 (2007)

[MBN⁺10]   Mechael, P., Batavia, H., Kaonga, N., Searle, S., Kwan, A., Goldberger, A., Fu, L., Ossman, J.: Barriers and gaps affecting mhealth in low and middle income countries. In: A Policy White Paper commisioned by The mHealth Alliance (2010)

[ML97]   Myers, A.C., Liskov, B.: A Decentralized Model for Information Flow Control. In: ACM Symp. on Operating Systems Principles, pp. 129–142 (1997)

[ML98]   Myers, A.C., Liskov, B.: Complete, safe information flow with decentralized labels. In: Proceedings of the 1998 IEEE Symposium on Security and Privacy, pp. 186–197 (May 1998)

[OKOG12]   Otieno, C.F., Kaseje, D., Ochieng, B.M., Githae, M.N.: Reliability of community health worker collected data for planning and policy in a peri-urban area of kisumu, kenya. Journal of Community Health 37, 48–53 (2012)

[PPM⁺13]   Prasad, A., Peterson, R.A., Mare, S., Sorber, J., Paul, K., Kotz, D.: Provenance framework for mhealth. In: Fifth International Conference on Communication Systems and Networks, COMSNETS 2013, Bangalore, India, January 7-10, pp. 1–6 (2013)

[Pri11]   Priyedarshi, A.: Caching and Distributed Data for Cloud-Style Computation. Master's thesis, Department of Computer Science & Engineering, IIT Delhi (2011)

[SL13]   Schultz, D.A., Liskov, B.: IFDB: decentralized information flow control for databases. In: Proc. of the 8th ACM European Conf. on Computer Systems, pp. 43–56. ACM (2013)

[SMK⁺01]   Stoica, I., Morris, R., Karger, D., Kaashoek, M.F., Balakrishnan, H.: Chord: A scalable peer-to-peer lookup service for internet applications. In: Proceedings of the 2001 Conference on Applications, Technologies, Architectures, and Protocols for Computer Communications, SIGCOMM 2001, pp. 149–160. ACM, New York (2001)

[SPBZ11]   Shapiro, M., Preguiça, N.M., Baquero, C., Zawirski, M.: Conflict-free replicated data types. In: Défago, X., Petit, F., Villain, V. (eds.) SSS 2011. LNCS, vol. 6976, pp. 386–400. Springer, Heidelberg (2011)

[SRC84]   Saltzer, J.H., Reed, D.P., Clark, D.D.: End-to-end arguments in system design. ACM Trans. Comput. Syst. 2(4), 277–288 (1984)

[Swa12]   Swasthya Slate of Public health foundation of India (2012), http://www.swasthyaslate.org

[WHO11]   WHO. mhealth: New horizons for health through mobile technologies Global Observatory for eHealth Series, 3 (2011)

[WHO12]   WHO. Management of patient information: Trends and challenges in member states. Global Observatory for eHealth Series, 6 (2012)

[ZBWKM06]   Zeldovich, N., Boyd-Wickizer, S., Kohler, E., Mazières, D.: Making Information Flow Explicit in HiStar. In: USENIX Conf. on Operating Systems Design and Implementation, pp. 263–278 (2006)

Host Trait Prediction of Metagenomic Data for Topology-Based Visualization

Laxmi Parida[1,*], Niina Haiminen[1], David Haws[1], and Jan Suchodolski[2]

[1] Computational Biology Center, IBM T.J. Watson Research,
Yorktown Heights, NY, USA
[2] Veterinary Medicine & Biomedical Sciences, Texas A&M University,
College Station, TX, USA
parida@us.ibm.com

Abstract. Microbiome and metagenomic research continues to grow as well as the size and complexity of the collected data. Additionally, it is understood that the microbiome can have a complex relationship with the environment or host it inhabits, such as in gastrointestinal disease. The goal of this study is to accurately predict a host's trait using only metagenomic data, by training a statistical model on available metagenome sequencing data. We compare a traditional Support Vector Regression approach to a new non-parametric method developed here, called PKEM, which uses dimensionality reduction combined with Kernel Density Estimation. The results are visualized using methods from Topological Data Analysis. Such representations assist in understanding how the data organizes and can lead to new insights. We apply this visualization-of-prediction technique to cat, dog and human microbiome obtained from fecal samples. In the first two the host trait is irritable bowel syndrome while in the last the host trait is Kwashiorkor, a form of severe malnutrition.

1 Introduction

In recent years there has been an explosion of interest in microbiomes and metagenomics, which has been coupled with a dramatic increase in data to process and analyze. The microbiome is understood to be the community of microorganisms that inhabit some environment, such as the human gut, the soil surrounding plant roots, sewage treatment, etc. Metagenomics is the study of the genetic material of the microbes inhabiting some microbiome. Some studies focus on whole genomic sequencing of all organisms in the microbiome, providing massive amounts of data to analyze. Often though, many studies focus primarily on the diversity and specific abundance of each type of microorganism in one or many samples. To this end, sequencing typically targets the 16S rRNA gene which is present in most organisms. Equipped with 16S rRNA sequences, researchers are able to estimate which microorganisms are present in the environmental sample and classify the them from coarser to finer categories by

---

* Corresponding author.

R. Natarajan et al. (Eds.): ICDCIT 2015, LNCS 8956, pp. 134–149, 2015.
© Springer International Publishing Switzerland 2015

phylum, class, order, family, and genus, with a loss of accuracy as one moves from coarser to finer classification.

It is understood that the microbiome plays a crucial role in the environment it inhabits, and may have a complicated relationship with the host or organism of interest. For example, the microbiome surrounding plant soil can have a dramatic effect on drought resistance [1], and conversely plants can effect the microbiome of the soil they inhabit [2] and changes in the health of a human host can directly impact the microbiome in the gut [3,4]. However, many microbiome collection efforts are focused on collecting samples from some environment and do not consider information about the environment or host, such as host disease status or other host phenotypes. As such, many studies and data sets contain an abundance of microbiome samples from multiple hosts, with little or no data on the host itself. Additionally, it is often difficult to understand and compare multiple microbiomes with respect to host traits. Nevertheless, we are interested in the relationship of a microbiome with respect to its associated host's traits.

The goal of this study is two-fold. First, to quantify the host status (e.g. disease status or some phenotype) by training a statistical model on available host and metagenomic data. From this, one can then attempt to predict a host's trait using only metagenomic data. This study is focused on Operational Taxonomic Unit (OTU) information for each microbiome and binary host traits. Second, provide a low-dimensional visualization of multiple host's microbiomes using tools from topological data analysis. The visualization is able to break down multiple microbiomes with respect to the host traits as well as highlight differences seen only at the microbiome level. The visualization is able to retain important structures of the high-dimensional data with the goal of leading to new insights and understanding of the otherwise opaque complicated data.

2 Methods

Quantifying Host Trait. All datasets that we studied contain multiple microbiome samples across multiple hosts. For each microbiome, OTU tables and the host's binary trait ($\{0, 1\}$) were obtained. The first step involves the training of a statistical model on available OTU and host trait data. Two approaches were used for this step, widely used Support Vector Regression (SVR) – a parametric approach – and a new non-parametric algorithm called **P**rediction through **K**ernel density **E**stimation of **M**etagenomic data, or PKEM for short. Both approaches are described below.

Support Vector Machines (SVMs) have been utilized in microbiome data analysis [5,6] due to their observed empirical performance on this type of data, as well as due to several theoretical considerations as summarized in [5]: SVMs perform well in data with limited sample size, are relatively insensitive to high dimensionality of the data, prevent overfitting by using regularization techniques, and can learn both simple and complex decision functions. Hence we also included SVMs as a state of the art method in our comparison.

The topological data analysis visualization then uses the above predictions of the host trait, as well as a distance measure between OTU tables. If available, the weighted UniFrac [7] distance was used. The output is a low-dimensional representation of the microbiome data and is described below.

UniFrac distance is also used by existing microbial community analysis systems such as QIIME [8] that employs Random Forests for trait classification. Here we focus on SVM as the benchmark method for classification, for the above mentioned reasons.

Support Vector Regression. SVR [9,10,11,12,13] attempts to model the relationship between the explanatory and response variables by finding a hyperplane (high-dimensional generalization of a 3d-plane), where all the data points lay either on the hyperplane or as close as possible to it. The real trick here is that the data are first mapped to a different high-dimensional space using possibly a non-linear kernel.

Following [14], given a training set $(\mathbf{x}_i, y_i)$, $i = 1, \ldots l$, where $\mathbf{x}_i \in \mathbb{R}^n$, the goal of ε-SV regression is to find a function $f(\mathbf{x})$ that is at most ε deviation from the explanatory variable y_i over the response variable $\mathbf{x}_i$, while remaining as flat as possible in the feature space. In our case, the response variables will be OTU data, and the explanatory variable will be the host trait associated with the microbiome. Training an SVR requires solving

$$\min_{\mathbf{w}, b, \xi} \quad \frac{1}{2}\mathbf{w}^\top \mathbf{w} + C \left(\sum \xi_i + \sum \xi_i^*\right)$$

$$\text{subject to} \begin{cases} y_i - \mathbf{w}^\top \phi(\mathbf{x}_i) - b \leq \varepsilon + \xi_i \\ \mathbf{w}^\top \phi(\mathbf{x}_i) + b - y_i \leq \varepsilon + \xi_i^* \end{cases} \tag{1}$$

$$\xi_i, \xi_i^* \geq 0.$$

The data vectors $\mathbf{x}_i$ are mapped to another space via the function ϕ, and SVR attempts to fit the data in this higher dimensional space. Thus, the choice of ϕ, referred to as the *kernel*, has a large impact. The de-facto SVR software `libsvm` [15] provides four kernels:

$$\text{Linear:} \quad \mathbf{u}^\top \mathbf{v},$$
$$\text{Polynomial:} \quad (\gamma \mathbf{u}^\top \mathbf{v} + r)^d, \ \gamma > 0,$$
$$\text{Radial:} \quad exp(-\gamma \|\mathbf{u} - \mathbf{v}\|^2), \ \gamma > 0,$$
$$\text{Sigmoid:} \quad tanh(\gamma \mathbf{u}^\top \mathbf{v} + r).$$

Conversely, *Support Vector Machine* (SVM) attempts to find a hyperplane separating a set of data points and is used for binary classification. In this case the inequalities in Equation 1 are reversed and thus data points are penalized for being too close to the separating hyperplane via the ξ and ξ^* parameters appearing the cost function. The CRAN `e1071` [16] R [17] package was used for all SVR and SVM computations.

PKEM. A second non-parametric prediction method was developed called **P**rediction through **K**ernel density **E**stimation of **M**etagenomic data, or PKEM for short. It combines a dimensionality reduction step with multivariate kernel density estimation. The dimensionality reduction step is often required since kernel density estimation can lead to improper fitting of the data when sample sizes are small relative to the dimension of the data. Classical principal component analysis is used for the dimensionality reduction step.

Principal Component Analysis (PCA) [18,19] is a well-established method which uses orthogonal transformations such that the first principal component contains the largest variance, the second principal component contains the second largest variance, and so on. PCA is often used on high-dimensional data to transform and truncate the data to a lower dimensional space, while attempting to preserve as much variance as contained in the original data. That is, PCA reformulates the data according to the principal components, ranking from most important to least important. By truncating the least important principal components, one retains the most important parts of the original data while reducing its dimension.

PCA can be accomplished using a singular value decomposition. Any real $m \times n$ matrix M can be written $M = U\Sigma V^\top$. Here, U is an $m \times m$ *unitary* $(U^\top U = UU^\top = I)$ matrix, Σ is an $m \times n$ rectangular diagonal matrix containing the singular values from largest (upper left) to smallest (lower right), and $V^\top$ is the transpose of an $n \times n$ unitary matrix. The PCA transformation is given by $U\Sigma$, and the pth PCA truncation is given by $U_p \Sigma_p$ where U_p and Σ_p are the first p rows of U and Σ respectively.

Kernel density estimation (KDE) [20,21] is a non-parametric approach to estimate the probability distribution of a random variable. That is, if one has a sample of a random variable, kernel density estimation can be used to find an approximation of the unknown distribution underlying the random variable. Conceptually, kernel density estimation is similar to a histogram of the sample data, but with a smoothing out operation.

In the univariate case, if $(x_1, \ldots, x_n)$ are sampled identically and independently from a distribution with some unknown density function f, the goal of kernel density estimation is to estimate f via some function $\hat{f}_h$. It does this by giving a little bit of weight to each sample and is formulated as

$$\hat{f}_h(x) := \frac{1}{nh} \sum_{i=1}^{n} K(x - x_i).$$

The function $K(\cdot)$ is the *kernel* and it is assumed to be symmetric and integrates to 1. The parameter h is called the *bandwidth* and is chosen as small as the data will allow. Typically a Gaussian kernel is used for $K(\cdot)$. One way to visualize kernel density estimation is to imagine that for each data point on the real line, a handful of dirt is dropped (which makes a nice Gaussian dirt hill). Thus, if a group of data points are close on the real line, then a large mound of dirt accumulates around the group of data points since one dropped many handfuls of dirt around there. See Figure 1 for an example.

Multivariate kernel density [22] estimation is nearly identical to the above univariate case, except the kernel is almost always a multivariate Gaussian and

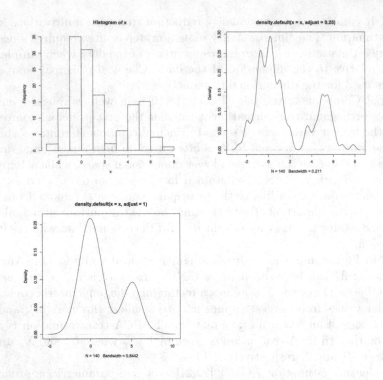

Fig. 1. Histogram of 140 data points (top left) sampled from some unknown distribution. Kernel density estimation using 0.25 of normal bandwidth (top right). Kernel density estimation using normal bandwidth (bottom).

the bandwidth parameter h is replaced by a bandwidth matrix H which is symmetric and positive definite. The bandwidth matrix H determines the shape of the multivariate Gaussian kernel $K(\cdot)$.

The PKEM algorithm can be summarized:

1. Let $\mathbf{X}$ be a matrix where the rows are the OTU fractions and the columns are the N hosts being studied.
2. Let $\mathbf{Y}$ be the $\{0, 1\}$ host traits.
3. Let p be the user-input truncation dimension.
4. Perform PCA on the subsets of columns of X with host trait Y equal to 0 (or 1). Use obtained PCA transformation on all data X, call transformed data B.
5. Train a multivariate kernel density estimation function F using columns of B with host trait Y equal to 0 (or 1).
6. Output kernel density estimation function F which takes as input any OTU table data and outputs an estimate of its density estimation of the associated host trait to be 0 (or 1).

The PKEM algorithm can be trained on either the OTU data taken from hosts with traits valued 0 or valued 1, which may lead to different results depending on the data. The `prcomp` function in the `stats` base package of R [17] was used to compute PCA and the `np` [23] R package was used to perform multivariate kernel density estimation. Additionally, the function F output by KDE is normalized by the largest estimated value, yielding values in $[0, 1]$.

2.1 Topological Data Analysis

Topology is the mathematical study of spaces and their qualities, such as properties of spaces that are preserved under continuous deformations. Topological Data Analysis (TDA) is the application of the mathematically rigorous field of algebraic topology towards understanding large and high-dimensional data. Recently there has been a rapid growth in interest in TDA and its many applications [24,25,26,27,28].

One exciting application of TDA is forming reliable low-dimensional representations of high-dimensional data, with the ambition that the low-dimensional representation maintains important relationships and can be easier to interpret, leading to new insights on the otherwise opaque high-dimensional data. One recently introduced popular approach called `mapper` [29] has been successfully applied in many additional studies [28,26]. The fundamental concept of `mapper` is that the output is a combinatorial graph, as opposed to a set of data points or some subspace. Additionally, TDA is more robust to noise, can handle large data sets, and can handle any notion of distance. That is, one does not need to use Euclidean distance of data and may choose a more appropriate measure of distance. Lastly, `mapper` requires a *filter function* on the high-dimensional data, which is some real-valued function. That is, the filter function f assigns some real value for each high-dimensional data point.

The `mapper` approach works roughly as follows: The filter function is applied to the input high-dimensional data $\mathbf{X}$ and the filter values are saved. Then the range of filter values are divided up into k overlapping intervals. For each interval of filter values, the subset of data from $\mathbf{X}$ corresponding to the current filter interval is clustered. This clustering is performed for each filter interval. Once all the clusters have been formed, a graph is drawn with a node for each cluster. Since the filter intervals were overlapping, two clusters may share a data point from $\mathbf{X}$ in common. Thus, if two nodes (clusters) share at least one data point then an edge is drawn between the nodes. This completes the original `mapper` algorithm, but additional visualization can be performed such as coloring each node based on the average filter values as well as plotting any additional meta data about the data points in each node. For an example of `mapper` see Figure 2.

It must be emphasized that the output of `mapper` is highly dependent on the filter function chosen, the amount of overlap in the filter intervals, and the distance used for clustering as well as the clustering method. However, the output low-dimensional representation will often reflect the properties of the original high-dimensional data.

For this study, the PKEM and SVR algorithms were used to compute filter values. If the host trait was disease (0 healthy, 1 disease), than each algorithm estimates a host's disease status from 0 to 1 depending on its associated microbiome

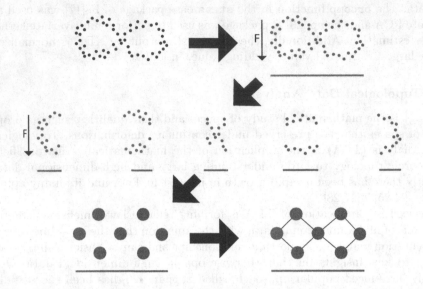

Fig. 2. Example of mapper algorithm. First a filter function F is applied to the data. In this case, data are given a high value if they are to the left (red) and a low value if they are to the right (green). Second, the range of filter values are formed into overlapping intervals, creating corresponding collections of the original data. Third, each collection of data is independently clustered. Lastly, an edge is drawn between two clusters if they have at least one element of the data in common.

OTU data. The distance between OTU tables was either the weighted UniFrac distance if available, or the Euclidean distance. Clustering was performed using hierarchical clustering and the Ward method. Further, the number of clusters was determined in an unsupervised way by choosing the number of clusters which maximized the mean silhouette score [30].

2.2   Data

Cat and Dog Data. All samples were from dogs and cats that lived in home environments and were collected by veterinarians who evaluated the animals for their GI disease. Healthy animals were owned by students and staff at Texas A&M University. All samples were stored frozen at -80°C until processing of samples for DNA extraction. A 100mg (wet weight) aliquot of feces was extracted by a bead-beating method using a commercial DNA extraction kit (ZR Fecal DNA Kit™, Zymo Research Corporation) following the manufacturer's instructions. The bead beating step was performed on a homogenizer (FastPrep-24, MP Biomedicals) for 60 s at a speed of 4 m/s. The collection and analysis of fecal samples was approved by the institutional Clinical Research Review Committee of the college of Veterinary Medicine, Texas A&M University.

Cat Data. Fecal samples were obtained from healthy cats ($n = 23$) and cats with diarrhea ($n = 76$). Diseased cats were further compared based on the duration of their diarrhea: duration < 21 days ($n = 32$) vs. duration > 21 days ($n = 44$). None of the animals received antibiotics within 3 months of sample collection. Sequencing was performed targeting the V4 region of the 16S rRNA gene using forward and reverse primers: 515F (5'-GTGCCAGCMGCCGCGGTAA-3') and 806R (5'- GGACTACVSGGGTATCTAAT-3') using the Ion Torrent platform at a depth of 15,000 sequencing reads per sample. Operational taxonomic units (OTUs) were assigned based on at least 97% sequence similarity using QIIME v1.7. The sequences were deposited in SRA under accession number SRP047088. A similar data collection and analysis process is described also elsewhere [31].

Dog Data. Fecal samples were collected from healthy dogs ($n = 98$), dogs with chronic enteropathy (IBD, $n = 79$), and dogs with acute hemorrhagic diarrhea ($n = 15$). All dogs with CE were evaluated by endoscopic examination and intestinal inflammation was confirmed by histopathology. Dogs with acute diarrhea were worked up for the GI disease and were all diagnosed with uncomplicated diarrhea that resolved with routine symptomatic treatment within one week of presentation. None of the animals received antibiotics within 3 months of sample collection. Sequencing was performed targeting the V4 region of the 16S rRNA gene using forward and reverse primers: 515F (5'-GTGCCAGCMGCCGCGGTAA-3') and 806R (5'- GGACTACVSGGGTATCTAAT-3') using the Illumina platform at a depth of 5,000 sequencing reads per sample. Operational taxonomic units (OTUs) were assigned based on at least 97% sequence similarity using QIIME v1.7. A similar data collection and analysis process is described also elsewhere [32].

Kwashiorkor Data. Publicly available data was taken from a study of gut microbiomes of Malawian twins suffering from Kwashiorkor, a form of sever acute malnutrition [33] [1]. In the study, 317 Malawian twin pairs were followed for three years during which 43% became discordant (Kwashiorkor). In such discordant cases, both twins were fed ready-to-use therapeutic food (RUTF). The authors of the above study observed that the consumption of RUTF by discordant individuals eventually led to an improved health of the individuals' microbiome, and if RUTF was stopped prematurely the microbiomes regressed to their discordant state. Additionally, when the authors transplanted discordant microbiomes into gnotobiotic mice and provided a Malawian diet, the kwashiorkor microbiome lead to drastic weight loss as well as changes in their metabolism.

   Phylum, class, order, family, and genus level 16S OTU data was taken from the original study for all individuals. Additional data was included here, specifically *weight-for-height* z (WHZ) score, RUTF consumption, and age. Multiple microbiome samples were available for each individual, each labeled with the state *healthy* or *kwashiorkor*. All *kwashiorkor* samples were included in the anal-

---

[1] Data retrieved from Jeffrey Gordon website:
   http://gordonlab.wustl.edu/SuppData.html

ysis presented here, however, if an individual had multiple *healthy* microbiome samples, only the sample with the highest WHZ score was included.

3 Results

3.1 Prediction Accuracy

The ability of SVR, SVM, and PKEM to accurately predict the host's trait was tested by tenfold cross validation. That is, OTU and host trait data were split into ten evenly sized sets. Then SVR, SVM, and PKEM were trained on 90% of the available data and each method was used to predict the remaining 10% of the data. Both SVR and PKEM can be coerced to output a $[0, 1]$ continuous estimate of the host's binary trait. Thus a threshold is used to determine if the predicted host trait is 0 or 1. Figure 3 show the false positives vs. true positives as the threshold for the $\{0, 1\}$ classification varies. The parametric SVR outperforms the non-parametric PKEM. However, PKEM does remain viable as a classifier, as long as the threshold is low (approximately 0.2–0.3). Note, the linear, polynomial, and sigmoid SVR kernels were also studied but did not perform as well as the radial kernel.

Thresholds were set to 0.25 for PKEM and 0.50 for SVR and the F-score and accuracy of SVR, SVM, and PKEM were computed, see Table 1. Accuracy is reported in term of the *F-score* (F1) and the *accuracy* (ACC). Let TP=True Positives, TN=True Negatives, FP=False Positive, FN=False Negatives, P=Positive instances, and N=Negative instances, then $F1 := 2TP/(2TP + FP + FN)$ and $ACC := (TP + TN)/(P + N)$. Notice that the F1 score is primarily influenced by the TP.

In the Dog data, PKEM (truncation dimension 6) is comparable to SVR (linear) and SVM (linear) in terms of best accuracy 0.60. However, PKEM suffers from fewer TP, and thus has a lower F1 score. SVM slightly outperforms SVR in terms of F1, but not by a large margin, likely due to a poor choice of threshold for SVR (0.50).

In the Cat data, SVR (radial) and SVM (radial) have highest accuracy (0.81), while PKEM (truncation dimension 6) is slightly behind (0.78). Again, PKEM under performs in the F1 score due to low TP, although it has better F1 score than SVR (linear, polynomial) and SVM (polynomial, radial). In this case, SVM seems to suffer from very low TP and thus low F1 scores.

In the Kwashiorkor data, SVM (radial, sigmoid) ties for highest accuracy (0.64) and SVM (radial) has the highest F1 (0.76). The Kwashiorkor data set presents the largest difference in F1 and accuracy between SVM versus SVR and PKEM. It is good to note that, in this case, SVR and PKEM perform similarly.

Across all data, SVM attains the highest accuracy, or is at least as good as SVR and PKEM. Although, SVM performs poorly in terms of F1 score on the cat data. It is clear that all methods are able to use OTU microbiome data alone in order to predict the host's trait value. Additionally, the linear and radial kernel often perform best. For this reason, the radial kernel was chosen for use in the TDA visualization. PKEM performs well in terms of accuracy, although it does

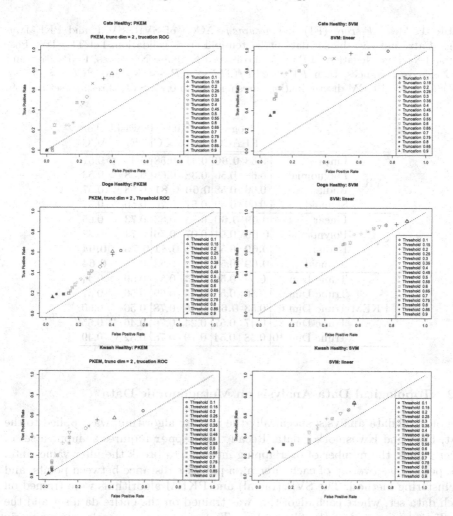

Fig. 3. Receiver of Operator Curves (ROC). The threshold to decide the $\{0, 1\}$ host trait was varied and the false positive vs. true positive rates were recorded. An ideal classifier would have ROC points in the upper left. The diagonal reflects a random classifier.

fall behind in terms of F1 score due to low TP. However, PKEM does not suffer from a choice of a kernel, since it is non-parametric.

Although SVM has high accuracy, the fact that it gives a binary $\{0, 1\}$ classification does not allow its use in the Topological Data Analysis described herein, whereas SVR and PKEM both give an estimate of the host trait value in the range of $[0, 1]$.

Table 1. Mean *F-score* (F1) and *accuracy* (ACC) of SVR, SVM, and PKEM on Dogs, Cats, and Kwashiokor data under ten-fold cross validation. Let TP=True Positives, TN=True Negatives, FP=False Positive, FN=False Negatives, P=Positive and N=Negative instances, then $F1 := 2TP/(2TP + FP + FN)$ and $ACC := (TP + TN)/(P + N)$. PKEM discrimination threshold set to 0.25. SVR threshold set to 0.50.

		Dog		Cat		Kwashiorkor	
		F1	ACC	F1	ACC	F1	ACC
SVR	Linear	0.68	**0.60**	0.41	0.58	0.49	0.51
	Polynomial	0.68	0.56	0.38	0.68	0.58	0.53
	Radial	0.66	0.58	**0.66**	**0.81**	0.58	0.57
	Sigmoid	0.66	0.59	0.57	0.76	0.60	0.57
SVM	Linear	**0.69**	**0.60**	0.58	0.83	0.73	0.65
	Polynomial	**0.69**	0.54	0.07	0.76	0.74	0.62
	Radial	**0.69**	0.54	0.33	**0.81**	**0.76**	**0.64**
	Sigmoid	**0.69**	0.54	0.49	0.83	0.74	**0.64**
PKEM	Trunc Dim 2	0.59	0.56	0.43	0.52	0.50	0.44
	Trunc Dim 4	0.56	0.58	0.45	0.69	0.56	0.57
	Trunc Dim 6	0.53	**0.60**	0.46	0.78	0.56	0.60
	Trunc Dim 8	0.47	0.57	0.24	0.76	0.46	0.55
	Trunc Dim 10	0.38	0.54	0.10	0.78	0.32	0.49

3.2   Topological Data Analysis on Metagenomic Data

Topological data analysis, specifically the `mapper` algorithm, was applied to the Cat, Dog, and Kwashiorkor data. Recall that `mapper` requires as input a set of filter values, the number of overlapping intervals to break the filter values into, the percentage overlap of each interval, a pairwise distance between points, and a clustering method. The SVR (radial) and PKEM algorithms were trained on each data set, where each algorithm was trained on the entire data set and the prediction was used as the filter values. The number of intervals was set to six with an overlap of 90%.

For clustering, the hierarchical method was used with Ward criteria for joining two clusters, which merges two clusters that minimize the resulting within-cluster variance. Here an unsupervised approach was taken by cutting the hierarchical clustering dendogram at 1.0, which in effect does hierarchical clustering using the Ward criteria and merges clusters as long as the within-cluster variance does not exceed 1.0. In the case of the Cat and Dog data the weighted UniFrac distance was used as input to the `mapper` algorithm in order to perform the cluster analysis. Whereas in the Kwashiorkor data the Euclidean distance between OTU samples was used as the distance measure.

Figure 4 shows the output of `mapper` applied to the Cat, Dog, and Kwashiorkor data. Additionally recall that `mapper` connects two nodes (two clusters) if they share an individual in common. In Figure 4 the number of overlapping individuals is given on the edge in orange. Lastly, summaries of metadata for each dataset

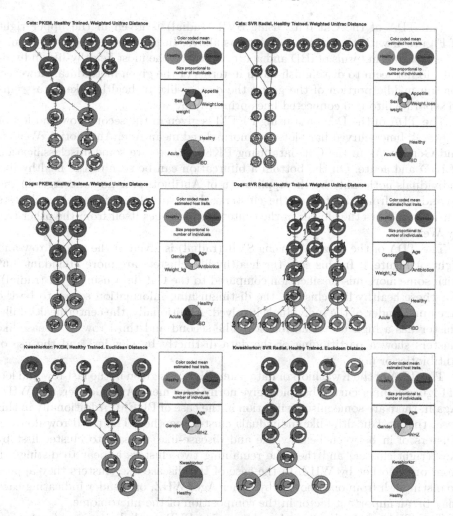

Fig. 4. Output of mapper applied to the Cat, Dog, and Kwashiorkor data. Left, the PKEM algorithm is used to compute the filter values where on the right the SVR algorithm with a radial kernel is used. Both used the weighted UniFrac distance.

and each cluster are also presented in Figure 4 and the details of each figure are discussed below.

The TDA of the Cat data using PKEM is given in the upper left of Figure 4. Inner curved bar plots give normalized mean Age, Appetite, Sex, Weight, and Weight Loss. In the bottom a bifurcation of the healthy-like cats appears where on the left the individuals appear to have higher weight and higher weight loss. The healthy-like individuals on the right contain some mis-classified individuals with IBD. The middle portion of clusters that are between healthy and disease also shows a splitting of the data, where sex and appetite may play a role.

The TDA of the Cat data using SVR (radial) is given in the upper right of Figure 4, with the same meta-data as above. In this case there are few misclassifications in terms of IBD and acute. However, the most healthy-like individuals do not seem to distinguish much in terms of the given meta data. However, for the middle portion of the graph the disease-like to healthy-like data seems to separate into two connected lines primarily by sex.

The TDA of the Dog data using PKEM is given in the second row and left of Figure 4. Inner curved bar plots give normalized mean Age, Antibiotics, Weight, and Gender. As in the Cat data using PKEM, there are some misclassification of IBD and acute. On the bottom a bifurcation can be seen of the healthy-like individuals noticeably by the application of Antibiotics or not and Age. In the second row from the top of the clusters, there are three disease-like clusters where it appears the cluster in the center distinguishes itself from the other two by Weight.

The TDA of the Dog data using SVR (radial) is given in the second row and right of Figure 4. In this case the healthy-like clusters are more abundant, but with some more misclassification compared to the Cat data using SVR (radial). For these healthy-like clusters, the distinguishing information seems to be the Age and Gender of the individuals involved. Additionally, the center healthy-like cluster has a high use of antibiotics. The second and third row of disease-like clusters show a partitioning of the data distinctly by Gender, and the use of Antibiotics or not.

The TDA of the Kwashiorkor data using PKEM is given in the last row and left of Figure 4. Inner curved bar plots give normalized mean Age, Gender, and WHZ. Again, there are some misclassification in the case of PKEM. Additionally in this case, the most healthy-like individuals cluster together. The third row down of clusters of in between healthy-like and disease-like appears to cluster first by Age (right cluster) and then the remaining two clusters appear to distinguish from one another by WHZ. In the case of the disease-like clusters they appear to distinguish from one another by either Age, WHZ, or Gender indicating each may be an important factor in the composition of the microbiome.

The TDA of the Kwashiorkor data using SVR (radial) is given in the last row and right of Figure 4. In this case, the healthy-like individuals are quite separated into multiple clusters where Gender and Age may play the biggest role. In the middle section of clusters in between healthy-like and disease-like there is a bifurcation of individuals primarily by Age and a Gender. In the case of the most disease-like surprisingly Gender, and to a lesser degree WHZ, appears to be a large factor in distinguishing microbiomes

4   Discussion

Research into microbiomes and metagenomics will only continue to grow, as well as the size and complexity of the available data. Additionally, the connection between host traits and the microbiome is only beginning to be elucidated and needs further study. We demonstrated here that, in fact, statistical models can be trained on OTU metagenomic data and applied to accurately predict host traits.

Gastrointestinal disease is most likely a combination of various environmental factors and therefore it is not possible to define a clear cut host trait. Thus while feces would have lower sensitivity for separation, intestinal biopsies may have a much higher rate. This is also corroborated in Crohn's disease [34] where the authors observed a lower sensitivity when classifying disease status using fecal samples (See Figure 4) as compared to using tissue samples.

Finally there is a need to visualize and understand the ever-growing complex metagenomic data. Combining traditional prediction algorithms or novel non-parametric prediction methods such as PKEM with powerful topological data analysis can lead to improved insights into the data. For example, visualizing the data along with annotations such as antibiotic usage, age, and weight can assist in understanding the separation between healthy and afflicted individuals.

References

1. Zolla, G., Badri, D.V., Bakker, M.G., Manter, D.K., Vivanco, J.M.: Soil microbiomes vary in their ability to confer drought tolerance to Arabidopsis. Applied Soil Ecology 68, 1–9 (2013)
2. Badri, D.V., Quintana, N., El Kassis, E.G., Kim, H.K., Choi, Y.H., Sugiyama, A., Verpoorte, R., Martinoia, E., Manter, D.K., Vivanco, J.M.: An ABC transporter mutation alters root exudation of phytochemicals that provoke an overhaul of natural soil microbiota. Plant Physiology 151(4), 2006–2017 (2009)
3. Devaraj, S., Hemarajata, P., Versalovic, J.: The human gut microbiome and body metabolism: implications for obesity and diabetes. Clinical Chemistry 59(4), 617–628 (2013)
4. Koren, O., Knights, D., Gonzalez, A., Waldron, L., Segata, N., Knight, R., Huttenhower, C., Ley, R.E.: A guide to enterotypes across the human body: Meta-analysis of microbial community structures in human microbiome datasets. PLoS Computational Biology 9(1), e1002863 (2013)
5. Statnikov, A., Alekseyenko, A.V., Li, Z., Henaff, M., Perez-Perez, G.I., Blaser, M.J., Aliferis, C.F.: Microbiomic signatures of psoriasis: Feasibility and methodology comparison. Scientific Reports (3) (2013)
6. Statnikov, A., Henaff, M., Narendra, V., Konganti, K., Li, Z., Yang, L., Pei, Z., Blaser, M., Aliferis, C., Alekseyenko, A.: A comprehensive evaluation of multicategory classification methods for microbiomic data. Microbiome 1(1) (2013)
7. Lozupone, C., Knight, R.: UniFrac: a new phylogenetic method for comparing microbial communities. Applied and Environmental Microbiology 71(12), 8228–8235 (2005)
8. Caporaso, J.G., Kuczynski, J., Stombaugh, J., Bittinger, K., Bushman, F.D., Costello, E.K., Fierer, N., Peña, A.G., Goodrich, J.K., Gordon, J.I., et al.: QIIME allows analysis of high-throughput community sequencing data. Nature Methods 7(5), 335–336 (2010)
9. Boser, B.E., Guyon, I.M., Vapnik, V.N.: A training algorithm for optimal margin classifiers. In: Proceedings of the 5th Annual ACM Workshop on Computational Learning Theory, pp. 144–152 (1992)

10. Guyon, I., Boser, B., Vapnik, V.: Automatic capacity tuning of very large VC-dimension classifiers. Advances in Neural Information Processing Systems, 147–155 (1993)
11. Cortes, C., Vapnik, V.: Support-vector networks. In: Machine Learning, pp. 273–297 (1995)
12. Schölkopf, B.: Support vector learning (1997), http://www.kernel-machines.org
13. Vapnik, V., Golowich, S.E., Smola, A.: Support vector method for function approximation, regression estimation, and signal processing. Advances in Neural Information Processing Systems 9, 281–287 (1996)
14. Smola, A.J., Schölkopf, B.: A tutorial on support vector regression. Statistics and Computing 14(3), 199–222 (2004)
15. Chang, C.C., Lin, C.J.: LIBSVM: A library for support vector machines. ACM Transactions on Intelligent Systems and Technology 2, 27:1–27:27 (2011), Software available at http://www.csie.ntu.edu.tw/~cjlin/libsvm
16. Dimitriadou, E., Hornik, K., Leisch, F., Meyer, D., Weingessel, A.: e1071: Misc Functions of the Department of Statistics (e1071), TU Wien (2011) R package version 1.6
17. R Core Team: R: A Language and Environment for Statistical Computing. R Foundation for Statistical Computing, Vienna, Austria (2014)
18. Hotelling, H.: Analysis of a complex of statistical variables into principal components. Journal of Educational Psychology 24(6), 417 (1933)
19. Pearson, K.: LIII. on lines and planes of closest fit to systems of points in space. The London, Edinburgh, and Dublin Philosophical Magazine and Journal of Science 2(11), 559–572 (1901)
20. Parzen, E.: On estimation of a probability density function and mode. The Annals of Mathematical Statistics, 1065–1076 (1962)
21. Rosenblatt, M.: Remarks on some nonparametric estimates of a density function. The Annals of Mathematical Statistics 27(3), 832–837 (1956)
22. Simonoff, J.S.: Smoothing methods in statistics. Springer, London (1996)
23. Hayfield, T., Racine, J.S.: Nonparametric econometrics: The np package. Journal of Statistical Software 27(5) (2008)
24. Zomorodian, A., Carlsson, G.: Computing persistent homology. Discrete & Computational Geometry 33(2), 249–274 (2005)
25. Carlsson, G.: Topology and data. Bulletin of the American Mathematical Society 46(2), 255–308 (2009)
26. Nicolau, M., Levine, A.J., Carlsson, G.: Topology based data analysis identifies a subgroup of breast cancers with a unique mutational profile and excellent survival. Proceedings of the National Academy of Sciences 108(17), 7265–7270 (2011)
27. Chan, J.M., Carlsson, G., Rabadan, R.: Topology of viral evolution. Proceedings of the National Academy of Sciences 110(46), 18566–18571 (2013)
28. Bartlett, C.W., Cheong, S.Y., Hou, L., Paquette, J., Lum, P.Y., Jäger, G., Battke, F., Vehlow, C., Heinrich, J., Nieselt, K., et al.: An eQTL biological data visualization challenge and approaches from the visualization community. BMC Bioinformatics 13(suppl. 8), S8 (2012)
29. Singh, G., Mémoli, F., Carlsson, G.E.: Topological methods for the analysis of high dimensional data sets and 3D object recognition. In: SPBG, pp. 91–100 (2007)
30. Rousseeuw, P.J.: Silhouettes: a graphical aid to the interpretation and validation of cluster analysis. Journal of Computational and Applied Mathematics 20, 53–65 (1987)

31. Bell, E.T., Suchodolski, J.S., Isaiah, A., Fleeman, L.M., Cook, A.K., Steiner, J.M., Mansfield, C.S.: Faecal microbiota of cats with insulin-treated diabetes mellitus. PLoS ONE 9(10) (2014)
32. Suchodolski, J.S., Markel, M.E., Garcia-Mazcorro, J.F., Unterer, S., Heilmann, R.M., Dowd, S.E., Kachroo, P., Ivanov, I., Minamoto, Y., Dillman, E.M., Steiner, J.M., Cook, A.K., Toresson, L.: The fecal microbiome in dogs with acute diarrhea and idiopathic inflammatory bowel disease. PLoS ONE 7(12) (2012)
33. Smith, M.I., Yatsunenko, T., Manary, M.J., Trehan, I., Mkakosya, R., Cheng, J., Kau, A.L., Rich, S.S., Concannon, P., Mychaleckyj, J.C., Liu, J., Houpt, E., Li, J.V., Holmes, E., Nicholson, J., Knights, D., Ursell, L.K., Knight, R., Gordon, J.I.: Gut microbiomes of Malawian twin pairs discordant for kwashiorkor. Science 339(6119), 548–554 (2013)
34. Gevers, D., Kugathasan, S., Denson, L.A., Vázquez-Baeza, Y., Van Treuren, W., Ren, B., Schwager, E., Knights, D., Song, S.J., Yassour, M., et al.: The treatment-naive microbiome in new-onset Crohns disease. Cell Host & Microbe 15(3), 382–392 (2014)

Gappy Total Recaller:
Efficient Algorithms and Data Structures
for Accurate Transcriptomics

B. Mishra

Courant Institute, NYU, New York
mishra@nyu.edu
http://cs.nyu.edu/mishra/

Abstract. Understanding complex mammalian biology depends crucially on our ability to define a precise map of all the transcripts encoded in a genome, and to measure their relative abundances. A promising assay depends on RNASeq approaches, which builds on next generation sequencing pipelines capable of interrogating cDNAs extracted from a cell. The underlying pipeline starts with base-calling, collect the sequence reads and interpret the raw-read in terms of transcripts that are grouped with respect to different splice-variant isoforms of a messenger RNA. We address a very basic problem involved in all of these pipelines, namely accurate Bayesian base-calling, which could combine the analog intensity data with suitable underlying priors on base-composition in the transcripts. In the context of sequencing genomic DNA, a powerful approach for base-calling has been developed in the TotalReCaller pipeline. For these purposes, it uses a suitable reference whole-genome sequence in a compressed self-indexed format to derive its priors. However, TotalReCaller faces many new challenges in the transcriptomic domain, especially since we still lack a fully annotated library of all possible transcripts, and hence a sufficiently good prior. There are many possible solutions, similar to the ones developed for TotalReCaller, in applications addressing de novo sequencing and assembly, where partial contigs or string-graphs could be used to boot-strap the Bayesian priors on base-composition. A similar approach would be applicable here too, partial assembly of transcripts can be used to characterize the splicing junctions or organize them in incompatibility graphs and then provided as priors for TotalReCaller. The key algorithmic techniques for this purpose have been addressed in a forthcoming paper on Stringomics. Here, we address a related but fundamental problem, by assuming that we only have a reference genome, with certain intervals marked as candidate regions for ORF (Open Reading Frames), but not necessarily complete annotations regarding the 5' or 3' termini of a gene or its exon-intron structure. The algorithms we describe find the most accurate base-calls of a cDNA with the best possible segmentation, all mapped to the genome appropriately.

1 Introduction and Motivations

To obtain key insights into biological problems – especially, those with important biomedical implications – one may need to observe how a population of cells of

R. Natarajan et al. (Eds.): ICDCIT 2015, LNCS 8956, pp. 150–161, 2015.
© Springer International Publishing Switzerland 2015

heterogeneous types behave over time. By identifying and quantifying the full set of transcripts in a small number of cells at different time-points and under different conditions, and further aided by sophisticated systems-biology inference tools, the scientists have attempted to fill in the gaps in our understanding of complex biological processes — for instance, those involved in disease progression. In a recent article, entitled: *"Broad Applications of Single-cell Nucleic Acid Analysis in Biomedical Research,"* by Michael Wigler [Wigler, 2012] the author discusses the hurdles posed by both the heterogeneity and temporality in cancer as detected by single cell genomic assays that could be easily carried over different stages of cancer progression. A complex picture has emerged from these studies: Namely, that a tumor is a highly heterogeneous mixture of many different cell-types [1] and that each cell assumes different cell-states in response to the micro-environment, signaling, metabolic needs with different strategies in different cell-types. Thus an important problem faced by the cancer biotechnologists is that of collecting and interpreting massive amount of transcriptomic data just from a single patient assuming that "in the near future assessing both DNA and RNA content simultaneously from hundreds to thousands of single cells will be quantitatively accurate, as complete as needed, and affordable."

1.1 Challenges of RNA-Seq

In attempting to achieve these goals, one still faces enormous computational and statistical challenges:

Sequence-Based Transcriptomic Data is Complex. (a) Genes can be expressed with wildly varying copy numbers that change rapidly, (b) the same gene can have multiple splice variants whose structures remain unannotated and are expressed in unknown and varying proportions, and (c) many genes belong to gene-families sharing high-degree of homology. See [Gingeras, 2009], [Batut *et al.*, 2013], [Tilgner *et al.*, 2012], [Dunham *et al.*, 2012], [Djebali *et al.*, 2012].

Short Read Sequencing Technologies Have Limitations. Base-calling errors tend to be rather high for next generation sequencing platforms (more than 1% error in the initial 100bp read, with the error rate rising further with the read-length), which further confounds the analysis of already complex transcriptomic data.

Single-Cell RNA-Seq Presents Additional Hurdles. Firstly, the data quality is lowered by the need for enzymatic pre-amplification. This process significantly truncates the 5' region of the transcript, resulting in an unavoidable loss of sequence information. Secondly, due to the small amount mRNA present in a single cell at any one time, the number of obtainable reads per cell is much smaller than that obtainable from bulk samples (typically < 40 million vs. 150 million+), making rare transcripts harder to detect. See [Bartfai *et al.*, 2012], [Tariq *et al.*, 2011], [Levsky *et al.*, 2002].

---

[1] Certain cell-types such as Cancer Stem Cells, Circulating Tumor Cell, Tumor Initiating Cells, appear to be rare, though they assume disproportionately dominant roles in the fate of the tumor.

Existing sequence analysis technologies fail to adequately address these problems [Dobin *et al.*, 2013], [Grant *et al.*, 2011], [Wu and Nacu, 2010], [Wang *et al.*, 2010], [Trapnell *et al.*, 2009], significantly limiting the effectiveness of single cell RNA-Seq. A superior base-calling approach, such as the one proposed here, could alleviate the situation considerably, for example, by correctly re-calling 'poor quality' bases will effectively 'salvage' extra reads that would have been discarded due to low quality. This approach significantly increases the number of reads per run in cases where the sample is of limited quantity (single cells) or is degraded (preserved tissue).

1.2   TotalRecaller: Base-Calling Innovation

TotalReCaller (TRC, [Menges *et al.*, 2011]) is a rapid base-calling and resequencing platform for NGS (next-generation sequencing), originally created to be versatile in handling various genomics applications. Currently, alternative re-sequencing approaches use multiple modules in a serial pipeline (i.e., without feedback) to interpret raw sequencing data from next-generation sequencing platforms, while remaining oblivious to the genomic information until the final alignment step [Dobin *et al.*, 2013], [Grant *et al.*, 2011], [Wu and Nacu, 2010], [Wang *et al.*, 2010], [Trapnell *et al.*, 2009], [Menges *et al.*, 2011], [Bona *et al.*, 2008]. Such approaches fail to exploit the full information from both raw sequencing data and the reference genome that can yield better quality sequence reads, SNP-calls, variant detection, as well as an alignment at the best possible location in the reference genome. TRC addressed this unmet need for novel reference-guided bioinformatics algorithms for interpreting raw analog signals representing sequences of the bases (A, C, G, T), while simultaneously aligning possible sequence reads to a source reference genome.

The resulting base-calling algorithm, TotalReCaller (TRC), achieves demonstrably improved performance in all genomic domains, wherever it has been tested. A linear error model for the raw intensity data, coupled with Burrows-Wheeler transform (BWT) and FM-index based alignment create a Bayesian score function, which is then globally optimized over all possible genomic locations using an efficient branch-and-bound approach. The algorithm has been implemented in soft- and hardware [field-programmable gate array (FPGA)] to achieve real-time performance. Empirical results on real high-throughput Illumina data were used to evaluate TotalReCaller's performance relative to its peers Bustard, BayesCall, Ibis and Rolexa based on several criteria, particularly those important in clinical and scientific applications [Menges *et al.*, 2011]. Namely, it has been evaluated for (*i*) its base-calling speed and throughput, (*ii*) its read accuracy, (*iii*) its specificity and sensitivity in variant calling and (*iv*) its effect on FRC (Feature-Response Curve) analysis, as used in genome assembly (see [Mishra, 2012]).

If our genomic and transcriptomic knowledge was complete and correct (i.e., we have *high quality* references genomes along with its *complete* annotations) then the existing TotalReCaller can derive and use a Bayesian prior efficiently to achieve similar order of high accuracy also in RNASeq applications as in its genomic version [Menges *et al.*, 2011]. However, more than 50% of the RNA sequences are estimated to be unannotated [Tilgner *et al.*, 2012], [Djebali *et al.*, 2012], and complicating the matter, not only are many genes expressed in multiple splice-variant isoforms (whose structures are unknown), but also in cancer, pseudo-genes are often transcribed. These structural variations need to be learned and encoded in the prior used by RNASeqTRC (while allowing for self-index to carry out rapid searches). Two important modifications – one in alignment and the other in data-structures – play a key role in achieving this goal and are described in this paper: namely, (a) branch-and-bound for "gappy" alignment (to reference genome) and (b) a compressed "stringomics" data structure that generalizes BWT to a family of strings (e.g., isoforms). The specific innovative attributes of RNASeqTRC that make it ideal for single cell transcriptomic profiling are summarized:

High Accuracy. RNASeqTRC's empirical Bayesian approach can yield high
specificity and sensitivity.

Robustness Against Incomplete Information. Encoding the priors by
"gappy" references and Stringomics data-structures allows RNASeqTRC to
deal with the uncertainty of unannotated genes with no significant loss of
performance (compressibility and fast queries).

High Speed. RNASeqTRC's simplicity of structure makes it amenable to hardware acceleration.

2   Approach

The proposed approach to transcriptomic assays follows the standard protocols, which have been categorized into the following classes: (1) *Align-then-assemble*, (2) *Assemble-then-align* and (3) *Hybrid Approach* [Martin and Wang, 2011]. Since TRC performs simultaneous base-calling and alignment, even when it is used in the *de novo* fashion, it possesses a significant amount of information about the alignments, although this information may vary from transcript-to-transcript. These variations may depend on whether the transcript has been annotated or not, and for unannotated transcript, whether it can be inferred from the reference by a 'gappy' alignment. In order to describe the full algorithm precisely and clearly, we have organized the rest of the section, in terms of various building blocks.

2.1   Base-Calling without a Reference

The simplest base calling process at the core of TRC involves certain standard pre-processing steps and may vary from technology to technology: for Illumina's HiSeq technology, we developed linear models addressing crosstalk, fading and cycle synchronous lagging [Menges *et al.*, 2011]. It mainly uses a dynamic transition matrix in order to filter the raw intensity channels. The model is derived from modeling crosstalk and fading and then extended to include lagging. Since the models are described in great details elsewhere [Menges *et al.*, 2011], we omit them here.

For simplicity, it is assumed that in each cycle, the sequencing proceeds with one new base at a time (e.g., no lagging in a cycle asynchronous manner). In other words, after the first cycle, there are four possible sequences of length one; after two cycles there are 16 possible sequences each of length two; and after k-cycles there are 4^k possible sequences each of length k and so on, which can be represented in a quaternary tree of depth k. Among these exponentially many possibilities, a small subset (ideally one unique string represented by a path in the tree) is desired to be identified as the ones very likely to be the correct (or closest-to-the-correct) base-sequence of the DNA. For this purpose, TRC solves a combinatorial optimization problem using Branch and Bound (B&B), which statistically estimates the correctness of a solution by an associated score.

The B&B algorithm [Lawler and Wood, 1966], [Land and Doig, 1960] is an iterative algorithm based on three consecutive steps. Each cycle performs an iterative process consisting of:

Branching: Explore the solution space by adding new leafs to the tree.

Bounding: Evaluate the solution space by weighing the leafs of the tree with respect to a suitably chosen *score function*.

Pruning: Constrain the solution space by pruning all but the best $b \leq$ const, $b \geq 1$ solutions: b is the beam-width of the underlying beam-search algorithm. When $b = 1$, note that this is just a *greedy algorithm*. Subpaths of the resulting tree can be augmented with the computed score function, as well as a p-value either using a known null-model for the score function or by empirical Bayes method, where null model itself is estimated from the data (e.g., ordering over the score functions of the best b solutions computed so far).

Note that an MLE (maximum likelihood estimator) score functions can be computed from the precomputed linear models quite easily using calibrating data (or all the solutions computed so far), without modeling exact chemistry or optimally estimating the parameters of the underlying technology. We recommend a data-driven score-function for this purposes, as it makes the resulting TRC algorithm *technology-agnostic*.

Following the pre-processing step, we may assume that we have a model for following conditional probabilities for the observations: namely, $P_k(X_B|B) =$ conditioned to the underlying base being $B \in \{A, T, C, G\}$, it is the probability of estimating the normalized intensity on B's channel to assume a value X_B in the kth cycle; $P_k(X_B|\neg B) =$ conditioned to the underlying base being $\neg B = \{A, T, C, G\} \setminus B$, it is the probability of estimating the normalized intensity on B's channel to assume a value X_B in the kth cycle. They may be approximated as Gaussian distributions with the parameters μ_B, σ_B, $\mu_{\neg B}$ and $\sigma_{\neg B}$:

$$X_B|B \sim \mathcal{N}(\mu_B, \sigma_B), \qquad X_B|\neg B \sim \mathcal{N}(\mu_{\neg B}, \sigma_{\neg B}).$$

Thus,

$$P_k(X_B|B) = \frac{1}{\sqrt{2\pi}\sigma_B} \exp\left(-\frac{(X_B - \mu_B)^2}{2\sigma_B^2}\right).$$

Similarly,

$$P_k(X_B|\neg B) = \frac{1}{\sqrt{2\pi}\sigma_{\neg B}} \exp\left(-\frac{(X_B - \mu_{\neg B})^2}{2\sigma_{\neg B}^2}\right).$$

Combining the previous results and computing the log likelihood, we get a score function as shown below:

$$f_{\text{score}}(X_B; k) = \ln\left(\frac{P_k(X_B|B)}{P_k(X_B|\neg B)}\right)$$

$$= \ln\left(\frac{\sigma_B}{\sigma_{\neg B}}\right) + \frac{1}{2}\left(\frac{X_B - \mu_{\neg B}}{\sigma_{\neg B}} + \frac{X_B - \mu_B}{\sigma_B}\right)\left(\frac{X_B - \mu_{\neg B}}{\sigma_{\neg B}} - \frac{X_B - \mu_B}{\sigma_B}\right).$$

2.2 Base-Calling with Gappy Alignment to a Reference Genome

While the approach described earlier, with well-chosen score function extracts as much information as possible to call each base accurately and provides b-optimal solutions (b = beam-width parameter), ordered according to their scores (or their p values or quality scores), it can be further improved in the presence of a Bayesian prior that also provides the marginal probabilities $P_k(B)$ and $P_k(\neg B)$. In the absence of any prior information about the underlying biological system, the most non-informative prior can be chosen to make all $P_k(B)$'s equiprobable for all $B \in \{A, T, C, G\}$, taking the value $1/4$ (in which case $P_k(\neg B) = 3/4$); the values can be modified suitably when the CG-bias for the reference genome(s) is known, or when the di-neucleotide, tri-neucleotide biases for the reference genome are known (from the reference genome), or when the distribution of k-mers over the genome are known. A better solution may be derived from Markov-model of the reference genome (e.g., derived from an estimated HMM), which can be inferred from an assembled reference (genotypic/haplotypic) genome(s), an assembled genome with a single reference along with all the population poly-morphisms (e.g., SNP's, indels, breakpoints, structural variants), or a semi-assembled reference genome with a set of un-phased contigs, or even from just a collection of sequence reads (possibly error-corrected, and organized in a de-Bruijn graph). A more direct solution can be devised by avoiding pre-processing altogether and simply following a "lazy-evaluation" scheme where $P_k(B)$ (and $P_k(\neg B)$) are estimated in real-time by aligning the $(k-1)$-prefix of the sequence, analyzed and 'called' so far, to all the locations in the reference genome using efficient compressed and searchable data structures (e.g., BWT, Burrows-Wheeler Transform and FMI, Ferragina-Manzini Index and its variants, see the survey by Navarro and Makinen [Navarro and Mäkinen, 2007]). Thus the composite score function is:

$$f_{\text{score}}(X_B; k) + w_{\text{align}}(\cdot)f^*_{\text{score}}(B; k, sp_k, ep_k, sp_{k-1}, ep_{k-1})$$

with

$$f^*_{\text{score}}(B; k, sp_k, ep_k, sp_{k-1}, ep_{k-1}) = \ln\left(\frac{P_k(B)}{P_k(\neg B)}\right)$$

$$= \ln(ep_k - sp_k + 1) - \ln(ep_{k-1} - sp_{k-1} - ep_k + sp_k),$$

where the FMI's sp_k and ep_k define the interval in the FMI-dimension corresponding to all the aligned matches in the reference for B in the kth cycle, which translates in a very straightforward manner to the number of occurrences of the sequences in the reference up to cycle $(k-1)$, which can be calculated by $ep_k - sp_k + 1$. Since the equivalent value after $(k-1)$ cycle is $ep_{k-1} - sp_{k-1} + 1$, the corresponding number for "non-matches" to B (or matches to $\neg B$) is the difference $(ep_{k-1} - sp_{k-1} - ep_k + sp_k)$. The estimator can be suitably modified to a "shrinkage estimator," for instance, one using pseudo-counts, which also avoids various degenerate situations.

It is also straightforward to further generalize the TRC base-callers to more general class of alignments that include "indels," by simply expanding the 4-character alphabet from $\{A, T, C, G\}$ to a 6-character alphabet $\{A, T, C, G, \iota, \delta\}$, where ι represents an insertion and δ a deletion. Of course, the score function appropriate for a runs of insertion and deletion is more complex, and also requires some amount of "look-ahead" before employing the "pruning" step in the branch-and-bound algorithm. A very naïve way to account for the effect of a 'gap' is to introduce another operation γ, which indicates that the score function needs to account for a gap in the alignment by restarting a new subtree rooted at a node labeled γ. The simplest implementation we describe here lets a new alignment to restart (anywhere in the genome: the FMI's being recalculated *ab initio*). In order to avoid trivial gaps, there should be an appropriate gap penalty, and the putative 'gaps' will need to be checked (using the FMI's for substrings between the gaps) in post-processing step. The performance of the 'gappy' alignments can be improved significantly, by making sure that the alignment process is sufficiently localized: For instance, in the case of RNASeq applications, it makes sense to limit the alignments only to ORF's or to run several alignment processes in parallel, with each process using a set of 'pools' of ORF's, where all the ORF's in the same pool are sufficiently uncorrelated from each other.

However, once such a base-caller is used with priors resulting in 'gappy' alignment, the resulting base-calls are expected to be superior to what can be inferred by the traditional base-callers that have been developed for RNASeq applications. But more importantly, from the base call and the 'gappy' alignment (the correct one being inferred from the FMI values), one could also infer the locations of exons and splice sites, providing an annotation for the intron-exon structure as well as the splicing isoforms that the data represent.

2.3   Base-Calling with Alignment to an Annotated Reference Genome: "Stringomics"

In addition, for RNASeq applications, TRC can also take advantage of the annotated portions of the reference genome, by using a novel data-structure, recently developed by Ferragina and Mishra [Ferragina and Mishra, 2013]. In this structure, the exon-intron structures and the multiple splicing-isoforms are encoded efficiently such that the scheme described earlier (for the whole genome) can be extended and generalized easily without sacrificing space and time efficiency. Thus, this *"stringomics"* data-structure supports, as would be expected, the complex topology encoded by the splice junctions connecting groups of exons and is represented as a directed-acyclic graph DAG. Its main function is to align the sequence seen so far as a path in the graph and provides the needed information about the next anticipated base efficiently (e.g., in terms of indices similar to FMI). We sketch the basic ingredients of the "*stringomics*" data structure below, and encourage the reader to consult the full paper [Ferragina and Mishra, 2013].

We define a "stringome" to be a family of strings that can be obtained by concatenation of a small number of shorter elemental strings – "stringlets," which may (or may not) additionally share many common structures, patterns and similarities or homologies. Study of such combinatorial objects have been referred to as "*stringomics*," as in [Ferragina and Mishra, 2013]. The stringomics approach aims to solve various algorithmic problems related to a special case of pattern matching on hypertext. It is built on an underlying graph, which is directed and acyclic (DAG, Directed Acyclic Graph); furthermore, the nodes are assumed to be partitioned into groups, whose strings may have certain additional structures that allow them to be highly compressed.

To be precise, our problem consists of k groups of variable-length strings $K_1, K_2, \ldots, K_k$, providing the building blocks for the "stringomes." The strings are n in number, have a total length of N characters, and are further linked in a pair-wise fashion by m links, defined below more precisely. Each group K_i consists of n_i strings $\{s_{i1}, s_{i2}, \ldots, s_{in_i}\}$, possibly similar to each other. In many situations of practical interest to us, it could be assumed that $|s_{ij}| \leq S_{\max}$ and n_i is bounded from above by a small constant. The indicator function, $\mathbb{1}_{s',s''}$ is 1, if there is a link (edge) between the pair of strings (s', s'') and 0, otherwise. It is, then, $n = \sum_{i=1}^{k} n_i$, $N = \sum_{i=1}^{k} \sum_{j=1}^{n_i} |s_{ij}|$, and $m = (n_1 + n_k) + \sum_{i=1}^{k-1} \sum_{s' \in K_i} \sum_{s'' \in K_{i+1}} \mathbb{1}_{s',s''}$. Several complexity bounds can be derived in terms of the parameters N and m, resorting subsequently to the k-th order empirical entropy $H_k(K)$ of the string set $K = \cup_i K_i$ when dealing with compressed data structures [Navarro and Mäkinen, 2007].

These groups of strings are interconnected to form a multi-partite DAG $G = (V, E)$ defined as follows. The set V consists of $n + 2$ nodes, one node per string s_{ij} plus two special nodes, designated s_0 and s_{n+1}, which constitute the "source" and the "sink" of the multi-partite DAG and contain empty strings (in order to avoid generating spurious hits). The set E consists of m edges which link strings of adjacent groups, namely we can have edges of the form $(s_{ij'}, s_{(i+1)j''})$, where $1 \leq j' \leq n_i$ and $1 \leq j'' \leq n_{i+1}$. In addition, the source s_0 is connected to all strings of group K_1 and the sink s_{n+1} is linked from all strings in K_k.

The main algorithmic question, to be addressed, is the following: Build an index over G in order to efficiently support two basic pattern queries:

Counting: Given a pattern $P[1, p]$, we wish to count the *number occ* of pattern occurrences in G.

Reporting: Same as the previous query, but here we wish to *report* the positions of these *occ* occurrences.[2]

Various versions of the "Stringomics," can be created using basic building blocks for: D_K (to keep track of the indexing), T_K (to organize the underlying strings and stringlets) and P_K (to perform $2d$-range queries in an index-space).

Theorem 1. *Listed below are three possible implementations of the "Stringomics" ensemble of data structures, which address three different contexts of use.*[3]

I/O-efficiency: *The following implementation built upon, the String B-trees for D_K and for T_K, the external-memory Range-Tree for P_K, uses $O(N/B + (m/B)(\log m/\log\log_B m))$ disk pages, which we can safely assume to be $O(N/B)$, hence $O(N\log N)$ bits of space.*

Compressed Space: *The following implementation built upon, the FM-index for D_K, two Patricia tries for T_K, the Range-Tree for P_K, uses $NH_k(K) + o(N) + m\log^2 m$ bits of space.*

I/O + compression: *The following implementation built upon, the Geometric BWT for D_K, the String B-tree for T_K, a blocked compression scheme for the strings in K, an external-memory Range-Tree for P_K, uses $O(N + m\log m)$ bits of space.* $\square$

We remark that, for various RNASeq applications of immediate interest, any suffix-array like data structure is likely to satisfy our algorithmic needs; nonetheless, we prefer a somewhat more complex implementation based on FM-index as we foresee rapidly growing needs for the technology to scale.

2.4   Putting it all Together

Base Calling. The RNAseqTRC algorithm works in real-time in the standard manner, but without the fore-knowledge of whether the underlying cDNA (being read currently) corresponds to an annotated gene (in which case the prior is already encoded in the "Stringomics" data structure) or to an unannotated gene, pseudo-gene or a contaminant (in case the prior is available from a possibly 'gappy' alignment to the reference genome). Thus TRC runs, in parallel, two (or multiple) branch-and-bound algorithms to call bases with the two sets of priors

---

[2] It is clear that the identification of a pattern occurrence may involve in our DAG setting three integers: one to identify the source string, (optional) one to identify the destination string, and one to specify the offset of the pattern occurrence in the source string.

[3] We note parenthetically that these are not necessarily the best possible combinations but only offer a good trade-off between simplicity and efficiency.

and compares the resulting score values at the end to decide whether the cDNA examined corresponds to an annotated or unannotated gene.

Additionally, as TRC collects a new dictionary of unannotated genes, it can compile a dictionary of isoforms of genes and pseudo-genes, along with their structural descriptions in terms of exons, introns, and splicing junctions. Periodically, in a "garbage-collection-like" step, this dictionary will be examined serially to filter out contaminants (chimeras and sterile transcripts, pseudo-genes, etc.), leaving only the newly discovered genes, rank-ordered by their score functions (or p-values). The validated newly discovered genes are then inserted into the existing "Stringomics" data-structure, which will involve modifying the three data-structures: D_K (to keep track of the indexing), T_K (to organize the underlying strings and stringlets) and P_K (to perform $2d$-range queries in an index-space). The frequency of this "garbage-collection," step can be determined as the one that optimizes the computational complexity of "dynamization."

Note that, at this point, the role of TRC can be easily abstracted away (and hence hidden) from the rest of the RNASeq pipeline, as it can treat TRC as just a base-calling module – except that it has the ability to produce better-quality base-calls, and that it can be tuned suitably to take the best advantage of the trade-off between false-positive and negative errors.

Transcriptome Profiling. If our focus was only on the set of transcripts associated with the annotated genes, as would be the case, in many clinical transcriptomic applications, then the simplest strategy would be to keep track of the splice-junctions (i.e., the edges in the Stringomics graph) corresponding to the reads seen from the entire set of reads. The paths in the Stringomics data-structure induced by the edges, labeled by the tracking of splice-junctions, correspond to the splice-variants isoforms, and a rough estimate of such paths can be inferred by a max-flow algorithm running on the graph. However, a much better estimate for the expressed transcripts and their copy number can be obtained from a Bayesian algorithm that, in its prior, models the distributions of the data that correspond to a particular hypothesized transcriptomic profiling.

Transcriptome Assembly. In certain applications, in addition to transcription profiling, it would be necessary to discover mutational changes to transcripts, transcript-editing, new transcripts, new splice-variant isoforms of known/ annotated transcripts, or even sterile transcripts (e.g., resulting from pseudo-genes). For such applications, the reads would need to be accurately assembled, which is complicated by the read-lengths, quality of base-calling, and various subtle statistical issues, related to variable coverage, estimation of optimal parameters, strand-specificity, etc. The advantage provided by RNASeqTRC are manifold: (1) base-calling accuracy, (2) longer reads, (3) information from alignments to stringomics and reference (that are stored by FM-indices or D_K/P_K structure in Stringomics). These information provide important ingredients to check local correctness of the string-overlaps, and can be summarized by a global score function. Overlap-Layout-Consensus-based global-optimizing algorithm, such as SUTTA [Narzisi and Mishra, 2011], can be used with these information to assemble the reads and count the coverage in each transcript-assembly to create a transcriptional profile for all transcripts (sterile or otherwise), and to discover those assemblies that fail to match any of the known annotated transcripts (or fail to align to the reference by a 'gappy' alignment).

As discussed earlier, the strategies for whole genome transcript-analysis are usually categorized in terms of three related approaches: (1) Align-then-assemble, (2) Assemble-then-align, and (3) Hybrid [Martin and Wang, 2011]. In terms of these categories, the approach described here would be considered a hybrid approach as the underlying base-caller, TRC, automatically aligns to all the known information, such as references, annotations and variations (provided in its prior), and uses these information in base-calling, assembly, validation and discovery.

3   Conclusions

This paper initiates the study of transcriptional analysis using very accurate and efficient algorithms, that can be eventually implemented in hardware to run in real-time. Our algorithm efficiently uses Bayesian priors to improve accuracy, and since it obtains these priors from the reference genome and its annotations, it would be appropriate to classify it to be a "reference-guided strategy." As always, the success of reference-guided assemblers depends on the quality of the reference genome being used, but since TRC can optimize the w_{align} parameter in its score function, TRC trades off errors (false positives and negatives) in the best possible manner. TRC will not thus be affected very strongly by the "hundreds to thousands of mis-assemblies and large genomic deletions, which may lead to misassembled or partially assembled transcriptomes," existing in many extant reference assemblies. Another issue, not directly addressed in this paper, arises from certain trans-spliced genes, in which two pre-mRNAs are spliced together into a single mature mRNA, and requires TRC's stringomics data structure to be complicated further. In the simplest description provided here, such trans-spliced genes (or those with RNA-editing) will show up as uninterpretable new transcripts. Their status: as new discoveries, as chimeras or as contaminants, will have to be determined in a post-processing step.

References

Bartfai et al., 2012. Bartfai, T., Buckley, P.T., Eberwine, J.: Drug targets: single-cell transcriptomics hastens unbiased discovery. Trends in Pharmacological Sciences 33(1), 9–16 (2012)

Batut et al., 2013. Batut, P., Dobin, A., et al.: High-fidelity promoter profiling reveals widespread alternative promoter usage and transposon-driven developmental gene expression. Genome Research 23(1), 169–180 (2013)

Bona et al., 2008. De Bona, F., Ossowski, S., et al.: Optimal spliced alignments of short sequence reads. Bioinformatics 24(16), I174–I180 (2008)

Djebali et al., 2012. Djebali, S., Davis, C.A., et al.: Landscape of transcription in human cells. Nature 489(7414), 101–108 (2012)

Dobin et al., 2013. Dobin, A., Davis, C.A., et al.: Star: ultrafast universal rna-seq aligner. Bioinformatics 29(1), 15–21 (2013)

Dunham et al., 2012. Dunham, I., Kundaje, A., et al.: An integrated encyclopedia of dna elements in the human genome. Nature 489(7414), 57–74 (2012)

Ferragina and Mishra, 2013. Ferragina, P., Mishra, B.: Pattern matching against 'stringomes'. BIORXIV 2014(001669), 11 (2013)

Gingeras, 2009. Gingeras, T.R.: Implications of chimaeric non-co-linear transcripts. Nature 461(7261), 206–211 (2009)

Grant et al., 2011. Grant, G.R., Farkas, M.H., et al.: Comparative analysis of rna-seq alignment algorithms and the rna-seq unified mapper (rum). Bioinformatics 27(18), 2518–2528 (2011)

Land and Doig, 1960. Land, A.H., Doig, A.G.: An automatic method of solving discrete programming problems. Econometrica: Journal of the Econometric Society 28(3), 497–520 (1960)

Lawler and Wood, 1966. Lawler, E.L., Wood, D.E.: Branch-and-bound methods: A survey. Operations Research 14(4), 699–719 (1966)

Levsky et al., 2002. Levsky, J.M., Shenoy, S.M., et al.: Single-cell gene expression profiling. Science 297(5582), 836–840 (2002)

Martin and Wang, 2011. Martin, J., Wang, Z.: Next-generation transcriptome assembly. Nature Reviews Genetics 12, 671–682 (2011)

Menges et al., 2011. Menges, F., Narzisi, G., Mishra, B.: Totalrecaller: improved accuracy and performance via integrated alignment and base-calling. Bioinformatics 27(17), 2330–2337 (2011)

Mishra, 2012. Mishra, B.: The genome question: Moore vs. jevons. Computer Society of India: Journal of Computing (2012)

Narzisi and Mishra, 2011. Narzisi, G., Mishra, B.: Scoring-and-unfolding trimmed tree assembler: Concepts, constructs and comparisons. Bioinformatics 27(12), 153–160 (2011)

Navarro and Mäkinen, 2007. Navarro, G., Mäkinen, V.: Compressed full-text indexes. ACM Computing Surveys 39(1) (2007)

Tariq et al., 2011. Tariq, M.A., Kim, H.J., et al.: Whole-transcriptome rnaseq analysis from minute amount of total rna. Nucleic Acids Research 39(18) (2011)

Tilgner et al., 2012. Tilgner, H., Knowles, D.G., et al.: Deep sequencing of subcellular rna fractions shows splicing to be predominantly co-transcriptional in the human genome but inefficient for incrnas. Genome Research 22(9), 1616–1625 (2012)

Trapnell et al., 2009. Trapnell, C., Pachter, L., Salzberg, S.L.: Tophat: discovering splice junctions with rna-seq. Bioinformatics 25(9), 1105–1111 (2009)

Wang et al., 2010. Wang, K., Singh, D., et al.: Mapsplice: Accurate mapping of rna-seq reads for splice junction discovery. Nucleic Acids Research 38(18) (2010)

Wigler, 2012. Wigler, M.: Broad applications of single-cell nucleic acid analysis in biomedical research. Genome Medicine 4(10) (2012)

Wu and Nacu, 2010. Wu, T.D., Nacu, S.: Fast and snp-tolerant detection of complex variants and splicing in short reads. Bioinformatics 26(7), 873–881 (2010)

Finding RkNN Set in Directed Graphs

Pankaj Sahu[1], Prachi Agrawal[2], Vikram Goyal[1], and Debajyoti Bera[1]

[1] Indraprastha Institute of Information Technology-Delhi (IIIT-D), India
{pankaj1244,vikram,dbera}@iiitd.ac.in
[2] LNM Institute of Information Technology, Jaipur, India
happyprachi.1@gmail.com

Abstract. The *reverse k-nearest neighbors* of a query data point q characterizes the influence set of q, and comprises of data points which consider q among their k-nearest neighbours. This query has gained considerable attention due to its importance in various applications involving decision support systems, profile-based marketing, location based services, etc. Although this query is reasonably well-studied for scenarios where data points belong to Euclidean spaces, there has not been much work done for non-Euclidean data points, and specifically, for large data sets with arbitrary distance measures. In this work, a framework has been proposed for performing RkNN query over data sets that can be represented as directed graphs. We present a graph pruning technique to compute the RkNN of a query point which significantly reduces the search space. We report results of extensive experiments over some real-world data sets from a social network, a product co-purchasing network of Amazon, the web graph, and study the performance of our proposed heuristic in various settings on these data sets. These experiments demonstrate the effectiveness of our proposed technique.

1 Introduction

A common problem that arises in many marketing and decision support systems is to determine the "influence" of a data point on other data points of a database. Korn, Flip and Muthukrishnan introduced the concept of *reverse nearest neighbor*[4] in 2000 to compute the set of influenced points for datasets with a notion of "closeness" between the points. The underlying idea is that a nearby point have a larger influence than a point farther away, which immediately leads to the concept of reverse nearest neighbor (RNN), and its generalisation reverse k-nearest neighbor (RkNN).

The most common application of reverse nearest neighbor query for computation of influential sets can be illustrated by a facility location scenario. Suppose a company is exploring the option of opening a new restaurant in a location and wants to find likely customers – people who would be "more likely" to use this restaurant compared to another one; in our terminology, we say these people are influenced by the location and profile of this restaurant.

The important issue, therefore is to efficiently compute the data points influenced by a query point. Technically, the reverse nearest neighbor (RNN) of a query point consists of all those data points for which the query point is their nearest neighbor (NN). Reverse k-nearest neighbor (RkNN) is a generalisation of RNN, where kNN is used in the place of NN in the earlier definition.

R. Natarajan et al. (Eds.): ICDCIT 2015, LNCS 8956, pp. 162–173, 2015.

Efficient algorithms for computing RkNN have been designed for various types of data [2,3] and several variants of nearest neighborhood query. Majority of these works have focused on data with a well-defined concept of distance or similarity, such as Euclidean distances, similarity measures for word vectors, and other distances that are metric in nature. However, the problem becomes fundamentally different for data points with arbitrary distances between the points such as people, products, movies, etc. Data with an arbitrary notion of distance is well represented by a weighted graph. The focus of this paper are data which can be represented as such graph, and furthermore, as weighted directed graphs. The nodes in the graph are the data points, and the weighted and directed edges represent the distance and relation, respectively, between related points.

Given such a graph, it is often meaningful to consider the shortest-path distance as the distance between two points. There are a few major hurdles in computing RkNN of a query point in such a graph. First similar to the general problem, the concept of nearest neighborhood is not symmetric, so we cannot simply run one single-source shortest path query from the query point.

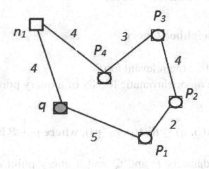

Fig. 1. Nearest Neighborhood using Shortest-path Distance

For example, in Fig. 1, P_1 is the nearest neighbor of query point q but P_2 is the NN of P_1 and not of q. This also implies that the points in RNN need not be in the immediate vicinity of the query point, and a large segment of the graph may have to be traversed. This presents a major challenge for large graphs because we cannot benefit from locality conditions. A solution based on running a Dijkstra's algorithm from every point (to compute the kNN of each point) would be correct, but computationally very expensive. Secondly, we are interested in a non-index based solution; index/pre-processing based techniques are often not much efficient or directly possible for situations where k is not fixed and due to relationship constraints present in graphs.

An interesting application of RkNN query in directed graphs can be seen in social networks; here, RkNN can be used to determine the influence set of any person. The weights on the directed edges of such network can represent the influence of one person on another, say, regarding forwarding of messages, and the RkNN query for a person would then give a set of individuals who would play an important role in diffusing any information initiated or forwarded by the query person.

In an earlier work, a graph-pruning based algorithm was designed by Papadias et al.[11] for undirected graphs. However their technique does not work for directed graphs. The main contribution in this paper is an approach for computing reverse nearest neighborhood for directed graphs. We give two algorithms, Directed Eager (D_M) and an optimized version for large graphs, Directed Eager Materialization (D_EM) for processing (monochromatic) RkNN for arbitrary k. Another important contribution is extensive experimentation on large directed networks coming from real datasets including that of a social network, a product co-purchasing network from Amazon and a web network of Berkeley-Stanford university.

The rest of the paper is organized as follows: Section 2 presents the necessary background and related work. Section 3 discusses our algorithm. Section 4 reports our experimental results on some real world data sets including performance comparisons with respect to various parameters. Section 5 concludes the paper suggesting some directions for future work.

2   Background and Related Work

2.1   Reverse Nearest Neighbor Query

We will now formally define the relevant terms.

Given a dataset P, the monochromatic RkNN of a query point q not in P is defined as:

RkNN (q) = {p∈P | dist(p, q) ≤ dist(p, p$_k$(p)), where p$_k$∈P is the kth NN of p}

Similarly, given two datasets P and Q and a query point q∈Q, the bi-chromatic RkNN of a query point q returns all those data points $p \in P$ which are nearer to q than any other points of Q.

bRkNN (q) = {p∈P | dist(p, q) ≤ dist(p, q$_k$(p)), where q$_k$∈Q is the kth NN of p}

In this paper, we are interested in only monochromatic RkNN.

Furthermore, like [11], we consider a generalized scenario where not all nodes in the graph are data points. For instance, not every author in a co-authorship graph works in some specified field. Such networks are called *restricted* networks. Consider the example in Fig. 2(a). Suppose it represents a DBLP co-authorship (collaboration) network. An (monochromatic) R1NN query for query point q will return authors whose 1NN is q, among authors of his same field $\{P_1, P_2, P_3, P_4\}$. Other nodes, such as n_1, n_2 and n_3 represent the authors which are not working in the author's field and, thus, are irrelevant for this query.

In this figure, RNN(q)=$\{P_4\}$, because P_4's NN is q, and R2NN(q)=$\{P_1, P_2, P_4\}$. The other type of network, where the data and query points can be any node of the graph, is called an unrestricted network. However, we give a solution for the more general restricted network.

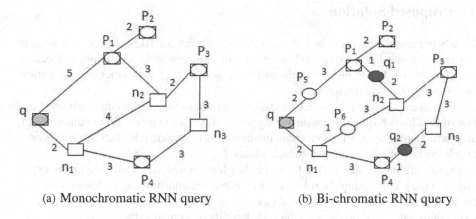

(a) Monochromatic RNN query   (b) Bi-chromatic RNN query

Fig. 2. Types of RNN Queries

2.2 Related Work

A lot of work has been done on RNN queries. The work was started by a paper [4] in 2000 where the authors define the notion of influence set and show that nearest neighbour set of a point is different from a reverse nearest neighbour set of the point. They show multiple applications of RNN query whereas finding a facility location is one of them. To solve RNN query efficiently, the authors propose to have a pair of R-tree structures on spatial objects and MBR regions of objects containing their nearest neighbour, respectively. Subsequently, there has been more work [7,10] on providing efficient solutions using better data structures or methods constraining the search to a well defined set of candidates. Our work focuses on finding RkNN set for weighted directed graphs and uses network distances as well relationship of nodes for search.

The other work for RNN query has been done on Road networks [8,5,11,9,6] and for continuous RNN queries [1,3]. In continuous RNN queries case, the problem is to continuously report the RkNN set of a moving query point. The brute force solution of computing RNN set afresh would not be good and hence an incremental solution was proposed by the authors. The approach is based on the concept of safe region that defines the boundary around a query point, crossing which there is a need to recompute the RNN set.

The work on RNN query over road network was done in [8,5]. Safar et al. [5] used a network Voronoi diagram (NVD) for efficiently processing the RNN queries over road networks. The NVD uses the Voronoi cell that has the nodes & the edges which are nearer to the generator point of the cell compare to other points in the network. The authors in [11] model the road network as an undirected graph and presents two versions of problem, restricted case where data objects/points can be only at intersection nodes and unrestricted case where objects can be anywhere on the edges. The authors gave two different algorithms called eager and lazy approaches that use heuristic rules to prune the search space.

3 Proposed Solution

Here we present our proposed algorithms for solving an RkNN query for a given directed graph (digraph) G, and edge weight function $d(\cdot)$. As explained earlier, our algorithm is based on the results of Papadias et al.[11] with crucial modifications necessary to handle directed networks.

We maintain two graphs, one G_M and another graph G_R whose edges are reverse of that of G. This is required because our algorithm traverses in a best-first manner starting at q (which uses G_M), but to ascertain the inclusion of a node p in RkNN(q) we need to check the neighborhood of p for which we use G_R.

Our algorithm is based on the following key lemma which is used to optimize exploration of the graph. Using the rule given in the lemma, unpromising nodes are identified those need not be further explored. As exploring them further would not be useful due to the reason that if a successor of the node have its short path to the query point through the node, it would not be in RkNN.

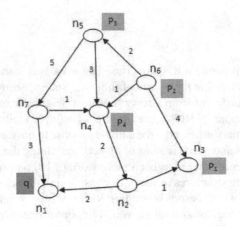

Fig. 3. Lemma

Lemma 1. *For a query point q, a data point p and a node n, if $d(n,q) > d(n,p)$ and there is another data point p$\prime \neq$ p whose shortest path to q passes through n, then point p$\prime$ is not in the RNN set of q.*

Proof. The proof is really straight forward.
$d(p\prime,q) = d(p\prime,n)+d(n,q) > d(p\prime,n)+d(n,p) \geq d(p\prime,p)$.
Since, $d(p\prime,p) < d(p\prime,q)$, p$\prime \notin$ RNN(q). $\square$

Therefore, in such a situation, the node n can be pruned and need not be further expanded. As an illustration, refer to Fig. 3. There, $d(n_2, q) = 2 > d(n_2, p1) = 1$. According the lemma, any data point (in Fig. 3 p_4) whose shortest path to q passes through n_2 cant be the RNN of q as the data point p_4 is nearer to p_1. In this case, node n_2 will be pruned and need not be expanded further.

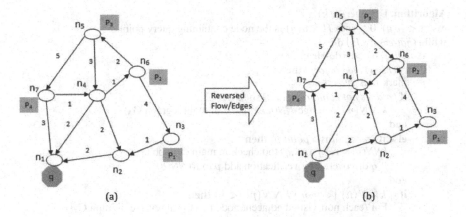

Fig. 4. Example of Directed Eager (a) Main Graph G_M (b) Reverse Graph G_R

Similar to [11], we use two subroutines *range-NN* query and *verify* query. A straight forward modification of these subroutines given in their paper turn out to be sufficient for directed graphs, so we skip their implementation details in our paper. The *range-NN(n,k,q)* query returns (at most) k nearest data points with shortest-path distance smaller than $d(n,q)$. The query *verify(n,k,q)* is similar to *range-NN(n,k,d(n,q))*, except that it stops as soon as q is encountered.

3.1 Directed Eager(D_E) Algorithm

Our main algorithm traverses the reverse graph G_R starting from the query point q, in a best-first manner, and every encountered node n in G_R is inserted into a min-heap H. H is also used to select the next node to explore. For every point node n deheaped from the queue, we proceed as given below. The range-NN and verify queries are executed on the main digraph G_M and all other operations are done on the reverse graph G_R. The only difference between the range-NN query and the verify query is that range-NN returns the set of k nodes whereas verify returns boolean value to decide whether to explore the node further.

– If the node contains a data point p∈P, then we need to take two decisions:
  1. Whether $p \in$ RkNN(q)? This we determine by running *range-NN(p,k,q)*.
  2. Whether p should be explored further? This we determine using Lemma 1 by using *verify(p,k,q)*. If k (or more) points are found, then there is no need to explore further the neighbors of p.
– If the node does not contain a data point, then we only need to determine whether that node should be explored further. We employ the same treatment as (2) above.
– In the case of node is not to be explored further, no adjacent nodes of the currently explored node with respect to G_R are enqueued in the heap H.

We now illustrate our algorithm on Fig. 4, on which we run a query RNN(q) for k=1. The algorithm starts its traversal from node n_1 (source node which contains the query point q) and insert $< n_1(q),0>$ into H (currently empty). After this, n_1 is deheaped.

Algorithm. D_Eager(q, k)
insert $< n(q), 0 >$ into H // $n(q)$ is the node containing query point q
while *(not-empty(H)* **do**
    $< n, d(q,n) >$:= de-Heap(H);
   if *(n is not visited before)* **then**
      mark n as visited
      if *(n does not contain a point)* **then**
         $kNN(n) = $ *range-NN(n,k,d(q,n))* in main digraph G_M.
      end
      else if *(n contains a point p)* **then**
         $kNN(p) = $ *verify(p,k,q)* too check in main digraph G_M.
         if q discovered by verification add p to *RkNN(q)*
      end
      if $(| kNN(n) |< k$ *or* $| kNN(p) |< k)$ **then**
         For (each non-visited adjacent node n_i of n in reverse digraph G_R)
         insert $< n_i, d(q,n) + w(n,n_i) <$ into H
      end
    end
  end
end
return RkNN(q)

Since it does not contain any data point, and since $d(n_1,q)=0$, range-NN returns the empty set trivially. Therefore, it's adjacent nodes in reverse graph G_R, $<n_2, 2>$ $<n_4, 2>$ and $<n_7, 3>$, are now inserted into H.

The next deheaped node is n_2 which also does not contain a data point. A range-NN($n_2,1,2$) query in G_M again does not return any point within distance 2 from n_2. Similar to the previous case, its adjacent node $< n_3, 3>$ in G_R is inserted into H.

The subsequent deheaped node is n_4, which too, does not contain a data point. However, a range-NN($n_4,1,2$) in G_M returns a data point p_2, because $d(n_4, p_2) = 1 < d(q, n_4) = 2$. Hence node n_4 can be pruned, and so its adjacent nodes are not inserted into H.

Next node n_7 is deheaped which contains a data point p_4. We run a *range-NN($n_7,1,3$)* query that returns p_4 itself, however running *verify($p_4,1,q$)* in G_M returns the data point p_2. Therefore, neither p_4 belongs to RkNN(q), nor should p_4 be explored further. In case of verify query at a node, data point located at the node itself is not considered.

At last node n_3, containing data point p_1, is deheaped and *range-NN($n_3,1,3$)* returns point p_1. The *verify($p_1,1,q$)* query in G_M finds q and returns true. So p_1 is added into RkNN(q) and no adjacent of n_3 is added in heap H.

At this stage, H is empty which means that our algorithm is terminated with final result containing RNN(q)=$\{p_1\}$.

3.2 Directed Eager Materialization

Materialization is the technique of pre-computing the shortest distances between all pairs of nodes and store it in a lookup table. A naïve approach for materialization is to apply the kNN query on each node, but this method is not scalable for large graph.

Therefore, an *all-NN* algorithm is proposed that accessed the network only once to compute the distance value for different values of k for each node.

The algorithm is as given below.

Algorithm. Directed_All-NN (k)
for *(each node n those contains point p in main digraph G_M)* **do**
    insert $< n, p, 0 >$ into H
end
while *(not-empty(H))* **do**
    $< n, p, d(p, n) >$:= de-Heap(H)
    if *(| $kNN(n)$ |$< k$ and $p \notin kNN(n)$)* **then**
        add $< p, d(p, n) >$ to kNN(n)
        for *(each adjacent node n_i of n in reverse graph G_R)* **do**
            if *(| $kNN(n_i)$ |$< k$ and $p \notin kNN(n_i)$)* **then**
                insert $< n_i, p, d(p, n) + w(n, n_i) >$ into H
            end
        end
    end
end
return kNN

Our directed eager materialization algorithm (Directed_EM or D_EM) utilizes the materialized lookup table build above to retrieve the kNN of any n in constant time. This replaces the costly range-NN and verify operations to constant time table look-up operation.

4 Experimental Evaluation

In this section, we show our experimental results for processing RkNN query over directed graphs. In the graph |V| represents number of nodes in the graph, |P| represents data points cardinality and D=|P| / |V| represents data density. However, if $D = 1$ then R1NN query returns a point situated on the query node itself. For providing more meaningful results, we restricted value of D from 0.1 to 0.4. All the experimental results show the average value of 50 queries generated randomly from all the data points in the network. All algorithms are implemented in Java and experiments are run on an Intel Xenon 2.00 GHz machine with Windows environment. In our experiments, we evaluate the performance of the algorithms in terms of (i) computation time in milliseconds(ms), (ii) number of accessed nodes, (iii) number of accessed points. We study the performance with respect to the size of requested data points (k), and the density (D) of a graph. The value of $k <<| P |$.

4.1 Directed Graph

We study the performance of directed eager (D_E), directed eager materialization (D_EM) and the naïve approach on different datasets.

The first set of experiments has been performed on a social network dataset of Facebook [1]. The dataset contains 1862 users and 20k directed edges among the users. A user is represented as a node n and an edge direction between two users e(i,j) refers, if a user 'i' has sent at least one online message to a user 'j'. The strength measure or weight on the edge e(i,j) represents the 1/(number of messages) between users 'i' to 'j'.

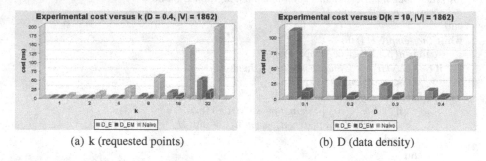

(a) k (requested points)   (b) D (data density)

Fig. 5. Facebook Social Network (a) Effect of K on Computation Time (ms) (b) Effect of D (data density) on Computation Time

In the first experiment, we measure the effect of query parameter k on computation time when density D is 0.4. Figure 5(a) shows the result. When k increases, the computation cost also increases. It is because of the increase in the number of accesses of nodes/points with increase in k. In the second experiment, effect of density D on the computation cost is evaluated. Fig. 5(b) shows the results. It is seen that when D increases (value of K is set to 10 as a default value), the computation time cost decreases. It is due to the fact that increase in density of points in the graph makes availability of data points near to the query points as well as increases the proximity of data points to each other and other graph nodes. The probability of finding k data points within the distance d(n,q) from a node increases and hence the adjacent nodes of the node need not be put in the heap. This results in better pruning and less graph is searched for RkNN.

It can be seen that when the data density D is very low, D_E performs worse as compared to the naïve approach. It is because of non-pruning of nodes. Most of the nodes in the graph do not find k data points and hence their adjacent nodes are enqueued in the heap, and the algorithm D_E ends up in accessing more nodes for retrieving k points. When D increases, the computation cost of algorithm D_E drastically decreases and performs better than the naïve approach. During this experiment, we also observe that when D increases, then the number of accesses nodes decreases and the number of points increases, because more points need to be verified.

The second set of experiment has been performed on product co-purchasing network of Amazon [2]. The dataset contain 410,235 nodes and 3.3 million edges. Each node represents the product which was purchased by a customer from the Amazon sites. Two products i and j are linked by a directed edge from i to j if the product j is

---

[1] (http://toreopsahl.com/datasets/#online_social_network)
[2] http://snap.stanford.edu/data/amazon0505.html

purchased after product i. The edge can be interpreted as a causal relation, i.e., if item i is purchased then item j is also purchased. All the edge weights are assigned randomly for our experiments.

Table 1. Effect of K on Computation Time, $D = 0.4$, Amazon Dataset

K	D_E	D_EM	Naive
1	0.56	0.32	1424.08
2	0.64	0.36	2460.92
4	1.18	0.52	5138.54
8	3.36	1.62	11371.42
16	9.94	4.28	24444.34
32	37.68	13.74	48922.28

Table 2. Effect of D on Computation Time, $K = 10$, Amazon Dataset

D	D_E	D_EM	Naive
0.1	64.06	7.32	16852.38
0.2	19.1	4.2	15140.12
0.3	9.56	3.2	14445.6
0.4	4.58	2.08	13986.24

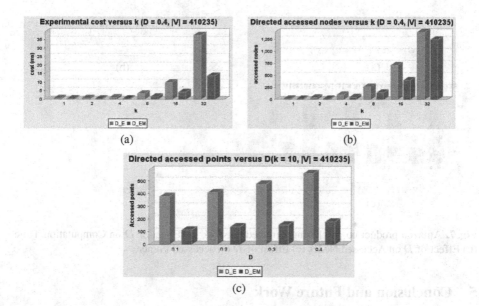

(a)   (b)

(c)

Fig. 6. Amazon product co-purchasing Directed network (a) Effect of k on Computation Time (b) Effect of k on Accessed Nodes (c) Effect of k on accessed Points

Table 1 shows the computation cost for different values of k when D is 0.4. The experimental results show that when k increases, then computation time increases. The naïve algorithm takes too much time as compared to D_E. It is because of early pruning of the search space by algorithm D_E and exploring only few nodes. Fig. 6 shows the performance of the directed_eager materialized (D_EM) algorithm with respect to the directed eager(D_E) algorithm. (D_EM) algorithm performs much better due to its constant time cost for verification step (Naïve showed worst amongst all and not shown in the graph). However the graph for the value of D as 1 are not shown, in this case D_E would perform best as the probability of finding k data points is very high within k hops from the node. As we will go farther from the query point, their probability of being in RkNN set would decrease.

Next experiment shows the effect of D, given in Table 2. It shows that when D increases the computation cost decreases. It is because of the reason that the algorithm D_E finds more points near around the query point and expansion happens to a small set of nearby nodes. Figure 7 shows this experimental result for D_E and D_EM algorithms. Figure 7(b) & 7(c) show qualitative results in terms of accessed nodes and accessed points. It may be noted that we do not count an accessed node twice.

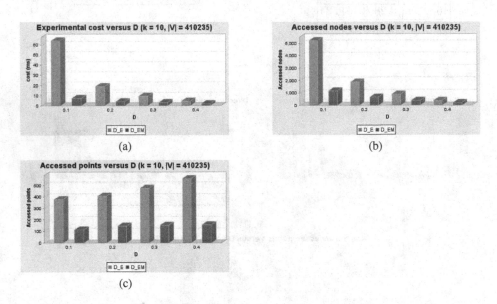

(a)

(b)

(c)

Fig. 7. Amazon product co-purchasing Directed network (a) Effect of D on Computation Time (b) Effect of D on Accessed Nodes (c) Effect of D on accessed Points

5   Conclusion and Future Work

We have presented two algorithms for RkNN query on directed graphs in the paper. The optimized version, D_EM algorithm, performs best amongst all and takes very less time for finding out an RkNN set. We have performed an extensive set of experiments on three real graphs to study the performance of the algorithms. Results show that the pruning rule we have proposed in the paper is very effective.

Acknowledgement. Authors will like to acknowledge the support provided by ITRA project, funded by DEITy, Government of India, under grant with Ref. No. ITRA/15(57)/ Mobile/HumanSense/01

References

1. Cheema, M., Zhang, W., Lin, X., Zhang, Y., Li, X.: Continuous reverse k nearest neighbors queries in euclidean space and in spatial networks. The VLDB Journal 21(1), 69–95 (2012)
2. Goyal, V., Likhyani, A., Bansal, N., Liu, L.: Efficient trajectory cover search for moving object trajectories. In: Proceedings of the 2013 IEEE Second International Conference on Mobile Services, MS 2013, pp. 31–38. IEEE Computer Society, Washington, DC (2013)
3. Goyal, V., Navathe, S.B.: A ranking measure for top-k moving object trajectories search. In: Proceedings of the 7th Workshop on Geographic Information Retrieval, GIR 2013, Orlando, Florida, USA, pp. 27–34 (November 5, 2013)
4. Korn, F., Muthukrishnan, S.: Influence sets based on reverse nearest neighbor queries. SIGMOD Rec. 29(2), 201–212 (2000)
5. Safar, M., Ibrahimi, D., Taniar, D.: Voronoi-based reverse nearest neighbor query processing on spatial networks. Multimedia Systems 15(5), 295–308 (2009)
6. Shang, S., Yuan, B., Deng, K., Xie, K., Zhou, X.: Finding the most accessible locations: reverse path nearest neighbor query in road networks. In: GIS 2011, pp. 181–190 (2011)
7. Stanoi, I., Agrawal, D., Abbadi, A.E.: Reverse nearest neighbor queries for dynamic databases. In: ACM SIGMOD Workshop on Research Issues in Data Mining and Knowledge Discovery, pp. 44–53 (2000)
8. Tran, Q.T., Taniar, D., Safar, M.: Reverse k nearest neighbor and reverse farthest neighbor search on spatial networks. In: Hameurlain, A., Küng, J., Wagner, R. (eds.) Transactions on Large-Scale Data- and Knowledge-Centered Systems I. LNCS, vol. 5740, pp. 353–372. Springer, Heidelberg (2009)
9. Wang, Y., Xu, C., Gu, Y., Chen, M., Yu, G.: Spatial query processing in road networks for wireless data broadcast. Wirel. Netw. 19(4), 477–494 (2013)
10. Yang, C., Lin, K.-I.: An index structure for efficient reverse nearest neighbor queries. In: ICDE, pp. 485–492 (2001)
11. Yiu, M.L., Papadias, D., Mamoulis, N., Tao, Y.: Reverse nearest neighbors in large graphs. IEEE Transactions on Knowledge and Data Engineering 18(4), 540–553 (2006)

Gathering Asynchronous Swarm Robots under Nonuniform Limited Visibility

Avik Chatterjee[1], Sruti Gan Chaudhuri[2], and Krishnendu Mukhopadhyaya[3]

[1] Techno India, Hoogly, India
[2] Jadavpur University, Kolkata, India
[3] Indian Statistical Institute, Kolkata, India
cavik81@gmail.com, srutiganc@it.jusl.ac.in, krishnendu@isical.ac.in

Abstract. This paper proposes a distributed algorithm for gathering a group of autonomous, homogeneous, oblivious, asynchronous mobile robots having limited visibility (sensing) ranges. To the best of our knowledge, all reported results have assumed that the visibility ranges are uniform for all the robots. In contrast, we consider that the visibility ranges of the robots are not uniform. Moreover, the robots have no knowledge about the visibility ranges of other robots. However, a lower bound on the visibility range of all the robots is known to all the robots.

Keywords: Asynchronous robots, Nonuniform limited visibility, Gathering.

1 Introduction

A swarm of robots is a collection of small, inexpensive, identical, autonomous mobile robots working together to execute a task. Distributed algorithms for swarm robots is an emerging field of research where the interest is to realize the fact that, these swarm robots though having minimal capabilities can be as powerful as expensive big robots. Under the basic distributed model of swarm robots [3], that we use in this paper, the robots are represented by points on the 2D plane. Each robot considers itself as the origin of its local coordinate system. They agree on the directions of X and Y axes. The robots operate on executing a cycle *wait-look-compute-move* repeatedly. In *wait* phase they remain idle, in *look* phase they sense or observe the positions of the other robots in their surroundings, up to a certain range (known as visibility range), with the help of some sensing devices. The robots plot the positions of other robots in their local coordinate systems. In *compute* phase, depending upon what they have observed and the requirement of the given task the robots compute destinations to move to. Finally, in *move* phase, the robots move to their destinations. The robots are oblivious, i.e., after completing a cycle, the robots remove all computations related to that cycle. The robots execute the cycles following asynchronous scheduling, where, all robots do not observe at the same time. All robots may not be active at a time to execute the cycles. Some robots may observe other robots in motion. The robots can not differentiate between a static robot and a moving robot. Thus, different robots compute on different data. In move phase, a

R. Natarajan et al. (Eds.): ICDCIT 2015, LNCS 8956, pp. 174–180, 2015.

robot may stop before reaching its destination. And it may again start the cycle. However, if it moves, it travels at least a distance δ in each move step. Robots do not communicate explicitly through wired or wireless medium. In look phase a robot can observe a finite range, known as visibility range, around itself. The visibility range may be different for different robots (in our case)[1]. The robots have no knowledge about the visibility ranges of the other robots. The minimum visibility range of all the robot, say $\Delta > 0$ is fixed and known to all the robots. The robots do not know the total number of robots and they can not identify if a point contains more than one robot.

Gathering of point robots (collecting the robots at a point not fixed in advanced) under unlimited visibility has been investigated by many researchers [1,2,4,6] for a long time. It has been proved [3] that gathering is not possible for oblivious robots without any extra assumptions. To study the solvability of gathering problem the traditional model has been modified by various aspect such as providing constant amount of memory or implicit message communication by the robots [5] or allowing the robots to have limited range of vision [4]. Flocchini et al.[4] first proposed a gathering algorithm under limited visibility for oblivious, asynchronous robots. They consider that all the robots have equal visibility range. In many real time situation, it many not be possible for all the robots to sense uniform range of visions. It may happen due to some internal hardware error or external environment issues. Algorithms considering nonuniform ranges of vision will make the system more general. In this paper, we have modified the algorithm by Flocchini et. al. [4], for gathering the robots with limited nonuniform visibility ranges.

2   Terminology

Let $R = \{r_1 \ldots, r_n\}$ be a finite set of robots. r, describes the position of a robot $r \in R$ on a 2D plane. Let V_r denote the visibility range of r. Let $G_R(V, E)$ be a directed graph formed by the robots in R, defined as follows. V is the set of n robots in R. If a robot r_i can see another robot r_j, then there exists an edge e_{ij} connecting r_i and r_j having direction from r_i to r_j. Note that if r_i and r_j are mutually visible then both e_{ij} and e_{ji} exist. We assume that if r_i can see r_j then r_j can also see r_i and vice versa.

A directed graph G is known as *strongly connected* when, there is a path from any node u to any other node v if and only if there is a path from v to u also.

Definition 1. *A directed graph is called Strong Edge Connected Graph (SECG) if there is an edge from u to v if and only if there exist an edge from v to u, where u and v are any two vertex in G.*

---

[1] Traditionally it is uniform for all the robots.

Note that every SECG is also strongly connected graph but every strongly connected graph is not SECG. The robots in R form a SECG denoted as G_R. We assume that initially G_R is connected. We use the following notations in this paper, $Min(a,b)$: the minimum between a and b; $Dist(a,b)$: the distance between a and b; V_r: the vertical line drawn through r; H_r: the horizontal line drawn through r; Δ: the minimum visibility radius of the robots in R; VC_r: The circle centered at r, v_r (the visibility range of r);

3   Gathering Algorithm

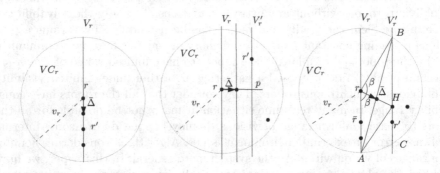

Fig. 1. Down move   **Fig. 2.** Right move   **Fig. 3.** Diagonal move

if *r sees robots only below on V_r (Fig. 1.)* **then**
    r' : the robot nearest to r on V_r; $\bar{\Delta} = Min(\Delta, Dist(r,r'))$;
    Compute a point T_r on V_r such that $Dist(r,T_r) = \bar{\Delta}$;
    r moves to T_r;

Algorithm 1. Down Movement

if *r sees robots only to its right (Fig. 2.)* **then**
    r' : the robot nearest to r and lies on the vertical line just next to V_r.
    p : is the projection of r' on H_r; $\bar{\Delta} = Min(\Delta, Dist(r,p))$;
    Compute a point T_r on H_r such that $Dist(r,T_r) = \bar{\Delta}$;
    r moves to T_r;

Algorithm 2. Right Movement

if *r sees robots both below on V_r and on its right (Fig. 3.)* **then**

r' : the robot nearest to r on the vertical line just next to V_r;

$B :=$ Upper intersection point between $VC(r)$ and $V_{r'}$;

$C :=$ Lower intersection point between $VC(r)$ and $V_{r'}$;

$A :=$ Point on V_r at distance v_r below r;

$2\beta := A\hat{r}B$;

if $\beta < 60°$ **then**

Rotate B around r such that $\beta = 60°$;

Let B' be the position of B after rotation;

$H :=$ The point on V_B [a] and on the diagonal of the parallelogram with sides rB and rA;

$\bar{\Delta} = Min(\Delta, Dist(r, H))$;

Compute a point T_r along the ray rH such that $Dist(r, T_r) = \bar{\Delta}$;

r moves to T_r;

Algorithm 3. Diagonal Movement

---

[a] vertical line through B

4   Correctness of the Algorithm

Lemma 1. *G_R remains connected during down movements of any robot $r \in R$.*

Proof. If r finds a robot r' below on V_r, r moves down $\bar{\Delta}$ distance. Note that r' can not be in motion. If r' is static, r moves down $Dist(r, r')$ decreases. Thus r and r' remains mutually visible. Hence, connectivity does not break. There exists no other robot on upper or right or left side of r, in VC_r. Any arbitrary robot inside or on the VC_r can only lie on V_r or right-down side of r. These robots can not move according to our algorithm. Let r'' be a robot on V_r or at right-down side of r, such that r'' is inside or on VC_r. As r executes a down movement, $Dist(r, r'')$ reduces. Thus, r does not lose connectivity with any arbitrary robot inside or on VC_r. □

Lemma 2. *Every internal chord of a triangle has length less or equal to the longest side of the triangle.*

Lemma 3. *G_R remains connected during right movements of any robot $r \in R$.*

Proof. If r sees robots only in its right side, then it decides to move right. r moves to the nearest vertical line $V_{r'}$ passes through r' such that r' is a robot nearest to r on V'_r. Since, r' can not move by our algorithm, when r moves towards r' along H_r, if r' lies below or above H_r, r will perform right movement by distance $\bar{\Delta}$ along H_r towards $h =$ projected point of r' on H_r. Let T_r be the computed destination of r. Let p be any arbitrary position of r towards T_r. $Dist(p, r') \le Dist(r, r')$ (lemma 2). Thus, $Dist(r, r')$ reduces as r moves to T_r. If r' lies on H_r, r will perform side movement towards r' along H_r. $Dist(r, r')$ decreases. Thus the distance between r and r' decreases during side movement of r. r and r' remains mutually visible. Therefore connectivity does not break.

Note that when r is executing side movement, there exists no robot at its up, left and down. All robots in VC_r lies at right side of r. Thus, this lemma is also true if we replace r' by any arbitrary robot r'' in VC_r at right side of r.   □

Lemma 4. G_R *remains connected during diagonal movements of any robot* $r \in R$ *(Fig. 4).*

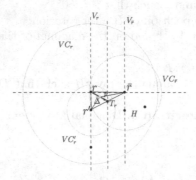

Fig. 4. Examples of diagonal movement of r (lemma 4)

Proof. r decides to move diagonally if it sees a robot say r' below on V_r and a robot say $\bar{r}$ in its right side. Note that r' and $\bar{r}$ can not move. As r moves diagonally $Dist(r, r')$ and $Dist(r, \bar{r})$ reduce (from lemma 2). Thus the mutual connectivity between r, r' and $r, \bar{r}$ remains intact during diagonal movements of r. If r' and $\bar{r}$ are replaced with any arbitrary robots on below r and right side of r, this lemma holds.   □

Combining lemmas 1, 3, and 4 we can state that:

Theorem 1. *The graph* G_R *remains connected during the execution of the algorithm.*

Now we will show that the robots will gather in finite time. (for the lack of space we will present only some of the proofs of the lemmas.)

Lemma 5. *Let* $V_{\mathcal{L}}{}^2$ *be the left most vertical line, i.e., no robots lie to its left. Either (i) one of the robots on* $V_{\mathcal{L}}$ *will leave, or (ii) all the robots on* $V_{\mathcal{L}}$ *will be gathered to the bottom-most robot on* $V_{\mathcal{L}}$, *in finite time.*

Corollary 1. *If there exists any robot at the right side of* $V_{\mathcal{L}}$, *then all robots on* $V_{\mathcal{L}}$ *will leave* $V_{\mathcal{L}}$ *in finite time.*

Let $V_{\mathcal{R}}{}^3$ be the right most vertical line of R.

---

[2] The vertical line passes through the left most robot(s) in R.
[3] The vertical line passes through the right most robot(s) in R.

Lemma 6. *The robots in R will not cross $V_\mathcal{R}$.*

Note that $V_\mathcal{L}$ changes due to robots movement, but $V_\mathcal{R}$ is fixed.

Lemma 7. *Distance between $V_\mathcal{L}$ and $V_\mathcal{R}$ reduces by a finite amount in finite number of movements of the robots.*

Proof. Suppose at time t, $V_\mathcal{L}$ is the left most vertical line for R. If $V_\mathcal{L} \neq V_\mathcal{R}$, then all the robots leave $V_\mathcal{L}$ after finite time and moves towards $V_\mathcal{R}$ (corollary 1). Note that if the robots perform right or diagonal movements to leave $V_\mathcal{L}$, the distances of the robots from $V_\mathcal{R}$ reduces. Suppose at time $t' > t$, when all the robots moves from $V_\mathcal{L}$ (at t), $V'_\mathcal{L}$ is the new left most vertical line. Since all the robots have been moves towards $V_\mathcal{R}$, the left most vertical line is also shifted towards $V_\mathcal{R}$. Thus, the distance between $V'_\mathcal{L}$ and $V_\mathcal{R}$ is less than the distance between $V_\mathcal{L}$ and $V_\mathcal{R}$. □

Following lemma 7 we can state that:

Lemma 8. *After a finite time there exists no vertical line between $V_\mathcal{L}$ and $V_\mathcal{R}$.*

Lemma 9. *All the robots in R will reach $V_\mathcal{R}$ in finite time.*

Proof. Suppose from lemma 8, at some time there exist only $V_\mathcal{L}$ and $V_\mathcal{R}$. The robots from $V_\mathcal{L}$ will leave after a finite time (corollary 1) and the distance between $V_\mathcal{L}$ and $V_\mathcal{R}$ reduces (lemma 7). Suppose, after some time the maximum distance between a robot in $V_\mathcal{L}$ and a robot in $V_\mathcal{R} \leq \Delta$. At this stage when the robots on $V_\mathcal{L}$ leave, they directly move on $V_\mathcal{R}$. Since, there are finite number of robots, all the robots reach $V_\mathcal{R}$ in finite time. □

Lemma 10. *If $V_\mathcal{L} = V_\mathcal{R}$, all the robots gather on down most robot in finite time.*

Finally we can state the following theorem.

Theorem 2. *The robots in R will gather in finite time.*

5   Conclusion

In this paper, we have proposed a gathering algorithm for a swarm of oblivious, asynchronous robots having nonuniform visibility ranges. Till now (both in [4] and this paper), for gathering robots in limited visibility, it have been assumed that the robots are mutually visible (though having unequal visibility ranges) and they have agreement in the direction of $X-Y$. The immediate open questions of this work would be as, (i) is gathering possible if the robots are not mutually visible? (ii) is gathering possible if the robots have agreement in one axis?

References

1. Cieliebak, M., Flocchini, P., Prencipe, G., Santoro, N.: Distributed computing by mobile robots: Gathering. SIAM Journal on Computing 41(4), 829–879 (2012)
2. Dieudonné, Y., Petit, F.: Self-stabilizing gathering with strong multiplicity detection. Theoretical Computer Science 428(0), 47–57 (2012)
3. Flocchini, P., Prencipe, G., Santoro, N.: Distributed Computing by Oblivious Mobile Robots. Synthesis Lectures on Distributed Computing Theory. Morgan & Claypool Publishers (2012)
4. Flocchini, P., Prencipe, G., Santoro, N., Widmayer, P.: Gathering of asynchronous robots with limited visibility. Theoretical Computer Science 337(1-3), 147–168 (2005)
5. Flocchini, P., Santoro, N., Viglietta, G., Yamashita, M.: Rendezvous of two robots with constant memory. In: Moscibroda, T., Rescigno, A.A. (eds.) SIROCCO 2013. LNCS, vol. 8179, pp. 189–200. Springer, Heidelberg (2013)
6. Prencipe, G.: Impossibility of gathering by a set of autonomous mobile robots. Theoretical Computer Science 384(2 - 3), 222–231 (2007); In: Pelc, A., Raynal, M. (eds.) SIROCCO 2005. LNCS, vol. 3499, pp. 222–231. Springer, Heidelberg (2005)

A Routing Calculus with Flooding Updates

Manish Gaur[1,2,*], Simon J. Gay[2], and Ian Mackie[3]

[1] Department of Computer Sc and Engg, IET Lucknow, India
[2] School of Computing Science, University of Glasgow, Glasgow, UK
[3] LIX, École Polytechnique, 91128 Palaiseau Cedex, France

Abstract. We propose a process calculus which explicitly models routing in a distributed computer network. We define a model which consists of a network of routers where the topology of routers is fixed. The calculus has three syntactic categories namely processes, nodes and systems. Processes reside in nodes which are connected to a specific routers which forms a system. Upon creation of new nodes, the routing tables are updated using flooding method. We show that the proposed routing calculi is reduction equivalent to its specification asynchronous distributed pi-calculus (ADpi). We believe that such modeling helps in prototyping the distributed routing algorithms.

Keywords: Routing, Process Calculi, Flooding, Specification, Computational Cost.

1 Introduction

In the last decade, we have witnessed the birth of many calculus intended to support programming of global distributed systems. These formalisms, in [7,12,6,4,11,1,2,10], in general provide constructs and mechanisms at different abstraction levels. These models don't consider the actual topology or routing of the process communication as the Internet connectivity is neither a clique nor a forest of trees. We present a name passing calculus, DR_π, (an elaboration of ADpi calculus [7]) with a realistic topology of nodes with routers to act as functions in determining the path from a source node to the destination node. We characterise the cost of communication to prove certain properties, such as path determination, about the routers with an aim to show their impact on the quality of service of the network. We develop the calculus for describing distributed computations explicitly in the presence of routers in an Internet like network. The new concept is that of a site for computational activity. It consists of named routers which host computational entities called *nodes*. Each node is directly connected to specific router. These sites run in parallel to form a large distributed network called a *system*. The communication between processes of any two nodes in this network is possible only through their respective routers. In Fig.1 we present a very simple network for the purpose of illustration. This network consists of three *routers* R_1, R_2 and R_3.

* We gratefully acknowledge the support received from commonwealth scholarship commission, UK (Ref: INCS-2005-145 and INCF-2012-252).

R. Natarajan et al. (Eds.): ICDCIT 2015, LNCS 8956, pp. 181–186, 2015.

The nodes l, m, n, o, p, q and r are connected to their respective *routers* R_1, R_2 and R_3 as shown. The routers are connected through a fixed topology. There connectivity is a directed graph and is defined as Γ_c. We shall view the routers as named functions which map set of node names to router names. Therefore the entries in the router function form a table called a *routing table*. The routing table at a router R is expressed as $\langle R \rangle$. The routing tables at each router are used to determine the path of communication between the communicating processes.

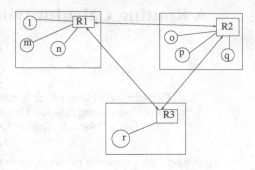

Fig. 1. A Simple Distributed Network with Routers

In DR_π, we describe a method for routing table update where upon creation of a new node we update all the routing tables in the network. The fundamental approach followed is very similar to *breadth first traversal* [3] of a graph. In DR_π, we use two types of messages. One called as control messages which are involved in propagating the update information and updating the routing tables about newly created nodes in the network. The other is a value propagating message which is used to propagate and deliver values to the waiting input processes. Whenever a new node is created a set of control messages propagate in a breadth first search manner across the network of routers to update all the routing tables. As soon as all the routing tables are updated the control messages are automatically discarded by the semantics of the language. This method of routing table update is known as Flooding[13]. We use two types of control messages; one for propagating the update information to all the connected routers and another for updating the router tables. The control messages don't participate in the communication of values between the processes.

A typical system in DR_π looks like $\langle R \rangle [\![n[P]]\!]$ where a process is P is located at node n. The node n is directly connected to the router R. The systems reduce with respect to the router connectivity Γ_c and therefore the reductions are defined on configurations. A configuration $\Gamma_c \rhd S$ consists of router connectivity Γ_c and system S.

In Sections 2 and 3 we describe the syntax and semantics of DR_π. Section 4 discusses the equivalence between DR_π and its specification. Section 5 is the conclusion.

2 Syntax

We will use $v, u, \ldots$ to describe values which may be a name or a variable. We use variables $a, b, c, \ldots$ to range over channel names C or node names $\mathcal{N}$. $n, m, \ldots$ are used to range over node names $\mathcal{N}$ and we use $R, R_1, R_2, \ldots$ to range over set of router names $\mathcal{R}$. The variables $k, l, \ldots$ range over integers to represent the cost of communication.

Further, we assume that sets of channel names, node names and router names are disjoint from each other. We also assume that router and node names are unique. There are three syntactic categories in the calculus: Systems, Nodes and Processes. The syntax of this calculus is described in Fig. 2.

We describe a system as $\langle R \rangle[\![M]\!]$ where R is a router and M is a nodes. All components in M are directly connected to the router R. Concurrency between two systems is expressed as $S \mid T$. $[R]M_{sg}^k(n, m, v@c)$ is a message at router R. This message propagates a value v sent by a process at node n to another process located at destination node m. Value v is supposed to be delivered at channel c of a waiting process at node m. k is an integer representing the number of hops the message has crossed on its way to the destination.

The control messages are categorised as update and propagate messages which we denote as $[R]M_{sg}(\text{update}, m, R')$ and $[R]M_{sg}(\text{prop}, m)$ respectively. The

S, T	$::=$		**Systems**
		$\langle R \rangle[\![M]\!]$	Router
		$S \mid T$	Concurrency
		$[R]M_{sg}^k(n, m, v@c)$	Value Messages
		$[R]M_{sg}(\text{update}, m, R')$	Update message
		$[R]M_{sg}(\text{prop}, m)$	Propagate message
		$(\text{new } d)\, S$	New name
		ε	Identity
M, N	$::=$		**Nodes**
		$m[T]$	Named processes
		$M \mid N$	Concurrency
		$(\text{new } d)\, M$	New name
		0	Identity
T, U	$::=$		**Process terms**
		$c?(x)\, T$	Input
		$m!\langle v@c \rangle$	Output
		if $u = v$ then T else U	Matching
		$(\text{new } b)\, T$	Channel name creation
		newnode m with P in Q	New node creation
		$T \mid U$	Concurrency
		$* T$	Repetition
		stop	Identity

Fig. 2. Syntax of DR_π

update message $[R]M_{sg}(\text{update}, m, R')$ is used to update the routing table $\langle R \rangle$ with an entry $\{m \to R'\}$ about the newly created node m. For example the message $[R]M_{sg}(\text{update}, m, R')$ will update the routing table at R with an entry $\{m \to R'\}$ provided the router R does not know about the node name m. If R already knows about m then this message at R is discarded. In this calculi we use a notation $\langle R \rangle(m) \downarrow$ to denote that node m is defined at the router R. Similarly we use $\langle R \rangle(m) \uparrow$ to denote that node m is undefined at router R.

The propagate message $[R]M_{sg}(\text{prop}, m)$ is used to propagate the new node name m across the network. The propagate message $[R]M_{sg}(\text{prop}, m)$ generates set of update messages at all the routers which are directly connected to R with an update entry $\{m \to R\}$.

We call these messages, update and propagate, *control messages*. Since control messages don't deliver any values therefore they are not used in determining the quality of services in delivery of values. For this reason the superscript representing the number of hops a message has already crossed in a routers network has been left blank in control messages whereas in the value carrying message $[R]M_{sg}^k(n, m, v@c)$, which is different than control messages, it has been represented as k. The term $(\text{new } d) S$ is a scoping mechanism for names as usual [9,7]. The syntax for nodes are described in [7]. Similarly the process terms are very similar to the terms in [7,9]. The definitions of bound variables and names in [7,9] are extended in a similar way in this calculus as well. Since names of routers and nodes are fixed and disjoint therefore they can't be renamed in this calculi. However α-conversion may be applied to channel names. We use a formal relation between the systems called *structural equivalence*, intuitively to represent the systems as same computational entities. This is defined in a conventional way [7,9]. We use the notion $\equiv$ to represent this relation. Structural equivalence is defined for each syntactic categories. However, the process equivalence is inherited by the node equivalence and the node equivalence is inherited by the system equivalence. For example $\langle R \rangle [\![N]\!] \equiv \langle R \rangle [\![S]\!]$ is true provided $N \equiv S$ where N and S are nodes at router R. There are certain axioms which are standard and applicable to all syntactic categories. These standard axioms are similar to standard pi-calculus structural equivalence axioms [7,9]. The standard axioms for structural equivalence, which is applicable at all syntactic categories, is same as described in the conventional manner at [7]. We use two additional notations; one as $Adj(R_1)$ to represent $Adj(R_1) = \{R_2 \mid (R_1, R_2) \in \Gamma_c\}$ and the other $\Gamma_c \triangleright \prod_{Adj(R_1)} [R]M_{sg}(\text{update}, k, R_1)$ to mean $[R_2]M_{sg}(\text{update}, k, R_1) \mid [R_3]M_{sg}(\text{update}, k, R_1) \mid \ldots \mid [R_n]M_{sg}(\text{update}, k, R_1)$ where $Adj(R_1) = \{R_2, \ldots, R_n\}$.

3   Reduction Semantics

The reduction semantics of DR_π are defined on configurations $\Gamma_c \triangleright S$. A typical configuration reduction step is described as $\Gamma_c \triangleright S \longrightarrow^k \Gamma_c \triangleright S'$ where the cost of this reduction is k and a system S reduces to S' with respect to the router connectivity Γ_c. The reduction rules for DR_π are given in Figures 3 and 4. The reduction rules (R-CONTX), (R-STRUCT) in Figure 4 are about compositional reductions and reductions that are defined upto structural equivalence. These rules are directly inherited from [7]. The rules (R-OUT) and (R-IN) in Figure 3 are about message creation and delivery. We have only one rule for message forwarding for those messages which carry a value for delivery to a waiting input process at some node. For example in a configuration $\Gamma_c \triangleright [R_1]M_{sg}^k(n, m, v@c) \mid \langle R_2 \rangle [\![N]\!] \mid S$, suppose $\langle R_1 \rangle (m) = R_2$ then this message is hopped to router R_2. This means that the configuration $\Gamma_c \triangleright [R_1]M_{sg}^k(n, m, v@c) \mid \langle R_2 \rangle [\![N]\!] \mid S$ is reduced to $\Gamma_c \triangleright [R_2]M_{sg}^{k+1}(n, m, v@c) \mid \langle R_2 \rangle [\![N]\!] \mid S$. Note that the superscript k is incremented by one to record the number of hops the message has travelled so far. This reduction is irrespective of the knowledge of the routing table $\langle R_2 \rangle$ about the $n(v)$ if $v \in \mathcal{NN}$. This is because, in case $\langle R_2 \rangle(v) \uparrow$, there are separate control messages which will eventually update the router table of R_2 about $n(v)$.

The reduction rules about new node creation and routing table updates are significant and they follow flooding mechanism (in a breadth first traversal mechanism [3]) to update the routing tables about the newly created nodes. These rules, (R-NEWNODE − CREATION), (R-UPDATE − I), (R-UPDATE − II) and (R-PROPAGATE), are self explanatory in Figure 3.

(R-OUT)
$$\Gamma_c \triangleright \langle R \rangle [\![n[m!\langle v@c \rangle \mid P] \mid N]\!] \longrightarrow \Gamma_c \triangleright [R] M_{sg}^0(n, m, v@c) \mid \langle R \rangle [\![n[P] \mid N]\!]$$

(R-MSG−FWD)
$$\frac{(R_1, R_2) \in \Gamma_c \quad \langle R_1 \rangle(m) = R_2}{\Gamma_c \triangleright [R_1] M_{sg}^k(n, m, v@c) \mid \langle R_2 \rangle [\![N]\!] \mid S \longrightarrow \Gamma_c \triangleright [R_2] M_{sg}^{k+1}(n, m, v@c) \mid \langle R_2 \rangle [\![N]\!] \mid S}$$

(R-IN)
$$\frac{\langle R \rangle(m) = R}{\Gamma_c \triangleright [R] M_{sg}^k(n, m, v@c) \mid \langle R \rangle [\![m[c?(x) P] \mid N]\!] \longrightarrow^k \Gamma_c \triangleright \langle R \rangle [\![m[P\{v/x\}] \mid N]\!]}$$

(R-NEWNODE−CREATION)
$$\Gamma_c \triangleright \langle R \rangle [\![n[\text{newnode } m \text{ with } P \text{ in } Q]]\!] \longrightarrow \Gamma_c \triangleright (\text{new } m) \langle R \rangle [\![n[Q] \mid m[P]]\!] \mid [R] M_{sg}(\text{update}, m, R)$$

(R-MATCH)
$$\Gamma_c \triangleright \langle R \rangle [\![n[\text{if } v = v \text{ then } P \text{ else } Q]]\!] \longrightarrow \Gamma_c \triangleright \langle R \rangle [\![n[P]]\!]$$

(R-MISMATCH)
$$\Gamma_c \triangleright \langle R \rangle [\![n[\text{if } v_1 = v_2 \text{ then } P \text{ else } Q]]\!] \longrightarrow \Gamma_c \triangleright \langle R \rangle [\![n[Q]]\!] \quad v_1 \neq v_2$$

(R-UPDATE−I)
$$\frac{\langle R_1 \rangle(m) \uparrow}{\Gamma_c \triangleright \langle R_1 \rangle [\![N]\!] \mid [R_1] M_{sg}(\text{update}, m, R_2) \longrightarrow \Gamma_c \triangleright \langle R_1 \{m \to R_2\} \rangle [\![N]\!] \mid [R_1] M_{sg}(\text{prop}, m)}$$

(R-UPDATE−II)
$$\frac{\langle R_1 \rangle(m) \downarrow}{\Gamma_c \triangleright \langle R_1 \rangle [\![N]\!] \mid [R_1] M_{sg}(\text{update}, m, R_2) \longrightarrow \Gamma_c \triangleright \langle R_1 \rangle [\![N]\!]}$$

(R-PROPAGATE)
$$\Gamma_c \triangleright [R_1] M_{sg}(\text{prop}, m) \mid S \longrightarrow \Gamma_c \triangleright \prod_{Adj(R_1)} [R] M_{sg}(\text{update}, m, R_1) \mid S \quad Adj(R_1) \in S$$

Fig. 3. Reduction semantics for DR$_\pi$

How do we know that the reduction semantics is reasonable and does not introduce inconsistencies in the system? We know because we can prove that if a configuration is "coherent" before we apply a reduction it remains "coherent". "Coherence" will mean a series of properties, which summed together gets us the notion of a well-formed configuration. As an example all the routing tables must have knowledge of the propagating node names. Therefore this should be

(R-STRUCT)
$$\frac{S \equiv S', \ \Gamma_c \triangleright S' \longrightarrow^k \Gamma_c \triangleright R', \ R' \equiv R}{\Gamma_c \triangleright S \longrightarrow^k \Gamma_c \triangleright R}$$

(R-CONTX)
$$\frac{\Gamma_c \triangleright S_1 \longrightarrow^k \Gamma_c \triangleright S_1'}{\Gamma_c \triangleright S_1 \mid S_2 \longrightarrow^k \Gamma_c \triangleright S_1' \mid S_2}$$
$$\Gamma_c \triangleright S_2 \mid S_1 \longrightarrow^k \Gamma_c \triangleright S_2 \mid S_1'$$
$$\Gamma_c \triangleright (\text{new } d) S_1 \longrightarrow^k \Gamma_c \triangleright (\text{new } d) S_1'$$

Fig. 4. contd...Reduction semantics for DR$_\pi$

a condition on a well formed configurations. The notion of well formed configurations in DR$_\pi$ is adapted from the established theory of typed behavioural equivalence [8,5]. It's easy to show that conditions on well-formed configurations are preserved by semantic reductions.

4   Equivalence between DR$_\pi$ and its Specification

We shall now try to establish an equivalence of DR$_\pi$ with a specification of it. ADpi [7] like language where located processes are called nodes, and each pair of nodes are directly connected can be a specification for DR$_\pi$. In [7], as all pair of nodes are directly connected they form a clique of the graph of connected nodes. Intuitively, D$_\pi$ is a top level view of DR$_\pi$.

We show that both languages, DR$_\pi$ and D$_\pi$, are reduction equivalent after abstracting away the details of routers and paths from DR$_\pi$. For the purpose of abstraction of routers and paths from DR$_\pi$ we define a function, $\Im$, over DR$_\pi$ system to a D$_\pi$ system. Function $\Im$ abstracts away the routers from a DR$_\pi$ term.

5   Conclusion

We described the routing calculi DR$_\pi$, where the crucial role of routers in determining the quality of communication services in a distributed network is demonstrated. We justified this model by showing that this is, in fact, implementation of ADpi [7]. The basic design of the model itself shows that it is closer to the real distributed networks.

References

1. Barbanera, F., Bugliesi, M., Dezani-Ciancaglini, M., Sassone, V.: A calculus of bounded capacities. In: Saraswat, V.A. (ed.) ASIAN 2003. LNCS, vol. 2896, pp. 205–223. Springer, Heidelberg (2003)
2. Cardelli, L., Gordon, A.D.: Mobile ambients. Theor. Comput. Sci. 240(1), 177–213 (2000)
3. Cormen, T.H., Leiserson, C.E., Rivest, R.L., Stein, C.: Introduction to Algorithms, 2nd edn. MIT Press (2003)
4. Gaur, M., Hennessy, M.: Counting the cost in the picalculus (extended abstract). Electronic Notes in Theoretical Computer Science (ENTCS) 229(3), 117–129 (2009)
5. Gay, S.J., Hole, M.: Subtyping for session types in the pi-calculus. Acta Inf. 42(2-3), 191–225 (2005)
6. Griffin, T.G., Sobrinho, J.L.: Metarouting. In: SIGCOMM, pp. 1–12 (2005)
7. Hennessy, M.: A distributed Pi-Calculus. Cambridge University Press (2007)
8. Hennessy, M., Rathke, J.: Typed behavioural equivalences for processes in the presence of subtyping. Mathematical Structures in Computer Science 14(5), 651–684 (2004)
9. Milner, R.: Communicating and mobile systems: The π-Calculus. Cambridge University Press (1999)
10. Nicola, R.D., Gorla, D., Pugliese, R.: Basic observables for a calculus for global computing. Inf. Comput. 205(10), 1491–1525 (2007)
11. Orava, F., Parrow, J.: An algebraic verification of a mobile network. Formal Asp. Comput. 4(6), 497–543 (1992)
12. Sewell, P., Wojciechowski, P.T., Pierce, B.C.: Location-independent communication for mobile agents: A two-level architecture. In: Bal, H.E., Cardelli, L., Belkhouche, B. (eds.) ICCL 1998 Workshop. LNCS, vol. 1686, pp. 1–31. Springer, Heidelberg (1999)
13. Tanenbaum, A.S.: Computer Networks. Pearson Education, Inc., Upper Saddle River (2003)

k-Distinct Strong Minimum Energy Topology Problem in Wireless Sensor Networks

Bhawani Sankar Panda[1], D. Pushparaj Shetty[2], and Arti Pandey[1]

[1] Computer Science and Application Group
Department of Mathematics
Indian Institute of Technology Delhi, Hauz Khas
New Delhi 110016, India
{bspanda,artipandey}@maths.iitd.ac.in
[2] Department of Mathematical and Computational Sciences
National Institute of Technology Karnataka 575025, India
prajshetty@nitk.edu.in

Abstract. Given a set of sensors, the strong minimum energy topology (SMET) problem is to assign transmit power to each sensor such that the resulting topology containing only bidirectional links is strongly connected and the total energy of all the nodes is minimized. The **SMET** problem is known to be NP-hard. Currently available sensors in the market support a finite set of transmission ranges. So we consider the k-DISTINCT-SMET problem, where only k transmission power levels are used. We prove that the k-DISTINCT-SMET problem is NP-complete for $k \geq 3$. However, on the positive side, we show that the 2-DISTINCT-SMET problem can be solved in polynomial time. The energy cost of transmitting a bit is higher than the cost of computation, and hence it may be advantageous to organize the sensors into clusters and form a hierarchical structure. This motivated the study of k-**Distinct-rStrong Minimum Energy Hierarchical Topology** (k-**Distinct-rSMEHT**) **problem:** Given a sensor network consisting of n sensors, and integers k and r, assign transmit powers to all sensors out of the k distinct power levels such that (i) the graph induced using only the bi-directional links is connected, (ii) at most r sensors are connected to two or more sensors by a bidirectional link and (iii) the sum of the transmit powers of all the sensors is minimum. We Propose a $\frac{r+1}{2}$- approximation algorithm for the k-Distinct-rSMEHT problem for any fixed r and arbitrary k.

Keywords: Wireless Sensor Network, Topology Control Problem, Transmission Power Assignment, Graph Theory, NP-complete, Heuristics.

1 Introduction

A wireless sensor network (WSN) consists of a collection of autonomous devices, each of which consists of a digital circuitry, radio transceiver, transmission amplifier and a small battery. The communication among these nodes is based on radio propagation. Since the battery of each sensor is of limited capacity

R. Natarajan et al. (Eds.): ICDCIT 2015, LNCS 8956, pp. 187–192, 2015.

and it is not possible to replace the battery always, energy conservation is a critical issue in order to increase the lifetime of a sensor network. Each sensor node u has an omni-directional antenna, which can transmit signal within a certain specified range $r(u)$. Node u can directly communicate with other nodes located within its range. In general, communication is *multi-hop* in nature, where intermediate nodes are used to relay the transmission until destination is reached.

Given a set of sensors S, and a connectivity constraint Π, the minimum range assignment problem, MIN-RANGE(Π) is to assign transmission range f, to the nodes in S such that given connectivity constraint Π is satisfied and $cost(f)$ is minimum. The connectivity constraint Π could be simple connected, strongly connected or bi connected (see [4]). The symmetric connectivity is the strong form of connectivity among all, as it contains only bidirectional links. The bidirectional/symmetric edges are preferred in wireless sensor networks, because the signal transmitted over a link are to be acknowledged. Bidirectional links also simplify routing protocols. The current MAC layer protocols such as IEEE 802.11 and S-MAC take into account only bidirectional links. The bidirectional range assignment is studied by cheng *et al.* [3] and they named this problem as *Strong Minimum Energy Topology* (SMET) problem. The SMET problem is known to be NP-hard [3].

Currently available sensors in the market support a finite set of transmission ranges. So we consider k-DISTINCT-SMET problem, where only k transmission power levels are used. We prove that the k-DISTINCT-SMET problem is NP-complete for $k \geq 3$. However, on the positive side, we show that the 2-DISTINCT-SMET problem can be solved in polynomial time. The energy cost of transmitting a bit is higher than the cost of computation, and hence it may be advantageous to organize the sensors into clusters and form a hierarchical structure. This motivated the study of k-**Distinct** r **Strong Minimum Energy Hierarchical Topology** (k-**Distinct-rSMEHT**) **problem:** Given a sensor network consisting of n sensors and an integer r, assign transmit powers to all sensors out of the k distinct power levels such that (i) the graph induced using only the bi-directional links is connected, (ii) at most r sensors are connected to two or more sensors by a bidirectional link and (iii) the sum of the transmit powers of all the sensors is minimum. We propose a $\frac{r+1}{2}$- approximation algorithm for the k-Distinct-rSMEHT problem for any fixed r and arbitrary k.

The rest of the paper is organized as follows. In Section 2, we present a summary of related work. In Section 3, we define the SMET problem and the special cases of the SMET problem. In Section 4, we propose an efficient algorithm for the 2-DISTINCT-SMET problem. In Section 5, we present the k-Distinct-rSMEHT problem for arbitrary r and k and propose a $(\frac{r+1}{2})$-approximation algorithm for the k-Distinct-rSMEHT problem for fixed r and arbitrary k. Finally, Section 6 concludes the paper.

2   Previous and Related Work

A WSN is modeled as a complete weighted undirected graph $G = (V, E, c)$, where $c : E \to \mathbb{R}$ is the cost function. Given a spanning sub graph H of G, the cost of H is defined as $C(H) = \sum_{e \in E(H)} c(e)$. For a vertex $u \in V$, the power of u is the maximum cost of an edge in H, incident on u, i.e $P_H(u) = \max_{uv \in E(H)} C(uv)$. The power of a graph is the sum of powers of its nodes. We are interested in the minimum energy spanning subgraph problem where the subgraph is a spanning tree. Minimum energy spanning tree problem is NP-hard for the sensors on a 2-dimensional plane (see [3]).

The minimum energy symmetric connectivity problem is studied in [3]. For more details about topology control in WSN, we refer to [8].

Prim-incremental heuristic for the SMET problem was proposed by [3]. Valley-free heuristic for the SMET problem was proposed by [1]. Panda and Shetty proposed Kruskal-incremental based heuristic algorithm [5] and local search based heuristic algorithm [6] for the SMET problem. A 2-hop strong minimum energy rooted topology (2*h*-SMERT) and its algorithmic aspects are presented in [7].

3   Special Cases of Strong Minimum Energy Topology Problem

Definition 1 (SMET). *Given a set of sensors in the plane, compute the transmit power of each sensor such that there exists at least one bidirectional path between any pair of sensors and the sum of transmit powers of all the sensors is minimized.*

Let $T = (V, E')$ be a spanning tree of a weighted graph $G = (V, E,)$ having cost function w. Let $P_T(v) = \max\{w(uv) | uv \in E(G)\}$ and $P(T) = \sum_{v \in V} P_T(v)$. The SMET problem now reduces to the problem of finding a spanning tree T of G such that $P(T)$ is minimum. Formally, we define the SMET problem as follows:

Problem: SMET

Instance: (K_n, w, M), where K_n is a complete graph with n nodes, $w : E(K_n) \to \mathbb{R}^+$ is the weight function, and M is a positive real value.

Question: Does there exist a spanning tree T of K_n such that $P(T) \leq M$?

As the status of the SMET problem is known to be NP-hard [3], we examine the computational complexity of the following special cases of the SMET problem.

1 *k*-DISTINCT-SMET Problem: The SMET problem with the restriction that the admissible range of a node is one of the *k*-distinct power threshold values. This special case is important as the currently available sensors in the market supports a discrete set of power ranges.

2 *k-Distinct r Strong Minimum Energy Hierarchical Topology (k-Distinct-rSMEHT) problem:* Given a sensor network consisting of *n* sensors and integers *k* and *r*, assign transmit powers to all sensors out of the *k* distinct power

levels such that (i) the graph induced using only the bi-directional links is connected, (ii) at most r sensors are connected to two or more sensors by a bidirectional link and (iii) the sum of the transmit powers of all the sensors is minimum.

4 k-Distinct-SMET Problem

In practice, it is usually impossible to assign arbitrary power levels to the transmitters of a radio network. Instead one can only choose from a constant number of pre-set power levels corresponding to a constant number of ranges [2]. In this context, we study the decision version of the k-DISTINCT-SMET problem which is formally defined below:

Problem: k-DISTINCT-SMET-D
Instance: (K_n, w, M), where K_n is the complete graph with n nodes, $w :$
$E(K_n) \rightarrow \{c_1, c_2, \ldots, c_k\}$ is a weight function, and M is a positive real number.
Question: Does there exist a spanning tree T of K_n such that $P(T) \leq M$?

Theorem 1. *The k-DISTINCT-SMET-D problem is NP-complete.*

Proof. The proof is omitted due to space constraint.

4.1   The 2-Distinct-SMET Problem

Consider the case where only two power threshold levels, say, high and low are used. We call this problem 2-DISTINCT-SMET problem. Power assignment in radio networks with two power levels is studied by Carmi and Katz [2].

Let c_1 and c_2 be the two distinct edge costs assigned to K_n. Let $E(c_i) = \{e | w(e) = c_i\}$, $1 \leq i \leq 2$.

Theorem 2. *An optimal solution for 2-DISTINCT-SMET problem can be found in polynomial time.*

Proof. The proof is omitted due to space constraint.

5 k-Distinct-rSMEHT Problem

Most wireless networks are structured hierarchically, where some nodes play the role of cluster heads and others as ordinary nodes. So we a study a topology control problem where there are k distinct power levels and at most r sensors are connected to two or more sensors by a bidirectional link and the total power of the network is minimized. The k-Distinct-r SMEHT Problem is formally defined as follows.

Problem: k-DISTINCT-r SMEHT-D
Instance: (K_n, w, r, M), where K_n is a complete graph with n nodes, $w :$

$E(K_n) \to \{c_1, c_2, \ldots, c_k\}$ is a weight function, r and M are positive real numbers.

Question: Does there exist a spanning tree T of K_n such that $P(T) \leq M$ and T has at most r non-pendent vertices?

Theorem 3. *The k-DISTINCT-r SMEHT-D problem is NP-complete.*

Proof. The proof is omitted due to space constraint.

5.1 Approximation Algorithm for the *k*-Distinct-*r*SMEHT Problem for Fixed *r*

Given a weighted complete graph (K_n, w) and a fixed positive integer constant r, we propose a $\frac{r+1}{2}$-approximation algorithm for the k-Distinct-rSMEHT problem. In order to explain our algorithm we define, the extension of a tree as follows:

Definition 2 (Extension of a Tree). *Let $T^l = (V_l, E^l)$ be any tree such that $V_l \subset V(K_n)$. Let $V_l = \{v_1, v_2, \ldots, v_l\}$. Let $X_1 = \{x \mid x \in V \setminus \{v_1, v_2, \ldots, v_l\}$ and $w(xv_1) \leq w(xv_j)\ 2 \leq j \leq l\}$. Let $X_i = \{x \mid x \in V \setminus \{v_1 \ldots v_l\} \cup (\cup_{j=1}^{i-1} X_j)$ and $w(xv_i) \leq w(xv_j)\ 1 \leq j \leq l, j \neq i\}$, for $i > 1$. Let $E_i = \{v_i x \mid x \in X_i\}, 1 \leq i \leq l$. The extension of T^l, denoted as $Ex(T^l)$, is defined by $Ex(T^l) = (V, Ex(E^l))$, where $Ex(E^l) = E^l \cup (\cup_{i=1}^l E_i)$.*

Let T^l be tree of K_n. If T^l is not a spanning tree, then extension of tree T^l is used to construct a spanning tree T of the complete graph K_n.

Lemma 1. *Let T be a minimum energy tree of an instance (K_n, w, r) of the k-Distinct-rSMEHT problem. Let $v_1, v_2, \ldots, v_l, l \leq r$, be the non-pendant vertices of T and $v_{l+1}, v_{l+2}, \ldots, v_n$ be the pendant vertices of T. Let $T' = T[\{v_1, v_2, \ldots, v_l\}]$. Let T'' be the extension of T'. Then, $P(T'') \leq \frac{k+1}{2} P(T)$.*

Proof. The proof is omitted due to space constraint.

Algorithm 1. Algorithm k-Distinct-rSMEHT

    Input: (K_n, w, r), where K_n is a complete graph having cost function
            $w : E(K_n) \to \{c_1, c_2, \ldots, c_k\}$, and r is a fixed integer constant.
    Output: A spanning tree T with at most r non-pendant vertices.

```
1  begin
2  |    Let T be any arbitrary spanning tree of K_n having exactly r non-pendant
   |    vertices.
3  |    for each subset V_r of V(K_n) of r elements do
4  |    |    for each spanning trees T_r of K_n[V_r] do
5  |    |    |    if P(Ex(T_r)) ≤ P(T) then
6  |    |    |    |    T = Ex(T_r);
7  |    |    |    end
8  |    |    end
9  |    end
10 |    output(T),
11 end
```

Note that $Ex(T^l)$ is a spanning tree of K_n and can be computed in $O(nl)$ time. Let $K_n[V_r]$ denote the subgraph of K_n induced by vertices in $V_r \subset V$. We now propose an algorithm to construct a minimum energy spanning tree T of K_n with at most r non-pendent vertices.

Theorem 4. *The algorithm k-Distinct-rSMEHT is a $\frac{r+1}{2}$-approximation algorithm.*

Proof. The proof is omitted due to space constraint.

6   Conclusion

In this paper we study the k-Distinct-SMET problem and the k-Distinct-rSMEHT problem. We proved that the k-Distinct-SMET problem is NP-complete for $k > 2$. We proposed a polynomial time solution for the k-Distinct-SMET problem, for $k = 2$. We proposed a $\frac{r+1}{2}$- approximation algorithm for the k-Distinct-rSMEHT problem for any fixed r and arbitrary k.

References

1. Aneja, Y.P., Bari, A., Jaekel, A., Chandrasekaran, R., Nair, K.P.K.: Minimum energy strong bidirectional topology for ad hoc wireless sensor networks. In: IEEE International Conference on Communications, ICC 2009, pp. 1–5. IEEE (2009)
2. Carmi, P., Katz, M.J.: Power assignment in radio networks with two power levels. Algorithmica 47(2), 183–201 (2007)
3. Cheng, X., Narahari, B., Simha, R., Cheng, M.X., Liu, D.: Strong minimum energy topology in wireless sensor networks: Np-completeness and heuristics. IEEE Transactions on Mobile Computing 2(3), 248–256 (2003)
4. Fuchs, B.: On the hardness of range assignment problems. Networks 52(4), 183–195 (2008)
5. Panda, B.S., Pushparaj Shetty, D.: An incremental power greedy heuristic for strong minimum energy topology in wireless sensor networks. In: Natarajan, R., Ojo, A. (eds.) ICDCIT 2011. LNCS, vol. 6536, pp. 187–196. Springer, Heidelberg (2011)
6. Panda, B.S., Pushparaj Shetty, D.: A local search based approximation algorithm for strong minimum energy topology problem in wireless sensor networks. In: Hota, C., Srimani, P.K. (eds.) ICDCIT 2013. LNCS, vol. 7753, pp. 398–409. Springer, Heidelberg (2013)
7. Panda, B.S., Pushparaj Shetty, D.: Strong minimum energy 2-hop rooted topology for hierarchical wireless sensor networks. Journal of Combinatorial Optimization, 1–18 (2013), http://dx.doi.org/10.1007/s10878-013-9683-z
8. Santi, P.: Topology Control in Wireless Ad Hoc and Sensor Networks. John Wiley & Sons Ltd (2005)

Path Planning Algorithm for Mobile Anchor in Connected Sensor Networks

Kaushik Mondal[1], Arindam Karmakar[2], and Partha Sarathi Mandal[1]

[1] Indian Institute of Technology Guwahati, India
[2] Tezpur University, India

Abstract. Path planning is an important issue for localization with mobile anchor in wireless sensor networks as movement of the mobile anchor consumes more energy compared to static anchor. Most of the works available in the literature either looks into the aspect of reducing path length of the mobile anchor or tries to increase localization accuracy. In this paper we propose a cost-effective movement strategy i.e., path planning for a mobile anchor which reduces path length and at the same time localization can be done using localization scheme [3], which yields good accuracy. Simulation results show improvement over existing work [4] in terms of both path length and localization accuracy.

Keywords: Path Planning, Connected Networks, Mobile Anchor, Range-free Localization, Wireless Sensor Networks.

1 Introduction

Generally several static anchors are used to localize sensor networks, whereas one mobile anchor with a suitable path planning can substitute those static anchors. There are localization schemes [3,6,7] in literature which use mobile anchor for localization. One can save large number of anchors with deployment cost in the expense of the mobility of the mobile anchor. So, path planning of the mobile anchor has become an important issue in the area of localization. In most of the existing works [2,4] where path planning has been done for connected network, ranging techniques have been used. Our aim is to propose a movement strategy which uses connectivity information only for anchors next step of movement while adapting with existing range-free localization schemes which yields better accuracy. Topology-based path planning problems can be viewed as a graph traversal problem. Sensors have information about their neighbors which they send to the mobile anchor for determining the path. Kim et al. proposed a path planning in [2] for randomly deployed sensors using trilateration method for localization. Mitton et al. in [4] proposed a depth first traversal scheme *DREAMS* by the mobile anchor to localize the sensors. Both these works need range estimations. Mobile anchor first visits a sensor in *DREAMS*, using random movement before performing depth-first traversal on the network. An already visited localized sensor provides information to the anchor about it's next destination. Algorithm stops when anchor returns to the first sensor.

R. Natarajan et al. (Eds.): ICDCIT 2015, LNCS 8956, pp. 193–198, 2015.

During depth-first traversal, anchor performs distance-based heuristic movement using received signal strength (RSS) from sensors. Chang et al. proposed another path planning algorithm of the mobile anchor in [1] mobile sensor calculates its trajectory by moving around already localized sensors.

Our Contribution. In this paper we provide a hexagonal movement strategy for mobile anchor. Our proposed distributed range-free movement strategy localizes all sensors within $r/2$ error-bound in a connected network, where r is the transmission range of the sensors and the mobile anchor. To the best of our knowledge, this is the first work where localization and path planning both have been done using connectivity of the network without any range estimation. Simulation results show improvement over existing work [4] in terms of both path length and localization accuracy.

2   Path Planning for Connected Network

In this section we discuss path planning to localize an arbitrary connected network of any number of sensors. The mobile anchor broadcasts beacon with its position information after every t time interval. Distance traveled by the mobile anchor between two consecutive broadcasts of beacon is called *beacon distance* and is denoted by u. The circle with radius r centering at the sensor, where r is the communication range of the sensor. Largest regular hexagon inscribed within the communication circle of any sensor is defined as LRH. Definition of beacon point is given below.

Definition 1. (*Beacon point*) *The position of the anchor that is extracted from the beacon received by a sensor at time x is denoted as a beacon point for the sensor if and only if the sensor does not receive any beacon either in time interval $[x - t_0, x)$ or in time interval $(x, x + t_0]$, where t_0 is the waiting time such that $t < t_0 < 2t$ and t is time interval of periodical broadcasts of beacon by the anchor.*

The algorithm begins with localizing a sensor by random movement of the anchor. The localized sensor broadcasts its position which is received by the anchor and according to our movement strategy, the anchor reaches at any point on the communication circle of the localized sensor. Then anchor computes the LRH inscribed within the communication circle with that point as a vertex. At the same time all the other vertices of LRH are also computed by the anchor. Then the anchor starts moving along the LRH and broadcasting beacons with its current position along with all vertices of the LRH at regular interval so that any sensor which receives a beacon, knows the LRH. At the same time all the neighbors of the localized sensor marks at least two beacon points which help them to compute two probable positions of themselves according to the scheme [3]. In our work we do not need three beacon points to localize the sensor like the scheme [3]. Hexagonal movement strategy helps to reduce the requirement of beacon points from three to two. One may find the detail description in [5] along with the proofs of the theorems stated in this paper.

We have found conditions in the following theorem to make the error bound of the scheme [3] less than $r/2$. This error bound ensures localization of all sensors within $r/2$ error according to our proposed path planning as we have used the scheme [3] for localization.

Theorem 1. *Using the localization scheme [3], if $l \geq (r-u)$ then the localization error remains less than $r/2$ for beacon distance $u < r/7.5$, where l is the distance between two beacon points and r is the communication range.*

Theorem 2. *If an anchor completes its movement along the LRH around a sensor Q, then all other sensors lying inside the circle of radius $3r/2$ centering at Q can be localized with error less than $r/2$ for suitable beacon distance u, if Q has been localized within $r/2$ error.*

Theorem 3. *If a mobile anchor completes its movement along the LRH around a sensor which is localized within $r/2$ error, then all its neighbors are localized within $r/2$ error.*

3   Distributed Algorithm for Path Planning

We assume sensors form a connected network. The number of sensors in the network is not an input of our algorithm. Each sensor has unique id and knows the id of its one hop neighbors. Set of one hop neighbors of a sensor i is denoted by $nbd(i)$. We define *NLN-degree(i)* as the number of non-localized neighbors of a sensor i. Initially NLN-degree(i) = $|nbd(i)|$, where $|nbd(i)|$ is the cardinality of the set $nbd(i)$. Mobile anchor decides its path according to the Algorithm 1: HEXAGONALLOCALIZATION.

Algorithm 1. HEXAGONALLOCALIZATION

---

1. Mobile anchor localizes a sensor by its random movement then PUSH id of the sensor into the STACK.
2. Computes LRH centering at sensor i which is at the TOP of the STACK and broadcasts beacons with period t until the LRH movement completes.
3. The anchor moves $r/2$ distance towards i and sends a message to i for next destination of its movement.
4. Sensor i sends a message to all $j \in nbd(i)$ for NLN-degree(j) with their positions.
5. On receiving the replies, sensor i selects a neighbor sensor j' that achieves the value max{NLN-degree(j)$|j \in nbd(i)$} and sends position of j' with NLN-degree(j') to the anchor for next destination of movement.
6. If NLN-degree(j') > 0 then the anchor PUSH j' into the STACK and moves to the closest point of the communication circle of j' and executes step 2, otherwise POP from the STACK.
7. The algorithm terminates if STACK is empty, otherwise the anchor revisits the sensor whose id is at the TOP of the STACK and executes step 3.

Algorithm 1 ensures localization of all sensors in a connected network. Time complexity of the proposed algorithm is same with complexity of Depth First Search in a connected graph.

4   Simulation Results

We have used MATLAB platform to study the performances of our proposed schemes. We have randomly generated connected graphs of sensors in a 50 meter × 50 meter square region. According to the section 2, we have taken values of beacon distance $u < r/7.5$. Following Fig. 1 shows the hexagonal movement path of a mobile anchor through the network during localization, where black thick lines are transition path between LRHs. The blue crosses and red circles are the actual and calculated positions of the sensors respectively and pairs are joined by dotted lines. The number of sensors n, communication ranges r, path length D and average positioning error are given in the caption of each figure. All the values showing in the tables and figures are in meters. As the area remains fixed and connectivity is maintained by increasing number of sensors along with decreasing communication range of sensors and the anchor, path length does not increase much with the number of sensors. We have also simulated path lengths of the mobile anchor for different number of sensors with communication range 10 meter. As number of sensors varies from 100 to 300, path length varies from 1490 to 1754 meter as shown in Table 2. As average degree increases with the number of sensors in a fixed region, one LRH movement localizes more number of sensors (approximately equal to the average degree), so path length does not increase much with the number of sensors. By average degree, we mean average number of one hop neighbors each node have.   In Table 1, we have shown localization

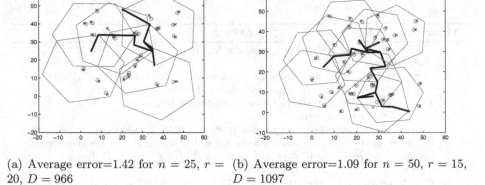

(a) Average error=1.42 for $n = 25$, $r =$ (b) Average error=1.09 for $n = 50$, $r = 15$,
20, $D = 966$ $D = 1097$

Fig. 1. Hexagonal movement pattern in a connected network

error for different communication ranges r and beacon distances u. Localization error decreases as beacon distance decreases for any fixed communication range. Here, $u = r/k$, where $k > 7.5$ according to Theorem 1 and Theorem 2. We have compared path length and average error of our algorithm with [4]. For comparison, we have considered same parameters as in [4]. Sensors are randomly

Table 1. Showing average error (in meters) for different communication range and beacon distance

Beacon distance → Communication range(↓)	$r/10$	$r/15$	$r/20$	$r/25$	$r/30$
10	1.47	1.10	0.61	0.42	0.33
15	2.35	1.36	1.01	0.73	0.54
20	2.74	1.90	1.28	0.93	0.62
25	4.35	2.38	1.53	1.22	0.94
30	5.89	3.14	2.12	1.64	1.13

Table 2. Average path length (in meters) of our scheme varying number of sensors

No. of sensors	100	150	200	250	300
Average path length (meter)	1490	1550	1640	1675	1754

deployed over a square region of side length 1000 meter forming a connected graph. Average degree of vertices in the connected graph is varied from 7 to 35 by increasing number of sensors, where a sensor represents a vertex. We have compared path length of our proposed algorithm with $DREAMS - LMST - Closest$ as it provides minimum path length among the methods proposed in [4]. Simulation results show that, path length of our technique is higher than $DREAMS - LMST - Closest$ for average degree 7 and 10 as shown in Fig. 2. But as average degree increases, our method outperforms [4] in terms of path length. We have compared average error with $DREAMS - Random$ [4] as $DREAMS - Random$ yields minimum average error among the methods proposed in [4]. Lesser localization errors are shown in Fig. 3 for different beacon distances 1 meter and 0.5 meter where $r = 100$ meter.

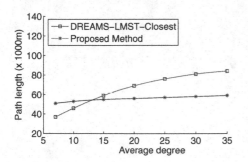

Fig. 2. Path length comparison

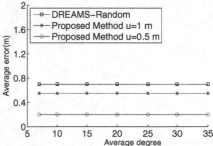

Fig. 3. Average error comparison

5   Conclusion

Our movement strategy reduces the requirement of three beacon points for localization to two beacon points. In a connected network, once a sensor is localized, our path planning is able to localize all its neighbors with one hexagonal movement around the sensor. After completing one hexagonal movement, anchor decides its next destination depending upon received information from the neighboring sensors and localizes all sensors along the way it moves. The novelty is that without knowing the boundary of the network, our distributed algorithm localizes all sensors using connectivity without any range estimation. In future we will try to investigate path planning in presence of obstacles.

Acknowledgement. The first author is thankful to the Council of Scientific and Industrial Research (CSIR), Govt. of India, for financial support during this work.

References

1. Chang, C.T., Chang, C.Y., Lin, C.Y.: Anchor-Guiding Mechanism for Beacon-Assisted Localization in Wireless Sensor Networks. IEEE Sensors Journal 12(5), 1098–1111 (2012)
2. Kim, K., Jung, B., Lee, W., Du, D.-Z.: Adaptive path planning for randomly deployed wireless sensor networks. J. Inf. Sci. Eng. 27(3), 1091–1106 (2011)
3. Lee, S., Kim, E., Kim, C., Kim, K.: Localization with a mobile beacon based on geometric constraints in wireless sensor networks. IEEE Trans. on Wireless Communications 8(12), 5801–5805 (2009)
4. Li, X., Mitton, N., Simplot-Ryl, I., Simplot-Ryl, D.: Dynamic beacon mobility scheduling for sensor localization. IEEE Trans. Parallel Distrib. Syst. 23(8), 1439–1452 (2012)
5. Mondal, K., Karmakar, A., Mandal, P.S.: Designing path planning algorithms for mobile anchor towards range-free localization. CoRR, abs/1409.0085 (2014)
6. Ssu, K.-F., Ou, C.-H., Jiau, H.C.: Localization with mobile anchor points in wireless sensor networks. IEEE Trans. Vehicular Technology 54(3), 1187–1197 (2005)
7. Xiao, B., Chen, H., Zhou, S.: Distributed localization using a moving beacon in wireless sensor networks. IEEE Trans. Parallel Distrib. Syst. 19(5), 587–600 (2008)

SMCDCT: A Framework for Automated MC/DC Test Case Generation Using Distributed Concolic Testing

Sangharatna Godboley, Subhrakanta Panda, and Durga Prasad Mohapatra

Department of CSE, National Institute of Technology,
Rourkela-769008, Odisha, India
sanghu1790@gmail.com, {511cs109,durga}@nitrkl.ac.in

Abstract. In this paper we propose a framework to compute MC/DC percentage for distributed test case generation. MC/DC stands for Modified Condition/Decison Coverage [1]. This approach uses several client nodes to generate the non-redundant test cases in a distributed and scalable manner. To achieve an increase in MC/DC, we transform the input C program, P, into its transformed version, P', using Ex-NCT. A coverage analyzer accepts P along with the generated test cases as input from SCORE framework and outputs the MC/DC percentage. The experimental studies show that SMCDCT approach achieves 6.5 % (approx.) of average increase in MC/DC. This increase in MC/DC percentage is achieved in an average computation time of 7.1622715 seconds.

Keywords: MC/DC, Distributed Concolic Testing, Coverage Analyser.

1 Introduction

We propose an approach to calculate MC/DC percentage using *SMCDCT (Scalable MC/DC percentage Calculator using Distributed Concolic Testing)* for structured C programs. SMCDCT consists of mainly three modules: i) *Code Transformer (Ex-NCT)* [2], ii) *Concolic Tester (SCORE)* [3], and iii) *Coverage Anlyser (CA)* [2]. The experimental studies in [2] shows that Ex-NCT gives better MC/DC percentage as compared to Program Code Transformer (PCT). Hence, in SMCDCT we use Ex-NCT for code transformation of the target programs. In this approach, we use SCORE in SMCDCT to improve the effectiveness and efficiency of the framework, as compared to traditional concolic testing. SCORE is based on distributed concolic testing to generate test cases for the program under consideration. This process reduces the computation time for measuring MC/DC percentage. The coverage analyser takes the non-transformed program and the generated test cases to calculate the MC/DC percentage.

2 SMCDCT Framework

First we present an overview of the proposed SMCDCT framework in Section 2.1, then discuss the steps of our proposed approach in Section 2.2.

R. Natarajan et al. (Eds.): ICDCIT 2015, LNCS 8956, pp. 199–202, 2015.
© Springer International Publishing Switzerland 2015

2.1   Overview of SMCDCT Framework

As the CREST concolic tester supports only linear-integer arithmetic (LIA) formulae, the non linear arithmetic operations in a target C program may not be analyzed symbolically [4,5]. The concolic testing consumes a significant amount of time in exploring the possible execution paths, and this forms a big challenge in its reification. We have proposed a framework to overcome some of the above mentioned limitations. Our main objective is to achieve an increase in MC/DC percentage without affecting the time value. We have used six distributed computing nodes connected through network in order to decrease the time cost of traditional concolic testing. To achieve high scalability, SMCDCT framework enables distributed nodes to generate test cases independently. SMCDCT consists of three modules these are discussed below:

Code Transformer. The Code Transformer (Ex-NCT [2]) uses transformation technique to instrument the C program by augmenting it with additional nested if-else conditional statements. This augmentation of code with additional statements causes MC/DC to vary.

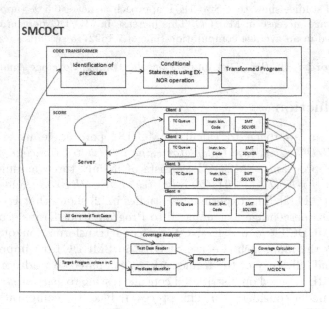

Fig. 1. Schematic representation of the proposed SMCDCT Framework

SCORE. SCORE consists of the *library code* and *symbolic execution engine* modules to achieve full path coverage without generating any redundant test cases. SCORE supports the bit vector symbolic path formulae by using Z3 2.19

SMT Solver [6] to solve the non-linear arithmetic operations symbolically. A distributed concolic algorithm in SCORE decreases the communication overhead among the distributed nodes and increases the speed of test case generation [3].

Coverage Analyser (CA). The module CA [2,7] accepts original C program under test and set of test cases generated from concolic tester as inputs to compute the MC/DC percentage.

As SMCDCT is based on SCORE, so it overcomes the limitations of traditional concolic testing. Therefore, SMCDCT is efficient to effectively perform a distributed and scalable concolic testing in less time.

2.2   Steps of Our Proposed Approach

In this section, we describe in detail the steps of our proposed approach to compute the MC/DC percentage difference. These steps are as follows:

Step1: Generate Test_Suite1 for the target program P.
Step2: Compute MC/DC_1 percentage.
Step3: Transform P into P'.
Step4: Generate Test_Suite2 for P'.
Step5: Compute MC/DC_2 percentage.
Step6: Compare MC/DC_1 percentage and MC/DC_2 percentage.

3   Experimental Study

In this section, we discuss the experimental analysis of the obtained results. The experimentation is carried out on two benchmark C programs (sed and grep) taken from SIR repository [8]. The results are presented under four different experimental scenarios as described below:

  i. The first scenario corresponds to the experimentation carried out with the *CREST tool* that ran on a stand-alone machine.
 ii. The second scenario corresponds to the experimentation carried out with *Ex-NCT* and *CREST tool* that ran on a stand-alone machine.
iii. The third scenario corresponds to the experimentation carried out with *SCORE tool* that ran on a client-server architecture implemented with six distributed nodes.
 iv. The fourth scenario corresponds to the experimentation carried out with *Ex-NCT* and *SCORE tool* that ran on a client-server architecture implemented with six distributed nodes.

The readings in Table 1 show that we achieve 6.5 % (approx.) of average increase in MC/DC for both the experimental programs. The Table 2 shows, the different timing results for the two experimental programs. From Table 2, it can be observed that the average of total computation times for the two experimental programs is 7.1622715 seconds.

Table 1. Comparison of MC/DC percentages

S.No	Program	MCDC %(CREST)	MCDC %(Ex-NCT + CREST)	MCDC %(SCORE)	MCDC %(Ex-NCT + SCORE)	MCDC %(difference)
1	sed	58.5 %	79.7%	82.4%	89.7%	7.3%
2	grep	53.8%	76.2%	79.68%	85.37%	5.69%

Table 2. Timing Reqiurements

S.No	Program	Ex-NCT (Sec)	SCORE (Sec)	CA (Sec)	Total Time (Sec)
1	sed	2.213746	0.871246	3.812357	6.897349
2	grep	2.523712	1.114357	3.789125	7.427194

4   Conclusion and Future Work

We proposed a framework for distributed test case generation named SMCDCT that is based on coverage analysis of C programs. We discussed the detailed steps of our proposed approach along with the working principles of the modules (Code transformer, SCORE, and Coverage Analyzer) of SMCDCT. The experimental results show that the proposed approach achieves better MC/DC in comparison to the existing approaches. SMCDCT approach achieved 6.5 % of average increase in MC/DC. This increase in MC/DC percentage is achieved in an average computation time of 7.1622715 seconds. In future, we will aim at developing an approach to find MC/DC of OOPs.

References

1. Hayhurst, K.J., Veerhusen, D.S., Chilenski, J.J., Rierson, L.K.: practical tutorial on modified condition/decision coverage, Tech. rep. (2001)
2. Godboley, S.: Improved modified condition/ decision coverage using code transformation techniques, M. tech thesis. NIT Rourkela (2013)
3. Kim, Y., Kim, M.: Score: A scalable concolic testing tool for reliable embedded software. In: Proceedings of the 19th ACM SIGSOFT Symposium and the 13th European Conference on Foundations of Software Engineering, pp. 420–423. ACM (2011)
4. Kim, M., Kim, Y., Rothermel, G.: A scalable distributed concolic testing approach: An empirical evaluation. In: Software 2012 IEEE Fifth International Conference on Testing, Verification and Validation (ICST), pp. 340–349 (2012)
5. [link], http://www.code.google.com/p/crest
6. de Moura, L., Bjørner, N.: Z3: An efficient SMT solver. In: Ramakrishnan, C.R., Rehof, J. (eds.) TACAS 2008. LNCS, vol. 4963, pp. 337–340. Springer, Heidelberg (2008)
7. Godboley, S., Mohapatra, D.P.: Time analysis of evaluating coverage percentage for c program using advanced program code transformer. In: Computer Society of India, 7 th CSI International Conference on Software Engineering, pp. 91–97 (2013)
8. Do, H., Elbaum, S., Rothermel, G.: Supporting controlled experimentation with testing techniques: An infrastructure and its potential impact. Empirical Softw. Engg. 10(4), 405–435 (2005)

On-the-Fly Symmetry Reduction of Explicitly Represented Probabilistic Models

Reema Patel[1], Kevin Patel[2], and Dhiren Patel[1]

[1] Computer Engineering Department, NIT Surat, India
{reema.mtech,dhiren29p}@gmail.com
[2] Department of Computer Science and Engineering, IIT Bombay, India
kevin.patel@cse.iitb.ac.in

Abstract. Quantitative analysis of concurrent systems becomes intractable due to searches over the enormous state space. Since these systems often contain many identical processes consisting of symmetrical and interchangeable components, this problem can be tackled using symmetry reduction. In this paper, we present an on-the-fly symmetry reduction technique that is applicable to explicitly represented models in the probabilistic setting. We have performed the experiments by integrating our technique into PRISM probabilistic model checker. Experimental results are very encouraging with considerable reductions in both the time taken for property evaluation and the associated memory usage.

Keywords: Probabilistic Model Checking, Explicit State Representation, On-the-fly Symmetry Reduction.

1 Introduction

Probabilistic model checking is an automated formal procedure intended to verify the quantitative properties of stochastic system. The system is modeled as either a Discrete Time Markov Chain(DTMC), a Markov Decision Process(MDP) or a Continuous Time Markov Chain(CTMC) [6] to verify its desired properties. The model of a system can itself be represented in either symbolic or explicit [2] form.

One of the major problems associated with model checking is the state space explosion, i.e., as the number of components increases in the system, the state space associated with the system model grows exponentially. This problem is more intense with concurrent system analysis.

Concurrent system frequently contains replicated components in form of identical processes. Replication of processes induces symmetry in the state space associated with the system model. As a consequence, model checking may involve redundant search over the equivalent areas of the state space. To overcome this state space explosion in concurrent system, symmetry reduction is well suited. It exploits the presence of replicated components in the system. Key challenge in symmetry reduction is to find out the states that belong to the same equivalence class.

R. Natarajan et al. (Eds.): ICDCIT 2015, LNCS 8956, pp. 203–206, 2015.

Symmetry reduction constructs a smaller model known as quotient model in which sets of equivalent states in the original model are replaced with respective single equivalence class representatives. Model checking of the system can then be performed on a quotient model, thus avoiding redundant searching over equivalent area of the state space.

On-the-fly symmetry reduction has successfully applied onto non-probabilistic model checking [1]. In this paper, we present an on-the-fly symmetry reduction algorithm to build a quotient model at the time of exploration of reachable states. Our algorithm is applicable to explicitly represented probabilistic models. Major problem with explicit state representation is to list out all reachable states. Hence explicit model cannot be built with enormous state space. Using an on-the-fly symmetry reduction, we are able to build an explicit quotient model of an original model with extensive state space. We also explore integration of our proposed on-the-fly symmetry reduction method into PRISM [3] for explicitly represented system.

2   Related Work

Survey paper [7] explain different approaches of symmetry reduction for symbolic and explicit-state representation. Here we focus onto the symmetry reduction techniques applied on explicit representation of probabilistic models.

Thesis entitled "Probabilistic symmetry reduction" by Christopher power [5] has presented a new probabilistic model specification language PSS (Probabilistic Symmetric System). The author has also built a tool to generate the quotient model of explicitly represented system model and set of properties formulas which can be analyzed using PRISM. But the main hurdle of using this tool is that it is not freely available for other users.

3   On-the-Fly Symmetry Reduction

Here, we discuss our proposed on-the-fly symmetry reduction algorithm which is applicable to explicitly represented probabilistic models. Input of the algorithm is the probabilistic model (represented in language form) of a given system to be analyzed. And output of the algorithm is quotient model where S_Q and P_Q contains reduced states and transitions respectively. The representative state which required further for transition computation is stored into set Explore.

The algorithm 1 begins by adding the initial state s_0 into S_Q and Explore. Start with exploring s_0 and computes the number of transitions and successor state for each transition. Now for each successor state of s_0, algorithm computes the representative and check if it has been encountered before. If the representative of successor state has not been encountered then it is added to S_Q and Explore. The transitions of the representative state are added into P_Q. Now algorithm extract the next state from Explore set and proceed further. Once the Explore set is empty, the state space has been fully explored. Here, S_Q and P_Q contains the states and transitions of quotient model.

Algorithm 1. On-the-fly Symmetry Reduction

// Initialization
$S_Q := \{representative(s_0)\}$;
$P_Q := \emptyset$;
$Explore := \{representative(s_0)\}$;

while $Explore \neq \emptyset$ **do**
    remove a state s from $Explore$;
    //compute transitions for state s
    for each transition $s \rightarrow \hat{s}$ **do**
        $s' = representative(\hat{s})$;
        if $s' \notin S_Q$ **then**
            insert s' into S_Q and $Explore$;
        end if
        insert $s \rightarrow s'$ into P_Q;
    end for
end while

We have to compute the representative of each state. Let $I = \{1, 2, \ldots, n\}$ be the set of component identifiers. A state $s \in S$ has the representation $s = (g, l_1, l_2, \ldots, l_n)$, where l_i denotes the local state of component i and g indicates global variables if any. The usual lexicographical ordering of vectors provides a total ordering on S. From the equivalence class of a state, we have chosen lexicographically smaller state as a representative of that state. Here, once the state is generated, we sort that state component-wise. This sorted state is lexicographically smaller and considered as the representative.

Note that our proposed algorithm bypasses the major limitation of explicit models - the requirement to enumerate all reachable states and transitions. The algorithm computes the representative of a state at the time of exploration itself. So those states, whose representative is already explored, need not be stored. This frees up the storage space. Also, such states are not even explored, thereby saving time. In the next section, we present our experimental results.

4   Experimental Results

Our contribution extends the functionality of PRISM's explicit engine by providing it with a mechanism for symmetry reduction. Here we present experimental results for PRISM benchmark case study - the randomized consensus shared coin protocol from [4].

Table 1 shows the comparison between original and symmetry reduced explicit model. For "Consensus" case study, N denotes the number of symmetric processes in the system. Columns 3-4 give the state space size of original and quotient explicit model. As expected, using symmetry reduction we obtain a large reduction in state space size and it increases with N. Next two columns show the time taken for building the each model. Last two columns shows the time

Table 1. Experimental Results of Original and Quotient Explicit Model

Case Study	N	Model size (States)		Explicit Model Build Time (in Seconds)		Model Checking Time (in Seconds)	
		Original	Quotient	Full explicit model	Quotient explicit model (proposed)	Full explicit model	Quotient explicit model (proposed)
Consensus shared coin protocol	2	272	154	0.123	0.068	0.058	0.048
	4	22656	2e+3	0.704	0.562	2.812	0.371
	6	1.2e+6	1e+4	38.17	2.134	373.77	3.856
	8	6.1e+7	4e+4	memory out	6.379	-	28.483
	10	2.8e+9	1.3e+5	memory out	21.568	-	155.864

required to performing probabilistic model checking on each of the two models. In "consensus", using full explicit model, we cannot build a model with more than 6 number of processes. However, using an on-the-fly symmetry reduction, we were able to build a model with more number of processes. Time required to perform model checking on quotient model is much less compare to original model. Thus, the proposed on-the-fly symmetry reduction technique speeds up the model checking task and also enables the verification of systems with larger number of processes.

References

1. Barner, S., Grumberg, O.: Combining symmetry reduction and under-approximation for symbolic model checking. In: Brinksma, E., Larsen, K.G. (eds.) CAV 2002. LNCS, vol. 2404, pp. 93–106. Springer, Heidelberg (2002), http://dx.doi.org/10.1007/3-540-45657-0_8
2. Burch, J., Clarke, E., McMillan, K., Dill, D., Hwang, L.: Symbolic model checking: 10^{20} states and beyond. Information and Computation 98(2), 142–170 (1992)
3. Hinton, A., Kwiatkowska, M., Norman, G., Parker, D.: PRISM: A tool for automatic verification of probabilistic systems. In: Hermanns, H., Palsberg, J. (eds.) TACAS 2006. LNCS, vol. 3920, pp. 441–444. Springer, Heidelberg (2006)
4. Kwiatkowska, M., Norman, G., Segala, R.: Automated verification of a randomized distributed consensus protocol using Cadence SMV and PRISM. In: Berry, G., Comon, H., Finkel, A. (eds.) CAV 2001. LNCS, vol. 2102, pp. 194–206. Springer, Heidelberg (2001)
5. Power, C.: Probabilistic symmetry reduction. Phd thesis, University of Glasgow (2012), http://theses.gla.ac.uk/3493/
6. Rutten, J., Kwiatkowska, M., Norman, G., Parker, D.: Mathematical Techniques for Analyzing Concurrent and Probabilistic Systems. CRM Monograph Series, vol. 23. American Mathematical Society (2004)
7. Wahl, T., Donaldson, A.: Replication and abstraction: Symmetry in automated formal verification. Symmetry 2(2), 799–847 (2010)

Time and Cost Aware Checkpointing
of Choreographed Web Services

Vani Vathsala Atluri and Hrushikesha Mohanty

CVR College of Engineering and University of Hyderabad
Hyderabad, India
atlurivv@yahoo.com, mohanty.hcu@gmail.com

Abstract. Complex business processes can be realized by composing two or more web services into a composite web service. Due to the widespread reachability of Internet, more and more web services are becoming available to the consumers. Quality aware consumers look for resilience in services provisioned on Internet. This paper proposes message logging based checkpointing and recovery for web services to make them resilient to faults. It presents an algorithm that checkpoints services participating in a choreography in such a way that the execution time and cost of service constraints are always met. It identifies checkpoint locations by considering the costs involved in checkpointing, message logging and replaying for service recovery. The cost estimation is carried out using service interaction patterns and QoS values of the services involved. Performance of the proposed checkpointing strategy is corroborated with the results obtained from experiments.

Keywords: Web services, choreography, checkpointing, QoS.

1   Introduction

There are several algorithms that are proposed in literature for checkpointing distributed applications. Any checkpointing scheme has to satisfy the requirement of resilient service provisioning [13]. Checkpointing a choreographed web service needs special care so that recovery does not need a chain of restarts of component services. Hence checkpointing web services is of interest. We propose to perform checkpointing of choreographed web services at three different stages of web service development: 1. Design time 2. Deployment time 3. Run time.

A group of web services interacting with each other by means of message exchanges, to accomplish a business task are called as a choreographed web services. Choreographed web services have the information about their sequence of message based interactions, and actions to be performed by each of them, documented in a design time artefact called as **choreography** document. Using this document, we have proposed a **design time** checkpointing approach in our previous work [12] that introduces checkpoint locations in a choreography, at places where non repeatable actions are performed. In the event of transient

R. Natarajan et al. (Eds.): ICDCIT 2015, LNCS 8956, pp. 207–219, 2015.
© Springer International Publishing Switzerland 2015

failures(temporary failures) this checkpoint arrangement avoids chain of rein-vocation of web services, specifically when a non repeatable action is executed. But, it does not handle the issue of meeting deadlines in case of transient fail-ures. This paper addresses this issue using Quality of Service(QoS) values (like response time, reliability, cost of service etc.) and other quantities like check-pointing time, message logging time etc which can be measured at the time of **deployment**. We propose a time and cost aware checkpointing algorithm that introduces minimum number of checkpoints so that execution time and cost con-straints are met even in the event of transient failures. The trade-off between number of checkpoints and recovery time is experimentally analysed. As part of our future work we intend to take up revision of checkpoint locations at **run time** using dynamically predicted QoS values and dynamic composition of web services. We have presented our approaches on response time prediction of web services in our previous works [11] [14].

This paper is organised as follows: in section 2 we discuss existing checkpoint-ing approaches and compare them with our approach, in section 3 we give an overview of our choreography model and three stage checkpointing approach, in section 4 we brief on our proposed approach for deployment time checkpointing. Checkpointing algorithm is given in section 5 along with experimental results. Conclusion and future work are discussed in section 6.

2   Related Work

Well understood techniques[6] for checkpointing and recovery of distributed ap-plications are not readily applicable for that of web services. This is because a recovery strategy for distributed applications requires other processes also, in addition to failed process, to rollback. Such a strategy is not suitable for com-posite web services since requiring chain of rollbacks of the remaining services leads to a compromise in quality of the composite service.

Fault handling strategies proposed in the field of web services are of two types [13]: Checkpointing and recovery [2], [10], [9], and Substitution [4], [3], [5]. In the proposed checkpointing and recovery strategies [2],[10], responsibility of specifying checkpointing locations in the design document is bestowed on the user. Success of such strategies lies in the knowledge and skillset of the users. In another checkpointing strategy[9], checkpointing is used to save the work of constituent services that have not failed but, the faulty constituent service has to restart from the beginning. Substitution approaches proceed by substituting the faulty web service with a functionally equivalent one. The main drawback of this approach can be seen when the invoking service itself fails. The failed instances would have to be reexecuted from the beginning. This implies recalling the invoked services again resulting in increased execution times.

QoS aware checkpointing has been proposed in various areas like embedded systems [1], and mobile computing [8]. In [1] authors propose QoS aware message logging based checkpointing of embedded and distributed systems. They formu-late the problem of finding an optimal checkpoint interval, in a process, that maximizes systems overall quality as a Mixed Integer Non-Linear Programming (MINLP) problem and provide an algorithm for finding the solution. They do not consider QoS values of other processes participating in the composition, in checkpointing decisions. In [8], authors work on mobile computing environment where in hosts going out of range transfer their checkpointed data to other hosts. It uses link reliability values to dynamically maintain superior checkpointing arrangement.

Considering QoS values of the constituent services while taking checkpointing decisions for a choreographed web service is pivotal in meeting promised deadlines. In our survey we have not come across any web service checkpointing strategy that focuses on this issue. Hence in this paper we advocate time and cost aware checkpointing strategy that makes use of QoS values of constituent services, to decide on checkpoint locations while meeting the promised deadlines.

In the next section we present concepts [12] required here for putting the proposed strategy at right perspective.

3   Checkpointing Choreographed Web Services

A choreography of web services describes in a document, called choreography document, series of interactions that are to be performed by constituent web services to accomplish common business goals. A choreography of web services is modelled as a composition of interaction patterns in our previous work. We use this model to aid in checkpointing decisions. In the following subsection we give a brief on our model, details can be obtained from [12].

3.1   Modelling Choreographed Web Services

Each participant ξ of a service choreography performs some local actions and communicates necessary information with other participants. Thus, broadly, **operations** of a service are classified into two categories: *local action* and *interaction*. An **interaction pattern**, or a **pattern** in short, is defined as a sequence of operations wherein the first operation in the sequence is an interaction. In our previous paper [12] we have proposed different types of interaction patterns and detailed on modelling service choreographies using these patterns.

To make the description in this paper self-contained, and to keep up with the space requirements, we use only one of our proposed patterns, pattern P_2 (Chose P_2 as it has maximum number of interactions) in this paper. In P_2, the initiator ξ sends an invoke message and continues to execute a sequence of operations, before getting a reply from ξ_r. Upon receiving the invoke message, ξ_r executes a sequence of operations and sends a reply message back to ξ (refer to Fig 1(a)).

In [12] we propose that service interaction patterns may be combined in different ways using composition operators to give composite patterns. We proposed four kinds of composite patterns: sequential pattern, nested pattern, iterative pattern, and concurrent pattern whose operators are ".",[ ],* and | respectively. Fig 1(f) depicts an example choreography which is modelled as a composition of

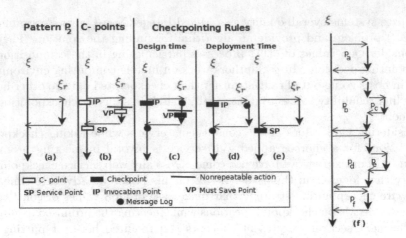

Fig. 1. Modelling service choreographies and checkpointing rules

our patterns. A composite web service is compactly represented in text using a pattern string. A **pattern String** represents a choreographed web service whose composition is expressed in terms of patterns and composition operators. The pattern string for the example choreography is $p_a.p_b[p_c].p_d[p_e].p_f$

In a step towards identifying possible checkpoint locations in a given choreography, we associate each pattern with what are called as C-points. A **C-point** is a probable checkpointing location. We define three types of C-points: service point, must save point and invocation Point. Fig 1(b) depicts C-points in pattern P_2. A *service point* is marked in the initiator of the pattern after the reply message is received. An *invocation point* is marked in the initiator of the pattern after it sends the invoke message. A *must Save point* is marked in a participant of a pattern after a nonrepeatable action, if any.

The example choreography depicted in Fig 1(f) is used to assist in illustration of concepts. In this example, web service ξ interacts with few other web services resulting in a composite web service. **We illustrate checkpointing the web service ξ in this paper, which is applicable to other constituent web services.**

To start with, we define what are called as sequential components. The part of pattern string which is delimited by "." operator is called as a **sequential component** *"s"* . The sequential components in our example are p_a, $p_b[p_c]$, $p_d[p_e]$, p_f which are named as s_1, s_2, s_3, s_4 respectively (Fig 2(a)).

Each sequential component is a pattern(can be either atomic or composite) and hence has C-points associated with it. Sequential components are referred to as **components** for ease of writing from here on. If the web service ξ initiates n_s number of components we have a maximum of $2n_s$ C-points to be converted into checkpoints. It may not be possible to convert all these C-points since conversion of all the C-points might result in violation of deadlines.

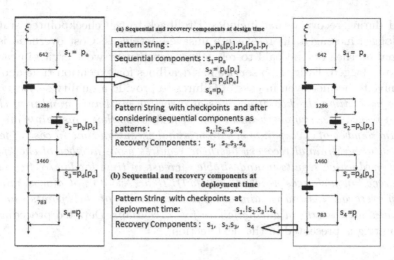

Fig. 2. A choreography and its recovery components

3.2 Recovery Components

A recovery component is defined as an execution unit that is delimited by checkpoints. A failure at anywhere in a recovery component results in rollback to the checkpoint placed at the beginning of the recovery component. In case checkpoints are inserted into a web service either at design time or later, the pattern string that reflects the choreography must reflect the checkpoint locations also. Hence we use the following notation: For a component s if its invocation point is converted to a checkpoint then symbol "!" is added to the left of it, if its service point is converted to a checkpoint then symbol "!" is added to the right of it and if both the C-Points of a component are checkpointed then the component is removed from the pattern string along with its two "!" marks. **A recovery component** is that part of a pattern string which is delimited by "!" mark.

Fig 2(a) depicts the example choreography with checkpoints inserted at design time. It's pattern string annotated with "!" marks at design time is given by $s_1.!s_2.s_3.s_4$. Thus we have initially two recovery components $s_1, s_2.s_3.s_4$ for the example choreography. Fig 2(b) depicts the choreography and its recovery components after a service point is converted into checkpoint at deployment time. By this time we have three recovery components $s_1, s_2.s_3, s_4$.

3.3 Proposed Approach on Deployment Time Checkpointing

We assume that occurrence of transient failures in a web service follow Poisson distribution with the mean failure rate given by λ. It is assumed that failures do not occur during recovery time. Each failure has to be followed by recovery of the failed service for successful completion of its execution.

Recovery of a web service has the following two overheads: **execution time overhead and cost overhead**. Execution overhead is the additional time required during recovery that includes: i)rollback to the checkpointed state ii) replay logged messaged iii) re-execute unsaved activities. Cost overhead is the additional overhead to be paid to reinvoke a constituent web service in case its reply is not logged. Every web service has deadlines for execution time and cost which have to be met even in case of failures to provide a quality service.

Deployment time checkpointing aims at inserting minimum number of checkpoints to reduce recovery overhead in case of failures so that constraints are met. Minimum number of checkpoints ensure minimal execution time in case of failure free executions. Minimal recovery overhead requires more number of checkpoints to be inserted which results in undesirable increase in time for failure free executions (execution instances which do not fail). Hence we do not aim at minimal recovery overhead, instead we aim at minimum number of checkpoints which result in minimum overhead during failure free executions. Detailed procedure for checkpointing is presented in the next section.

4   Procedure for Deployment Time Checkpointing

Deployment time checkpointing is performed in three stages. 1) Measurement of execution time and other quantities at deployment time. 2)Collection of QoS values of constituent services. 3)Computation of recovery overhead and placement of checkpoints.

4.1   Measurement of Quantities

Initially all the participants of a choreography should insert checkpoints in their code at the locations according to design time checkpointing policy. Let ξ be the participant which is currently being checkpointed. Let T_C, T_L, T_R and T_{CR} represent checkpointing time, message logging time, message replay time and time to restore ξ to a saved state, respectively. These quantities have to be determined experimentally at deployment time. Let C_D represent the cost of service charged by ξ when service is provided with in the promised maximum execution time T_D.

4.2   Collection of QoS Values

We have identified and modeled those QoS attributes which play a crucial role in checkpointing decisions. The considered QoS attributes are response time, vulnerability and cost of service provision.

Let ξ_r be the service provider in a component s initiated by ξ. **Response time** $s.t_{rt}$ of s, is defined as the response time of ξ_r. **Vulnerability** $s.vl$ of s to failures is defined as vulnerability of ξ_r which in turn is defined using reliability of ξ_r. **Reliability** rl is defined as the success rate of the service i.e. the ratio of number of times the service is successfully delivered to total number of service invocations. $\xi_r.vl = 1 - (\xi_r.rl)$. Cost of a service is defined as the price to be paid for providing the requested service. **Cost of service** $s.ct$ of s is defined as cost of service provided by ξ_r of the component.

4.3   Computation of Recovery Overhead

Recovery overhead is measured in terms of additional execution time and cost of service to be paid, to recover ξ from failures. Recovery overhead for each of the recovery components is computed using the quantities measured at deployment time and QoS attributes defined above.

4.3.1   Execution Time Overhead

For each of the components s, initiated by the participant ξ, let $s.t_{at}$ and $s.t_{rt}$ represent average local activity time and response time of the callee. These values are determined experimentally at deployment time. For every component s, there can be only one invocation point, one service point, and one or more must save points in ξ. According to our design time checkpointing policy[12], only invocation point and must save points of a component may be converted into checkpoints, service points cannot be. Let $s.n_{mp} \geq 0$ and $s.n_{ip} \in (0,1)$ represent number of must save points and invocation points which are converted into checkpoints at design time. Let $s.n_{sp} \in (0,1)$ represent number of service points which are converted into checkpoints. According to the design time policy, $s.n_{sp} = 0$ indicating that zero service points are checkpointed yet.

Let $T_{pure}(s)$ represent pure execution time of a component s without including any of checkpointing and message logging times. $T_{pure}(s) = max(s.t_{at}, s.t_{rt})$. Let $T_{fixed}(s)$ represent the fixed execution time of component s after including checkpointing and message logging times for checkpoints and logs inserted at design time. Checkpointing time is given by $(s.n_{mp} + s.n_{ip}) * T_C$. These checkpoints are never revised at deployment time and run time. Hence we call it as $T_{fixed}(s)$. If an invocation point or a must save point is converted into checkpoint, the reply message received by ξ has to be logged, refer [12]. Let $s.n_{ml} \in (0,1)$ represent number of message logs at design time for component s. $T_{fixed}(s) = T_{pure}(s) + (s.n_{mp} + s.n_{ip}) * T_C + s.n_{ml} * T_L$.

We use the notation $\alpha_0(s)$ to represent $T_{fixed}(s)$, 0 indicates that 0 C-points of s are converted into checkpoint in deployment stage. Let $T_{fixed}(\xi)$ represent fixed execution time of the participant ξ before converting any of the C-points of ξ into checkpoints in deployment stage. It is in short represented as $\alpha_0(\xi)$ where 0 indicates that 0 C-points are already converted into checkpoints in deployment stage. $T_{fixed}(\xi) = \alpha_0(\xi) = \sum_{i=1}^{n_s} \alpha_0(s_i)$ where n_s is number of components initiated by ξ.

$\alpha_k(\xi)$ represents **failure free execution time** of ξ after k C-points are converted into checkpoints and lg messages are logged in deployment stage. $\alpha_k(\xi) = \sum_{i=1}^{n_s} \alpha_0(s_i) + k * T_C + lg * T_L$.

Let $T_W(\xi)$ represent **worst case execution time** of the participant ξ which is defined as follows: $T_W(\xi) = \alpha_k(\xi) + T_{rec}(\xi)$, which includes $\alpha_k(\xi)$, and time $T_{rec}(\xi)$ to recover the web service in case of its failure. To satisfy the promised maximum execution time, $T_W(\xi)$ must be $\leq T_D$. In the next subsection we describe recovery time $T_{rec}(\xi)$ computation.

Recovery Time Computation. In a component if its invocation point is check-pointed, then the service $s.\xi_r$ is not invoked again and hence $T_{rec}(s)$ includes i) the time taken, T_{CR}, to restore the web service from its latest checkpoint, ii) message replay time T_R and iii) time to execute unsaved local activities. Maximum unsaved work in a component results when a failure occurs almost at the end of the component, i.e just before receiving reply. If s's invocation point is converted into checkpoint at design time $T_{rec}(s) = T_{CR} + T_R + s.t_{at}$, else $T_{rec}(s) = max(s.t_{at}, s.t_{rt})$. Table 2 (fifth column) gives recovery time values for the example choreography. $T_{rec}(r) = \sum_{s \in r} f(s) * T_{rec}(s)$, where $f(s) = (\lambda * T_{rec}(s))$ gives average number of failures in the component s. $T_{rec}(\xi) = \sum_{i=1}^{n} T_{rec}(r_i)$ where n is the number of recovery components of ξ.

Relative recovery time of component s is defined as: $T_{rrec}(s) = \frac{T_{rec}(s)}{T_{rec}(r)}$.

Relative recovery time of recovery component r is: $T_{rrec}(r) = \frac{T_{rec}(r)}{T_{rec}(\xi)}$.

4.3.2   Cost Overhead

Let C_{total} indicate failure free cost of service for all the components of ξ, $C_{total} = \sum_{i=1}^{n_s} s_i.ct$. Let $C_{rec}(s)$ indicates additional cost incurred in component s during recovery in case of a failure.

In a component if its invocation point is checkpointed, then the service ξ_r is not invoked again and hence there is no additional cost of invocation. Thus, $C_{rec}(s) = 0$ if $s.n_{ip} = 1$, else $C_{rec}(s) = s.ct$.
$C_{rec}(r) = \sum_{s \in r} f(s) * C_{rec}(s)$. and $C_{rec}(\xi) = \sum_{i=1}^{n} C_{rec}(r_i)$.

Relative recovery cost for s is defined as: $C_{rrec}(s) = \frac{C_{rec}(s)}{C_{rec}(r)}$.

Relative recovery cost for r is defined as: $C_{rrec}(r) = \frac{C_{rec}(r)}{C_{rec}(\xi)}$.

Let $C_W(\xi)$ indicate worst case cost of service which is defined as $C_W(\xi) = C_{total} + C_{rec}(\xi)$. Cost constraint is satisfied if $C_W(\xi) \leq C_D$.

4.3.3   Checkpointing Score

Checkpointing score cs of a component s quantifies suitability of the component for checkpointing. It is defined as the following weighted sum. Higher values of cs indicate greater need for checkpointing the component.

$$s.cs = W_1 * T_{rrec}(s) + W_2 * s.vl + W_3 * C_{rrec}(s)$$

where $\sum_{i=1}^{3} W_i = 1$ and they represent weights to be used to alter the effects of individual components on the checkpointing score. Similarly, checkpointing score cs of a recovery component r is defined as:

$$r.cs = W_1 * T_{rrec}(r) + W_2 * r.vl + W_3 * C_{rrec}(r).$$

4.3.4   Deciding on Checkpoint Locations

Recovery component r_j which has the highest checkpointing score is selected for checkpointing. From among all components of r_j, the component s_o that has got maximum checkpointing score is selected for placing the checkpoint. Further, if local activity time of s_o is greater than or equal to s_o's response time the next checkpoint is placed at service point of s_o. Else the next checkpoint is placed at invocation point of s_o, i.e if s_o's response time is larger, the service provider of s_o is not reinvoked in the event of failure of ξ by placing a checkpoint at the invocation point (refer to Fig 1 (d,e)).

5   Time and Cost Aware Checkpointing Algorithm

We propose Time and Cost aware Checkpointing algorithm [Algorithm 1] that incrementally converts C-points into checkpoints, one at a time. It takes as input all the quantities measured and collected at deployment stage, and pattern string representing the composition with checkpoints inserted at design stage (line no 1). Algorithm starts by computing recovery overhead of all components (line nos 4,5). In each iteration it finds out recovery components and computes their execution cost and time overhead (line nos 12,14). It then computes worst case execution cost $C_W(\xi)$ and time $T_W(\xi)$ (line nos 13,16). Then it checks to see if $T_W(\xi)$ is within T_D and $C_W(\xi)$ is within C_D. If so, it terminates. Generally $T_W(\xi)$ is large and is greater than T_D. After conversion of a C-point into checkpoint, $T_W(\xi))$ decreases. Also, total checkpointing time increases. We continue converting C-points into checkpoints until time and cost constraints are met. Exact checkpointing location is decided using the deployment checkpointing strategy presented in subsection 4.3. Due to space constraints we do not present the algorithm $RecoveryComponents(ps, \xi)$ that extracts recovery components from a given pattern string.

5.1   Experimental Results

To illustrate the effectiveness of our approach, we have developed, tested and monitored the performance of sample web services using Oracle SOA suite 11g [7]. We have used weblogic server which is configured to work as SOA server. Oracle JDeveloper is used for development and deployment of web services. Oracle Enterprise Manager which is also a part of Oracle SOA suite, is used to collect performance related metrics. The weblogic server is hosted on a machine using 4GB RAM, 2.13GHz CPU and J2SDK5. Oracle 11g Database is installed on a machine having 4GB RAM and 3.00GHz CPU. All the PCs run on Windows 7 OS and are connected via high speed LAN through 100Mbps Ethernet cards.

To aid in our experimental results, we have developed the following web services: *WS1:* web service which invokes *currency converter* web service and then *calculator* web service. *WS2:* web service which invokes *currency converter* web service. *WS3:* web service which invokes *calculator* web service. *WS4:* web service takes an Indian state and returns its capital. *WS5:* web service which returns the Indian state to which a given capital city belongs. *WS6:* web service which invokes four web services in the order: WS4, WS3,WS2,WS5. For testing the efficiency of the proposed algorithm, we have used web service WS6, the

Algorithm 1. Time and Cost aware Checkpointing Algorithm

1 Input: Read $T_C, T_L, T_R, T_{CR}, T_D, C_D, \lambda$ and QoS values of components, pattern
   string ps.
2 $k = 0 // k$ indicates number of C-points checkpointed at deployment time
3 $lg = 0 // ml$ indicates number of messages logged at deployment time
4 **for** *each component s* **do**
5 $\quad |$ Compute $C_{rec}(s)$, $T_{rec}(s)$
6 $C_{total} = \sum_{i=1}^{n_s} s_i.ct$
7 $R = RecoveryComponents(ps, \xi)$
8 **while** *R is not Null* **do**
9 $\quad n = |R| //$ Number of recovery components
10 $\quad$ **for** *each recovery component $r \in R$* **do**
11 $\quad\quad |$ Compute $C_{rec}(r)$, $T_{rec}(r)$
12 $\quad C_{rec}(\xi) = \sum_{i=1}^{n} (C_{rec}(r_i))$
13 $\quad C_W(\xi) = C_{total} + C_{rec}(\xi)$
14 $\quad T_{rec}(\xi) = \sum_{i=1}^{n} (T_{rec}(r_i))$
15 $\quad \alpha_k(\xi) = \alpha_0(\xi) + k * T_C + lg * T_L$
16 $\quad T_W(\xi) = \alpha_k(\xi) + T_{rec}(\xi)$
17 $\quad$ **if** $(T_W(\xi) \leq T_D)$ *and* $(C_W(\xi) \leq C_D)$ **then**
18 $\quad\quad |$ break. // deadlines can be met
19 $\quad$ //else select a component from recovery component r for checkpointing
20 $\quad$ **for** *each recovery component $r \in R$* **do**
21 $\quad\quad C_{rrec}(r) = \frac{C_{rec}(r)}{C_{rec}(\xi)}$
22 $\quad\quad T_{rrec}(r) = \frac{T_{rec}(r)}{T_{rec}(\xi)}.$
23 $\quad\quad r.cs = CHS(r)$ //CHS computes checkpointing score of r
24 $\quad$ j = index of recovery component whose cs is returned by $\max_{i=1}^{n}(r_i.cs)$
25 $\quad$ Let the recovery component r_j consist of sequential components from index
   l to l+h where $1 \leq h \leq n_s - l$
26 $\quad$ **for** *each component $s \in r$* **do**
27 $\quad\quad |$ $s.cs = CHSP(s)$ //CHSP computes checkpointing score of s
28 $\quad$ o = index of component whose cs is returned by $\max_{i=l}^{l+h}(s_i.cs)$
29 $\quad$ **if** $s_o.tat \geq s_o.trt$ **then**
30 $\quad\quad |$ $s_o.n_{sp} = 1$ //Place the next checkpoint at service point of s_o
31 $\quad$ **else**
32 $\quad\quad$ $s_o.n_{ip} = 1$ //Place the next checkpoint at invocation point of s_o
33 $\quad\quad$ $s_o.n_{ml} = 1$ //log the reply message received
34 $\quad\quad$ $lg = lg + 1$
35 $\quad$ k=k+1
36 $\quad R = RecoveryComponents(ps, \xi)$
37 Print no of checkpoints inserted = k

Table 1. Execution Time Parameters for WS6

Quantity	Value Time in msec, Cost in units
T_C	78
T_L	24
T_R	15
T_{CR}	36
$T_{pure}, \alpha_0(\xi)$	4171, 4171+78+24=4273
T_D, C_D	6000,150
W_1, W_2, W_3, λ	0.333,0.333,0.333,.001

Table 2. Checkpointing score calculation for constituent web services

s	**WS**	$s.t_{at}$	$\alpha_0(s)$	$T_{rec}(s)$	$s.vl$	$s.ct$	$C_{rec}(s)$	cs	$f(s)$
s_1	WS4	125	642	642	0.43	25	25	(0.2533+0.43+0.555) *0.333=0.413	0.642
s_2	WS3	240	1286	$240 + 36 + 15 = 291$	0.56	30	0	(0.115+0.56+0)* 0.333=0.225	0.291
s_3	WS2	1024	1460	1460	0.38	25	25	(0.576+0.38+0.555)* 0.333=0.504	1.460
s_4	WS5	245	783	783	0.24	20	20	(0.308+0.24+0.444)* 0.333=0.330	0.783

Table 3. Algorithm 1 Trace for k=1

Quantity	Value
Q, Q_0	$\{s_1, s_2, s_3, s_4\}$
$R = \{r_1, r_2\}$	$r_1 = s_1, r_2 = s_2.s_3.s_4$
$C_{rec}(\xi)$	$\sum(C_{rec}(r_1), C_{rec}(r_2)) = \sum(25 * 0.642, 0 + 25 * 1.46 + 20 * 0.783) = 68$
$T_{rec}(\xi)$	$\sum(T_{rec}(r_1), T_{rec}(r_2)) = \sum(642 * .642, 291 * .291 + 1460 * 1.46 + 783 * .783) = 3241$
$\alpha_k(\xi), T_W(\xi)$	4273 +0 = 4273, 4273+3241=7514
$C_{total}(\xi), C_W(\xi)$	100,68
r_1	$T_{rrec} = \frac{642}{3241} = 0.198, vl = 0.43, C_{rrec} = \frac{25}{68} = .5555, cs = .367$
r_2	$T_{rrec} = \frac{2534}{3241} = .8727, vl = 0.81, C_{rrec} = \frac{45}{68} = .661, cs = .780$
k, j, l, h	0, 2, 2, 2
$\max(s_2.cs, s_3.cs, s_4.cs)$	$\max(0.225, 0.504, 0.330) = 0.504$
o	3, Place checkpoint at ip of s_3 and log reply message.

choreography document of which is depicted in Fig 2(a). Numbers in the figure depict fixed execution time, $\alpha_0(s)$, of each of the components.

Table 1 depicts the values of various required quantities that are recorded and read into the algorithm. Table 2 shows checkpointing score calculation for components. Table 3 gives a trace of the algorithm for $k = 1$. According to computations component s_3 is selected for converting its invocation point into checkpoint.

Graphs in Fig 3 depict variation of important quantities computed by the algorithm with increase in k value. It can be seen that T_W and C_W cross time deadline for $k = 0$ (Fig 3(c),(d)). T_W and C_W decrease considerably after converting a C-point into checkpoint. Also, failure free execution time increases due to this checkpoint. But conversion of another C-point into checkpoint is not taken up because deadline is already met with $k = 1$ and also failure free execution time increases further with $k = 2$ (Fig 3(b)). Hence the algorithm terminates when k=1.

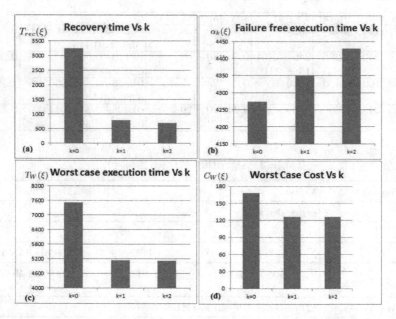

Fig. 3. Plots of important quantities in three iterations of algorithm

6   Conclusion and Future Work

In this paper we have detailed on time and cost aware checkpointing algorithm that has to be adopted at deployment stage for resilient execution of choreographed web services. We define units of execution called as recovery components and compute their checkpointing score by using execution time and other quantities measurable at deployment time and QoS values of constituent services. It aims at introducing minimum number of checkpoints in a web service so that time and cost constraints are met during both failure free executions and failed and recovered executions. Web services operate in highly dynamic Internet where response times are bound to vary from the advertised values. We intend to take up run time revision of checkpoint locations as part of our future work. It is mainly intended to consider actual values of all response times and revise checkpoint locations accordingly.

References

1. Chen, N., Yu, Y., Ren, S.: Checkpoint interval and system's overall quality for message logging-based rollback and recovery in distributed and embedded computing. In: ICESS 2009 (2009)
2. Elnozahy, E.N(M.), Alvisi, L., Wang, Y.-M.: A survey of rollback-recovery protocols in message-passing systems. ACM Comput. Surv. (2002)
3. Ezenwoye, O., Sadjadi, S.M.: Trap/bpel: A framework for dynamic adaptation of composite services. In: Proc. WEBIST 2007 (2007)
4. Mansour, H.E., Dillon, T.: Dependability and rollback recovery for composite web services. IEEE Transactions on Services Computing (2011)
5. Liu, A., Qing, L., Huang, L., Xiao, M.: Facts: A framework for fault-tolerant composition of transactional web services. IEEE Transactions on Services Computing (2010)
6. Elnozahy, E.N.(M.), Alvisi, L., Wang, Y.-M.: A survey of rollback-recovery protocols in message-passing systems. ACM Comput. Surv. (2002)
7. Oracle White Paper, editor. Oracle SOA Suite 12c A Detailed Look. Oracle (2014)
8. Darby, P.J., Tzeng, N.-F.: Decentralized qos-aware checkpointing arrangement in mobile grid computing. IEEE Transactions on Mobile Computing (2010)
9. Rukoz, M., Cardinale, Y., Angarita, R.: Faceta*: Checkpointing for transactional composite web service execution based on petri-nets. Procedia Computer Science (2012)
10. Urban, S.D., Gao, L., Shrestha, R., Courter, A.: Achieving recovery in service composition with assurance points and integration rules. In: Meersman, R., Dillon, T.S., Herrero, P. (eds.) OTM 2010. LNCS, vol. 6426, pp. 428–437. Springer, Heidelberg (2010)
11. Vani Vathsala, A., Mohanty, H.: Using hmm for predicting response time of web services. In: Proceedings of the CUBE International Information Technology Conference. ACM (2012)
12. Vani Vathsala, A., Mohanty, H.: Interaction patterns based checkpointing of choreographed web services. In: Proc of the 6th International Workshop on Principles of Engineering Service-Oriented and Cloud Systems. ACM (2014)
13. Vathsala, A.V., Mohanty, H.: A survey on checkpointing web services. In: Proc of the 6th International Workshop on Principles of Engineering Service-Oriented and Cloud Systems. ACM (2014)
14. Vathsala, A.V., Mohanty, H.: Web service response time prediction using hmm and bayesian network. In: Jain, L.C., Patnaik, S., Ichalkaranje, N. (eds.) Intelligent Computing, Communication and Devices. AISC, vol. 308, pp. 327–335. Springer, Heidelberg (2015)

A Preprocessing of Service Registry:
Based on I/O Parameter Similarity

Lakshmi H.N. and Hrushikesha Mohanty

University of Hyderabad, Hyderabad, India
hnlakshmi@gmail.com, hmcs_hcu@yahoo.com

Abstract. For registry based web services, finding a service for a given input and output, can be improved by registry preprocessing, that groups services of similar input and output parameters, to a cluster. This paper proposes a Wordnet based similarity detection technique for service I/O parameter clustering and also demonstrates the uses of the technique with experimental result.

1 Introduction

The increasing availability of web services within an organization and on the Web demands for an efficient search mechanism to find services satisfying user requirements. Various approaches can be used for service search, such as, searching in UDDI, Web and Service portals. Universal Description, Discovery and Integration (UDDI) is an industry standard for service registries,developed to solve the web service search problem. In this paper we take up the issue of searching at service registries for its practicality in business world as providers would like to post their services centrally, for searching there is less time consuming than searching on world wide web. Further in many business domains, privacy is a concern and that drives implementation towards registry based service provision.

Among different techniques for service composition and service search, input/output parameter matching is a technique of often use [18,7,6,4,12,14]. The input and output parameters of a web service represents its functionality and can be utilized for finding similar and composable services. Most of the current approaches for service search and service composition use semantic web services that have semantic tagged descriptions[12], e.g., OWL-S, WSDL-S [2,15].

However, these approaches have many limitations: it is impractical to expect all services to have semantic tagged descriptions and descriptions of majority of existing web services are specified using WSDL and do not have associated semantics. Approaches that use non-semantic services[7,18,16] often refer to domain ontology that could be at times large and complex enough for the purpose. Further, from the consumer's perspective, the consumer may be unaware of the domain and the exact terms to be used in the service request. As a result, such

R. Natarajan et al. (Eds.): ICDCIT 2015, LNCS 8956, pp. 220–232, 2015.
© Springer International Publishing Switzerland 2015

a search may overlook many relevant services. In order to address these limitations a generic input/output parameter matching approach, not tied to a specific service description language, needs to be developed.

A parameter name,(eg: FlightInfo, CheckHotelCost), is typically a sequence of concatenated words,(eg: Flight,Check,Hotel,Cost), referred to as terms. For effectively matching I/O parameters of web services, it is essential to consider their underlying semantics. However, this is hard since parameter names are not standardized and are usually built using terms that are highly varied due to the use of synonyms, hypernyms, and different naming conventions. Hence, to widen the scope of I/O parameter matching, it is useful to cluster service I/O parameters based on their similarity.

We exploit the semantic similarity and co-occurrence of terms in parameter names, computed using wordnet as the underlying ontology, to cluster service parameters into semantic groups. We propose a semantic similarity measure for computing similarity of parameters and an approach for clustering service parameters based on the classical DBSCAN algorithm[3]. The parameter clustering serves as a pre-processing step for I/O parameter based web service search. Experimental evidence shows that the clusters generated by our algorithm has a better Precision and Recall values when compared with the clusters generated by K-means algorithm[10].

The rest of the paper is organized as follows. In section 2 we describe the semantic similarity measure for computing similarity of service I/O parameters. Section 3 describes the procedure for clustering service parameters into semantic groups. In Section 4 we essay the related work. Section 5 discusses our experimental results. We conclude our work in Section 6.

2   Similarity Measure for Clustering Service Parameters

The similarity/distance measure reflects the degree of closeness/separation between a symbolic description of two objects into a single numeric value and hence should correspond to the characteristics that distinguish the clusters embedded in a dataset. The similarity metrics like edit distance etc. mostly measure a kind of structural similarity with scant regard to semantic similarity. For this application semantic based search is wishful for providing a number of alternative web services to a user on need. A cluster of web services is formed on the basis of similarity of their I/O parameters. Then for a given set of query I/O parameters, corresponding set of alternative services can be picked from a cluster that is selected by matching of query I/O parameters to I/O parameters of a cluster. Thus, in general measuring similarity between two parameters has an importance for preprocessing of service registry to find clusters of services. Clustering of parameters based on similarity is a two-step method. First,a parameter is tokenized to terms and second, the parameter similarity is computed.

2.1   Tokenizing Web Service I/O Parameters

A parameter name,(eg: FlightInfo, CheckResortCost), is typically a sequence of concatenated words like Flight,Check,Resort,etc., referred to as terms. For widening the scope of matching I/O parameters of web services, it is essential to consider their underlying semantics. However, this is hard since parameter names are not standardized and are usually built using terms that are highly varied due to the use of synonyms, hypernyms, and different naming conventions. We hence exploit the semantic similarity of the terms in service registry to form clusters of parameter names. Further these clusters are used for searching webservices for a given query I/O parameters.

Due to the nature of the parameter names normally included in a WSDL, we first apply a tokenization process to produce the set of terms to be actually matched before applying the parameter name similarity function. For eg., parameter names included in a Web service could be like HotelName or FlightCost which are difficult to find in a general purpose ontology. On the contrary, we can find the terms composing these names: e.g., hotel, cost, name, flight, in the ontology. Hence, we tokenize a parameter name to obtain the terms to be used for similarity calculation. A parameter name P_i is tokenized to a term vector T_{P_i} according to a set of rules inspired by common naming conventions, taking care of case change, presence of underscore and hyphenation, etc.

2.2   Parameter Similarity Function ($pSim$)

The Parameter Similarity Function, $pSim$, calculates the semantic similarity between two parameters and returns a value in $[0\ldots1]$. The higher the value of $pSim$, the higher the similarity between the two parameters. In particular $pSim(P_1, P_2) = 1$ iff P_1 is semantically similar to P_2, whereas, $pSim(P_1, P_2) = 0$, iff P_1 and P_2 are semantically unrelated. The $pSim$ function relies on a maximization function called $maxMeas$ that computes the maximum measure between the two term vectors we are comparing.

Maximization Function ($maxMeas$). On inspecting many web services in dataset[1], we observed that most of the Parameter names are built of domain dependent terms. Table 1 lists a few example parameter names that can be used to get the cost of a hotel or room. It can be seen that though the terms are similar, their placement in the parameters differ from one to another. For ex: looking for the term $Hotel$ in all the parameter names listed in Table 1, we observe that it is the first term in 5, second term in 1, third term in 7 and 8, parameters 2 and 4 have synonymn $Room$ as second term and parameters 3 and 6 have synonymn $Resort$ as second and sixth term respectively. Given a set of terms for parameters, they can be placed anywhere based on the naming conventions used by the provider. Hence, given the term vectors T_{P_i} and T_{P_j}, we compare each term in a parameter T_{P_i} with all terms in T_{P_j}.

The maximization function is formulated as a maximum weighted bipartite matching problem. Given a graph G = (V,E), a matching M $\subseteq$ E, is a set of

Table 1. Different placements of *Hotel* in Parameters

Par No	Parameter Names	Placement for *Hotel*
1	GetHotelCost	second
2	FetchRoomPrice	second (Synonymn)
3	CheckResortCost	second (Synonymn)
4	RequestRoomRate	second (Synonymn)
5	HotelCostEnquiry	first
6	ResortPrice	first (Synonymn)
7	RequestForHotelRate	third
8	CostOfHotel	third

pairwise non-adjacent edges; that is, no two edges share a common vertex. A maximum weighted bipartite matching is defined as a matching where the sum of the values of the edges in the matching have a maximal value.

Let A and B be set of vertices representing the term vectors that need to be matched, with an associated edge weight function given by measuring function $mf : (A, B) \rightarrow [0 \ldots 1]$. The maximization function $maxMeas : (mf, A, B) \rightarrow [0 \ldots 1]$ returns the maximum weighted bipartite matching, i.e., a matching so that the average of the edge weights is maximum. Expressing the maximization function using Linear Programming model, we have :

$$maxMeas\,(mf, A, B) = \frac{\max \left[\sum_{i \in I, j \in J} mf\,(A_i, B_j) \cdot x_{ij}\right]}{\max\{\|A\|, \|B\|\}}$$

subject to,

$$\sum_{j \in J} x_{ij} = 1, \quad \forall i \in I, \quad \sum_{i \in I} x_{ij} = 1, \quad \forall j \in J \tag{1}$$

$$0 \le mf\,(A_i, B_j) \le 1, \quad i \in I, \quad j \in J$$

$$I = [1 \ldots \|A\|], \quad J = [1 \ldots \|B\|]$$

$\|A\| < \|B\|$ implies that the number of terms in A is lesser than the number of terms in B; so, for each term in A, we may find a similar term in B. On the contrary, $\|A\| > \|B\|$ always evaluates to a $maxMeas < 1$. Since our approach aims to compute the similarity between A and B, we divide the result of the maximization by the maximum cardinality of A and B. Hence, the function $maxMeas$ is symmetric , i.e., $maxMeas\,(mf, A, B) = maxMeas\,(mf, B, A)$. Apart from $\|A\|$ and $\|B\|$, the $maxMeas$ function is affected by $mf : (A, B)$ values.

Fig 1 illustrates the computation in $maxMeas$ function , where the bold lines constitute the maximum weighted bipartite matching.

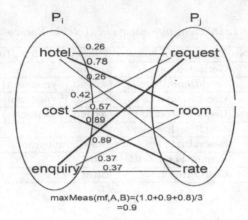

maxMeas(mf,A,B)=(1.0+0.9+0.8)/3
=0.9

Fig. 1. Illustration of $maxMeas$ function

Given two parameters P_A and P_B and their term vectors T_A and T_B, their semantic similarity is evaluated using the $maxMeas$ function introduced above as:

$$pSim\,(P_A, P_B) = maxMeas\,(simMeas, T_A, T_B) \tag{2}$$

The weights of the edges are given by $simMeas : (term_{Ai}, term_{Bj}) \rightarrow [0..1]$.

Wordnet for Similarity Computation. Several approaches are available for computing semantic similarity among terms, by mapping terms (concepts) to an ontology and by examining their relationships in that ontology. Some of the popular semantic similarity methods are implemented and evaluated using WordNet as the underlying reference ontology [13]. We use jcn (Jiang and Conrath) measure for computing the semantic similarity between two terms.

Note that the following properties hold for the Parameter Similarity Function ($pSim$):

1. $0 \leq pSim(P_A, P_B) \leq 1$. $pSim(P_A, P_B) = 1$ iff the two parameters are totally similar and fully replacable and $pSim(P_A, P_B) = 0$ iff the two parameters are totally unrelated.
2. $pSim$ is symmetric , i.e., $pSim(P_A, P_B) = pSim(P_B, P_A)$.

3   Similarity Based Clustering of Service Parameters (SCSP)

Our clustering is based on the following heuristic : *"parameters tend to express the same concept if the terms in their names are semantically similar"* and is validated by experimental results. The clustering algorithm, Similarity Based Clustering of Service Parameters(SCSP), is based on the classical DBSCAN

Algorithm[3]. DBSCAN is a density based clustering algorithm, designed to discover clusters of arbitrary shape and capable of handling noise and outliers effectively. The key idea in DBCAN is that for each data object of a cluster, the neighbourhood of a given radius(Eps) has to contain at least a minimum number(MinSP) of objects.

3.1 Definitions

The following definitions are used in our clustering algorithms :

1. ϵ **Semantic Neighborhood of a Parameter:** We define ϵ Semantic Neighborhood of a parameter P_i in a set of parameters P, as follows:

$$SN_\epsilon(P_i) = \{P_j \in P | pSim(P_i, P_j) \geq \epsilon\} \tag{3}$$

where ϵ is the minimum parameter similarity value defined to form clusters.

2. **Core Parameter(CP):** A parameter is a Core Parameter, iff,

$$|SN_\epsilon(CP)| \geq MinSP \tag{4}$$

where $MinSP$ is the minimum number of similar parameters required to make a cluster.

3. **Noise:** Let $C_1, \ldots, C_k$ be the clusters of parameters in P wrt. ϵ and $MinSP$. We define the noise as the set parameters in P not belonging to any cluster C_i , i.e.,

$$Noise = \{p \in P | \forall i : p \notin C_i\} \tag{5}$$

3.2 SCSP Algorithm

To find a cluster, SCSP starts with an arbitrary parameter P_i in P and retrieve all parameters that are in ϵ Semantic Neighborhood of P_i. If P_i is a Core Parameter, as defined in eqn 4, then this set of parameters yields a cluster with respect to ϵ and $MinSP$. If P_i is not a Core Parameter, then the algorithm continues by searching for another Core Parameter in P. This procedure is continued till all the clusters and $Noise$ in P are generated. Algorithm 1 and Procedure 2 provides the psuedocode for the clustering algorithm and the procedure for selecting a Core Parameter.

3.3 Cluster Validation

Ideally, clusters generated by SCSP Algorithm should have the following features:

1. Rare parameters should be left unclustered.
2. The cohesion of a cluster(the similarity between parameters inside a cluster) should be strong; the correlation between clusters(the similarity between parameters in different clusters) should be weak.

Algorithm 1. Similarity Based Clustering of Service Parameters

---

    Input: $pSim$ for P, ϵ, $MinSP$
    Output: Parameter Clusters
1 **foreach** P_i *in* P **do**
2   nextP=P_i
3   **if** $CoreParameter(nextP, \epsilon, MinSP)$ **then**
4   Create a cluster with $nextP$ as $CoreParameter$
5   **else**
6   Mark $nextP$ as $Noise$

Procedure `Core Parameter`

    Input: nextP,$pSim$ for P, ϵ, $MinSP$
    Output: Boolean value
1 count:=0
2 **foreach** P_i *in* P **do**
3   **if** $pSim(P_i, nextP) \geq \epsilon$ **then**
4   count:=count +1
5 **if** $count \geq MinSP$ **then**
6   return true
7 **else**
8   return false

Traditionally, cohesion is defined as the sum of squares of Euclidean distances from each point to the center of the cluster it belongs to; correlation is defined as the sum of squares of distances between cluster centers[5]. Clearly, these measures cannot be applied to our context because of the similarity measure utilised for clustering. We hence quantify the cohesion and correlation of clusters based on parameter similarity function defined for clustering.

Given a cluster C_I, we define the cohesion of C_I as the percentage of closely associated parameter pairs over all term pairs,i.e.,

$$Coh(C_I) = \frac{\|(P_i, P_j) \mid P_i, P_j \in C_I, i \neq j, pSim(P_i, P_j) > \epsilon\|}{\|C_I\| \cdot \|C_I - 1\|} \tag{6}$$

Given two cluster C_I and C_J, we define the correlation between C_I and C_J as the similarity measure between the Core Parameters of the two clusters,i.e.,

$$Cor(C_I, C_J) = pSim(CP(C_I), CP(C_J)) \tag{7}$$

An ideal clustering has a high average Cohesion value while maintaining a low average correlation value. Our goal is to obtain a parameter clustering with such properties.

4   Related Work

Specifications for web services fall into two main categories viz. ontology based and keyword based. A web service of former category is built with domain ontology whereas of latter case keywords are used for specifying inputs and outputs. Though, semantic webservices are versatile in arture still keyword based service specification is popular for its fast response avoiding reference to domain ontology that could be at times large and complex enough for the purpose. Hence we have taken keyword based service specification and are interested in I/O Parameter based search that correspond to service functionality which user may find interesting. In this paper we propose to cluster I/O parameters to widen the scope of I/O parameter based service search.

A great deal of research has been done in recent years on wordnet based approaches[18,11,9,8,17] to enhance the efficiency of semantic service matching and on I/O parameter based web service search[18,16,14] in a service registry. In this section we summarize these approaches for non-semantic web services.

4.1   Wordnet Based Approaches for Service Matching

Zeina et al[17] propose an approach for tagging Web services automatically. Text mining and machine learning techniques are used for extraction of candidate tags and for selection of relevant tags. The extracted set of tags is then enriched with semantically related tags using WordNet. Cheng et al.[18] present a matching algorithm SMA between web services of multiple input/output parameters, which considers the semantic similarity of concepts in parameters based on WordNet. They propose a service composition algorithm Fast-EP based on their storage strategy.

Shao et al.[8] propose a web service discovery method that combines Word-Net and domain ontologies along with SWRL (Semantic Web Rule Language) rules. They use WordNet to extend queries,whereas domain ontology is used to store services descriptions, service name and service attributes. Shang et al.[9] propose a method that uses domain ontologies in conjunction with WordNet to evaluate functional similarity between queries and web service descriptions, based on WSDL and SAWSDL. WordNet is also exploited to expand the query for increasing accuracy of service search.

4.2   I/O Parameter Based Approaches for Service Search and Composition

Xin Dong et.al.[16] develop a clustering based web service search engine, Woogle. They extract a set of semantic concepts, by exploiting the co-occurrence of terms in Web service inputs and outputs of operations, from the set of Web services that match a given user query. This makes it possible to combine the original keywords with the extracted concepts and compare two services on a keyword and concepts level to improve precision and recall. This approach leads to significantly better results than a plain keyword-based search. Paliwal et.al[12] propose an ontology guided categorization of Web Services into functional categories for efficient service discovery.

Pablo et.al.[14] present an A* algorithm for matching semantic input-output message structure for web service composition. A service dependency graph is dynamically generated for a given request from services in a repository and a minimal composition satisfying the request is found using A* search algorithm. Daewook Lee et.al [7] propose an relational database approach to build a scalable and efficient I/O parameter based web services composition search system. The compositions are pre-computed and stored in tables, along with the ontology information extracted from web services.

Most of the current approaches discussed above for I/O parameter based service search and composition either use semantic services or domain ontology for finding services having similar I/O parameters. These approches have many limitations: it is impractical to expect all services to have semantic tagged descriptions and descriptions of majority of existing web services are specified using WSDL and do not have associated semantics. The domain ontology referred to could be at times large and complex enough for the purpose. In order to address these limitations a generic input/output parameter matching approach, not tied to a specific service description language, needs to be developed. Hence, to widen the scope of I/O parameter matching we propose to cluster service I/O parameters based on their similarity, computed using wordnet as the underlying ontology.

5   Experimental Results

In this section, we present an experimental evaluation of the proposed approach by measuring:

1. Quality of Service Parameter clustering.
2. Performance of I/O parameter clustering.

Experimental Setup. To evaluate the performance of Algorithm $SCSP$, as discussed in section 3.2, we conducted experiments on QWS dataset[1]. We ran our experiments on a 1.3GHz Intel machine with 4 GB RAM running Microsoft Windows 7. Our algorithms were implemented with JDK 1.6, Eclipse 3.6.0 and Oracle 10g. The values for the parameters ϵ and $MinSP$ for $SCSP$ Algorithm is set as 0.75 and 3 respectively. The experiments were initially conducted for 200 parameters in the registry and then repeated for all the 500 I/O parameters of 1000 web services in the registry.

5.1   Evaluating Quality of Service Parameter Clustering

To evaluate the Quality of $SCSP$ clustering algorithm, we introduce two metrics Cluster Cohesion and Correlation as defined in section 3.3. We compare the

performance of our approach with clusters generated by K-means[10] clustering approach. K-means is a widely adopted clustering algorithm that is simple
and fast. Its drawback is that the number of clusters has to be predefined manually before clustering. On applying $SCSP$ and K-means algorithm on 200 service
I/O parameters, 5 clusters were obtained, for which cluster cohesion was calculated. Repeating the same process for 500 service I/O parameters yielded 10
clusters. Figure 2 compares the cluster cohesion values obtained for the clusters
generated by $SCSP$ algorithm with those generated by K-means clustering. The
average cluster cohesion for $SCSP$ algorithm is 0.295 whereas for K-means algorithm is 0.623 for 500 service I/O parameters, as seen in Figure 2b. It can
be inferred from the results that our approach generates clusters with higher
Cluster Cohesion values, thus generating clusters of better quality.

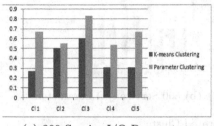
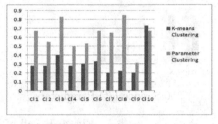

(a) 200 Service I/O Parameters   (b) 500 Service I/O Parameters

Fig. 2. Cluster Cohesion of Generated Clusters

5.2 Performance of Service Parameter Clustering

We use two standard metrics: *Precision* and *Recall*, widely adopted in information retrieval domain, to measure the overall performance of $SCSP$ clustering
algorithm. The performance of our approach is compared with clusters generated
by the standard K-means[10] algorithm. Let $SP(C_i)$ be the number of parameters that are correctly placed in the cluster C_i, $MP(C_i)$ be the number of
parameters that are misplaced in the cluster C_i and $MSP(C_i)$ be the number of
parameters that should have been placed in C_i but has been placed in another
cluster. Then *Precision* and *Recall* of a cluster C_i is defined as below :

$$Precision\,(C_i) = \frac{SP\,(C_i)}{SP\,(C_i) + MP\,(C_i)} \tag{8}$$

$$Recall\,(C_i) = \frac{SP\,(C_i)}{SP\,(C_i) + MSP\,(C_i)} \tag{9}$$

Figures 3 and 4 compares the values of Precision and Recall of clusters generated by $SCSP$ algorithm versus that of K-means clustering, for 200 and 500
service I/O parameters respectively. The average Precision and Recall values obtained is summarized in Table 2 It can be inferred from the results obtained that
our approach outperforms the traditional K-means approach both in Precision
and Recall.

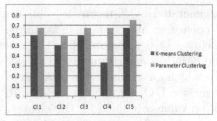
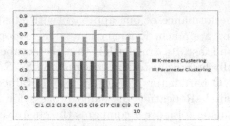

(a) 200 Service I/O Parameters   (b) 500 Service I/O Parameters

Fig. 3. Precision of Generated Clusters

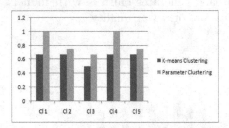
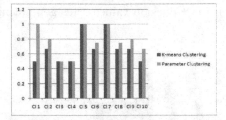

(a) 200 Service I/O Parameters   (b) 500 Service I/O Parameters

Fig. 4. Recall of Generated Clusters

Table 2. Average Precision and Recall of Clusters

Number of I/O Parameters	Performance Measure	Algorithm SCSP	Algorithm K-means
200	Precision	0.672	0.54
200	Recall	0.834	0.636
500	Precision	0.66	0.38
500	Recall	0.777	0.668

6   Conclusion

I/O Parameter based web service matching is an important issue, especially for non-semantic Web service search and composition. For this application semantic based search is wishful for providing a number of alternative web services to a user on need. A cluster of web services is formed on the basis of similarity of their I/O parameters. Then for a given set of query I/O parameters, corresponding set of alternative services can be picked from a cluster that is selected by matching of query I/O parameters to I/O parameters of a cluster.

Thus, in general measuring similarity between two parameters has an importance for preprocessing of service registry to find clusters of services. Hence in order to widen the scope of search for a web service with a given set of I/O parameters, it is useful to cluster services having similar I/O parameters. In this paper, we propose an approach for clustering service I/O parameters on their similarity, using wordnet as the underlying ontology.

Algorithm $SCSP$ in section 3.2 generates Parameter Clusters of I/O parameters of the web services in a registry. The cluster selection in the algorithm is governed by the values of ϵ and $minSP$, as discussed in section 3.1. We have simulated the algorithms on QWS Dataset[1]. Experimental evidence shows that the clusters generated by our algorithm has a better Precision and Recall values when compared with the clusters generated by K-means algorithm[10]. We would further like to utilize these parameter clusters for clustering services with similar I/O parameters to enable Parameter based web service search in service registries.

References

1. Al-Masri, E., Mahmoud, Qusay, H.: Discovering the best web service: A neural network-based solution. In: IEEE International Conference on Systems, Man and Cybernetics, SMC 2009, pp. 4250–4255 (October 2009)
2. David, M., Massimo, P., et al.: Bringing semantics to web services: The OWL-S approach. In: Cardoso, J., Sheth, A.P. (eds.) SWSWPC 2004. LNCS, vol. 3387, pp. 26–42. Springer, Heidelberg (2005)
3. Ester, M., Kriegel, H.-P., Sander, J., Xu, X.: A density-based algorithm for discovering clusters in large spatial databases with noise. In: KDD, vol. 96, pp. 226–231 (1996)
4. Lakshmi, H.N., Mohanty, H.: RDBMS for service repository and composition. In: Fourth International Conference on Advanced Computing (ICoAC), pp. 1–8 (December 2012)
5. Hand David, J., Padhraic, S., Heikki, M.: Principles of Data Mining. MIT Press, Cambridge (2001)
6. Kwon, J., Lee, D.: Non-redundant web services composition based on a two-phase algorithm. Data and Knowledge Engineering 71, 69 (2012)
7. Lee, D., Kwon, J., Lee, S., Park, S., Hong, B.: Scalable and efficient web services composition based on a relational database. J. Syst. Softw. 84(12) (2011)
8. Lu, S.Y., Hsu, K.-H., Kuo, L.-J.: A semantic service match approach based on wordnet and SWRL rules. In: 2013 IEEE 10th International Conference on e-Business Engineering (ICEBE), pp. 419–422 (September 2013)
9. Ma, S.-P., Li, C.-H., Tsai, Y.-Y., Lan, C.-W.: Web service discovery using lexical and semantic query expansion. In: 2013 IEEE 10th International Conference on e-Business Engineering (ICEBE), pp. 423–428 (September 2013)
10. MacQueen, J., et al.: Some methods for classification and analysis of multivariate observations. In: Proceedings of the Fifth Berkeley Symposium on Mathematical Statistics and Probability, California, USA, pp. 281–297 (1967)
11. Maher, M., Hamza, H.S., Mohamed, R.M.: Service composition recovery using formal concept analyst & wordnet similarity. In: 2011 IEEE International Conference on Information Reuse and Integration (IRI), pp. 123–128. IEEE (2011)
12. Paliwal, A.V., Shafiq, B., Vaidya, J., Xiong, H., Adam, N.: Semantics-based automated service discovery. IEEE Transactions on Services Computing 5(2), 260–275 (2012)
13. Pedersen, T., Patwardhan, S., Michelizzi, J.: Wordnet:similarity: Measuring the relatedness of concepts. In: Demonstration Papers at HLT-NAACL 2004, HLT-NAACL–Demonstrations 2004, pp. 38–41. Association for Computational Linguistics (2004)

14. Rodriguez-Mier, P., Mucientes, M., Lama, M.: Automatic web service composition with a heuristic-based search algorithm. In: 2011 IEEE International Conference on Web Services (ICWS), pp. 81–88 (July 2011)
15. McIlraith, S.A., Martin, D.L.: Bringing semantics to web services. IEEE Intelligent Systems 18(1), 90–93 (2003)
16. Xin, D., Alon, H., Jayant, M., Ema, N., Jun, Z.: Similarity search for web services. In: Proceedings of the Thirtieth International Conference on Very Large Data Bases, VLDB 2004, vol. 30. VLDB Endowment (2004)
17. Azmeh, Z., Falleri, J.-R., Huchard, M., Tibermacine, C.: Automatic web service tagging using machine learning and wordNet synsets. In: Filipe, J., Cordeiro, J. (eds.) WEBIST 2010. LNBIP, vol. 75, pp. 46–59. Springer, Heidelberg (2011)
18. Zeng, C., Ou, W., Zheng, Y., Han, D.: Efficient web service composition and intelligent search based on relational database. In: 2010 International Conference on Information Science and Applications (ICISA), pp. 1–8 (April 2010)

Financial Risk Management in e-commerce Using Executable Business Process Modeling Notation

Ramkumar Iyer and Sanjeevi Moorthy

Paypal India Private Limited
{rriyer,smoorthy}@paypal.com

Abstract. In e-commerce systems like online auction houses or online stores, there are financial transactions involving buyers and sellers. At large payment processing firms, there is significant risk of fraud (upto 0.9 %). This fraud can be prevented before the actual transaction phase through risk scoring models. In the post transactions phase, measures like withholding or reserving funds of the seller, or asking for additional supporting material from the seller to release the funds can be done. There are numerous variations based on different geographies or different seller classes or different holding mechanisms of these measures.

It was found that the software being developed for a payment system was combining both infrastructural software (database, queue, logs) as well the actual risk business process. Subsequently, prototypes were created for different risk measures in the post transaction phase using executable BPMN2 (using Activiti engine). For example, a certain amount of money may be withheld from the seller for a configurable time period which can be edited in the graphical BPMN2.

In this paper, we discuss the numerous types of transactions, the numerous measures for financial risk and how BPMN2, can be used to model the same and at the same time form a performant executable component reducing development time. It is also possible that such models can be standardized and exchanged in the industry.

1   Introduction

E-commerce is one of the rapidly growing businesses in the world with revenues expected to be in the range of 1.5 trillion dollars as of 2014. The average fraud rate in e-commerce has been estimated to range around 0.9% (approx. 3.5 billion dollars) which is a significant number due to risks like credit card fraud, identity theft, spoofing and other sophisticated attacks. The classic risk model has 4 major ways of dealing with risk: Avoidance, Reduction, Transference or Acceptance. Each of these concepts is applicable at a certain stage of the transaction being conducted between a buyer and seller. The transaction stages are typically split into pre-transaction, transaction and post-transaction stage. Pre-transaction risk avoidance strategies can be adopted based on payment history or whether the person conducting the transaction is on a blacklist or if the credit card is under dispute or there is a sudden location change. In post

R. Natarajan et al. (Eds.): ICDCIT 2015, LNCS 8956, pp. 233–238, 2015.

transaction, holding a payment in the sellers account and releasing it only after certain duration so as to avoid any disputes or asking for additional information if fraud is suspected is an accepted method. This paper primarily focuses on modeling post transaction risk in an executable fashion however pre-transaction risk can also be modeled.

The software achieving the objective under study is highly complex, distributed with real-time elements and asynchronous components. It is primarily developed for post transaction risk management. The nature of variations handled in the software could be geography specific or seller specific or product specific or mechanism specific. Further, in the software, there is close coupling between the infrastructural code (say accessing the database, queueing system, mailing system, logging system) and the actual business process for post-transaction risk handling. Also, software requires multiple changes in code and business logic level to introduce changes and there is a lot of duplicate cut and copy code. By segregating the software into infrastructural and post transaction business process models that can be executed it is possible to achieve ease of comprehension, rapid configurability, simplified service composition and orchestration, ease of deployment, and standardized versioning.

2   Brief Review of Business Process Modeling and Risk

There has been a lot of work on risk and business; as risk forms a fundamental component. Business process modeling has been used for tasks ranging from program planning to program execution [1]. In the current context, program execution is one the key parameters for realizing it benefits technically. Typically flow charts, data flow diagrams, control flow diagrams are some of the traditional methods. BPEL (Business Process Execution Language) and BPMN2 (Business Process Modeling Notation) are some of the more modern methods. The modeling element of choice if BPMN2 primarily because it is friendly towards business personnel as well as technical personnel, the tool support for BPMN2 is rapidly growing and variety of training materials are available for free from the concept to execution cycle [2, 3, 4].

In e-commerce, there have been numerous attempts to integrate BPM. For example, the work [5] addresses web service composition in e-business. In [6], BPM is introduced as a technology for collaborative commerce (C-Commerce) with applications for e-procurement. In, [7], workflow management systems and their types are elucidated with a production work flow having high business value, low uniqueness, high complexity and high task structure. This paper is one of the first to address production workflows in e-commerce live systems. With regards to financial risk, [8, 9] model financial risk based elements.

The research problem addressed in this paper is how executable BPMN2 models can be used for financial risk management in e-commerce and the investigating the technical areas like performance and usability where there can be future improvements. This will also form the basis of full-fledged adoption in the financial risk domain both at organization and industry level. Activiti [10, 11] was chosen as the experimental open source BPMN2 process execution platform due to the availability of an integrated modeling tool, management tool, larger specification support, community support, open source nature and Java interoperability.

3   A Brief Review of Introducing BPMN2 within an Organization

A step by step model is required to make BPMN2 successful [12]. The steps followed in migration of the post transaction risk software are in Fig 1.

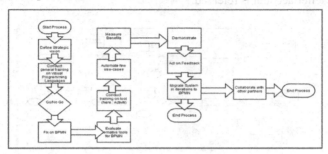

Fig. 1. Process for introducing BPMN2 within an organization

4   Use Cases

In this section, use cases are provided to prove the applicability of financial risk systems in e-commerce and how executable BPMN2 was applied.

4.1   Holds and Reserves

All transactions are placed under a hold or a reserve when the buyer pays the seller for a specific good. These holds are auto-released after a configurable period. An executable BPMN2 diagram models the same.

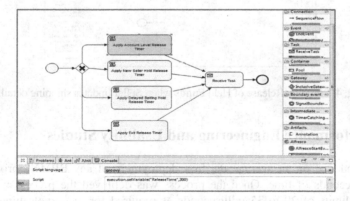

Fig. 2. Release Timers for Hold Types

4.2   Buyer Confirmation and Buyer Rating

In certain cases, if the buyer confirms the receipt of a product or if the buyer rates the seller highly after the transaction is completed in post-transaction phase, the hold placed on the seller account is released.

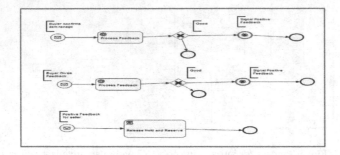

Fig. 3. Release mechanisms when buyer gives positive feedback or confirms receipt

4.3   Shipping Release

Sometimes, the seller may not be able to wait till the hold amount is released after the specified configurable period. Hence, they would provide proof that the item has been shipped.

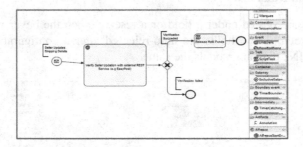

Fig. 4. Shipping Release of Held Funds when Seller updates shipping details

5   Performance Engineering and Usability Studies

It was found that on an average the first deployment of any BPMN2 process took around 4 seconds of time. Once the process was deployed the process was within acceptable limits of 20 to 35 milliseconds as required for the simple timer process discussed in 4.1.   Further load testing is being carried out to validate the same with live traffic. The deployment time of the solution was also considerably reduced.

6   Conclusions and Future Works

This paper looked at financial risk management in the post transaction phase and how executable BPMN2 can be used in software to segregate framework and business process level concerns and improve productivity especially when the software has multiple simple variations on a common theme. A model was presented on how to introduce BPMN2 based solutions. The existence of an overarching strategy in the model and gradual rather than top down introduction of BPMN2 is a criteria for success discovered.

Executable BPMN2 models for financial risk management in e-commerce can be standardized across the industry, only allowing for company or service specific variation. This will allow for uniform buyer and seller experience when dealing with a plethora of e-commerce solutions and also allow them cognitive insight into the actual process. For example consider a shareable Know Your Customer executable model. This is termed as multi-tenancy. Future benchmarking with other approaches like BPEL or proprietary is also planned.

Mathematically, BPMN2 has been modeled as graph rewrite rules [13]. One of the applicable emerging areas for modeling e-commerce risk in post transaction phase is artificial immune theory [14] which was validated with senior risk professionals in the organization. Further, complexity theory [15] can be used to model the external environmental changes. The exploration of mathematical foundation of the executable modeling with these theories is also planned.

Acknowledgements. We thank our organization and Risk Product Development participants in our training and ideation programs for all their feedback and encouragement.

References

1. Dufresne, T., Martin, J.: Process Modeling for E-Business. In: Methods for Information Systems Engineering: Knowledge Management and E-Business (2003)
2. Shapiro, R., Fischer, L., Silver, B.: BPMN2 2.0 Handbook (2010)
3. Freund, J., Rucker, B.: Real-Life BPMN2: Using BPMN2 2.0 to Analyze, Improve, and Automate Processes in Your Company (2012)
4. BPM 2013, http://bpm2013.tsinghua.edu.cn/wp-content/uploads/2013/09/From-Conceptual-to-Executable-BPMN2-Process-Models.pdf
5. Zhang, D.: Web services composition for process management in E-Business. Journal of Computer Information Systems XLV (2), 83–91 (2005)
6. Chen, M., Zhang, D., Zhou, L.: Empowering collaborative commerce with Web services enabled business process management systems, Decision Support Systems (2005)
7. Menztas, C., Halaris, C.: Workflow on the Web: Integrating E-Commerce and Business Process Management. International Journal of E-Business Strategy Management 1(2), 147–157 (1999)

8. Marcinkowski, B., Kuciapski, M.: A Business Process Modeling Notation Extension for Risk Handling. In: Cortesi, A., Chaki, N., Saeed, K., Wierzchoń, S. (eds.) CISIM 2012. LNCS, vol. 7564, pp. 374–381. Springer, Heidelberg (2012)
9. Altuhhov, O., Matulevičius, R., Ahmed, N.: An Extension of Business Process Model and Notation for Security Risk Management. Int. Journal of Information System Modeling and Design (2013)
10. Activiti, http://activiti.org/
11. Rademakers, T.: Activiti in Action: Executable Business Processes in BPMN2 2.0. Manning Publications Co., Greenwich (2012)
12. BPTrends, BPM Critical Success Factors Lessons Learned from Successful BPM Organizations (2011)
13. Dijkman, R., Van Gorp, P.: BPMN 2.0 execution semantics formalized as graph rewrite rules. In: Mendling, J., Weidlich, M., Weske, M. (eds.) BPMN 2010. LNBIP, vol. 67, pp. 16–30. Springer, Heidelberg (2010)
14. Zeng, Z., Wang, J.: Advances in Neural Network Research and Applications, pp. 106–107 (2010)
15. Liu, H., Tian, Z., Guan, X.: Analysis of Complexity and Evolution of E-commerce System. International Journal of u-and e-Service, Science and Technology 6(6) (2013)

DILT: A Hybrid Model for Dynamic Composition and Execution of Heterogeneous Web Services

Kanchana Rajaram[1], Chitra Babu[1], and Akshaya Ganesan[2]

[1] Department of Computer Science and Engineering, SSN College of Engineering,
Anna University, Chennai - 603110, Tamil Nadu, India
{rkanch,chitra}@ssn.edu.in
[2] St. Joseph's College of Engineering, Anna University, Chennai, Tamil Nadu, India
akshaya1988@gmail.com

Abstract. Business applications in domains such as e-Governance, require collaboration among both Governmental and non Governmental departments, which raises the need for composing SOAP-based as well as RESTful services. Existing works address this objective using static composition alone. However, it would be beneficial if users can specify the requirements during run-time, based on the outcome of the previous services executed. In general, business applications follow a predefined order and consequently the composition process can follow a template of business activities. Existing works on dynamic web service composition either separate the composition and execution phases distinctly or perform them in an interleaved fashion. The former approach cannot adapt to changes in run-time whereas the latter can select services based on the outcome of previous service executions. However, the interleaved approach does not support business activities that have a specific ordering among them. Hence, a novel hybrid model - Dynamic InterLeaved Template (DILT) - that enables interleaved composition and execution of web services based on predefined workflow templates has been proposed in this paper. This hybrid model lends itself naturally for composing both SOAP-based and RESTful services.

Keywords: Web Services, Dynamic composition, Service Oriented Architecture, SOAP services, RESTful Services.

1 Introduction

Applications in e-Governance are increasingly becoming widespread which require handling transactions across the various governmental as well as private departments. Whenever a single service is not sufficient for implementing a business process, multiple services need to be suitably composed. The web services are heterogeneous in nature and the two prominent types are SOAP-based and RESTful services. In general, SOAP-based web services are predominantly used in business applications where multiple competing providers exist for a single

R. Natarajan et al. (Eds.): ICDCIT 2015, LNCS 8956, pp. 239–244, 2015.

functionality. RESTful web services are preferred for Governmental department web services since, RESTful services are light-weight and less prone to security attacks.

Existing works on web service composition provide solutions for static composition of SOAP-based web services using Existing language standard for composition - Business Process Execution Language (BPEL), static composition of RESTful services [1], and semi automated solution for both types. In e-Governance business applications, the component services of a composition need input values from the end-user. Sometimes, the end-user might want to decide the service parameter values based on the outcome of the previous service execution. Several authors have surveyed and compared different approaches for web service composition [2]. Interleaved approach [3] supporting dynamic composition interleaves composition and execution of component services of a composite service. However, in enterprise applications, the business is conducted in a predetermined manner and hence the template based composition [3] is more suitable wherein the control flow among the business activities is captured. Existing works on composition of SOAP and RESTful services together [4,5], follow either static composition or severely restrict the interaction between heterogeneous services. The existing dynamic composition frameworks [6,7,8] do not allow the interleaving of composition and execution steps. Existing works on interleaved composition and execution [9,10] do not follow a specific ordering among business activities. Hence, *a novel **Dynamic InterLeaved Template** model (DILT) is proposed in this paper, that dynamically interleaves composition and execution steps associated with component services of a composite business process, based on predefined control flow.* This hybrid model lends itself naturally for composing heterogeneous services.

2   Existing Work

Peng et al., proposed REST2SOAP [4] framework that integrates RESTful web services with SOAP-based services by converting them into SOAP services. In this work, the advantages of RESTful services such as lightweight nature and security are lost. Another hybrid orchestration approach of He et al. [5] is effective only when the interactions among different types of services are minimal. The MDCHeS [11] approach used BPEL engine to compose SOAP-based services, JOpera visual composition language to compose RESTful services, and BPEL for REST extension for composing heterogeneous services. All these works are semi-automatic approaches and do not address dynamic composition. An approach proposed by De Giorgio et al. [12], supported alternate service selection at run-time from a pre-discovered set of SOAP-based and RESTful services which is not truely dynamic.

A-DynamiCoS [13] framework supports user-centric interleaved service composition. However, it is not suitable for business applications where the activities follow a specific order. In Ardagna et al.'s [14] adaptive composition approach, web service selection as well as optimization and web service execution are interleaved. However, selection of each service is not interleaved with its execution, which makes specification of user requirements based on the outcome of the previous service execution, impossible. Ozorhan et al., [15] proposed an abductive event calculus framework that can be used to formalize the interleaved and template-based approach [3] separately. This framework does not address combining interleaved and template based approaches. All these three works do not address composition of heterogeneous web services.

3 Proposed Hybrid Model for Web Service Composition and Execution

The proposed hybrid model, DILT combines the features of interleaved and template based approaches for composing and executing web services. Figure 1 depicts the approach adapted by DILT model. This model involves three steps namely, dynamic selection, binding, and execution of services. The web services are selected from the respective service registry based on their type at run-time by matching the functional requirements specified by the user and the capabilities of the services advertised in the registry. Since, this paper does not focus on semantic discovery of services, it is assumed that the activity as well as the corresponding services are named similarly. The services from different service providers corresponding to a given activity are named as activity name followed by the name os the service provider. When several service providers deploy services for the same functionality, service selection involves comparing their non-functional capabilities which is outside the scope of this paper. The three steps involved in the composition are interleaved for each activity present in the template. Hence, the response of the previous service execution is useful for deciding the selection of services from the registry, for a subsequent activity in the workflow template. The process flow of the proposed DILT model is shown in Figure 2. The services are composed in sequence or in parallel based on the workflow patterns. The workflow patterns such as Sequence, AND-Split, AND-Join, XOR-Join, and XOR-Split have been considered in the schema. The approach adapted by the DILT model is depicted in Figure 3. A set of following middleware services have been designed and deployed.

- *WFParser* for parsing the workflow template
- *WSSelection* for selecting a SOAP-based web service from *WSRegistry* and *SOAPBinding* for binding them
- *URIRetrieval* for selecting RESTful web services from *RESTfulRepository* and *RESTBinding* for binding them

4 Case Study

The proposed DILT model is illustrated using an e-Governance application of Land Registration (LR) as depicted in Figure 4 . which involves searching, selecting and buying a residential plot that suits the user preferences and registering

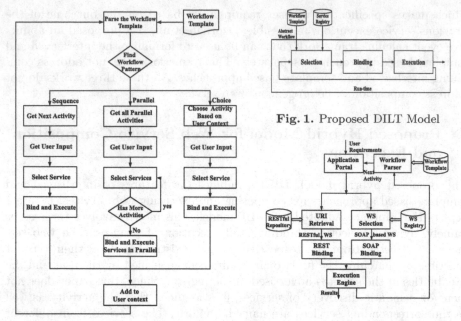

Fig. 1. Proposed DILT Model

Fig. 2. Process flow of DILT model

Fig. 3. Composition and Execution of Heterogeneous Web Services

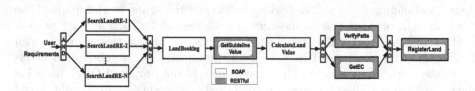

Fig. 4. Workflow for Land Registration System

the sale deed with the government department for registration.The LR application involves collaboration among the various real estate providers as well as Government departments such as the registration and the revenue departments. The business workflow for Land Registration depicted in Figure 4 involves sequential composition of searching for a land with specific requirements, selecting the land, obtaining the land value fixed by Government, calculating the total land cost, validating land details, and registering the land.

5   Experimentation

The LR application is implemented using the proposed DILT model. The application is implemented using the technologies, JAX-WS for SOAP-based web services and JAX-RS for RESTful services. The impact of DILT model on the

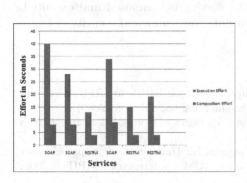

	Automated Composition	Dynamic WS Discovery	Support for SOAP and RESTful WS	Interleaved Composition	Template based Composition	User Centric Composition
REST2SOAP	X	X	✓	X	X	X
He's Hybrid Architecture	X	X	✓	X	X	X
MDCHeS	X	X	✓	X	X	X
De Giorgio et al.'s work	X	X	✓	X	X	X
DynamicCoS	✓	✓	X	✓	X	✓
Ozorhan et al.'s work	✓	✓	X	✓	✓	X
Ardagna et al.'s work	✓	✓	X	✓	X	✓
Proposed DILT Model	✓	✓	✓	✓	✓	✓

Fig. 5. Execution Effort versus Composition Effort

Fig. 6. Comparison of DILT Model with the Existing works

performance of LR application is studied by measuring the effort involved in executing the various activities. The execution effort for obtaining the results of an activity, (EE_i) includes the efforts involved in composing a suitable service i, (CE_i) and then executing it. RT_i represents the response time of a service. $EE_i = CE_i + RT_i$. The composition effort involved in dynamically composing a service i, (CE_i) consists of the time incurred in selecting a suitable service (ST_i) and binding the service based on its type (BT_i). $CE_i = ST_i + BT_i$. The execution effort involved in the case of SOAP based services is high compared to RESTful services, since SOAP messages need to be prepared whereas in case of RESTful message, it involves only a HTTP request.

The percentage of additional effort spent in dynamic service selection by the proposed approach in DILT model, has been measured and shown in Figure 5. It is observed that on an average, 26% of execution effort is incurred in service selection during run-time. Though dynamic selection, adapted in the DILT model incurs an additional overhead, the advantages of the proposed approach such as adapting to new services/providers, service selection based on the outcome of previous service execution, and dynamic composition of heterogeneous services justify the overhead.

A comparison of the proposed DILT model with the existing works discussed in Section 2 is presented in Figure 6.

6   Conclusion

The major contribution of this research work is to compose heterogeneous web services *dynamically*. By interleaving the composition and execution steps, the outcome of the service saved as user context becomes useful in specifying the user preferences for selecting the subsequent services. Since e-Governance applications follow a predefined ordering among the activities of the business process, the template based approach adapted in the proposed DILT model suits such applications. The proposed model requires the user to specify the input parameter values for any service, only when the service is composed and executed. Thus, the user can preserve the privacy of data and can avoid security risks.

References

1. Pautasso, C.: Restful Web Service Composition with BPEL for REST. International Journal on Data and Knowledge Engineering 68, 851–866 (2009)
2. Schahram, D., Wolfgang, S.: A Survey on Web Services Composition. Int. J. Web and Grid Services 1(1), 1–30 (2005)
3. Agarwal, V., Chafle, G., Mittal, S., Srivastava, B.: Understanding approaches for Web Service Composition and Execution. In: ACM Conference COMPUTE 2008, pp. 1:1–1:8 (2008)
4. Peng, Y.-Y., Ma, S.-P., Lee, J.: REST2SOAP: A framework to integrate SOAP services and RESTful services. In: 2009 IEEE International Conference on Service-Oriented Computing and Applications (SOCA), pp. 1–4 (2009)
5. He, K.: Integration and Orchestration of Heterogeneous Services. In: IEEE Joint Conferences on Pervasive Computing (JCPC), pp. 467–470 (2009)
6. Chan, P.P.W., Lyu, M.R.: Dynamic Web Service Composition: A New Approach in Building Reliable Web Service. In: 22nd International Conference on Advanced Information Networking and Applications, pp. 20–25 (2008)
7. Wang, X., Yue, K., Huang, J.Z., Zhou, A.: Service Selection in Dynamic Demand-Driven Web Services. In: IEEE Int. conference on Web Services (ICWS), pp. 376–383 (2004)
8. Zeng, L., Ngu, A.H., Benatallah, B., Podorozhny, R., Lei, H.: Dynamic Composition and Optimization of Web Services. International Journal on Distributed and Parallel Databases 24, 45–72 (2008)
9. Fan, X., Umapathy, K., Yen, J., Purao, S.: An Agent-based Approach for Interleaved Composition and Execution of Web Services. In: Atzeni, P., Chu, W., Lu, H., Zhou, S., Ling, T.-W. (eds.) ER 2004. LNCS, vol. 3288, pp. 582–595. Springer, Heidelberg (2004)
10. Maamar, Z., Sheng, Q.Z., Benatallah, B.: Interleaving Web Services Composition and Execution using Software Agents and Delegation. In: Workshop on Web Services and Agent-Based Engineering (WSABE 2003), pp. 51–59 (2003)
11. Farokhi, S., Ghaffari, A., Haghighi, H., Shams, F.: MDCHeS: Model-Driven Dynamic Composition of Heterogeneous Service. International Journal of Communications, Network and System Sciences, 249–259 (1987)
12. De Giorgio, T., Ripa, G., Zuccalà, M.: An Approach to Enable Replacement of SOAP Services and REST Services in Lightweight Processes. In: Daniel, F., Facca, F.M. (eds.) ICWE 2010. LNCS, vol. 6385, pp. 338–346. Springer, Heidelberg (2010)
13. da Silva, E.G., Pires, L.F., van Sinderen, M.: A-DynamiCoS: A Flexible Framework for User-centric Service Composition. In: IEEE 16th International Conference on Enterprise Distributed Object Computing (EDOC), pp. 81–92 (2012)
14. Ardagna, D., Pernici, B.: Adaptive Service Composition in Flexible Processes. IEEE Transactions on Software Engineering 33(6), 369–384 (2007)
15. Ozorhan, E.K., Kuban, E.K., Cicekli, N.K.: Automated Composition of Web Services with the Abductive Event Calculus. International Journal on Information Sciences 180(19), 3589–3613 (2004)

Application of Soft Computing Technique for Web Service Selection

Debendra Kumar Naik, Smita Kumari, and Santanu Kumar Rath

Department of Computer Science and Engineering,
National Institute of Technology,
Rourkela, India 769008
{debendrakunaik,Smitu2410}@gmail.com,
skrath@nitrkl.ac.in

Abstract. One of the main challenges in service oriented architecture is the optimal selection and ranking of web services. The process of selecting relevant services from a service repository in a heterogeneous environment is a difficult task. Use of different search engines help in selection process by efficiently searching the service repository (like UDDI), peer-to-peer networks, service portals etc. Fixing up appropriate services is necessary because composition of these services leads to the development of a particular application. In this paper, soft computing technique such as ANN and Fuzzy logic are employed for optimal selection of web service with the help of the requisite attributes related to quality of service. A comparative study of performance of both the techniques based on error parameter has been made in order to help in critical assessment.

Keywords: Web Service, QoS, BPN algorithm, RBFN, PNN, Fuzzy logic.

1 Introduction

Web service is the basic building block of Service Oriented Architecture(SOA). It provides interoperable, reusable and loosely coupled services to client. Web service consists of three main component. i.e, Service Consumer, Service Provider, and Service Registry. Interaction between components occur through publish, find and bind operation [2]. Service provider builds the services and publish it in to service registry. Service consumer search services in service registry. Services are described using WSDL(webservice description language) [2].

The objective of this paper is to select the appropriate web service from the repository like UDDI using fuzzy logic [5] [4] and Artificial Neural Network [7]. Back Propagation Network (BPN) using gradient descent method [3]. Radial Basis Function network (RBFN) using Pseudo inverse Technique, and Probablistic Neural Network (PNN) for classification of web service have been applied [6]. In both the techniques i.e, fuzzy logic and ANN, web services are classified based on quality of service attribute. Accuracy of result obtained from both the methods is compared in order to critically access the performance.

R. Natarajan et al. (Eds.): ICDCIT 2015, LNCS 8956, pp. 245–248, 2015.
© Springer International Publishing Switzerland 2015

2   Literature Survey

There are quite a number of approaches available for QoS(quality of service) based discovery. Entropy Based discretization method is used for webservice selection [4]. Other approaches based on artificial neural network is used for ranking of web service but this paper provides the better result [1].

3   Methodology

Web service description and discovery is realized using universal description discovery and integration(UDDI). To define the QoS, nine QOS parameter such as Response Time(RT), Availability(AV), Throughput(TP), Success ability(SA), Reliability(RB), Compliance(CP), Best Practices(BPT), Latency(LC), Documentation(Doc) are considered.

Based on these nine QoS parameters service classification is done separately such as fuzzy logic and ANN [4]. The techniques considered are based on concept such as:

Fuzzy Logic is the multivalued logic. It consist of three phases i.e, Fuzzification, Fuzzy inference system, and DeFuzzification.

BackPropagation Network is a multilayer feed forward network. Network is trained using supervised learning Algorithm.

Radial Basis Function Network(RBFN). In RBFN weight as well as center both are learned and each hidden layer unit is represented as radial center $C_1, C_2, C_3, C_4......, C_h$.

Probablistic Neural Network(PNN). Probablistic neural network(PNN) is inherently a classifier. PNN is based on the Bayesian network and principle of statistical algorithm.

4   Results and Analysis

4.1   Fuzzy Logic

A set of nine attributes of QoS are used as a quality of service. That is used as input in inference system and the output is found as quality of web service(QoS). Each attributes is classified with four membership functions (Triangular Membership Function) i.e, Low, Medium, High, VeryHigh as input and poor, average, good, best respectively as output i.e, ranges form 0 to 1.

From the Fuzzy Rule based approach, web service is classified by the giving input value to the rule viewer that can generate the output.

The output is finally computed by defuzzification mechanism. The centroid method is applied to convert fuzzy set obtained from aggregation into crisp result. MatLab Tool is used for above calculation. It can generate the output of the above system in Rule Viewer.

4.2   Artificial Neural Network

ANN algorithms like BPN, RBFN and PNN used in this study consider nine QoS attributes as input. These nine inputs corresponds to input layer nodes in each ANN algorithm. However, number of hidden layers differs for each network.

In BPN, number of nodes present in hidden layer is considered to be greater than nodes of input layers. So number of hidden nodes considered to be fifteen in BPN.

In RBFN, hidden layer consisting of four radial center is taken. Since there are four different classes, Euclidian distance of a web service input vector(nine QoS attribute) from these radial center is calculated.

In PNN, hidden layer consisting of four hidden unit and each hidden unit corresponds to each class. In the summation layer, sum of output from each unit is calculated. Then at the output layer, maximum of all the output from summation layer is taken. Maximum value corrsponds to output class to which a particular web service belong. Calculated value is compared with the actual value (DataSet [1]) for the performance evaluation.

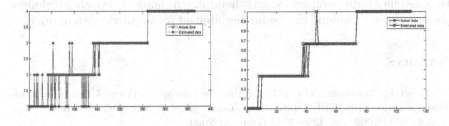

Fig. 1. Comparison of actual and estimated value of DATA in a. Fuzzy Logic and b. BPN

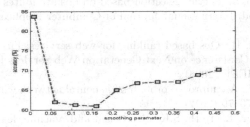

Fig. 2. Accuracy of PNN

Performance of Fuzzy logic and ANN are shown in figure 1 and 2. Matlab tool is used for calculating the Performance of Fuzzylogic and Python programming language is used for performance evaluation of ANN. Finally, Comparison of different technique are given in Table 1.

Table 1. Performance of Different Algorithm

Performance Evaluation Parameter	ANN	RBFN	Fuzzy Logic
MAE	0.0182	0.204	0.0687
MARE	0.0795	0.56	0.0358
RMSE	0.0779	0.26	0.2621
SEM	0.0234	0.06	0.0478

5   Conclusion

In this paper a method of optimal web service selection using soft computing technique like ANN and Fuzzy logic has been proposed. BPN, RBFN and PNN are used for classification of web services. Among these Neural networks accuracy obtained by the BPN is best. Accuracy obtained using PNN is moderate and RBFN accuracy is less than PNN. Rule based Fuzzy logic approach is used for classification of web services and it provides the accuracy better than RBFN. Problem with this approach is that as the no of attribute increase, service classification becomes more complex. Some other different machine learning technique like Neuro Fuzzy technique can be further applied for improving accuracy.

References

1. Al-Masri, E., Mahmoud, Q.H.: Discovering the best web service: A neural network-based solution. In: IEEE International Conference on Systems, Man and Cybernetics, SMC 2009, pp. 4250–4255 (October 2009)
2. Brenner, M.R., Unmehopa, M.R.: Service-oriented architecture and web services penetration in next-generation networks. Bell Labs Technical Journal 12(2), 147–159 (2007)
3. Kamalahhasan, M.: Applications of neural networks for ranking of web services using qos metrics. SSRG-IJECE 1, 4–8 (2014)
4. Susila, S., Vadival, S.: Service selection based on qos attributes using entropy discretization method. International Journal of Computer Applications 30(2), 47–53 (2011)
5. Tran, V.X., Tsuji, H.: Qos based ranking for web services: Fuzzy approaches. In: 4th International Conference on Next Generation Web Services Practices, NWESP 2008, pp. 77–82. IEEE (2008)
6. Yang, H., Yang, Y.: An improved probabilistic neural network with ga optimization. In: ICICTA, pp. 76–79 (2012)
7. Suresh, Y., Kumar, L., Rath, S.K.: Statistical and machine learning methods for software fault prediction using ck metric suite. ISRN Software Engineering 2014, 1–15 (2011)

Weighted Load Balanced Adaptive Gateway Discovery in Integrated Internet MANET

Rafi U. Zaman[1], Khaleel Ur Rahman Khan[2], and A. Venugopal Reddy[3]

[1] Department of Computer Science and Engineering, Muffakham Jah College of Engineering
and Technology, Hyderabad, India
rafi.u.zaman@mjcollege.ac.in
[2] Department of Computer Science and Engineering, Ace Engineering College,
Hyderabad, India
khaleelrkhan@aceec.ac.in
[3] Department of Computer Science and Engineering, University College of Engineering,
Osmania University, Hyderabad, India
avgreddy@osmania.ac.in

Abstract. An Integrated Internet MANET (IIM) is a heterogeneous network which is an interconnection of the wired Internet and the wireless MANET. Two of the issues which arise in Integrated Internet-MANET are gateway load balancing and efficient gateway discovery. These two issues have been addressed separately in the literature. In this paper, a mechanism is presented which incorporates gateway load balancing and adaptive gateway discovery together. The proposed mechanism uses the Maximal Source Coverage algorithm for dynamically adjusting the proactive range of the IIM while using the WLB-AODV routing protocol for gateway load balanced routing of packets in the MANET. Simulation results using ns-2 network simulator show that the proposed protocol gives better performance in terms of packet delivery ratio and end to end delay than the existing approach.

1 Introduction

An interconnection of MANET and Internet is called an Integrated Internet MANET (IIM) [1]. This interconnection is achieved through intermediate gateways. Mobile nodes in the MANET discover and register with the gateways in order to access Internet connectivity. Strategies for integrating mobile ad hoc networks with the Internet have been proposed which address the issue of routing of packets from one network to the other [1]. The issue of gateway load balancing has been addressed in the literature [2] [3] and also that of efficient adaptive gateway discovery [4] [5]. But none of the authors have addressed these two issues together. In this paper, the issues of gateway load balancing and gateway discovery are addressed together as part of a single mechanism. In the proposed approach, WLB-AODV [3] routing protocol is used for load balanced routing of packets between mobile nodes within the MANET, and between mobile nodes and gateways. The maximal source coverage gateway discovery mechanism is used to dynamically adjust the proactive zone of the IIM. The proposed algorithm has been simulated in network simulator ns-2. Its performance has been compared to the WLB-

R. Natarajan et al. (Eds.): ICDCIT 2015, LNCS 8956, pp. 249–252, 2015.

AODV approach which does not use adaptive gateway discovery. It is observed that the proposed approach gives better performance delivery ratio and end to end delay than the existing approach.

2   Adaptive WLB-AODV Protocol

The features of gateway load balancing and adaptive gateway discovery are combined to give the adaptive WLB-AODV protocol based on the maximal source coverage algorithm. The mobile nodes in the ad hoc network run the WLB-AODV routing protocol in order to facilitate gateway load balancing. The maximal source coverage adaptive gateway discovery is used to achieve dynamic adjustment of the proactive range of gateway advertisements. The proactive ranges of all the gateways in the IIM have been initialized to 2 hops. In fig1, mobile node MN6 is an active source which is outside the proactive range in the current gateway advertisement cycle. MN6 receives gateway advertisements from two different gateways viz. gateway1 and gateway2 via the paths MN1-MN3 and MN1-MN4-MN8. MN6 registers with gateway 2 since the path MN1-MN4-MN8 is lightly loaded when compared to MN1-MN3 which is heavily loaded. Initially, MN6 was 3 hops away from both the gateways. Now, since MN6 has become an active source of gateway2, the TTL value of the gateway 2 is adjusted to 3 hops in the next gateway advertisement cycle to increase the proactive range and include MN6 into the proactive range.

In this way, the advantages of load balanced routing of packets and adaptive gateway discovery are combined into a single protocol.

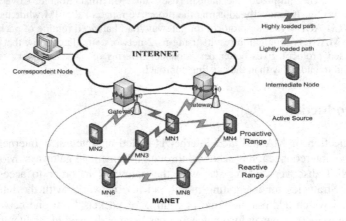

Fig. 1. Working of the proposed Adaptive WLB-AODV protocol

3   Performance Evaluation

The proposed protocol has been simulated in the network simulator ns-2.34 [7]. Its performance is compared with the integration strategy running WLB-AODV routing protocol without any adaptive gateway discovery mechanism. For the integrated Internet-MANET framework, we use the AODV+ routing protocol [6]. The parameters for the simulation scenarios are given in table I. The variable parameter is speed of mobile node which varies between 1 mt/sec to 6 mts/sec. The performance of the proposed routing protocol is analyzed with respect to the following performance metrics:

Table 1. Simulation Parameters

Simulation Parameter	Value
Number of Mobile Nodes	15
Number of gateways	2
Toplogy	800 X 500
Mobile node radio range	250m
Simulation time	900 sec
Number of traffic sources	5
Traffic Type	CBR
Mobility Model	Random Waypoint
Node Speed	1-6 Mts/Sec
Packet Sending Rate	5 packets/ sec
Number of destination nodes	2
Pause Time	60 seconds
Ad Hoc Routing Protocol	AODV+

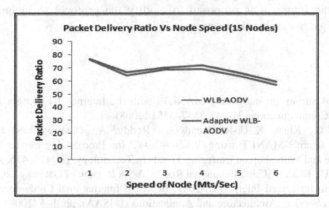

Fig. 2. Packet Delivery Ratio Vs. Node Speed for 15 Nodes

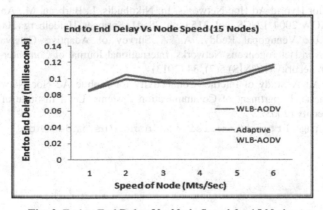

Fig. 3. End to End Delay Vs. Node Speed for 15 Nodes

Packet Delivery Ratio: It is the percentage of the number of packets received by the destination to the total number of packets sent by the source.

End-to-End Delay: It is the average overall time taken (delay) for a packet to traverse from a source node to a destination node.

From figures 2 and 3, we observe that the proposed protocol performs better than the existing approach in terms of packet delivery ratio and end to end delay. Thus we observe that for lightly loaded MANET with 15 mobile nodes, the proposed protocol outperforms the existing approach in terms of packet delivery ratio and end to end delay.

4   Conclusion

In this paper, a protocol to implement gateway load balancing and adaptive gateway discovery, called Adaptive WLB-AODV was proposed which addressed these issues together. The proposed mechanism has been simulated in the network simulator ns-2. The simulation results show that the proposed protocol gives better performance than the existing approach in terms of packet delivery ratio and end to end delay. In the proposed approach, only the gateway advertisement proactive zone is dynamically adjusted. In the future, it is proposed to modify the protocol to include dynamic adjustment of gateway advertisement periodicity.

References

[1] Ding, S.: A survey on integrating MANETs with the Internet: Challenges and designs. Computer Communications 31(14), 3537–3551 (2008)
[2] Zaman, R.U., Khan, K.-U.-R., Venugopal Reddy, A.: Gateway load balancing in integrated internet-MANET using WLB-AODV. In: Proceedings of the International Conference and Workshop on Emerging Trends in Technology, pp. 411–416. ACM (2010)
[3] Zaman, R.U., Khan, K.U.R., Venugopal Reddy, A.: A Review of Gateway Load Balancing Strategies in Integrated Internet-MANET. In: IEEE International Conference on Internet Multimedia Services Architecture and Applications (IMSAA), pp. 1–6 (2009)
[4] Ruiz, P.M., Gómez-Skarmeta, A.F.: Maximal Source Coverage Adaptive Gateway Discovery for Hybrid Ad Hoc Networks. In: Nikolaidis, I., Barbeau, M., An, H.-C. (eds.) ADHOC-NOW 2004. LNCS, vol. 3158, pp. 28–41. Springer, Heidelberg (2004)
[5] Zaman, R.U., Venugopal Reddy, A.: A Survey of Adaptive Gateway Discovery Mechanisms in Heterogeneous Networks. International Journal of Computer Network and Information Security (IJCNIS) 5(7), 34 (2013)
[6] Hamidian, A.: A Study of Internet Connectivity for Mobile Ad Hoc Networks in NS2, Masters Thesis, Department of Communication Systems, Lund Institute of Technology, Lund University (2003)
[7] Ns 2 Home page, http://www.isi.edu/nsnam/ns/index.html

Slice Based Testing of CGI Based Web Applications

Madhusmita Sahu and Durga Prasad Mohapatra

Department of CSE, National Institute of Technology, Rourkela-769008
Odisha, India
{513CS8041,durga}@nitrkl.ac.in

Abstract. We propose a slice based testing technique to generate test paths for web applications. Our web application is based on *Common Gateway Interface* (CGI) and we have used *PERL* programming language. Our technique uses slicing criterion for all variables defined and used in the program. Then, it computes the slices for each of these criteria and generates test paths. Finally, we generate test cases using these test paths.

Keywords: Program Slicing, CGI, PERL, Test Case.

1 Introduction

Mark Weiser [1] introduced technique of program slicing. In this paper, we propose an algorithm named Web Slice Testing (WST) Algorithm to generate test paths for web applications using slicing [3]. Rest of paper is organized as follows. In Section 2, slice based testing of CGI programs is discussed. Section 3 concludes paper.

2 Proposed Work

Let u be a node corresponding to statement s in a program P and $slice(u)$ be static slice w.r.t. slicing criterion $< s, v >$ where v is a variable defined or used at s.

Web Slice Testing (WST) Algorithm

1. Construct the Web Application Dependence Graph (WADG) statically once.
2. Compute static slices with respect to each slicing criterion $< s, v >$ using two-phase algorithm proposed by Horowitz et al. [2].
3. Let $slice(u_1)$ and $slice(u_2)$ be two slices.
   (a) If $slice(u_1) \subset slice(u_2)$, then discard $slice(u_1)$ and retain $slice(u_2)$.
4. Generate the test paths. Let node u correspond to statement s.
   (a) Perform Breadth First Search (BFS) starting from the node present in the $slice(u)$ whose indegree is zero.

R. Natarajan et al. (Eds.): ICDCIT 2015, LNCS 8956, pp. 253–256, 2015.

```
h1   <html>
h2   <head><title>Triangle Type</title></head>
h3   <body>
     <!--<center>-->
h4   <h2>Triangle Categorization</h2>
     <br><br>
h5   <ul>
h6   <li>Invalid triangle</li>
h7   <li>Obtuse angled triangle</li>
h8   <li>Acute angled triangle</li>
h9   <li>Right angled triangle</li>
h10  <li>Input values are out of range</li>
     </ul>
     <br><br>
h11  <h4>Enter values between 1 and 100</h4>
     <br><br>
h12  <form action="http://localhost/trgcgi/
     trg.cgi" method=POST>
h13  <table>
h14  <tr>
h15  <td>First Side</td>
h16  <td><input type=text name="a"></td>
     </tr>
h17  <tr>
h18  <td>Second Side</td>
h19  <td><input type=text name="b"></td>
     </tr>
h20  <tr>
h21  <td>Third Side</td>
h22  <td><input type=text name="c"></td>
     </tr>
     </table>
     <br><br><br><br>
h23  <input type=reset value="Clear">
h24  <input type=submit value="Categorize">
     </form>
     <!--</center>-->
     </body>
     </html>
```

```
c1   #!C:\Dwimperl\perl\bin\perl.exe
c2   use strict;
c3   use CGI qw(:standard);
     #print "Content-type: text/html\n\n";
c4   print header(), start_html("Type of Triangle");
c5   print "<center>";
c6   print h2("Result");
     print "</center>";
c7   my $valid=0;
c8   my $a=param("a");
c9   my $b=param("b");
c10  my $c=param("c");
c11  $valid=&check_validity($a,$b,$c);
c12  if($valid==1){
c13  find_category($a,$b,$c);}
c14  elsif($valid==-1){
c15  print h3("Invalid triangle");}
c16  else{
c17  print h3("Input values are out of range");}
c18  print end_html();
c19  sub check_validity{
c20  if($_[0]>0 && $_[0]<=100 && $_[1]>0 && $_[1]<=100
     && $_[2]>0 && $_[2]<=100){
c21  if(($_[0]+$_[1])>$_[2] && ($_[1]+$_[2])>$_[0] &&
     ($_[2]+$_[0])>$_[1]){
c22  $valid=1;}
c23  else{
c24  $valid=-1;}}
c25  return $valid;}
c26  sub find_category{
c27  my $a1=($_[0]*$_[0]+$_[1]*$_[1])/($_[2]*$_[2]);
c28  my $a2=($_[1]*$_[1]+$_[2]*$_[2])/($_[0]*$_[0]);
c29  my $a3=($_[2]*$_[2]+$_[0]*$_[0])/($_[1]*$_[1]);
c30  if($a1<1 || $a2<1 || $a3<1){
c31  print h3("Obtuse angled triangle");}
c32  elsif($a1==1 || $a2==1 || $a3==1){
c33  print h3("Right angled triangle");}
c34  else{
c35  print h3("Acute angled triangle");}}
```

Fig. 1. An example HTML code to input values of 3 sides of a triangle (trg.html)

Fig. 2. CGI code to determine the category of triangle based on the values of 3 sides (trg.cgi)

(b) During traversal, perform the followings:

    i. Traverse the ancestor nodes of u whose outdegree is zero.

    ii. Let k be a descendant node of u whose outdegree is zero. Then, discard k if $k \notin slice(u)$.

    iii. Let k be an ancestor node of u whose outdegree is zero. Then, discard k if $k \notin slice(u)$.

    iv. Let k be an ancestor node of u representing the end of the program. Then discard k if $k \notin slice(u)$.

5. Repeat Steps 3 to 4 for all slices computed in Step 2.

6. Design test cases randomly to exercise all test paths obtained in Step 5.

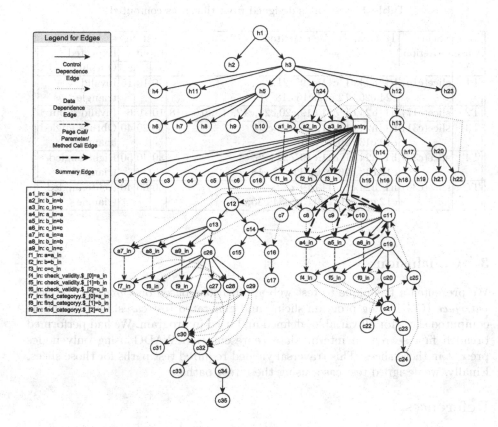

Fig. 3. WADG of the programs given in Fig. 1 and Fig. 2

Working of the Algorithm: Triangle Classification Problem. Consider a program for classification of a triangle. Its input is a triplet of positive integers (say a,b and c) and $1 \leq a \leq 100$, $1 \leq b \leq 100$ and $1 \leq c \leq 100$. The output may have one of the following words: [Acute angled triangle, Obtuse angled triangle, Right angled triangle, Invalid triangle, Invalid Input].

Fig. 1 gives HTML code to input values for 3 sides of the triangle and Fig. 2 shows CGI code to solve the above Triangle Classification Problem. The WADG of programs given in Fig. 1 and Fig. 2 is shown in Fig. 3. We compute static slices for all variables defined and used at some statements and then compare two slices to find whether one slice is subset of another. Then, we perform BFS starting from a node present in retained slice whose indegree is zero. Applying Step 4 of WST algorithm, we find test path for that slice. Table 1 shows test paths to be executed in each slice and test cases for example program given in Fig. 1 and Fig. 2. Symbol p~q denotes all nodes present on path between nodes p and q.

Table 1. Test cases designed from the slices computed

Test Case ID	Slicing Criterion	Test path to be executed	Test cases Input a	b	c	Expected Output
T1	slice(c15)	h1~h24,c1~c11,c19~c21,c23, c24,c25,c12,c14,c15,c18	30	10	15	Invalid triangle
T2	slice(c17)	h1~h24,c1~c11,c19,c20,c25,c12,c14,c16~c18	10	-1	6	Invalid input
T3	slice(c31)	h1~h24,c1~c11,c19~c22,c25, c12,c13,c26~c31,c18	30	20	40	Obtuse angled triangle
T4	slice(c33)	h1~h24,c1~c11,c19~c22,c25, c12,c13,c26~c30,c32,c33,c18	30	40	50	Right angled triangle
T5	slice(c35)	h1~h24,c1~c11,c19~c22,c25, c12,c13,c26~c30,c32,c34,c35,c18	50	60	40	Acute angled triangle

3   Conclusion

We presented a technique to test web applications based on *Common Gateway Interface* (CGI) using program slicing and generated test cases. Our technique computed slices for all variables defined and used in program. We had performed breadth first search on intermediate representation WADG using only nodes present in those slices. This traversal yielded required test paths for those slices. Finally, we designed test cases using these test paths.

References

1. Weiser, M.: Program Slicing. IEEE Transactions on Software Engineering 10(4), 352–257 (1984)
2. Horwitz, S., Reps, T., Binkley, D.: Inter-Procedural Slicing Using Dependence Graphs. ACM Transactions on Programming Languages and Systems 12(1), 26–60 (1990)
3. Li, X., Wang, F., Wang, T., Wang, M.: A Novel Model for Automatic Test Data Generation Based on Predicate Slice. In: Proceedings of 2nd Int. Conf. on Artificial Intelligence, Management Science and Electronic Commerce, pp. 1803–1805 (2011)

A Fuzzy Computationally Intelligent System
for Resource Allocation in WiMAX

Akashdeep Sharma

UIET, Panjab University Chandigarh
akashdeep@pu.ac.in

Abstract. WiMAX is an upcoming technology gaining grounds day by day that has inherent support for real and non real time applications. Distribution of resources in such networks has always been a challenging phenomenon. This problem can be solved by designing intelligent and adaptive systems. This paper proposes an application of fuzzy logic by virtue of which an intelligent system for distribution of resources has been defined. The system works adaptively to allocate bandwidth to traffic classes according to incoming traffic in their queues. The results demonstrate significance of the proposed method.

Keywords: Fuzzy Logic, WiMAX, Quality of service.

1   Introduction

The theories of fuzzy logic are very useful at places where defining exact and precise mathematical modeling is very difficult. Fuzzy logic based system can be used in such situation where vagueness of fuzzy can help to write applications for these scenarios. One such place is distribution of resources in WiMAX networks. WiMAX stands for World Wide Interoperability for Metropolitan Area Networks which is popularized and licensed by WiMAX Forum in compliance with IEEE 802.16 standard [1]. Incoming traffic in WiMAX network is categorized into five different service classes namely UGS(unsolicited grant service), ertPS(extended real time polling service), rtPS(real time polling service), nrtPS(non real time polling service) and BE(best effoert). IEEE 802.16 standard specifies only priority to these classes and does not specify any fixed mechanism for allocation of resources to these classes. Equipment manufacturers are free to design and implement their own algorithms.

Increasing number of multimedia applications makes process of resource allocation a very complex and tedious process as real time applications are always hungry for more and more resources. This puts lots of pressure on scheduler serving these service classes and maintaining relatively good quality of service levels gets more difficult with rise in number of packets in network. This requires scheduling system to be intelligent and powerful so that it can adapt itself to incoming traffic pattern of various applications. This paper discusses one such intelligent system developed using fuzzy logic. The fuzzy logic system works according to the changes in traffic patterns of incoming traffic and adapts itself to these changes so that appreciable performance level can be maintained for all service classes. Design of intelligent

R. Natarajan et al. (Eds.): ICDCIT 2015, LNCS 8956, pp. 257–260, 2015.

systems for WIMAX networks has started gaining popularity very shortly as number of papers in this direction is still limited. Few of these studies are available at [3]-[10]. Fuzzy logic has been employed by Tarek Bchini et. al. [2] and Jaraiz Simon et al.[3] in handover algorithms. Use of fuzzy logic for implementing inter-class scheduler for 802.16 networks had been done by Yaseer Sadri et al.[5]. Authors had defined fuzzy term sets according to latency for real time applications and throughput for non real time applications. Shuaibu et al.[4] has developed intelligent call admission control (CAC) in admitting traffics into WiMAX. Mohammed Alsahag et al.[6] had utilized uncertainty principles of fuzzy logic to modify deficit round robin algorithm to work dynamically on the basis of approaching deadlines. Similar studies have also been proposed by Hedayati[7], Seo[8] and Akashdeep[9] et al.

2   System Design

Different nodes/subscribers(SS) in WiMAX network request resources from BS and these requests are classified into different queues by classifier of IEEE 8021.6. The scheduler at BS listens to these request and serves these queues by performing two different functions:- allocating resources to different request made by SS and transmission of data to different destinations. Presently IEEE 802.16 does not specify any algorithms for resource allocation and numbers of schedulers are available in literature with weighted fair queuing(WFQ) being one of them. Real time classes have high priority as a result of which low priority non real time classes tend to suffer increased delays in WFQ algorithm. This can be improved by devising strategy that could adapt itself to changing requirements of incoming traffic.

The proposed system works as component of base station(BS) consuming two input variables and outputting a single output variable. The input variables are taken as follows:- Since real time traffic classes have strict time constraints and demand service before expiry of time limits therefore latency of real time applications is taken as first input variable. Throughput is another desired parameter for non real traffic and is taken as second input variable. The output of fuzzy system is taken as weight of queues serving real time traffic. Membership functions for these variables have been defined utilizing knowledge of domain expert for which substantial amount of data has been explored. Five different linguistic levels are defined for input and output variables .The membership function are defined as NB(Negative Big), NS(negative small), Z(Zero), PS (Positive small) and PB(positive big). The nature of variables forces their dynamics to range between 0 and 1. The rule base consists of 25 rules. The rule base has been defined considering the nature and dynamism of input traffic and is considered to be sufficiently large.

The initial weight for any flow (i) is calculated from following equation

$$w_i = \frac{R_{min(i)}}{\sum_{i=0}^{n} R_{\min (i)}} \tag{1}$$

where $R_{min(i)}$ is the minimum reserved rate for flow(i) and All flows shall satisfy the constraint of equation 2.

$$\sum_{i=0}^{n} w_i = 1 \qquad 0.001 \leq w_i \leq 1 \tag{2}$$

Equation (2) enables system to allocate a minimum value of bandwidth to all flows as weights of queues cannot be zero. Whenever new bandwidth request is received by BS, BS calls fuzzy inference system. The fuzzy system reads values of input variables, fuzzifies these values and inputs it to the fuzzy scheduler component at BS. Fuzzy reasoning is thereafter applied using fuzzy rule base and a value in terms of linguistic levels is outputted. At last, de-fuzzification of output value is performed to get final crisp value for weight. De-fuzzification is performed using centre of gravity method and inference is applied using Mamdami's method. The outputted value is taken as the weight for real time traffic. The bandwidth allocation to different queues is made on basis of weight assigned to that queue using desired bandwidth allocation formula.

3   Results and Discussion

The proposed scheme is tested by designing a WiMAX network consisting of one BS and a number of SS and performing two different experiments to validate scheduler performance. First experiment was implemented by increasing SS from 10 to 120. The inter service number of connections were also varied to admit traffic pertaining to all applications. Obtained results in terms of delay, throughput and jitter for all five scheduling services indicate that proposed system was able to provide required quality of service levels for all service classes. This is because fuzzy system was able to adapt itself to requirements of incoming traffic and was able to modify weight of queues to suit incoming traffic requirements.

Another experiment was conducted by increasing number of UGS connections in scenario while keeping number of rtPS, ertPS and nrtPS connections fixed. Scenario consists of 10 ertPS, 10 rtPS, 25 nrtPS connections and 25 BE connections and number of active UGS connections were varied from 10 to 40. Values of delay incurred by real time and non real time classes with increase in number of UGS connections were plotted. The variation in delay of UGS connections is minimal while delay for ertPS and rtPS classes shows an increase when number of UGS connections approaches above 30 which is understandable as more resources are consumed to satisfy high priority UGS traffic class. The delay for nrtPS and BE traffic classes shows steep rise when amount of traffic increases in the network, this was expected since these classes have minimum priority amongst all traffic classes. In spite of this increase delay values are considerably manageable considering amount of traffic in network. Values of throughput were also observed under same experiment. Throughput obtained for UGS are maximum since periodic grants are made to this class by scheduler. Throughput for ertPS and rtPS was quite good until number of UGS connection increased beyond a limit after which throughput for nrtPS started to decrease but throughput for ertPS still remained competitive enough. nrtPS throughput shows small oscillations and scheduler provides minimum bandwidth to achieve minimum threshold levels for nrtPS class. The BE service enjoys same throughput as enjoyed by nrtPS service for small number of active connections since scheduler have allocated residual bandwidth to this service. When number of connections is high, throughput for BE decreases as this is least prioritized class.

Throughput of both non real time classes was good in the start as there were enough resources available but increased amount of UGS led to degradation of performance levels of these classes.

4   Conclusion and Future Scope

This study has proposed an application of fuzzy logic for allocation of resources in WiMAX networks. The system is intelligent as it adapts itself to requirements of incoming traffic. Results indicate that system was able to provide desired quality of service levels to all traffic classes. Increase in relative traffic of UGS was also not able to deteriorate system performance. The system can further be improved by incorporating more input parameters to fuzzy system and one such parameter can be the length of queues of various traffic classes.

References

1. IEEE, Draft.: IEEE standard for local and metropolitan area networks. 727 Corrigendum to IEEE standard for local and metropolitan area networks—Part 16: 728 Air interface for fixed broadband wireless access systems (Corigendum to IEEE Std 729 802.16- 2004). IEEE Std P80216/Cor1/D2. 730 (2005)
2. Bchini, T., Tabbane, N., Tabbane, S., Chaput, E., Beylot, A.: Fuzzy logic based layers 2 and 3 handovers in IEEE 802.16e network. J. Com. Comm. 33, 2224–2245 (2010)
3. Simon, J., Maria, D., Juan, A., Gomez, P., Miguel, A., Rodriguez, A.: Embedded intelligence for fast QoS-based vertical handoff in heterogeneous wireless access networks. J. Per Comp. (2014),
   http://dx.doi.org/10.1016/j.pmcj.2014.01.009
4. Shuaibu, D.S., Yusof, S.K., Fiscal, N., Ariffin, S.H.S., Rashid, R.A., Latiff, N.M., Baguda, Y.S.: Fuzzy Logic Partition-Based Call Admission Control for Mobile WiMAX. ISRN Comm. and Netw. 171760, 1–9 (2010)
5. Sadri, Y., Mohamadi, S.K.: An intelligent scheduling system using fuzzy logic controller for management of services in WiMAX networks. J. Sup. Com. 64, 849–861 (2013)
6. Mohammed, A., Borhanuddin, A., Noordin, A.M., Mohamad, N.K., Fair, H.: uplink bandwidth allocation and latency guarantee for mobile WiMAX using fuzzy adaptive deficit round robin. J. Net. Com. Appl. 39, 17–25 (2014),
   http://dx.doi.org/10.1016/j.jnca.2013.04.004i
7. Hedayati, F.K., Masoumzadeh, S.S., Khorsandi, S.: SAFS: A self adaptive fuzzy based scheduler for real time services in WiMAX system. In: 2012 9th International Conference on Communications (COMM), June 21-23, pp. 247–250 (2012)
8. Seo, S.S., Kang, J.M., Agoulmine, N., Strassner, J., Hong, J.W.-K.: FAST: A fuzzy-based adaptive scheduling technique for IEEE 802.16 networks. In: 2011 IFIP/IEEE International Symposium on Integrated Network Management (IM), May 23-27, pp. 201–208 (2011), doi:10.1109/INM.2011.5990692
9. Akashdeep, K.K.S.: An Adaptive Weight Calculation based Bandwidth Allocation Scheme for IEEE 802.16 Networks. J. Emer. Tech. Web Inte. 6(1), 142–147 (2014)

Improving Activity Prediction and Activity Scheduling in Smart Home Networks for Enhanced QoS

Koteswara Rao Vemu

Samsung R & D Institute India-Bangalore
koti.vemu@samsung.com

Abstract. This paper proposes an algorithm, to enhance the prediction accuracy of inhabitant activities in smart home networks. This work is an enhancement to SPEED [1], which was earlier drawn upon [2,3]. It works with the nested episodes of activity sequences along with the innermost episodes to generate user activity contexts. For a given sequence, our approach on an average predicts 86 percent accurately, which is much better than SPEED's 59 percent accuracy.

1 Introduction

The daily routines of inhabitants generate activity sequences in Smart Home Networks, which follow a pattern for each inhabitant. Historic activity sequences can be used to predict user behavior and give reminders about upcoming activities. We have adopted an algorithm SPEED [1], which is drawn from [2,3]. SPEED categorizes sequence of user activities into episodes and generate contexts. These contexts are used for predicting inhabitants activities using prediction by partial matching algorithm (PPM). For details about PPM one can refer to [1].

In a sequence, where multiple nested episodes are possible, SPEED only considers the inner most episode for identifying context frequencies, which results in reduced prediction accuracy. Our proposed algorithm overcomes the limitations mentioned above and results in better prediction with a faster convergence rate. Also, resource management and concurrent activity scheduling is an important functionality of any multi-resource Smart Home solution, having more resources of same type (multiple TV sets). The better the resource management, the better is user experience in a Smart Home. For example, consider a smart home solution deployed in a 2 user ($User1$, $User2$) environment . Assume there are 2 TV sets installed in a smart home, one in living room and another in bed room of $User1$. Consider that based on the past history of $User1$ activities, there is a prediction that Sunday $7:30pm$, a scheduled TV show to be watched by $User1$. At the same time $User2$ has a weekly show scheduled at $7:30pm$ on Sunday. So in this situation, smart home should be able to allocate living room TV set to $User2$ and suggest $User1$ to watch show in bed room. This idea provides an algorithm to handle concurrent activities in Smart Home environment through resource management.

R. Natarajan et al. (Eds.): ICDCIT 2015, LNCS 8956, pp. 261–264, 2015.

2 Predicting and Scheduling User Activities in Smart Home

In this section, we propose our algorithm to improve prediction accuracy of inhabitant activities and we use inhabitant and resident interchangeably. Using the activity sequence, we can predict inhabitant's activities based on certain parameters, such as day and time. SPEED [1] categorizes sequence of events of inhabitant into episodes, we use the same approach here as well. And we represent start of an activity with a capital letter and finishing of an activity with a small letter, same as SPEED [1]. A sample activity sequence can be represented as $KCRrckAaKRCcrk$, we will use this sequence to compare our results with SPEED. An episode is defined as all activities between starting an activity and ending an activity both inclusive. For Example $KCRrck$ is an episode, $CRrc$ is another episode. Once the episodes are identified, our approach as that of SPEED [1] uses them to generate contexts, which will be used to create context trees. These context trees are used for predicting inhabitant's activities using PPM as below.

$$P_k(\psi) = p_k(\psi) + e_k(\psi).P_{k-1}(\psi) \qquad (1)$$

Where, ψ is the symbol to predict, $P_k(\psi)$ is the final probability of symbol ψ, k is the length of the phase, $p_k(\psi)$ is the probability of seeing the ψ symbol after the k length phase, $e_k(\psi)$ is the escape probability (probability of null outcomes) of symbol ψ. Using SPEED algorithm, the contexts are getting generated from smallest episode, which is available in window, refer [1] for algorithm and generated contexts for an episode. In our example sequence $KCRrckAaKRCcrk$, SPEED considers only Aa episode for generating contexts, even though there are other episodes, such as $KCRrck$ and $CRrc$. It treats the remaining episodes as noise data generated in smart home. Our approach considers outer episodes along with inner episodes, results in extracting more contexts from a given sequence. While considering nested episodes, we ensure de-duplication of episodes. Also we propose a model to allocate resources to inhabitant in a multi-inhabitant and multi-resource environments [4,5]. Nowadays, it is quite common to have multiple appliances/resources of same kind in homes; e.g., having a TV set in living room, bed room and drawing room. All these having restricted access for users, e.g., all users can have access to living room TV set, but access is restricted for TV sets that are installed in bedrooms. We form a bipartite graph between inhabitants and resources by constructing edges between inhabitant and accessible resource. While predicting the activity, the smart home controller is able to find out what are all the available resources to allocate and inform to the user.

3 Simulation and Results

For simulations, we considered user sequence as $KCRrckAaKRCcrk$, which is already mentioned in previous section. We have generated list of all possible contexts using SPEED and our approach, Table 1 represents the comparison of all possible contexts along with their frequencies.

Table 1. Comparison of all possible contexts using SPEED and Our Approach

Possible Contexts using SPEED	Possible Contexts using Our Approach
R(1),r(1),A(1),a(1), C(1),c(1),Cc(1), Aa(1),Rr(1)	A(1),a(1),K(2),k(2),C(2),c(2),R(2),r(2),Rr(1),rc(1),KC(1), ck(1),Aa(1),Cc(1),RC(1),cr(1),KR(1),rk(1),Rrc(1),KCR(1), rck(1),CRr(1),RCc(1),Ccr(1),crk(1),KRC(1),CRrc(1),KCRr(1), Rrck(1),RCcr(1),KRCc(1),Ccrk(1),KCRrc(1),CRrck(1), KRCcr(1),RCcrk(1),KCRrck(1),KRCcrk(1)

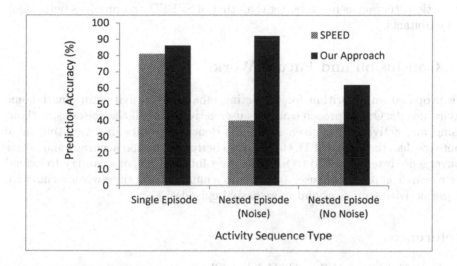

Fig. 1. Comparison of SPEED and our approach

3.1   Example

Now let us see an example of how to calculate the probability of events using both the approaches using the previous sequence $KCRrckAaKRCcrk$. Assume that our current window state is K and we try predicting an event from current window state. We assume all of the suffixes of window $(K, null)$ to calculate the probability of the next event. Suppose that we have to estimate the probability of the next event of switching on Coffee Machine (C). **Using SPEED**, there are two contexts $(K, null)$, from which we can estimate the probability of event C. From context K, probability of event C after context $K = 0$, escape probability is 0. From context $null$, probability of event C after context $null = 1/6$. The total probability of event r occurring after window sequence K is $0 + 0(1/6) = 0$. **Using Our Approach**, there are two contexts $(K, null)$, from which we can estimate the probability of event C. From context K, probability of event C after context $K = 1/2$, escape probability is 0. From context $null$, probability of event C after context $null = 2/14$. The total probability of event r occurring after window sequence R is $1/2 + 0(2/14) = 0.5$. In this example, the probability of predicting C from Sequence K is not 0 as in SPEED, because after K there is at least one instance of C happened. In this example, our algorithm predicts the probability of events more accurately than that of SPEED. The comparison of both the approaches for various activity sequences are shown in Fig. 1. In Fig. 1 both SPEED and our approach results in almost equal prediction accuracy in case of sequence having single episode (with or without noise data), where as in nested episode sequences with noise data our approach is performing much better than SPEED. Even in Nested episodes with no noise data also, our algorithm is predicting more accurately than SPEED. Overall our algorithm's prediction accuracy is much better than that of SPEED and provides better QoS to inhabitants.

4 Conclusion and Future Work

We proposed an algorithm for predicting inhabitant activities in smart home environments. Our approach considers user activities in all the episodes, without losing any activity in a given sequence. Hence it results in generating more contexts than that of SPEED, this leads to better prediction accuracy and better convergence rate compared to SPEED. As a future work, one can try to extend the research on predicting user activities in a multi-inhabitant environments with bigger activity sequences and more nested episodes.

References

1. Alam, M.R., Reaz, M.B.I., Ali, M.A.M.: SPEED: An inhabitant activity prediction algorithm for smart homes. IEEE Transactions on Systems, Man, and Cybernetics, Part A 42(4), 985–990 (2012)
2. Gopalratnam, K., Cook, D.J.: Active lezi: an incremental parsing algorithm for sequential prediction. International Journal on Artificial Intelligence Tools 13(4), 917–930 (2004)
3. Gopalratnam, K., Cook, D.J.: Online sequential prediction via incremental parsing: The active lezi algorithm. IEEE Intelligent Systems 22(1), 52–58 (2007)
4. Roy, N., Misra, A., Cook, D.: Infrastructure-assisted smartphone-based ADL recognition in multi-inhabitant smart environments. In: PerCom, pp. 38–46. IEEE Computer Society (2013)
5. Crandall, A.S., Cook, D.J.: Using a hidden markov model for resident identification. In: Callaghan, V., Kameas, A., Egerton, S., Satoh, I., Weber 0001, M.(eds.) Sixth International Conference on Intelligent Environments, IE 2010, Kuala Lumpur, Malaysia, July 19-21, pp. 74–79. IEEE Computer Society (2010)

Repetition Pattern Attack
on Multi-word-containing SecureString
2.0 Objects

Günter Fahrnberger

University of Hagen, North Rhine-Westphalia, Germany
guenter.fahrnberger@fernuni-hagen.de

Abstract. Cloud computing appeals to private individuals and particularly enterprises at a progressive rate, but a noticeable percentage of them refuse it due to mistrust or missing commitment to security. The cryptosystem SecureString 2.0 was designed to outweigh these deficits through the support of blind computations on character strings. Repetition pattern attacks count among the most hazardous enemies of SecureString 2.0 objects because reoccurring ciphergrams within them may reveal linguistic identifying features of the correspondent plaintext. This paper analyzes and compares the success probability of repetition pattern attacks on the following three sorts of SecureString 2.0 objects: single-word-containing ones, multi-word-containing ones with a known number of words plus unknown delimiter positions, and multi-word-containing ones with an unknown number of words plus unknown boundary locations. The latter type is expected to provide the highest privacy.

Keywords: Blind computing, Character string, Character string function, Character string operation, Cloud, Cloud computing, Dictionary Attack, Repetition Pattern, Repetition Pattern Attack, Secure computing, String, String function, String operation.

1 Introduction

These days, private individuals and particularly enterprises have to administer and process huge masses of data. Either they house and compute their binary goods in their private computer centers respectively in their home workstations, or they resort to outsourced virtual environments – well-known as (public) cloud computing. While in-house solutions let their owners know where their data reside, redundancy through geographical replicas and scalability lack or demand expensive expansions. Cloud computing offers the opposite with great flexibility and resilience, but the detention of sensitive data as well as reading or writing activities on them become nontransparent and thus probably dangerous.

The resulting challenge consists in the maximum yield of the advantages of both paradigms accompanied by the eradication or mitigation of the disadvantages. An imaginable approach could focus on costly enhancements of the own physical IT-infrastructure to a private cloud to achieve all benefits. The cheaper

R. Natarajan et al. (Eds.): ICDCIT 2015, LNCS 8956, pp. 265–277, 2015.

way is taken by bringing (convenient) security to a public cloud. Security poses as a coarse term and needs further specification. Privacy, integrity, authenticity and resilience represent intersubjective desirable security goals that shall be maintained at all.

Many scientific disquisitions have proposed ways to sustain data security in outsourced unconfident or semiconfident domains. These ones for secure numeric calculations try to explore feasible homomorphic functions. Most of those ones for secure string computations tackle issues in enciphered databases and keyword search in encrypted documents, mainly by dint of trapdoor functions. Both function types – homomorphic and trapdoor ones – form the heart algorithms of blind computing. Blind computing indicates that a cloud application computes ciphertext data without becoming aware of the meaning of input, output and intermediate results. A comparative overview of state-of-the-art published work about blind computing can be found in [7].

SecureString 1.0 [6] belongs to the kind of cryptosystems for blind computing on nonnumerical data. It bases upon a topical underlying symmetric cryptosystem and polyalphabetical encryption. The ciphering scheme encrypts each n-gram (substring of length n) of a word together with the beginning position of the n-gram within the word. Thereby, the start index of each n-gram stipulates the applied alphabet on it. SecureString 1.0 brings the ciphertext n-grams out of sequence after their encryption without losing the possibility to operate on them because their order can be restored after their decryption through their enveloped position information. Due to the finiteness of character string lengths that can be fully supported through querying and replacing operations, every SecureString 1.0 object intendedly contains exactly one word. Disadvantageously, this discloses the string boundaries and abets repetition pattern attacks on them.

Among other improvements, the succeeding SecureString 2.0 [7,8] overcame this limitation to permit an arbitrary number of cohered words per SecureString 2.0 object. In detail, SecureString 2.0 heads for monoalphabetical (substitutional) encryption within each character string, but every utilized alphabet (alphabet = encryption transformation) must not become effective for more than one word. Normally, each encryption transformation depends on a dedicated key, but SecureString 2.0 enciphers each character of the same plaintext character string together with an identical salt (salt = arbitrary nonce). If the salt always transmutes from word to word, then the encryption transformation also changes from word to word, even in case the same key would be employed for all character strings. Automatic salt updating [1,9] is applicable, which means that each salt serves as input for a hash function that outputs the salt for the encryption of the successive plaintext word. This non-size-preserving behavior of SecureString 2.0 entails the advantage that the decryption scheme can simply ignore salts rather than care about them. Optionally for flow control, the salts can be shortened to make room for an appended sequential number that becomes verified during the decryption scheme.

Howsoever SecureString 2.0 ensures a unique encryption transformation for each character string, this treatise examines the first time how the success probability of repetition pattern attacks varies according to the foe's knowledge respectively nescience of the amount of enclosed words in SecureString 2.0 objects whose delimiters (e.g. blanks or full stops) appear as ciphertext characters of ordinary words. The answer for this first inquiry strongly correlates with the upshot of the following second raised question: Does the recognizability of the proper word boundaries, whereupon each of them shares the salt with its left-neighbored character string, abate if an opponent is unaware of the amount of included words in SecureString 2.0 objects? The detectability of the genuine delimiters and hence the success probability of repetition pattern attacks are anticipated to recede if the quantity of ciphered character strings in Secure-String 2.0 objects stays unclear for an opponent. The findings of these research questions allow to assess the privacy of SecureString 2.0 objects for various repetition pattern attack scenarios.

Apart from the introductive section, this paper is structured as follows: Section 2 treats of preliminaries that are to be found in related work about repetition pattern attacks. While Section 3 embodies a formal view on repetition pattern attacks on single-word-containing SecureString 2.0 objects, Section 4 does the same for multi-word-containing ones. Ultimately, Section 5 summarizes the obtained examination results and suggests worthwhile future work.

2   Preliminaries

2.1   Repetition Patterns

A repetition pattern characterizes regularities of an observed text through mapping its characters to natural numbers. Appearing equal numbers indicate reoccurring characters. Definition 1 expresses the generator function of a monographic repetition pattern for an arbitrary input text.

Definition 1. *Let Σ be an alphabet, let $v \in \Sigma^l$ be plaintext of length $l \in \mathbb{N}$, and let $v_j \in \Sigma | j \in \mathbb{N} \wedge 1 \leq j \leq l$ be the jth character of v.*

Then $rp(v_j)$ computes the jth number of the repetition pattern of v as follows.

$$rp(v_j) := \begin{cases} 1 & \text{if } j = 1 \\ rp(v_i) & \text{if } (\exists i \in \mathbb{N} | 1 \leq i < j)(v_i = v_j) \\ 1 + max\{(rp(v_1), \cdots, rp(v_{j-1}))\} & \text{if } (\nexists i \in \mathbb{N} | 1 \leq i < j)(v_i = v_j) \end{cases}$$

The complete repetition pattern of v emerges from the ordered set $RP(v) := \{rp(v_j) | 1 \leq j \leq l\}$.

For example, the word "cabbages" causes the repetition pattern "12332456", just as the the character string "guttural" ends in. Evidently, the generator function for repetition patterns is not injective. "Idiomorphs" denote text particles with the same repetition pattern [2]. Cryptanalysts name instantiations of patterns without repetitions as pangrams [5]. The theoretical maximum of distinct repetition patterns with length l equals the count of partitions of a set with

Table 1. Bell numbers

l	0	1	2	3	4	5	6	7	8	9	10	11	12	13	14
B(l)	1	1	2	5	15	52	203	877	4140	21147	115975	678570	4213597	27644437	190899322

cardinality l [2], the Bell number $B(l) := \sum_{k=0}^{l-1} \binom{l-1}{k} B(k)$ [3,4]. Table 1 depicts the exponential growth of the Bell numbers. The most recent publication about SecureString 2.0 [8] inadvertently supposed the Catalan numbers as upper limits for producible differing repetition patterns that are growing more slowly than the Bell numbers.

An encryption scheme behaves monoalphabetically if it substitutes each occurrence of a specific plaintext character or of an n-gram with the same ciphertext. This statement even holds for contemporary ciphers with large block sizes (256 bits or more), but the odds (for hackers) look bad that such long plaintext blocks recur. Even if plaintext block repetitions happen, more sophisticated operation modes than ECB (Electronic Code Book) mode [10] impede the use of just one alphabet and therefore ciphertext recurrences. Anyway, if a cryptosystem (such as SecureString 2.0) deliberately processes shorter block lengths (e.g. 7, 8 or 16 bits at monographical substitutional encryption) to maintain the viability of string operations directly on encrypted texts, then repetitive ciphertexts become more probable. For this reason, the incorporated volatile salt in SecureString 2.0 grants ciphertext repeats within character strings only. Nonetheless, recurring plaintext characters or n-grams induce related ciphertext repetitions. The first invariance theorem in [2] confirms that all monoalphabetical substitutions preserve identical repetition patterns between plaintexts and their counterpart ciphertexts. Shannon divides all plain- and ciphertexts into residue classes on the basis of their repetition patterns [14]. In contrast, homophonic and polyalphabetical substitutions as well as transpositions destroy this heredity of repetition patterns [2]. SecureString 2.0 exploits polyalphabetism to avert repeating ciphertext in different words and therefrom deductions of relationships between them.

2.2 Repetition Pattern Attacks

A repetition pattern attack stands out as a subtype of dictionary attacks. To conduct a dictionary attack, an offender requires a repository with an exhaustive list of potentially occurring words [15]. A conventional dictionary attacker tries to break (a secret password of) an authorization mechanism by testing it out with one repository word after another until they reveal the correct element [12]. A repetition pattern attack on a sole ciphertext character string differs from a traditional dictionary offense against an authorization mechanism in two points.

Firstly, only the repetition patterns of a subset of repository words coincide with the repetition pattern of the attacked character string and come into consideration as plaintext candidates. One could assume that a dictionary comprehends $|\Sigma|^l$ words with length l and thus $|\Sigma|$ times more than such ones with with length $l - 1$ (corresponding to $\frac{|\Sigma|^l}{|\Sigma|^{l-1}} = |\Sigma|$). Additionally, it is assumable that the repetition patterns of the $|\Sigma|^l$ character strings with length l split into the $B(l)$ maximally possible alternatives equably. Both assumptions seldom persist in practice. Already the recent survey about SecureString 2.0 [8] remarked that the frequency scale of natural language words with various lengths resembles almost normal distribution rather than equipartition. Also, only the minority of the potential $B(l)$ repetition patterns per length l matches for the vocables of a natural language. The extremely rare incidence of more than two identical letters in a row describes one obvious cause therefor.

Secondly, there exists no primitive deciding algorithm to unambiguously determine the correct candidate. In case of natural languages, programs can decide on orthographical and grammatical mistakes at the best rather than on the meaningfulness of sentences or texts. Computers can combinatorially assemble all candidate combinations and perform rudimentary preselections, but only humans possess sufficient feel for language to can make the final decision on useful text constructs. In case of repetition pattern attacks on character strings that do not appertain to a natural language, solely the evaluation of the most frequently occurrent candidate could help.

If an assailant expects certain words or phrases (ideally such ones without known idiomorphs) in a monoalphabetically enciphered cryptotext, then they can look there for the appearance of the accordant repetition pattern and save a lot of time instead of attempting to link all ciphered character strings to appropriate candidates in the dictionary. Each such discovered cryptotext fragment together with the probable word forms a "crib" [2]. The prosperous detection of cribs claims the normalization of all search positions in the ciphertext as detailed in example 1.

Example 1. Let Σ be an alphabet, let $v :=$ "Hide the bomb near the pump" be the targeted plaintext and $w \in \Sigma^{27}$ its monographically monoalphabetically encrypted counterpart, let $u :=$ "bomb" be the sought keyword and $q \in \Sigma^4$ its monographically monoalphabetically enciphered counterpart, then the function in Definition 1 generates the same repetition pattern $RP(v) = RP(w) :=$ "1 2 3 4 _ 6 7 4 _ 8 9 10 8 _ 11 4 12 13 _ 6 7 4 _ 14 15 10 14" for v and w respectively the same repetition pattern $RP(u) = RP(q) :=$ "1 2 3 1" for u and q.

Subsequently, $RP(q)$ must be compared with each repetition pattern of all six embraced character strings of w as follows: "1 2 3 4", "1 2 3", **"1 2 3 1"**, "1 2 3 4", "1 2 3" and **"1 2 3 1"**. The bold repetition patterns label the two idiomorphic substrings "bomb" and "pump". The keyword "bomb" poses as a suboptimal example due to a bulk of coexisting idiomorphic English expressions for the repetition pattern $RP(q)$, but quests for words with inimitable repetition patterns would promise better success.

Even if the spaces in v would become ciphered monograms in w rather than staying invariant and thence exposed, the comparison of $RP(q)$ with each of the following 24 repetition patterns (which reflect all four characters long substrings of w) identifies "bomb" and "pump": "1 2 3 4", "1 2 3 4", "1 2 3 4", "1 2 3 4", "1 2 3 4", "1 2 3 4", "1 2 3 4", "1 2 3 4", "1 2 3 4", **"1 2 3 1"**, "1 2 3 4",

"1 2 3 4", "1 2 3 4", "1 2 3 4", "1 2 3 4", "1 2 3 4", "1 2 3 4", "1 2 3 4", "1 2 3 4", "1 2 3 4", "1 2 3 4", "1 2 3 4", "1 2 3 4" and "**1 2 3 1**".

(Especially long) terms with unique repetition patterns can also be spotted through those of their subpatterns that are unique as well. Queries for shorter words respectively their resultant repetition patterns skimp on time. For the same purpose, ciphergram look-ups for the nominative case of nouns respectively for infinitive verbs may take place before continuing with their declined or conjugated variants.

3   Repetition Pattern Attack on Single-word-containing SecureString 2.0 Objects

In case of the SecureString 2.0 cryptosystem, the most easily breakable cipher-text accrues if an opponent has the knowledge that it only incorporates such SecureString 2.0 objects whereupon each of them comprises of exactly one encrypted dictionary entry. If a plaintext includes a dictionary word $v_m | m, o \in \mathbb{N} \wedge 1 \leq m \leq o$ with an unrivaled repetition pattern, and a SecureString 2.0 object merely consists of v_m's ciphered form w_m in accordance with Theorem 1, then $|U_m| = 1$ and thence $p(v_m) = p(w_m) = \frac{1}{1} = 1 \Rightarrow$, i.e. a repetition attack can uncover w_m very easily. Consequently, the probability of exposing one character string of w attains the maximum value 1 with $1 - \prod_{k:=1}^{o} 1 - p(w_k) = 1 - 0 = 1$ because the factor $1 - p(w_m) = 1 - 1 = 0$ zeros the entire product $\prod_{k:=1}^{o} 1 - p(w_k)$.

Theorem 1. *Let Σ be an alphabet, let $v \in \Sigma^*$ be a plaintext with $o \in \mathbb{N} | o > 0$ delimited character strings, let $v_k \in \Sigma^* | k \in \mathbb{N} \wedge 1 \leq k \leq o$ be the kth word of v and $w_k \in \Sigma^*$ its correspondent SecureString 2.0 object, let $w := \{w_k | 1 \leq k \leq o\}$ be the ordered set of all SecureString 2.0 objects (each with an enciphered word of v), let the function in Definition 1 generate the correct repetition pattern $RP(v_k) = RP(w_k)$ for each v_k respectively w_k, let $Q \subseteq \Sigma^*$ be a dictionary with at least all o words that occur in v, and let $\Omega_k \subseteq Q$ be the probability space with all events (dictionary words) that precisely own the repetition pattern $RP(w_k)$.*

1. *Then*

$$p(w_k) := \frac{1}{|\Omega_k|} | (\forall u \in \Omega_k)(RP(w_k) = RP(u))$$

   is the probability of choosing the right dictionary item for w_k,

2.

$$1 - \prod_{k:=1}^{o} 1 - p(w_k)$$

   is the probability of guessing the true dictionary word for at least one character string of w,

3. *and*

$$p(w) := \prod_{k:=1}^{o} p(w_k)$$

is the probability of choosing the right dictionary item for each character string of w.

Proof:

1. w_k encapsulates only a single event. Therefore, the set $A_k \in \mathcal{P}(\Omega_k)$ with the correct events must be singleton and incloses just v_k. The incidence rate $p(A_k) = p(v_k) = p(w_k)$ can differ from text to text and hence is presumed equally as that of the other members of Ω_k with $p(u)|(\forall u \in \Omega_k)(u \neq v_k)$. If all events in a finite probability space resemble uniform distribution, then the incidence rate for each of them is $p(u) = p(A_k) = p(v_k) = p(w_k) = \frac{|A_k|}{|\Omega_k|} = \frac{1}{|\Omega_k|}$ referred to Laplace's formula.

2. On the contrary, the probability of selecting not the correct event in Ω_k arises from the probability of picking one of the mutually exclusive, complementary events $p(\Omega_k \backslash A_k) := 1 - p(A_k)$. The probability of opting the wrong event for each element of w results from the product of the individual converse incidence rates $\prod_{k:=1}^{o} 1 - p(w_k)$. The converse probability of this product $(1 - \prod_{k:=1}^{o} 1 - p(w_k))$ shows the chances of choosing not all events wrongly, i.e. at least one event correctly.

3. The probability of guessing the proper event for each element of w is the product of the individual incidence rates $\prod_{k:=1}^{o} p(w_k)$.   □

A SecureString 2.0 object, which embraces all o units of w with recognizable boundaries, implies just a single data structure with the equivalent vulnerability magnitude as o SecureString 2.0 objects, each with one item of w. The successional subsection investigates the implications of wrapping all elements of w in one SecureString 2.0 object while keeping their boundaries covertly.

4   Repetition Pattern Attack on Multi-word-containing SecureString 2.0 Objects

Malicious parties that snap up a multi-word-containing SecureString 2.0 object with concealed character string delimiters interest themselves in the recognition of these boundaries in order to seek dictionary words with the repetition patterns of the segregated words. Foremost, an evildoer must designate all possible positions of a targeted repetition pattern that suit as delimiter candidates. If multi-word-containing SecureString 2.0 objects do not imbed additional delimiters or miscellaneous characters to create intentional confusion for villains, then Theorem 2 itemizes the characteristics of potential word boundary candidates in repetition patterns.

Theorem 2. *Let Σ be an alphabet, let w be a SecureString 2.0 object that secures a plaintext $v \in \Sigma^l$ without additional confusing delimiters or miscellaneous* *characters, whereupon each word boundary shares the salt with its left-neighbored character string, let $w_j \in \Sigma | j \in \mathbb{N} \wedge 1 \leq j \leq l$ be the jth encased character in w and $rp(w_j)$ its number in the repetition pattern $RP(w)$ agreeable to Definition 1.*

Then each $rp(w_j)$ represents a potential word delimiter candidate if it fulfills all of the following requirements.

1. $1 < rp(w_j) < l$
2. $(\forall i \in \mathbb{N} | 1 \leq i < j)(rp(w_i) < rp(w_j))$
3. $(\forall i \in \mathbb{N} | j < i \leq l)(rp(w_i) > rp(w_j))$

Proof:

1. Supposedly, if the jth encased character of w tags a word delimiter with $rp(w_j) = 1$ respectively $rp(w_j) = l$, then $j = 1$ respectively $j = l$ in agreement with Definition 1. The first respectively the last character of w as word delimiter contradicts the presumption that w does not embed additional confusing delimiters or miscellaneous characters. On account of this, $1 < rp(w_j) < l$ must be valid for a word delimiter candidate w_j.

2. Assuming that the jth encased character of w marks a word delimiter and an $i | 1 \leq i < j$ with $rp(w_i) \geq rp(w_j)$ exists, then at least one $f \in \mathbb{N} | 1 \leq f \leq i$ with $rp(w_f) = rp(w_j)$ must occur in $RP(w)$, because $(\forall rp(h) \in \mathbb{N} | rp(f) < rp(h) \leq rp(i))(\exists g | rp(g) + 1 = rp(h)$ in compliance with Definition 1. The validity of $rp(w_f) = rp(w_j)$ contravenes the premise that only a non-repetitive number in a repetition pattern can flag a word boundary, because each delimiter shares the salt with its left-neighbored character string and each word exhausts a unique salt. On that account, a word boundary candidate w_j demands that $(\forall i \in \mathbb{N} | 1 \leq i < j)(rp(w_i) < rp(w_j))$.

3. Granted that the jth encased character of w typifies a word delimiter and an $i | j < i \leq l$ with $rp(w_i) \leq rp(w_j)$ exists, then at least one $f \in \mathbb{N} | 1 \leq f \leq j$ with $rp(w_f) = rp(w_i)$ must appear in $RP(w)$, because $(\forall rp(h) \in \mathbb{N} | rp(f) < rp(h) \leq rp(j))(\exists g | rp(g) + 1 = rp(h)$ pursuant to Definition 1. Plural existences of the same ciphertext character connote that they adhere to the same salt. Therefrom, $rp(w_f)$ and $rp(w_i)$ and all interjacent enciphered characters belong to the identical word. Accordingly, the also-intermediary $rp(w_j)$ is surrounded by characters of the same character string and cannot act as word boundary anymore. That is why $(\forall i \in \mathbb{N} | j < i \leq l)(rp(w_i) > rp(w_j))$ must have validness for a character string delimiter w_j. □

There may be void combinations of word delimiter candidates. In particular, those ones are invalid in which adjacent candidates deny character strings betwixt them. For this reason, upon ascertainment of the potential word boundaries, all valid combinations of them must be descried in order to calculate the success probability of a repetition pattern attack on each of them and to derive an overall success probability.

4.1   Repetition Pattern Attack on a SecureString 2.0 Object That Contains a Known Number of Multiple Words

If a miscreant becomes aware how many separate character strings a targeted SecureString 2.0 object protects and reckons that exactly one delimiter symbol divides contiguous words, they can stint expenses and continue only with such word delimiter combinations that contain one item fewer than the set of separated words. The number of scrutinized boundary combinations ensues from the amount of all potential delimiters $|D|$ and the quantity of o character strings in a SecureString 2.0 object. Theorem 3 displays the case for a SecureString 2.0 object without a punctuation mark as the last character, i.e. one with o words and $o-1$ boundaries. Furthermore, the Theorem excludes all combinations with adjoining delimiter candidates.

Theorem 3. *Let Σ be an alphabet, let w be a SecureString 2.0 object that secures all $o \in \mathbb{N} | o > 0$ delimited character strings of a plaintext $v \in \Sigma^*$, let $D \subsetneq RP(w)$ be the ordered set of all potential word boundary candidates subject to the outcome of Theorem 2, let $D_m \subseteq D | m \in \mathbb{N} \wedge 1 \leq m \leq \binom{|D|}{o-1}$ be the mth combination of $o-1$ character string delimiter candidates out of D, and let $b_m \in \{1, \infty\}$ be a dichotomous flag that indicates if D_m constitutes a valid word boundary combination.*
Then

$$b_m := \begin{cases} 1 & \text{if } (\nexists d, e \in D_m)(|d - e| = 1) \\ \infty & \text{otherwise} \end{cases}$$

Proof: Due to the familiar fact of o shielded words inside w, an iniquitous cryptographer may presume $o-1$ delimiter symbols that divide them. The binomial coefficient determined by $|D|$ and $o-1$ gives the number of subsets of D with $o-1$ elements. All of these subsets with conterminal boundaries, i.e. such ones with an arithmetic difference of 1, are invalid and hence their binary marks set to infinite. The flags of unobjected combinations are assigned to 1.   □

Eventually, a wretch executes a repetition pattern attack in virtue of Example 1 for the o words of each valid boundary combination. Theorem 4 pursues Theorem 3 and outlines his overall success probability of breaking w with it.

Theorem 4. *Let Q be defined as in Theorem 1, let $\Sigma, v, o, w, D, m, D_m, b_m$ be defined as in Theorem 3, let $w_{k,m} \in \Sigma^* | k \in \mathbb{N} \wedge 1 \leq k \leq o$ be the kth encapsulated word in w if the elements of D_m act as character string delimiters in w, and let $p(w_{k,m})$ be the probability of choosing the right item for $w_{k,m}$ in Q.*
Then

$$p(w) := \cfrac{1}{\sum_{m:=1}^{\binom{|D|}{o-1}} \cfrac{1}{b_m * \prod_{k:=1}^{|D_m|+1} p(w_{k,m})}} = \cfrac{1}{\sum_{m:=1}^{\binom{|D|}{o-1}} \cfrac{1}{b_m * \prod_{k:=1}^{o} p(w_{k,m})}}$$

is the probability of revealing the right word delimiters and the correct dictionary item for each character string of w.

Proof: As proved in Theorem 1, the probability of tipping the right event for each element of w is the product of the individual incidence rates $\prod_{k:=1}^{o} p(w_{k,w})$ if the elements of D_m act as character string delimiters in w. The multiplicative inverse $\frac{1}{b_m * \prod_{k:=1}^{o} p(w_{k,m})}$ counts the quantity of suitable dictionary word combinations. If D_m encompasses an invalid word boundary combination, then Theorem 3 returns $b_m := \infty$ by what the amount of fitting dictionary word combinations becomes zeroed. Each valid combination of character string delimiters contributes such a quantity of matching dictionary word combinations. As a result, all these quantities must be summated to a total amount of suited dictionary word combinations $\sum_{m:=1}^{\binom{|D|}{o-1}} \frac{1}{b_m * \prod_{k:=1}^{o} p(w_{k,m})}$. The reciprocal value $\frac{1}{\sum_{m:=1}^{\binom{|D|}{o-1}} \frac{1}{b_m * \prod_{k:=1}^{o} p(w_{k,m})}}$ is the prob-ability of culling the right character string boundaries and the correct dictionary item for each word of w.   □

Despite a criminal's lore about o for a multi-word-containing SecureString 2.0 object, they need to look up the repetition patterns of $\sum_{m:=1}^{\binom{|D|}{o-1}} b_m * o$ ciphertext words instead of o look-ups in summary for o comparable single-word-containing SecureString 2.0 objects. On these grounds, the usage of one o-word-containing SecureString 2.0 object in place of o single-word-containing SecureString 2.0 objects improves privacy rather than abides it.

4.2   Repetition Pattern Attack on a SecureString 2.0 Object That Contains an Unknown Number of Multiple Words

This subsection deals with the success probability of repetition pattern attacks on SecureString 2.0 objects which conceal their amounts and positions of pro-tected words and boundaries. For that reason, a felon must check all subsets of the list with the potential word delimiter candidates D for validity rather than only those with $o-1$ items as demonstrated in Theorem 3. Theorem 5 copies the principle from Theorem 3 how to differentiate between valid and void boundary combinations, but significantly more subsets than in Theorem 3 can incur that need to be processed.

Theorem 5. *Let Σ, v, o, w, D be defined as in Theorem 3, let $D_m \subseteq D | m \in \mathbb{N} \wedge 1 \leq m \leq 2^{|D|}$ be the mth combination of string delimiter candidates out of D, whereby each of the $|D|$ bits of the binary representation of $m - 1$ decides the incorporation of a particular candidate of D in D_m, and let $b_m \in \{1, \infty\}$ be a dichotomous flag that indicates if D_m constitutes a valid word boundary combination.*

Then

$$b_m := \begin{cases} 1 & \text{if } (\nexists d, e \in D_m)(|d - e| = 1) \\ \infty & \text{otherwise} \end{cases}$$

Proof: In addition to the proof of Theorem 3, it needs an evidence that an m for each subset of D exists, so that D_m equates the subset. $\mathcal{P}(D)$ is the power set of D and enfolds all $2^{|D|}$ diverse subsets of D (inclusive the empty subset with nary a potential character string delimiter candidate and D with all potential word boundary candidates). Let m be stored in an array with as many binary elements as candidates in D, whereupon each bit of m determines the presence of a dedicated candidate in D_m. A bit can adopt one of $2^1 = 2$ states. An array with $|D|$ bits can adopt one of $2^{|D|}$ states. Accordingly, m possesses barely enough states to enumerate all $2^{|D|}$ items of $\mathcal{P}(D)$. □

Finally, a delinquent can move on to execute a repetition pattern attack on the character strings of all valid word delimiter combinations as shown in Theorem 6.

Theorem 6. *Let Q be defined as in Theorem 1, let Σ, v, o, w, D be defined as in Theorem 3, let m, D_m, b_m be defined as in Theorem 5, let $\Delta(b_m, 0)$ be the Hamming weight [11,13] of b_m, i.e. the number of ones in b_m, let $w_{k,m} \in \Sigma^* | k \in \mathbb{N} \wedge 1 \le k \le \Delta(b_m, 0) + 1$ be the kth encapsulated word in w if the elements of D_m act as character string delimiters in w, and let $p(w_{k,m})$ be the probability of choosing the right item for $w_{k,m}$ in Q.*

Then

$$p(w) := \cfrac{1}{\sum_{m:=1}^{2^{|D|}} \cfrac{1}{b_m * \prod_{k:=1}^{|D_m|+1} \frac{1}{p(w_{k,m})}}} = \cfrac{1}{\sum_{m:=1}^{2^{|D|}} \cfrac{1}{b_m * \prod_{k:=1}^{\Delta(b_m,0)+1} \frac{1}{p(w_{k,m})}}}$$

is the probability of revealing the right word delimiters and the correct dictionary item for each character string of w.

Proof: Further to the proof of Theorem 4, the differing upper bounds of the product and of the summation sign require to be proved.

Like in Theorem 3, it is assumed that the last wrapped character in w concludes the closing word rather than being a punctuation mark. Thence, each surmised character string of w is followed by a delimiter symbol except the last word. Thereby, w shields $|D_m| = \Delta(b_m, 0)$ boundaries and $|D_m| + 1 = \Delta(b_m, 0) + 1$ character strings. This explains the product of $|D_m| + 1 = \Delta(b_m, 0) + 1$ word incidence rates.

The upper bound of the summation sign $2^{|D|}$ follows from the number of vetted subsets as per Theorem 5. □

The deficiency of knowing the amounts and positions of safeguarded character strings and boundaries in SecureString 2.0 objects aggravates the odds to break them. In the most secure case, v is a pangram, i.e. in obedience to the first condition of Theorem 2, $|v| - 2 = l - 2$ (all but the first and the last) guarded characters in w qualify for potential word delimiters and entail

$$p(w) := \cfrac{1}{\sum_{m:=1}^{2^{|v|-2}} \cfrac{1}{b_m * \prod_{k:=1}^{\Delta(b_m,0)+1} \frac{1}{p(w_{k,m})}}} = \cfrac{1}{\sum_{m:=1}^{2^{l-2}} \cfrac{1}{b_m * \prod_{k:=1}^{\Delta(b_m,0)+1} \frac{1}{p(w_{k,m})}}}.$$

5   Conclusion

Repetition pattern attacks stick out as the most striking measure to break SecureString 2.0 objects because repetitive ciphertext characters may occur in them. On these grounds, this paper provides an investigation over the success probability of such offensives.

After an introduction of the cryptosystem SecureString 2.0 and its predecessor SecureString 1.0, the preliminaries set out with Definition 1 that specifies and exemplifies how to generate and offend a monographic repetition pattern for an arbitrary input text.

Thereafter, Theorem 1 handles the success probability of repetition pattern attacks on SecureString 2.0 objects if an assaulter knows that they just shelter single words. The privacy of such objects becomes highly vulnerable if their repetition patterns merely mesh with few dictionary elements, or, more seriously, only with a lone one.

If a SecureString 2.0 object allegedly harbors several character strings, then the potential boundaries between them can be figured out with the aid of Theorem 2 which presents the necessary properties that a number of a repetition pattern must have to become a candidate.

The Theorems 3 and 4 clarify the two research questions of Section 1 for a known amount of unknown words and their unknown boundaries in SecureString 2.0 objects. Expectedly, such objects proffer harder recognizability compared to single-word-containing ones.

The Theorems 5 and 6 treat the two research questions of Section 1 in case a thug is even not aware of the number of character strings (and of their delimiters) in SecureString 2.0 objects. Such objects come along with the most difficult detectability in comparison with the other two settings but still do not cope modern privacy needs.

The finding of the last attack scenario notably is that the aim of stronger secrecy could be reached with SecureString 2.0 objects that convert every arbitrary plaintext into pangram ciphertext, i.e. ciphergrams never reoccur. The advancement of SecureString 2.0 to accomplish this goal would be valuable future work.

Acknowledgments. Many thanks to Bettina Baumgartner from the University of Vienna for proofreading this paper!

References

1. Anderson, R.J.: Security engineering - a guide to building dependable distributed systems, 2nd edn. Wiley (2008)
2. Bauer, F.L.: Decrypted Secrets: Methods and Maxims of Cryptology, 4th edn. Springer Publishing Company, Incorporated (2010)
3. Bell, E.T.: Exponential polynomials. Annals of Mathematics 35(2), 258–277 (1934)
4. Bell, E.T.: The iterated exponential integers. Annals of Mathematics 39(3), 539–557 (1938)
5. Eckler, A.R.: Pangram variations. Word Ways 10(1), 17 (1977)
6. Fahrnberger, G.: Computing on encrypted character strings in clouds. In: Hota, C., Srimani, P.K. (eds.) ICDCIT 2013. LNCS, vol. 7753, pp. 244–254. Springer, Heidelberg (2013)

7. Fahrnberger, G.: Securestring 2.0 - a cryptosystem for computing on encrypted character strings in clouds. In: Eichler, G., Gumzej, R. (eds.) Networked Information Systems. Fortschritt-Berichte Reihe 10, vol. 826, pp. 226–240. VDI Düsseldorf (June 2013)

8. Fahrnberger, G.: A second view on securestring 2.0. In: Natarajan, R. (ed.) ICDCIT 2014. LNCS, vol. 8337, pp. 239–250. Springer, Heidelberg (2014)

9. Fahrnberger, G.: Sims: A comprehensive approach for a secure instant messaging sifter. In:2014 13th IEEE International Conference on Trust, Security and Privacy in Computing and Communications (TrustCom) (September 2014)

10. Ferguson, N., Schneier, B.: Practical cryptography. Wiley (2003)

11. Hamming, R.W.: Error detecting and error correcting codes. Bell System Technical Journal 29(2), 147–160 (1950)

12. Pinkas, B., Sander, T.: Securing passwords against dictionary attacks. In: Proceedings of the 9th ACM Conference on Computer and Communications Security, CCS 2002, New York, NY, USA, pp. 161–170 (2002)

13. Reed, I.S.: A class of multiple-error-correcting codes and the decoding scheme. Transactions of the IRE Professional Group on Information Theory 4(4), 38–49 (1954)

14. Shannon, C.E.: Communication theory of secrecy systems. Bell System Technical Journal 28(4), 656–715 (1949)

15. Soroka, E.V., Iracleous, D.P.: Social networks as a platform for distributed dictionary attack. In: Proceedings of the 5th WSEAS International Conference on Communications and Information Technology, CIT 2011, pp. 101–106. World Scientific and Engineering Academy and Society (WSEAS), Stevens Point (2011)

Computationally Secure Cheating Identifiable Multi-Secret Sharing for General Access Structure*

Partha Sarathi Roy[1], Angsuman Das[2], and Avishek Adhikari[1]

[1] Department of Pure Mathematics,
University of Calcutta, Kolkata, India
{royparthasarathi0,avishek.adh}@gmail.com
[2] Department of Mathematics,
St. Xavier's College, Kolkata, India
angsumandas054@gmail.com

Abstract. Secret sharing scheme is a key component of distributed cryptosystems. In its basic form, secret sharing schemes can tolerate honest but curious adversary. But, in modern open system environment, adversary can behave maliciously i.e., the adversary can do anything according to his available computational resources. To get rid of such adversary, cheating identifiable (multi) secret sharing scheme plays an important role. Informally, cheating identifiable (multi) secret sharing scheme can identify the cheating participants, who are under the control of malicious adversary, and recover the correct secret whenever possible. However, to achieve unconditional security against such adversary, share size should be at least equal to the size of the secret. As a result, the need for computational notion of security of such schemes, which can accommodate smaller share size, has been felt over the years, specially in case of multi-secret sharing schemes. In this paper, we propose a notion of security for computationally secure cheating identifiable multi-secret sharing scheme for general access structure along with a construction which is secure under this new notion.

Keywords: cheating identifiable secret sharing, general access structure, computational security.

1 Introduction

Secret sharing scheme is a corner stone of secure distributed cryptographic protocols. It is also an essential building block for *encryption* schemes (specially *identity based encryption scheme*). Informally speaking, a *secret sharing scheme* (SSS) allows a dealer $\mathcal{D}$ to split a secret s into different pieces, called *shares*, which are given to a set of players $\mathcal{P}$, such that only certain qualified subsets

* Research supported in part by National Board for Higher Mathematics, Department of Atomic Energy, Government of India (No 2/48(10)/2013/NBHM(R.P.)/R&D II/695).

R. Natarajan et al. (Eds.): ICDCIT 2015, LNCS 8956, pp. 278–287, 2015.

of players can recover the secret using their respective shares. The collection of those qualified set of players is called *access structure* Γ_s corresponding to the secret s.

Blakley [2] and Shamir [16], in 1979, independently, introduced the notion of secret sharing scheme with a construction for threshold access structure. Presently, there exists a rich literature of secret sharing schemes with advanced features like general access structures (where qualified subsets are not all of same size t), multiple secrets (when number of secrets to be shared is more than one), verifiability, multi-usability (reconstruction of one secret does not endanger the security of the other secrets). But, some important issues remain open after extensive work of last three decades. In this paper, we deal with one of them. We consider cheating identifiable multi-secret sharing for general access structure which is an enhanced version of multi-secret sharing for general access that can tolerate any number of malicious participants and capture more realistic scenarios. In this scenario, the dealer is assumed to be honest and the goal is to identify the cheaters and to recover the correct secret whenever possible. In this work, we focus on public cheater identification, where reconstruction of the secret and cheater identification can be performed by a third party.

Most of the cheating identifiable secret sharing schemes proposed and analysed so far enjoy unconditional (or information-theoretic) security. Though there is an advantage that information theoretically secure scheme can tolerate computationally unbounded adversary, but there are some crucial drawbacks, such as requirement of honest majority, large amount of secret information. An alternative solution can be relying on computational security, by which tolerance of arbitrary number of dishonest participants is possible with lower share size (secret information), that serves well in practical purposes.

1.1 Related Work

The idea and construction of computationally secure secret sharing schemes came into existence with various proposals [1, 8, 6, 15, 4, 3, 11]. In 1994, He-Dawson [8] proposed a multi-stage (t, n) threshold secret sharing scheme. In 2007, Geng *et al.* [6] proposed a multi-use threshold secret sharing scheme using one-way hash function and pointed out that the He-Dawson scheme was actually an one-time-use scheme and can not endure conspiring attacks. A SSS is said to be *multi-use* if even after a secret is reconstructed by some players, the share remain hidden from the adversary. Generally, to make a scheme multi-use, the players do not broadcast the original share but a shadow or image of that share, which is actually an entity that depends on the original share. This image or shadow is known as the *pseudo-share*. Multi-use multi-secret sharing for general access structure was first introduced in [15, 4].

Herranz *et. al.* [9], [10] formalize the computational notion of security for multi-secret sharing schemes with a concrete construction. In [12], authors discussed formal security notion for cheating identifiable threshold (single) secret sharing scheme. But, up to the best of our knowledge, there does not exists any formal security notion for computationally secure cheating identifiable multi secret sharing scheme for general access structure.

1.2   Our Contribution

In this paper, we introduce a formal notion of security for computationally secure cheating identifiable multi secret sharing scheme for general access structure and propose a multi secret sharing scheme which is secure under the proposed notion in random oracle model. In this context, it is worth mentioning that there is a simple way (see [13]) to construct computationally secure cheating identifiable secret sharing scheme from secret sharing scheme by using signature of the dealer on the shares and thereby preventing any tampering of shares. But, this technique is not applicable for multi-use multi-secret sharing schemes, as in multi-use multi secret sharing schemes, secrets are reconstructed with the help of pseudo-shares which are generated by the participants. As a result, dealer's signature may not be useful any more.

1.3   Organization of the Paper

In Section 2, we describe the adversarial model and communication model on which our construction and analysis are based. The detailed construction is given in Section 3 and its security analysis is done in Section 3.1. Finally we conclude in Section 4.

2   Model and Definition

In this section, we specify the adversarial and communication model used in the rest of the paper. We also propose formal definitions of construction and security of cheating identifiable multi-secret sharing scheme for general access structure.

Adversarial Model. The dealer $\mathcal{D}$ is assumed to be honest. The dealer delivers the shares to respective players over point-to-point private channels. We assume that $\mathcal{A}$ is computationally bounded and malicious. Once a player P is corrupted, the adversary learns his share and internal state. Moreover from that point onwards, $\mathcal{A}$ has full control over P. By being *malicious*, we mean that $\mathcal{A}$ can deviate from the protocol in an arbitrary manner.

Communication Model. We assume synchronous network model. There are point to point secure channels among the dealer and the players. Moreover, all them have an access of a common broadcast channel.

Definition 1. *A Cheating Identifiable Multi Secret Sharing Scheme (CI-MSSS) Ω consists of three probabilistic polynomial time algorithms (Setup, Dist, Reconst) as follows:*

1. *The setup protocol, Setup, takes as input a security parameter $\lambda \in \mathbb{N}$, the set of players $\mathcal{P}$ and the k access structures $\Gamma_1, \Gamma_2, \ldots, \Gamma_k$, where $\Gamma_i =$*

$\{A_{i1}, A_{i2}, \ldots, A_{it_i}\}$ *is the access structure for the ith secret and* A_{ij} *is the jth qualified subset of the access structure for the ith secret* s_i, *and outputs some public and common parameters* pms *for the scheme (such as the access structures and set of players, mathematical groups, hash functions, etc.). We implicitly assume that* pms *also contains the descriptions of* $\mathcal{P}$ *and the access structures.*

2. *The share distribution protocol,* Dist, *(run by the dealer* $\mathcal{D}$*) takes as input* pms *and the global secret* $\vec{s} = (s_1, s_2, \ldots, s_k)$ *to be distributed, and produces the set of shares* $\{x_\alpha\}_{P_\alpha \in \mathcal{P}}$, *possibly some public output* out_{pub} *and a set of public verification values* $\mathcal{V} = \{V_{\varphi(x_\alpha, A_{ij})} : P_\alpha \in A_{ij} \in \Gamma_i\}$. *(Note:* $\varphi(x_\alpha, A_{ij})$ *is a public function used to generate pseudo-shares from the share* x_α *and the qualified set* A_{ij}.*)*

3. *The secret reconstruction protocol,* Reconst, *takes as input* $\mathsf{pms}, \mathsf{out}_{pub}, \mathcal{V}$ *and the possible pseudo-shares* $\{\varphi^*_\alpha\}_{P_\alpha \in A_{ij}}$ *of the players belonging to some subset* $A_{ij} \in \Gamma_i$ *and outputs either a possible value of the secret* s^*_i *for the i-th secret or a special symbol* $\perp$ *along with a list of cheating participants* $\mathsf{CheatList} = \{P_\alpha \in A_{ij} : V_{\varphi(x_\alpha, A_{ij})} \neq V_{\varphi^*_\alpha}\}$.

For correctness, we require that, for any index $i \in \{1, 2, \ldots, k\}$ *and any subset* $A_{ij} \in \Gamma_i$, *it holds*

$$\mathsf{Reconst}(\mathsf{pms}, \mathsf{out}_{pub}, \{\varphi(x_\alpha, A_{ij})\}_{P_\alpha \in A_{ij}}) = s_i$$

if $\{x_\alpha\}_{P_\alpha \in A_{ij}} \subset \{x_\alpha\}_{P_\alpha \in \mathcal{P}}$ *and* $(\mathsf{out}_{pub}, \{x_\alpha\}_{P_\alpha \in \mathcal{P}}) \leftarrow \mathsf{Dist}(\mathsf{pms}, \vec{s})$ *is a distribution of the secret* $\vec{s} = (s_1, \ldots, s_i, \ldots s_k)$ *and the setup protocol has produced* $\mathsf{pms} \leftarrow \mathsf{Setup}(1^\lambda, \mathcal{P}, \{\Gamma_i\}_{1 \leq i \leq k})$.

The computational security and cheating identifiablity of CI-MSSS Ω is defined by the games described in Definition 2 and Definition 3 respectively.

Definition 2. (Indistinguishability of Shares against Chosen Secret Attack). *Indistinguishability of shares of a CI-MSSS under chosen secret attack* **(IND-CSA)** *is defined by the following game* $\mathcal{G}$ *between a challenger* $\mathcal{C}$ *and an adversary* $\mathcal{A}$ *as follows:*

1. *The adversary* $\mathcal{A}$ *publishes the set of players* $\mathcal{P}$ *and the k access structures* $\Gamma_1, \Gamma_2, \ldots, \Gamma_k \subset 2^\mathcal{P}$.

2. *The challenger* $\mathcal{C}$ *runs* $\mathsf{pms} \leftarrow \mathsf{Setup}(1^\lambda, \mathcal{P}, \{\Gamma_i\}_{1 \leq i \leq k})$ *and sends* pms *to* $\mathcal{A}$.

3. $\mathcal{A}$ *outputs a subset* $\tilde{B} \subset \mathcal{P}$ *of unqualified players (unqualified means* $\exists i \in \{1, 2, \ldots, k\}$ *such that* $\tilde{B} \notin \Gamma_i$*) and two different global secrets* $\vec{s}^{(0)} \neq \vec{s}^{(1)}$ *with the restriction:*

$$s_i^{(0)} = s_i^{(1)}, \forall i \in \{1, 2, \ldots, k\}, \text{ such that } \tilde{B} \in \Gamma_i.$$

4. *The challenger* $\mathcal{C}$ *chooses at random a bit* $b \in_R \{0, 1\}$, *runs* $\mathsf{Dist}(\mathsf{pms}, \vec{s}^{(b)}) \rightarrow (\mathsf{out}_{pub}, \mathcal{V}, \{x_\alpha\}_{P_\alpha \in \mathcal{P}})$ *and sends* $(\mathsf{out}_{pub}, \mathcal{V}, \{x_\alpha\}_{P_\alpha \in \tilde{B}})$ *to* $\mathcal{A}$.

5. *Finally,* $\mathcal{A}$ *outputs a bit* b'.

The advantage of $\mathcal{A}$ in breaking the CI-MSSS Ω is defined as $\mathsf{Adv}_{\mathcal{A}}(\lambda) = |\Pr[b' = b] - \frac{1}{2}|$.

The scheme Ω is said to be computationally IND-CSA secure if $\mathsf{Adv}_{\mathcal{A}}(\lambda)$ is negligible for all polynomial-time adversaries $\mathcal{A}$.

Definition 3. (Cheating Identifiability). *Cheating Identifiability of a CI-MSSS Ω is defined by the following game $\mathcal{G}$ between a challenger $\mathcal{C}$ and an adversary $\mathcal{A}$ as follows:*

1. *The adversary $\mathcal{A}$ chooses the set of players $\mathcal{P}$, a secret vector $\vec{s} = (s_1, s_2, \ldots, s_k)$ and the corresponding k access structures $\Gamma_1, \Gamma_2, \ldots, \Gamma_k \subset 2^{\mathcal{P}}$. Then $\mathcal{A}$ runs $\mathsf{pms} \leftarrow \mathsf{Setup}(1^{\lambda}, \mathcal{P}, \{\Gamma_i\}_{1 \leq i \leq k})$ and sends $(\mathsf{pms}, \vec{s})$ to $\mathcal{C}$.*
2. *The challenger $\mathcal{C}$ runs $\mathsf{Dist}(\mathsf{pms}, \vec{s}) \rightarrow (\mathsf{out}_{pub}, \mathcal{V}, \{x_\alpha\}_{P_\alpha \in \mathcal{P}})$ and sends $(\mathsf{out}_{pub}, \mathcal{V}, \{x_\alpha\}_{P_\alpha \in \mathcal{P}})$ to $\mathcal{A}$.*
3. *For each secret s_i, $\mathcal{A}$ outputs one qualified subset of Γ_i and a corresponding set of pseudo-shares (may or may not be honestly generated) of each participant in that qualified set, i.e.,*

$$\forall i \in \{1, 2, \ldots, k\}, \mathcal{A} \text{ outputs some } A_{ij} \in \Gamma_i \text{ and } \{\varphi_\alpha^*\}_{P_\alpha \in A_{ij}}$$

4. *The challenger $\mathcal{C}$ runs $\forall i \in \{1, 2, \ldots, k\}$*

$$\mathsf{Reconst}(\mathsf{pms}, \mathsf{out}_{pub}, \mathcal{V}, \{\varphi_\alpha^*\}_{P_\alpha \in A_{ij}}, A_{ij} \in \Gamma_i) \rightarrow Out_i,$$

where $Out_i = \begin{cases} s_i, & \text{if } V_{\varphi(x_\alpha, A_{ij})} = V_{\varphi_\alpha^*}, \forall P_\alpha \in A_{ij} \\ \{\bot, \mathsf{CheatList} = \{P_\alpha \in A_{ij} : V_{\varphi(x_\alpha, A_{ij})} \neq V_{\varphi_\alpha^*}\}\}, & \text{otherwise} \end{cases}$

5. *If for any $i \in \{1, 2, \ldots, k\}$, for some $P_\alpha \in A_{ij}$, $\varphi(x_\alpha, A_{ij}) \neq \varphi_\alpha^*$, but $V_{\varphi(x_\alpha, A_i)} = V_{\varphi_\alpha^*}$, i.e., $P_\alpha \notin \mathsf{CheatList}$, the challenger $\mathcal{C}$ sets $b = 1$, else sets $b = 0$. Finally, $\mathcal{C}$ outputs the bit b.*

The scheme Ω is said to be computationally cheating identifiable if $\Pr[b = 1]$ is negligible for all polynomial-time adversaries $\mathcal{A}$.

3   A Cheating Identifiable Multi-Secret Sharing Scheme

In this section, we modify the MSSS for general access structure proposed by [15] and analyse its security in the computational model of IND-CSA and cheating identifiability. (It is worth mentioning that the scheme in [15] lacked formal security analysis.) The scheme $\Omega = (\mathsf{Setup}, \mathsf{Dist}, \mathsf{Reconst})$ consists of three basic phases,

1. **Setup:** On a input security parameter λ, the set of n players or participants $\mathcal{P} = \{P_\alpha : \alpha \in \{1, 2, \ldots, n\}\}$ and k-access structures $\Gamma_1, \Gamma_2, \ldots, \Gamma_k$ for k secrets, where $\Gamma_i = \{A_{i1}, A_{i2}, \ldots, A_{it_i}\}$ is the access structure for the i-th secret and A_{ij} is the jth qualified subset of the access structure of ith secret s_i and $|A_{ij}| = r_{ij}$,

(a) Choose a $q = q(\lambda)$-bit prime p.

(b) Choose a hash function $H : \{0,1\}^{q+l+m} \to \mathbb{Z}_p \subseteq \{0,1\}^q$, where $l = [log_2 k] + 1, m = [log_2 t] + 1$ such that $t = max\{t_1, t_2, \ldots, t_k\}$.

(c) Choose distinct identifier $ID_\alpha \in_R \mathbb{Z}_p^*$ corresponding to each of the participant $P_\alpha, \alpha \in \{1, 2, \ldots, n\}$

(d) Choose a hash function $G : \{0,1\}^q \to \{0,1\}^{u(\lambda)}$. [This is needed for cheating identifiability.]

(e) Set as pms $= (p, q, k, l, m, H, G, ID_\alpha, \mathcal{P}, \Gamma_1, \Gamma_2, \ldots \Gamma_k)$.

2. **Dist:** On input pms $= (p, q, k, l, m, H, ID_\alpha, \mathcal{P}, \Gamma_1, \Gamma_2, \ldots \Gamma_k)$ and k secrets $s_1, s_2, \ldots, s_k \in \mathbb{Z}_p \subseteq \{0,1\}^q$,

(a) Choose $x_\alpha \in_R \{0,1\}^q$, $\alpha = 1, 2, \ldots, n$.

(b) For A_{ij} where $i = 1, 2, \ldots, k; j = 1, 2, \ldots, t_i$, choose $d_1^{ij}, d_2^{ij}, \ldots, d_{r_{ij}-1}^{ij}$ $\in_R \mathbb{Z}_p \subseteq \{0,1\}^q$ and set

$$f_{ij}(x) = s_i + d_1^{ij} x + d_2^{ij} x^2 + \cdots + d_{r_{ij}-1}^{ij} x^{r_{ij}-1}$$

(c) For each $P_\alpha \in A_{ij}$, compute

 - $\varphi(x_\alpha, A_{ij}) = H(x_\alpha || i_l || j_m)$ where i_l denotes the l-bit binary representation of i, j_m denotes the m-bit binary representation of j and '$||$' denotes the concatenation of two binary strings.
 - $\mathcal{B}_{ij}^\alpha = f_{ij}(ID_\alpha)$ and $\mathcal{M}_{ij}^\alpha = \mathcal{B}_{ij}^\alpha - \varphi(x_\alpha, A_{ij})$.
 - the public verification values $V_{\varphi(x_\alpha, A_{ij})} = G(\varphi(x_\alpha, A_{ij}))$. [needed for cheating identifiability]

(d) Output $\{x_\alpha\}_{1 \leq \alpha \leq n}$ as shares, out$_{pub} = \{\mathcal{M}_{ij}^\alpha : P_\alpha \in A_{ij}, 1 \leq i \leq k; 1 \leq j \leq t_i\}$ as public output.

(e) Output $\mathcal{V} = \{V_{\varphi(x_\alpha, A_{ij})} : P_\alpha \in A_{ij}, 1 \leq i \leq k; 1 \leq j \leq t_i\}$ as public verification value. [needed for cheating identifiability]

3. **Reconst:**

(a) **Participant Phase:** On input pms, out$_{pub}$ and $A_{ij} \in \Gamma_i$, each participant $P_\alpha \in A_{ij}$ computes and broadcast $\varphi(x_\alpha, A_{ij}) = H(x_\alpha || i_l || j_m)$, $\forall A_{ij} \in \Gamma_i$.

(b) **Verification Phase:** On input $\mathcal{V}$ and $\{\varphi(x_\alpha, A_{ij}) : \forall P_\alpha \in A_{ij} \in \Gamma_i\}$,

 - participants check $G(\varphi(x_\alpha, A_{ij}) \overset{?}{=} V_{\varphi(x_\alpha, A_{ij})}), \forall P_\alpha \in A_{ij}$.
 - compute CheatList $= \{P_\alpha : G(\varphi(x_\alpha, A_{ij}) \neq V_{\varphi(x_\alpha, A_{ij})}\}$.

(c) **Secret Reconstruction Phase:**

 - if CheatList $= \emptyset$, then compute $f_{ij}(ID_\alpha) = \mathcal{B}_{ij}^\alpha = \mathcal{M}_{ij}^\alpha + \varphi(x_\alpha, A_{ij})$, $\forall P_\alpha \in A_{ij}$. Then compute and output s_i from $\{f_{ij}(ID_\alpha) : P_\alpha \in A_{ij}\}$ using Lagrange's Interpolation.
 - otherwise, output $\{\bot, \text{CheatList}\}$.

3.1 Security Analysis of Ω

Theorem 1. Ω *satisfies correctness condition.*
Proof : As correctness is considerable only when all the participants are honest, it is obvious that, using Lagrange's Interpolation, every qualified set of honest participants can reconstruct corresponding secret.   □

Theorem 2. Ω *is IND-CSA secure CI-MSSS in random oracle model.*
Proof : Let $\mathcal{A}_\Omega$ be an adversary against IND-CSA security of Ω. Let $\mathcal{C}$ be the challenger of the security game. $\mathcal{A}_\Omega$ starts the game by choosing a set of participants $\mathcal{P} = \{P_1, P_2, \ldots, P_n\}$ and k access structures $\Gamma_1, \Gamma_2, \ldots, \Gamma_k$. $\mathcal{C}$ runs Setup of Ω to generate pms and send everything in pms except the hash functions G, H to $\mathcal{A}_\Omega$.

$\mathcal{A}_\Omega$ outputs a set $\tilde{B} \subset \mathcal{P}$ of corrupted players and two different global secrets $\vec{s}^{(0)} \neq \vec{s}^{(1)}$ with the restriction:

$$s_i^{(0)} = s_i^{(1)}, \forall i \in \{1, 2, \ldots, k\}, \text{ such that } \tilde{B} \in \Gamma_i.$$

$\mathcal{C}$ chooses pairwise distinct $x_\alpha \in_R \{0, 1\}^q$, $\alpha = 1, 2, \ldots, n$.

Simulation of H-queries: $\mathcal{C}$ starts with two empty lists namely H-list and R-list. When $\mathcal{A}_\Omega$ submits a hash query of the form $x||i||j$ (In this proof, for simplicity, we write i_l, j_m as i, j only.), $\mathcal{C}$ checks whether $x = x_\alpha$ for some $P_\alpha \in \mathcal{P}$.

If $x \neq x_\alpha, \forall \alpha \in \{1, 2, \ldots, n\}$

do $\begin{cases} \text{Choose } \gamma \in_R \{0,1\}^q \\ \text{Add } (x||i||j, \gamma) \text{ to the R-list} \\ \text{Return } \gamma. \end{cases}$

If $x = x_\alpha$ for some α,

If $x = x_\alpha$ & $P_\alpha \in \tilde{B}$,

do $\begin{cases} \text{If } P_\alpha \in A_{ij} \in \Gamma_i \\ \text{Choose } h_{\alpha,i,j} \in_R \{0,1\}^q. \\ \text{Add } (x_\alpha||i||j, h_{\alpha,i,j}) \text{ to H-list} \\ \text{Return } h_{\alpha,i,j}. \\ \text{If } P_\alpha \notin A_{ij} \in \Gamma_i \\ \text{Choose } \gamma \in_R \{0,1\}^q. \\ \text{Add } (x_\alpha||i||j, \gamma) \text{ to the R-list} \\ \text{Return } \gamma. \end{cases}$

If $x = x_\alpha$ & $P_\alpha \notin \tilde{B}$,

do $\begin{cases} \text{If } P_\alpha \in A_{ij} \in \Gamma_i \\ \text{Choose } h_{\alpha,i,j} \in_R \{0,1\}^q. \\ \text{Add } (x_\alpha||i||j, h_{\alpha,i,j}) \text{ to H-list} \\ \text{Return } h_{\alpha,i,j}. \\ \text{If } P_\alpha \notin A_{ij} \in \Gamma_i \\ \text{Choose } \gamma \in_R \{0,1\}^q. \\ \text{Add } (x_\alpha||i||j, \gamma) \text{ to the R-list} \\ \text{Return } \gamma. \end{cases}$

If a hash query $x||i||j$ by $\mathcal{A}_\Omega$ is already in H or R-list, the stored value is sent back to $\mathcal{A}_\Omega$. It is to be noted that the entries in R-list are not required in the actual execution of the MSSS, whereas H-list will be used by the challenger $\mathcal{C}$ to simulate the out_{pub}.

Simulation of G-queries: $\mathcal{C}$ starts with two empty lists namely G-list and G'-list. When $\mathcal{A}_\Omega$ submits a hash query of the form h^*, $\mathcal{C}$ checks whether $h^* = h_{\alpha,i,j}$ for some $h^* \in H$-list.

If $h^* = h_{\alpha,i,j} \in H$-list, $\qquad\Big\|$ If $h^* \notin H$-list,

do $\left\{\begin{array}{l} \text{Choose } V_{\alpha,i,j} \in_R \{0,1\}^u. \\ \text{Add } (h_{\alpha,i,j}, V_{\alpha,i,j}) \text{ to G-list} \\ \text{Return } V_{\alpha,i,j}. \end{array}\right.$ $\Big\|$ do $\left\{\begin{array}{l} \text{Choose } \eta \in_R \{0,1\}^u. \\ \text{Add } (h^*, \eta) \text{ to G'-list} \\ \text{Return } \eta. \end{array}\right.$

If a hash query h^* by $\mathcal{A}_\Omega$ is already in G or G'-list, the stored value is sent back to $\mathcal{A}_\Omega$. It is to be noted that it may happen that $\mathcal{A}_\Omega$ queries the hash function G with h^* such that at that stage $h^* \notin H$-list, but h^* was latter added to the H-list as some $h_{\alpha,i,j}$. In that case, the entry (h^*, η) is shifted from G'-list to G-list and renamed as $(h_{\alpha,i,j}, V_{\alpha,i,j})$. Observe that the entries in the final G'-list are not required in the actual execution of Dist algorithm. Only the entries in G-list are used by the challenger $\mathcal{C}$ to simulate the $\mathcal{V}$.

$\mathcal{C}$ chooses a bit $b \in_R \{0,1\}$ and do the following:

- $\forall A_{ij} \in \Gamma_i$ where $i = 1, 2, \ldots, k; j = 1, 2, \ldots, t_i$, choose $d_1^{ij}, d_2^{ij}, \ldots, d_{r_{ij}-1}^{ij} \in_R \mathbb{Z}_p \subseteq \{0,1\}^q$ and set

$$f_{ij}(x) = s_i + d_1^{ij} x + d_2^{ij} x^2 + \cdots + d_{r_{ij}-1}^{ij} x^{r_{ij}-1}$$

- For each $P_\alpha \in A_{ij}$, compute $\mathcal{B}_{ij}^\alpha = f_{ij}(ID_\alpha)$, $\mathcal{M}_{ij}^\alpha = \mathcal{B}_{ij}^\alpha - h_{\alpha,i,j}$.

The values of $h_{\alpha,i,j}$ are either recollected from H-list, if they exist, or they are chosen randomly from $\{0,1\}^q$. In the latter case, the entry is added to the H-list for answering further hash queries. Moreover, $\mathcal{C}$ generates a simulated set $\mathcal{V} = \{V_{\alpha,i,j} : P_\alpha \in A_{ij} \in \Gamma_i\}$ where $V_{\alpha,i,j}$'s are either collected from G-list, if they exists, or randomly chosen from $\{0,1\}^u$ and added in the G-list.

$\mathcal{C}$ returns the public output $\text{out}_{pub} = \{\mathcal{M}_{ij}^\alpha : P_\alpha \in A_{ij}, 1 \leq i \leq k; 1 \leq j \leq t_i\}$, $\mathcal{V} = \{V_{\alpha,i,j} : P_\alpha \in A_{ij} \in \Gamma_i\}$ and the shares $\{x_\alpha : P_\alpha \in \tilde{B}\}$ of the corrupted participants to $\mathcal{A}_\Omega$. Finally, $\mathcal{A}_\Omega$ outputs its guess b' for b.

Therefore, to compute the probability that $\mathcal{A}_\Omega$ outputs the correct bit, we distinguish between two cases, depending on whether $\mathcal{A}_\Omega$ somehow manages to get the pseudo-share $h_{\alpha,i,j}$ for some non-corrupted participant $P_\alpha \notin \tilde{B}$ and $P_\alpha \in A_{ij} \in \Gamma_i$ or not. If $\mathcal{A}_\Omega$ gets $h_{\alpha,i,j}$ for some $P_\alpha \notin \tilde{B}$, say with probability δ, this is the best case for $\mathcal{A}_\Omega$ and he can correctly guess the secret bit. On the other hand, if $\mathcal{A}_\Omega$ is not able to output any pseudo-share corresponding to a non-corrupted participant, which happens with probability $1 - \delta$, then the probability of $\mathcal{A}_\Omega$ guessing the correct bit is exactly $1/2$. Hence, in any case, the probability of $\mathcal{A}_\Omega$ guessing the correct bit is $\delta + \frac{1}{2}(1 - \delta) = \frac{\delta}{2} + \frac{1}{2}$ i.e., $\text{Adv}_{\mathcal{A}_\Omega}(\lambda) = |(\frac{\delta}{2} + \frac{1}{2}) - \frac{1}{2}| = \frac{1}{2}\delta$.

Now, let E_1 be the event that $\mathcal{A}_\Omega$ makes a hash query $x_\alpha\|i\|j$, where x_α is the share of $P_\alpha \in \mathcal{P} \setminus \tilde{B}$ and $P_\alpha \in A_{ij} \in \Gamma_i$ and $|\tilde{B}| = \tilde{t}$. The probability that a single H query leads to E_1 is $\dfrac{n - \tilde{t}}{2^q - \tilde{t}}$. Now, taking Q_H to be the total number of H-queries, we get

$$\Pr[E_1] = 1 - \left(1 - \frac{n - \tilde{t}}{2^q - \tilde{t}}\right)\left(1 - \frac{n - \tilde{t}}{2^q - \tilde{t} - 1}\right) \cdots \left(1 - \frac{n - t}{2^q - \tilde{t} - Q_H + 1}\right)$$

$$\leq 1 - \left(1 - \frac{n - \tilde{t}}{2^q - \tilde{t}}\right)^{Q_H} \approx \frac{Q_H(n - \tilde{t})}{2^q - \tilde{t}} \leq \frac{n \cdot Q_H}{2^q - \tilde{t}} \approx \frac{n \cdot Q_H}{2^q}$$

as $\tilde{t}, Q_H$ are negligible compared to 2^q. Let E_2 be the event that $\mathcal{A}_\Omega$ guesses the $h_{\alpha,i,j}$ for some $P_\alpha \notin \tilde{B}$ and $P_\alpha \in A_{ij} \in \Gamma_i$ from the publicly available $V_{\alpha,i,j}$. Since, $V_{\alpha,i,j}$ is randomly chosen and letting Q_G to be the total number of G-queries, we get,

$$\Pr[E_2] = 1 - \left(1 - \frac{1}{2^u}\right)^{Q_G} \approx \frac{Q_G}{2^u}$$

Now, $\delta = \Pr[E_1 \cup E_2] \leq \Pr[E_1] + \Pr[E_2] \approx \dfrac{n \cdot Q_H}{2^q} + \dfrac{Q_G}{2^u}$. Thus,

$$\mathsf{Adv}_{\mathcal{A}_\Omega}(\lambda) \approx \frac{1}{2}\left(\frac{n \cdot Q_H}{2^q} + \frac{Q_G}{2^u}\right).$$

$\square$

Theorem 3. Ω *is cheating identifiable, if G is collision resistant.*

Proof : The adversary $\mathcal{A}$ chooses the set of players $\mathcal{P}$, a secret vector $\vec{s} = (s_1, s_2, \ldots, s_k)$ and the corresponding k access structures $\Gamma_1, \Gamma_2, \ldots, \Gamma_k \subset 2^{\mathcal{P}}$. Then $\mathcal{A}$ runs $\mathsf{Setup}(1^\lambda, \mathcal{P}, \{\Gamma_i\}_{1 \leq i \leq k}) \rightarrow \mathsf{pms} = (p, q, k, l, m, H, G, ID_\alpha)$ and sends $(\mathsf{pms}, \vec{s})$ to $\mathcal{C}$. The challenger $\mathcal{C}$ runs $\mathsf{Dist}(\mathsf{pms}, \vec{s})$ to output the shares $\{x_\alpha\}_{P_\alpha \in \mathcal{P}}$, public outputs $\mathsf{out}_{pub} = \{\mathcal{M}_{ij}^\alpha : P_\alpha \in A_{ij}, 1 \leq i \leq k; 1 \leq j \leq t_i\}$ and public verification value $\mathcal{V} = \{V_{\varphi(x_\alpha, A_{ij})} : P_\alpha \in A_{ij}, 1 \leq i \leq k; 1 \leq j \leq t_i\}$ and sends $(\mathsf{out}_{pub}, \mathcal{V}, \{x_\alpha\}_{P_\alpha \in \mathcal{P}})$ to $\mathcal{A}$.

For each secret s_i, $\mathcal{A}$ outputs one qualified subset of Γ_i and a corresponding set of pseudo-shares (may or may not be honestly generated) of each participant in that qualified set, i.e.,

$$\forall i \in \{1, 2, \ldots, k\}, \mathcal{A} \text{ outputs some } A_{ij} \in \Gamma_i \text{ and } \{\varphi_\alpha^*\}_{P_\alpha \in A_{ij}}.$$

Finally, the challenger $\mathcal{C}$ runs $\forall i \in \{1, 2, \ldots, k\}$

$$\mathsf{Reconst}(\mathsf{pms}, \mathsf{out}_{pub}, \mathcal{V}, \{\varphi_\alpha^*\}_{P_\alpha \in A_{ij}}, A_{ij} \in \Gamma_i) \rightarrow Out_i,$$

where $Out_i = \begin{cases} s_i, & \text{if } V_{\varphi(x_\alpha, A_{ij})} = V_{\varphi_\alpha^*}, \forall P_\alpha \in A_{ij} \\ \{\bot, \mathsf{CheatList} = \{P_\alpha \in A_{ij} : V_{\varphi(x_\alpha, A_{ij})} \neq V_{\varphi_\alpha^*}\}\}, & \text{otherwise} \end{cases}$

Now, let us consider the case when $\mathcal{A}$ wins the game i.e., when $\mathcal{C}$ outputs $b = 1$. Note that $b = 1 \Rightarrow \exists$ at least one $i \in \{1, 2, \ldots, k\}$ such that $\exists P_\alpha \in A_{ij}$ with $\varphi(x_\alpha, A_{ij}) \neq \varphi_\alpha^*$, but $V_{\varphi(x_\alpha, A_i)} = V_{\varphi_\alpha^*}$, i.e.,

$$\varphi(x_\alpha, A_{ij}) \neq \varphi_\alpha^* \text{ but } G(\varphi(x_\alpha, A_{ij})) = G(\varphi_\alpha^*),$$

i.e., we find a collision for G.

Let us denote the event of finding collision for G by Col_G and let $\Pr[\mathsf{Col}_G] = \delta_G$. Thus, the adversary wins the game if Col_G occurs, i.e., $\Pr[b = 1] \leq \delta_G$.

Since, G is collision resistant, δ_G is negligible and as a result, $\Pr[b = 1]$ is negligible.

$\square$

4 Conclusion

In this paper, the notion of computational cheating identifiability for multi-secret sharing schemes for general access structure is established. We also provide construction and proofs of security of a cheating identifiable MSSS for general access structure. As a topic of future research, one can think of more efficient construction of cheating identifiable multi-secret sharing schemes for general access structure.

References

1. Bellare, M., Rogaway, P.: Robust computational secret sharing and a unified account of classical secret-sharing goals. In: Proceedings of the 14th ACM Conference on Computer and Communications Security, pp. 172–184 (2007)
2. Blakley, G.R.: Safeguarding cryptographic keys. In: The National Computer Conference 1979. AFIPS, vol. 48, pp. 313–317 (1979)
3. Damgård, I., Jakobsen, T.P., Nielsen, J.B., Pagter, J.I.: Secure key management in the cloud. In: Stam, M. (ed.) IMACC 2013. LNCS, vol. 8308, pp. 270–289. Springer, Heidelberg (2013)
4. Das, A., Adhikari, A.: An efficient multi-use multi-secret sharing scheme based on hash function. Applied Mathematics Letters 23(9), 993–996 (2010)
5. Dehkordi, M.H., Mashhadi, S.: An efficient threshold verifiable multi-secret sharing. Computer Standards and Interfaces 30, 187–190 (2008)
6. Geng, Y.J., Fan, X.H., Hong, F.: A new multi-secret sharing scheme with multi-policy. In: The 9th International Conference on Advanced Communication Technology, vol. 3, pp. 1515–1517 (2007)
7. He, J., Dawson, E.: Multi-secret sharing scheme based on one-way function. Electronic Letters 31(2), 93–95 (1994)
8. He, J., Dawson, E.: Multi-stage secret sharing based on one-way function. Electronic Letters 30(19), 1591–1592 (1994)
9. Herranz, J., Ruiz, A., Saez, G.: New results and applications for multi-secret sharing schemes. In: Design, Codes and Cryptography, pp. 1–24. Springer (2013)
10. Herranz, J., Ruiz, A., Saez, G.: Sharing many secrets with computational provable security. Information Processing Letters 113, 572–579 (2013)
11. Huang, Z., Li, Q., Wei, R., Li, Z.: A Generalized Multi-secret Sharing Scheme to Identify Cheaters. Journal of the China Railway Society (July 2006)
12. Ishai, Y., Ostrovsky, R., Seyalioglu, H.: Identifying cheaters without an honest majority. In: Cramer, R. (ed.) TCC 2012. LNCS, vol. 7194, pp. 21–38. Springer, Heidelberg (2012)
13. Martin, K.M.: Challenging the adversary model in secret sharing schemes. Coding and Cryptography II. In: Proceedings of the Royal Flemish Academy of Belgium for Science and the Arts, pp. 45–63 (2008)
14. McEliece, R., Sarwate, D.: On sharing secrets and reed-solomon codes. Communications of the ACM 24(9), 583–584 (1981)
15. Roy, P.S., Adhikari, A.: Multi-Use Multi-Secret Sharing Scheme for General Access Structure. Annals of the University of Craiova, Mathematics and Computer Science Series 37(4), 50–57 (2010)
16. Shamir, A.: How to share a secret. Communications of the ACM 22, 612–613 (1979)

S-Gossip: Security Enhanced Gossip Protocol for Unstructured P2P Networks

Sumit Kumar Tetarave[1], Somanath Tripathy[1], and Sathya Peri[2]

[1] Indian Institute of Technology Patna, India
{sktetarave,som}@iitp.ac.in
[2] Indian Institute of Technology Hyderabad, India
sathya_p@iith.ac.in

Abstract. Peer to Peer (P2P) is one of the most popular technology which paved a way to new structures in many applications including content searching, file sharing etc. On the other hand, inclusion of a few malicious peers, the entire network could be disrupted without proper security measures. This paper presents a very simple but an effective security mechanism for gossip based P2P networks. In the proposed protocol, each gossiping node observes its peers closely to ensure that no malicious nodes will actively participate in the gossip protocol. To achieve this, each peer builds trust information about other nodes in the system and exchanges with its neighbours. Using the trust information, each node is able to identify and blacklist malicious nodes in its view. Thus, each node gossips only with nodes it deems as non-malicious. The efficiency of the proposed protocol is far ahead of existing security protocols such as TooLate. Our simulation results show the effectiveness of the proposed work.

1 Introduction

The Internet has grown in an uncontrolled manner over the years, while providing wide variety of useful services. The idea of providing centralized services over Internet may lead to serious service level agreement (SLA) violations due to long latencies and one or more single point failures. Clearly, centralized services can not scale to the size of Internet. So, the only way to provide fast services on such large sized network is Peer to Peer (P2P) computing. In P2P model, nodes not only consume resources passively, but they also participate, interact and contribute to the services that they make use of. This participatory nature of computing has been exploited for supporting a large number of efficient large-scale distributed applications. P2P model combines scalability and high resilience to the network dynamics.

A striking feature of P2P network is that its membership changes dynamically with time. Nodes may join and leave a network in an unrestricted manner. Interestingly, the dynamicity also leads to many difficulties in implementation of non-trivial services over P2P networks. In order to tackle the issue of dynamicity and unstructured nature of P2P model, overlays were proposed. P2P overlay networks are organized in regular structures known as distributed hash tables (DHT). DHTs are important in P2P systems as they offer an effective means

R. Natarajan et al. (Eds.): ICDCIT 2015, LNCS 8956, pp. 288–298, 2015.

of performing exhaustive and exact search through efficient routing in large-scale systems. This structured P2P overlay networks provide efficient lookups by organized architectures and precisely placing links between nodes across the network [8, 1, 14].

Gossip based mechanisms in unstructured P2P overlays have drawn attention of researchers for development of efficient protocols [16]. It has been showed that gossip based protocols can ensure connectivity even with high degrees of churn (rate of nodes joining and leaving). In these protocols, nodes periodically gossip with other nodes to exchange data and/or membership information. Such protocols achieve different topologies depending on how the views get exchanged. Structurally, different topologies are generated in the form of random graphs through random peer sampling (RPS) protocols [13].

RPS service is a basic building block in gossip based systems to deploy and maintain connected overlays even in the presence of high churn. RPS can be employed in a wide variety of settings such as information dissemination [2,13], load balancing [10] and overlay bootstrapping [11]. RPS is also a generic tool that acts as a source of randomness to guarantee both connectivity and convergence to weakly structured overlays like the ones built through peer clustering [15]. Such overlays provide an efficient support for keyword-based or range queries. For example, Cyclon [16] is an RPS protocol in which nodes swap random links (exchange a subset of their neighbours) in order to shuffle the overlay. This policy prevents the duplication of links and ensures that the in-degree of nodes remains balanced, and the overlay remains connected even if 70% nodes become dead or leave at suddenly.

But, the major drawback of RPS gossip protocols is that a few cooperating malicious nodes (MNs) can easily fool the protocol and become important. Later those malicious nodes can get the other nodes to connect them and in this way create a hub. Then, after some time all the malicious nodes leave the system and thus partition the network. This form of attack is called *hub attack* and the effect of the attack has been shown in SPSS [6] and TooLate [7].

Both these works [6, 7] also described solutions to prevent hub attack. The idea behind these protocols is to maintain blacklist and whitelist of node descriptors for each node. TooLate protocol is a distributed protocol whereas SPSS is centralized. A node (say A), monitors other nodes in the system. If A realizes that some node (say X) has high in-degree, then A believes X to be malicious and blacklists X. To identify this, TooLate protocol runs multiple instances of gossip with its few selected neighbours. If intersection of the view of the node A and the view of any of the selected gossip peer X crosses a threshold, then X is placed in the local blacklist of A.

Recently some papers described and analysed different attack scenarios, which are also focused on in-degree of a node. The paper [4] described a protocol for uniform and ergodic sampling with malicious nodes. Brahms [5] described a protocol to work against byzantine attacks in gossip protocols.

In this paper we augment the basic RPS protocol with a mechanism to detect malicious nodes. Each node, in the augmented protocol, maintains three more data-structures: Genuine Table (GT), Suspicious Table (ST) and Malicious Table

(MT) in addition to view table. These tables contain descriptors of other nodes in the system. In the course of gossip, each node populates these tables. A node believes that the nodes in its genuine table to be honest and does not gossip with the nodes in the malicious tables believing them to be malicious.

The simulation results show that the non-malicious nodes are able to detect the malicious nodes, and assists their neighbors not to gossip with such malicious nodes. The protocol has been simulated over *PeerSim* simulator [3], and the results were compared with TooLate protocol.

The organisation of the rest of this paper is as follows. The Hub attack in a common gossip based protocol is described in Section 2. The proposed solution (S-Gossip) is described in Section 3, which includes its data structures and gossiping mechanism. Experiments are analysed in Section 4 while Section 5 concludes the work.

2 Hub Attack in Traditional Gossip Protocols

Gossip based protocols usually form a random graph with the help of a set of neighbours. These set of neighbours referred as view. The view of each node are exchanged and update own view with fresh peers. This activity produces a random graph after each gossip.

Gossip based routing protocols are preferred for unstructured networks, as they have proved to be inherently scalable, fault tolerant and robust. Also these protocols are highly adaptable to network changes and dynamic environments. They can exhibit the property of graceful degradation in case of huge failure of nodes.

In such gossip mechanism each update depends on the current view of a peer and received peers from its neighbours. Figure 1 shows a sample of different view conditions. A view may be full of non-malicious peers, malicious peers or combination of them. A1, A2, A3 and B1, B2, B3 are sample of different view condition of peer A and the received view from a gossiping peer, say B, respectively. Cases (A1 and B1), (A2 and B1), and (A3 and B1) represent full of non-malicious peers inside their views. In this case, view of A always filled non-malicious peers. In contrast, case (A1 and B3), (A2 and B3), (A3 and B2), and (A3 and B3) are full of malicious peers and the resulting view of A is always converted into full of malicious peers. The figure also reflects that the view of A turns completely malicious in those cases which have B3 received view. This is also depicted that if view is completely filled with malicious peer, such as A3, may be recovered with non-malicious nodes when it receives non-malicious peer, such as B1. Case (A2 and B2) may fill partially or fully malicious peers into the resulting update view of A. Suppose the received malicious nodes are same as exist malicious nodes inside view. In this case only malicious nodes are updated. But the received malicious nodes are different, it may fill completely malicious nodes inside view.

The Hub attack is very simple and straight forward. In this attack, the malicious peers send the descriptors of malicious peers and update own view with non-malicious peers. Thus, after a few cycles the view of a genuine node contains only malicious nodes and gossip with those only. Therefore, these nodes could be completely disconnected if all the malicious nodes leave out. To bypass

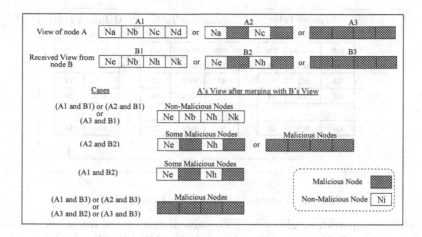

Fig. 1. A sample of S-Gossip architecture

the security mechanism i.e., to hide from being detected the malicious nodes gossip periodically rather continuously. They can target only those nodes which are very active in the overlay rather all the nodes. Those modifications in Hub attack can strengthen the attack and it becomes difficult to detect for a security scheme.

To prevent from these damages, we proposed secure gossip (S-Gossip) protocol verifies the in-degree of the suspected node while gossip. Verification is based on trust among the neighbours. This property focuses about in-degree of suspicious nodes with the help of information given by gossiping nodes that whether the nodes having that suspicious nodes are present in their View or not.

3 The Proposed Solution (S-Gossip)

S-Gossip detects a malicious peer by a non-malicious peer after executing a few gossip cycles and prevent the overlay from the disruption. In this section we present S-Gossip technique emphasizing the way it detects the malicious nodes attempting for Hub attack.

3.1 Data Structure Used in S-Gossip

As in traditional RPS gossip protocol like Cyclon, S-Gossip also uses a data structure named View. View Table has two descriptors for each nodes, NodeID (NID) and Age. Node ID is a unique identification of the node and assumed to be remaining unchanged throughout. Age shows the oldness of a node within its corresponding view. Apart from View, S-Gossip uses three more data structures named Genuine Table (GT), Suspicious Table(ST) and Malicious Table(MT). GT contains three descriptors named NID, Suspicious Count (SCount) and Time-to-Live (TTL). SCount descriptor reflects the same occurrence of that

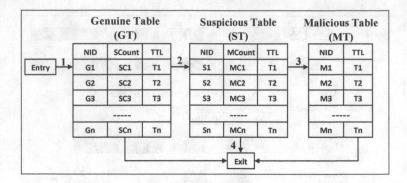

Fig. 2. A sample architecture of the tables

node while gossip with neighbours. TTL value indicates the liveliness of a node within the tables. ST has three descriptors NID, Malicious Count(MCount) and TTL and MT has NID and TTL only. The fields used in each table is as depicted in figure 2.

Among four tables VT uses for gossiping while GT, ST and MT for detecting Malicious nodes and isolating thereafter. The nodes of GT, ST and MT are treated as non-malicious, suspicious and malicious nodes respectively. The three tables (GT, ST, MT) maintained in such a way that no common nodes exist in either of two tables at any instance.

$$\forall i(GT.NID_i \cap ST.NID_i \cap MT.NID_i) = \phi \tag{1}$$

But VT includes the NID from GT only, so

$$(VT \subset GT). \tag{2}$$

3.2   Gossiping in S-Gossip

The Gossiping in S-Gossip is carried out as follows and depicted in Algorithm 1. This technique uses Genuine Table(GT), Suspicious Table(ST) and Malicious Table(MT) to detect and confirm the malicious nodes. To start with, each node (say A) keeps its peers in GT. A node chooses a peer (say B) for gossiping (with maximum age value) from the GT and initiate gossiping by sending its gossip sequence (GS). GS contains its view appended with β number of suspicious node-ids. Initially due to lack of suspicious nodes the said could be 0s. The identical operation is also being executed by peer B. Now both the peers A and B update their view considering the received view in GS from their peer. This operation is called as *maintain_view()*. Let A receives C_i in the view of GS received from B. This leads to different cases as C_i may or may not exist in the tables of A. The action corresponding to each case is highlighted in table 1.

Thus the exchange while gossiping is performed in the similar fashion to that of the traditional gossiping mechanism except a few suspicious NIDs are piggybacked. These NIDs are used to conform a node malicious or not by its peers. For this purpose after each cycle the tables are updated as discussed in the next section.

ALGORITHM 1: Gossiping in S-Gossip

---

forever do
> *wait(T time units)*
> *incr. VT Age and decr. TTL of (GT, ST & MT)by 1*
> $Q \leftarrow select\_peer();$
> *neighbor_to_send ← select_to_send();*
> *ext_neighbor_to_send ← piggybacking;*
> *send ext_neighbor_to_send to B*
> *receive ext_neighbor_to_send from B*
> $View \leftarrow maintain\_view();$

end

Table 1. Actions as per Ci's position

Options	Actions of receiving node C_i
A's View	Insert node C_i into GT table.
A's GT	Update node C_i SCount.
A's ST	Update node C_i MCount.
A's MT	Reinitialised TTL value with max.
No where	Insert node C_i into View. Update SCount of node C_i, if present.

Table Update. The main purpose of this phase is to take out the conformed malicious nodes to MT from ST and suspicious nodes from GT to ST. Thus S-Gossip uses three level of filtering they are SCount in GT, MCount in ST and TTL in MT table as summarized in table 2.

In each cycle each node updates their tables as follows. The SCount of GT is updated accordingly the characteristic of the corresponding node. Here to accomplish with Hub attack the SCount value increases if the same NID exists in the view filed of GS received from neighbor peer.

Table 2. Updating Tables

Entry/Exit	Cause	Update
1	Receiving node only presents in View.	Insert in to GT.
2	$GT.Node_{SCount} > GT(\mu + \sigma)$	Declared as suspicious and move inside ST table.
3	$ST.Node_{MCount} > STthr$	move inside MT
4	$GT.Node_{TTL} = 0$ or $ST.Node_{TTL} = 0$ or $MT.Node_{TTL} = 0$	Remove from the table.

To demote a node from GT to ST, GT computes an upper threshold $\delta(= \mu_{SCount} + \sigma_{SCount})$. Where, μ_{SCount} and σ_{SCount} denote respectively for Mean and Standard Deviation on SCount in GT, defined as in equations 3 and 4.

$$\mu_{SCount} = \frac{1}{|N|} \sum_{i=0}^{(N-1)} node_{i.(SCount)} \tag{3}$$

and

$$\sigma_{SCount} = \sqrt{\frac{\sum_{i=0}^{(N-1)}(node_{i.(SCount)} - (\mu_{SCount}))^2}{|N|}} \tag{4}$$

Here N is the size of the network i.e., number of active nodes in the considered P2P system. Any node with SCount value more than δ is shifted to ST initializing MCount to 0 and TTL to view length (vl). The said entry is deleted from GT.

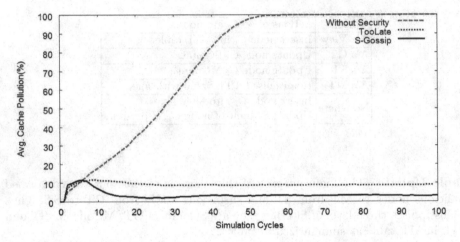

Fig. 3. With and without security mechanism: 2% Malicious Nodes

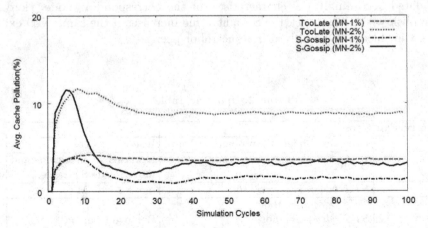

Fig. 4. 1% and 2% Malicious Nodes in 1,000 nodes

Note that the TTL in GT decrements in each cycle and the said entry from GT can be deleted if the corresponding TTL reaches to 0.

The MCount value of corresponding NID increments if the said NID exists in the Suspicious field of GS. Once the MCount reaches to vl, the said NID is shifted to MT (initializing the TTL to a maximum value) deleting the corresponding entry from ST. The TTL decrements on each cycle and the said entry is deleted from the MT (to avoid the indefinite growth of MT) once the TTL reaches to 0.

4   Experimental Analysis

To evaluate the efficiency of S-Gossip, the simulations are performed through PeerSim [3] simulator. We consider the Hub attack as a case study and compared its efficiency with TooLate, the existing security protocol. This is because

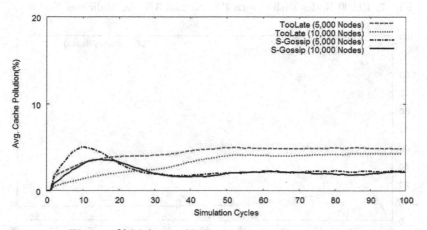

Fig. 5. 2% Malicious Nodes in 5,000 and 10,000 nodes

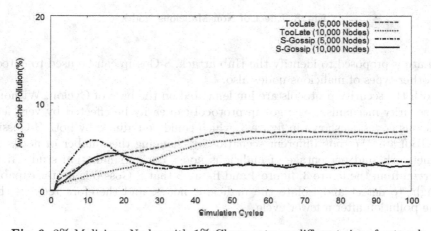

Fig. 6. 2% Malicious Nodes with 1% Churn rate on different size of network

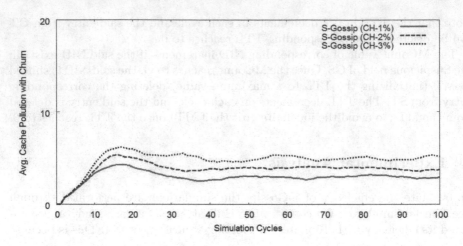

Fig. 7. 10,000 Nodes with Churn 1%, 2% and 3%: 2% Malicious Nodes

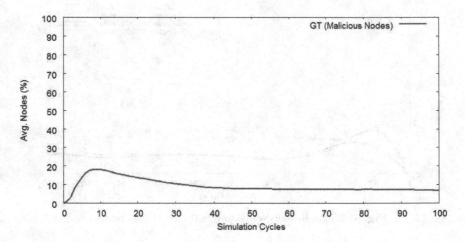

Fig. 8. Effect of Non-Malicious Nodes

TooLate is proposed to identify the Hub attack. S-Gossip can be used to detect any other types of malicious nodes also.

Both the security protocols are implemented on the base of Cyclon. Without any security mechanism, the gossip protocol can easily be effected by very few malicious nodes, as shown in figure 3, which could be reduced by both S-Gossip and TooLate. We took different scenarios by changing the number of nodes in the network, and percentage of malicious nodes during simulation study. It is observed from the figure 3, figure 4 and figure 5 that S-Gossip is better capable enough, to detect and isolate the malicious nodes, and therefore reduces the cache pollution after a fewer cycle.

Also, the experiments are performed for different churn rates. The results have been shown for 1% and 2% respectively in figure 6 and figure 7. It is conformed that for different churn rates also S-Gossip is more effective than that of TooLate.

The figure 8 shows that after a few cycles (around 10)almost all the malicious nodes are detected and isolated as they shifted into MT.

5 Conclusion

This paper presented a security enhanced gossip based mechanism named S-Gossip for unstructured P2P networks. Each node in S-Gossip observes the characteristic of its neighbors and conforms maliciousness of a peer based on the feedback obtained from other peers. The protocol isolates the malicious peer preventing to gossip with it. For evaluation we have simulated the Hub attack in the PeerSim simulator and compared with the existing solution TooLate. The result conforms that S-Gossip is more effective then TooLate. On the top, the proposed mechanism can be used to thwart against other malicious attacks also.

References

1. Rowstron, A., Druschel, P.: Pastry- Scalable, decentralized object location and routing for large-scale peer-to-peer systems. In: Guerraoui, R. (ed.) Middleware 2001. LNCS, vol. 2218, pp. 329–350. Springer, Heidelberg (2001)
2. Demers, A., Greene, D., Hauser, C., Irish, W., Larson, J., Shenker, S., Sturgis, H., Swinehart, D., Terry, D.: Epidemic algorithms for replicated database maintenance. In: Proc. of the 6th ACM Symposium on Principles of Distributing Computing (PODC 1987), pp. 1–12 (1987)
3. Montresor, A., Jelasity, M.: PeerSim: A scalable P2P simulator. In: IEEE Ninth International Conference, pp. 99–100 (2009)
4. Anceaume, E., Busnel, Y., Gambs, S.: Uniform and Ergodic Sampling in Unstructured Peer-to-Peer Systems with Malicious Nodes. In: Lu, C., Masuzawa, T., Mosbah, M. (eds.) OPODIS 2010. LNCS, vol. 6490, pp. 64–78. Springer, Heidelberg (2010)
5. Bortnikov, E., Gurevich, M., Keidar, I., Kliot, G., Shraer, A.: Brahms: byzantine resilient random membership sampling. In: Proceedings of the twenty-seventh ACM Symposium on Principles of Distributed Computing (PODC 2008), Canada, pp. 145–154 (2008)
6. Jesi, G.P., Montresor, A., van Steen, M.: A Secure Peer Sampling. Computer Networks 54(12), 2086–2098 (2010)
7. Jesi, G.P., Hales, D., van Steen, M.: Identifying Malicious Peers Before its TooLate: A Decentralized Secure Peer Sampling Service. In: First International Conference on Self-Adaptive and Self-Organizing Systems (SASO), Boston, MA, USA, pp. 237–246 (2007)
8. Stoica, I., Morris, R., Liben-Nowell, D., Karger, D.R., Kaashoek, M.F., Dabek, F., Balakrishnan, H.: Chord- A Scalable Peer-to-Peer Lookup Service for Internet Applications. IEEE/ACM Transactions on Networking 11(1), 17–32 (2003)
9. Kleinberg, J.: The small-world phenomenon: An algorithmic perspective. In: Proc. of the 32nd ACM Symposium on Theory of Computing (STOC 2000), pp. 163–170 (2000)

10. Jelasity, M., Montresor, A., Babaoglu, O.: A modular paradigm for building self-organizing peer-to-peer applications. In: Di Marzo Serugendo, G., Karageorgos, A., Rana, O.F., Zambonelli, F. (eds.) ESOA 2003. LNCS (LNAI), vol. 2977, pp. 265–282. Springer, Heidelberg (2004)
11. Jelasity, M., Montresor, A., Babaoglu, O.: The bootstrapping service. In: Proc. Of the 26th IEEE International Conference Workshops on Distributed Computing Systems (IDCSW 2006), pp. 11–16. IEEE Computer Society (2006)
12. Bertier, M., Bonnet, F., Kermarrec, A.M., Leroy, V., Peri, S., Raynal, M.: D2HT-The Best of Both Worlds, Integrating RPS and DHT. In: European Dependable Computing Conference, pp. 135–144 (2010)
13. Eugster, P.T., Guerraoui, R., Kermarrec, A.M., Massouli, L.: Epidemic information dissemination in distributed systems. IEEE Computer 37(5), 60–67 (2004)
14. Rhea, S., Geels, D., Roscoe, T., Kubiatowicz, J.: Handling churn in a DHT. In: Proc. of the USENIX Annual Technical Conference, pp. 10–23. USENIX Association, Berkeley (2004)
15. Voulgaris, S., van Steen, M.: Epidemic-style management of semantic overlays for content-based searching. In: Cunha, J.C., Medeiros, P.D. (eds.) Euro-Par 2005. LNCS, vol. 3648, pp. 1143–1152. Springer, Heidelberg (2005)
16. Voulgaris, S., Gavidia, D., van Steen, M.: Cyclon- Inexpensive membership management for unstructured P2P overlays. Journal of Network and Systems Management 13(2), 197–217 (2005)

k-degree Closeness Anonymity: A Centrality Measure Based Approach for Network Anonymization

Debasis Mohapatra[1] and Manas Ranjan Patra[2]

[1] Deptt. of Computer Science & Engg, PMEC, Berhampur, 761003, India
devdisha@gmail.com
[2] Deptt. of Computer Science, Berhampur University, Berhampur, 760007, India
mrpatra12@gmail.com

Abstract. Social network data are generally published in the form of social graphs which are being used for extensive scientific research. We have noticed that even a k-degree anonymization of social graph can't ensure protection against identity disclosure. In this paper, we have discussed how closeness centrality measure can be used to identify a social entity in the presence of k-degree anonymization. We have proposed a new model called k-degree closeness anonymization by adopting a mixed strategy of k-degree anonymity, degree centrality and closeness centrality. The model has two phases, namely, construction and validation. The construction phase transforms a graph with given sequence to a graph with anonymous sequence in such a manner that the closeness centrality measure is distributed among the nodes in a smooth way. The nodes with the same degree centrality are assigned with a closer set of closeness centrality values, making re-identification difficult. Validation phase validates our model by generating 1-neighborhood graphs. Algorithms have been developed both for the construction and validation phases.

Keywords: k-degree anonymity, k-degree closeness anonymity, closeness centrality, Social network.

1   Introduction

Two common approaches in privacy preserving data mining are secure multiparty computation [1] and data obscuration [2]. Randomization and anonymization are the two most important data obscuration methods. The anonymization problem is widely studied in the context of relational tables but less amount of work is found in the field of graph anonymization. Among various anonymity models such as k-anonymity [3, 4], l-diversity [5], (α,k) anonymity [6], and anatomy [7], the k-anonymity model has emerged as the most popular model where the focus is on generalization and suppression[8] of quasi-identifiers [4,8]of relational tables. Authors of [9] have proved that two general version of optimal k-anonymization of relations are NP-hard. Generalization and Suppression can be applied to anonymize the node label and edge label in a social graph, but will not fruitfully work against identity disclosure. Even the removal of labels and assignment of random numbers to nodes of the graph, called naïve anonymization [10] cannot serve the purpose. Establishment of k-anonymity is challenging in case of social graphs because social dependencies exist among the

R. Natarajan et al. (Eds.): ICDCIT 2015, LNCS 8956, pp. 299–310, 2015.

social entities, thus any modification may cause a ripple effect to other social entities present in the social graph [11].

An interesting anonymization model is k-degree anonymization [12]. This approach realizes the degree sequence to generate a graph that satisfies the same degree for at least k nodes. Random perturbation of graphs to assure structural automorphism is also a strong model [10]. But ensuring automorphism is not possible in all cases. K-anonymity social network can be designed by using edge addition, edge deletion, swapping, vertex addition etc. In the edge addition problem the k-label sequence anonymity of arbitrary labeled graph is hard [13]. To achieve k-anonymity by addition of minimum vertices, on vertex-labeled graph is NP-complete [14].

Attack models are used for re-identification. To protect against the neighborhood attack, combination of k-anonymity and l-diversity model is useful [15]. The node and link data from other domain can be correlated with the anonymized network to re-identify the anonymized nodes [16]. Structural attack threatens re-identification by analyzing structure of the network. Authors of [17] have proposed k-symmetry model, which modifies a naïve anonymized network such that for any vertex in the network, there are at least $k-1$ structurally equivalent counterparts. In another powerful attack called 1^*-neighborhood attack [18], the adversary has a prior knowledge about the 1-neighborhood graph along with degrees of the target's one-hop neighbors. HIGA scheme with probability indistinguishability property is used against this attack [18].

In most of the previous works centrality measures are not used during anonymization, which may be used by an adversary to re-identify a node. Our approach is based on the integration of three different approaches: k-degree anonymization, degree centrality measure and closeness centrality measure. We have introduced a k-degree closeness anonymity model and weighted closeness centrality measure. We have devised an algorithm that transforms a given original graph G into a k-degree closeness anonymous graph G_1, which sets priority of the nodes by considering a balance between degree and closeness centrality. The performance of the model is measured by using closeness centrality and weighted closeness centrality. Our model is validated through 1-neighborhood graphs.

2   Basic Concepts

In this section we have provided some basic definitions and formulae that are used in the subsequent sections. Related concepts are explained with examples for better understanding.

2.1   Naïve Anonymization

Definition 1 (Naïve Anonymization). *A graph $G(V,E)$ is mapped to an isomorphic graph $G_1(V_1,E_1)$, such that Label(V)is mapped to Label(V_1),where Label(V_1) ϵ RS(Random Set).*

Fig.1 shows an original social graph G. Fig.2 is a naïve anonymized version of G, by using one-to-one random mapping {Alice→1 Bob→2 Sastri→3 Yang→4 Zen→5 Srinivash→6 Doglous→7}.

2.2   K-degree Anonymization

Definition 2 (K-degree Anonymization). *A graphic degree sequence ds(G) is k-degree anonymous if* $|ds(G)|/|ud(G)| \geq k$, $k=min(F)$. *where ud(G)is the sequence of unique degrees and* $F=f_1, f_2, ..., f_n$ *is the frequency sequence of those degrees in ds(G), if ds(G) is k-degree anonymous then G is also k-degree anonymous.*

Fig.3 represents a 2-degree anonymous graph of *NG*. Degree sequence of graph *D* is {2, 2, 3, 2, 3, 2, 2} which is enumerated according to the numeric order.

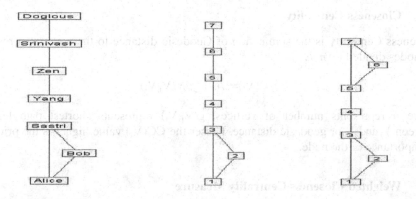

Fig. 1. OriginalGraph(OG)   **Fig. 2.** Naïve Graph(NG)   **Fig. 3.** 2-Degree(D)

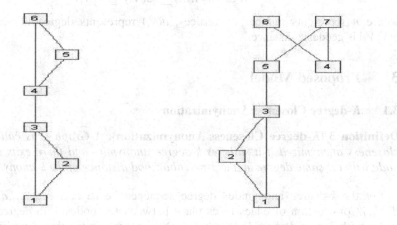

Fig. 4. 2-degree closeness(CD)   **Fig. 5.** 2-degree closeness anonymous graph

2.3   Degree Centrality

Degree Centrality is a basic measure that allocates high importance to vertex with high degree. This is obtained by counting the number of 1 present in i^{th} row of adjacency matrix A.

$$DC(V_i)=deg(V_i). \tag{1}$$

where $deg(V_i)$ is degree of vertex V_i.

2.4   Closeness Centrality

Closeness Centrality is the summation of Geodesic distance to the node from rest of the nodes divided by $n-1$.

$$CC(V_i)=1/n-1\sum_{j\neq i}g(V_j,V_i) \tag{2}$$

where n represents number of vertices, $g(V_j,V_i)$ represents shortest path length between V_j and V_i or geodesic distance. Lesser the $CC(V_i)$ value higher is the priority or importance of the node.

2.5   Weighted Closeness Centrality Measure

This metric assigns a high value to vertex V_i that is present far away from the vertices with higher degrees.

$$WC(V_i)=1/n-1\sum_{j\neq i}d(V_i)*g(V_j,V_i) \tag{3}$$

where n represents number of vertices, $d(V_i)$ represents degree of vertex V_i and $g(V_j,V_i)$ is geodesic distance.

3   Proposed Model

3.1   *K*-degree Closeness Anonymization

Definition 3 (*K*-degree Closeness Anonymization). *A Graph G is called k-degree closeness anonymized if it satisfies k-degree anonymity and there exits at least one node with the same degree in the 1-neighborhood distance of the k-anonymous nodes.*

Let the k-degree anonymous degree sequence be $ds<d_1,d_2,d_3,......,d_n>$ such that $d_i \geq d_{i+1}$. Construction of edges takes place between the nodes with degree d_i and the nodes with degree d_l where $i+1 \leq l \leq i+d_i-1$. During this construction d_i is eliminated and ds is updated to $<d_x-1,......,d_y-1,...d_n>$ where $x=i+1,y= i+d_i-1$. Degree sequence is not rearranged after an iteration. It forms clusters of d_i-nearest neighbors where d_i varies from node to node. It ensures that a node with degree d_i contains at least one node with degree d_i in its *1-neighborhood distance* for $k \geq 2$. This is applicable to both the nodes x_i and x_j between which an edge is placed as the graph is undirected.

Example: Graph D in fig. 3 is 2-degree anonymous but not 2-degree closeness anonymous. Let us consider a graphic degree sequence {3, 3, 2, 2, 2, 2} that corresponds to the graph CD in fig.4. Graph CD is 2-degree closeness anonymous because for degree 3, node 3 and node 4 are present in *1*-neighborhood distance. For degree 2, node 2 and node 1, node 5 and node 6 are in *1*-neighborhood distance.

3.2   Identity Disclosure

In identity disclosure, the identity associated with the social entity representing a node in a social graph is disclosed. In naïve anonymization approach the simple background knowledge along with the published anonymized graph can re-identify the social entity. If the adversary knows that degree of *Sastri* is 3, then he can easily identify *Sastri* as node 3 in fig.2. So a better approach can be a *k*-degree anonymous approach. Fig. 3 is a 2-degree anonymous graph of fig. 1. So probability of finding out *Sastri* as node 3 is ½. But if the adversary is modeled to access both degree and closeness centrality value then re-identification becomes easier. Suppose the adversary knows that degree of *Yang* is 2 and having closeness centrality value 1.83 (as computed by equ.2). Then in 2-degree anonymous graph in fig. 3 the adversary finds all 2 degree nodes {1, 2, 4, 6, 7} with closeness centrality {2.5, 2.5, 1.66, 2.5, 2.5}, so he can re-identify *Yang* as node 4 with a closer value 1.66 to the value1.83. To avoid this problem we have constructed a 2-degree closeness anonymous graph of fig.1 shown in fig.5 where all nodes with degree 2 {1, 2, 4, 6, 7} having closeness centrality {2.3, 2.3, 2.5, 2.0, 2.0}, which makes re-identification of *Yang* difficult.

3.3   Adversary Model

In this section we discuss an adversary model against which our proposed model works. In our adversary model the adversary is allowed to query on the original graph. An adversary is modeled for degree query and closeness centrality query where he is provided with a prior knowledge of degree and closeness centrality of the nodes respectively. Adversary is assumed to be a passive attacker. By acquiring the prior information about the network through query, the adversary tries to disclose the identity of the social entity. Here adversary is only concerned about identity disclosure.

3.4   Problem Definition

We have proposed a model called *k*-degree closeness anonymization which works considerably well against the adversary model. Our objective is to hide the identity of the social entity by distorting the social graph. *Given a graph G with degree sequence d(G) and a k-degree anonymous degree sequence d. Graph G is converted into k-degree closeness anonymous graph G₁ that satisfies d.*

4   Design of the Algorithms

In this section we present our algorithms that serve our problem definition. We have proposed *DegreeToGraph* and *GraphTransformation* algorithms for construction of the *k*-degree anonymous graph and *OneNeighborhood* algorithm to validate the resultant graph.

4.1   Degree to Graph Conversion Algorithm

In fig.6 we explain the *DegreeToGraph* conversion algorithm. Input *ds* is a *k*-degree anonymous sequence which is converted into *k*-degree closeness graph. Variable *s* stores the size of the degree sequence *ds*. *Name* assigns the numbers to the nodes of the graph. The adjacency matrix *mat* is initialized with zeroes. All the nodes are then arranged according to their respective degree sequences. The edges of the graph are traced out and the corresponding locations of matrix *mat* are set to binary 1. During edge tracing the node *X* with degree *n* forms *n* different edges with *n* subsequent nodes of *X*. This process is repeated |*ds*| times.

Algorithm. DegreeToGraph(ds)
Input: k-degree anonymous sequence
Output: k-degree closeness Graph

1. $s \leftarrow size(ds)$
2. $Name[] \leftarrow 1$ to s
3. $t \leftarrow 1, k \leftarrow 1$
4. $mat[1$ to $s, 1$ to $s] \leftarrow 0$
5.   **while** $k < s$ **do**
6.   **for** $i \leftarrow k$ to s **do**
7.   **for** $j \leftarrow i+1$ to s **do**
8.   **if** $d[i] < d[j]$ **then**
9. $Swap(d[i], d[j])$
10. $Swap(Name[i], Name[j])$
11.   **end if**
12.   **end for**
13.   **end for**
14.   **for** $m \leftarrow t+1$ to s **do**
15.   **if** $d[t]!=0$ **then**
16. $mat[Name[t], Name[m]] \leftarrow 1$
17. $mat[Name[m], Name[t]] \leftarrow 1$
18. $d[t] \leftarrow d[t]-1$
19. $d[m] \leftarrow d[m]-1$
20.   **end if**
21.   **end for**
22. $k \leftarrow k+1, t \leftarrow t+1$
23. **end while**
24. $return(mat)$

Fig. 6. DegreeToGraph Algorithm

4.2   Graph Transformation Algorithm

Fig.7 depicts the *GraphTransformation* algorithm. The algorithm is implemented by using some set theoretic operations to the adjacency matrix of the graph that is a consequence of edge addition and deletion operation in the corresponding graph. Steps 1 and 2 generate *k*-degree closeness anonymous graph and a complete graph from a *k*-degree anonymous sequence and complete graph sequence respectively. Steps 3 and 4 find the complement of Graphs *G* and *G_1* respectively. Steps 5 and 6 define edge deletion. Steps 7 and 8 explain edge addition. Graph *G* is converted into *G_1*.

Algorithm: GraphTransformation(G)

Input: Original Graph(G) and k-degree anonymous sequence d(G1).

Output: G converted to *k*-degree closeness anonymous graph.

1. $G_1 \leftarrow DegreeToGraph(d(G1))$.
2. $CG \leftarrow DegreeToGraph(v)$.
3. $COMPG \leftarrow CG\text{-}G$
4. $COMPG_1 \leftarrow CG\text{-}G_1$
5. $INTER_1 \leftarrow COMPG_1 \cap G$
6. $G \leftarrow G\text{-}INTER_1$
7. $INTER_2 \leftarrow COMPG \cap G_1$
8. $G \leftarrow G\text{+}INTER_2$

Fig. 7. GraphTransformation Algorithm

4.3   Validation Algorithm

We validate the *k*-degree closeness anonymity by finding out *1*-nighborhood graphs of all nodes through the *OneNeighborhood* algorithm explained in fig.8. The input to the algorithm is a graph *G* and a *node* for which *1*-neighborhorhood graph is to be generated. It returns a matrix *tart* which is the adjacency matrix of *1*-neighborhood graph. This algorithm is invoked *n* number of times to generate *1*-neighborhood graphs of all *n* vertices.

4.4   Complexity Analysis

In *DegreeToGraph* algorithm lines 6-13 can be computed in $O(n^2)$ time for *n* times. Lines 14-21 can be computed in n-1, n-2,....,1 times. So the time complexity of *DegreeToGraph* is $O(n^3)+O(n^2) \approx O(n^3)$. However, the lines 6-13 can be computed in $O(n \log n)$ time by using merge sort. So the time complexity of *DegreeToGraph* is reduced to $O(n^2)$. In *GraphTransformation* algorithm all lines except lines 1 and 2 can be computed in $O(n^2)$ time because the set theoretic operations are implemented on the adjacency matrix of the graph. Lines 1 and 2 can be computed in $O(n^2)$ time. So the time complexity of *GraphTransformation* is $O(n^2)$. The complexity of *OneNeighborhood* is dominated by the computation of lines 18-28. Lines 18-28 can be computed in $O(m^2)$ where m is number of nodes present in the *1*-neighbourhood distance of *node* . The *OneNeighborhood* algorithm is invoked n times for the purpose of validation and the time complexity turns out to be $O(n(max(m))^2)$.

Algorithm. OneNeighborhood(G,node)

Input: G is the adjacency matrix of Graph G, *node* is a node for which 1-neighborhood graph is to be generated.

Output: OneNeighborhood Graph .

  1. s ← size(G)
  2. t ← 0
  3. **for** *i ← 1 to s* **do**
  4.   **if** *G[node,i]==1* **then**
  5.   *t ← t+1;*
  6.   *m[t] ← i;*
  7.   **end if**
  8. **end for**
  9. s1 ← size(m)
  10. tart[1 to s1+1 , 1 to s1+1] ← 0
  11. p ← 2
  12. **for** *j ← 1to s1* **do**
  13.   *tart[1,p] ← 1*
  14.   *tart[p,1] ← 1*
  15.   *p ← p+1;*
  16. **end for**
  17.   *l ← 1*
  18. **for** *i ← 1 to s1-1* **do**
  19.   *l ← l+1*
  20.   *k ← l+1*
  21.   **for** *j ← i+1 to s1* **do**
  22.   **if** *G[m[i],m[j]]==1* **then**
  23.   *tart[l,k] ← 1*
  24.   *tart[k,l] ← 1*
  25.   **end if**
  26.   *k ← k+1*
  27.   **end for**
  28. **end for**
  29. return(tart)

Fig. 8. OneNeighborhood Algorithm

5   Experimental Setup

Experiments are carried out using both synthetic and real data sets. All the algorithms are implemented in MATLABR2009b. The real datasets like CSphd and Kohonen are gathered from the UCI Network Data Repository. We have converted CSphd and Kohonen graphs into undirected graphs. Self-loops are removed from Kohonen graph to make it as simple graph. Experimental results show that our proposed model works much more efficiently in distorted homophily networks. The nodes with same degree centrality are placed closer to each other and assigned with a closer set of closeness centrality. We have observed that if the network is having n nodes which is divided into clusters $C_1, C_2, \ldots C_m$, then C_i contains at least 2 and at most $n\text{-}2*(m\text{-}1)$ nodes. Also, if n nodes are present with degree d then at most $ceil(n/2)$ and at least 1 clusters of same degree d are present. We have seen that our all k-degree closeness anonymized graphs pass through the validation phase.

5.1   Result Analysis

We have compared our proposed model of k-degree closeness anonymization with the existing k-degree anonymization model [12]. Our comparison is based on two centrality measures: closeness centrality and weighted closeness centrality. We have shown the closeness centrality comparisons in fig.9 and fig.10 for the synthetic graphs Synth1 and Synth2 respectively where $k=2$. We have observed that the distribution of both closeness centrality and weighted closeness centrality are uniform in our model in comparison to the existing model. Fig.11 shows weighted closeness centrality distributions for Synth1. The closeness and weighted closeness centrality are measured with the help of all pair shortest path evaluation methods.

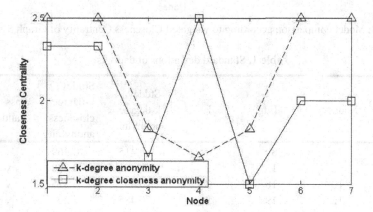

Fig. 9. Model comparison according to Closeness Centrality of Graph Synth1

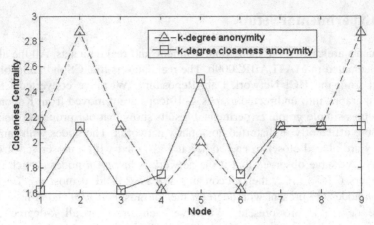

Fig. 10. Model comparison according to Closeness Centrality of Graph Synth2

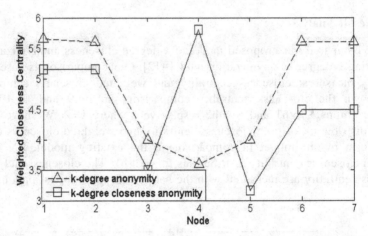

Fig. 11. Model comparison according to weighted Closeness Centrality of Graph Synth1

Table 1. Standard deviations of datasets

Graph	Nodes	Edges	k	Stddev k-degree anonymity	Stddev k-degree closeness anonymity	Pass through Validation
Synth1	7	8	2	0.415	0.369	√
Synth2	9	13	2	0.449	0.298	√
Synth3	10	18	3	0.492	0.325	√
Synth4	12	19	3	0.485	0.201	√
Synth5	13	24	3	0.5	0.302	√
CSphd	1882	1740	4	3.214	2.567	√
Kohonen	4470	12731	4	4.68	3.97	√

Graphs with different nodes, edges and k values are converted into k-degree anonymous and k-degree closeness anonymous graph. All k-degree closeness anonymous graphs are validated by 1-neighbourhood test. The standard deviations of closeness centrality of these two versions of each graph are tabulated in Table 1, and the comparison is shown in fig.12. We have noticed, if G is a k-degree anonymous graph and G_1 is a k-degree closeness anonymous graph then $Std_{cc}(G) \leq Std_{cc}(G_1)$, where $Std_{cc}(X)$ is the standard deviation of closeness centrality measure of graph X. The re-identification of a node in a k-degree closeness anonymous graph is difficult because the nodes with the same degree are assigned with nearer closeness centrality values.

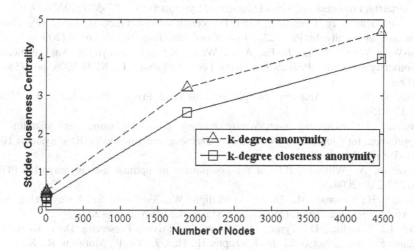

Fig. 12. Model comparison according to standard deviation of closeness centrality

6   Conclusions

In this paper, we have proposed a model called k-degree closeness anonymity to protect against identity disclosure in social networks. Algorithms have been designed for the construction and validation of the model which are computed in $O(n^2)$ and $O(n(max(m))^2)$ time respectively. We have analyzed the algorithms based on closeness centrality and weighted centrality measures. Further, it is shown that our proposed model is efficient in comparison to existing k-degree anonymity model with respect to our adversary model. The proposed model ensures uniform distribution of centrality measures with less standard deviation with respect to k-degree anonymity model.

References

1. Lindell, Y., Pinkas, B.: Secure Multiparty Computation for Privacy-Preserving Data Mining. The Journal of Privacy and Confidentiality 1, 59–98 (2009)
2. Hann, J., Kamber, N.: Data mining: Concepts and techniques. MorganKanfmann Publishers, San Francisco (2001)
3. Aggarwal, G., Feder, T., Kenthapadi, K., Motwani, R., Panigrahy, R., Thomas, D., Zhu, A.: Anonymizing tables. In: Eiter, T., Libkin, L. (eds.) ICDT 2005. LNCS, vol. 3363, pp. 246–258. Springer, Heidelberg (2005)
4. Sweeney, L.: k-ANONYMITY: A Model for Protecting Privacy, International Journal on Uncertainty. Fuzziness and Knowledge-based Systems 10(5), 557–570 (2002)
5. Machanavajjhala, A., Gehrke, J., Kifer, D., Venkitasubramaniam, M.: l-diversity: Privacy beyond k-anonymity. In: Proc. 22nd Intnl. Conf. Data Engg (ICDE), p. 24 (2006)
6. Chi-Wing Wong, R., Li, J., Fu, A.W., Wang, K.: (α,k)Anonymity: An Enhanced k-Anonymity Model for Privacy Preserving Data Publishing. In: KDD 2006, pp. 754–759 (2006)
7. Xiao, X., Tao, Y.: Anatomy: Simple and Effective Privacy Preservation. In: VLDB, pp. 139–150 (2006)
8. Sweeney, L.: Achieving k-anonymity privacy protection using generalization and suppression. Int'l Journal on Uncertainty, Fuzziness, and Knowledge-Base Systems 10(5), 571–588 (2002)
9. Meyerson, A., Williams, R.: On the complexity of optimal k-anonymity. In: PODS, pp. 223–228 (2004)
10. Michael, H., Gerome, M., David, J., Philipp, W., Siddharth, S.: Anonymizing social networks. Technical report, University of Massachusetts Amherst (2007)
11. Kun, L., Kamalika, D., Tyrone, G., Hillol, K.: Privacy-Preserving Data Analysis on Graphs and Social Networks. In: Kargupta, H., Han, J., Yu, P., Motwani, R., Kumar, V. (eds.) Next Generation of Data Mining, ch. 21, pp. 419–437. Chapman & Hall/CRC (2008)
12. Kun, L., Evimaria, T.: Towards identity anonymization on graphs. In: Proceedings of ACM SIGMOD, Vancouver, Canada, pp. 93–106 (2008)
13. Kapron Bruce, M., Gautam, S., Venkatesh, S.: Social Network Anonymization via Edge Addition. In: ASONAM 2011, pp. 155–162 (2011)
14. Sean, C., Kapron Bruce, M., Ganesh, R., Gautam, S., Alex, T., Venkatesh, S.: k-Anonymization of Social Networks by Vertex Addition. In: ADBIS (2) 2011, pp. 107–116 (2011)
15. Bin, Z., Jian, P.: Preserving privacy in social networks against neighborhood attacks. In: Proceedings of the 24th International Conference on Data Engineering (ICDE 2008), pp. 506–515 (2008)
16. PedarsaniPedram, G.M.: On the Privacy of Anonymized Networks. In: KDD 2011, pp. 1235–1243 (2011)
17. Wu, W., Xiao, Y., Wang, W., He, Z., Wang, Z.: K-Symmetry Model for Identity Anonymization in Social Networks. In: Proceedings of the 13th International Conference on Extending Database Technology (EDBT 2010), pp. 111–122 (2010)
18. Wang, G., Liu, Q., Li, F., Yang, S., Wu, J.: Outsourcing Privacy-Preserving Social Networks to Cloud. In: 2013 Proceedings IEEE INFOCOM, pp. 2886–2894 (2013)

A Chinese Remainder Theorem Based Key Management Algorithm for Hierarchical Wireless Sensor Network

Pranave Kumar Bhaskar and Alwyn R. Pais

Department of Computer Science and Engineering, NITK Surathkal, India
pkbls.10@gmail.com
alwyn@nitk.ac.in

Abstract. Wireless Sensor Networks (WSN) are network of sensors having low computation, storage and battery power. Hierarchical WSN are heterogeneous network of sensors having different capabilities which form a hierarchy to achieve energy efficiency. Key management algorithms are center of the security protocols in WSN. It involves key pre distribution, shared key discovery, key revocation, and refreshing. Due to resource constraints in WSN achieving a perfect key management scheme has been quite challenging. In this paper a new key management scheme for Hierarchical WSN based on Chinese Remainder Theorem has been proposed. An experimental setup is created to evaluate this scheme. The results indicate that it establishes the key with minimum computation, communication, storage cost at each node, also it is scalable and resilient to different attacks.

1 Introduction

Since the evolution of practical cryptography, key management has been subject of attention. This is mainly because prior to any secure communication, encryption/decryption key must be obtained. Key exchange generally uses public key cryptography, however for a WSN it becomes infeasible, for want of resources. Thus a key management scheme is needed. In this paper a key management algorithm for hierarchical sensor network based on Chinese remainder theorem is proposed.

The organization of this paper is as follows. Section 1 introduces the topic in general. In Section 2 popular existing schemes for sensor network key management are discussed. At the end of this section their respective pros and cons are analyzed. Section 3 discusses the architecture of sensor network and proposed scheme in detail. In Section 4 experimental setup and simulation parameters are explained in brief. In Section 5 the result of the experiments are presented with a detailed discussion on these results and finally an analysis is made. Section 6 provides conclusion and scope for future work.

2 Existing Schemes

This section gives a brief account of different popular schemes for key management with their pros & cons. There are many key management algorithms proposed in literature for WSN [6]. Table 1 presents a comparative analysis of the schemes based

R. Natarajan et al. (Eds.): ICDCIT 2015, LNCS 8956, pp. 311–317, 2015.
© Springer International Publishing Switzerland 2015

on different parameters such as scalability, resilience, process load, communication load and storage load. From Table 1 it is seen that all these algorithms have their respective limitations. Some algorithms provide connectivity but require either heavy computation [3] or they have large storage and communication requirements [2], [4]. Some algorithms do provide key distribution without these shortcomings but they have their own requirements like prior deployment knowledge [5]. The hybrid schemes have other issues such as scalability and lack of resilience to common attacks.

Table 1. Comparison of different key management algorithms for WSN

Protocol	Theory	Resilience	Process Load	Comm. Load	Storage Load
Pure Probabilistic [1]	Random Graph	Medium	Medium	Medium	High
Q Composite [2]	Random Graph	Good	Medium	High	High
Polynomial based [3]	t-degree polynomial	Good	High	Medium	High
Matrix based [4]	Symmetric Matrix	Good	Medium	Medium	High
Deployment Info based [5]	Random Graph	Excellent	Medium	Medium	Medium

Thus there is a need for a novel key management scheme which overcomes the above discussed limitations. A scheme for key management in HSN based on CRT was presented in [7], which discussed the theoretical idea. In this paper this idea is extended and evaluated to make it practical in a real sensor network environment.

3   Proposed Scheme

3.1   Architecture

The sensor network architecture for which the key management algorithm is proposed is HSN (Hierarchical Sensor Network). A HSN is organized into groups called clusters with a CH (cluster head). All communication to base station (BS) happens via this CH. CH generally have larger computation power and memory. Individual sensor nodes in a cluster are responsible to accumulate the sensing data and send it at regular time interval to the CH. Each of these clusters has a group key (GK) which is used for all communication within the cluster. The CH sends these sensed data to BS on request basis. The communication between CH and BS is encrypted via a key that is exclusively shared by each CH and BS. This key is called BGK. Typical architecture of HSN is as shown in Fig. 1.

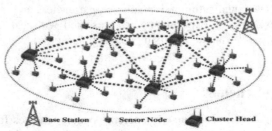

Fig. 1. Hierarchical Sensor Network Architecture

The total numbers of nodes considered in this experiment are 128, 256, 512 and 1024 i.e. total four setups. The number of nodes in each cluster is taken to be 8 and 12.

3.2   Scheme Details

This section explains establishment of group key and rekeying in HSN architecture using CRT. The best algorithm to solve CRT congruence takes m $(\log n)^3$ operations, where m being total equations and n, bit size of keys. In pre-distribution phase each of the sensor node get their private key K_i from the BS's key pool, each of these keys are relatively prime to each other. The BS and CH maintains ID↔K pair in its database for each node. In running phase the cluster is formed by sending HELLO message by the CH, the sensor nodes in the proximity respond to this message and forms the cluster. Once the cluster is formed the CH deletes keying information of nodes not in its cluster. In each of these clusters, the CH now chooses a randomly generated group key GK and forms a congruence system as follows

$X \equiv a_1 \pmod{K_1}$
$X \equiv a_2 \pmod{K_2}$
$:$
$X \equiv a_n \pmod{K_n}$

Where $a_i = GK \oplus K_i$ and K_i is the secret key of sensor SN_i. The CH solves this congruence to find X. The CH then broadcast this X value to sensor nodes in its group. The sensor nodes will calculate the group key by formula GK = $(X \bmod K_i) \oplus K_i$.

XOR Overflow. While creating the congruence the residuals of congruence is calculated by XOR of node keys with group key i.e. $a_i = GK \oplus K_i$. These a_i some times are greater than K_i. So while creating the congruence instead of using a_i, use $a_i \% K_i$ (i.e. reminder of a_i divided by K_i). Viz. if K_i= 17 and GK = 53 then a_i= GK $\oplus$ K_i =36. In this case the congruence equation becomes:

~~X = 36 (mod 17)~~ => X $\equiv$ 2 (mod 17)

So, while calculating GK at node the value of a_i is taken as 2 instead of 36. Thus the divisor value should be preserved for each congruence equation to get original a_i. For this purpose divisor value d_i is stored for each node and unicasted to individual nodes separately. The formula for calculating group key at node level now changes as follows:

X mod K_i = a'_i(This is not actual a_i)
a_i= $d_i * K_i$ + a'_i
And finally GK = $a_i \oplus K_i$.

Key Selection. There are two stages in key selection. In first stage the key pool (KP) is selected from a set of strong primes N, in second phase individual node keys are chosen from this key pool. The key pool size depends on size of the network. Initially the key pool is selected randomly and then refreshed regularly. New keys are selected from N using following formula:

$$K_i \text{ (new)} = N[K_i \text{ (old)} * F \bmod |N|]$$

Where F is no. of refresh and |N| is size of set N. These key pools (KP) are stored in a 2D array of size nxn. Individual keys K_i for nodes are selected from the key pool based on following formula:

$$K_i = KP[q][r],$$

Where q = (A*22 + C) mod n and r = (B*22 + D) mod n and A, B, C and D are each decimal representation of 8 bit parts taken from four equal division of 32 bit ID.

4   Experimental Setup

As explained in the architecture section, there are four different setups considered for this experiment i.e. sensor networks having 128, 256, 512 and 1024 total nodes (CH+SN). The number of nodes in each cluster is taken to be 8 and 12 for each case. Different specifications for these nodes are used as simulation parameter that are listed in Table 2.

Table 2. Generic simulation parameters

Parameter name	Value
Number of sensor nodes	128/256/512/1024
Max nodes in cluster	8 /12
Key pool	20X20/30X30/40X40/60X60 with max key size 16 bit
Area size (A)	200 m x 200 m (for 128 nodes and accordingly)
Radio range in open air	200 m
Bandwidth	20kbps
Max Packet size	512 bits
Initial battery capacity	200 J (for Sensor Node), 4000J (for CH)
Min Simulation time	600 sec

5   Results and Analysis

The criteria for evaluating key management schemes include processing complexity (T_p), communication complexity (T_c), storage complexity (T_s), resilience, rekeying cost and scalability. Different results and their analysis w.r.t. these evaluation criteria are as follows:

Computation Cost (T_p). The time taken to calculate the CRT congruence is close to 3.2 and 5 μsec (Fig. 2) for clusters of size 8 and 12 respectively. The theoretical value of time consumed are 3 and 4.8 μsec respectively. These theoretical values are approximately same as obtained in the experiment.

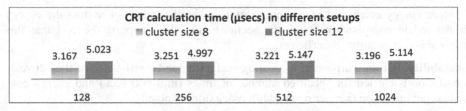

Fig. 2. Number of nodes Vs. CRT calculation time (μsec)

If the energy (battery power) consumed in CRT computation is considered, it is approximately 1.26and 2.02μJ (Fig. 3) for clusters of size 8 and 12 respectively. This is slightly greater than theoretical values which are 1.15 and 1.82 μJ respectively.

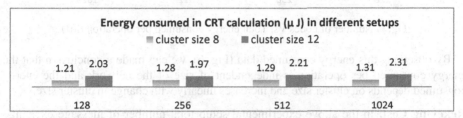

Fig. 3. Number of nodes Vs. Energy consumed in CRT calculation (μJ)

Communication Cost (T_c). In this scheme to establish group key the CH broadcasts the cluster key X (i.e. one transmit) and sensor nodes receive the cluster key.

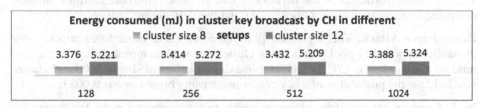

Fig. 4. Number of nodes Vs. Energy consumed (mJ) in cluster key broadcast by CH

The results from Fig. 4 indicate that the energy consumed at CHs are approximately 3.4mJ and 5.2mJ respectively for clusters of size 8 and 12. This is very close to theoretical values which are 3.2 and 5.0mJ. Similarly from Fig. 5, the energy consumed per node for cluster key receive is 58 and 90 μJ for clusters of size 8 and 12 respectively.

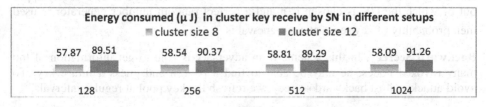

Fig. 5. Number of nodes Vs. Energy consumed (μJ) in cluster key receive by SN

Here energy consumed in communication is significantly higher than the energy consumed in computation (see prev. section); this also supports the fact that this scheme is computationally efficient.

Scalability. For the purpose of evaluating scalability and consistence of the network, simulation is carried for specified number of times (min 600 secs) and energy consumed per operation (i.e. per node addition/deletion) is noted.

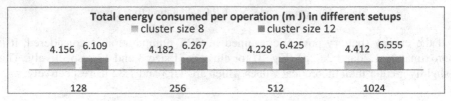

Fig. 6. Number of nodes Vs. Total energy consumed per operation (mJ)

By observing this energy consumed data (Fig. 6), we can made a conclusion that the energy consumed per operation is independent of size of the network and the energy consumed depends on cluster size and increases linearly with change in cluster size.

Rekeying Cost. In the above experimental setup total number of message exchange per operation (including broadcast and unicast messages) is also measured. This gives the rekey cost calculation.

Security Analysis. Here we discuss resilience of proposed algorithm to different attacks. The performance of the network in case of node removal/addition is already discussed in previous section. Other attacks and their effects are further discussed.

Brute Force Attack. This algorithm is designed to make brute force attacks very difficult. Suppose key pool size is P and cluster size is C then probability of compromise of a group key is C/P. In this setup maximum key pool size is 3600 and cluster size is 12, so the probability of a key compromise using brute force is 0.0033.

Node Capture Attack. If an adversary is able to compromise a node, the keying information is revoked from that node, and whole congruence is recalculated excluding that node to establish a new group key.

Collusion Attack. This scheme is full collusion resistant i.e. if an adversary is able to compromise k nodes he can't establish a GK with other nodes or get keying information of an uncompromised node.

Forward Secrecy. This scheme provides forward secrecy as the group key GK is chosen by CH at random and it has no relation with older keys. If size of key space out of which the GK is chosen is n and a perfect random number generator is used then probability of key reuse at next renewal is $\frac{1}{n}$.

Backward Secrecy. In this scheme if an adversary is able to get information of too many revoked nodes, he may be able to find a pattern and guess a future key. To avoid attack against backward secrecy, we refresh the key pool at regular intervals.

6   Conclusion and Scope for Future Work

This paper discusses a new key management technique for Hierarchical Sensor Network which is based on Chinese Remainder Theorem. This scheme provides key establishment in a cluster like environment with minimal computation, storage and communication cost. Experimental result also suggests that it is highly scalable and consistent. The resilience to different attacks was also analyzed and it can be concluded that it is protected from most common attacks that may happen in clustered architecture of HSN. Future work may include combining the CRT based scheme with distributed architecture in a hybrid scheme.

References

1. Eschenauer, L., Gligor, V.: A Key-Management Scheme for Distributed Sensor Networks. In: Proc. of ACM CCS (2002)
2. Chan, H., Perrig, A., Song, D.: Random Key Pre distribution Schemes for Sensor Networks. In: IEEE Symposium on Research in Security and Privacy (2003)
3. Liu, D., Ning, P.: Establishing Pairwise Keys in Distributed Sensor Networks. In: 10th ACM CCS, Washington D.C (2003)
4. Blom, R.: An optimal class of symmetric key generation systems. In: Beth, T., Cot, N., Ingemarsson, I. (eds.) EUROCRYPT 1984. LNCS, vol. 209, pp. 335–338. Springer, Heidelberg (1985)
5. Du, W., Deng, J., Han, Y., Chen, S., Varshney, P.: A Key Management Scheme for Wireless Sensor Networks Using Deployment Knowledge. In: IEEE Infocom (2004)
6. Akyildiz, F., Su, W., Sankarasubramaniam, Y., Cyirci, E.: Wireless Sensor Networks: A Survey. Computer Networks 38(4), 393–422 (2002)
7. Bhaskar, P.K., Sahoo, S.: A Novel Key Establishment Scheme for Hierarchical Sensor Network based on Chinese Remainder Theorem. In: National Workshop on Cryptology, SITE, VIT University (2012)

An Evolutionary Computation Based Classification Model for Network Intrusion Detection

Ashalata Panigrahi and Manas Ranjan Patra

Department of Computer Science, Berhampur University, Berhampur 760007, India
ashalata.panigrahi@yahoo.com
mrpatra12@gmail.com

Abstract. Current techniques used for network intrusion detection have limited capabilities in coping with the dynamic and increasingly complex nature of security threats. In this paper, we propose a classification model for detecting intrusions based on Genetic Programming, Artificial Immune Recognition Systems (AIRS1, AIRS2), and Clonal Selection Algorithm (CLONALG). Further, six Rank based, viz., Information Gain, Gain ratio, Symmetrical Uncertainty, Chi squared Attribute Evaluator, Relief-F, and one-R; and five search based feature selection methods, viz., PSO Search, Genetic Search, Best First Search, Greedy Stepwise, and Rank Search have been employed to select the most relevant attributes before classification. The performance of the model has been evaluated in terms of accuracy, precision, detection rate, F-value, false alarm rate, and fitness value.

1 Introduction

A genetic or evolutionary algorithm [1] applies the principles of evolution found in nature to the problem of finding an optimal solution to a problem. Genetic programming (GP) is a rule evolution approach for detecting novel attacks. Four genetic operators, namely reproduction, mutation, crossover, and dropping condition operators are used to evolve new rules. Initial rules are selected based on background knowledge and can be represented as parse trees. New rules are used to detect novel or known attacks. Intrusion detection systems require that the system be able to change over time to accommodate new information and new attacks.

Artificial immune systems [2] are new class of algorithms inspired by how the immune system recognizes attacks and the intruders. The immune system is sometimes called the "second brain" for its abilities to recognize new intruders and remember past occurrences. The role of the biological immune system is to provide the organisms with an effective mechanism against pathogenic infections. The biological immune system mainly consists of two defensive lines, one is the innate immune system, and the other is the adaptive immune system. These two systems perform the defensive tasks complementarily. The important characteristic of the immune system is learning. The learning ability of the immune system lies primarily in the Clonal expansion [3]. The core of the adaptive immune response is the Clonal selection theory.

R. Natarajan et al. (Eds.): ICDCIT 2015, LNCS 8956, pp. 318–324, 2015.

2   Evolutionary Computation Based Classification Techniques

2.1   Genetic Programming (GP)

Genetic programming is an evolutionary computation (EC) based technique that automatically solves problems without requiring the user to know or specify the form or structure of the solution in advance [4]. GP randomly generates an initial population of solutions which is then manipulated using various genetic operators such as reproduction, crossover, mutation, and dropping condition.

Genetic Programming Algorithm
```
 Input: Populationsize, nodes func, nodesterm, Pcrossover, Pmutation, Preproduction, Palteration
 Output: Sbest
 begin
    Population  ←  InitializePopulation (Populationsize, nodes func, nodesterm)
    EvaluatePopulation (Population), Sbest  ←  GetBestSolution (Population)
      while StopCondition () do
                        Children ← Ø
              while Size (Children) < Populationsize  do
              Operator  ←  SelectGeneticOperator(Pcrossover, Pmutation, Preproduction, Palteration)
              if Operator ≡ CrossoverOperator then
                Parent1, Parent2 ← selectParents (Population, Populationsize )
                Child1, Child2 ← Crossover (Parent1, Parent2), Children ← Child1, Children ← Child2
              else if Operator ≡ MutationOperator  then
                Parent1 ← SelectParents (Population, Populationsize),
                Child1 ← Mutate (Parent1), Children ← Child1
              else if Operator ≡ ReproductionOperator then
                        Parent1 ← SelectParents (Population, Populationsize)
                        Child1 ← Reproduce (Parent1),   Children ← Child1
              else if Operator ≡ AlterationOperator then
                        Parent1 ← SelectParents (Population, Populationsize)
                        Child1 ← AlterArchitecture(Parent1), Children ← Child1
            end
        end
        EvaluatePopulation(Children)
        Sbest ← GetBestSolution (children, Sbest), Population ← Children
        return Sbest
    end
```

2.2   The AIRS Algorithm

The Immune System (IS) is a complex system comprising of cells, molecules and organs that represent an identification mechanism capable of perceiving and combating dysfunction of our own cells (infectious self) and the action of exogenous infectious microorganisms (infectious non-self) [5]. Artificial Immune Recognition Systems (AIRs) refer to a class of algorithms inspired by the human immune system. The AIRS algorithm has five basic steps, viz., Initialization, Antigen training, Competition for limited resources, Memory cell selection, and Classification. The classification performance of AIRS algorithm depends on user defined parameters such as affinity threshold scalar, clonal rate, hyper-mutation rate, initial memory cell pool size, number of instances to compute the affinity threshold, number of nearest neighbors, and total resources.

AIRS2 Algorithm.

Input: InputPatterns, $Clone_{rate}$, $mutate_{rate}$, $stim_{thresh}$, $resources_{max}$, $affinity_{thresh}$

Outputs: $Cells_{memory}$

begin

    $Cells_{memory}$ ← InitializeMemoryPool(Input Patterns)

    for ($InputPattern_i$ ∈ InputPatterns)

        Stimulate($Cells_{memory}$,InputPatterns), $Cell_{best}$ ← GetMostStimulated($InputPattern_i$, $Cells_{memory}$)

        if ($Cell_{best}^{class}$ ≠ $InputPattern_i^{class}$)

            $Cells_{memory}$ ← CreateNewMemoryCell($InputPattern_i$)

        else

            $Clones_{num}$ ← $Cell_{best}^{stim}$ × $Clone_{rate}$ × $mutate_{rate}$, $Cells_{clones}$ ← $Cell_{best}$

            for (i to $Clone_{sum}$)

                $Cells_{clones}$ ← CloneAndMutate($Cell_{best}$)

            end

            while(AverageStimulation($Cells_{clones}$ <= $stim_{thresh}$)

                for ($Cell_i$ ∈ $Cells_{clones}$)

                    $Cells_{clones}$ ← CloneAndMutate($Cell_i$)

                end

                Stimulate($Cells_{clones}$, InputPatterns),

                ReducePoolToMaximumResources($Cells_{clones}$, $resources_{max}$)

            end

        $Cell_c$ ← GetMostStimulated($InputPattern_i$, $Cells_{clones}$)

        endif

        if ($Cell_c^{stim}$ > $Cell_{best}^{stim}$)

            $Cells_{memory}$ ← $Cell_c$

            if(Affinity($Cell_c$, $Cell_{best}$) <= $affinity_{thresh}$)

                DeleteCell($Cell_{best}$, $Cell_{memory}$)

        endif endif

    end

    return ($Cells_{memory}$)

end

2.3   CLONALG: Clonal Selection Algorithm

The CLONALG is based on Clonal selection theory as proposed in [6]. Its goal is to develop a set of antibodies that represents a solution for a specific problem.

CLONALG Algorithm.

Input: Populationsize, Selectionsize, Problemsize, Randomcellsnum, Clonerate, Mutationrate

Output: Population

begin

    Population ← CreateRandomCells (Populationsize, Problemsize)

    while StopCondition() do

      for each pi ∈ Population do

          Affinity(pi)

      end

      Populationselect ← Select(Population, Selectionsize), Populationclones ← ∅

      for each pi ∈ Populationselect do

          Populationclones ← Clone (pi, Clonerate)

      end

      for each pi ∈ Populationclones do

          Hypermutate(pi, Mutationrate), Affinity(pi)

      end

      Population ← Select (Population, Populationclones, Populationsize)

      Populationrand ← CreateRandomCells (Randomcellsnum), Replace(Population, Populationrand)

    end

    return Population

end

3   Proposed Hybrid Model

The hybrid classifier techniques enhance the accuracy of classification. The objective of the proposed model is to combine different techniques to build a hybrid intrusion detection system which can exhibit low false alarm rate and high detection rate. The model as depicted in figure 1 comprises of two levels. The first level consists of feature selection methods with an objective of identifying, and removing irrelevant and redundant attributes from the intrusion dataset. Five search based methods namely, PSO search, Genetic search, Best First search, Greedy Stepwise, Rank Search; and six rank based methods namely, Information gain, Gain Ratio, Symmetrical Uncertainty, Chi Squared attribute evaluator, Relief-F, and One-R, have been applied for selection of relevant attributes. In the second level the reduced data set obtained from level-1 is classified using four evolutionary computation techniques viz., Genetic Programming (GP), Artificial Immune Recognition System algorithms (AIRS1, AIRS2) and the Clonal Selection Algorithm (CLONALG).

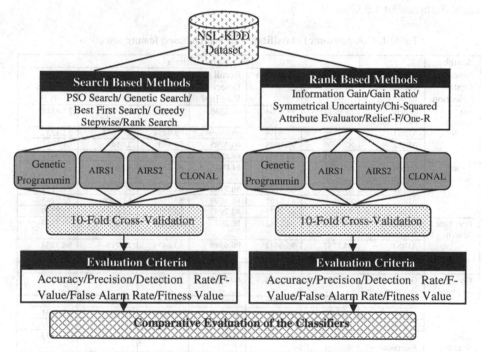

Fig. 1. Evolutionary Computation Based Classification Model

4   Experimental Setup and Result Analysis

The NSL-KDD intrusion dataset [7] which consists of 41 feature attributes has been used for our experimentation. The total number of records in the data set is 125973 out of which 67343 are normal and 58630 are attacks. First, the dataset is subjected to pre-processing using two different categories of feature selection methods [8]. Then, the training and testing of the classifiers are done using 10-fold cross-validation.

Table 1 and 2 depict the performance of four Evolutionary Computation based classification techniques with five different search methods and six rank based feature selection methods respectively. We have compared the accuracy, precision, detection rate, F-value, false alarm rate, and fitness value of all four techniques. AIRS1 technique with Best First Search feature selection method gives the highest accuracy of 94.2757% and the highest detection rate of 90.6549%. AIRS1 technique with Greedy Stepwise Search feature selection method gives the lowest false alarm rate of 2.2289%. Similarly, AIRS1 technique with Relief-F rank feature selection method gives the highest accuracy of 93.8391% and the highest detection rate of 92.323%. Further, AIRS2 technique with Gain Ratio feature selection method gives the lowest false alarm rate of 1.332%.

Table 1. Comparison of classifiers with Search based feature selection

Search based Feature Selection	Classifier Techniques	Evaluation Criteria					
		Accuracy in %	Precision in %	Recall or Detection Rate in %	F-Value in %	False Alarm Rate in %	Fitness Value in %
PSO Search	Genetic Programming	89.027	94.4064	81.2366	87.3278	4.1905	**77.8323**
	AIRS1	72.7688	71.9058	68.0965	69.9494	23.1635	52.323
	AIRS2	82.7709	**95.1948**	66.3295	78.183	**2.9144**	64.3961
	CLONALG	**89.0691**	89.3274	**86.8958**	**88.0948**	9.0388	79.0414
Genetic Search	Genetic Programming	88.9611	**94.4502**	81.0438	87.2349	**4.1459**	77.6838
	AIRS1	**89.6819**	86.4729	**90.7160**	**88.5437**	12.5655	**79.3171**
	AIRS2	85.2508	81.6161	88.1699	84.7665	17.2906	72.9248
	CLONALG	87.0496	84.8923	87.7997	86.3216	13.6035	75.8559
Best First Search	Genetic Programming	90.2026	92.1582	86.292	89.1287	6.3926	80.7756
	AIRS1	**94.2757**	**96.8442**	**90.6549**	**93.6474**	**2.5719**	**88.3234**
	AIRS2	91.2076	94.3799	86.2442	90.1289	4.4711	82.3881
	CLONALG	87.6108	84.5805	89.7407	87.0842	14.2435	76.9585
Greedy Stepwise	Genetic Programming	87.7077	92.2138	80.3752	85.8885	5.9086	75.6262
	AIRS1	91.1878	**97.0295**	83.6261	89.8306	**2.2289**	81.7622
	AIRS2	**91.4609**	96.8086	84.4363	**90.2001**	2.4234	**82.3901**
	CLONALG	89.7518	89.0529	**88.9101**	88.9814	9.5155	80.4499
Rank Search	Genetic Programming	88.1641	**93.7638**	79.8823	86.2682	**4.6256**	76.1873
	AIRS1	87.6672	89.1863	83.6432	86.3259	8.8294	76.258
	AIRS2	89.1159	92.5055	83.3686	87.6997	5.88	78.4662
	CLONALG	**88.846**	88.0101	**88.0266**	**88.0183**	10.4406	**78.8361**

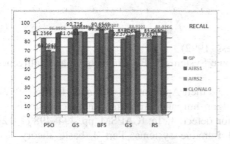

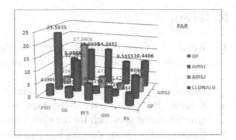

Fig. 2. Comparison of Detection Rate/Recall   **Fig. 3.** Comparison of False Alarm Rate

Table 2. Comparison of classifiers with Rank based feature selection

Rank based Feature Selection	Classifier techniques	Evaluation Criteria					
		Accuracy %	Precision %	Recall/ Detection %	F-Value %	False Alarm %	Fitness Value %
Information Gain	Genetic Program	88.746	93.8921	81.095	87.0256	4.5929	77.3704
	AIRS1	93.0572	**96.3968**	88.3865	92.218	**2.8763**	85.8442
	AIRS2	**93.2359**	96.2542	88.9272	**92.4457**	3.0129	**86.2478**
	CLONALG	88.896	86.9198	**89.6299**	88.2541	11.7429	79.1048
Gain Ratio	Genetic Program	87.5592	93.8257	78.4308	85.4404	4.4934	74.9066
	AIRS1	68.7925	64.3405	73.912	68.7945	35.6637	47.5516
	AIRS2	84.6681	**97.818**	68.5877	80.6356	**1.332**	67.6742
	CLONALG	**88.307**	87.7161	**87.0698**	**87.3917**	10.6158	**77.8266**
Symmetrical Uncertainty	Genetic Program	89.4882	**94.181**	82.5124	87.9614	**4.4385**	78.8501
	AIRS1	88.9524	86.0478	91.0216	88.4649	12.8491	79.3261
	AIRS2	**91.6522**	90.6547	**91.4958**	**91.0733**	8.2117	**83.9825**
	CLONALG	88.7579	86.7686	89.4917	88.1091	11.881	78.8592
Chi-Squared Attribute Evaluator	Genetic Program	90.2741	**94.3656**	84.1259	88.952	**4.3731**	80.4469
	AIRS1	**91.6371**	92.5627	89.1984	**90.8494**	6.2397	**83.6327**
	AIRS2	90.0883	88.2189	**90.834**	89.5074	10.5608	81.2412
	CLONALG	87.7505	85.2386	89.1131	87.1328	13.4357	77.1401
Relief-F	Genetic Program	90.4329	**95.465**	83.4061	89.0291	**3.4495**	80.529
	AIRS1	**93.8391**	94.3195	**92.323**	**93.3106**	4.8409	**87.8538**
	AIRS2	92.1078	91.655	91.3611	91.5078	7.242	84.7447
	CLONALG	83.8672	86.7087	77.1653	81.6591	10.298	69.2188
One-R	Genetic Program	89.1143	94.9521	80.9125	87.3719	3.745	77.8823
	AIRS1	**93.3756**	**96.7741**	88.7242	**92.5745**	**2.5749**	**86.4397**
	AIRS2	90.7631	90.4762	89.6691	90.0708	8.2231	82.2955
	CLONALG	88.9119	86.7214	**89.9488**	88.3056	11.9908	79.1632

5   Conclusion

In this paper, we have proposed a hybrid intrusion detection model based on four evolutionary computation based classifiers and two different categories of feature selection methods. The performance of the model was analyzed along different evaluation criteria on the intrusion dataset. It was observed that the AIRS1 classifier with Best First Search feature selection gives the highest accuracy and with Relief-F feature selection gives the highest detection rate whereas AIRS2 classifier with Gain Ratio rank feature selection gives the lowest false alarm rate.

References

1. Koza, J.R.: Genetic Programming. MIT Press (1992)
2. Dasgupta, D.: Advances in Artificial Immune Systems. IEEE Computational Intelligence Magazine (2006)
3. Dasgupta, D.: Artificial Immunity Systems and their Applications. Springer, Berlin (1999)
4. Sridevi, R., Chattemvelli, R.: Genetic algorithm and Artificial immune systems: A combinational approach for network intrusion detection. In: ICAESM, pp. 494–498 (2012)
5. Castro, L.D., Von Zuben, F.: Artificial immune systems: Part 1 basic theory and applications. DCA 01/99, Tech. Rep. (1999)
6. Castro, L.D., Von Zuben, F.: Learning and optimization using the clonal selection principle. IEEE Trans. on Evolutionary Computation 6, 239–251 (2002)
7. Tavallaee, M., Bagheri, E., et al.: A detailed analysis of the KDD CUP 99 data set. In: IEEE Symposium on Computational Intelligence in Security and Defense Applications (2009)
8. Gong, S.: Feature selection method for network intrusion based on GQPSO attribute reduction. In: Int. Conference on Multimedia Technology (ICMT), pp. 6365–6368 (2011)

Intrusion Detection in a Tailor-Made Gaussian Distribution Wireless Sensor Networks

Amrita Ghosal and Subir Halder

Department of CSE, Dr. B.C. Roy Engineering College, Durgapur, India
ghosal_amrita@yahoo.com, sub.halder@gmail.com

Abstract. Node deployment strategy plays a crucial role in determining the intrusion detection capability of a wireless sensor network (WSN). In this paper, we investigate the intrusion detection problem in a tailor-made Gaussian distributed network considering multiple-sensing detection scenario. Exhaustive simulation is performed primarily to validate the correctness of modeling and analysis. Effects of different network parameters on the detection probability are also examined. Finally, the effectiveness of the proposed approach is confirmed by comparing with its counterpart Gaussian deployment strategy under the considered scenarios.

Keywords: Energy-hole problem, Gaussian distribution, Intrusion detection.

1 Introduction

Intrusion detection is one of the fundamental applications in WSNs and has significant importance in practice. Generally, it is defined as a monitoring system for detecting the existence and movement of any malicious intruder that is invading the network domain within pre-defined distance or time period [1]. A WSN for intrusion detection can be implemented for diverse security scenarios, ranging from small apartment to a large battlefield.

Distributed intrusion detection in WSNs has been extensively studied by many researchers. In one such work, Wang *et al.* [2] formulated the intrusion detection probability for both homogeneous and heterogeneous uniformly random distributed WSNs while in [3] Wang *et al.* examined the intrusion detection problem in a truncated Gaussian distributed WSN. In [1], Wang and Lun derived analytical formula for detection probability considering multi-level sensing model. Although, it is observed that the uniformly distributed [3], Gaussian distributed [1], truncated Gaussian distributed [3] WSN ensured the improved detection quality, however all of them suffers from energy-hole problem [4]. To alleviate the energy-hole problem, a customized Gaussian distribution based node deployment strategy is proposed in [4]. Since customized Gaussian deployment mitigates the energy-hole problem, thereby, one can obtain enhanced network lifetime compared to both uniform and Gaussian deployments.

In view of the above said benefits, in this paper, we investigate the intrusion detection problem exploring customized Gaussian distribution based node deployment strategy. Further, we mathematically derive the detection probability with respect to network parameters e.g., number of deployed nodes, sensing range etc., employing

R. Natarajan et al. (Eds.): ICDCIT 2015, LNCS 8956, pp. 325–330, 2015.

multiple-sensing detection model. The effectiveness of the proposed approach is confirmed by comparing with its counterpart Gaussian deployment strategy.

The rest of this paper is organized as follows. The system model and definitions considered for the present work is described in Section 2. Section 3 examines the intrusion detection probability in a customized Gaussian distributed WSN for multiple-sensing detection model. Section 4 illustrates and explains both the theoretical and simulation results. Finally, the paper is concluded with some mention about the future scope of the work in Section 5.

2   System Model

In this section, we describe the network model. This section also presents network deployment model, sensing and detection models, and the performance evaluation metrics considered for this work.

2.1   Network Model

We consider a square shaped network area which is covered by a set of uniform-width coronas or annuli [4]. Each such annulus is designated with width r as layer. The sink is considered to be located at the centre of the network area and responsible for collecting data from the nodes. Nodes are placed in different layers surrounding the sink where the area of a layer-i is equal to $\pi(2i-1)r^2$ for $i=1,...,N$.

2.2   Network Deployment Model

We assume nodes deployed in different layers around the sink use two dimensional customized Gaussian distribution [4]. In customized Gaussian distribution, the probability density function (PDF) that a node resides at point (x, y) of layer-i with respect to deployment point (x', y') is given in (1), where σ_{ix} and σ_{iy} are standard deviations along X and Y dimensions of layer-i. Since, we consider layered network architecture where the sink is located at centre i.e., at co-ordinate (0, 0) therefore, in our case mean value is (0, 0) i.e., standard deviations for X and Y dimensions of layer-i are equal i.e., $\sigma_{ix} = \sigma_{iy} = \sigma_i$. The PDF given in (1) is used in this work for node deployment as given in (2), where σ_i^2 is the variance for $i=1,...,N$.

$$f_i(x, y) = \frac{1}{2\pi\sigma_{ix}\sigma_{iy}} e^{-\left(\frac{(x-x')^2}{2\sigma_{ix}^2} + \frac{(y-y')^2}{2\sigma_{iy}^2}\right)}. \tag{1}$$

$$f_i(x, y) = \frac{1}{2\pi\sigma_i^2} e^{-\left(\frac{x^2+y^2}{2\sigma_i^2}\right)}. \tag{2}$$

2.3   Sensing and Detection Models

We consider the network comprises of static nodes equipped with sensing and communication units. Let each node has a sensing/detection range of r_s. Further, we consider a realistic probabilistic sensing model [5] in which the probability that the node detects a target depends on the relative position of the target. Equation (3) shows the probabilistic sensing model where r_e $(r_e < r_s)$ is a measure of the uncertainty in detection, l is the distance between node and target, λ and β are parameters that measure detection probability [1].

In a WSN, there are two detection models single-sensing and multiple or m-sensing detection models [3]. We consider m-sensing detection model where an intruder has to be sensed by at least m (>1) nodes and m depends on an application.

$$p = \begin{cases} 0, & if \ r_s + r_e \leq l \\ e^{-\lambda a^\beta}, & if \ r_s - r_e < l < r_s + r_e \ . \\ 1, & if \ r_s - r_e \geq l \end{cases} \tag{3}$$

2.4 Evaluation Metrics and Definitions

In order to evaluate the performance of intrusion detection in WSNs, intrusion distance and detection probability have been considered as metrics. Similar to [3], we define the intrusion distance (D) as the distance between the point where the intruder enters the WSN and the point where the intruder gets detected by any node(s). Following the definition of intrusion distance, the maximal intrusion distance (denoted by d, $r > d > 0$) is the maximal distance allowable for the intruder to move before it is detected by the WSN. On the contrary, detection probability $P[D \leq d]$ is defined as the probability that an intruder is detected within the maximal allowable intrusion distance d, specified by a WSN application.

As an intrusion strategy model, we assume that the intruder enters the network domain at an arbitrary point and moves toward the centred target along a linear path [1, 3] for compromising purpose.

3   Theoretical Analysis on Intrusion Detection

In this section, we theoretically derive the detection probability for customized Gaussian deployed WSN under m-sensing detection scenario. In case of $d > 0$, the intruder is allowed to travel some distance within the WSN and is therefore referred to as relaxed intrusion detection [3]. On the contrary, if $d = 0$, the intruder has to be detected before it can make any movement inside the WSN and is therefore referred to as immediate intrusion detection [3]. For theoretical analysis purpose, we build a Cartesian coordinate system as illustrated in Fig. 1. Without loss of generality, (0, 0) is set as the target, and $(R, 0)$ is the starting position of the intruder, where $(i-1)r < R < (i+1)r$. The intruder is moving towards (0, 0) along the X-axis.

Theorem 1: The probability $P_d[D \leq d]$ that an intruder can be detected within the maximal allowable intrusion distance d under the m-sensing detection is given as:

$$P_d[D \leq d] = 1 - \left| \sum_{q=1}^{m} \binom{S}{q} \left(1 - p_1 - p_2 e^{-\lambda e^\beta}\right)^{(S-q)} \left(p_1 + p_2 e^{-\lambda e^\beta}\right)^{q} \right|.$$

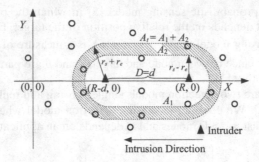

Fig. 1. Intrusion detection area in a customized Gaussian deployed network area for $d > 0$

Proof: In order to detect the intruder within d, there should be at least m nodes deployed in the intrusion detection area A_t where $A_t = A_1 + A_2$ (Fig. 1). Let p_1, p_2 and p_t be the probability that a node is deployed in the intrusion detection area A_1, A_2 and A_t, respectively. Hence, the probability that q numbers of nodes (out of total S nodes) are deployed in the area A_1 is $(1 - p_t)^{(S-q)} p_t^q$. The probability that q nodes exactly located in the area A_t is $\binom{S}{q}(1 - p_t)^{(S-q)} p_t^q$. The probability that less than m (where $m > 1$) nodes are placed in the intrusion detection area A_t is $\sum_{q=1}^{m} \binom{S}{q}(1 - p_t)^{(S-q)} p_t^q$. Consequently, the probability that at least m nodes are placed in the area A_t can be determined as: $1 - \left[\sum_{q=1}^{m} \binom{S}{q}(1 - p_t)^{(S-q)} p_t^q \right]$. According to our probabilistic sensing model, a node located in the area A_2 can detect the intruder with probability $e^{-\lambda e^\beta}$. Therefore, the probability that at least a node detects the intruder in the area A_t is $p_t = p_1 + p_2 e^{-\lambda e^\beta}$. Hence, the intruder to be detected when it enters the network domain under m-sensing detection scenario is given as:

$$P_d[D \leq d] = 1 - \left[\sum_{q=1}^{m} \binom{S}{q}\left(1 - p_1 - p_2 e^{-\lambda e^\beta}\right)^{(S-q)} \left(p_1 + p_2 e^{-\lambda e^\beta}\right)^q \right].$$

Theorem 2: The probability $P_i[D = 0]$ that an intruder can be immediately detected once it enters network area under the m-sensing detection is given as:

$$P_i[D = 0] = 1 - \left[\sum_{q=1}^{m} \binom{S}{q}(1 - p_1)^{(S-q)} p_1^q \right].$$

Proof: For immediate intrusion detection, intrusion detection area is confined within A_1 i.e., $d = 0$ and $p_2 = 0$. Therefore, from Theorem 1, the probability that the intruder can be detected immediately after it enters the network area is derived as:

$$P_i[D = 0] = 1 - \left[\sum_{q=1}^{m} \binom{S}{q}(1 - p_1)^{(S-q)} p_1^q \right].$$

From both theorems, it is revealed that S, r_s, R, and the node distribution play an important role in determining the intrusion detection probability of a customized Gaussian distributed WSN for both immediate and relaxed intrusion detections.

4 Simulation and Verification

In this section, the effectiveness of the developed analytical model for intrusion detection, reported in Section 3, is evaluated through simulation using MATLAB (version 7.1). Monte-Carlo simulation is performed to validate the correctness of our proposed model and analysis.

4.1 Simulation Arrangement

Simulation results of our Customized Gaussian Distributed (CGD) WSN scheme is compared with Gaussian Distributed (GD) WSN [3] scheme. During simulation, we assume (100×100) m^2 network area where an intruder enters the network domain at an arbitrary point $(100, 0)$ and moves towards the centre $(0, 0)$ along a linear path. Further, we assume $r = 10$ m, $r_s = 10$ m, $r_e = 5$ m, $\sigma=25$, $\lambda=0.5$, $\beta=0.5$ and $d=20$ m. Due to page limitations, effects of S and r_s on the detection probability are only examined. Extensive simulation has been performed with a confidence level of 95% and 5% accuracy.

4.2 Effect of the Number of Deployed Nodes

Fig. 2(a) illustrates the analytical and simulation results on detection probability for the CGD and GD under immediate and relaxed intrusion detection scenarios when S is varied from 10 to 200. It is clear from the plot (Fig. 2(a)), that simulation results are well matched with the analytical results. The detection probability for both the scenarios keeps increasing with the increase in S and the CGD performs better compared to the competing scheme GD for both scenarios. This is because CGD provides enhanced node density [4] in monitored areas that are around the border compared to GD. This supports the effectiveness of the CGD in terms of relieving the drawback of GD when the intruder starts from the network boundary.

4.3 Effect of the Sensing Range

Fig. 2(b) illustrates the effect of r_s on the intrusion detection probability in both CGD and GD. While simulating, we consider 200 nodes are deployed. It is observed from Fig. 2(b), similar to Fig. 2(a), that the detection probability for both the scenarios keeps increasing with the increase of r_s as increasing r_s improves the network coverage leading to a higher detection probability. Further, under the given network parameters, the detection probability approaches towards 1 while r_s is increased to a certain threshold. For example, for CGD (Fig. 2(b)), threshold of r_s is 30 m for 4-sensing detection. This also supports the effectiveness of the CGD in terms of relieving the drawback of GD when the intruder starts from the network boundary.

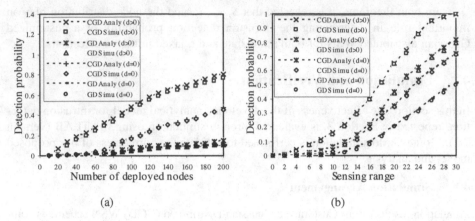

(a)   (b)

Fig. 2. Simulation and analytical results under immediate (d=0) and relaxed (d>0) intrusion detection scenarios. (a) Varying number of deployed nodes. (b) Varying sensing range.

5   Conclusion and Future Work

In this work, we have devised an analytical model for intrusion detection by exploring customized Gaussian distribution based node deployment strategy. The intrusion detection probability is mathematically formulated as a function of network parameters (e.g. number of deployed nodes, sensing range) for multiple-sensing detection scenario. Exhaustive simulation is performed to validate the correctness of modeling and analysis. The results show dominance of our proposed approach over the competing scheme [3] in terms of detection probability under various network parameters. As a future extension of our work, the effect of realistic probabilistic sensing model on the detection probability may be analyzed considering different values of λ and β.

References

1. Wang, Y., Lun, Z.: Intrusion Detection in a K-Gaussian Distributed Wireless Sensor Network. Journal of Parallel and Distributed Computing 71(12), 1598–1607 (2011)
2. Wang, Y., Wang, X., Xie, B., Wang, D., Agrawal, D.P.: Intrusion Detection in Homogeneous and Heterogeneous Wireless Sensor Networks. IEEE Trans. on Mobile Computing 7(6), 698–711 (2008)
3. Wang, Y., Fu, W., Agrawal, D.P.: Gaussian Versus Uniform Distribution for Intrusion Detection in Wireless Sensor Networks. IEEE Trans. on Parallel and Distributed Systems 24(2), 342–355 (2013)
4. Halder, S., Ghosal, A.: Is Sensor Deployment using Gaussian Distribution Energy Balanced? In: Kołodziej, J., Di Martino, B., Talia, D., Xiong, K. (eds.) ICA3PP 2013, Part I. LNCS, vol. 8285, pp. 58–71. Springer, Heidelberg (2013)
5. Ababnah, A., Natarajan, B.: Optimal Control-based Strategy for Sensor Deployment. IEEE Trans. on Systems, Man and Cybernetics, Part A: Systems and Humans 41(1), 97–104 (2011)

SecureString 3.0
A Cryptosystem for Blind Computing on Encrypted Character Strings

Günter Fahrnberger[1] and Kathrin Heneis[2]

[1] University of Hagen, North Rhine-Westphalia, Germany
guenter.fahrnberger@fernuni-hagen.de
[2] University of Vienna, Austria
kathrin.heneis@gmx.at

Abstract. If (electronic) computations need to be undertaken, then mostly performance or commercial aspects lead to the selection for an optimal executing computer. In case the beneficiary of the computation upshots does not wholly confide in any computers except his ones, trust becomes his major decision criterion instead. Blind computing can do the trick to (re)win the beneficiary's confidence. This paper ameliorates the well-known cryptosystem SecureString 2.0 concerning privacy through pangram ciphertexts and referring integrity through secret sharing. The emerging cryptosystem of this amelioration is called SecureString 3.0 that facilities blind computing on encrypted character strings through an untrusted host.

Keywords: Blind computing, Character string, Character string function, Character string operation, Cloud, Cloud computing, Secret Sharing, Secure computing, String, String function, String operation.

1 Introduction

Blind operations on numerical values have emerged since the introduction of the homomorphic cryptosystem RSA (Rivest Shamir Adleman) in 1978 [9]. Blind computing on character strings turns out to be a double-edged sword.

On the one hand, (key)words and fragments of scrambled texts can be tied and covertly sought with characterizing hash values with the aid of a searchable encryption scheme easily (see Definition 1).

Definition 1. *Let Σ be an alphabet, let $h : \Sigma^* \to \Sigma^*$ be a (trapdoor) hash function, let $u \in \Sigma^*$ be a sought plaintext keyword and $h(u)$ its hash value, let $E : \Sigma^* \to \Sigma^*$ be an encryption function that enciphers not only an input plaintext $v \in \Sigma^*$ but additionally attaches the hash values of encrypted keywords by dint of h to its output, and let $f(v, u) : \Sigma^* \times \Sigma^* \to \{false, true\}$ be a search function that decides if v contains one occurrence of u at least.*

Then the homomorphic function $g(E(v), h(u)) : \Sigma^* \times \Sigma^* \to \{false, true\}$ forms a searchable encryption scheme, if $(\forall v)(\forall u)g(E(v), h(u)) = f(v, u)$.

R. Natarajan et al. (Eds.): ICDCIT 2015, LNCS 8956, pp. 331–334, 2015.

On the contrary, secure modifying character string operations prove to be more difficult because too easy replacements or cutting-outs of ciphertext parts abet successful replay or cut and splice attacks [1,5]. However, if a key customer mistrusts the security of an in-house computer center of a business partner for modifications on his crucial character strings, then they may claim to face up to the hard problem of safely swapping out these operations to an external provider supported by an adequate cryptosystem.

Two versions of an innovative cryptosystem named SecureString tried to offer safe modifying computations on ciphered character strings [3,4,5,7]. Each of the two recent treatises about the second edition (SecureString 2.0) addressed another improvement opportunity in its concluding section. "A second view on SecureString 2.0" calls for better integrity of SecureString 2.0 objects [5]. The most recent treatise about SecureString 2.0 suggested to develop an advancement of the cryptosystem that converts every arbitrary plaintext into pangram ciphertext and thereby impedes any recurrences of ciphergrams [7].

On these grounds, this paper incorporates both advices in order to introduce SecureString 3.0 as the next generation of the cryptosystem.

The main Section 2 delves into the principles of the third SecureString edition. The last Section 3 recaps the merits of this disquisition and recommends ideas for worthwhile future work.

2   SecureString 3.0

While the assignment for smarter privacy can be prudently coped with pangram ciphertext, the assurance of integrity (especially against cut and splice attacks) in SecureString 3.0 objects puzzles one's head. An offender can malevolently garble SecureString 2.0 objects by eradicating, duplicating or displacing parts of them, possibly even remaining undetected. For example, SafeChat [8] and SIMS (Secure Instant Messaging Sifter) [6] require a trustable mechanism that annihilates illicit terms in messages before they reach their consignees, and apart from the designated senders and receivers, no parties (such as online filters) may acquire awareness about message contents.

Obviously at first glance, the consigner or particularly the addressee of a message could take over the sieving process and permit the establishment of a contemporary end-to-end encryption instead of wasting computing time and space by employing a homomorphic cryptosystem. In case a receiver suspects a sender's censor quality, an engaged TTPG (Trusted Third Party Generator) can restore confidence by securely double-checking the sender's sieve outcome with a searchable encryption scheme. Unfortunately, a rule-based set of expressions (inclusive their declined or conjugated variants) intended for excision may vary from day to day (similar to virus databases). For that reason, an serviced online repository with deprecated vocables must be periodically polled and downloaded as necessary by the decentralized filters.

If these bandwidth-incriminatory transfers shall be avoided, then no alternative to an online sifter remains, but the task of maintaining integrity must be accomplished anyhow. The most promising resolution would be if an online sieve echoes its clean (yet ciphered) results to their source. The originator inspects the cleaned messages and decides either to reject the amendments by completely dropping them or to confirm them by fingerprinting them with irreversible hash values, signing the fingerprints and conveying the signatures to the online filter. The sifter forwards the messages and their signed fingerprints to the target and thence demonstrates the addresser's consent to the executed modifications.

This thought is going to affect the successional principles of SecureString 3.0.

2.1 Principles

SecureString 3.0 acts as a revised continuation of its predecessors that perpetuates their approved attributes rather than reinvents the wheel. The listing given below specifies the established and the novel characteristics of the cryptosystem:

- **Underlying Replaceable Symmetric Cryptosystem:** SecureString 3.0 performs each ciphering by means of a topical underlying exchangeable symmetric cryptosystem that becomes unquestionably exchanged if its vulnerability exceeds any observable modern security norms.
- **Monographic Encryption [2]:** SecureString 3.0 monographically substitutes plaintext to circumvent time-consuming inter-ciphertext-polygram operations.
- **Message Authentication Code (MAC):** Despite the employment of monographic encryption, the integrity of an altered SecureString 3.0 object abides, because its creator signs its hash value upon inspection and thus enables the recipient to perceive possible malicious alterations, e.g. caused through cut and splice attacks.
- **Public Key Infrastructure (PKI):** Each signature of a MAC bases upon its signer's private key for a state-of-the-art asymmetric cryptosystem. The corresponding public key must be signed by a trustworthy CA (Certification Authority).
- **Polyalphabetism [2]:** SecureString 3.0 utilizes the same encryption transformation as long as it does not have to create recurring ciphertext. Just before repetitive ciphertext would arise, a new encryption transformation becomes operative. That is why such a transformation change may happen within a word just as well.
- **Salting:** SecureString 3.0 obtains different encryption transformations by suffixing diverse salts to plaintext characters. Each salt indicates another encryption transformation.
- **Automatic Salt Updating [1,6]:** In compliance with SecureString 2.0, each salt serves as input for a hash function that outputs the salt for the encryption transformation of the successive plaintext word. Every use case with high data throughput is urged to employ a $TTPG$ that demands just a starting salt in order to prepare the homomorphic computations for an untrustworthy (external) node.

3   Conclusion

Business partners' or customers' suspiciousness of the security of in-house data processing centers can force a corporation to outsource applications to an external hosting solution (such as a public cloud). Generally, such external surroundings proffer amplified resilience but inferior authenticity, integrity and privacy. Blind computing finds a remedy to maintain the latter, in particular with the help of homomorphic cryptosystems in narrow sense for blind computations on ciphered numeric values.

This disquisition advances SecureString 2.0, a cryptosystem for blind computing on ciphertext character strings, to SecureString 3.0. The new release pledges improved privacy through pangram ciphertexts and stronger integrity through cognizance division between a trusted sender, a trusted third party generator and an untrusted host.

Related future work should focus on algorithmic implementation details, on a security analysis based on an appropriate adversarial model, and on a comparative performance analysis for SecureString 3.0.

References

1. Anderson, R.J.: Security engineering - a guide to building dependable distributed systems, 2nd edn. Wiley (2008)
2. Bauer, F.L.: Decrypted Secrets: Methods and Maxims of Cryptology, 4th edn. Springer Publishing Company, Incorporated (2010)
3. Fahrnberger, G.: Computing on encrypted character strings in clouds. In: Hota, C., Srimani, P.K. (eds.) ICDCIT 2013. LNCS, vol. 7753, pp. 244–254. Springer, Heidelberg (2013)
4. Fahrnberger, G.: Securestring 2.0 - a cryptosystem for computing on encrypted character strings in clouds. In: Eichler, G., Gumzej, R. (eds.) Networked Information Systems. Fortschritt-Berichte Reihe 10, vol. 826, pp. 226–240. VDI, Düsseldorf (2013)
5. Fahrnberger, G.: A second view on securestring 2.0. In: Natarajan, R. (ed.) ICDCIT 2014. LNCS, vol. 8337, pp. 239–250. Springer, Heidelberg (2014)
6. Fahrnberger, G.: Sims: A comprehensive approach for a secure instant messaging sifter. In: 2014 13th IEEE International Conference on Trust, Security and Privacy in Computing and Communications (TrustCom) (September 2014)
7. Fahrnberger, G.: Repetition pattern attack on multi-word-containing securestring 2.0 objects. In: Natarajan, R., Barua, G., Patra, M.R. (eds.) ICDCIT 2015. LNCS, vol. 8956, pp. 265–277. Springer, Heidelberg (2015)
8. Fahrnberger, G., Nayak, D., Martha, V.S., Ramaswamy, S.: Safechat: A tool to shield children's communication from xplicit messages. In: 2014 14th International Conference on Innovations for Community Services (I4CS), pp. 80–86 (June 2014)
9. Rivest, R.L., Shamir, A., Adleman, L.: A method for obtaining digital signatures and public-key cryptosystems. Commun. ACM 21(2), 120–126 (1978)

A Secure Image Hashing Technique for Forgery Detection

Tanmoy Kanti Das[1] and Piyush Kanti Bhunre[2]

[1] Academy of Technoogy, India
dastanmoy@gmail.com
[2] National Institute of Science and Technology, India
kbpiyush@gmail.com

Abstract. Nowadays most of the multimedia contents are in digital form. With the increased use of powerful computer and image processing software, along with wide availability of digital cameras have given rise to huge numbers of doctored images. Several forgery detection algorithms are available. However, these techniques do not address the issue from cryptographic point of view. As a result, even if an image or video is identified as doctored, most of the time it is not possible to track the actual offender. Here, we present a perceptual hash function which can be used for both detection of forged images as well as tracking of forgers.

1 Introduction

Analog photos and video images have always been accepted as a "proof of occurrence" of the depicted event. For that very reason, courts have set high standard to ensure the integrity of those images. Advent of digital images raises additional concerns, because the images can so easily be manipulated and in many occasions, forged images are used to influence the naive people. Although digital watermarks have been proposed as a tool to provide authenticity of images, it is a fact that most of the images that are captured today do not contain any watermark. And we expect this situation will not change in immediate future. Hence, it is required to develop techniques those can detect the tampering of digital images. Some of the well known digital image tempering techniques can be found in [2]. In light of these problems, the subject of digital forensics has been developed to find the answers to the following questions [5].

- Is this an original image or manipulated image?
- What is the processing history of the image?
- What parts of the image has undergone processing and up to what extent?
- Was the image acquired by the device as claimed by the producer?
- Did this image originate from a source X as claimed?

These are just a few questions that are routinely faced by forensic experts and law enforcement agencies. Most of the existing research in this area is based on image processing techniques and lack a proper cryptographic framework. And it is well known that, once an image processing based forgery detection methodology is developed, the forgers will find new ways to circumvent it. Here, we propose a new perceptual hashing algorithm which use cryptographic framework for both authentication of digital images and tracking of the forgers.

R. Natarajan et al. (Eds.): ICDCIT 2015, LNCS 8956, pp. 335–338, 2015.

2   Image Hashing Technique

In general, cryptographic hash functions or message authentication functions are used to ensure data integrity. However, these functions are key dependent and sensitive to change in every bit of information. We know that minor changes in image information (i.e. pixel values) do not change the image visually. For example, one can generate some image I' form original image I by applying lossy image compression over I and both I' and I remain visually indistinguishable. In this scenario, we want the hash function to produce same hash values for I and I' as long as these images remain visually indistinguishable. Several image hash functions [1,6] were proposed in the existing literature. But they mostly depend on complex image processing techniques. Here we propose a new image hashing technique which is inspired by the ideas presented in [4]. Our technique is based on *wavelet transform* and uses basic statistical features like *mean, standard deviation, kurtosis, skewness* etc. to generate the hash value.

Before we proceed further, let us first discuss about wavelet transform using an example. Consider the following one dimensional signal $I = [11, 5, 7, 15]$ consisting of four samples. After applying Haar wavelet transform [7], the coefficients look like $I_{wav}^{L=1} = [\frac{11+5}{2}, \frac{7+15}{2}, \frac{11-5}{2}, \frac{7-15}{2}] = [8, 11, 3, -4]$. In the next level of wavelet transform, low frequency coefficients (here, first two coefficients) are subjected to further processing. Thus, $I_{wav}^{L=2} = [\frac{8+11}{2}, \frac{8-11}{2}, 3, -4] = [9.5, -1.5, 3, -4]$. As, in this example, there is only one low frequency component, we can not proceed further. To extend these ideas to images, we consider an image as a 2D signal and apply wavelet transform separately, first along the rows and then along the columns. In each level of wavelet transform four different bands are generated and they are denoted as LL_n, HL_n, LH_n, HH_n, where n is the level number. Let us now describe the hashing algorithm.

1. Pre-process the original image O to get I.
2. Compute wavelet transform of the image I upto n^{th} level. So there will be $n \times 3 + 1$ bands. Exclude band LL_n from further processing.
3. For each band, compute *mean, median ,mode, range, standard deviation, kurtosis, skewness* and represent the result in a matrix form. So, there will be 7 columns, each representing one statistical feature and there will be $n \times 3$ rows.
4. We convert all the values obtained in the last step to a 3 bit integer number and apply gray coding [3] to get a bit sequence.
5. The bit sequence is decoded using $(7, 3)$ Reed-Solomon code to get the hash value.
6. Encrypt the hash value H using the private key of the owner X using RSA algorithm or any other suitable public key algorithm to form the digital signature D_X. Now X can publish the image along with the digital signature D_X.

Here, we always choose LL band for next level of wavelet transform. Though one can choose any of the available bands i.e. LL, LH, HL, HH for next level of wavelet transform. In fact, the choice of band for the next level of wavelet transform can be made *key* dependent to introduce randomness. In this scenario, one cannot compute the hash value without the knowledge of the key. Thus the hash value becomes a keyed-hash message authentication code (**HMAC**). Now, after receiving an image I along with the digital signature D_X from X, one can can check whether the image is authentic or not, using the following steps:

1. Generate the hash value H' using the received image I
2. Decrypt the hash value D_X to get H using public key of X.
3. If *normalized hamming distance* between H and H' is less than threshold, then
   (a) Image is authentic as the hash values match.
   (b) X is the owner of the image as we can decrypt D_X using the public key of X.
4. Else the image is not authentic.

Security Analysis

Security of image hashing technique is not well defined and an active area of research. In this context, Swaminathan et al. proposed a security metric based on differential entropy of the hash value in their paper [6]. In simple terms, one can describe differential entropy is the amount of effort an adversary has to put to compute the correct image hash without the knowledge of the key. So, larger value of differential entropy is better for security. Our algorithm when used in HMAC mode performs very well in this regard.

Suppose we compute the k features $M_1^{(p)}, M_2^{(p)}, M_3^{(p)}, \cdots, M_k^{(p)}$ from a wavelet band at p^{th} level, where $p = 1, 2, \cdots, n$. At p^{th} level, one of the wavelet bands $LL^{(p)}, LH^{(p)}, HL^{(p)}, HH^{(p)}$ is chosen at random for the computation of the wavelet bands in the next level. In the proposed scheme, the wavelet bands are chosen with equal probabilities. Note that, as the wavelet bands are chosen randomly, the computed features will also take random values. Let us first consider the probability distribution of the ith feature at the 2nd level. The ith feature $M_i^{(2)}$ have four possible values depending upon the choice of wavelet band at the first level to generate the wavelet bands at the 2nd level and they are equally likely. Therefore the entropy of $M_i^{(2)}$ is $log(4)$. Hence the entropy of k random features, denoted by a vector $M^{(2)} = [M_1^{(2)}, M_2^{(2)}, \cdots, M_k^{(2)}]$ at the 2nd level is $klog(4)$. The wavelet band that is chosen for next level of wavelet computation can be represented as follows.

$$B^{(p)} = \delta_{LL}^{(p)} LL^{(p)} + \delta_{LH}^{(p)} LH^{(p)} + \delta_{HL}^{(p)} HL^{(p)} + \delta_{HH}^{(p)} HH^{(p)} \tag{1}$$

where, $\delta_{LL}^{(p)}, \delta_{LH}^{(p)}, \delta_{HL}^{(p)}, \delta_{HH}^{(p)}$ are delta-functions associated with each wavelet band and its value can be either 0 or 1. The value of delta-function is 1 only when the corresponding wavelet band is chosen for next level of wavelet transform. Therefore, value of random variable $M_i^{(2)}$ can also be written as:

$$M_i^{(2)} = \delta_{LL}^{(1)} M_i^{(2)}(LL^{(1)}) + \delta_{LH}^{(1)} M_i^{(2)}(LH^{(1)}) + \delta_{HL}^{(1)} M_i^{(2)}(HL^{(1)}) + \delta_{HH}^{(1)} M_i^{(2)}(HH^{(1)}) \tag{2}$$

In level 3, the randomly chosen wavelet band, denoted by $B^{(2)}$, is further decomposed into four wavelet bands. The randomly chosen wavelet band and the extracted feature can be written as follows.

$$B^{(2)} = \delta_{LL}^{(2)} LL^{(2)} + \delta_{LH}^{(2)} LH^{(2)} + \delta_{HL}^{(2)} HL^{(2)} + \delta_{HH}^{(2)} HH^{(2)} \tag{3}$$

$$M_i^{(3)} = \delta_{LL}^{(2)} M_i^{(3)}(LL^{(2)}) + \delta_{LH}^{(2)} M_i^{(3)}(LH^{(2)}) + \delta_{HL}^{(2)} M_i^{(3)}(HL^{(2)}) + \delta_{HH}^{(2)} M_i^{(3)}(HH^{(2)}) \tag{4}$$

From equation 1-4, it follows that at level 3, the ith feature can take 4^2 many different values due to different choices of δ's at level 1 and 2. Each of those values of the feature is equally likely. Hence the entropy for the ith feature in the 3rd level is $log(4^2)$ and the entropy for k independent features is $klog(4^2)$. Following a similar argument, the entropy of a feature at n^{th} level will be $log(4^{n-1}) = (n-1)log(4)$. Then the entropy of k many independent features at n^{th} level is $k(n-1)log(4)$.

It is observed that the random vectors $M_i^{(p)}, p = 2, 3, \cdots, n$ are not independent. In fact, for any fixed i, it is obvious that the sequence of random variables $M_i^{(2)}, M_i^{(3)}, ... M_i^{(n)}$ will form a markov chain of order 1 and the conditional distribution of the random variable $M_i^{(p+1)}$ given $M_i^{(p)}$ is a discrete uniform distribution with probabilities $\frac{1}{4}$ for each of its four distinct values. Hence, the joint entropy of the ith feature for all levels of the wavelet tree is as follows.

$$E(M_i^{(2)}, M_i^{(3)}, \cdots, M_i^{(n)}) = E(M_i^{(2)}) + E(M_i^{(3)}|M_i^{(2)}) + \cdots + E(M_i^{(n)}|M_i^{(n-1)})$$

i.e., $E(M_i^{(2)}, M_i^{(3)}, \cdots, M_i^{(n)}) = log(4) + log(4) + \cdots + log(4) = (n-1)log4$

Considering k many independent features, we can obtain the joint entropy of all features at all levels as $k \times (n-1) \times log(4)$ which is same as the entropy of the feature vector at the last level. This result shows that the joint entropy of the features is a linear function of both the level (p) of the wavelet tree and the number of features (k) is used for computation of the hash value. Now, considering $n = 6$ and $k = 7$, the *entropy* of our algorithm is 70. Though we cannot compare it directly with the results obtained by Swaminathan et. al. [6] as they have reported the *differential entropy*; however, the best value of differential entropy obtained by them is 16.39.

3   Conclusion

In this paper, we have proposed a secure and robust image hashing algorithm. The proposed technique possesses very good discriminating property and is very much sensitive to malicious image processing operations like object insertion. It is robust against the content preserving image processing operations such as JPEG compression, filtering, small rotation etc.. Nevertheless, further improvement is desired against the geometric operations such as rotation, scaling, translation.

References

1. Birajdar, G.K., Mankar, V.H.: Digital image forgery detection using passive techniques: A survey. Digital Investigation 10(3), 226–245 (2013)
2. Goldfarb, B.: Digital deception, http://brucegoldfarb.com/larrysface/deception.shtml (accessed on June 2014)
3. Gray, F.: Pulse code communication. U.S. Patent 2,632,058; (filed on November 13, 1947) (issued March 17, 1953)
4. Kailasanathan, C., Naini, R.S., Ogunbona, P.: Image authentication surviving acceptable modifications. In: Proc. of IEEE-EURASIP Workshop on Nonlinear Signal and Image Processing, Baltimore, MD (2001)
5. Sencar, H.T., Memon, N.: Overview of state-of-the-art in digital image forensics. In: Indian Statistical Institute Platinum Jubilee Monograph series titled 'Statistical Science and Interdisciplinary Research', pp. 325–348. World Scientific Press (2008)
6. Swaminathan, A., Mao, Y., Wu, M.: Robust and secure image hashing. IEEE Transactions on Information Forensics and Security 1(2), 215–230 (2006)
7. Vetterli, M., Kovacevic, J.: Wavelets and subband coding. Prentice-Hall (1995)

Design and Development of Secure Cloud Architecture for Sensor Services

R.S. Ponmagal, N. Dinesh, and Uma Rajaram

Department of Computer Science and Engineering,
Dr. M.G.R. Educational and Research Institute University, Chennai, India
rsponmagal@gmail.com, dineshnagambaram@icloud.com,
umarajaram1@yahoo.com

Abstract. This paper is aimed at the design and development of secure cloud architecture for the Wireless Sensor Networks (WSN), in which the sensor data are represented as services and are accessed by the client applications in a secure manner with a simple authentication solution for sensors (SASS). Currently, sensor system needs an intelligent middleware to integrate with the cloud. Service Oriented Architecture (SOA), which makes use of the web services and XML technologies, will provide a solution to meet the current demands. Web services provide a mechanism for open and flexible interaction between heterogeneous systems with loosely coupled service endpoints. Further a technique based on formal specification is utilized which reduces the data volume of xml documents at a level that can be handled by the resource constrained environment of the wireless sensors. The proposed architecture will provide a scalable infrastructure for integrating heterogeneous sensor networks using a small set of powerful abstractions.

Keywords: secure cloud, sensor, service, intelligent middleware, SOA, SASS, formal specification, xml.

1   Introduction

Wireless Sensor Networks consists of energy constrained sensor nodes and a Sink node with higher processing capabilities. The heterogeneous sensors to sense different process parameters are networked together to form a distributed sensor network [1]. The gathered data can be made accessible to other nodes, including a specialized one called sink through a variety of means [2]. Sensor networks are distributed event based systems that focus on simple data gathering applications and operate notably differently from that of traditional computer networks. The sensor information can be transmitted to the requesting client as [3] SOAP messages, which is accessed through the Cloud.

Currently, the cloud system demands an intelligent middleware that can be interoperable in a secure way with different entities to fulfill the client application requirements. This paper proposes an advanced middleware solution namely Service-Oriented Architecture based on web services for WSN applications. In this paper, the SOA is a middleware which acts as an agent, translating application requirements into

R. Natarajan et al. (Eds.): ICDCIT 2015, LNCS 8956, pp. 339–344, 2015.

WSN configuration parameters and provides an abstraction layer between applications and the underlying network infrastructure. Data provided by the sensors are represented as Services. Hosting a web service [4] challenges battery life, bandwidth, processing power constraints of low power sensor nodes. Clients access the sensor network by submitting queries to those services. The proposed Sensor Profiles which is based on formal specification, reduces the verbosity of XML messages embedded with SOAP, hence occupies less bandwidth during data transmission.

Sensor networks collect information about the physical environment, but typically lack the resources to store and process the collected data over long periods of time. Cloud computing elastically provides the missing storage and computing resources. Specifically, it allows to store and access the collected sensor data effectively via Cloud-based services. As an additional benefit, storage and processing in the Cloud enable the efficient aggregation and analysis of information from different sensor data sources. However, sensor data often contain sensitive information. As the volume of users accessing the cloud data is also increasing heavily, the vulnerability of the data, which is an invaluable asset for any organization, is also increasing proportionally. For current Cloud platforms, the data owner loses control over the data once it enters the Cloud. Hence, a Cloud design is required that the data owner can trust to handle the sensitive data securely. A trusted Cloud design is analyzed and security architecture of Sensor Cloud [5] is presented. This architecture enforces end-to-end data access control by the data owner reaching from the sensor network to the Cloud storage and processing subsystems as well as strict isolation up to the service-level.

In this paper a security solution called Simple Authentication Solution for Sensors (SASS) for sensor accessing through a Cloud environment is proposed based on [6], in which message to be authenticated is also encrypted, with secure encryption algorithm, to append a short random string to be used in the authentication process.

2   Service Oriented Sensor Network Architecture with Secure Cloud Architecture

An advanced middleware solution to the problem of integrating a Wireless Sensor Network into the information system of an enterprise, such as cloud at a high abstraction level is proposed through the Service Oriented Sensor Networks (SOSN). The SOSN model has three elements namely Sensor Service Provider, Sensor System Registry and Sensor Systems Client. The sensor system services are categorized in to Pressure service, Temperature service, and Level service. A sensor Service provider offers the above services and describes the interface information of the services in interface description language called SSDL (Sensor Services Description Language) which is in the form of XML that makes the services available in the Sensor System Registry. Services are the key building blocks of SOA. A service is usable function that can be invoked by another component through a well-defined interface. Services are loosely coupled, that is, they hide their implementation details and only expose their interfaces. In this manner, sensor system client need not be aware of any underlying technology or programming language which the service is used. The sensor system clients discover the service available in the registry by service names and acquire the interface information by Sensor SDL of the sensor services. Based on this information, the clients have a binding with the sensor service provider and can invoke services using Simple Object Access Protocol (SOAP).

The sensed data such as temperature is measured through WSN-EDU2110CB Wireless Sensor Network Educational Kit operating at 2.4 GHz with Data Acquisition boards with temperature (MDA100) sensor and PC Interface Boards (MIB520).The sensor data are obtained through TinyOS simulator (TOSSIM). This simulator runs on TinyOS1.7. NesC is the language used to simulate the sensor nodes. The TOSSIM itself got the packages to simulate real time sensors. A sensor node is simulated and its sensed parameters are written into tossim.txt file in the following path: C:\ProgramFiles\UCB\ cygwin\opt\tin yos-1.x\apps\Sense\tossim.txt. The sense folder also contains two NesC files called configuration (Sense.nc) file and Module (SenseM.nc) file.

The XML representation of sensor data is essential for web service deployment. Moreover, XML is a key feature to build SOSN. Using XML in sensor networks encourages the interchangeability of different types of sensors and systems. The general verbosity of XML conflicts with the limited energy and memory capacities of sensor nodes. In this proposed work, sensor profiles are written in XML, to be transported with SOAP request and response messages.

J2EE 1.4 Sun App Server is used as the service provider. The J2EE 1.4 platform provides comprehensive support for web services through the JAX-RPC 1.1 API, which can be used to develop service endpoints based on SOAP. The interface and implementation files for the process parameters such as temperature, pressure, and flow are written. Configuration files are written to specify the XML namespace and target namespace. These files are compiled to generate Sensor Services Description Language (contains possible inputs and server's address) for client reference and mapping file (port number and service endpoint location) for the server reference. With deployment tool war files are generated from the services written and deployed in the server. To facilitate orchestration and aggregation of services into processes and applications, registry (data base) is used. To publish the services, the eb-XML registry available with tomcat50-java web services developer package is used. The SSDL files for sensor services are used and the appropriate service bindings are set to register the services on tomcat server.

The data which comes from the sensor node is in SOAP format. Inside the SOAP message sensor profiles - xml is used. In order to reduce the power consumption of the sensor nodes, the normal SOAP message is optimized into reduced format. This optimized SOAP is sensed from the sensor node to sink node. The sensor data which are sensed from the sensor node is also updated on sensor base. This will be useful for performing the future statistical analysis. The client application sends a SOAP request for a specific service to sink by the application running on the Sun App Server. The sink uses the XSLT based transformation and mapping algorithm to transform the data in a suitable format for internet accessing. This is accomplished through web service provided by the Sun App Server.

Sensor resources do not have direct connection with cloud. Hence, a framework is necessary to manage the data from the sensor network and take it over long environment. Hence SOSN is extended to cloud by using Integration Controller which acts as a bridge between the two technologies. The Integrated architecture of SOSN with Cloud is shown in Figure 1. In this architecture the Integration Controller (IC) will upload the sensed data to the IBM Bluemix Cloud.

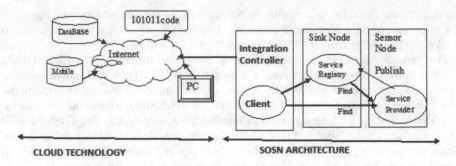

Fig. 1. Integrated Cloud Architecture with SOSN

The collected data only leaves the network domain of the sensor service provider on distinct and controlled paths. Cloud computing allows sharing of sensor resources by different users and applications under flexible scenario. In this scenario security of the sensor data is to be considered. Sensor data access is an application in which messages that need to be exchanged are short and both their privacy and integrity need to be preserved. The SOAP with sensor profiles-xml message which is to be authenticated is also encrypted, with any secure encryption algorithm, to append a short random string to be used in the authentication process. Since the random strings used for different operations are independent, the authentication algorithm can benefit from the simplicity of unconditional secure authentication to allow for faster and more efficient authentication, without the difficulty to manage one-time keys. The used encryption algorithm is a block cipher based to further improve the computational efficiency of the authentication technique.

In the proposed architecture, the authentication of the message transmitted is taken care of in the IC module, the end user is able to access the sensor data by performing a simple step of providing user name and password, and is represented as mobile client in Figure 2.

3   Performance Analysis

3.1   Web Service Message Sizes for Different Encapsulations

The web services implementation is centered on the WSDL standard. WSDL supports several encapsulation protocols for sending the method calls to the web service host device. Currently supported encapsulation protocols are SOAP, HTTP, and MIME. The binding section of the WSDL file describes which one of these standards is used for accessing methods. The SOAP envelope is very verbose and also needs significant radio bandwidth. The web service message sizes for different encapsulations are shown in Table 1. The proposed SOAP message with sensor profiles-xml encapsulation, occupies less size compared to the previous SOAP encapsulations, which are taken from the previous research [7]. This is due to the fact that the proposed messages are well compressed SOA messages. When this message is transferred over the wired or wireless link it occupies only less bandwidth; hence the performance is improved.

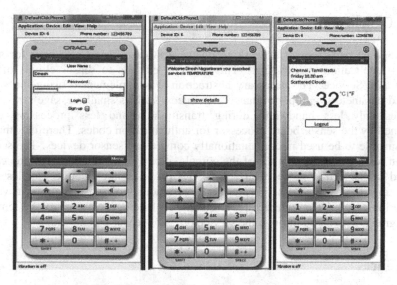

Fig. 2. Temperature service at mobile client

Table 1. Web service message sizes for various encapsulations

Method name	SOAP 1.1	SOAP 1.2	HTTP	SOAP with Sensor profiles-xml
GetTemperature	491	442	162	426
GetTemperatureResponse	479	499	258	482

3.2   Optimization in the Proposed Authentication Code

Since in sensor based applications messages are short, eliminating the need to perform such a cryptographic operation will have a significant impact on the performance of the MAC operation. For instance, while the cryptographic hash functions SHA-256 and SHA-512 run in about 23.73 cycles/byte and 40.18 cycles/byte, respectively [8], the modular multiplication   used in the proposed scheme runs on the used data acquisition boards with temperature (MDA100) sensor in about 2.5 cycles/byte, which illustrates the significance of removing the cryptographic phase from the proposed authentication code. Another significant advantage of the proposed method, especially for low-power devices, is hardware efficiency. The hardware (memory) required to perform modular multiplication is less than the hardware required to perform sophisticated cryptographic operations.

4   Conclusion

The proposed paper aimed at working on the service oriented paradigm for sensor network application engineering. This solution extends to sensor clouds offering Sensor as a Service. The necessary abstraction was implemented using the service oriented parameters with performance guarantees, such as small message sizes which occupies only less bandwidth during transmission and less processing cycles consumed by the sensor board processor for authentication codes. Therefore, they are more suitable to be used in computationally constrained sensor devices. The security solution remains simple as most of the complexities of the authentication process are handled at the sensor node level itself. The proposed architecture enables client applications to easily access and process large amounts of sensor data from various applications. Hence the architecture is scalable as heterogeneous sensor systems can be integrated with cloud through the service oriented sensor parameters.

References

1. Weiss, B., Truong, H.L., Schott, W., Scherer, T., Lombriser, C., Chevillat, P.: Wireless Sensor Network for Continuously Monitoring Temperatures in Data Centers. IBM Research Report, RZ 3807 (June 2011)
2. Lombriser, C., Hunkeler, U., Truong, H.L.: Centrally controlled clustered wireless sensor networks. IBM Research Report, RZ 3811 (November 2011)
3. Rajesh, V., Gnanasekar, J.M., Ponmagal, R.S., Anbalagan, P.: Integration of Wireless Sensor Network with Cloud. In: International Conference on Recent Trends in Information, Telecommunication and Computing, pp. 321–323 (2010)
4. Ghobakhlou, A., Kmoch, A., Sallis, P.: Integration of Wireless Sensor Network and Web Services. In: 20th International Congress on Modelling and Simulation, Adelaide, Australia, December 1-6 (2013)
5. Hummen, R., Henze, M., Catreiny, D., Wehrle, K.: A Cloud Design for User-controlled Storage and Processing of Sensor Data. In: The Sensor Cloud Project is Funded by the German Federal Ministry of Economics and Technology (2012)
6. Alomair, B., Poovendran, R.: Efficient Authentication for Mobile and Pervasive Computing. IEEE Transactions on Mobile Computing 13(3) (2014)
7. Nissanka, B., Aman, K., Michel, G., Feng, Z.: Tiny web services: design and implementation of Interoperable and evolvable sensor networks. In: 6th ACM Confeence on Embedded Network Sensor Systems (SenSys 2008), pp. 253–266 (2008)
8. Nakajima, J., Matsui, M.: Performance analysis and parallel implementation of dedicated hash functions. In: Knudsen, L.R. (ed.) EUROCRYPT 2002. LNCS, vol. 2332, pp. 165–180. Springer, Heidelberg (2002)

Cloud Federation Formation
Using Coalitional Game Theory

Benay Kumar Ray[1], Sunirmal Khatua[2], and Sarbani Roy[3]

[1] SMCC, Jadavpur University, India
roy.binay@gmail.com
[2] Department of CSE, University of Calcutta, India
skhatuacomp@caluniv.ac.in
[3] Department of CSE, Jadavpur University, India
sarbani.roy@cse.jdvu.ac.in

Abstract. Cloud federation has been emerged as a new paradigm in which group of Cloud Service Providers (SP) cooperate to share resources with peers, to gain economic advantage. In this paper, we study the cooperative behavior of a group of cloud SPs. We present broker based cloud federation architecture and model the formation of cloud federation using *coalition game theory*. The objective is to find most suitable federation for Cloud SPs that maximize the satisfaction level of each individual Cloud SP on the basis of Quality of Service(QoS) attributes like availability and price.

Keywords: Cloud federation, Coalition game, satisfaction level, cloud broker, Cooperative game.

1 Introduction

Delivering cloud services are often a delicate balancing act where service provider (SP) has to balance resource request traffic, maximize resource utilization and accommodate spikes in demand while satisfying service consumer's service level agreements (SLAs). With more awareness and growth in the cloud market, demand for cloud resources has increased and it will become difficult for individual SPs to fulfill all resource requests without violating SLAs. Hence this necessitates cloud SPs to form federation for seamless provisioning of resource requests across different cloud providers. Cloud federation is the practice of interconnecting the cloud computing environments of two or more SPs where each SP can share resources with peers to gain economic advantages. In the last few years, many cloud service providers are moving into federation, some relevant research works in this field can be found in [1],[2],[3],[4],[5]. However, none of these works in the literature considered the cloud federation formation based on cloud SP QoS attributes, from the game theoretic perspective. The major contribution of this paper is to formulate the cloud federation as a coalitional game. The proposed cloud federation mechanism is based on satisfaction level of cloud service provider QoS attributes (availability and price).

R. Natarajan et al. (Eds.): ICDCIT 2015, LNCS 8956, pp. 345–350, 2015.

2   Cloud Federation Architecture

In this section, we propose a broker based cloud federation architecture, which is an extension of the cloud service broker architecture [6]. It finds the best federation from a set of federations $fd = \{fd_1, fd_2, \cdots fd_y\}$ where each $fd_j = \cup SP^i$, $SP^i \in \eta$ where $\eta = \{SP^1, SP^2, SP^3, \cdots\cdots SP^Z\}$ denotes set of cloud service providers. The components of cloud federation architecture are (a) *Service Provider Broker (SPB):* administers a set of registered cloud SP and set of federation formed by different cloud SP, (b) *Broker Coordinator (BC):* handles all internal request for fd_j and intimate every update to SPB, (c) *Virtual machine instance type (VMIT$_{I_x}$):* keep homogeneous types of instances information of different SP in fd_j where $I = \{I_A, I_B, \cdots\cdots I_y\}$, define the particular type of instances and (d) *Sub Broker Coordinator (SBC):* is part of each $VMIT_{I_x}$ and maintain records of all virtual machine and simultaneously handles all request received by BC.

Two important QoS attributes for a cloud SP are the price and availability. Availability is defined as the uptime of the service and price is defined as the amount of charge that a cloud Service Consumer (SC) has to pay to use the service. It is assumed that a SP with high availability will charge high price for its services. Let availability and price of SP be $a = \{a_1, a_2, \cdots a_\eta\}$ and $p = \{p_1, p_2, \cdots p_\eta\}$. Then we can formulate the relation between price and availability as $p_i = \rho * a$, where we consider ρ as a proportionality constant and its value denotes price of SP whose availability is 1, here the assumption is that all SP with same availability will have same price to offer.

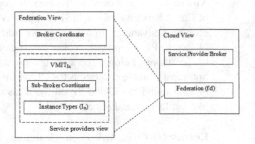

Fig. 1. Cloud federation architecture

3   Formation of Cloud Federation as a Coalition Game

In this section we model cooperation among autonomous rational cloud service provider based on coalition game theory, and design a systematic approach that helps SP to form a set of coalition or federation fd. A cooperative game or a coalition game with transferable utility is defined as a pair (η, v), where η is a set of players and $v : 2^\eta \to \Re$ is a characteristic function (value), with $v(\emptyset) = 0$ and $v(\eta) \geq \sum_{i=1}^z SP^i$. Here value represent the profit achieve by federation when different cloud SP work as a group [7].

Availability of a service (here $VMIT_{I_x}$) in a federation is very important and is achieved by the cooperation among members in a federation and their individual availability. The cooperation among SP in federation are managed by BC, according to optimal arrangement order, $\alpha = \{E_j^{SP^i} | j = 1, 2, \cdots z$ and $SP^i \in \eta\}$. Request of SC is processed based on arrangement order of SP in α. Therefore based on conditional probability, unavailability of $VMIT_{I_x}$ of federation fd_j is given by $U_{fd_j}^{VMIT_{I_x}}(\alpha) = \prod_{i=1}^N u_{I_x}^{sp^i}$.

Therefore availability will be given as $A_{fd_j}^{VMIT_{I_x}}(\alpha) = 1 - U_{fd_j}^{VMIT_{I_x}}(\alpha)$, where $u_{I_x}^{sp^i}$ are the event of unavailability of I_x and $U_{fd_j}^{VMIT_{I_x}}(\alpha)$ and $A_{fd_j}^{VMIT_{I_x}}(\alpha)$ denotes unavailability and availability of $VMIT_{I_x}$ in federation fd_j. Here it shows that availability of $VMIT_{I_x}$ arranged in pre-defined order of SP, based on availability of independent elements with equivalent distribution in a federation is the product of availability of each instance $I_x^{sp^i}$ of SP^i.

We consider a set of rational Cloud Provider as η which will form federation among them. Suppose SP^i offers $I_x^{SP^i}$ where each instances are differentiated based on specific number of cores $Co_{I_x}^{sp^i}$, amount of compute unit $Cu_{I_x}^{sp^i}$, amount of storage $m_{I_x}^{sp^i}$ and amount of memory $s_{I_x}^{sp^i}$. Each cloud SP^i incurs cost when providing resources. The respective cost of $I_x^{SP^i}$ type of instance of SP^i can be derived as follows $c_{I_x}^{sp^i} = Co_{I_x}^{sp^i} \cdot p_C + Cu_{I_x}^{sp^i} \cdot p_{Cu} + m_{I_x}^{sp^i} \cdot p_m + s_{I_x}^{sp^i} \cdot p_s$, where p_C is the cost of each core, p_{Cu} is the cost of one compute unit, p_m is the cost of one GB of memory and p_s is the cost of one GB of storage. In cloud federation, the cost of federation is based on availability of each $VMIT_{I_x}$. The cost of each $VMIT_{I_x}$ in federation relies on the cost(offered price) and availability of individual instance $I_x^{sp^i}$ of SP^i. The cost of federation fd_j will be the sum of cost of each instance I_x of federation fd_j provided by SP^i is defined as:

$$C_{fd_j}(\alpha) = \sum_{I_x \in I} \sum_{i=1}^{N} \prod_{k=1}^{i-1} u_{I_x}^{sp^k} \cdot a_{I_x}^{sp^i} \cdot c_{I_x}^{sp^i} \tag{1}$$

where $a_{I_x}^{sp^i}$ denotes the availability of service provider SP^i of instance type I_x. The total chargeable price of instance I_x in federation fd_j is defined as:

$$P_{fd_j}(\alpha) = \sum_{I_x \in I} \rho_{I_x}^{sp^i}(\alpha) \cdot A_{fd_j}^{VMIT_{I_x}}(\alpha) \tag{2}$$

where $\rho_{I_x}^{sp^i}(\alpha)$ is the price of instance I_x whose availability is 1 and $A_{fd_j}^{VMIT_{I_x}}(\alpha)$ is the availability of instance I_x in federation fd_j. The payoff of federation formed among cloud SP is composed of the total gain obtained by the group of cooperative SP in Federation fd_j. The payoff function for any cloud federation fd can be expressed as $v_\alpha(fd_j) = P_{fd_j}(\alpha) - C_{fd_j}(\alpha)$, where $v_\alpha(fd_j)$ is the total payoff obtained by federation fd_j, which is equal to difference between the revenue received $P_{fd_j}(\alpha)$ from the cloud service consumer and the cost $C_{fd_j}(\alpha)$ incurred by cloud SP. All cloud SP produces the extra payoff through forming federation. Therefore for fair distribution of possible payoff, we choose Shapley value to decide a fair allocation in a cooperative game theory [7].

In this paper we have defined satisfaction level as in [6] (i) to measure satisfaction $sat^{SP^i}(fd_j)$ of SP^i in federation fd_j and satisfaction $sat^{SP^i}(I(SP^i))$ $(I(SP^i))$ (denotes the identity federation i.e federation consisting of single SP) of SP^i without being in any federation and (ii) to measure satisfaction $sat(fd_j)$ of federation. In our research satisfaction level $sat^{SP^i}(fd)$ and $sat^{SP^i}(I(SP^i))$ are calculated based on service provider two QoS attributes profit and availability. Whereas satisfaction level $sat(fd_j)$ of federation are calculated based on value and availability of federation. Thus the total satisfaction level $sat^{SP^i}(fd_j)$ for SP^i in federation fd_j is given by sum of $sl^{SP^i}_{fd_j}(G) \cdot w^{SP^i}_G$ and $sl^{SP^i}_{fd_j}(A) \cdot w^{SP^i}_A$, where weight w represent the factor of importance of corresponding attributes satisfaction level. We have assume equal value of weights w ($w_G + w_A = 1$).

Distributed approach of coalition formation *algorithm* for cloud federation is presented here. It is assumed that at any time any SP or any formed coalition can join a new coalition or leave a current coalition. SPB on receiving merge or split request from any SP or coalition, it first evaluates the request and then perform required actions. Other than this SPB at every time interval checks for availability of $VMIT_{I_x}$ type of resource for every federation (coalition). If any type of $VMIT_{I_x}$ of any federation is below threshold value (predefined) then SPB intimates BC of following federation. BC on receiving SPB intimation, it acknowledges that with new request to merge with new SP or federation. In order to form a federation, we define some set of preference rules based on satisfaction level over possible federation(coalition) partition λ [8], where (i) a service provider will merge any federation if it's individual satisfaction level increases in federation otherwise will split, (ii) federation will merge with other federation or service provider only if it get some gain in terms of satisfaction level.

4 Simulation Result

In this section we analyze how SPB help different SP to form federation based on defined preference rules. We have considered twelve cloud SP. Each cloud SP provide three types of instances namely small, medium and large as specified in Amazon EC2 [9]. The details of cloud SP based on small instance, are provided in Table 1. We have evaluated four scenarios (Figure 2) of federation formation as shown in Table 2. Figure 2(a) compare average satisfaction level of individual SP in identity federation for two different cases. From Figure 2(b), it is noticed that federation $fd(SP-6, SP-2)$

Table 1. Profit obtained by each service provider on each instance

Service Provider	Availability	Instance cost	Chargeable Price	Profit	Satisfaction level
SP-1	.95	148	250	102	0.60636
SP-2	0.90	140	200	60	0.53966
SP-3	0.85	130	194	64	0.51521
SP-4	0.80	124	190	66	0.48893
SP-5	0.77	120	185	65	0.47113
SP-6	0.75	117	178	61	0.43621
SP-7	0.70	109	165	56	0.42349
SP-8	0.65	101	160	59	0.398125
SP-9	0.60	93	148	55	0.36632
SP-10	0.55	85	140	55	0.33820
SP-11	0.50	78	115	37	0.29354
SP-12	0.45	70	100	30	0.25899

Table 2. Four scenarios of federation formation

Scenario	Description
Request by identity federation(single SP) to merge with other identity federations	Four different identity federations, say, $fd(I(SP-2)), fd(I(SP-7)), fd(I(SP-9)), fd(I(SP-11))$ send request to SPB for federation formation. These identity federations form a new federation among themselves as shown in Figure 2(a).
Request by federation to merge with new identity federation(single SP)	Federation $fd(SP-6, SP-2)$ send a request to form a federation with identity federation. SPB will find best identity federation, Figure 2(b) shows that federation $fd(SP-6, SP-2)$ receives improved satisfaction level when it merges with $fd(I(SP-3))$. Thus the new federation is $fd(SP-6, SP-2, SP-3)$.
Request by SP to split from current federation to merge with new federation	Identity federation $fd(I(SP-9))$ will merge with federation $fd(SP-8, SP-5, SP-9)$ because satisfaction level of $fd(I(SP-9))$ increases in this new federation, in compared to its satisfaction level in existing federation as shown in Figure 2(c).
Request by federation to merge with new federation	A federation $fd(SP-10, SP-4)$ sends request to SPB to find a suitable federation, such that it gives rise in satisfaction level as shown in Figure 2(d).

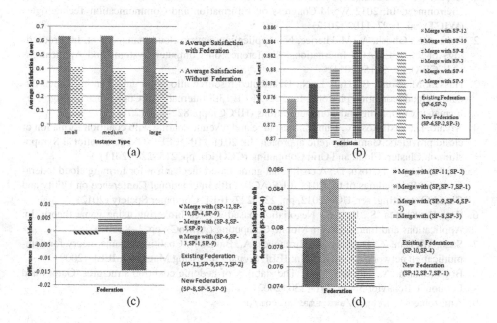

Fig. 2. Satisfaction level in (a) scenario 1 (b) scenario 2 (c) scenario 3 (d) scenario 4

will achieve highest satisfaction level when it merge with fd(I(SP-3)). Figure 2(c) shows satisfaction level difference between existing federation and new federation of SP-9 and Figure 2(d) shows difference in satisfaction level of federation $fd(SP-10, SP-4)$ with other new federation.

5 Conclusion

The main objective of this paper is to study the cooperative behavior of group of cloud service provider in federation. First we present broker based cloud federation architecture. Then a coalitional game model has been proposed to obtain cooperation decision of the cloud service provider in different cloud federation. In this paper we design a scheme of coalition formation of cloud SPs based on their individual QoS attributes like availability and price. SPB makes decision to merge or split based on satisfaction level of service provider and federation. Based on cloud federation framework, we show how federation can be formed between different cloud service providers. The simulated result presents four different scenarios of federation formation.

Acknowledgment. This research is supported by the project: *UGC UPE Phase II. Mobile Computing and Innovative Applications* at Jadavpur University, funded by UGC.

References

1. Lu, Z., Wen, X., Sun, Y.: A game theory based resource sharing scheme in cloud computing environment. In: 2012 World Congress on Information and Communication Technologies (WICT), pp. 1097–1102 (2012)
2. Khatua, S., Ghosh, A., Mukherjee, N.: Application-centric cloud management. In: Proceedings of 9th IEEE/ACS International Conference on Computer Systems and Applications (AICCSA), pp. 9–15 (2011)
3. Hassan, M., Song, B., Huh, E.-N.: Distributed resource allocation games in horizontal dynamic cloud federation platform. In: 2011 IEEE 13th International Conference on High Performance Computing and Communications (HPCC), pp. 822–827 (2011)
4. Niyato, D., Vasilakos, A., Kun, Z.: Resource and revenue sharing with coalition formation of cloud providers: Game theoretic approach. In: 2011 11th IEEE/ACM International Symposium on Cluster, Cloud and Grid Computing (CCGrid), pp. 215–224 (2011)
5. Mashayekhy, L., Grosu, D.: A coalitional game-based mechanism for forming cloud federations. In: Proceedings of the 2012 IEEE/ACM Fifth International Conference on Utility and Cloud Computing, ser. UCC 2012, pp. 223–227. IEEE Computer Society (2012)
6. Ray, B., Khatua, S., Roy, S.: Negotiation based service brokering using game theory. In: Applications and Innovations in Mobile Computing (AIMoC), pp. 1–8 (2014)
7. Saad, W., Han, Z., Debbah, M., Hjrungnes, A., Basar, T.: Coalitional game theory for communication networks: A tutorial. In: IEEE Signal Processing Magazine. IEEE (2009)
8. Bogomolnaia, A., Jackson, M.O.: The stability of hedonic coalition structures. Games and Economic Behavior 38(2), 201– 230 (2002)
9. Amazon.com., http://aws.amazon.com/ec2

An Efficient Resource Allocation Algorithm
for IaaS Cloud

Sanjaya K. Panda[1] and Prasanta K. Jana[2]

[1] Department of Information Technology
Veer Surendra Sai University of Technology, Burla, India
[2] Department of Computer Science and Engineering
Indian School of Mines, Dhanbad, India
sanjayauce@gmail.com, prasantajana@yahoo.co.in

Abstract. Infrastructure as a Service (IaaS) cloud provides access to computing resources by forming a virtualized environment. The resources are offered by means of leases. However, it is not possible to satisfy all the leases due to finite capacity of resources (or nodes). Mapping between all the leases and the available nodes referred as resource allocation problem is very challenging to IaaS cloud. In this paper, we propose a resource allocation algorithm for IaaS cloud which is based on a novel approach of alert time. First, it uses alert time to assign the leases and then employs swapping to reschedule the already accommodated leases in case a lease is not schedulable by the alert time. This makes resource allocation superior to support the deadline sensitive leases by minimizing the lease rejection in contrast to two existing algorithms by Haizea [3] and Nathani [2]. We perform extensive experiments on several synthetic data sets and the results show that the proposed algorithm outperforms both the algorithms in terms of accepted leases and rejected leases.

Keywords: Resource Allocation, IaaS Cloud, Alert Time, Swapping, Haizea.

1 Introduction

Resource allocation in IaaS cloud is very challenging. The resources are provided to the user on pay-per-use basis [1] and provisioned in the form of virtual machines (VMs) which are deployed on physical machines. The users request such computational resources in the form of leases. The leases are submitted in one of the modes, i.e., AR (advanced reservation), BE (best effort), immediate or DS (deadline sensitive). In AR and immediate mode, resources are non-preemptable and the corresponding leases are time constraint. The BE and DS leases are preemptable and flexible in time constraint. The resource allocation between leases and the VMs (also called nodes) is a well known NP-Complete problem [2]. Therefore, several attempts [2-6] have been made to find a near optimal solution. However, the problem in resource allocation is very crucial and not well studied.

In this paper, we address the same resource allocation problem as described in [2] for IaaS cloud and propose an algorithm called alert time based resource allocation

R. Natarajan et al. (Eds.): ICDCIT 2015, LNCS 8956, pp. 351–355, 2015.

(ALT-RA). The algorithm uses a novel concept based on alert time to assign the resources. The algorithm is tested rigorously with synthetic data sets. The experimental results show that the proposed algorithm performs better than the existing algorithms [2] and [3] in terms of accepted leases and rejected leases.

In the recent years, many resource allocation algorithms [2-6] have been developed for *Cloud Computing*. Nathani et al. [2] have proposed policy based resource allocation for DS leases in Haizea. But rescheduling and preemption are the major overhead of this system. The algorithm presented in this paper is an improvement over [2] with respect to the following aspects. 1) Our algorithm uses start time and alert time to assign the resource in contrast to submit time and start time as used by [2] and as a result prevention of lease rejection is more. 2) The algorithm uses a novel swapping approach to reschedule the leases (as and when required) instead of sorting the leases in descending order of their resources as used by [2] and this leads reduction of lease swapping.

The remainder of the paper is organized as follows. We describe the resource allocation problem in Section 2. We present the proposed scheme in Section 3 followed by the experimental results in Section 4. Finally, we conclude the paper in Section 5.

2   Problem Statement

We assume here that each lease is a 6-tuple $\{ID, AT, ST, D, P, |N|\}$ where ID denotes the unique identification number, AT is the arrival time, S is the start time, D is the deadline, P is the period, $|N|$ is the number of nodes. Given a set of m resources (called nodes) $N = \{N_1, N_2, N_3, ..., N_m\}$ and a set of n leases $L = \{L_1, L_2, L_3,..., L_n\}$, the problem of resource allocation is to map the leases onto the available nodes such that the lease rejection is minimized.

Table 1. Submitted leases with their 6-tuple

	ID	AT	ST	D	P	N	ALT
G_1	L_1	08:30	09:00	10:30	40	1	09:50
	L_2	08:35	09:00	10:30	30	3	10:00
	L_3	08:45	09:00	10:40	30	2	10:10
	L_4	08:55	09:00	10:30	40	4	09:50
G_2	L_5	09:25	10:00	11:00	10	1	10:50

We illustrate it with an example as follows. Suppose there are five leases as shown in Table 1. These leases are required to be scheduled with four available nodes. For instance, consider the lease L_3 which requires 2 nodes. The lease can be assigned with one of the following pairs: (N_1, N_2), (N_1, N_3), (N_1, N_4), (N_2, N_3), (N_2, N_4) or (N_3, N_4) where order of nodes in each pair is immaterial.

3   Proposed Scheme

The proposed algorithm is based on the alert time (ALT) of the leases which is calculated by using the following Equation.

$$x = D - ST$$
$$ALT = ST + (x - P) - \alpha \qquad (1)$$

where α is the overhead time. For example, consider the lease L_1 (refer Table 1) in which the D and ST values are 10:30 and 09:00 respectively. So, the x value is 10:30 – 09:00 = 90. The lease requires a period of 40. Therefore, the ALT time is 09:00 + (90 – 40) – 0 = 09:50 assuming that the value of α is zero. The basic idea of the proposed algorithm is as follows. First, it sorts the leases in the ascending order of their ST. Then, it divides the whole set of the leases into groups (See Table 1). The leases with the same ST are kept in the same group. Next it calculates the alert time of the leases within each group and allocates the leases such that the lease with earliest ALT is assigned first. However if there is a tie with the same ALT value, then the lease with maximum |N| value, i.e., the lease with maximum number of node requirement is assigned first. Note that this approach has two basic advantages over the existing algorithms by Haizea [3] and Nathani et al. [2]: 1) it prevents the deadline of the leases and 2) it utilizes the resources properly. From here onwards we will refer the algorithm of Haizea as HAIZEA and the algorithm of Nathani et al. (without backfilling) as DPS (dynamic planning based scheduling).

3.1   A Typical Case: Resource Allocation with Swapping

This scenario is occurred when the proposed algorithm cannot accommodate a newly arrived lease. Swapping is used to make space for the upcoming leases. So, we propose here a novel swapping approach to reschedule the leases. We first define some terminologies as follows.

Definition 3.1 (ST-ALT lease_set): We define it as the set of all already accommodated leases whose duration between ALT and ST intersects with the duration between ALT and ST of a newly arrived lease.

Definition 3.2 (ALT-D lease_set): This is the set of all already accommodated leases whose duration between D and ALT intersects with the duration between D and ALT of a newly arrived lease.

The proposed scheme with swapping reschedules the leases by forming two lease_sets, i.e, ST-ALT and ALT-D. Then, it checks whether the intersection of these lease_sets, i.e., {ST-ALT} ∩ {ALT-D} is empty or not. If the intersection is not empty then it finds the difference of these lease_sets using following Equation.

$$\{ST\text{-}ALT\} = \{ST\text{-}ALT\} - \{ALT\text{-}D\} \qquad (2)$$

Note that this difference actually makes $\{ST\text{-}ALT\} \cap \{ALT\text{-}D\}$ empty. Next, each lease of $\{ST\text{-}ALT\}$ is compared with the lease of $\{ALT\text{-}D\}$ to decide whether they can be swapped or not.

Remark. If two lease_sets have m leases and l leases, the above comparison takes $O(ml)$ time by the proposed algorithm.

They can only be swapped when the following two conditions are met. First, each $\{ST\text{-}ALT\}$ lease has less requested resources than $\{ALT\text{-}D\}$. Second, interchange of $\{ST\text{-}ALT\}$ and $\{ALT\text{-}D\}$ lease does not violate their deadline constraints. However, if the newly arrived lease is not allocated after swapping, then it rollbacks the rescheduling.

Remark. If the lease_sets has n leases $(n = l + m)$, the DPS algorithm takes $O(n^2)$ time in contrast to $O(lm)$ time required by the proposed algorithm.

4   Experimental Results

We tested the proposed algorithm through simulation run with numerous synthetic data sets. The experiments were carried out using MATLAB R2010b on an Intel Core 2 Duo processor, 2.20 GHz CPU and 4 GB RAM running on the platform Microsoft Windows 7. We took four nodes with equal specifications. The numbers of leases were taken as 11, 22, 33 and 44 respectively. However, the parameters of the leases were taken manually. We measured the performance in terms of accepted leases and rejected leases as used by [2]. The accepted and rejected leases are the total number of leases accepted/rejected in a data set. Figs. 1-2 show the comparison of proposed algorithm with the two existing algorithms HAIZEA [3] and DPS [2].

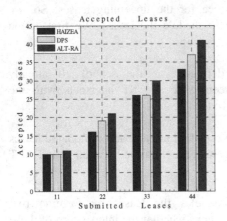

Fig. 1. Accepted leases

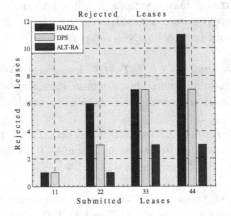

Fig. 2. Rejected leases

5   Conclusion

We have presented a resource allocation algorithm for IaaS clouds. The algorithm is based on alert time of the leases. It was experimented extensively on several synthetic data sets. The experimental results have been compared with two well known existing resource allocation algorithms. The comparison results show that the proposed algorithm outperforms both the algorithms in terms of two performance metrics namely, accepted leases and rejected leases.

References

1. Buyya, R., Yeo, C.S., Venugopal, S., Broberg, J., Brandic, I.: Cloud Computing and Emerging IT Platforms: Vision, Hype and Reality for Delivering Computing as the 5th Utility. Future Generation Computer Systems 25, 599–616 (2009)
2. Nathani, A., Chaudhary, S., Somani, G.: Policy Based Resource Allocation in IaaS Cloud. Future Generation Computer Systems 28, 94–103 (2012)
3. Haizea, http://haizea.cs.uchicago.edu/whatis.html (accessed on January 9, 2014)
4. Vora, D., Chaudhary, S., Bhise, M., Kumar, V., Somani, G.: Allocation of Slotted Deadline Sensitive Leases in Infrastructure Cloud. In: Ramanujam, R., Ramaswamy, S. (eds.) ICDCIT 2012. LNCS, vol. 7154, pp. 242–252. Springer, Heidelberg (2012)
5. Beloglazov, A., Abawajy, J., Buyya, R.: Energy-Aware Resource Allocation Heuristics for Efficient Management of Data Centers for Cloud Computing. Future Generation Computer Systems 28, 755–768 (2012)
6. Akhani, J., Chuadhary, S., Somani, G.: Negotiation for Resource Allocation in IaaS Cloud. In: 4th ACM Conference COMPUTE (2011)

Genetic Algorithm Framework for Bi-objective Task Scheduling in Cloud Computing Systems

A.S. Ajeena Beegom[1] and M.S. Rajasree[2]

[1] Dept. of Computer Science and Engineering
College of Engineering Trivandrum, India
ajeena@cet.ac.in
[2] IIITM-K, Trivandrum, India
rajasree.ms@iiitmk.ac.in

Abstract. Cloud computing gives an excellent opportunity for business enterprises as well as researchers to use the computing power, over Internet, without actually owning the infrastructure, there by reducing establishment and management cost. Task scheduling in cloud systems is challenging due to the conflicting objectives of end users and the cloud service providers. Running time and cost are two key factors that determine the optimal service from the cloud. In this paper, we focus on two objectives, makespan and cost, to be optimized simultaneously using genetic algorithm framework. Finding an optimal schedule, considering both of these conflicting objectives, is a search problem under NP-hard category. We have considered the scheduling of independent tasks and the proposed frame work can be used in public or hybrid cloud.

Keywords: Cloud Computing, Task Scheduling, Pareto Optimality, Genetic Algorithm.

1 Introduction

Cloud computing refers to leasing computing resources over Internet for meeting the computing / storage requirements of an individual, small scale companies and research organization. In order to achieve maximum economy for the cloud service provider, jobs or tasks has to be scheduled in an optimal way. Most of the existing research work in the literature for task scheduling in cloud systems are either running time optimal or budget oriented. Pareto optimal modelling is addressed by Riza et.al [1] for hybrid cloud scheduling where the objectives are to optimize both cost and makespan using a posteriori approach to find optimal schedule. A hybrid Genetic Algorithm (GA) technique is used to address the issue of scheduling precedence constrained parallel applications in heterogeneous environment by M Mezmaz [5]. They have attempted to optimize both energy consumption at the processor level and makespan. The work in [3] uses Genetic algorithm to solve task scheduling problem in cloud computing for single objective optimization. Genetic algorithm frame work has been used in [6] and [2] to solve the dynamic load balancing problem for distributed systems and

R. Natarajan et al. (Eds.): ICDCIT 2015, LNCS 8956, pp. 356–359, 2015.

for workflow scheduling in hybrid cloud[1]. Our proposed system is modeled as a constraint bi-objective optimization problem and uses Genetic algorithm to solve the same. We assume that the tasks are independent and can be executed in parallel on different virtual machines(VMs).

2   Proposed System

Assume an application consists of N independent tasks, n out of N are scheduled at each time window, where the value of n is limited by the number of available VMs m and $k = \frac{N}{n}$ similar epochs are needed to complete the execution of all tasks. For each type of VM instance $I = [small, medium, large, ...]$, the associated cost of usage and the computing power are different. Let Pf_j represent the processing power of jth VM instance type where j ranges from 1 to $|I|$ and C_j represents its cost for unit time. The task length T_i of each task $TASK_i$ is precomputed which represents the time needed to execute each task in 'small' type VM. The optimization objectives for N tasks are :

$$Minimize \quad Makespanfn = \sum_{p=1}^{k}\sum_{i=1}^{n} T_i * Pf_j * x_{ij} \quad for \quad some \quad j\epsilon I \quad (1)$$

$$Minimize \quad Costfn = \sum_{p=1}^{k}\sum_{i=1}^{n} C_j * T_i * Pf_j * x_{ij} \quad for \quad some \quad j\epsilon I \quad (2)$$

subject to constraints:

$$n \leq m \quad (3)$$

$$x_{ij} = \begin{cases} 1 & if \ TASK_i \quad scheduled to \quad VM_j \\ 0 & otherwise \end{cases} \quad (4)$$

and

$$\sum_{i=1}^{n} x_{ij} = m \quad (5)$$

2.1   Pareto Optimality

A multi objective optimization problem consists of optimizing a vector of n_{obj} where the objective function is $F(x) = (f_1(x), f_2(x), ..., f_{n_{obj}}(x))$. We have used weighted sum approach to solve the same, which in essence convert a multi-objective optimization problem to a single objective optimization problem with weights representing preferences among objectives by the decision maker[4]. Hence our bi-objective optimization problem can be represented using the formula:

$$Minimize \quad \theta * Costfn + (1 - \theta) * Makespanfn \quad (6)$$

where θ represent the relative weight or preference of one objective over the other. When $\theta = 0$, the optimization problem becomes that of minimizing $Makespanfn$ and when $\theta = 1$, the problem becomes minimizing $Costfn$.

2.2   Genetic Algorithm Modelling

Genetic algorithms[5] are meta-heuristics based on the iterative application of stochastic operators in a population of candidate solutions. At each iteration, solutions are selected from the population. The selected solutions are recombined in order to generate new ones. The new solutions replace other solutions selected either randomly or according to a replacement strategy. Here permutation encoding technique is used to represent each solution. Every VM is assigned a number from 1 to n and solutions are represented by a sequence of assigned nodes in task order. The sequence (5, 2, 1, 3, 4) means that assign Task 1 to PM 5, Task 2 to PM 2, etc. and the corresponding makespan and cost is estimated for the given schedule. Initial populations are randomly generated.

3   Results and Discussion

Each solution is evaluated to find its fitness based on cost of execution, makespan of the current assignment and on both the objectives together with the preference parameter θ set on different values as well as for different sets and types of VMs and tasks (Performance Analysis in Fig. 1(a) to Fig. 1(d)). Since make span and cost of execution are represented in different scales, they are normalised initially. For experiments, the population size is fixed as $|P| = 5$, $\theta = 0.9$ and uses classic Roulette wheel selection technique. The crossover probability is fixed at 0.9 and mutation rate at 0.02. The cross over strategy used is single point

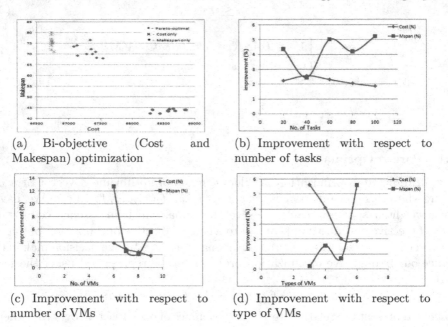

(a)   Bi-objective   (Cost   and Makespan) optimization

(b) Improvement with respect to number of tasks

(c) Improvement with respect to number of VMs

(d) Improvement with respect to type of VMs

Fig. 1. Performance Analysis

cross over technique where the cross over point is varied at random on each iteration, which intensifies the search process.

An off-spring chromosome, the position of gene and the value to be replaced is also determined randomly, which will enable an existing task assignment to another VM in an arbitrary way so as to enable maximum diversification, implementing mutation operator. Generational replacement with elitism is used and the termination criterion is fixed as 500 generations, outputting a single best solution for 9 task. The same is repeated for 11 times to find schedule for 99 tasks. Each of these solutions are tested to see that all the constraints are satisfied. If m is less than n in any epoch, dummy task sets of zero length are supplied. From the figures, it is clear that proposed framework achieves better value of cost and make span for all the scenarios considered.

4   Conclusion

Scheduling tasks in the cloud is challenging as the same involves many factors such as cost and profit considerations, execution time, SLAs, QoS parameters and power considerations. Also the task arrival rate is highly unpredictable and dynamic in nature. We have addressed this problem through an IP modeling and used genetic algorithm to solve the same. The results are compared for different scenarios such as pareto-optimal scheduling, cost optimal scheduling and makespan optimal scheduling and for different sets and types of VMs and tasks.

References

1. Farahabady, R.H., Lee, Y.C., Zomay, A.Y.: Pareto optimal cloud bursting. Accepted for Publication in IEEE Transactions on Parallel and Distributed Systems (2013)
2. Gonnade, P., Bodkhe, S.: An efficient load balancing using genetic algorithm in hierarchical structured distributed systems. International Journal of Advanced Computer Research 6(2), 69 (2012)
3. Jang, S.H., Kim, T.Y., Kim, J.K., Lee, J.S.: The study of Genetic Algorithm Based Task Scheduling for Cloud Computing. International Journal of Control and Automation 5(4), 157–162 (2012)
4. Marler, R.T., Arora, J.S.: The weighted sum method for multi-objective optimization: New insights. Springer (2009)
5. Mezmaz, M., Melab, N., Kessaci, Y., Lee, Y.C., Talbi, E.G., Zomaya, A.Y., Tuyttens, D.: A parallel bi-objective hybrid metaheuristic for energy-aware scheduling for cloud computing systems. Journal of Parallel and Distributed Computing, 1497–1508 (2011)
6. Zomaya, A.Y., Teh, Y.-H.: Observations on using genetic algorithms for dynamic load balancing. IEEE Transactions on Parallel and Distributed Systems 12(9), 899–913 (2001)

Optimal Cloud Resource Provisioning:
A Two-Criteria Formulation

Geetika Mudali[1], Manas Ranjan Patra[2], K. Hemant Kumar Reddy[1],
and Diptendu Sinha Roy[1]

[1] Department of Computer Science and Engineering
National Institute of Technology, Berhampur, India - 761008
geetika_nist@hotmail.com, khemant.reddy@gmail.com,
diptendu.sr@gmail.com
[2] Department of Computer Science
Berhampur University, Berhampur, India
mrpatra12@gmail.com

Abstract. Federated resource provisioning in an on-demand, instantly procurable fashion with the flexibility of a pay as you go model for pricing has led the path for cloud computing to be the computing technology of the future. However, resource provisioning technology needs to be well-supported by appropriate optimization strategies for sustainability purposes. In this paper, therefore, an efficient resource provisioning strategy has been proposed that arrives at optimal provisioning solution with minimal cost and SLA violation rate. To this end, an optimal cloud resource provisioning model has been formulated using the Stochastic Integer Programming (SIP) problem which has been solved by assuming customers' cloud demand for resources as Poisson's distribution to accommodate for uncertainties pertaining to user demand.

Keywords: Resource Provisioning, QoS, Poisson distribution, Stochastic Programming.

1 Introduction

In cloud computing, resources providers amass stockpiles of computing resources, like servers, disks and random access memory (RAM) for future allocation among users in a federated manner. Virtualization is the backbone technology that allows creation of independent virtual machines (VM) which are provisioned as a resource to cloud users as and when required with requisite quanitites of memory, disk and CPU capacities. Major cloud providers, like Amazon, Google, Microsoft provide cloud services like Amazon's Elastic Cloud 2 (EC2) [1], Google Apps Engine [2], Microsoft's Azure [3] respectively and so on, to their clients. Moreover, these major players offer flexible pricing options to their clients for using resources. Owing to diverse variation of resource prices set by the cloud providers and also due to dynamic nature of cloud users' demand, provisioning accurate amount of resources at minimal cost is a very difficult, nay improbable problem. The stochastic model for cloud resource provisioning at optimal cost is a well-known NP hard problem [4, 5].

R. Natarajan et al. (Eds.): ICDCIT 2015, LNCS 8956, pp. 360–364, 2015.

Quality of Service (QoS) fulfillment is another important parameter that needs to be taken care of in cloud parlance. Thus, cloud resource provisioning with QoS requirements is an even more challenging problem. In this paper, in order to calculate the optimal solution to the cloud resource provisioning problem, cost of cloud provisioning has been taken as one of the objective functions and the other objective function has been considered to be an utility function that is calculated based on deadline. In order to attain warranted service, we propose a Quality of service Analyzer (QoSA) model to be inserted within the cloud broker that is based on 0-1 dynamic Knapsack [6] that incorporates a standard incentive-penalty scheme.

Research pertaining to optimal provisioning could be traced as early as in the early 1980s in the context of computer networks [7]. Resource provisioning for SaaS and Paas levels have been addressed addressed in [8]. However, it does not consider any mechanism for allocation of VM to meet SLA or any management associated with violation of risks. In this paper, a cloud resource provisioning algorithm has been presented to meet the QoS requirements, by means of utility function for SLA violations, if any in addition to cost of provisioning. In [9], [10], [11] different approaches of resource provisioning were developed.

The remainder of the paper is organized as follows: Section 2 presents the system model and summarizes the assumptions made therein. It also presents the QoS Aware Resource Provisioning algorithm. In section 3, the experimental setup for testing the efficiay of the proposed provisioning algorithm has been delineated along with a summary of results obtained. Finally, the conclusions have been summarized in section 4.

2   System Model and Problem Formulation

Figure 1 depicts the system model for the cloud resource provisioning. The major components of the system are: cloud users (CU), the Quality of Service Analyzer (QoSA), the QoS-Aware Resource Provisioning (QARP) algorithm, VM repository, cloud provider (CP).

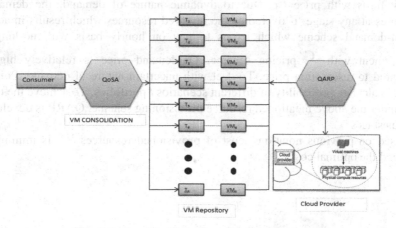

Fig. 1. System Model for Resource Provisioning

Table 1. Notation and Terminology

Parameter	Definition	P(s)	Probability of scenario 's'
$V, v \in V$	VM Instance type	d(s)	Demand of customer for scenario 's'
$R, r \in R$	Advance Reservation Contract	S	Scenarios/portfolio
$T, t \in T$	Total number of Stages	M	Max no. of instances that can be allotted
$C^a(r, v)$	Cost of Advance reservation contract	$C^o(v)$	Cost of On-demand scheme per hour
$C^r(r, v)$	Cost of Using reservation contract per hour		
$N^r(r, v)$	Number of VM instances reserved in reservation contract R		
$\eta_h{}^r(r, t)$	Number of hours VMs used in reservation scheme in stage' t'		
$\eta_h{}^o(o, t)$	Number of hours VMs used in On-demand scheme		
$N^o(v)$	Number of VM instances in On-demand scheme		
$N^u(v)$	Number of VM instances utilized in reservation contract R		

First of all, estimation of parameters of demand data is done assuming Poisson's distribution from historical cloud demand data collected from [13]. Here, demand is taken as Poisson Variate X, using the data from scientific workload [13], parameter λ (Mean) is calculated, probability function is defined as:

$$f(n) = P(X = n) = \frac{e^{-\lambda} * \lambda^n}{n!}$$

(1)

Various types of VM instances are provided by cloud provider under different provisioning stages. To get the optimal cost for VM resources, it is necessary to know the approximate future demand of resources. For this, a simple algorithm based on the Job execution time and 0-1 dynamic Knapsack to meet SLA is used. Thus, the amount of resources, N^r is reserved in advance under different reservation contract, R with C^a pricing and using those VM instances under reservation scheme is charged on hourly basis with price Cr. Due to dynamic nature of demand, the demand for resources at any stage 't' overcome the reserved resources which results in adoption of On-demand scheme which let us to pay on hourly basis with no-long term commitment with C^o pricing scheme. On-demand price is relatively higher as compared to reservation price. To deal with uncertain nature of demand, Poisson is used to calculate probability of different scenarios / portfolios. To achieve the optimal cost under the above mentioned resource provisioning scheme, QARP is developed in various stages.

Based on previous notations, cost of provisioned resources 'C' is minimized to obtained the optimal cost

Minimize:

$$C = \sum_{t \in T} \sum_{v \in V} \sum_{r \in R} C^a N^r + \sum_{t \in T} \sum_{v \in V} \sum_{r \in R} \sum_{s \in S} P(s) C^r N^u \eta_h{}^r$$

$$+ \sum_{t \in T} \sum_{v \in V} \sum_{s \in S} P(s) C^o N^o \eta_h{}^o ----(2)$$

Subjected to: $N^r, N^o >= 0$ and $N^r, N^o \in N$ $----$ (3)

$$\sum_T \sum_V \sum_S (\sum_R N^r + N^o) \geq \sum_S d \ ---$$ (4)

$$\sum_T \sum_V \sum_S (\sum_R N^r + N^o) \leq m \ ---$$ (5)

$$\sum_t \sum_s N^u \leq \sum_t \sum_s N^r \ ---$$ (6)

In equation (3), constraint implies that the number of instances in reservation scheme and On-demand Scheme are non-negative integer values. The constraint in equation (4) specifies that the total number of resources provisioned fulfills the demand of user and job is completed. In (5), the constraint implies that the maximum possible number of instances the provider can provision. The constraint in (6) states that the number of resources utilized in reservation scheme must not exceed the reserved number of resources. The above formulation is deterministic equivalent of a multistage stochastic process. This can be solved by Programming in powerful LINGO API solvers using LINGO14 [14] comprehensive tool.

3   Performance Evaluation

Optimal cost is calculated using pricing scheme offered by Amazon EC2 [1] and obtained by solving the deterministic equivalent formulation by programming in LINGO14. Also the same is solved using nested decomposition method and the results are summarized in table 2.

Table 2. Comparison of solving the optimal resource provisioning using LINGO

Time in milli Seconds	Determinist Equivalent	Nested Decomposition	
	Optimal Cost	*Optimal Cost*	*Deviation*
25753	$35.8	$31.9	10.8%
32498	$47.5	$43.1	9.2%
40458	$50.8	$47.1	7.2%
48242	$59.7	$53.6	10.2%
54973	$62.7	$57.2	8.7%

4   Conclusion

The experimental results shows that optimal cost obtained is minimal as compared to other provisioning scheme along with satisfying the QoS parameter (i.e. finishing the job within given budget and deadline) and imposing penalty on delayed job which is minimized in our case.

References

1. Amazon EC2, http://aws.amazon.com/ec2/
2. Google App Engine, https://appengine.google.com/
3. Microsoft Azure, http://azure.microsoft.com/en-us/
4. Dyer, M., Stougie, L.: Computational complexity of stochastic programming problems. Mathematical Programmin 106(3), 423–432 (2006)
5. Stougie, L., Van Der Vler, M.H.: Stochastic integer programming. Institute of Actuarial Sciences & Econometrics, University of Amsterdam (1996)
6. Cormen, T.H., Leiserson, C.E., Rivest, R.L., Stein, C.: Introduction to algorithms, 3rd edn. (2009)
7. Yemini, Y.: Selfish optimization in computer networks processing. In: Proceedings of the 20th IEEE Conference on Decision and Control Including the Symposium on Adaptive Processes, San Diego, USA (1981)
8. Calheiros, R.N., Ranjan, R., Buyya, R.: Virtual machine provisioning based on analytical performance and QoS in cloud computing environments. In: 2011 International Conference on Parallel Processing (ICPP). IEEE (2011)
9. Hu, M., Jun, L., Wang, Y.: Practical Resource Provisioning and Caching with Dynamic Resilience for Cloud-Based Content Distribution Networks, pp. 1–1 (2013)
10. Zaman, S., Grosu, D.: Combinatorial auction-based dynamic vm provisioning and allocation in clouds. In: 2011 IEEE Third International Conference on Cloud Computing Technology and Science (CloudCom), pp. 107–114. IEEE (2011)
11. Khatua, S., Sur, P.K., Das, R.K., Mukherjee, N.: Heuristic-based Optimal Resource Provisioning in Application-centric Cloud. arXiv preprint arXiv:1403.2508 (2014)
12. Real workload data, http://www.cs.huji.ac.il/labs/parallel/workload/
13. Bertsekas, D.P.: Nonlinear Programming, 2nd edn. Athena Scientific, Belmont (1999)

Predicting Post Importance in Question Answer Forums Based on Topic-Wise User Expertise

Deepa Anand and Febin A.Vahab

CMR Institute of Technology, Bangalore, India
{deepa.anand,febin.s}@cmrit.ac.in

Abstract. Q & A forums on the web are aplenty and the content produced through such crowd-sourced efforts is generally of good quality and highly beneficial to novices and experts alike. As the community matures, however, the explosion in the number of posts/answers leads to the information overload problem. Many a times users having expertise in a particular area are not able to address quality issues raised in the area maybe due to the positioning of the question in the list displayed to the user. A good mechanism to assess the quality of questions and to display it to the users depending on their area of expertise, if devised, may lead to a higher quality answers and faster resolutions to the questions posted. In this paper we present the results of our investigations into the effectiveness of various mechanisms to represent user expertise to estimate a post score reflecting its quality/utility of the post. We follow three different approaches to building a user profile representing the user's areas of expertise: topic models based approach, tag-based approach and semantic user profiling approaches. We present the results of experiments performed on the popular Q&A Forum Stack Overflow, exploring the value add offered by these approaches. The preliminary experiments support our hypothesis that considering additional features in terms of user expertise does offer an increase in the classification accuracy even while ignoring features computable only after the first 24 hours. However, the proposed method to individually leverage on the semantic tag relations to construct an enhanced user profile did not prove beneficial.

Keywords: component, formatting, Discussion Forums, Q&A Forums, Semantic Profiling, Expertise Modelling, Prediction.

1   Introduction

Community forums for Q & A benefit a large population of the web users and are a great means for knowledge acquisition and troubleshooting. Many popular Q & A sites such as Stack Overflow (SO) [1] list the questions posed under different criteria such as time of posting, score, user interests etc. The posts within each area are chronologically ordered. However the rapidness of incoming posts may hamper the users' ability to browse through all posts of interest to him and highly important posts of impact to a vast majority of users may not get quality answers. Though these websites do have a scoring mechanism where users vote for/against questions and answers,

R. Natarajan et al. (Eds.): ICDCIT 2015, LNCS 8956, pp. 365–376, 2015.

new questions which enter the system don't have any associated scores and may get lost depending on the time at which it was posted and the other questions that were posted in the same time frame. There have been a few attempts in the past to quantify the level/usefulness of a post based on various parameters based on user features, community behavior, question content etc [2][3][4] and for various purposes such as predicting closed questions [2], directing questions to relevant experts [3] and to find the correlation between question and answer quality [4] etc. The authors in [4] propose a mechanism to score the quality of new questions and answers based on various features. Though the main aim of the paper is to show that question and answer quality are interdependent, they outline a mechanism to estimate a post quality based on various input parameters such as post length, user experience in posting questions in the forum in the past, number of comments received in the first 24 hours, number of answers received in the first 24 hours etc. Though such a mechanism produces reasonable accuracy for question and answers score prediction it relies on the data available after the first 24 hours. This means that the proposed approach would prove inadequate to evaluate fresh posts not past 24 hours for their appropriateness in the top posts lists. Moreover one of the parameters considered is the user overall reputation in the system.

We argue that not all users may possess expertise in all areas of interest but rather the level of knowledge in various subject areas may be varied. Consequently the level of user reputation alone may not be a good indicator of the quality of the post written by the user. An ability to evaluate subject area expertise of a user and to leverage the user expertise in estimating post scores would not only provide nuanced representation of the user knowledge but also would help mitigate the problem of unavailability of post features in the first 24 hours by supplementing the sparse features for a brand new post with the user expertise levels in the areas matching that of the post content. Modeling topic wise user expertise is a task that has been attempted previously albeit for a slightly different task of identifying expert users who may offer quality answers to a post. The current work differs in its aim which is to estimate the importance or quality of a post based on the match between the topic subject and the posting user's expertise in the same subject.

Previous attempts at modeling user expertise have employed variations of topic model based or clustering based algorithms to segregate the topics into clusters(with cluster sizes ≈ 10) and gauged user expertise in each of the clusters so formed. We argue that such an approach may lead to over-generalization since the clusters so formed may centre around more popular topics such as C#, Java, .NET etc and many technologies commonly used together may fall under the same cluster. The disadvantage is that topics which are less represented in terms of the number of posts related to them are forced into one of the pre-constructed categories which may defeat the purpose for which the approach was followed. For example posts relating to *Perl* may be grouped under the category *Python* and hence a user who has earned a reputation in answering and posing questions in the area of *Perl*-programming would be automatically deemed to be an expert in *Python*. On the other extreme each tag used to annotate posts may be viewed as a category unto itself and a score for each tag per user may be derived to assess the expertise of a user in the post domain. This approach suffers the disadvantage of specialization and scalability. For instance, a user who has answered several questions on *webforms* would most likely be proficient in *asp.net* since *webforms* is a part of the *ASP.NET* web application framework. Thus modeling expertise just on tags may not capture the inherent link between topics represented by tags. Moreover the tag space is huge and thus topics represented by them may run in tens of thousands. Estimating user experience in all these tag topics may not be feasible. In this paper we attempt to investigate the granularity at which the user expertise needs to be computed for aiding in the post score prediction task. Tags which are not well represented may require inputs from the semantic web to augment information about them.

The paper is organized as follows; the next section presents a background literature review of the area. The proposed approach is outlined in section 3 whereas section 4 presents the results of our experiments. We conclude with section 5 and point some directions for the future.

2   Background

2.1   Stack Overflow

Stack Overflow (SO) is a very popular Q & A community forum [1] which focuses on issues related to programming and software development. Different from discussion forums which encourage blog style discussion on various topics, SO posts are expected to be specific issues or concerns pertaining to programming languages/tools and are closely monitored for adherence to posting rules and deviation from the main essence of SO. The SO data is structured around several important entities such as posts, users, tags, votes and comments. A more detailed discussion on the data model used can be found in [5]. SO maintains the quality of posts to an extent by allowing users to vote questions and answers up or down. Other ways to express ones' opinion about a post is to accept an answer, mark a post as favorite etc. Based on the various activities of a user on the forum such as the number of quality question and answers, number of favorite posts etc, a user reputation score is computed. Posts are annotated using tags reflecting the subject of the post.

The availability of the entire SO data in various forms[5][6] has led to several recent research efforts to leverage data and perform mining tasks for purposes ranging from predicting when an answer would be deemed unfit for the forum[7] to assessing the quality of the crowd sourced API documentation produced through SO[8]. A burst of activity in this area is witnessed with several challenges being posed on SO data such as the one on Kaggle for predicting closed questions[9], to predict tags for posts and others[10]. A recent interesting work [4] attempts to predict the quality of question/answer pairs based on various input features gleaned from the dataset. The input parameters for questions and answers differ slightly and are based on criteria such as length of question body and question title, reputation of the person asking question/posting answers etc. SO offers a user friendly web interface through which it exposes the schema of the relations used and allows users to fire SQL queries on a copy of its database [5].

2.2   Approaches to User Expertise Assessment

The score for the user reputation computed though presents an overall picture of the user ability does not exactly indicate the areas of strengths and weaknesses of a particular user. Such a score is particularly useful for tasks such as identifying expert users to answer particular posts, or gauging the post quality of a new post etc.

Various efforts thus have been expended on quantifying the level of knowledge of a user under various domains by analyzing post text, tags, votes etc. The authors in [11] present a discussion on purposive social networks, using SO as an example, where people with similar interests and varied expertise come together and use crowd sourcing technique to solve a common problem. Though they outline a technique to use linked open data to augment the tag set for a post to find related more general tags denoting the category(such as databases for SQL etc.), the paper does not provide a detailed method on how exactly to extract and leverage the data. Moreover no experimental results are reported. Topic Expertise Model (TEM), a probabilistic generative model with GMM hybrid is used in [13] to jointly model topics and expertise by integrating textual content model and link structure analysis. The authors then use an approach called CQARank to measure user interestsand expertise score under different topics. Expertise areas represented by tags and post words are grouped into clusters and the user expertise and interest score for each topic is derived. This score then is used to match user expertise against the post topic and users most likely to answer the question well are identified. A Segmented Topic Model [13] for finding experts for a newly posted question is put forth. The topics are however seeded manually by choosing the top 21 best tags representing a range of topics. Topic models are then used to construct and refine the topic clusters. User expertise is modeled in a manner similar to [12].

The current work differs from the above approaches in the following points. Whereas the approaches discussed above are aimed at identifying expert users to answer posts the proposed approach is for predicting post score. Moreover the use of very few clusters (~10) means that several topics may be grouped under the same category. For e.g. [12] report C# and C++ falling in the same category. However, an expert C++ programmer may not at all be knowledgeable about C#. Similarly an expertise on clusters represented by generic tags such as "debugging" may not be of much use since a user may be very good at answering debugging questions in one tool whereas he may not even be aware of another.

3   User Profiles – Cluster Based, Tag Based and Semantics Based

In this section we describe techniques to model user expertise on various subject areas and subsequently outline the technique to leverage the expertise values for question quality estimation. We concentrate on devising techniques to find scores for questions and not for answer posts. Though the authors in [4] demonstrate that posts questions and the corresponding answers quality are correlated and hence use answer features as additional features to predict the question scores, here our main focus is to accurately predict the question quality when the question has received neither answers nor any votes.

The broad idea is to identify user strengths in terms of the area or domain in which the user can be considered an expert. If a user posted a question belonging to a domain and if the user expertise level in that domain is high then the question is expected to be of a high quality and hence garner more votes. SO does not have any classification of posts based on topics. It however allows the users to annotate questions with subject relevant tags. It is another matter that the tag annotations many a times do not fully capture the post content and in such cases post contents themselves may be analyzed to extract keywords which may be used as additional annotations. In this work we however restrict tags to the ones explicitly assigned to questions.

Let P be the set of question posts containing n_p questions and let T be the set of tags used to annotate the posts s.t. $|T| = n_t$. Let PT be the $n_p \times n_t$ matrix such that

$$PT(p,t) = \begin{cases} 1, & \text{if post p has been tagged with tag t} \\ 0, & \text{otherwise} \end{cases} \tag{1}$$

Each post p has a corresponding score s_p reflecting the general user sentiment as to the quality of the post and a user u_p who is the owner of the post. We investigate various means to model user expertise for a domain. In the simplest model we derive the score of a user for various tags by aggregating the scores of all the posts(question and answers) written by the user for that domain. The score of each question is weighted half whereas the score of the answer is considered as it is. The expertise of the user u for the domain denoted by tag t is computed as

$$TUP(u,t) = \tfrac{1}{2}\sum_{p \in Q_u} PT(p,t) \times score(p) + \sum_{p \in A_u} PT(p,t) \times score(p) \tag{2}$$

where Q_u and A_u are the set of question and answer posts written by user u. An alternative to the above formula could have been to compute the mean of the scores over all the posts related to a tag but then we lose the information about the number of posts related to the tag that were rated highly. The disadvantage of the formula proposed above is that the expertise score computed could be skewed by one post having a high number of votes. This direct approach would henceforth be referred to as the Tag based User Profile (TUP). Once the user profile is constructed, the estimate of user expertise in the question domain is computed as

$$TUE(p,u) = \mathcal{F}\left(TUP\left(u,t1_p\right), TUP\left(u,t2_p\right), ..., TUP\left(u,tn_p\right)\right) \tag{3}$$

where $\mathcal{F}$ is the aggregation function and $t1_p, t2_p ... tn_p$ are the tags associated with post p. The quantity so computed would henceforth be referred to as Tag based User Expertise (TUE). The TUE is computed for the author of a post and is taken as one of the features for question quality assessment (Feature 8 in Table 1).

We extend the approach proposed in [4] and the set of input features to estimate the post quality is listed in Table 1[4] for convenience. We note that the features such as which require data collected in the first 24hours would mean that the feature set cannot be constructed for the first day and hence the post quality during this duration cannot be estimated reliably. We propose to displace/supplement such features with the user expertise scores. The extended feature table is shown in the last part of Table 1 and the other features listed therein would be described further in this section.

Table 1. Question Features considered for score prediction

	Sl.No	Question Features
Basic Features	1	Questioner's reputation when the question is posted
	2	# of Questioner's previous questions when the question is posted
	3	The length of the question
	4	The length of the title
Features computable after 24 hours	5	# of answers received in 24 hours after the question is posted
	6	# of favorites received in 24 hours after the question is posted
	7	# of comments received in 24 hours after the question is posted
Proposed Features	8	Tag based User Expertise (TUE)
	9	Cluster based User Expertise (CUE)
	10	Extended Tag based User Expertise (ETUE)

The disadvantage of the first approach is that related tags may not be recognized and utilized for the purpose of matching post topic with user familiarity with the topic. For instance a post tagged with "Silverlight" (referring to Microsoft Silverlight which is a rich web application development tool) can be matched to a user having expertise in Rich-Internet-Applications (RIA) topic which contains both *Silverlight* as well as software such as *Adobe Flash* which is similar to *Silverlight* in function. Thus matching expertise and a question topic just on the basis of tags may not capture the inherent relationship. It can be argued that a simple co-occurrence count may help in performing this match but many a times due to unreliable tagging of posts by users the co-occurrence pattern does not reveal such relationships. For instance a glance through the most frequently co-occurring tags with Silverlight does not list RIA as one of the components. Moreover for tags which have recently been added a reliable estimate of related tags may not be possible due to the sparse usage of the tag.

For this purpose we utilize information available through semantic web for the expanding the tag base. SO contains a wiki post for most of the tags used therein which contain a brief description of the tag. The first paragraph in the wiki post was extracted and was fed as input to the *OpenCalais* tool to extract the entities and relations. The *OpenCalais* tool in addition to listing the entities also gives as output the topic associated and the confidence level. Since the information gathered from the Semantic Web is used to find associated tags to already existing tags there may be tags related to entities detected which may not be present in the current set of tags. Such tags are added to the tag set to form an expanded set of tags. A tag t1 which is detected while analyzing the wiki post of another tag t2 is added as an associated tag of t2 only when its topic is related to *Technology and Internet* and the confidence level of detection is above a certain threshold T. Some of the tags do not have any associated wiki posts. For such tags we extract the tag description from DBPedia through the SPARQL interface provided. To search for the Wikipedia and corresponding DBPedia entry for a tag we make use of the simple Wikipedia tool available. Once the record for the tag is extracted from DBPedia the first paragraph in the abstract is extracted and analyzed to find related tags. Let T' be the extended set of tags such that $|T'| = n'$ and let $A_{n' \times n'}$ be the tag association matrix. The entry $A(t1, t2) > 0$, if tag t2 is semantically associated with tag t1 and the entry $A(t1, t2)$ is set to a default value d. In our experiments we set the value of d to be 0.2. In addition to deriving tag associations through relations inferred through the semantic web the co-occurrence pattern can also reveal tag relations. The co-occurrence degree for tag *t2* with respect to tag *t1* is defined as

$$co\_occurence(t1, t2) = \frac{Number\ of\ posts\ tagged\ with\ t1\ and\ t2}{Number\ of\ posts\ tagged\ with\ t1} \qquad (4)$$

The tag association matrix A is updated as only if $co\_occurence(t1, t2)$ is greater than d:

$$A(t1, t2) = \max\left(A(t1, t2), co\_occurence(t1, t2)\right) \qquad (5)$$

Moreover a tag t1 can be considered a specialized version of another tag t2 if it is textually the same as t2 but with an additional version number, for instance "python" and "python-3.x". In such cases we make the entry $A(t1, t2) = 1$. The expertise of a user for a post using the extended tag set T' and the tag association matrix A, termed **Extended Tag based User Profile (XTUP)**, is derived as an extension to the equation (2):

$$XTUP(u, t) = \frac{1}{2}\sum_{p \in Q_u} score(p) \times max(\underset{t' \in T'}{sumK}(PT(p, t') \times A(t', t)), 1) +$$
$$\sum_{p \in A_u} score(p) \times max(\underset{t' \in T'}{sumK}(PT(p, t') \times A(t', t))) \qquad (6)$$

where *sumK(s1,s2,....,sn)* computes the sum of the K maximum elements in the set {*s1,...,sn*}. The above formula ensures that if several tags associated with the post are associated to tag *t* then the possibility of the indirect tag match of *t* with the post increases but doesn't increase beyond 1. The corresponding user expertise assessment for a post is computed by first accumulating an extended set of tags for a post. In addition to the set of tags assigned to a post the set of tags associated with the assigned tags along with their association degree can be deemed to be the actual extended set of tags assigned to the post. If T_p is the set of tags assigned to the post p, then the set of tags associations can be computed as:

$$PT'(p,t) = \max\left(\sum_{t'\in T} PT(p,t') \times A(t',t), 1\right) \tag{7}$$

where $t'_1, t'_2, \dots, t'_{n_p}$ are the set of tags associated with post p. The user expertise is calculated as follows and is referred to as Extended Tag based User Expertise (XTUE).

$$XTUE(p,u) =$$

$$\mathcal{F}(PT'(p,t1) \times XTUP(u,t1), \dots, PT'(p,t_{n_{p'}}) \times$$

$$XTUP(u,t_{n_{p'}})) \tag{8}$$

where $\mathcal{F}$ is the aggregation operator. The score computed for the owner of a post is considered as feature 10(Table 1). To compare the two user expertise models proposed above we compare it against already proposed means for expertise computation where the tags are clustered into a pre-set bunch of clusters (~10) and an expertise level is derived per-cluster. The clustering can be achieved using topic models such as LDA as proposed in [11][12]. If W is the matrix such that $W(t,c)$ denotes the degree to which the tag t belongs to the cluster c, then the user expertise of a user for a cluster can be derived as:

$$CUE(u,c) = \frac{1}{2}\sum_{p\in Q_u} score(p) \times \max_{t'\in T}(sumK(PT(p,t) \times W(t,c)), 1) +$$
$$\sum_{p\in A_u} score(p) \times \max_{t\in T}(sumK(PT(p,t) \times W(t,c))) \tag{9}$$

The user expertise using tag clusters can be calculated in a manner similar to Eq. (7) above and is termed Cluster based User Expertise (CUE) and considered as Feature 9(Table 1). Once the augmented feature set is constructed the weights for the features are learnt using linear regression as advocated in [4] and the scores for the question are predicted.

4   Experimental Evaluation

In this section we determine the effectiveness of the new features for question quality estimation proposed above by performing experiments comparing the results with the other attributes as suggested in [4]. The data is taken from SO by downloading the data dump made available at the website [14]. The dataset consisted of 6473505 posts posted by 3210608 users. We used the first 100000 question posts ordered chronologically for the experiments. To evaluate the effectiveness of the various methods the posts were randomly divided into training and test sets such that 50% of the posts are in the training and 50% are in the test set. While the training set is used to derive the weights for the various features, the test set is used to assess the quality of predictions offered by the various methods.

The quality of the predictions are gauged based on the actual error in prediction as well as precision and recall metrics. The relative prediction error is computed as

$$err = \frac{1}{n_p}\sum_{p\in P}\frac{|pr_p - sc_p|}{sc_p + 1} \tag{10}$$

where pr_p is the predicted score for post p and sc_p is the actual score for the post p. When the requirement is to have the higher scoring posts to be displayed to the user then the actual error in prediction does not matter as much as correctly classifying high and low quality posts. Precision and Recall metrics are used to assess the classification accuracy metrics. If L the is the length of the list of posts displayed to the user as being of high quality Precision measures the number of high quality posts among all the posts in the list whereas Recall measures the fraction of actual high quality posts to the ones displayed to the user. We deem a post p to be of high quality if $s_p > \mu + 2\sigma$, where μ is the mean σ is the standard deviation of post score across all posts.

When a post is introduced in the SO forum the features 5-7 cannot be computed. In such a case we compare the prediction accuracy excluding these features and compare the value add that the proposed features offer over using only the feature set 1-4. To do this we first evaluate each feature individually i.e. we attempt prediction with features 1-4 and 8, features 1-4 and 9 etc. The quality improvement, if any, is then attempted by including all the proposed features in addition to the features 1-4. We also investigate the value of augmenting all the features proposed in [4] (i.e. features 1-7, which can be estimated after 24 hours) with the proposed features.

To evaluate the prediction accuracy using the various methods, we perform several run of the experiments and the results obtained are shown in Fig.1. It is evident from the graph shown in Fig. 1 that across all runs the lowest prediction error is achieved by retaining the feature set proposed in [4] and not including any of the proposed features. Adding all the features (i.e. Feature 8-10) results in the worst performance. Augmenting the original feature set with feature 9, i.e. feature derived based on cluster user expertise performs better than individually adding the other proposed features.

This work is aimed at positioning posts in the list displayed to the user so that the high quality posts are positioned at the top. Here the interest is not to predict the score accurately but to be able to identify the top few posts. The results of comparing the precision of the various methods is shown in Fig 2.We demonstrate the results of our experiments by varying the size of L, the list size displayed to the user. It can be clearly seen that augmenting all the proposed features to the feature set 1-4 gives the best performance. In fact considering all the features gives a lower precision. Thus even after obtaining the features computable after the first 24 hours appending them only results in a reduced value of precision. The worst performer in this category is when only the basic features are considered. When adding individual proposed features (i.e. 8-10) to the basic feature set, it can be observed that addition of feature 8 based only on tags results in the maximum increase in the precision whereas the cluster based feature leads to the least increase.

A graph comparing the recall obtained using the various features is presented in Fig. 3. A trend similar to precision can be witnessed here too. As the list size increases the recall increases for all the methods. However utilizing all the proposed features along with the basic features works the best with the highest recall across all list sizes. Again using all the features slightly lowers the recall. The worst performance is obtained while using only the basic set of features and individually adding the feature 8 to the basic feature set results in the maximum increase in recall.

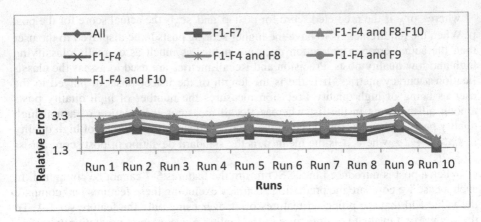

Fig. 1. Comparison of Prediction Accuracy for the various combinations with varying list sizes

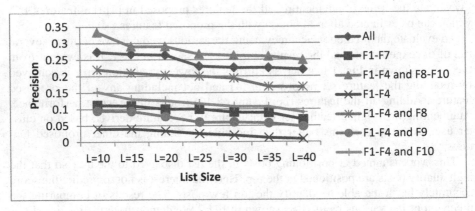

Fig. 2. Comparison of Precision for the various combinations with varying list sizes

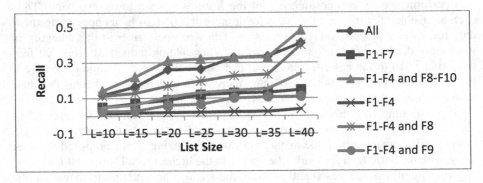

Fig. 3. Comparison of Recall for the various combinations with varying list sizes

5   Conclusions and Future Directions

The task of effectively assessing the quality of posts when they are introduced into a Q&A forum is addressed in this paper. This task is crucial since it leads to an increase in the visibility of high quality posts thus improving the likelihood of the corresponding issues to be addressed and benefitting a large user base. We extend the work presented in [4] by improvising on the input feature set used for question quality prediction in the absence of some of the features. We proposed a user expertise based model for constructing question features which are based on the intuition that a user possessing high skill sets in the subject area to which the question belongs may be expected to write posts of high quality. Tags assigned to questions are used for this approach and the tag-based method is extended to expand the tag set to contain semantically similar concepts related to the tags. Experiments reveal that the introduction of the new features do not result in any improvement in the prediction accuracy but rather cause the error to increase.

The current work did not find any significant benefits of applying the semantic similarity concepts to the domain expertise estimation and subsequently the question quality prediction but in the future we would explore other methods of exploiting the same. For instance, instead of expanding the tag sets, specific tags would be replaced by general tags. For instance "mysql2" may be replaced by "mysql" and "inheritance" by "oops". This would result in a more compact set of tags with the inherent links captured, but replacing specific tags with generic ones is not so straightforward and might require a more in-depth analysis of tag wikis/descriptions etc.

It is to be noted that a question voted with several votes need not necessarily be of "good quality" but may be more popular. For instance a question *"What is the difference between reference and pointer?"* is not really a novel or unique question but the vote count of the question is high maybe due to the popularity factor. An alternative would be to weight the votes for a question with the reputation or expertise of the user in the domain to which the question belongs. Thus a user's reputation is correlated to the number of high quality questions/answers he asks/answers and a question/answer is of high quality if it has been voted highly by reputed user. An argument for each case i.e. whether a question is to be displayed higher in the list if it is popular or of high quality can be made and is a question which can be taken up as a separate research direction.

It may also be noted that the text of the questions themselves are not explored in the proposed approach. The post text contains important information about the subject content or type of question not reflected by the tags themselves. Mining such a source could lead to greater insights and better matching of the posed questions with the experts and offers another possibility to work on.

References

1. Data Mining Reveals the Secret to Getting Good Answers,
   http://www.technologyreview.com/view/522171/data-mining-reveals-the-secret-to-getting-good-answers/
2. Correa, D., Sureka, A.: Fit or Unfit: Analysis and Prediction of 'Closed Questions' on Stack Overflow. In: Proceedings of the ACM Conference on Online Social Networks. ACM, Boston (2013)

3. Riahi, F., Zolaktaf, Z., Shafiei, M., Milios, E.: Finding Expert Users in Community Question Answering. In: Proceedings of the 21st International Conference Companion on World Wide Web, Lyon, France, April 16-20, pp. 791–798 (2012)
4. Yao, Y., Tong, H., Xie, T., Akoglu, L., Xu, F., Lu, J.: Want a Good Answer? Ask a Good Question First!, arXiv:1311.6876 (2013)
5. http://data.stackexchange.com/stackoverflow/
6. Fullerton, D.: Stack Exchange Creative Commons data now hosted by the Internet Archive, http://blog.stackexchange.com/category/cc-wiki-dump/ (January 23, 2014)
7. Correa, D., Sureka, A.: Fit or Unfit: Analysis and Prediction of 'Closed Questions' on Stack 'Overflow', arXiv:1307.7291 (2013)
8. Parnin, C., Treude, C., Grammel, L., Storey, M.: Crowd Documentation: Exploring the Coverage and the Dynamics of API Discussions on Stack Overflow, Georgia Tech Technical Report GIT-CS-12-05 (2013)
9. http://www.kaggle.com/c/predict-closed-questions-on-stack-overflow
10. http://2013.msrconf.org/challenge.php
11. Singh, P., Shadbolt, N.: Linked Data in Crowdsourcing Purposive Social Network. In: International World Wide Web Conferences Steering Committee, WWW Companion Volume, pp. 913–918. ACM (2013)
12. Yang, L., Qiu, M., Gottipati, S., Zhu, F., Jiang, J., Sun, H., Chen, Z.: CQARank: Jointly Model Topics and Expertise in Community Question Answering. In: Proceedings of the 22nd ACM International Conference on Conference on Information & Knowledge Management, pp. 99–108 (2013)
13. Riahi, F., Zolaktaf, Z., Shafiei, M., Milios, E.: Finding Expert Users in Community Question Answering. In: Proceedings of the 21st International Conference Companion on World Wide Web, Lyon, France, pp. 791–798 (2012)
14. https://archive.org/details/stackexchange

SQLiDDS: SQL Injection Detection Using Query Transformation and Document Similarity

Debabrata Kar[1], Suvasini Panigrahi[2], and Srikanth Sundararajan[3]

[1] Department of Computer Science and Engineering
Silicon Institute of Technology, Bhubaneswar, India
debabrata.kar@silicon.ac.in

[2] Department of Computer Science and Engineering
VSS University of Technology, Burla, Sambalpur, India
suvasini26@gmail.com

[3] Indian Institute of Technology Bhubaneswar, India
(currently at Helion Advisors, Bangalore, India)
sundararajan.srikanth@gmail.com

Abstract. SQL Injection Attack has been a major security threat to web applications since last 15 years. Nowadays, hackers use automated tools to discover vulnerable websites and launch mass injection attacks. Accurate run-time detection of SQL injection has been a challenge in spite of extensive research in this area. This paper presents a novel approach for real-time detection of SQL injection attacks using query transformation and document similarity measure. Acting as a database firewall, the proposed system named SQLiDDS, can protect multiple web applications using the database server. With additional inputs from human expert, SQLiDDS can also become more robust over time. Our experimental results confirm that this approach can effectively detect and prevent all types of SQL injection attacks with good accuracy yet negligible impact on system performance. The approach was tested on web applications built using PHP and MySQL, however it can be easily adopted in other platforms with minimal changes.

Keywords: sql injection detection, query transformation, sql injection prevention, document similarity, database firewall, phrase similarity.

1 Introduction

Web applications are exposed to various types of security threats among which SQL Injection attack is predominantly used against web databases. The Open Web Application Security Project (OWASP) ranks it on top among the Top-10 security threats [1]. According to TrustWave 2012 Global Security Report[2], SQL injection was the *number one* attack method for four consecutive years. Nowadays, attackers use sophisticated *Botnets*[3] which automatically discover vulnerable web pages from search engines like *Google* and launch mass SQL injection attacks from distributed sources. About 97% of data breaches across the world occur due to SQL injection alone [4].

R. Natarajan et al. (Eds.): ICDCIT 2015, LNCS 8956, pp. 377–390, 2015.
© Springer International Publishing Switzerland 2015

Research on SQL injection in the literature can be broadly categorized into: *defensive coding* practices, *vulnerability testing* approaches, and *prevention* based approaches. Defensive coding practices[5–7] consist of techniques applied during application development and require programming in a specific way, but in practice, programmers often ignore the security aspects. On the other hand, vulnerability testing approaches [8–10] rely on discovering possible SQL injection hotspots so that they can be fixed before deployment. The effectiveness of this approach is limited by the number of security issues identified. Majority of the research on SQL injection has been done under prevention based approaches. In general, prevention based approaches like [11–15] consist of preparing a model of SQL queries and/or the application's behavior during *normal-use* in a secured environment and then utilize the model at run-time to prevent SQL injection attempts. Any modifications or enhancements to the application code requires rebuilding the normal-use model, which is a major disadvantage of this approach. Further, these are mostly designed to protect a single web application and usually suitable for a specific language and database platform.

In this paper, we present a novel technique to detect SQL injection attacks by applying document similarity on transformed queries. Document similarity is typically used in information retrieval domain. We implemented the technique in a tool we named SQLiDDS (*SQL* *i*njection *D*etection using *D*ocument *S*imilarity) and validated the approach on five sample web applications. The query transformation scheme and application of document similarity concept for detecting SQL injection attacks are the main contributions of our work. Based on interesting observations made during the course of research, we postulate that, it is *sufficient* to examine only the WHERE clause part of run-time queries for detecting injection attacks, which is another significant contribution. SQLiDDS can protect multiple web applications interacting with a database server (as in shared hosting environments), which is an advantage over existing methods.

Rest of the paper is organized as follows. Section 2 explains the mechanism of SQL injection attack by example. Section 3 discusses our approach in detail covering the query transformation scheme, document similarity measure, and architecture of SQLiDDS. Experimental results are discussed in Sect. 4 along with assessment of performance overhead. Quoting related works in Sect. 5, we conclude the paper in Sect. 6 with future directions of research.

2   SQL Injection Attack

SQL injection attacks occur due to a commonly found vulnerability of using raw input data received through web forms or URL parameters without proper validation to construct dynamic SQL queries. Attackers exploit this vulnerability by inserting carefully crafted SQL keywords and values, effectively altering the semantics of dynamic queries, and causing them to return results intended by the attacker. To understand the basic mechanism, consider a product detail page of an E-commerce website accessed by clicking a link to the URL:

```
http://www.somewebstore.com/product_details.php?pid=24
```

The script `product_details.php` becomes vulnerable to SQL injection if the programmer uses the parameter `pid` to construct an SQL query without proper validation or type-checking. For example, in the following PHP code:

```
$query = "SELECT * FROM products WHERE prod_id = ".$_GET['pid'];
$result = mysql_query($query, $dbconn);
```

the parameter `pid` has been used directly for constructing the dynamic query assuming that an integer value (e.g., 24) will be always received. However, if an attacker adds " OR 1 = 1" to the URL then the string value "24 OR 1 = 1" will be used in the code which will generate the query as "SELECT * FROM products WHERE prod_id = 24 OR 1 = 1". Upon execution, it will return the entire *products* table as the query evaluates to *true* for all rows. This is an example of the simplest type of SQL injection known as *tautological attack*. There are several other types of SQL injection attacks[16], using which an attacker can steal sensitive information from other database tables.

Commercial Intrusion Detection Systems (IDS) and Web Application Firewalls (WAF) mostly rely on regular expression based filters created from known attack signatures. However, signature-based filters can be circumvented using a number of bypassing techniques [17, 18]. For example, consider the following attacks, showing only the injection code added by an attacker:

```
OR 'A' = 'A'
OR -5.24 = 17.43 - 22.67
OR 419320 = 0x84B22 - 0x1E52A
OR 'ABC' = CONCAT('A', 'B', 'C')
OR 'ABC' = CoNcAt(cHaR(0x28 + 25), cHaR(0x42), cHAr(80 - 0x0d))
OR 'XYZ' = sUbStRiNg(cOncAt('AB', 'CX', 'YZ', 'EF'), 4, 3)
OR 'XYZ' = /*!SuBsTrInG(*/CoNcAt('aB',/*!'cX','YZ',*/'eF')/*!,4,3)*/
```

All of these expressions evaluate to true, hence they are tautological attacks. Similar bypassing techniques can also be used in other types of SQL injection attacks. SQL injection attack expressions can be formed in a number of ways to the extent that constructing regular expression based filters becomes almost impossible. Signature based systems can be eluded by the attacker with creative changes to the injected expressions with a little effort.

3   Proposed Approach

Two key ideas, the query transformation scheme and application of document similarity measure, constitute the core of our approach. The system begins with an initial set of SQL injection attacks collected from honeypot web applications. These are converted into text form using a transformation scheme and then grouped into clusters by their document similarity. Attack vectors in each cluster are merged into a document. Each document thus contains a set of highly similar attack vectors. At run-time, SQL injection attacks are detected by comparing the document similarity of an incoming query with these documents. Rest of this section describes our approach and architecture of SQLiDDS in detail.

3.1   Query Transformation Scheme

We developed an extension of the transformation scheme proposed in [19], so that it normalizes an SQL query into a sentence-like form, and facilitates application of document similarity measure. The extended scheme uses only capital A-Z for all tokens and space character as token separator. All symbols and special characters are also transformed into words except the *underscore* (_) character, because it is frequently used in MySQL system databases, system tables and functions, e.g., `information_schema`, `table_priv`, `CURRENT_USER()`, `LAST_INSERT_ID()`, etc. Splitting such tokens at the underscore character would result in over tokenization and negatively affect the similarity values. The step-by-step process of transforming an SQL query has been detailed in Table 1.

Table 1. The Extended Query Transformation Scheme

Step	Token/Symbol	Transform
1.	Newline characters (\r or \n) if any	Remove
2.	Inline Comments (/*...*/) if any	Remove
3.	Anything within single/double quotes	
	(a) Hexadecimal value	HEX
	(b) Decimal value	DEC
	(c) Integer value	INT
	(d) IP address	IPADDR
	(e) Single alphabet character	CHR
	(f) General string (none of the above)	STR
4.	Anything outside single/double quotes	
	(a) Hexadecimal value	HEX
	(b) Decimal value	DEC
	(c) Integer value	INT
	(d) IP address	IPADDR
5.	System objects	
	(a) System databases	SYSDB
	(b) System tables	SYSTBL
	(c) System table column	SYSCOL
	(d) System variable	SYSVAR
	(e) System views	SYSVW
	(f) System stored procedure	SYSPROC
6.	User-defined objects	
	(a) User databases	USRDB
	(b) User tables	USRTBL
	(c) User table column	USRCOL
	(d) User-defined views	USRVW
	(e) User-defined stored procedures	USRPROC
	(f) User-defined functions	USRFUNC
7.	SQL keywords, functions and reserved words	To Uppercase
8.	Any token/word not transformed so far	
	(a) Single alphabet	CHR
	(b) Alpha-numeric without space	STR
9.	Other symbols and special characters	As per Table 2
10.	The entire query	To Uppercase
11.	Multiple spaces	Single Space

Each step of query transformation is a find-and-replace operation, done by appropriately using the `preg_replace()` and `str_replace()` built-in functions available in PHP. For example, `preg_replace("/\b0x[0-9a-f]+\b/i", "HEX", $query)` converts hexadecimal numbers in `$query` into `HEX` in a case-insensitive

Table 2. Transformation of Special Characters and Symbols

Symbol	Name	Transform	Symbol	Name	Transform
`	Backtick	Remove	(	Opening Parenthesis	LPRN
!= or <>	Not Equals	NEQ	)	Closing Parenthesis	RPRN
&&	Logical AND	AND	{	Opening Brace	LCBR
||	Logical OR	OR	}	Closing Brace	RCBR
~	Tilde	TLDE	[	Opening Bracket	LSQBR
!	Exclaimation	EXCLM	]	Closing Bracket	RSQBR
@	At-the-rate	ATR	\	Back Slash	BSLSH
#	Pound	HASH	:	Colon	CLN
$	Dollar	DLLR	;	Semi-colon	SMCLN
%	Percent	PRCNT	"	Double Quote	DQUT
^	Caret	XOR	'	Single Quote	SQUT
&	Ampersand	BITAND	<	Less Than	LT
|	Pipe or Bar	BITOR	>	Greater Than	GT
*	Asterisk	STAR	,	Comma	CMMA
-	Hyphen/Minus	MINUS	.	Stop or Period	DOT
+	Addition/Plus	PLUS	?	Question Mark	QSTN
=	Equals	EQ	/	Forward Slash	SLSH

manner. All symbols and special characters are transformed in Step–9 as per the scheme given in Table 2. The last two steps convert the transformed query to uppercase and reduce multi-spaces to single spaces. To visualize how the transformation scheme works, consider the following SQL queries, intentionally written in mixed-case to show the effect of transformation.

```
sEleCt * fRoM products wHeRe price > 10.00 aNd discount < 8
SeLeCt email FrOm customers WhErE fname LIKE 'john%'
```

By applying the transformation scheme, the above queries are transformed into the following form respectively:

```
SELECT STAR FROM USRTBL WHERE USRCOL GT DEC AND USRCOL LT INT
SELECT USRCOL FROM USRTBL WHERE USRCOL LIKE SQUT STR PRCNT SQUT
```

Consider an injected query generated due to a cleverly crafted attack to bypass detection (taken from the examples given in Sect. 2):

```
SELECT * FROM products WHERE prod_id = 24 OR 'ABC' = CoNcAt(cHaR(0x28 +
25), cHaR(0x42), cHAr(80 - 0x0d))
```

This query contains a number of symbols and operators, which is not suitable for application of a document similarity measure. The transformation scheme converts it completely into text form as:

```
SELECT STAR FROM USRTBL WHERE USRCOL EQ INT OR SQUT STR SQUT EQ CONCAT
LPRN CHAR LPRN HEX PLUS INT RPRN CMMA CHAR LPRN HEX RPRN CMMA CHAR LPRN
INT MINUS HEX RPRN RPRN
```

Any SQL query, irrespective of its complexity, is thus transformed into a series of words separated by spaces like a sentence in English. The structural form of the query is correctly maintained by the transformation scheme.

3.2   Document Similarity Measure

Several document similarity measures are available in the literature, out of which the vector space model (VSM) using term-frequency (TF) and inverse-document-frequency (IDF) weighting is widely used in information retrieval [20, Chap. 6]. In this model, two documents d_i and d_j are represented in vector form by the TF-IDF term weights as $\vec{d_i} = \langle w_{t_1,d_i}, w_{t_2,d_i}, \ldots, w_{t_n,d_i} \rangle$ and $\vec{d_j} = \langle w_{t_1,d_j}, w_{t_2,d_j}, \ldots, w_{t_n,d_j} \rangle$. Similarity between the documents is computed as the cosine of the angle θ between the document vectors. Formally,

$$Sim(d_i, d_j) = \cos(\theta) = \frac{\vec{d_i} \cdot \vec{d_j}}{\|\vec{d_i}\| \|\vec{d_j}\|} = \frac{\sum_{k=1}^{n} w_{t_k,d_i} w_{t_k,d_j}}{\sqrt{\sum_{k=1}^{n} w_{t_k,d_i}^2} \sqrt{\sum_{k=1}^{n} w_{t_k,d_j}^2}} \tag{1}$$

Although TF-IDF weighting is popular in information retrieval domain and has been used for intrusion detection in [21, 22], our experiments did not produce acceptable results using this measure. A major shortcoming of this measure is that it ignores the order of occurrence of terms in the document. For example, *"John is older than Mary"* and *"Mary is older than John"*, are determined as identical documents. The loss of term-order can be overcome by considering *phrases* instead of individual terms. By phrase, we mean a contiguous sequence of terms, not the syntactical or structural clauses of SQL. A phrase in this context is same as an N-gram where each *gram* corresponds to a term.

Considering that a document d is a sequence of terms $(t_1, t_2, \ldots, t_n)$, phrases are extracted by sliding a window of size w across the document, i.e., every phrase contains w terms. This is termed as *phrase length*. For example, if the phrase length is 2, then the phrases extracted are $(t_1 t_2, t_2 t_3, t_3 t_4, \ldots, t_{n-1} t_n)$. The number of phrases in a document therefore equals to $(n - w + 1)$. Let the phrases extracted from two documents d_i and d_j be $P_i = (p_{i_1}, p_{i_2}, \ldots, p_{i_m})$ and $P_j = (p_{j_1}, p_{j_2}, \ldots, p_{j_n})$ respectively. Then, the set of unique phrases in both the documents is $P = P_i \cup P_j = \{p_1, p_2, \ldots, p_k\}$ where $k \leq m + n$; the upper bound occurs when the documents are dissimilar. The documents can now be represented in vector form in k-dimensions by the frequency of the phrases they contain as $\vec{d_i} = \langle f_{p_1,d_i}, f_{p_2,d_i}, \ldots, f_{p_k,d_i} \rangle$ and $\vec{d_j} = \langle f_{p_1,d_j}, f_{p_2,d_j}, \ldots, f_{p_k,d_j} \rangle$. Following (1), phrase-based cosine similarity can be computed by:

$$Sim(d_i, d_j) = \frac{\sum_{q=1}^{k} f_{p_q,d_i} f_{p_q,d_j}}{\sqrt{\sum_{q=1}^{k} f_{p_q,d_i}^2} \sqrt{\sum_{q=1}^{k} f_{p_q,d_j}^2}} \tag{2}$$

The similarity computed by (2) is indirectly dependent on the phrase-length w. Taking $w = 1$ is same as computing similarity by unweighted term frequencies. A natural question arises – how to choose the appropriate phrase length? A rational answer is obtained by looking at the classic injection attack "OR 1 = 1" which gets transformed to "OR INT EQ INT" – containing four words. In rest of the paper, we adopt the phrase length $w = 4$ for computing similarity.

3.3 Detection Strategy of SQLiDDS

Design of SQLiDDS is strategically guided by two interesting observations which we were unable to find mentioned anywhere in the literature. The first observation surfaced while looking for an answer to *"where do SQL injections most commonly occur in an injected query?"* Looking at the general coding practices for developing web applications, we find that, dynamic SQL queries are usually constructed in two parts: (1) a static part hard coded by the programmer, and (2) a dynamic part produced by concatenation of SQL keywords, delimiters and received input values. Since the main objective of a dynamic query is to fetch different set of records depending on the input, the parameter values must be used in the WHERE clause to specify the *selection criteria*. This compulsive programming need as well as the de facto practice of using input values in the WHERE clause part of dynamic queries resolves that SQL injections happen after the WHERE keyword, almost in all cases. In fact, SQL injection before the WHERE keyword is extremely rare – not a single instance was found in over 16,500 queries containing SQL injection attacks we examined for this study.

The second interesting observation stems from the *basic intention* behind an SQL injection attack – stealing sensitive information from the back-end database, such as credit card numbers. By carefully formulating the injection code, the attacker tries to get the intended data displayed on the web page itself, which is the only method for data breach through SQL injection. Data is fetched by SELECT queries in SQL, which implies that unless the injectable parameter is used to construct a dynamic SELECT query that delivers data displayed on the web page, it is not useful for data breach. This points to another assertion that SQL injections mostly occur through dynamically generated SELECT queries.

The above observations lead to the strategic inference that, it is *sufficient* to examine the part of an SQL query after the WHERE keyword in order to detect the presence of any injection attack, which significantly narrows down the scope of processing. Another plausible strategy may be to intercept only SELECT queries for examination, however, this may enable the attacker to cause damage to the data, if not breach. As such, by considering the part of a query after the WHERE keyword, we automatically include UPDATE and DELETE queries in the investigation, because they also support a WHERE clause by SQL syntax.

A cognizant question may be raised concerning a special kind of attack, known as *Second Order SQL Injection*, which is initiated through INSERT queries. In this method, the attacker submits values containing injected code through form fields (e.g., a registration form) which is not executed at that time, but gets stored in the database as normal data. It takes effect when another part of the web application uses that stored value in a dynamic query. It is interesting to note that: 1) the victim dynamic query must be a SELECT query fetching data for display on the web page, and 2) the stored value containing injected code must be used in its WHERE clause. By detecting injection in the WHERE clause, the secondary attack would render ineffective. Therefore, the strategy to examine only the portion of queries after the WHERE keyword is correct and sufficient for detecting SQL injection attacks, including second order injections.

3.4   Architecture of SQLiDDS

Figure 1 shows the detail architecture of our approach. SQLiDDS operates in two phases: (1) offline phase, and (2) run-time phase. The offline phase begins with a collection of SQL injected queries (discussed in Sect. 4.1). The portion of the injected queries after the first WHERE keyword are extracted and converted to text form using the transformation scheme. A major advantage of the transformation scheme is that several queries get converted into the same form, which greatly reduces space and processing. The distinct transformed structures are stored in the *injected structures database.* The MD5 hash value of each structure is computed and stored separately in a *reference hash table,* which helps avoiding similarity computation for every incoming query at run-time. The distinct injected structures are also clustered into groups based on their phrase similarity (discussed in Sect. 4.2). Each cluster is merged into a single document and saved in a document repository. Each document thus contains a set of highly similar injection patterns against which queries will be compared at run-time.

The offline phase completes with creation of the reference hash table and the documents of injected structures, making SQLiDDS ready for deployment as a database firewall between the web server and database server. Two thresholds, (1) Rejection Threshold (R_{th}), and (2) Suspicious Threshold (S_{th}) are defined in SQLiDDS configuration, such that $R_{th} > S_{th}$.

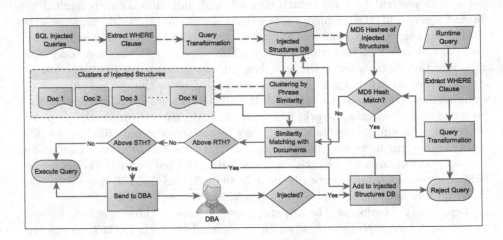

Fig. 1. Architecture of SQLiDDS (dashed: offline, solid: run-time)

At run-time, SQLiDDS intercepts queries issued by web applications to the database server. The portion of a run-time query after the first WHERE keyword is extracted and normalized using the query transformation scheme. If its MD5 hash is found in the reference hash table, it is confirmed as an injection attack and the query is rejected without any further check. When a match is not found, its phrase similarity with the documents is computed. If the similarity with any document is $\geq R_{th}$, the query is determined as an injection attack and rejected. It is added to the injected structures database and its MD5 hash is added to the reference hash table. As a new structure is added, clustering is redone and the set of documents is regenerated by merging structures of each cluster.

If the highest similarity with the documents is below R_{th} but $\geq S_{th}$, the query is allowed to execute, but tagged as *suspicious* and logged for scrutiny by the DBA. If the DBA marks the query as *malicious*, then its MD5 hash is added to the reference hash table, which ensures that next time the same attack is instantly detected. In addition, the pattern is added to the injected structures database, clustering process is repeated, and a fresh set of documents are generated by merging the injection patterns in each cluster. This increases the probability of detecting similar injection attacks in future. In this manner, the system learns new injection patterns and becomes more robust over time.

4   Experimental Setup and Evaluation

The experimental setup consisted of a standard desktop computer with Intel® Core-i3™ 2100 CPU @ 3.10GHz and 2GB RAM, running CentOS 5.3 Server OS, Apache 2.2.3 web server with PHP 5.3.28 configured as Apache module, and MySQL 5.5.29 database server. Five web applications; namely, Bookstore (e-commerce), Forum, Classifieds, NewsPortal, and JobPortal, developed using PHP and MySQL, were installed on the server computer simulating a shared hosting environment. Each web application was built with features similar to real websites, however the code was intentionally written *without* any input validation so that they are entirely vulnerable to SQL injection attacks.

4.1   Collection of Injected Queries

SQLiDDS requires an initial collection of injected queries to begin the offline phase. Due to unavailability of any standard real-world data set, we generated the same using a honeypot based technique. First, we switched on the General Query Log[1] option of the MySQL database server, which enables logging of every incoming SQL query. Three out of the five sample web applications, namely Bookstore, Classifieds, and JobPortal, were subjected to SQL injection attacks using a number of automated vulnerability scanners and SQL injection tools downloaded from the Internet, such as: HP Scrawler, WebCruiser Pro, Wapiti, Skipfish, NetSparker (community edition), SQL Power Injector, BSQL Hacker, NTO SQL Invader, sqlmap, sqlsus, The Mole, IronWasp, jSQL Injector, etc. An excellent penetration testing platform based on Debian, known as Kali Linux[2], comes bundled with several additional scanners and exploitation tools such as grabber, bbqsql, nikto, w3af, vega, etc., which were also applied.

Some SQL injection scripts were also downloaded from hacker and community sites such as Simple SQLi Dumper (Perl), darkMySQL (Python), SQL Sentinel

---

[1] http://dev.mysql.com/doc/refman/5.5/en/query-log.html
[2] Formerly known as BackTrack Linux: http://www.kali.org/

(Java), etc., and applied on the three websites. Each tool was applied multiple times with different settings to ensure that all possible types of SQL injection attack patterns are captured. We also applied injection attacks on the three websites using several tips and tricks collected from tutorials, forums, and black hat sites. During the entire process, all SQL queries generated by the web applications were recorded by MySQL server in the general query log.

Over 4.52 million lines were written into the log files from which 3.35 million SQL queries were extracted. After removing duplicates, INSERT queries, and queries without a WHERE clause, total 245,356 nos. of unique SELECT, UPDATE, and DELETE queries were obtained, containing genuine as well as injected queries. Each query was manually examined and the injected queries were separated. Out of the 49,273 injected queries identified, 16,702 unique queries were obtained, containing a natural mix of all types of SQL injection attacks. The portion after the first WHERE keyword of these queries were extracted and normalized using the transformation scheme producing 3,896 distinct injection attack patterns. The patterns were stored in the injected structures database and their MD5 hashes were stored in the reference hash table.

4.2   Clustering of the Injection Patterns

Various document clustering algorithms used in information retrieval have been described in [20, Ch.16-17]. Since the number of clusters cannot be guessed apriori, algorithms like k-means are not useful for our approach. Hierarchical clustering algorithm, on the other hand, does not require the number of clusters to be prespecified. Though it has at least $\Theta(n^2)$ complexity, it is not a bottleneck because: (1) the data set is not very large, (2) clustering is done once in the offline phase, and (3) re-clustering is required only when a new injection pattern is added to the database. We used Hierarchical Agglomerative Clustering (HAC) using the average-link method. The cutoff similarity was determined as 0.664 which yielded 106 clusters including 19 singletons. The injection patterns in each cluster were merged and saved as documents. The phrases of each document were pre-extracted for efficiency and stored in comma separated format.

4.3   Run-Time Results

The five sample web applications were used for run-time evaluation without any changes to their input handling. The thresholds R_{th} and S_{th} were empirically determined and set as 0.83 and 0.68 respectively. With SQLiDDS activated to intercept incoming queries, the web applications were attacked by using the automated tools and manual techniques mentioned in Sect. 4.1. The results of the first run (i.e., without DBA involvement) are shown in Table 3, where the numbers are unique instances of queries extracted from SQLiDDS logs.

The experimental results confirm that SQLiDDS exhibits good accuracy of detection for all test applications. The precision for all test applications is above 99% while the recall varies from 83.07% for NewsPortal to 94.66% for Classifieds. The false positive rate (FPR) is below 2% except for the Forum application.

Table 3. Results of SQL injection Detection by SQLiDDS

Web Application	# Queries Intercepted	TP	FN	FP	TN	TPR	FPR	Accuracy
Bookstore	4477	3862	52	6	557	98.67%	1.07%	98.70%
Forum	3580	2986	97	11	486	96.85%	2.21%	96.98%
Classifieds	1987	1587	21	7	372	98.69%	1.85%	98.59%
NewsPortal	1544	1223	54	2	265	95.77%	0.75%	96.37%
JobPortal	3114	2644	33	4	433	98.77%	0.92%	98.81%

Out of the false positives and negatives, total 162 queries (56.4%) were logged as *suspicious* queries for the DBA to examine. The overall accuracy of the system comes out as 98.05%. Interestingly, the accuracy for the Forum and NewsPortal are 96.85% and 95.77% respectively in the first run, even if they were *not* used as honeypots for collecting injection patterns (see Sect. 4.1). This is very encouraging and proves that injected queries collected from few honeypot applications can be used to protect multiple web applications, because input parameters are used in the WHERE clause of queries in similar manner across web applications.

4.4 Performance Overhead

Processing overhead by SQLiDDS consists of four components: (1) extracting the WHERE clause, (2) query transformation, (3) lookup of the reference hash table, and (4) similarity matching with clustered documents. Out of these, (1) and (3) consume negligible time and are ignored. Average time for query transformation and computing phrase based similarity were measured as 0.612 ms and 0.413 ms respectively. Considering that similarity with half of the documents needs to be computed on average, total processing overhead comes to 22.501 ms per incoming query. Assuming that a standard web page issues 10 queries on average, the total delay is $\simeq$ 225 ms per page. Since the page load times are generally in the order of several seconds over the Internet, a delay of 225 ms is insignificant and would not affect the end-users' browsing experience.

To assess impact on performance in practical usage scenario, load testing on the sample web applications was conducted using Pylot[3] with 10 to 100 concurrent user-agents, configured with request interval of 5 ms and 5 seconds ramp-up time, covering all public web pages as test cases. Each test was run for 30 minutes with and without SQLiDDS intercepting queries, and the difference in average response time of the web applications was measured. Figure 2 shows the delay introduced by SQLiDDS for each application. Clearly, the delay is proportional to the average number of queries issued per page and increases with the number of concurrent users. Overall, the delay introduced by SQLiDDS was found to account for 4.5–5.8% of the average response time of the web server, which is almost imperceptible in online environment over the Internet.

---

[3] Open source website performance testing tool: http://www.pylot.org/

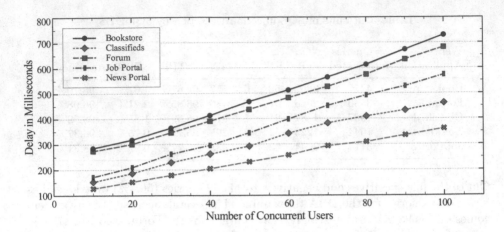

Fig. 2. Performance Overhead of SQLiDDS

5   Related Work

To the best of our knowledge, document similarity measures have not been so far proposed specifically for detection of injection attacks at the SQL query level in the literature. However, a few studies have used similarity measures on HTTP requests or payloads for classification of web attacks including SQL injection, which may be considered as related to our work to some extent.

Small et al. [23] used similarity measure and string alignment techniques for detecting malicious HTTP payloads. At the same time, Gallagher et al. [24] also used term frequency based similarity measure for classification of HTTP requests to identify and classify attacks. Ulmer et al. [25] used similarity on HTTP data for a configurable hardware classifier for web attacks. Later in [26], they proposed parallel acceleration for the document-similarity classifier on multi-core processor architecture, focusing mainly on hardware implementation. Choi et al. [27] used N-gram splitting and classification using Support Vector Machine (SVM) to detect SQL injection and XSS attacks. However, their approach to extract N-grams ignores the symbols and operators completely, which are important syntactic elements in a query. Application of document similarity measures in conjunction with query transformation for detecting SQL injection attacks is proposed for the first time in this paper to the best of our belief.

6   Conclusions and Future Work

This paper presented a novel approach to detect all types of SQL injection attacks by applying document similarity measure on normalized queries, implemented in a tool named SQLiDDS. We adopted the strategy to examine only the WHERE clause part of run-time queries and ignore INSERT queries, which was based on two interesting observations made during the course of research. The experimental results obtained on five fully vulnerable web applications developed with PHP and MySQL, are very encouraging and confirm effectiveness of our approach. The system acts as a database firewall and is able to protect multiple web applications hosted on a shared server, which is an advantage over existing methods. Though SQLiDDS requires an initial set of injected queries, these can be collected from few honeypot applications and reused for further deployments. The system can evolve with inputs from DBA and become more robust over time. Performance overhead of the system is almost imperceptible over Internet. The approach can also be ported to other web application development platforms without requiring major modifications.

Further research is required on four main aspects: (1) improving the query transformation scheme to harden against bypassing attempts, (2) evaluating other document similarity measures available in the literature and determine the best measure for accuracy and performance, (3) developing a weighting scheme for frequently occurring phrases in injected queries for lowering the false negative and false positive rates, and (4) using an efficient text clustering algorithm that produces less number of high quality clusters.

References

1. OWASP: Top 10 Security Threats 2013 (2013), https://www.owasp.org/index.php/Top_10_2013-A1-Injection (accessed: November 15 2013)
2. TrustWave: Executive Summary: Trustwave 2012 Global Security Report (2012), https://www.trustwave.com/global-security-report (accessed: June 24, 2013)
3. Maciejak, D., Lovet, G.: Botnet-Powered Sql Injection Attacks: A Deeper Look Within. In: Virus Bulletin Conference, pp. 286–288 (September 2009)
4. Curtis, S.: Barclays: 97 percent of data breaches still due to SQL injection (January 2012), http://news.techworld.com/security/3331283/barclays-97-percent-of-data-breaches-still-due-to-sql-injection/
5. Livshits, B., Erlingsson, Ú.: Using Web Application Construction Frameworks to Protect Against Code Injection Attacks. In: Proceedings of the 2007 Workshop on Programming Languages and Analysis for Security, pp. 95–104. ACM (2007)
6. Boyd, S.W., Keromytis, A.D.: SQLrand: Preventing SQL injection attacks. In: Jakobsson, M., Yung, M., Zhou, J. (eds.) ACNS 2004. LNCS, vol. 3089, pp. 292–302. Springer, Heidelberg (2004)
7. Johns, M., Beyerlein, C., Giesecke, R., Posegga, J.: Secure code generation for web applications. In: Massacci, F., Wallach, D., Zannone, N. (eds.) ESSoS 2010. LNCS, vol. 5965, pp. 96–113. Springer, Heidelberg (2010)
8. Benedikt, M., Freire, J., Godefroid, P.: VeriWeb: Automatically Testing Dynamic Web Sites. In: Proceedings of 11th International World Wide Web Conference (WWW 2002). Citeseer (2002)
9. Kals, S., Kirda, E., Kruegel, C., Jovanovic, N.: Secubat: A Web Vulnerability Scanner. In: Proceedings of the 15th International Conference on World Wide Web, pp. 247–256. ACM (2006)
10. Wassermann, G., Yu, D., Chander, A., Dhurjati, D., Inamura, H., Su, Z.: Dynamic Test Input Generation for Web Applications. In: Proceedings of the 2008 International Symposium on Software Testing and Analysis, pp. 249–260. ACM (2008)
11. Halfond, W., Orso, A.: AMNESIA: Analysis and Monitoring for NEutralizing SQL-Injection Attacks. In: Proceedings of the 20th IEEE/ACM International Conference on Automated Software Engineering, pp. 174–183. ACM (2005)

12. Buehrer, G., Weide, B., Sivilotti, P.: Using Parse Tree Validation to Prevent SQL Injection Attacks. In: Proceedings of the 5th International Workshop on Software Engineering and Middleware, pp. 106–113. ACM (2005)
13. Bisht, P., Madhusudan, P., Venkatakrishnan, V.: CANDID: Dynamic Candidate Evaluations for Automatic Prevention of SQL Injection Attacks. ACM Transactions on Information and System Security (TISSEC) 13(2), 14 (2010)
14. Lee, I., Jeong, S., Yeo, S., Moon, J.: A Novel Method for SQL Injection Attack Detection based on Removing SQL Query Attribute Values. Mathematical and Computer Modelling 55, 58–68 (2011)
15. Wang, Y., Li, Z.: SQL Injection Detection via Program Tracing and Machine Learning. In: Xiang, Y., Pathan, M., Tao, X., Wang, H. (eds.) IDCS 2012. LNCS, vol. 7646, pp. 264–274. Springer, Heidelberg (2012)
16. Halfond, W., Viegas, J., Orso, A.: A Classification of SQL-injection Attacks and Countermeasures. In: International Symposium on Secure Software Engineering (ISSSE), pp. 12–23 (2006)
17. Maor, O., Shulman, A.: SQL Injection Signatures Evasion (White paper). Imperva, Inc. (April 2004), http://www.issa-sac.org/info_resources/ISSA_20050519_iMperva_SQLInjection.pdf
18. Dahse, J.: Exploiting hard filtered SQL Injections (March 2010), http://websec.wordpress.com/2010/03/19/exploiting-hard-filtered-sql-injections/
19. Kar, D., Panigrahi, S.: Prevention of SQL Injection Attack Using Query Transformation and Hashing. In: Proceedings of the 3rd IEEE International Advance Computing Conference (IACC), pp. 1317–1323. IEEE (2013)
20. Manning, C.D., Raghavan, P., Schütze, H.: Introduction to Information Retrieval, vol. 1. Cambridge University Press, Cambridge (2008), http://nlp.stanford.edu/IR-book/pdf/irbookonlinereading.pdf
21. García Adeva, J.J., Pikatza Atxa, J.M.: Intrusion Detection in Web Applications using Text Mining. Engg. Appl. of Artificial Intelligence 20(4), 555–566 (2007)
22. Liao, Y., Vemuri, V.R.: Using Text Categorization Techniques for Intrusion Detection. In: USENIX Security Symposium, vol. 12, pp. 51–59 (2002)
23. Small, S., Mason, J., Monrose, F., Provos, N., Stubblefield, A.: To Catch a Predator: A Natural Language Approach for Eliciting Malicious Payloads. In: USENIX Security Symposium, pp. 171–184 (2008)
24. Gallagher, B., Eliassi-Rad, T.: Classification of HTTP Attacks: A Study on the ECML/PKDD 2007 Discovery Challenge. In: Center for Advanced Signal and Image Sciences (CASIS) Workshop (2008)
25. Ulmer, C., Gokhale, M.: A Configurable-Hardware Document-Similarity Classifier to Detect Web Attacks. In: 2010 IEEE International Symposium on Parallel & Distributed Processing, Workshops and Phd Forum (IPDPSW), pp. 1–8. IEEE (April 2010)
26. Ulmer, C., Gokhale, M., Gallagher, B., Top, P., Eliassi-Rad, T.: Massively parallel acceleration of a document-similarity classifier to detect web attacks. Journal of Parallel and Distributed Computing 71(2), 225–235 (2011)
27. Choi, J., Kim, H., Choi, C., Kim, P.: Efficient Malicious Code Detection Using N-Gram Analysis and SVM. In: 2011 14th International Conference on Network-Based Information Systems (NBiS), pp. 618–621. IEEE (2011)

Information Retrieval in Wikipedia
with Conceptual Directions

Julian Szymański

Department of Computer Systems Architecture,
Gdańsk University of Technology, Poland
julian.szymanski@eti.pg.gda.pl

Abstract. The paper describes our algorithm used for retrieval of textual information from Wikipedia. The experiments show that the algorithm allows to improve typical evaluation measures of retrieval quality. The improvement of the
retrieval results was achieved by two phase usage approach. In first the algorithm extends the set of content that has been indexed by the specified keywords
and thus increases the Recall value. Then, using the interaction with the user by
presenting him so-called *Conceptual Directions* the search results are purified,
which allows to increase Precision value. The preliminary evaluation on multi-
sense test phrases indicates, that the algorithm is able to increase the Precision,
within result set, without Recall loss. We also describe an additional method used
for extending the result set based on creating cluster prototypes and finding the
most similar, not retrieved content in text repository. In our demo implementation
in the form of web portal, clustering has been used to present the search results
organized in thematic groups instead of ranked list.

Keywords: information retrieval, Wikipedia, documents clustering.

1 Introduction

The basic approach to information retrieval from text repositories is based on finding
a content that contains specified keywords. This method is widely used in typical search
engines [1]. It uses inverted indexes [2] that allows to quickly find the web pages having
particular search phrases. Additionally, the search engines introduce mechanisms that
rank pages indexed with keywords, according to some relevance measures [3].

Despite successful applications the keyword-based retrieval has also some limitations. The main one is that this approach can not retrieve a content that is relevant to
the user requirements but does not contain keywords specified by the user. One of the
solutions to this issue is to provide a lexicon that introduces relations used to extend
the search phrases with additional, related words. Thus additional web pages (indexed
with related words) can be retrieved. This method allows to deal with synonyms but
frequently leads to introducing noise to the result set [4].

In spite of very useful applications, search engines based on keywords are still far
from user expectations. It should be stressed here that engines retrieve web pages that
contain specified keywords, but users usually want to have precise answer to his or her
query – not pages where that answer can be found. This task is a domain of question

R. Natarajan et al. (Eds.): ICDCIT 2015, LNCS 8956, pp. 391–402, 2015.

answering systems [5], where research is in progress. Despite some interesting results shown in that area, eg. with applying ontologies [6][7], the results are limited to domain-oriented repositories. The reason for this is the fact that machine can not understand the natural language, but it can only interpret the sequences of characters. Due to that natural language processing (and thus information retrieval) is mainly based on statistical text processing.

In our approach we propose a method for information retrieval improvement based on algorithm we call `Conceptual Sieve` [8]. In the next sections we describe a motivation for the algorithm, its functional components and preliminary results of its evaluation achieved within test repository based on Wikipedia. We conclude with discussion on achieved results and further directions of development.

2   Evaluation of Information Retrieval

If one retrieves information from a text repository (that can be for example digital library or WWW) the question arises how effective this retrieval is. The effectiveness of retrieval can be defined as a value that characterize how much of relevant information a system managed to retrieve and how pure retrieved information is. To describe the retrieval quality usually two main factors are considered:

- the first factor describes purity of retrieved information – in other words it is a value that characterize how much of the retrieved information is relevant from the user point of view,
- the second one describes amount of the retrieved information – in other words it is a fraction of information in the repository relevant to the user query that was actually retrieved.

These two factors can be described using typical Precision (1) and Recall (2) formulas.

$$
p = \begin{cases} \dfrac{|F \wedge I|}{|F|} & , \text{ if } |F| \neq 0 \\ 0 & , \text{ if } |F| = 0 \wedge |I| > 0 \\ 1 & , \text{ if } |F| = 0 \wedge |I| = 0 \end{cases} \tag{1}
$$

$$
r = \begin{cases} \dfrac{|F \wedge I|}{|I|} & , \text{ if } |I| \neq 0 \\ 0 & , \text{ if } |I| = 0 \wedge |F| > 0 \\ 1 & , \text{ if } |I| = 0 \wedge |F| = 0 \end{cases} \tag{2}
$$

where :

- F is a result set – documents/information that has been returned to the user and thus considered by the system as relevant,
- I is a relevance set – the documents/information that has been considered as significant by user.

It should be noticed that Precision and Recall measures are somehow opposite. If a system returns to the user whole information from the repository it ensures there will be all relevant information ($r = 1$), but it will contain much of additional information and thus it will contain much noise ($p \approx 0$). From the other hand if we do not retrieve any information the result set will be pure. These two border examples describe the expected case: we want to retrieve as much as possible and, at the same time, pure information. Thus, we want to maximize a unified measure that combines the two factors. This measure is called *F-measure* and is defined by (3). .

$$f^\beta = (1 + \beta^2) \cdot \frac{p \cdot r}{\beta^2 \cdot p + r},\tag{3}$$

where β parameter allows to put more stress on precision or on recall. If $\beta = 1$, the stress on two factors are kept in balance, and the measure is also called *F1-score*.

The goal of Conceptual Sieve algorithm is to increase F-measure of retrieval. We achieve it working in the following steps:

- the first, allows to increase Recall factor. It is achieved by gathering additional information that may be relevant to user requirements. This step is based on extending the set of specified keywords that has been used for retrieval,
- in the second phase, a user interactively narrows the result set to achieve more precise results and remove the information that is not related to his requirements,
- we also provide the functionality that enables to extend the result set with additional information based on proximity to the selected search results. This functionality allows to increase the Recall measure but it is performed using very different approach than in the first step. The extended (on user demand) set of results can be afterwards processed, using user interaction that narrows it to the subset fulfilling his or her requirements.

3 Conceptual Sieve Algorithm

In the Conceptual Sieve algorithm we distinguish the following steps:

A. Specification of user's requirements with a search phrases and extending them.
B. Narrowing the results with user's interaction.
C. Enhancing the set of results.

The aim of steps A and C is to increase Recall measure, step B allows to precise the results. Step A is performed only at the beginning of the search. Steps B and C can be performed on user demand. In our implementation each of the steps are performed by a separate module, thus the system can be modified flexibly. Below we describe each of the algorithm steps in detail.

3.1 Keywords Specification and Extension

The first operation in this step is the same as in typical search engines – keywords provided by user index the content that may be relevant to user's requirements. We extend this step by adding the content not directly indexed by specified keywords, but indexed with terms that are related to the provided phrases. These two sets – indexed with keywords and with related phrases – form an initial result set.

It should be noticed that extension of keyword-based retrieval can be performed using many different techniques. Methods widely used in search engines include: query expansion [9], synonyms analysis based on external dictionary (eg. WordNet [10]) or apply Latent Semantic Analysis [11]. These methods can be easily introduced to our system but in our approach we implemented a technique that capture word co-occurrences based on Hyperspace Analog to Language (HAL) model [12].

This approach analyses statistical co-occurrences of words in large text corpora. Using words co-occurrences two types of similarity can be found: paradigmatic and syntagmatic [13]. The first one analyses how often two particular words appear together in the same peace of text. The second analyze how often two words share the same context. In our method frequencies of co-occurring words only are calculated. The most co-occurring words form so called Context Vectors – the collection of words that are similar to a given one. The context vectors are used to extend search keywords provided by a user and they are incorporated to index additional content. The details of creating word co-occurrences and Context Vectors are described in [14].

3.2 Processing Results with User Interaction

Think about something – I'll try to guess it. This is an idea of popular word game where one is thinking about something and the other is asking the questions and tries to guess what his opponent has in mind. We implemented this game in the form of web portal[1] where users can play that game against a machine. In our game the machine asks questions to a human and tries to find what concept the human thought of. The game is implemented in the limited domain of animals where it shows the abilities to employ the knowledge model that approximates human semantic memory [15] for capturing commonsense relations between concepts [16]. The implementation of elementary linguistic competences using the cognitive model shows some abilities for human-machine interaction in a way more familiar to human-human interactions, but not based on mimicking the language understanding as it is in typical chatterbot conversations [17].

The idea of the game can be adopted to information retrieval. In typical retrieval systems a user asks the search engine and, as a response, he or she obtains a list of results that fits to the query. In our approach we switched the positions – it is the search engine who asks questions and tries to find out what the user is searching for. This reversion in the retrieval process allows to enhance the human-machine interaction. The interaction enables to narrow the search results and to precise it to a set with the most relevant content to the user requirements.

In a typical search engine, the requirements can be defined with search phrases only. In our system, besides search phrases we also provide a possibility of selecting so called conceptual directions that allows to describe how search will be continued. The conceptual direction is similar to an idea of dimension in Gardenfors Semantic

---

[1] http://diodor.eti.pg.gda.pl

Spaces [18]. It allows to aggregate some set of properties that are used to describe something.

In our experiments we used Wikipedia as a test-bed repository [19]. It approximates WWW nature well and additionally provides some structural information. To create conceptual directions we use the fact that Wikipedia articles are organized in categories and that articles are related one to another by hyper-references. The computational representation of an article is defined as a combination of article references and associations with categories they are related to. Each of them creates a feature that describes an article with a particular value. As both categories and references are associated to the others we were able to enhance representation with higher order associations that have been added with smaller weights.

Using associations between categories and article references we constructed the representation space where the proximity of articles is calculated as the reverse distances between the points. This representation space allows to perform computations on the text. In our approach we calculate the conceptual directions as thematic lines that separate the articles in terms of their differences. This differences are captured in the representation space as a category that is the most usable to differentiate sets of articles.

3.3   Calculation Conceptual Directions with Entropy

The first approach to conceptual direction selection has been based on calculating Entropy related to the particular representation dimension. Entropy, defined with (4), indicates the most usable dimension for articles separation.

$$H_d = -\sum_{i=1}^{I} p_i \log p_i, \qquad (4)$$

where H_d denotes Entropy calculated for a particular dimension in the representation space and p is a normalized value of sums of article weights. Formally, $p_i = \frac{|w_i|}{|A|}$, where $|A|$ is articles cardinality, $|w_i|$ is a cardinality of particular weight value and i denotes the number of unique w values in particular dimension d.

It should be noticed that H measure known from decision trees [20] is calculated for separation of the data set based on cardinality of objects belonging to the same class. Formula 4 performs partitioning that maximize division of the dataset into two parts as close to half as possible. Its usage in the experiments gave quite good results, but sometimes when there were significant differences in categories cardinality, Entropy resulted in a partition of a bigger conceptual set. We plan to reduce this influence by calculating conceptual directions on article prototypes that aggregate similar ones instead of calculation directly on articles.

The usage of Entropy measure for selecting conceptual directions allows to separate two sets: one that is related to it and the second that does not. To extend the number of possible ways the conceptual direction can be set up we present to the user top seven directions having the highest Entropy value (each of them described with a category most related to it). Wider number of possible combinations allows the user to select the direction more related to the search.

For now we only use a weights that relates articles with the features that are explicite defined in the Wikipedia. This produces sparse representation space and possibly can omit some important information. In future we plan to increase descriptive of representation space by mining new significant relations between categories [21]. Acquisition of this kind of knowledge can be also performed by interaction with the user (that selects particular conceptual directions). Such a interaction is particularly useful for evaluational and correcting automatically obtained relations [22].

3.4   Calculation Conceptual Directions with Partitioning Clustering

It should be noticed that Entropy allows to select the conceptual direction that is positively or negatively related to the user's answer. This requires to introduce additional functionality in the user interface that indicates "+" or "-" for the selected conceptual direction.

The simpler version for narrowing a result set has been tested by selecting conceptual directions based on clustering. This approach allows a user to select a conceptual direction that is related only positively to the search.

The main idea for calculation conceptual directions with clustering is to find the groups that accumulate the most similar search results. For that purpose we use k-means algorithm with adaptive selection of k parameter [23]. For selecting the cluster label – that is the most descriptive for that set – we use a measure that combines two factors: category popularity and its global inverse frequency.

The first one denotes how often a given category appears in cluster c. This number is a weighed sum of k category weights ($w_{k,c}$) and $n_{k,c}$ is the number of k category frequencies in cluster c. The cluster label based on frequency describes formula 5.

$$Cf_{k,c} = \sum n_{k,c} \cdot w_{k,c} \qquad (5)$$

The factor CF determines the importance of k category within the c cluster. The more often a category appears and has higher weights, the more important it is considered as characterizing the cluster suitably.

The inverse category frequency increases the weight of categories that occur in a small number of clusters. Thus this factor describes the importance of the category label in terms of its differentiating. Categories that appear in fewer number of clusters brings more information that is useful to differentiate them from others. This factor is computed using Formula 6.

$$ICf_k = log(\frac{|c|}{|k|}) \qquad (6)$$

where $|k|$ denotes the number of clusters that contain category k, and c is the total number of clusters.

The highest product of Cf and ICf_k factors indicates the most significant category that characterize particular cluster and it has been presented to the user for selection for narrowing search results.

The above presented two strategies for selecting conceptual direction allows to select category that is presented to the user and describes the direction in which the search process is continued. The interaction with the user by repeating this process allows to narrow the set of search results into the user's requirements and thus to improve the search precision.

3.5 Clustering for Result Set Presentation and Extension

A typical web search engine retrieves a content that contains specified keywords and returns results ranked according to some ranking function. Eg. Google ranks its list of results using Page Rank algorithm [24]. This approach causes user to focus on the results on top of the list and to leave other results unnoticed. To improve the effectiveness of results presentation we aggregate them into thematic groups that fulfill defined similarity. Content aggregation is performed by clustering the result set.

We examined many approaches to the text clustering [25] and found that the most usable for our task is the approach based on density analysis that is a modified version of DBSCAN [26]. The details of the modification has been described in [27]. Despite DBSCAN disadvantage in the computational $O(n^2)$ cost (where n denotes the number of clustered objects), the algorithm has many advantages over other approaches. The main one is that it does not require to determine the number of clusters explicitly, and it can create clusters having shapes other than convex. The computational resources of our machines allows to perform clustering process for a thousands of articles in run-time. Thus we are able to apply the approach to organize linear retrieval results into groups. This allows users to embrace the search result set more effectively and see its relevant and irrelevant elements.

The groups and similarity measure allows to introduce additional functionality. It enhances the set of results with additional information that is retrieved with calculating the similarity between information from the repository and a prototype of a particular group.

A modification of typical DBSCAN algorithm introduced to our system has been based on performing clustering three times, each time with a different *epsilon* parameter values. The DBSCAN *epsilon* parameter describes the similarity level between two objects to be classified as belonging to one cluster. The succeeding values of *epsilon* parameter we set up empirically to 0.7, 0.6, 0.5. Running DBSCAN three times allows to combine in each step articles such that at the very beginning very specific ones are combined together and then they form more general groups. The method resembles HAC algorithm [28] with the difference that we do not aggregate single articles but groups of thematically cohesive ones and at the end we do not create hierarchy but flat partitioned clusters. The pseudocode that realizes the above requirements has been presented in algorithm 1.

4   The System Prototype

In Figure 1 we present the system interface that has been deployed as a web portal and is available on-line at http://kask.eti.pg.gda.pl/bettersearch. In the interface we select the following features:

Algorithm 1. Agglomerative DBSCAN algorithm

$clusters \leftarrow cluster(documents, t_0)$
for all t_i in T **do**
  for all c in $clusters$ **do**
    if $|c| > maxClusterSize$ **then**
      $R \leftarrow R + cluster$
      $delete(cluster)$
    end if
  end for
  $clusters \leftarrow clusters + cluster(R, t_i)$
end for
for all $c in clusters$ **do**
  if $|c| > maxClusterSize \vee |c| < minClusterSize$ **then**
    $U \leftarrow U + c$
  else
    $cat \leftarrow FindRepresentative(c)$
    $docsByCategory[cat] \leftarrow docsByCategory[cat] + c$
  end if
end for

A. Edit box for entering a search phrase
B. List box for selecting a particular conceptual direction as well as buttons to indicate whether the direction is suitable for the user search or it is not related.
C. Include button that allows to incorporate to the search results additional articles that are related to the specified cluster.
D1. List of the clusters.
D2. Details of the cluster – the cluster label and the articles that belonging to that group.
E. The hyperlinks that allow to switch a type of view: list of results or clusters.

In the example given in Figure 1 for a specified search phrase *kernel* system retrieves all the articles that contains that word, then they have been organized in clusters. It can be noticed that the articles related to different thematic groups have been differentiated eg. articles related to *mathematics* have been assigned to different group then ones related to *operating systems*.

For now, the system is implemented to support Polish, English and Simple English Wikpiedias.

5   Results and Discussion

In our research we implemented algorithm presented in Section 3 to retrieve the information from Wikipedia. The usage of that repository has several advantages. The main one is the fact that Wikipedia is a good model of WWW nature. On the other hand it is limited and much better structuralized than WWW, thus it is a very good area to perform the experiments. The structuralization of Wikipedia offers the categories that organize its content. The categories have been used as a conceptual directions used as queries (in the word game) that allows to narrow the search results.

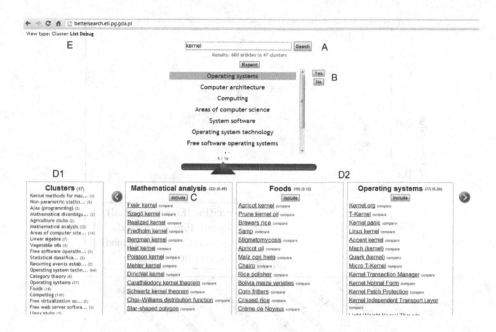

Fig. 1. Web interface of bettersearch system

The created platform has been used to perform experiments where we analyze how Conceptual Sieve algorithm allows to retrieve relevant content from Wikipedia. We performed series of test searches for 10 different multi-sense test phrases.

The aggregated results for retrieval of 27 different subjects indexed by 10 test phrases we present in Figure 2. The values on vertical axis denotes Precision and Recall values. The values on the horizontal axis denotes the following steps of the algorithm:

- 1 – entering the search phrase.
- 2 – extending the query using Context Vectors that were described in section 3.1.
- 3 - 6 – narrowing the results with user interaction. If for different test phrases there was no interaction, in the next step we assume it is the same as in the previous one.
- 7 – extending the result set with similarity based method.
- 8 - 9 – narrowing the results with user interaction.

Figure 2 presents the aggregated results of retrieval achieved by selection of conceptual directions using Entropy method (described in Section 3.3) as well as using Cluster method (described in Section 3.4). We can see that the Conceptual Sieve algorithm allows to improve results of retrieval for both strategies. The final values of Precision and Recall, greater then at the beginning of the search, indicate that the method allows to narrow the set of results. The initial result set indexed with multi meaning keywords has been narrowed into different (and more precise) final sets, according to user requirements. The results indicate the method can be adopted to extend typical retrieval based on keywords.

Also in the graphs there should be noticed expected degradation of Precision during the phases related to extending the result set. The extension allows to increase the Recall

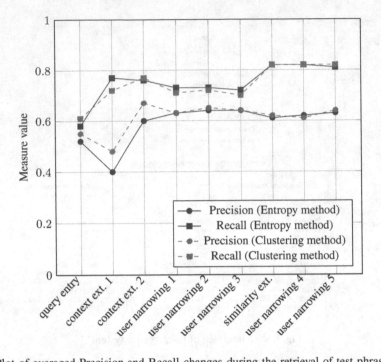

Fig. 2. Plot of averaged Precision and Recall changes during the retrieval of test phrases using Entropy and Clustering Methods

value and it does not decrease significantly during the interaction with the user that is intend to increase the Precision.

Both strategies of selecting conceptual directions gave similar final results. Entropy narrows the precision during the first interaction steps a little bit slower. Values of precision achieved in the next steps are very similar.

The available on-line implementation of our Conceptual Sieve algorithm serves as a system prototype and platform for performing further experiments. The results of its evaluation on test phrases using standard information retrieval measures indicate it can be useful for processing the search results as well as to find the content related to retrieved result set. The next step of our system development will be to increase data processing effectiveness. Solving this issue should allow us to scale-up the solution and run it on huge textual databases. We plan to extend the system to work not on closed repository of Wikipedia articles but on web pages in WWW. To do that we now create a web crawler that harvest the data from Polish Web. The main issue to apply our approach on unstructuralized data is conceptual direction creation. For that purpose we plan to use large scale classifier that would allow to categorize web content to Wikipedia categories [29]. To allow easy adaptation of the proposed algorithm to other than Wikipedia data sources we plan to be deploy it as a service in BeassyCluster environment [30].

References

1. Croft, W., Metzler, D., Strohman, T.: Search engines: Information retrieval in practice. Addison-Wesley (2010)
2. Scholer, F., Williams, H., Yiannis, J., Zobel, J.: Compression of inverted indexes for fast query evaluation. In: Proceedings of the 25th Annual International ACM SIGIR Conference on Research and Development in Information Retrieval, pp. 222–229. ACM (2002)
3. Agrawal, R., Gollapudi, S., Halverson, A., Ieong, S.: Diversifying search results. In: Proceedings of the Second ACM International Conference on Web Search and Data Mining, pp. 5–14. ACM (2009)
4. Buckley, C., Salton, G., Allan, J., Singhal, A.: Automatic query expansion using smart: Trec 3, p. 69. NIST SPECIAL PUBLICATION SP (1995)
5. Andrenucci, A., Sneiders, E.: Automated question answering: Review of the main approaches. In: Third International Conference on Information Technology and Applications, ICITA 2005, vol. 1, pp. 514–519. IEEE (2005)
6. Mann, G.: Fine-grained proper noun ontologies for question answering. In: Proceedings of the 2002 Workshop on Building and using Semantic Networks, vol. 11, pp. 1–7. Association for Computational Linguistics (2002)
7. Unger, C., Cimiano, P.: Pythia: Compositional meaning construction for ontology-based question answering on the semantic web. In: Muñoz, R., Montoyo, A., Métais, E. (eds.) NLDB 2011. LNCS, vol. 6716, pp. 153–160. Springer, Heidelberg (2011)
8. Szymański, J., Krawczyk, H., Deptuła, M.: Retrieval with semantic sieve. In: Selamat, A., Nguyen, N.T., Haron, H. (eds.) ACIIDS 2013, Part I. LNCS, vol. 7802, pp. 236–245. Springer, Heidelberg (2013)
9. Ogilvie, P., Voorhees, E., Callan, J.: On the number of terms used in automatic query expansion. Information Retrieval 12, 666–679 (2009)
10. Miller, G.A., Beckitch, R., Fellbaum, C., Gross, D., Miller, K.: Introduction to WordNet: An On-line Lexical Database. Cognitive Science Laboratory, Princeton University Press (1993)
11. Dumais, S.: Latent semantic analysis. Annual Review of Information Science and Technology 38, 188–230 (2004)
12. Lund, K., Burgess, C.: Hyperspace analog to language (hal): A general model of semantic representation. Language and Cognitive Processes (1996)
13. Jacquemin, C.: Syntagmatic and paradigmatic representations of term variation. In: Proceedings of the 37th Annual Meeting of the Association for Computational Linguistics on Computational Linguistics, pp. 341–348. Association for Computational Linguistics (1999)
14. Szymański, J.: Words context analysis for improvement of information retrieval. In: Nguyen, N.-T., Hoang, K., Jędrzejowicz, P. (eds.) ICCCI 2012, Part I. LNCS, vol. 7653, pp. 318–325. Springer, Heidelberg (2012)
15. Quillian, M.: Semantic memory. Semantic Information Processing 2, 227–270 (1968)
16. Szymański, J., Duch, W.: Information retrieval with semantic memory model. Cognitive Systems Research 14, 84–100 (2012)
17. Shawar, B., Atwell, E.: Chatbots: are they really useful? Zeitschrift für Computerlinguistik und Sprachtechnologie, 29 (2007)
18. Gärdenfors, P.: Semantics based on conceptual spaces. In: Logic and Its Applications, pp. 1–11 (2011)
19. Szymanski, J.: Comparative analysis of text representation methods using classification. Cybernetics and Systems 45, 180–199 (2014)
20. Quinlan, J.: Induction of decision trees. Machine Learning 1, 81–106 (1986)
21. Szymański, J.: Mining relations between wikipedia categories. In: Zavoral, F., Yaghob, J., Pichappan, P., El-Qawasmeh, E. (eds.) NDT 2010. CCIS, vol. 88, pp. 248–255. Springer, Heidelberg (2010)

22. Szymanski, J., Duch, W.: Semantic memory knowledge acquisition through active dialogues. In: Proceedings of the International Joint Conference on Neural Networks, IJCNN 2007, Celebrating 20 Years of Neural Networks, Orlando, Florida, USA, August 12-17, pp. 536–541 (2007)
23. Darken, C., Moody, J.: Fast adaptive k-means clustering: some empirical results. In: Int. Joint Conf. on Neural Networks, vol. 2, pp. 233–238 (1990)
24. Langville, A., Meyer, C.: Google page rank and beyond. Princeton Univ Pr. (2006)
25. Carpineto, C., Osiński, S., Romano, G., Weiss, D.: A survey of web clustering engines. ACM Computing Surveys (CSUR) 41, 17 (2009)
26. Ester, M., Kriegel, H., Sander, J., Xu, X.: A density-based algorithm for discovering clusters in large spatial databases with noise. In: Proceedings of the 2nd International Conference on Knowledge Discovery and Data Mining, vol. 1996, pp. 226–231. AAAI Press (1996)
27. Szymański, J.: Interactive information retrieval algorithm for wikipedia articles. In: Yin, H., Costa, J.A.F., Barreto, G. (eds.) IDEAL 2012. LNCS, vol. 7435, pp. 200–207. Springer, Heidelberg (2012)
28. Zhao, Y., Karypis, G., Fayyad, U.: Hierarchical clustering algorithms for document datasets. Data Mining and Knowledge Discovery 10, 141–168 (2005)
29. Draszawka, K., Szymanski, J.: Thresholding strategies for large scale multi-label text classifier. In: 2013 The 6th International Conference on Human System Interaction (HSI), pp. 350–355. IEEE (2013)
30. Czarnul, P.: Modeling, run-time optimization and execution of distributed workflow applications in the jee-based beesycluster environment. The Journal of Supercomputing 63, 46–71 (2013)

Query Execution for RDF Data
on Row and Column Store

Trupti Padiya, Minal Bhise, Sandeep Vasani, and Mohit Pandey

DA-IICT Gandhinagar
{padiya_trupti,minal_bhise,sandeep_vasani,
mohit_pandey}@daiict.ac.in

Abstract. This paper shows experimental comparison between various data storage techniques to manage RDF data. The work represents evaluation of query performance in terms of query execution time and data scalability, using row and column store for various data storage techniques. To demonstrate these ideas FOAF (Friend Of A Friend) data is used. The paper contributes experimental and analytical study for application of partitioning techniques on FOAF data which makes queries 168 times faster compared to traditional triples table. Materialized views over vertically partitioned data show an additional 8 times improvement in query performance against partitioned data for the frequently occurring queries. Vertical partitioning is executed on column store also, and as FOAF data size scales, an order of magnitude improved performance is observed over row store execution.

Keywords: Data Partitioning, Data Scalability, FOAF, Materialized Views, Query Execution, Semantic Web.

1 Introduction

Due to tremendous increase in RDF data, RDF applications need to retrieve data efficiently at the scale of web, which makes performance and scalability issues increasingly significant. Therefore, efficient query processing and efficient management of RDF data is an important factor to achieve goal of highly interactive semantic web applications. SQL query execution for relational data can be simpler and can take less time compared to SPARQL and there are tools available to convert RDF data to relational data.

RDF data can be stored in a relational model using various data stores. Triple Store- a three column simple and flexible representation suffers from a lot of performance issues [1], because as the number of join increases, query complexity increases which will result in serious performance issues in terms of execution time, and increase in data size will make query performance even worse.

Query performance is measured and analyzed for triples table and various other data storage techniques such as property table, horizontally and vertically partitioned tables using row store. We also use materialized views to increase query performance over vertically partitioned data. In addition we check repeatability of the experiment

R. Natarajan et al. (Eds.): ICDCIT 2015, LNCS 8956, pp. 403–408, 2015.

of vertically partitioned tables using column store to analyze query performance against row store [3]. Section 2 describes experimental details and Section 3 represents analysis and discussion of experimental results.

2   Experiment

FOAF is a project devoted to linking people and information using the Web. FOAF integrates three kinds of network: social networks of human collaboration, friendship and association. We are using FOAF [6] dataset from university of Maryland as a benchmark for our experiment. This Section highlights dataset and implementation of the experiment.

FOAF consists of 406540 triples. It has 550 properties out of which we have found 234 unique properties. We designed a query set of 15 real life frequently occurring queries on social web. These queries consist of multiple subject-object joins. We studied and analyzed query performance based on join types and other aggregate operations as depicted in Fig 1.

Query	Total Joins & Operation	Total Joins	Queries with Sub-Sub & Sub-Obj Joins			
			query	sub-sub	sub-obj	total
1	Type1 + Type2	2	1	1	1	2
2	Type2 + Intersection	1	11	1	1	2
3	Type2	1	12	1	2	3
4	Type2	1	Queries with Sub-Obj & Obj-Obj Joins			
5	Type4 + groupby	0	query	sub-obj	obj-obj	total
6	Type4 + groupby	0	14	3	1	4
7	Type 2 + Type2	2	15	2	1	3
8	Type4 + Intersection	0	Queries with only Sub-Obj			
9	Type4 + Union	0	query	sub-obj		total
10	Type1 + Intersection	1	2	1		1+Intersection
11	Type1 + Type2	2	3	1		1
12	Type1 + Type2 + Type2	3	4	1		1
13	Type1 + Type2 + Type3	3	7	2		2
14	Type2 +Type2 + Type2+ Type3	4	10	1		1+Intersection
15	Type2 + Type2 + Type3	3				

Queries with no Joins			Queries with Sub-Sub & Sub-Obj & Obj-Obj Joins				
5	groupby		query	sub-sub	sub-obj	Obj-Obj	total
6	groupby		13	1	1	1	3
8	Intersection						
9	Union						

Fig. 1. Join Analysis

We used Jena Parser to convert RDF data into triples and developed a tool to insert triples into a relational model; postgresql- a row store and MonetDB [5] - a column store. These RDBMS tools were installed on a machine having fedora as operating system, with 1 GB RAM and 0.6 GB swap memory, and 250 GB hard disk. This experiment uses Eclipse IDE, Java 1.6 SDK, Jena Parser 2.3, Postgres 8.2, and MonetDB.

FOAF data is stored in a triples table, a three column table consisting of subject, property and object. We use two clustered property tables and one left over triples table to experiment two specific queries. We study application of partitioning techniques on FOAF data and use vertical and horizontal data partitioning. For vertical partitioning, data is partitioned based on properties of a person. The dataset has 234 uniquely identified properties and therefore, there are total 234 tables for vertically partitioned FOAF data. For subject specific queries, FOAF data is partitioned using horizontal partitioning, based on subject names and thus it has 26 tables for names starting with (a-z) and 10 tables for names starting with numeric (0-9) having total 36 tables for horizontally partitioned FOAF data. A tool is developed using Eclipse and Java to partition FOAF data, and feed them in respective data stores. We create materialized views over vertically partitioned FOAF data, and compared and analyzed its query performance against vertically partitioned FOAF data without materialized views. Effect on query performance for a larger dataset is also experimented by performing data scaling on FOAF data. Initial size is gradually increased to 2 times, 4 times, 8 times and 10 times of actual data size. Query set of 15 queries is fired on all the data stores and query performance is measured in terms of query execution time. Hot and cold runs are taken for the experiment, which are averaged over three runs. For cold run we restarted database and flushed memory for every run. The same experiment for vertically partitioned data is repeated for column store.

3   Result and Discussions

We execute query set of 15 queries for various discussed data storage techniques on a row store. The same set of queries is executed for vertically partitioned data on a column store. We have taken hot and cold runs; however comprehensive analysis is presented based on cold runs as it helps us estimate the scenario when the database is up for the first time and gives the query execution time for the worst case. Details of cold run vs. hot run are given later in this section.

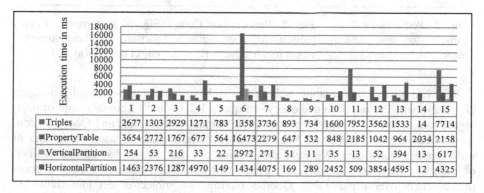

Fig. 2. Query Execution time on various data stores

Fig 2 plots the query execution time of various data storage techniques and Table 1 shows query performance gain using partitioning technique for all the queries over triples table. Various data storage technique occupies different disk storage space. FOAF data at the initial size occupied around 65 MB; property tables occupied 60 MB, and horizontal and vertically partitioned data stores occupied 53 MB and 35 MB respectively.

Table 1. n times gain using partitioning technique over triples table

Query	1	2	3	4	5	6	7	8	9	10	11	12	13	14	15
n x gain	11	25	14	39	36	1	14	18	67	46	612	69	4	1	13

3.1   Query Analysis for Scaled Data on Row Store

Data Scaling is performed chronologically by increasing number of triples to 2 times, 4 times, 8 times and 10 times of actual data size. So data size of resultant data stores were 813080, 1626160, 3252320 and 4065400 triples. The same experiment and analysis was performed for each data size on all data stores discussed in the previous subsection. We were able to find that partitioning techniques performed an order of magnitude better compared to all other data stores for scaled data.

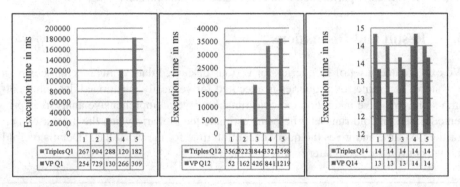

Fig. 3. Performance Comparison for one subject-object join for Query 1

Fig. 4. Performance Comparison for two subject-object join for Query 12

Fig. 5. Performance Comparison for three subject-object join for Query 14

Real life queries on semantic web generally have more number of subject-object (Type 2) joins. For our designed query set, query 1,2,3,4 and 11 contains one subject-object join, query 7, 12, and 15 contains two subject-object joins, and Query 14 contains three subject-object joins. We analyze query performance based on number of joins against scaled data. We were able to find out that queries having one subject-object join, when fired on vertically partitioned data store, shows 43 times average improvement over triples table. Queries having two subject-object join shows 36 times average improvement and queries having three subject-object join shows about nearly equal performance for triples table and vertically partitioned data.   Fig 3, 4, and 5 depicts query performance for vertically partitioned table against triples table for query 1, 12 and 14 having one, two and three subject-object join respectively. Number 1, 2, 3, 4, 5 on x-axis indicates data scaling of actual data, 2 times, 4 times, 8 times and 10 times respectively.

It is seen that vertically partitioned data outperforms other data storage techniques and hence we have implemented materialized view [6] over partitioned data to gain even better performance. Materialized views were created for every query listed in the query set. Based on the kind of joins, we studied queries and their performance with various data size on various data storage techniques. Query 3 has one subject-object join, whereas Query 6 has no joins. Vertical partitioning gives the best-case performance compared to all other storage techniques. The performance got enhanced after using materialized views for vertically partitioned data for query 3. Horizontal partitioning gives best-case performance for query 6. Since query 6 has no subject-object joins materialized views have not shown improvement in query execution time. Vertical partitioning and horizontal partitioning scales linearly, which shows that even with increases of data, partitioning technique leads to better performance compared to current storage techniques.

3.2   Query Analysis for Scaled Data on Column Store

The same experiment of vertical partitioning on a row store- postgresql experiment is executed on a column store- MonetDB [3]. The query set of 15 queries is fired on the column store and hot and cold runs are observed, which are averaged over three runs for both hot and cold runs. Data Scaling is performed chronologically same as done in row store experiment. Table 2 shows performance comparison (for cold runs) between row and column store results for vertically partitioned data with 4065400 triples. It is found that column store gives an order of magnitude better performance for query 1, 2, 3, 5, 6, 7, 10, 12, 13 and 15. For queries like query 4,8,9,11,14 it gives nearly equivalent performance as compared to row stores.

Table 2. Performance comparison between row store and column store for vertically partitioned data

Query	1	2	3	4	5	6	7
N x Gain	1.72	1.17	3.64	-0.97	2.18	18.12	6.58
8	9	10	11	12	13	14	15
-0.55	-0.28	1.41	-0.51	1.58	3.46	-0.01	57.45

3.3   Analysis – Cold Runs vs. Hot Runs

The query set of all the fifteen queries was fired on all the four data stores. We have taken hot and cold runs for all of them. Query execution was carried out for both cold and hot runs and the same runs were repeated. All runs are averaged over three runs for both hot and cold runs. Cold runs results in 1%, 4%, 17%, and 32% of fluctuation in query execution time for triples table, property table, vertical partitioning, and horizontal partitioning respectively. Whereas for hot runs the fluctuations were 47%, 46%, 43%, 92% of actual hot runs. To check the repeatability of these results, we performed the same experiment again and found that cold runs recline around the same percentage of fluctuation and hot runs gave fluctuation of 47%, 58%, 65%, and 91%. We were able to see from the data that execution time for hot runs were not stable.

In real life environment execution time of hot runs depend on the history of the accessibility of the data. In order to understand the phenomenon we need to understand the physical configuration and design of such systems. So we can not totally rely on the execution time using hot runs as it fluctuates more compared to cold runs, which was clearly visible from the observations. On the other hand, cold runs are the worst case scenario and shows remarkable repeatability.

4   Conclusion

We demonstrated that triples table performs and scales poorly compared to partitioned data due to increased number of self joins compared to partitioned data. Property tables are inefficient due to its complexity issues. In our query set, For 13 queries out of 15, vertical partitioning is giving best-case performance in terms of execution time, whereas for other 2 queries, horizontal partitioning gives best-case execution time. Queries which are user oriented and involved no joins, execute faster in horizontal partitioning and rest of the queries execute faster in vertically partitioned data. Queries for partitioned data, on an average executed 168 times faster compared to triples table. Queries that used to take execution time in thousands of milliseconds are now taking time in tens of milliseconds for partitioned data, which can help in making semantic web applications interactive. Queries in real life consists of subject-object join, and hence we have shown that depending on the type of join we can see 43 and 36 times performance improvement for vertically partitioned scaled data over triples table's scaled data, having one and two subject-object joins respectively. Queries which had subject-object join, on an average, executed 8 times faster, after using materialized views on vertically partitioned data. Frequent queries with more joins can be executed in even lesser time by creating materialized views on partitioned data. Cold runs showed remarkable repeatability where as hot runs shows considerable fluctuations comparatively.

References

1. Abadi, D.J., Marcus, A., Madden, S.R., Hollenbach, K.: SW-Store: a vertically partitioned DBMS for Semantic Web data management. The VLDB Journal — The International Journal on Very Large Data Bases 18(2), 385–406 (2009)
2. Abadi, D.J., Madden, S.R., Hachem, N.: Column-stores vs. row-stores: how different are they really? In: Proceedings of the 2008 ACM SIGMOD International Conference on Management of Data, Vancouver, Canada, June 09-12 (2008)
3. Sidirourgos, L., Goncalves, R., Kersten, M., Nes, N., Manegold, S.: Column-store support for RDF data management: not all swans are white. Proceedings of the VLDB Endowment 1(2), 1553–1563 (2008)
4. FOAF Dataset (February 23, 2013), http://ebiquity.umbc.edu/blogger/2005/01/25/foaf-dataset-available/
5. MonetDB Available: (March 1,2014), http://www.monetdb.org/Home
6. Vasani, S., Pandey, M., Bhise, M., Padiya, T.: Faster Query Execution for Partitioned RDF Data. In: Hota, C., Srimani, P.K. (eds.) ICDCIT 2013. LNCS, vol. 7753, pp. 547–560. Springer, Heidelberg (2013)

A Concept for Co-existence of Heterogeneous Recommender Systems Based on Blackboard Architecture

Rohit Gupta and Anil Kumar Singh

MNNIT Allahabad, Allahabad, U.P., India
{rohitatiiit,asbhadoria}@gmail.com
http://mnnit.ac.in

Abstract. This paper introduces the concept of software coordination, collaboration, moderation and visualization in the context of Recommender System (RS). The proposed concept assist to coordinates to execute multiple RSs and collaborates their respective outputs. It also moderates the top-n recommendation list generated by RSs. The multiple RSs can be heterogeneous in terms of their attributes, such as data mining algorithms & prediction techniques used for recommendation. These RSs may be developed by independent experts. The concept employs the notion of blackboard architecture for dealing with multiple RSs. Optimal results are expected to be achieved by feed-forward and feed-backward mechanism.

Keywords: Recommender System, Blackboard Architecture, Collaboration, Moderation, Visualization.

1 Introduction

Recommender Systems (RSs) are being increasingly employed to facilitate the users to make their choices of items (e.g. books, music videos, etc.) or services (e.g. airline ticket booking, medical treatment, etc.). A RS uses utility function that predict useful items to a set of users [15]. However, the concept of RS has evolved and now it focuses on optimization of experience of an individual user rather than on a group of users [5]. The functional requirement of RSs has evolved from simply rating based traditional system to the inclusion of domain experts and knowledge-base modern system. Similarly, the non-functional requirement has also evolved from the state of a simple recommender application to the consideration of issues like load balancing, scaling and QoS etc. [15]. With the beginning of Web 2.0, there is a pressure on RS to grow fast so as to keep up with the rate that web data is growing in the form of user generated content in the area of applications like e-commerce, entertainment systems, service based applications, digital libraries, etc.[15,2]. RSs that are independently developed for different specified domains using different approaches are likely to be heterogeneous. The heterogeneity poses a serious challenge in taking advantage

R. Natarajan et al. (Eds.): ICDCIT 2015, LNCS 8956, pp. 409–414, 2015.

of aggregation of the recommendation from various RSs [6]. The heterogeneity amongst RS can be observed in terms of:

1. Different format of input / output data (text, alphanumeric, multimedia data, etc.) from different domain (i.e. books, news, movies, music, etc.) is used;
2. Different algorithms used by RS to compute the recommendation (i.e. KNN, SVM, K-means, association rule, etc.);
3. The prediction techniques used to compute the recommendation (collaborative, content-based, demographic, Knowledge-based, etc.); and
4. Different form of GUI (i.e. comment box, images, rating in the form of number of stars to present their recommended data [12])used for RS.

Recommender systems go through continuous accuracy improvement for their recommendations, after their initial release. These system have a learning part which uses user feedback over its usage for long duration. Therefore RS software exhibits the kind of challenges that are unlike in a conventional software application. These challenges require to develop an adaptive, feedback based integrated software concept to present unified recommendations from various executing heterogeneous RSs to maintain high performance of RS. The proposed concept provides software coordination, collaboration, moderation and visualization for RSs. It employs blackboard architecture for dealing with multiple RSs. In Section 2, the various data mining algorithms used for RS, different techniques of RSs and challenges of RS are discussed. The need for a system of multiple RSs and the need for adaptive and feedback based RS is presented in section 3. Section 4 presents the concept of blackboard architecture, followed by a presentation of the architecture of proposed concept.

2   Data Mining Algorithms, Prediction Techniques and Challenges of RS

This section list various data mining algorithms that are frequently applied in RSs. The prediction techniques of RS and key challenges of RS are also touched upon.

2.1   Data Mining Algorithms

Data mining algorithms can detect meaningful patterns and rules from large amount of user and item data. These observed patterns and rules help in prediction of right choice of item for a focused user. Association rules, clustering, decision tree, k-Nearest neighbor, neural network, link analysis, regression and other heuristic methods are known algorithms of data-mining that are applied in RSs [14]. The selection of algorithm for a RS is strongly influenced by knowledgebase of application domain [6]. The social-knowledge, the individual-knowledge and the content-knowledge provide knowledge-base of domain.

2.2 Prediction Techniques of RS

The core function of any RS is to identify the useful items for a user. The RS identifies the target item by prediction method. The methodology used for prediction defines the class of RS. The well known traditional RSs are content-based filtering and collaborative filtering, whereas the modern RSs are context-aware based, demographic based, semantics based, cross-domain based and peer-to-peer based systems.

2.3 Recommender System Challenges

Cold-start, trust, scalability, sparsity and privacy are challenges in RSs. They have substantial influence on the performance of all the RSs ranging from classical to modern. These challenges occur due to lack of required training data.

3 System of Multiple Recommender Systems

This section describes the hybrid RS and their methods. The concept of adaptive and feedback RS is briefly discussed.

3.1 Hybrid Recommender System

The objective of any hybrid RS is to combine two or more RSs and get better performance as compared to individual one. A hybrid system removes the problem that a single RS may have. The output hybrid system could be the result of combined output of various RSs or a chain of RSs (for example output of content-based filtering is utilized as input to collaborative approach) [1]. Weighted, Switching, Mixed, Feature combination, Cascade, Feature augmentation, Meta-level are well know methods of hybrid RSs [5]. A hybrid system takes advantage of existing RSs for providing the desired improvement [5]. In any hybrid system, a component of RS would be either in training phase or candidate phase or in final phase. The performance is evaluated with respect to test data for each phase.

3.2 Adaptive and Feedback Based RS

The new trend of RS is more towards personalized RS. The objective of such system is to produce optimized result for one user as per profile of each user. It does not represent the consensus of a group. The satisfaction of user is more if recommendation matches with his profile and his expectation. The expectation of a user may be collected in implicit or explicit form. The user behavior is captured through his actions and profile.[18]. The tuning of RS with a user is a continuous process that required following operation :

1. The user response is feedback to the system on each recommendation.
2. The recommendation is generated by combination of different RSs.
3. Based on user profile and expectation, recommendation is generated.

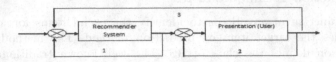

Fig. 1. The control structure diagram of proposed system

The heterogeneity poses a serious of challenge in taking advantage of aggregation of the recommendation from various RS [6]. Yet another challenge is that unlike a conventional software application, RSs go through continuous accuracy improvement in their recommendations because of the learning that takes place through user feedback over its usage for long duration, after their initial release [12]). The structure of proposed design is shown in figure 1. It is showing the following behavior of RS. Feedback loop at 1, helps system to improve the performance of RSs. Feedback loop at 2, helps system to improve its presentation. Feedback loop at 3, helps system improve the overall performance. All the feedback helps to improve the outcome of system as per user expectation. i.e it brings more personalized results for a user in each feedback loop.

4   Proposed Generic Framework for Heterogeneous RSs

This section describe the proposed framework for heterogeneous RSs that provides coordination and adaptability. The coordination mechanism includes feedforward and feed-backward so as to achieve optimal results. The concept helps to manage and collaborate the recommendation results from different RSs. It supports individual RS to update and handle the strategies of computation on their respective data. It moderates the top-n recommendation list of RS outcomes with feed-back mechanism. Figure 2 shows the architecture of proposed framework. It emphasizes on two aspects. First, it assures the co-existence of different heterogeneous RSs. Second, it shows how the coordination take place in feed-forward and feed-backward to optimize the results of RSs.

Heterogeneous RSs, Controller, Dashboard and Blackboard are granular level modules of proposed framework. Controller provides coordination among RSs and Blackboard provides shared memory space. The intermediate results are shown by Dashboard. The proposed framework ensure following objectives:

1. The different heterogeneous RSs can exist together.
2. The feed-forward and feed-backward provides coordination and optimization in output of RSs.
3. It supports individual RS to update their computation of data by applying control strategies.
4. It uses blackboard architecture for handling multiple RSs.
5. It manages to synthesize the results from multiple RSs.

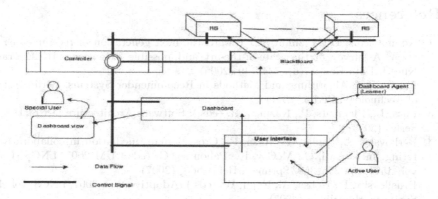

Fig. 2. The proposed framework for Heterogeneous RSs

6. It moderates top-n recommendation of RS by a feed-backward mechanism.
7. It uses learner component and feed-backward mechanism to reach to the desired recommendations for an active user.
8. It serves to customize the presentation, which is more suited for the active user to interact.
9. It has a layered architecture for RSs with the premise that each independent RS has its own interface.

In proposed framework, the structure of each RS has external layer which is called as "required interface" that is used to plug-in any RS However, each RS has default interface that is called as "internal layer" or "provided interface" of RS.

5 Conclusion

The paper has discussed the concept of RS and its challenges. It also looks on various data mining algorithms and different approaches of RS. The paper identify the need of a integrated system of multiple RSs that operate on the concept of feedback based adaptive system. The final section of paper discusses the proposed framework. The proposed framework could be refined for the issues of integrating database of heterogeneous RSs. The framework possess the scope of incorporating its component as intelligent agent. The future work is to develop a working prototype of proposed framework and verify it through mathematical model.

References

1. Adomavicius, G., Tuzhilin, A.: Toward the next generation of recommender systems: A survey of the state-of-the-art and possible extensions. IEEE Trans.+ Knowl. Data Eng. 17(6), 734–749 (2005)
2. Asanov, D.: Algorithms and Methods in Recommender Systems. Berlin Institute of Technology, Berlin (2011)
3. Bass, L., Clements, P., Kazman, R. (eds.): Software Architecture in Practice. SEI Series (2003)
4. Berkovsky, S., Kuflik, T., Ricci, F.: Cross-domain mediation in collaborative filtering. In: Conati, C., McCoy, K., Paliouras, G. (eds.) UM 2007. LNCS (LNAI), vol. 4511, pp. 355–359. Springer, Heidelberg (2007)
5. Brusilovsky, P., Kobsa, A., Nejdl, W. (eds.): Adaptive Web 2007. LNCS, vol. 4321. Springer, Heidelberg (2007)
6. Burke, R.D., Felfernig, A., Goker, M.H.: Recommender systems: An overview. AI Magazine 32(3), 13–18 (2011)
7. Carmel, D., Zwerdling, N., Guy, I., Ofek-Koifman, S., Har'El, N., Ronen, I., Uziel, E., Yogev, S., Chernov, S.: Personalized social search based on the user's social network. In: CIKM, pp. 1227–1236 (2009)
8. Claypool, M., Le, P., Waseda, M., Brown, D.: Implicit interest indicators. In: IUI, pp. 33–40 (2001)
9. Elgohary, A., Nomir, H., Sabek, I., Samir, M., Badawy, M., Yousri, N.A.: Wikirec: A semantic-based recommendation system using wikipedia as an ontology. In: ISDA, pp. 1465–1470 (2010)
10. Hayes-Roth, B.: A blackboard architecture for control. Artif. Intell. 26(3), 251–321 (1985)
11. Kanawati, R., Karoui, H.: A p2p collaborative bibliography recommender system. In: ICIW, pp. 90–96 (2009)
12. Knijnenburg, B.P., Willemsen, M.C., Gantner, Z., Soncu, H., Newell, C.: Explaining the user experience of recommender systems. User Model. User-Adapt. Interact. 22(4-5), 441–504 (2012)
13. Mordacchini, M., Baraglia, R., Dazzi, P., Ricci, L.: A p2p recommender system based on gossip overlays (prego). In: CIT, pp. 83–90 (2010)
14. Park, D.H., Kim II., H.K., Choi, Y., Kim, J.K.: A literature review and classification of recommender systems research. Expert Syst. Appl. 39(11), 10059–10072 (2012)
15. Ricci, F., Rokach, L., Shapira, B., Kantor, P.B. (eds.): Recommender Systems Handbook. Springer (2011)
16. Sarwar, B.M., Karypis, G., Konstan, J.A., Riedl, J.: Item-based collaborative filtering recommendation algorithms. In: WWW, pp. 285–295 (2001)
17. Sinha, R.R., Swearingen, K.: Comparing recommendations made by online systems and friends. In: DELOS Workshop: Personalisation and Recommender Systems in Digital Libraries (2001)
18. van Setten, M., Pokraev, S., Koolwaaij, J.: Context-aware recommendations in the mobile tourist application COMPASS. In: De Bra, P.M.E., Nejdl, W. (eds.) AH 2004. LNCS, vol. 3137, pp. 235–244. Springer, Heidelberg (2004)
19. Woerndl, W., Schlichter, J.: Introducing context into recommender systems, pp. 138–140. AAAI (2007)
20. Yang, C.-Z., Chen, I.-X., Wu, P.-J.: Cross-lingual news group recommendation using cluster-based cross-training. IJCLCLP 13(1) (2008)

Co-occurrence and Semantic Similarity Based Hybrid Approach for Improving Automatic Query Expansion in Information Retrieval

Jagendra Singh and Aditi Sharan

School of Computer and Systems Sciences,
Jawaharlal Nehru University, New Delhi-110067
jagendrasngh@gmail.com, aditisharan@mail.jnu.ac.in

Abstract. Pseudo Relevance feedback (PRF) based query expansion approaches assumes that the top ranked retrieved documents are relevant. But this assumption is not always true; it may also possible that a PRF document may contain different topics, which may or may not be relevant to the query terms even if the documents are judged relevant. In this paper our focus is to capture the limitation of PRF based query expansion and propose a hybrid method to improve the performance of PRF based query expansion by combining corpus based term co-occurrence information and semantic information of term. Firstly, the paper suggest use of corpus based term co-occurrence approach to select an optimal combination of query terms from a pool of terms obtained using PRF based query expansion. Second, we use semantic similarity approach to rank the query expansion terms obtained from top feedback documents. Third, we combine co-occurrence and semantic similarity together to rank the query expansion terms obtained from first step on the basis of semantic similarity. The experiments were performed on FIRE ad hoc and TREC-3 benchmark datasets of information retrieval. The results show significant improvement in terms of precision, recall and mean average precision (MAP). This experiments shows that the combination of both techniques in an intelligent way gives us goodness of both of them. As this is the first attempt in this direction there is a large scope of improving these techniques.

Keywords: Information Retrieval, Query Expansion, Pseudo Relevant Feedback, Term Co-occurrence, Semantic Similarity.

1 Introduction

The main objective of an information retrieval system is returning maximum number of relevant documents for corresponding user query. The most critical problem for retrieval effectiveness is the term mismatch problem. The indexers and the users do often not use the same words for the same concept or idea. Automatic query expansion widely used for handling such kind of term mismatch problem.

1.1 Term Co-occurrence Approaches for Query Expansion

According to Rijsbergen [1], the idea of using co-occurrence statistics is used to detect some kind of semantic relations between query and document terms and used it

R. Natarajan et al. (Eds.): ICDCIT 2015, LNCS 8956, pp. 415–418, 2015.

to expand the user's queries. Depth analysis of co-occurrence based query expansion shows mix chances of success or failure and it has scope with other approach.

1.2   Combining Semantics in Query Expansion

While dealing with natural language text, it is important to consider the meaning of text semantically as well as lexically. The main problem with traditional approaches used for information retrieval is that they only consider keyword or lexical based similarity and do not taken care of semantic meaning and relationship between words. To overcome from such limitations a new approach of semantic similarity introduced which considers keyword based similarity as well as semantics of word and relationship between them.

The main contributions of the proposed work are four fold

- First, co-occurrence based query expansion approach (CBQE) using co-occurring feedback information from top feedback documents is designed.
- Second, semantic based query expansion approach (SBQE) is developed utilizing the concept of WordNet based semantic similarity for solving the query semantic meaning related problem.
- Third, hybrid approach of co-occurrence and semantic notion, called co-occurrence and semantic based query expansion (CSBQE) is developed utilizing co-occurring feedback information and the concept of WordNet based semantic similarity for solving the query context related problem.
- Fourth, setting of different numbers of feedback documents and different numbers of top expansion terms are considered in our experiments. Finally mean average precision (MAP) based comparisons of our proposed approaches are explained and analyzed.

The rest of the paper is presented as follows: In Section 2, the proposed work is presented. Computational experiments and results are given in Section 3. Finally, in the last section we conclude our proposed work.

2   Proposed Approach

We used an efficient Okapi BM25 similarity measure [2] for selecting initial set of retrieved documents for a user query, which is more efficient then traditionally used Cosine similarity measure. Further, we used jaccard similarity coefficient [3] for selecting the co-occurring terms with the user query, we called it Co-occurrence Based Query Expansion (CBQE). Some top terms selected from co-occurrence form a term pool of candidate terms.

Next, we used the the concept of semantic similarity between the original query terms and the terms present in term pool to rank the expansion terms based on semantic similarity. Further, we combine the concepts of co-occurrence and semantic similarity together to rank the query expansion terms based on both approaches. The terms at the bottom are filtered to eliminate the noise. We call this approach as Co-occurrence and Semantic based Query Expansion (CSBQE). In order to present our proposed approaches in section 2.1 and 2.2, we discuss the CBQE and CSBQE respectively.

2.1   Algorithm for Co-occurrence Based Query Expansion

Once the tem pool is constructed for selecting the candidate terms, we present an algorithm of co-occurrence based query expansion in Table 1.

Table 1. Algorithm developed for selecting Expansion terms with co-occurrence

1. Select the query.
2. Find similarity value of all documents with query.
3. Sort documents according to their similarity value.
4. Find all unique terms of top n retrieved documents.
5. To find which of the terms are more suitable for query expansion, calculate co-occurrence between all the query terms individually with all the terms of top n retrieved documents using jaccard similarity measure.
6. Find similarity of whole query with all the terms giving a score to rank the co-occurring terms with entire query terms.
7. Form a term pool using original terms of query and top n terms from the ranked co-occurring terms.

2.2   Co-occurrence and Semantic Similarity Based Query Expansion

Once we obtained the terms using CBQE, we observed that some terms are noisy in the sense that they are very general and not related to query. In such cases these terms may retrieve some of the irrelevant documents. Thus it is important to filter these terms. In order to obtain a refined set of the terms, we tried using some background knowledge in form of Linguistic ontology called WordNet [4]. Semantic similarity represents semantic similarity between two words (query term and candidate term). This value can be calculated using a semantic similarity module/approach such as: Resnik [5], Wu Palmar [6] and Leacock & Chodorow [7], which takes two words/concepts as an input and returns semantic similarity between these two terms.

3   Experiment and Results

In our experiment, we use two well known benchmarks test collections: TREC disk 1&2 and FIRE adhoc dataset, which are different in size and genre (TREC disc 1&2 size is 6 Gb, while FIRE dataset is 3.4 Gb). Query numbers range from 126-175 are used for FIRE dataset and query numbers range from 151-200 are used for TREC dataset. In order to find the fair comparisons of our proposed approaches, we use okapi BM25 as a baseline model.

In table 2, we present the original results of our proposed approaches that represent the significant improvement of our proposed feedback methods CBQE, SBQE and CSBQE over baseline methods.

Table 2. Mean Average Precision values of proposed methods with baseline

Collection	Query no.	BM25	CBQE	SBQE	CSBQE
FIRE dataset	126-175	0.2287	0.2310	0.2368	0.2510
TREC disc1&2	151-200	0.2378	0.2495	0.2507	**0.2631**

We found that our proposed methods achieved significant improvement in term of MAP metric for both TREC and FIRE data collection, when the number of feedback documents is set 20. Further, we found when the number of top expansion terms is 30 the performance of our proposed feedback models with all three strategies is high for FIRE dataset. But, when the number of top expansion terms is 50, the performance of our proposed models with all three strategies is high for TREC dataset.

4   Conclusions

In this article, we propose a hybrid approach of co-occurrence and semantic similarity for PRF. PRF Based Query expansion is well studied research field in the area of Information Retrieval. However it has not been explored much from the point of using semantic similarity and co-occurrence based techniques together. Through extensive experiments on two representative TREC and FIRE collections, we evaluate the proposed approaches with baseline from different aspects, including its general performance, robustness and influence of important parameters. Specifically the paper suggests use of Co-occurrence Based Query Expansion (CBQE), Semantic Based Query Expansion (SBQE) and Co-occurrence and Semantic Based Query Expansion (CSBQE)   in order to improve retrieval efficiency of an Information retrieval system.

The comparison of the results has been done on the basis of mean average precision (MAP). Experimental results show motivating performance of the proposed feedback approaches, it was observed that CBQE is providing a more cohesive and better selection of expansion terms. In SBQE and CSBQE, semantic similarity was used to select those terms which are semantically similar to the query term present in top feedback documents and co-occurrence based term pool respectively.

References

1. Van Rijsbergen, C.J.: A theoretical basis for the use of co-occurrence data in information Retrieval. Journal of Documentation 33, 106–119 (1977)
2. Robertson, S.E., Walker, S., Beaulieu, M.H.: Okapi at TREC-7. In: Proceedings of the Seventh Text REtrieval Conference. Gaithersburg, USA (1998)
3. Kobayakawa, M., Kinjo, S., Hoshi, M., Ohmori, T., Yamamoto, A.: Fast Computation of Similarity Based on Jaccard Coefficient for Composition-Based Image Retrieval. In: Muneesawang, P., Wu, F., Kumazawa, I., Roeksabutr, A., Liao, M., Tang, X. (eds.) PCM 2009. LNCS, vol. 5879, pp. 949–955. Springer, Heidelberg (2009)
4. Miller, G.A., Beckwith, R., Fellbaum, C.D., Gross, D., Miller, K.: WordNet: An online lexical database. Int. J. Lexicograph. 3(4), 235–244 (1990)
5. Resnik, P.: Semantic Similarity in Taxonomy: An Information-Based Measure and its Application to Problems of Ambiguity in Natural Language. Journal of Artificial Intelligence Research 11, 95–130 (1999)
6. Wu, Z., Palmer, M.: Verb Semantics and Lexical Selection. In: Annual Meeting of the Associations for Computational Linguistic, Las Cruces, New, Mexico, pp. 133–138 (1994)
7. Leacock, C., Miller, G.A., Chodorow, M.: Combining Local Context and WordNet Similarity for Word Sense Identification. Journal of Computational Linguistic, 265–283 (1998)

Predicting User Visibility in Online Social Networks Using Local Connectivity Properties

Nemi Chandra Rathore, Somanath Tripathy, and Joydeep Chandra

Department of Computer Science and Engineering
Indian Institute of Technology Patna, India
{nemi,som,joydeep}@iitp.ac.in

Abstract. Recent developments in Online Social Network (OSN) technologies and services, added with availability of wide range of applications has paved the way towards popularity of several social network platforms. These OSNs have evolved as a major communication and interaction platform for millions of users worldwide. The users interact with their social contacts by using various types of available services like messaging, sharing pictures /videos, and many more. However, a major drawback of these platforms is that these activities might reveal certain private information about the users unintentionally. Whenever a user shares any information on OSN with his friends, the information is prone to leakage to other users. The probability of leakage increases with the visibility of the user himself (i.e. the number of users who would be interested on the information of the user) as well as the visibility of his/her friends. Therefore, it is important to measure the visibility of a user in the OSN community. This paper proposes a measure for the visibility of a user, by considering the connectivity properties of the users present in the network. The characteristics of the proposed measure is studied on a real Twitter network as well as a generated Erdős-Rényi network, where we observe the relation between visibility and certain topological parameters of the network. The results show that visibility of a user is determined by his/her direct social contacts, i.e. the number of followers in case of Twitter. However, evaluating the visibility of an user is practically difficult considering the immensely large size of the OSN's. These findings help us to generate simple mechanisms to estimate the visibility of a user using only its local connectivity properties.

Keywords: Online Social Networks, Privacy, Visibility, Topology.

1 Introduction

In recent years, evolution of mobile technology have provided wings to the growth of the number of Internet users. In March-2013, the number of Internet users have reached to 2.937 billions which is 40.7% of world's total population [17]. Nearly, half of these *Internet users* are members of some online social networks [5]. Only Facebook[1] has 1.3 billion monthly active users upto January 2014

---

[1] www.facebook.com

R. Natarajan et al. (Eds.): ICDCIT 2015, LNCS 8956, pp. 419–430, 2015.

who spend 18 minutes on average per visit [3]. According to statistics up to January, 2014, Twitter[2], a popular micro-blogging service has 645.75 million of total number of active users that generates 58 million tweets per day on average[4]. There are a number of other popular Social Networking sites like Google+[3], linkedIn[4] that have also drawn huge set of users. The OSN users represent themselves by their profiles where they share some of their attributes, including personal attributes like name, age, sex, education, location, places of study and many more. The users create new relationships on the basis of common interest, attributes, location, profession etc. They communicate with each other using wide range of information sharing and communication services offered by the OSNs.

However this flexibility of communication of users comes at the cost of risk upon his privacy. The users explicitly or implicitly share a lot of their personal and sensitive information with their friends over OSN through various means. This shared information are either visible to a group of their contacts or to every one depending on users privacy settings. An adversary can easily gather this personal and highly sensitive information to strengthen various type of attacks like recovering credentials of bank accounts, credit cards, phishing, de-anonymization, spamming etc. Moreover, hidden user attributes can also be inferred from the owner or his friends information. Mislove et. al. [15] have shown that if information of atleast 20% users are given, most of the other users information can be inferred with accuracy over 80%. A number of such attacks have been reported in literature which reveals users personal information. Different OSNs have taken different counter measures to thwart such attacks, but those have proved to be insufficient [6]. All the OSNs provide a set of security mechanisms to protect private information of their users. But, unfortunately, all of these current privacy protection mechanisms operate at syntactic level only and could be used to protect information from the users currently communicating [12].

The probability of leakage of private information of a user also depends on the position of the user in network topology. If the user himself is directly or indirectly connected to a large set of nodes in the network then the chances of information leakage through his neighbors increase. For example, if a user considers his birth date as a private information and shares only with his friends, it is highly likely that any one of his friends may share such information further with his friends, thereby causing an information leakage. The probability of this leakage will primarily depend on the number of users in his vicinity in one or more hops[5]. Although, it also depends on other factors like how active its neighbor nodes are in the OSN. We consider the number of such vicinity nodes of a user, who might be interested in the information about a user, as a measure of visibility of a user in the OSN. The visibility of a user can provide an idea about how much

---

[2] www.twitter.com

[3] www.plus.google.com

[4] www.linkedin.com

[5] Friends are assumed to be at hop-1, and friends of friends at hop-2.

a user is vulnerable to information leakage. In this paper, we propose a measure of the visibility of a user based on the topological properties of the network. We apply the proposed measure on real Twitter network and observe the relation between user visibility and various measurement parameters like the topology of the network. The results indicate that the visibility of the nodes is largely dependent on the local topological properties of a node like degree, clustering etc. These observations help us to generate simple mechanisms to estimate the visibility of a user using only his local topological characteristics.

The organization of the paper is as follows. We present related work in section 2. In section 3, we present our proposed measure to calculate user visibility. We study the characteristics of the proposed measure on real Twitter and Erdős-Rényi networks in section 4. In section 5, we discuss about the results of our experiments and finally, we conclude our work with possible future directions in section 6.

2 Related Work

Privacy is more prevalent issue on all OSN platforms. It attracts a number of researchers to find out techniques to address the issue. A major focus in the area is on inferring hidden user attributes either by exploiting available attributes of user or his social contacts and stopping such attacks. Liu et al. [14] proposed a framework to measure user privacy. Their work is inspired by Item Response Theory [1] and Information Propagation (IP) models [11]. In this work, visibility of any profile item is specified by user itself by providing an integer value, with higher value means higher visibility. But this work does not consider the impact of network structure on the visibility of any profile item. Gundecha et al. [9] proposed four indexes to quantify user privacy and how much a user's profile is public/visible to others. This work only focuses on the visibility of attributes only due to users or his friends profile settings but does not measure the visibility of any activities of user. Also, it does not take the structural aspects of social network into consideration. In [2] Becker et al. introduced a tool known as privAware to detect unintended leakage of user's information which infers the private or unspecified attributes using information of his direct social contacts. If it detects that certain private attributes can be inferred, then users can update their set of social contacts according to some suggested methods. Talukder et al.[18] have proposed a tool called *privometer* to measure user's privacy on Facebook. This tool measures the amount of information leakage based on the relationship and private information of his friends. But, in this work authors do not consider visibility of profile items, any shared message or activity revealing private information of user. To preserve user privacy two solutions called *Safebook* [7] that controls user privacy based on the trust between links, and Sybilguard [19] that controls Sybil attack on user privacy have been proposed.

All the existing approaches described above, just extract value of visibility of user attributes on the basis of privacy settings of user. No work to the best of our knowledge calculates user visibility using connectivity properties of user's local subgraph. In the next section, we have described our proposed method with required formal model of OSN to predict user visibility.

3   Proposed Methodology

In this section, we propose an analytical model to measure user visibility, considering network topology. The proposed model is based on the topological properties of a node like the degree and clustering coefficient.

3.1   Formal Model of an Online Social Network

Formally, an OSN can be represented as a directed graph $G = (V, E)$, where V, the set of vertices represents OSN users, E, the set of edges represents friendship links between OSN users. Further $v \in V$ represents a user by his profile which is a set of n ordered pairs of attributes and corresponding values (A_i, a_i) i.e.

$$v = \{(A_i, a_i) : i = 1, 2, ...n\}$$

A directed edge $e \in E$, is an ordered pair (v_1, v_2) with $v_1, v_2 \in V$, represents user v_1 as friend/follower of user v_2. The edge (v_2, v_1) also exists, if user v_2 is also the friend/follower of user v_1. Some OSNs like Facebook, consider friendship a bi-directional relation and automatically create link in other direction as soon as friendship request is accepted by other user. But, some OSNs like Twitter, Google+, create link only in one direction called as follower link.

3.2   Computing OSN User Visibility

The visibility of a user is measured by the number of nodes potentially connected to the user with respect to the degree of the highest degree node at each hop distance from it. Thus if the degree of a node A is d_A and d_{max} is the degree of highest degree node, then the visibility at hop-1 from the node is $\frac{d_A}{d_{max}}$. Further to find the visibility of the node A at subsequent hops, we formulate a recursive expression as follows:

If C_A, denote the clustering coefficient of node A, given as $k/\binom{d_A}{2}$, where k is the number of triangle formed at node A and $\binom{d_A}{2}$ represents the number of triplets at node A. Then, the visibility contributed of the neighbor V_j of node A is $(1 - C_A)V_j$. However, the number of nodes connected to node A, increase with the hop count, the actual interest on the information about node A will diminish with increase in hop count. So, we introduce a damping factor α, $(0 < \alpha < 1)$, that gets multiplied with the visibility contributed by the neighbor j. Hence the expression for visibility of node A can be written as follows;

$$V_A = \frac{d_A}{d_{max}} + \alpha(1 - C_A) \sum_{j \in N(A)} V_j \tag{1}$$

where $\alpha = \frac{1}{x}$ is a parameter called damping factor and x is an integer constant less than or equal to $\lceil f_{avg} \rceil$, the average number of followers in OSN.

If, we enable a user to know his visibility at different hops well in advance, then he can control the visibility of his any communication activity according to its sensitivity. Any attribute or information in user profile can be assigned a sensitivity value in interval $[0, 1]$. If $S_a = 0$, it indicates attribute can be made public without affecting privacy of user, but if $S_a = 1$, the attribute is treated to be highly sensitive and can't be disclosed to anyone. For example, if some information which is sensitive and can be disclosed to only friends then its visibility needs to be controlled such that its visibility is limited to one hop only. The visibility of any attribute or activity π with sensitivity S_π for user A can be calculated as follows:

$$V_\pi = S_\pi . V_A \tag{2}$$

Each user can set a threshold value V_T. If visibility of any of the user's activity crosses the set threshold, then any action like, commenting, sharing, liking will not be allowed further. In the next section, we present an analysis of our proposed formula over twitter followers dataset available at SNAP project's website of Stanford University [13]. We choose twitter dataset for our experiment as twitter have users having number of friends/follower with high variance. The objective of this study is to see how the number of connections (followers/friends) of a user affect his visibility in the online social network.

4 Experimental Observations

The experimental dataset consists of 81306 Twitter users with minimum and maximum in-degree (i.e. number of followers) 0, and 8660, respectively and average in-degree of 29.76582. The graph has 0 and 3373 as minimum and maximum out-degree respectively, with average out-degree 29.7618. Using this dataset, we created a directed graph of OSN users using Boost Graph Library (BGL)[10] in Ubuntu 14.04 environment on a machine equipped with OS Intel i7 Quad core processor, and 4GB RAM. We also consider an Erdős-Rényi (ER) graph [8] with same number of nodes and probability $p = 0.00037$ of any pair of nodes having any edge, to compare the observations with respect to the twitter network. This is because the node degrees in Erdős-Rényi network has much smaller variance as compared to the twitter graph. Since the Erdős-Rényi graph has symmetric links, the in-degree and out-degree of each of the nodes are considered to be same. The maximum in-degree and out-degree of nodes in the graph was 56, with average in-degree and out-degree of 30.1112. The graphs in figure 1, show followers distribution among users for both Twitter and Erdős-Rényi network. As stated earlier, it can be observed that the number of followers in Twitter (figure 1(b)) ranges from very low to very high, whereas for Erdős-Rényi network this variance is very low. In our experimental Twitter graph there was only one user who do not have any follower, and 12.566% users with only one follower. 90.02% users were having followers less than average. Only 0.2% users

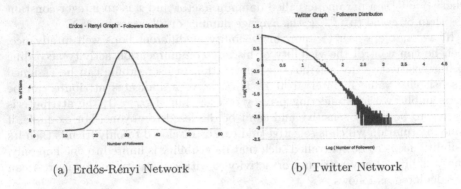

(a) Erdős-Rényi Network   (b) Twitter Network

Fig. 1. Follower distribution in Erdős-Rényi and Twitter network

have average number of followers and 9.97% of users having followers more than average. On the other hand, approximately 13.79% of users were not following any one, 75.026% users following between 1 and 59 users and 11.19% users following more than average number of users. A small number of users were having a large followers base, maximum upto 8660 followers.

We observe the variation of visibility of the users with respect to their number of followers, the number of hops considered for calculating the visibility and the damping factor. In the next few sections, we observe the effect of these parameters on the visibility of the nodes.

4.1   Effect of Followers

In this section we study the variation in the visibility of the nodes with respect to their follower count for different hop values with fix value of damping factor α.

To understand the relationship between number of followers and visibility at different hops, we plotted graph between number of followers verses user visibility at hop values $h = 1, 2, 3, 4$ while keeping α constant. Figure 2, shows the results for $\alpha = 0.2, 0.4, 0.6$ for both the networks. As can be observed in figure 2, for lower values of follower count in Twitter graph, the visibility of the nodes increases gradually with increasing number of followers. However, when the number of followers is high, the rate of increase in the visibility is very high with respect to the increase in the number of followers. Thus it can be observed that the number of followers of a node is a dominant factor in determining its visibility. Further, the rate of increase in visibility with respect to the number of followers is higher for Twitter networks as compared to the ER networks. This is because of the homogeneity in the node degrees in case of ER networks.

We next discuss the variation of node visibility with respect to the maximum hop count that we consider for evaluating the visibility of the nodes.

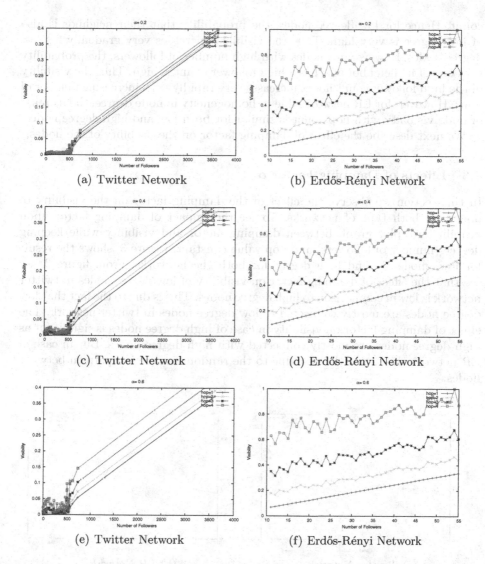

(a) Twitter Network

(b) Erdős-Rényi Network

(c) Twitter Network

(d) Erdős-Rényi Network

(e) Twitter Network

(f) Erdős-Rényi Network

Fig. 2. The variation of node visibility with respect to the number of followers at hop=1, 2, 3, 4 (for $\alpha = 0.2, 0.4, 0.6$) for Twitter and Erdős-Rényi networks

4.2   Effects of Maximum Hop Count

In this section we observe the effects of the maximum hop count on the visibility of the nodes. The results in figure 2, show that in Twitter network, the visibility of the low follower count nodes increases marginally with hop count. However, for large follower count nodes the increase in visibility is steep with increasing values of maximum hop count. The reason for such behavior is due to the fact that most of the nodes in the Twitter network is of low degree, i.e. low follower count. Hence for low degree nodes, the probability that their neighbor is also of low degree is very high. Thus the visibility increases very gradually for low degree nodes. However, for nodes with high number of followers, the probability that one of its neighbor also has a high follower count is high. Thus the visibility of the high follower count nodes increases very rapidly with increasing number of hops. However, for ER networks due to homogeneity in node degree, the increase of node visibility with hop count is similar for both low and high degree nodes.

We next describe the effect of damping factor on the visibility of the nodes.

4.3   Effects of Damping Factor α

In this section we observe the effect of the damping factor on the visibility of nodes for both type of networks. To see the impact of damping factor upon visibility, we plot graph between damping factor and visibility while keeping degree (number of followers) and hop value constant. Figure 3, shows the result for low, moderate and high degree for both the networks. From figure 3, we see that the effect of damping factor on visibility of low degree nodes in twitter network is low in comparison to high degree nodes. This is due to the fact that low degree nodes are mostly connected to low degree nodes in twitter network. The effect of damping factor on visibility in case of high degree nodes is significant as high degree nodes are mostly connected with high degree nodes. But in case of ER network this is not the case due to the random connection pattern between nodes.

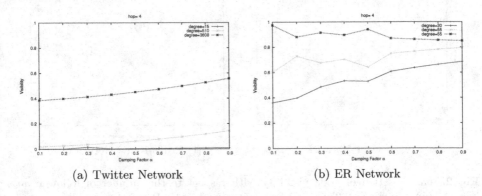

(a) Twitter Network   (b) ER Network

Fig. 3. The variation in node visibility for certain node degrees with respect to the damping factors in Twitter and Erdős-Rényi network. The value of the hop is considered as 4.

Thus, we find that follower count of the nodes play an important role in determining the visibility of the nodes. We next study the nature of the followers of the different nodes, i.e., whether high (low) follower users follow other users with similar follower count or otherwise. This is important as it would help us to understand how the visibility of the nodes depends on the nature of its followers.

4.4   The Mixing Nature of the Nodes

In this section, we study the assortative mixing property of the nodes based on their follower count. To distinguish between the nodes, we classify the nodes into three following categories depending upon their follower count and the nature of the followers.

1. Celebrity users: These are the users having number of followers higher than or equal to a threshold value.
2. Special users: These are the users having atleast one celebrity as their follower.
3. Normal Users: Users that are neither celebrity nor special nodes, are defined as normal users.

We study the nature of mixing among these users in the Twitter network. In this study, we consider 2500 as the node degree threshold value for being qualified as a celebrity node. The nodes having followers more than 2499 are called celebrity nodes. Approximately, 0.032% of the nodes qualified as celebrity nodes, 5.1% as special nodes and 94.85% as normal nodes. In case of Erdős-Rényi graph, no node qualified as celebrity node, as a result of it, there was no special node according to the chosen threshold value.

To understand, how different types of nodes are interconnected with each other, we calculate assortative mixing and assortativity coefficient using following formula given by Newman [16] for the dataset. Thus, if e_{ij} denotes the fraction of edges that connect nodes of type i with that of j, then the assortativity coefficient that measures the similarity of the connections among the node types is given as follows:

$$r = \frac{\sum_i e_{ii} - \sum_i a_i b_i}{1 - \sum_i a_i bi} \tag{3}$$

where $a_i = \sum_j e_{ij}$, $b_i = \sum_i e_{ij}$ and $\sum_{ij} e_{ij} = 1$. If r is nearer to 1 then it indicates assortative mixing, i.e. nodes preferentially connects to similar nodes, whereas a value of r nearer to -1 indicates that nodes preferentially connects to dissimilar nodes. A value of r near to 0 indicates that the connections are mostly random. Table 1 shows the mixing matrix e_{ji} i.e. $(v_i \leftarrow v_j)$ and values of a_i and b_i for interconnection between different node types in the Twitter follower network. The assortativity coefficient (r) for the graph happens to be 0.386406.

Table 1. The mixing matrix e_{ji} i.e. $(v_i \leftarrow v_j)$ and values of a_i and b_i for interconnection between different node types

Node Type	Special node	Celebrity node	Normal Node	a_i
Special Node	0.153854	0.00890998	0.148932	0.31169598
Celebrity Node	0.0733656	0.00181595	0.0218666	0.04206845
Normal Node	0.0665367	0	0.572869	0.6462346
b_i	0.2456055	0.01072593	0.7436676	-

This value of r, confirms that twitter graph is mostly assortative with respect to the node categories described. We observe that special nodes preferably connects with special nodes as compared to other node types. Same is true for normal nodes as well. It can be observed that 57.2% of normal nodes follow normal node only. However, celebrity nodes are connected to special nodes with a higher probability. Value b_i, for celebrity nodes shows that celebrity follows 0.1% of nodes only.

Thus these results indicate that with a very high probability, nodes are more likely to follow similar type of nodes. This observation can be used to estimate the visibility of the nodes by considering only its degree and the maximum node degree of the nodes in the nearby vicinity. We detail this in the next section.

5   Results and Discussion

In this section we interpret the results that we observe from our experimental analysis. Although we have proposed a measure to calculate the visibility of the users in the network, however the proposed mechanism requires exploring the entire topology and the connectivity properties of the nodes at several hops. Since present day social networks are immensely large, gathering such topological information about the entire network is difficult if not impossible. However, the observations made in the paper from the experiments can help the nodes to derive estimates about their visibility based on the local topological properties. We discuss the same in detail.

There are two major findings that we get from our experiments: first the visibility of a node is proportional to the number of followers it has and second the followers of the users have similar follower count as the user himself. Thus to estimate his visibility, a user, A, can modify equation 1 by replacing the visibility of its neighbor by its own visibility and iterating the same repeatedly.

$$\hat{V}_A^{(i)} = \frac{d_A}{d_{max}} + \alpha(1 - C_A) \sum_{j \in N(A)} \hat{V}_A^{(i-1)}, \qquad (4)$$

$$\hat{V}_A^{(0)} = \frac{d_A}{d_{max}}$$

where $\hat{V}_A^{(i)}$ is the estimate of the visibility of A in the ith iteration. In this case, the value of d_{max} can be estimated by considering the follower count of the highest degree node in its neighborhood.

Based on equation 4, we propose **algorithm-1**, that any node A can use to estimate its visibility. In the algorithm, we assume that node A knows its own clustering coefficient and wants to calculate its visibility upto a maximum number of hops h. Since the algorithm is intuitively based on the observed experimental results that we have discussed in earlier sections, we avoid stating the comparison of the same with the experimental result due to want of space.

Algorithm 1: Calculate_Visibility

Data: d_A: The degree of the node
Data: C_A: The clustering coefficient of node A
Result: Estimate of visibility of node A
for each $j \in N(A)$ **do**
    $d_j \longleftarrow Degree(j)$

$\hat{d}_{max} \longleftarrow max\{d_j \quad \forall j \in N(A)\}$
$\hat{V}_A^0 \longleftarrow \frac{d_A}{\hat{d}_{max}}$
$i \longleftarrow 1$
for $i <= h$ **do**
    $\hat{V}_A^{(i)} \longleftarrow \frac{d_A}{\hat{d}_{max}} + \alpha(1 - C_A)\sum_{j \in N(A)} \hat{V}_A^{(i-1)}$
    $i \longleftarrow i + 1;$

---

6 Conclusions and Future Work

In this paper, we proposed a method to measure the visibility of OSN users
based on topology of the online social network. We calculated the visibility of
user in case of a real OSN graph generated by followers dataset of Twitter.
Results show that visibility of an OSN user depends on user's degree (number
of followers/friends). We also showed that the network is assortative, similar
nodes with similar topological characteristics connect with each other with high
probability. Based on these observations we proposed an algorithm to estimate
the visibility of the users based on his local topological properties. Thus using this
mechanism the users can estimate their visibility and hence tune their privacy
settings accordingly. However, we have not taken into account user behavior (like
how much active he is in the social network) in the measurement of visibility.
As future work, we will study the role of user and his neighbor's behavior in
privacy measurement. Also we would like to see if other topological parameters
like closeness and betweenness can improve the results.

References

1. Baker, F.B., Kim, S.H.: Item Response Theory: Parameter Estimation Techniques.
   CRC Press, Marcel Dekker (2004)
2. Becker, J., Chen, H.: Measuring privacy risk in online social networks. In: Proceedings of W2SP 2009: Web 2.0 Security and Privacy, Oakland, CA, USA (May
   2009)
3. Statistics Brain. Statistics brain, facebook statistics (June 2013)
4. Statistics Brain. Statistics brain, twitter statistics (June 2013)
5. Pew Research Center. Global publics embrace social networking, pew research center (2010)
6. Chaabane, A., Acs, G., Kaafar, M.A.: You are what you like! information leakage
   through user's interests. In: NDSS (2012)
7. Cutillo, L.A., Molva, R., Strufe, T.: Safebook: A privacy-preserving online social network leveraging on real-life trust. IEEE Communications Magazine 47(12),
   94–101 (2009)

8. Erdös, P., Rényi, A.: On random graphs, i. Publicationes Mathematicae (Debrecen) 6, 290–297 (1959)
9. Gundecha, P., Barbier, G., Liu, H.: Exploiting vulnerability to secure user privacy on a social networking site. In: Proceedings of the 17th ACM SIGKDD International Conference on Knowledge Discovery and Data Mining, KDD 2011, pp. 511–519. ACM, New York (2011)
10. Lumsdaine, A., Siek, J., Lee, L.Q.: Boost graph library (2000)
11. Kempe, D., Kleinberg, J., Tardos, É.: Maximizing the spread of influence through a social network. In: Proceedings of the Ninth ACM SIGKDD International Conference on Knowledge Discovery and Data Mining, KDD 2003, pp. 137–146. ACM, New York (2003)
12. Krishnamurthy, B.: Privacy and online social networks: can colorless green ideas sleep furiously? IEEE Security Privacy 11(3), 14–20 (2013)
13. Leskovec, J., Krevl, A.: SNAP Datasets: Stanford large network dataset collection (June 2014), http://snap.stanford.edu/data
14. Liu, K., Terzi, E.: A framework for computing the privacy scores of users in online social networks. ACM Trans. Knowl. Discov. Data 5(1), 6:1–6:30 (2010)
15. Mislove, A., Viswanath, B., Gummadi, K.P., Druschel, P.: You are who you know: Inferring user profiles in online social networks. In: Proceedings of the Third ACM International Conference on Web Search and Data Mining, WSDM 2010, pp. 251–260. ACM, New York (2010)
16. Newman, M.E.J.: Mixing patterns in networks. Phys. Rev. E 67, 026126 (2003)
17. Internet World Stats. Internet world stats, usage and population statistics (January 2014)
18. Talukder, N., Ouzzani, M., Elmagarmid, A.K., Elmeleegy, H., Yakout, M.: Privometer: Privacy protection in social networks. In: 2010 IEEE 26th International Conference on Data Engineering Workshops (ICDEW), pp. 266–269 (March 2010)
19. Yu, H., Kaminsky, M., Gibbons, P.B., Flaxman, A.: Sybilguard: Defending against sybil attacks via social networks. SIGCOMM Comput. Commun. Rev. 36(4), 267–278 (2006)

Using KNN and SVM Based One-Class Classifier for Detecting Online Radicalization on Twitter

Swati Agarwal and Ashish Sureka

Indraprastha Institute of Information Technology, Delhi (IIIT-D)
New Delhi, India
{swatia,ashish}@iiitd.ac.in

Abstract. Twitter is the largest and most popular micro-blogging website on Internet. Due to low publication barrier, anonymity and wide penetration, Twitter has become an easy target or platform for extremists to disseminate their ideologies and opinions by posting hate and extremism promoting tweets. Millions of tweets are posted on Twitter everyday and it is practically impossible for Twitter moderators or an intelligence and security analyst to manually identify such tweets, users and communities. However, automatic classification of tweets into predefined categories is a non-trivial problem problem due to short text of the tweet (the maximum length of a tweet can be 140 characters) and noisy content (incorrect grammar, spelling mistakes, presence of standard and non-standard abbreviations and slang). We frame the problem of hate and extremism promoting tweet detection as a one-class or unary-class categorization problem by learning a statistical model from a training set containing only the objects of one class . We propose several linguistic features such as presence of war, religious, negative emotions and offensive terms to discriminate hate and extremism promoting tweets from other tweets. We employ a single-class SVM and KNN algorithm for one-class classification task. We conduct a case-study on Jihad, perform a characterization study of the tweets and measure the precision and recall of the machine-learning based classifier. Experimental results on large and real-world dataset demonstrate that the proposed approach is effective with F-score of 0.60 and 0.83 for the KNN and SVM classifier respectively.

Keywords: Mining User Generated Content, One-Class Classifier, Online Radicalization, Short-Text Classification, Social media analytics, Twitter.

1 Research Motivation and Aim

Twitter[1] is a popular social networking website and the largest micro-blogging platform on Internet. Twitter allows users to share ideas and information instantly by posting short messages of 140 characters called as Tweets. Research

---

[1] https://twitter.com/

R. Natarajan et al. (Eds.): ICDCIT 2015, LNCS 8956, pp. 431–442, 2015.

shows that Twitter has become a platform for online radicalization and posting hate and extremism promoting content due to low publication barrier, lack of stringent moderation, anonymity and wide penetration [2][4][9].

Automatic identification of hate and extremism promoting tweets is useful to intelligence and security informatics agents as well as Twitter moderators. Manual identification of such tweets and filtering information from raw data is practically impossible due to the large volumes of tweets (500 million) posted every day. Tweets consists of short text (maximum of 140 characters) and noise (incorrect grammar, spelling mistakes, slang and abbreviations) as a result of which automatic classification of tweets is a technically challenging problem. The motivation of the work presented in this paper is to investigate solutions to address the problems encountered by intelligence and security informatics agents and Twitter moderators for countering online radicalization on the largest micro-blogging platform on Internet. The research aim of the work presented in this paper is the following:

1. To investigate techniques to automatically identify hate and extremism promoting tweets. To identify linguistic and stylistic features and characteristics of hate and extremism promoting tweets.
2. To conduct empirical analysis on a large real-world dataset and demonstrate the effectiveness of the proposed Machine Learning based text classification approach. To examine the relative influence of each proposed feature for the task of identifying hate and extremism promoting tweets. To compare and contrast the performance of various Machine Learning algorithms (KNN and LibSVM) for the purpose of recognizing hate and extremism promoting tweets.

2   Related Work and Research Contributions

We conduct a literature survey in the area of online radicalization detection on Web 2.0 (refer to Table 1) and textual classification of microblogs (refer to Table 2). Online radicalization, hate and extremism has been studied on multiple topics and domains: terrorism, anti-black communities, nationalism, politics, jihad and anti-Islam. Table 1 and 2 also mentions the experimental dataset size used in each study. We characterize papers based on the linguistic features used for the classification task and highlight the tweet classification goal: humor [10], irony [10], sarcasm [7], spam [8], vulgarity [12] and sentiments. There are many categories in tweet classification but due to page limitation we discuss a few of them here. Table 3(a) and 3(b) shows the dimensions for reviewing these categories and features respectively. We conclude from the related work that there is a research gap in the area of hate and extremism promoting tweet classification (intersection of online radicalization on Web 2.0 and short text or micro-blog classification). In context to existing work, the study presented in this paper makes the following unique contributions extending our previous work ([1]):

Table 1. Summary of Literature Survey of 9 Papers on Detecting Various Forms of Radicalization on Twitter

Ref	Year	Study	Objective	Dataset Tweets	Nodes
[2]	2013	Nationalism	Identification of most influential, active and engaged hate promoting accounts on Twitter.	342K	3.5K
[4]	2013	Anti-Black	Classification of racist and non-racist conflicts in tweets by applying statistical measures.	24.5K	-
[9]	2013	Nationalism	Identification and analysis of extreme right communities on various social networking websites.	-	1697
[11]	2013	Terrorism	Content analysis of tweets in order to identify hidden groups related to a specific topic.	-	-

Table 2. Summary of Literature Survey of 11 Papers on Classifying Tweets

Ref	Year	Research Study C1	C2	C3	C4	C5	C6	C7	Objective	Features F1	F2	F3	F4	F5	F6	F7	F8	F9	F10	F11	Data
[7]	2013	✓							A linguistic analysis based approach to filter **sarcastic** tweets.					✓		✓	✓	✓			3.38M
[10]	2012	✓		✓	✓				Identifying **irony** and **humorous** message on Twitter.	✓	✓			✓			✓			✓	50K
[12]	2012	✓			✓				Identification of inappropriate and **vulgar** language in tweets.								✓			✓	696M
[8]	2012							✓	Language model to filter **spam** tweets in most trending topics.	✓	✓			✓	✓	✓	✓			✓	20M
[13]	2012						✓		Discovering valuable tweets with of **interest** to its audience.	✓				✓	✓	✓	✓				64M

Table 3. List of Tweet Classification Goals and Linguistic Features

(a) **Categories**

Symbol	Summary
C1	Sentiment Classification
C2	Sarcasm Classification
C3	Irony Classification
C4	Humor Classification
C5	Offensive Tweets
C6	Interestingness
C7	Spam Detection
C8	News & Public Opinion
C9	Software Related
C10	Political Preference
C11	Writing Style

(b) **Features**

Symbol	Summary
F1	Direct Message
F2	Shortened URLs
F3	Emoticons
F4	Punctuations
F5	Topics
F6	Hashtags
F7	Mentioned Entities
F8	N-grams
F9	+ve and -ve Comments
F10	Emphasis (CAPS)
F11	Terms

1. A one-class classifier for identifying hate and extremism promoting tweets. While there has been work done in the area of humor, sarcasm, irony, sentiment, vulgar and spam tweets, to the best of our knowledge, our study is the first work on hate and extremism promoting tweet identification using a one-class classifier framework.

2. An empirical analysis on real-world Twitter dataset investigating the influence of various linguistic features (discriminatory features) for the task of recognizing hate and extremism promoting tweets. We conduct a series of

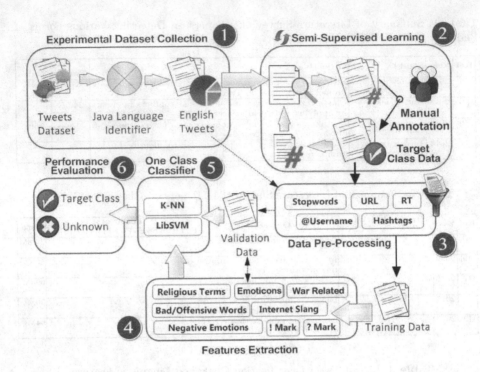

Fig. 1. A General Research Framework For Our Proposed Solution Approach

experiments to train a one-class SVM and KNN classifier and test its effectiveness for the given classification task.

3   Research Framework

Figure 1 illustrates the proposed solution approach. The proposed method is a multi-step process primarily consists of six phases: experimental dataset collection, training dataset creation, data pre-processing, feature extraction, one-class classification and performance evaluation. The six phases are labeled in the solution framework. In phase 1, we download two publicly available datasets [5] [6] (refer to Section 5.1 on experimental dataset) and combine them to form a single experimental dataset (a larger and diverse dataset to generalize our results). The dataset consists of tweets belonging to multiple languages. We use a language detection library[2] to filter English and non-English tweets. We conduct experiments only on English language tweets and discard non-English tweets. We notice that 85% of tweets are in English.

We require training dataset to create a statistical model for one-class classification task of identifying hate and extremism promoting tweets. We use

---

[2] https://code.google.com/p/language-detection/

Table 4. A Sample of Hate Promoting Tweets Leading to More Hashtags

Seed Hashtag	Tweet	Extended Hashtags
#Terrorism	Secret #recruitment British students #Muslim #extremists ? #islamophobia **#terrorism**	#islamophobia, #extremists
#Islamophobia	#NoJihad #Racism lowest form stupidity ! **#Islamophobia** height common sense ! #Quran	#NoJihad, #Racism
#Extremist	Engaging #AfPak Information War: Countering **#extremist** #propaganda with #mobile #technology	#propaganda
#Islam	**#Islam** evil according #GeertWilders one few islamophobic people Netherlands yet everywhere	#GeertWilders
#Terrorism	New: Al Qaeda Bomb Maker Video **#terrorism** #bomb #video #alqaeda #alquida	#bomb, #alqaeda, #alquida

Table 5. A Sample of Keywords Present in Hate Promoting Tweets

Hashtags	#islamophobia, #stealthjihad, #myjihad, #extremists, #NoJihad, #terrorism, #dreamact, #terrorist, #nativist, #GeertWilders, #alqaeda, #assassination
Religious	hijab, hizb, demon, jihad, god, maulana, kabba, azan, burka, prophet, koum, apostate, sikh, muhajir, immigrant, hijr, amen, hinduism, devil, atheist
War Related	LOC, Bomb, Blast, Attack, Holy war, Warfare, Tribute, Soldier, Jawan, Refugee, Enemies, Fighting, Patriot, Assassination, Expose, Army, Zindabad
-ve Emotions	endangered, enslaved, entangled, evaded, evasive, evicted, excessive, excluded, exhausted, exploited, exposed, fail, fake, hatred, regret, disgust, flaw
Emoticons	:), :-), :D, :-D, =], :], :), =P, :P, :-P, :*, :(, :-(, =(, :-S, :S, :O, :-O, :\, :-\, \-o, :-}X, :-(, =), :-E, :-F, :-C, 3:*>, :-(, :(, :-d, :->, :-@,)8-), 3:), O:), :'(
Internet Slangs	LOL, haha, ROFL, WT*, WTH, IMHO, OSM, AKA, BRB, 404, CC, TC, TT, Cya, Gr8, FAQ, FYI, Hw, L8r, N/A, W/O, B/W, BTW, NP, OMG, PLZ
Bad Words	ahole, ass, ba****d, bit*h, crap, f**k, gay, damned, hells, jackoff, sh**, pe***, sexy, sl*t, XXX, b17ch, s.o.b., wh**e, screw, bulls**t, d-bag, jerk-off

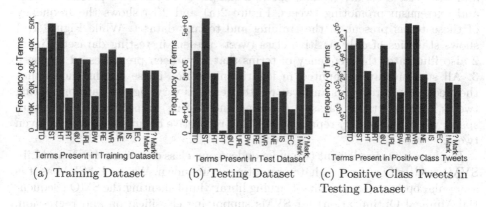

(a) Training Dataset	(b) Testing Dataset	(c) Positive Class Tweets in Testing Dataset

Fig. 2. Frequency Distribution of Various Terms Present in the Training and Testing Dataset. TD= Tweet Dataset, ST=Stopwords, HT= Hashtags, RT= Retweets, @U= @username Mentioned, URL= Hyperlinks, BW= Bad Words, RE= Religious Terms, WR= War Related Terms, NE= Negative Emotions, IS= Internet Slangs, EC=Emoticons.

a semi-supervised learning[3] approach to create our training dataset. Annotating Tweets is a time-consuming and tedious task (practically challenging to annotate a large dataset). Hence, we use semi-supervised learning making use of a small amount of labeled data and a large amount of unlabeled data. Hashtags are strong indicators of the topic of the tweet. We create a list of seed hashtags such as #Terrorism, #Islamophobia and #Extremist and identify tweets containing these hashtags. We manually analyze tweets containing such hashtags and identify hate and extremism promoting tweets. We extend the list of hashtags by extracting new hashtags (not already in the list) present in the positive class tweets. Table 4 illustrates a sample of some seed hashtags and their respective tweets leading us to new hashtags. We then identify tweets containing the new hashtags and manually analyze the tweets to identify hate promoting tweets. As a result of this, we extend the list of hashtags and our training dataset of size S. We repeat this process several times to collect training dataset. This dataset and list of hashtags is publicly available at https://sites.google.com/a/iiitd.ac.in/agrswati/datasets.

We make our experimental dataset publicly available so that our experiments can be replicated and used for benchmark purposes by other researchers. We perform a random sampling on English tweets and use a sample as our testing (or validation) dataset. We remove the term 'RT' (Re-Tweet), @username (username of the direct mention of a user in the tweet), URL (short URL) and hashtags. After removing these terms our problem becomes more challenging due to short text classification. In phase 4, we perform characterization and identification of various discriminatory features and compute the frequency (TF) of various terms. For example, religious, offensive, slang, negative emotions, punctuations and war related terms. Table 5 shows a sample of these terms present in hate and extremism promoting tweets. Figure 2(a) and 2(b) shows the frequency of these terms present in the training and testing dataset. While Figure 2(c) shows statistics of only positive class tweets present in testing dataset. Figure 2 also illustrates the frequency of terms that have been preprocessed in phase 3. All statistics are computed in logarithmic scale. These graphs shows that the frequency of religious and war related terms is very high in hate promoting tweets.We convert our datasets (training and testing) into a matrix of feature space; where each entity represents a TF of respective column feature in a given tweet.

In phase 5, we implement two independent one-class classifiers (KNN and LibSVM) to classify a tweet as hate promoting or unknown. We use LibSVM as it is a popular open-source machine-learning library implementing the SMO (Sequential Minimal Optimization) for SVMs supporting classification and regression. Algorithm 1 & 2 describes the procedure of KNN and LibSVM classifiers respectively. In last phase, we evaluate the performance of the two classifiers using standard confusion matrix.

---

[3] Semi-Supervised Learning: learning the classifier from a combination of both labeled and unlabeled data.

ALGORITHM 1: ONE CLASS K-NN ALGORITHM

Data: Training Dataset D_{tr}, Test Dataset D_{te}, Neighbors K, Threshold th
Result: List of class labels for test dataset C_{te}
Algorithm $OneClassKNN(D_{tr}, D_{te}, th, K)$

1   **for** *each instance* $I \in D_{te}$ **do**
2      $N1 \leftarrow NearestNeighbor(I, D_{tr})$
3      $D_1 \leftarrow Euclidean\_Distance(N, I)$
4   **if** *(K == 1)* **then**
5        $N2 \leftarrow NearestNeighbor(N1, D_{tr})$
6        $D_2 \leftarrow Euclidean\_Distance(N1, N2)$
     else
7        $ND_1 \leftarrow Euclidean\_Distance(D_{tr}), N1)$
8        $D_2 \leftarrow Average(ND_1, ND_2, ..., ND_K)$
     end
9   **if** *(D_1/D_2 > th)* **then**
10        $C_{te}.addClass(Unknown)$
     else
11        $C_{te}.addClass(TargetClass)$
     end
   end
12   return C_{te}

---

4 Solution Implementation

4.1 K-Nearest Neighbor Classifier

The proposed method (Algorithm 1) follows the standard one class KNN algorithm in order to classify a tweet as hate promoting or unknown. Inputs to this algorithm are pre-processed training dataset D_{tr}, testing dataset D_{te}, number of nearest neighbors K and a threshold measure th for accepting outliers. Each tweet in testing dataset is an arbitrary instance I that is represented by a feature vector $(f_1(I), f_2(I), ..., f_m(I))$ where $f_i(I)$ is an instance value for given feature and m is the number of discriminatory features. In steps 2 and 3, we compute euclidean distance[4] between an instance I of testing data and all instances of training datasets.

$$D = \sqrt[2]{\sum_{i=1}^{n} (f_i(I) \sim f_i(J))^2}, \text{ where } J \in D_{tr} \tag{1}$$

We create a distance matrix of size $n * 1$ for every instance $I \in D_{te}$, where n is the size of training dataset. Equation 1 shows the formula for computing euclidean distance between two instances. Based upon this distance matrix we find a nearest neighbor N_1 of I in training data. In steps 4 to 7, we find K nearest neighbors of N_1 in training dataset D_{tr}. Due to the large size of testing dataset we use $K = 100$. In step 8, we take an average of all K distances and name it as

---

[4] http://en.wikipedia.org/wiki/Euclidean_distance

D_2. Steps 9 to 11 perform unary classification. If the ratio of distances D_1 and D_2 comes out to be lower than threshold measure th, then instance I belongs to the target class otherwise it is classified as unknown. We compute an extent of similarity (euclidean distance) between all instances of training dataset D_{tr}. As a result of this, we get a distance matrix of size $n*1$. We take a harmonic mean of these distances and come up with the threshold value th.

4.2 Support Vector Machine Algorithm

One class SVM is a supervised learning technique that performs distribution estimation of given training dataset. We develop an algorithm that classifies most positive class tweets from outliers. In our research, we use LibSVM java library 3.18[5] for Weka 3.7.10[6], originally proposed by Chang et. al. [3]. LibSVM is a wrapper class that allows one class SVM classifier supported by LibSVM tool. In one class LibSVM, all SVM formulations are supported as quadratic minimization problem. Equation 2 shows the formulation of unconstrained dual form of standard SVM classifier, subject to a Lagrange multiplier α that varies between 0 & a constant value C. Q is an n*n matrix where n is the size of training vectors and e is a vector of all ones represented as [1,1,....,1]. To constraint in minimization we optimize margin hyperplane as $y^T \alpha = 0$. In one class LibSVM (Equation 3), we solve a scaled version of Equation 2 subject to α that varies between 0 & 1 [3]. Given training vectors x_i where $i = 0, 1, ..., n$, $v \in (0, 1)$, where 0 denotes a lower limit of support vectors and 1 denotes an upper limit on errors made in training a model. Equation 4 shows the kernel function Q_{ij} of one class LibSVM i.e. a dot product of two training vectors.

ALGORITHM 2: ONE CLASS LIBSVM ALGORITHM

Data: Training Dataset D_{tr}, Testing Dataset D_{te}
Result: List of class labels for test dataset C_{te}
Algorithm $OneClassLibSVM(D_{tr}, D_{te})$

```
1    Class_Label ← SVM.setTargetClass(D_tr)
2    Model ← SVM.buildClassifier(D_tr)
3    Preprocessed dataset T_p ← FilterTweets(D_te)
4    for each instance i ∈ T_p do
5        Class c ← Model.classifyTweets(i)
6        C_te ← c
     end
7    return C_te
```

Algorithm 2 describes basic modules of LibSVM that we implement in our classifier. We give an input of a training and testing dataset to the algorithm i.e. D_{tr} and D_{te} respectively. Training dataset contains a set of labeled feature vectors of only target class tweets. In steps 1 and 2, we set the target class label and build our model on training dataset. In step 3, we perform data pre-

---

[5] http://www.csie.ntu.edu.tw/~cjlin/libsvm/
[6] http://www.cs.waikato.ac.nz/ml/weka/

processing on testing dataset and remove all garbage data. Steps 4 to 6 performs classification and predicts most likely class for a given instance of testing dataset.

$$min_\alpha\{\tfrac{1}{2}\alpha^T Q\alpha - e^T\alpha\}, \quad 0 \leq \alpha \leq C, \quad y^T\alpha = 0 \tag{2}$$

$$min_\alpha\{\tfrac{1}{2}\alpha^T Q\alpha\}, \quad 0 \leq \alpha \leq 1, \quad e^T\alpha = vn \tag{3}$$

$$Q_{ij} \equiv K(x_i, x_j) = (x_i.x_j) \tag{4}$$

We also implement leave-p-out cross validation strategy in both KNN and Lib-SVM classifiers. We perform a column-wise partition on both training and testing datasets and remove p feature/s at a time. We repeat this process for all features and run our proposed classifiers $2 * {}^mC_p$ times, where m is the size of feature space and p is the number of features we remove per iteration, $p = 1$ in our case. As a result of this, we get a 1*m matrix for one classifier, where each instance shows the overall accuracy of respective classifier.

5   Empirical Analysis and Performance Evaluation

5.1   Experimental Dataset

We conduct experiments on publicly available dataset so that our results can be replicated or used for benchmarking or comparison purposes. We download two datasets: UDI-TwitterCrawl-Aug2012[7] and ATM-TwitterCrawl-Aug2013[8]. UDI-TwitterCrawl-Aug2012 consists of 50 million tweets approximately and was collected in May 2011 [6]. ATM-TwitterCrawl-Aug2013 consists of 5 million English tweets and was collected in June 2011 [5]. We use language detection library[9] for Java for language identification (supports 53 languages) of tweets and find 29 different languages in the dataset. There are 85% English and 15% non-English tweets present in the experimental dataset. Initially we have $53,234,567$ tweets in our dataset. In this paper, we focus only on English language tweets, therefore we discard all non-English ($7,889,609$) tweets and remain with a total of $45,344,958$ tweets. We perform a semi-supervised learning approach on experimental dataset and collect only hate & extremism promoting tweets. To avoid overfitting in classification we collect only $10,486$ labeled tweets for training dataset, which is a very small fraction of experimental dataset. We perform a random sampling on all 45.3 million tweets of experimental dataset and collect a random sample of 1 million tweets as testing (or validation) dataset. This dataset includes both hate promoting and unknown tweets.

---

[7] https://wiki.engr.illinois.edu/display/forward/
Dataset-UDI-TwitterCrawl-Aug2012
[8] https://wiki.engr.illinois.edu/display/forward/
Dataset-ATM-TwitterCrawl-Aug2013
[9] https://code.google.com/p/language-detection/

Table 6. Confusion Matrix And Accuracy Results

(a) KNN Classifier

		Predicted	
		Positive	Unknown
Actual	Positive	67,798	15,522
	Unknown	74,968	841,712

(b) LibSVM Classifier

		Predicted	
		Positive	Unknown
Actual	Positive	73,555	9,765
	Unknown	20,420	896,260

(c) Accuracy Results of Classifiers

Classifier	Precision	Recall	TNR	NPV	F-Score	Accuracy
KNN	0.48	0.81	0.92	0.98	0.60	0.90
LibSVM	0.78	0.88	0.98	0.99	0.83	0.97

5.2 Experimental Results

To evaluate the performance of our proposed solution approach, we use basic measures of relevance used in information retrieval and machine learning. We asked 4 graduate students to manually annotate each tweet in the dataset and based upon their decisions we validate our results (we gave them simple instructions to annotate a tweet as posiitve if they find it hate and extremism promoting). We compute accuracy of our classifier in terms of precision, recall and f-score. Table 6(a) and 6(b) shows the standard confusion matrix for KNN and LibSVM classifiers. We execute our classifiers on a testing dataset of size 1 million records containing tweets from both target class (positive) and outliers. One class KNN algorithm classifies $142,766$ ($67,798 + 74,968$) tweets as positive and $857,054$ ($15,522 + 841,712$) tweets as unknown. Table 6(a) reveals that there is a misclassification of 18.6% and 8.2% in predicting target (positive) class and outlier (unknown) instances. Similarly, given an input of 1 million tweets, one class LibSVM algorithm predicts $103,975$ ($73,555 + 20,420$) tweets as positive and $906,025$ ($9,765 + 896,260$) tweets as unknown.

Table 6(b) shows that 11.7% and 2.2% of tweets are wrongly classified as positive and unknown respectively. Table 6(c) shows accuracy results (precision, recall, f-score) for both KNN and LibSVM classifiers. Table 6(c) reveals that overall LibSVM classifier (accuracy of 97%) outperforms than KNN classifier (accuracy of 90%). Results shows that precision, f-score and accuracy of LibSVM classifier are much higher in comparison to KNN classifier and similarly recall is reasonably high for LibSVM classifier.

We apply leave-p-out strategy for both KNN and LibSVM classifiers ($p = 1$) and compute their accuracy. As discussed in Section 3, we use 8 discriminatory features to classify a tweet as hate promoting or unknown. Figure 3 shows

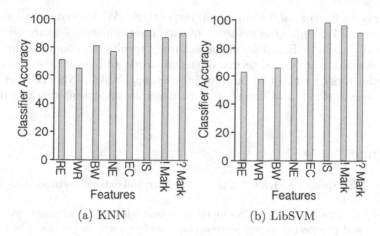

(a) KNN   (b) LibSVM

Fig. 3. Impact of Individual Feature on Overall Accuracy of A Classifier. RE= Religious, WR= War Related, BW= Bad Words, NE= Negative Emotions, EC= Emoticons, IS= Internet Slangs.

variance in overall accuracy of one class classifiers (KNN and LibSVM) after removing one feature vector at a time. Figure 3(a) reveals that if we remove religious or war related terms then the accuracy of KNN classifier decreases by 20 to 25%. Removing bad words or negative emoticons from feature vectors, accuracy falls down by 11 to 13%. Figure 3(a) reveals that internet slangs, emoticons and punctuations (! and ? marks) are less important features and doesn't affect the accuracy by a major difference but we can not neglect them completely because they affect the overall accuracy by 2 to 3%. Figure 3(b) reveals that in one class LibSVM classifier, presence of religious, war related terms, bad words and negative emotions plays an important role. And by removing any of these features, overall accuracy of classifier decreases by 20 to 45%. Ignoring presence of internet slangs and exclamation marks doesn't affect accuracy. Unlike KNN classifier, removing emoticons and question marks decreases the performance by a reasonable rate. The reason of this misclassification is the presence of noisy content and sparsity in datasets. Feature space of testing dataset is a matrix of size 1M*8, where 70% of entries are 0.

6   Conclusion

Hate and extremism promoting users and Tweets are prevalent on Twitter. We observe presence of tweets containing hashtags indicating hate and extremism and also tweets which do not contain such hashtags but are hate and extremism promoting. We conduct a manual analysis of tweets and identify linguistic features which can be used as discriminators for the task of identifying hate and extremism promoting tweets. We demonstrate a correlation between such tweets and features like presence of war, religious, negative emotions and offensive terms. We train a one-class SVM and KNN on 10,486 positive class tweets and observe an F-Score of 0.83 and 0.60 respectively. We implement a leave one out strategy and examine the influence of each discriminatory feature on overall accuracy of classifiers. Based upon the accuracy results, we conclude that presence of religious, war related terms, offensive words and negative emotions are strong indicators of a tweet to be hate promoting. Unlike KNN classifier, presence of internet slangs and question mark plays an important role in LibSVM classifier.

References

1. Agrawal, S., Sureka, A.: Learning to classify hate and extremism promoting tweets. JISIC (2014)
2. Berger, J., Strathearn, B.: Who matters online: Measuring influence, evaluating content and countering violent extremism in online social networks. The international centre for the study of radicalization and political violence (2013)
3. Chang, C.C., Lin, C.J.: LIBSVM: A library for support vector machines. ACM Transactions on Intelligent Systems and Technology 2, 27:1–27:27 (2011)
4. Kwok, I., Wang, Y.: Locate the hate: Detecting tweets against blacks. In: Twenty-Seventh AAAI Conference on Artificial Intelligence (2013)
5. Li, R., Wang, S., Chang, K.C.C.: Towards social data platform: automatic topic-focused monitor for twitter stream. Proceedings of the VLDB Endowment 6(14), 1966–1977 (2013)
6. Li, R., Wang, S., Deng, H., Wang, R., Chang, K.C.C.: Towards social user profiling: unified and discriminative influence model for inferring home locations. In: Proceedings of the 18th ACM SIGKDD International Conference on Knowledge Discovery and Data Mining, pp. 1023–1031. ACM (2012)
7. Liebrecht, C., Kunneman, F., van den Bosch, A.: The perfect solution for detecting sarcasm in tweets# not. Computational Approaches to Subjectivity, Sentiment and Social Media Analysis (2013)
8. Martinez-Romo, J., Araujo, L.: Detecting malicious tweets in trending topics using a statistical analysis of language. Expert Systems with Applications 40(8), 2992–3000 (2013)
9. O'Callaghan, D., Greene, D., Conway, M., Carthy, J., Cunningham, P.: Uncovering the wider structure of extreme right communities spanning popular online networks. In: Web Science Conference, pp. 276–285 (2013)
10. Reyes, A., Rosso, P., Buscaldi, D.: From humor recognition to irony detection: The figurative language of social media. Data & Knowledge Engineering 74, 1–12 (2012)
11. Wadhwa, P., Bhatia, M.P.S.: Tracking on-line radicalization using investigative data mining. In: NCC, pp. 1–5 (2013)
12. Xiang, G., Fan, B., Wang, L., Hong, J., Rose, C.: Detecting offensive tweets via topical feature discovery over a large scale twitter corpus. In: Proceedings of the 21st ACM International Conference on Information and Knowledge Management, pp. 1980–1984. ACM (2012)
13. Yang, M.C., Lee, J.T., Lee, S.W., Rim, H.C.: Finding interesting posts in twitter based on retweet graph analysis. In: SIGIR, pp. 1073–1074 (2012)

Data Mining on ICT Usage in an Academic Campus: A Case Study

Ajay Auddy and Sripati Mukhopadhyay

Department of Computer Science, Burdwan University, Burdwan, India
ajayauddy@rediffmail.com, dr.sripatim@gmail.com

Abstract. Nowadays, every higher education institution needs to assess the degree of utilisation of Information and Communication Technology (ICT) facilities installed in the campus. This study is based on the responses collected from the student and research communities via survey on ICT in the University of Burdwan. Data mining methodologies – Fuzzy-Rough Feature Selection (FRFS) to reduce the dimensions of survey dataset and subsequently different classification techniques such as J48, JRip, QuickRules Fuzzy-Rough rule induction, Fuzzy Nearest Neighbour, Fuzzy Rough Nearest Neighbour and Vaguely Quantified Nearest Neighbour (VQNN) are applied on this resultant dataset to build model for potential knowledge extraction. Fuzzy-Rough Feature Selection (FRFS) and then different classification algorithms are applied using WEKA 3.7.9 for analysis of the reduced dataset.

Keywords: ICT, Educational Data Mining (EDM), Feature Selection, Classification.

1 Introduction

In the sector of Higher Education, integrity of education and technology has created an opportunity for students and research communities to venture into knowledge outlook in new dimension. To keep in space with this new era, all educational institutions are implementing ICT infrastructure which is the prime ingredient to integrate the campus and the educational resources spread outside. Some of the advantages of ICT implementation are the virtual classroom, access to e-resources such as e-books, e-contents, e-journals, conduction of e-courses, creation of e-contents by faculties [14,15].

Educational Data Mining analyses data in educational repositories that has meaningful and understandable information which is unpredictable apparently [8,14,15]. Firstly, Fuzzy-Rough Feature Selection (FRFS) is applied on the dataset using WEKA to extract the relevant features to reduce the dimensionality of the feature space, to improve the predictive accuracy of the classification algorithms [18]. Subsequently different classification techniques such as J48, JRip, QuickRules Fuzzy-Rough rule induction, Fuzzy Nearest Neighbour, Fuzzy-Rough Nearest Neighbour and Vaguely Quantified Nearest Neighbour (VQNN) are applied to build model to extract meaningful knowledge [14,15].

R. Natarajan et al. (Eds.): ICDCIT 2015, LNCS 8956, pp. 443–447, 2015.

This paper is organized as follows: section 2 is devoted to the result obtained by using the data mining methodologies used for the ICT survey data obtained from research scholars and students of the university and section 3 is for the conclusion.

2   Results and Discussion

2.1   Implementation of Mining Model Using WEKA

Weka was developed at the University of Waikato in New Zealand. The name stands for Waikato Environment for Knowledge Analysis. The system is written in Java and runs on almost any platform. It provides an interface for data mining learning algorithms, encompassing the methods from beginning to the end phases of the data mining process and the evaluation of the result generated from this process can be applied on given dataset [17,21]. In this paper, an appropriate feature selection method is used to select the most appropriate set of features. Fuzzy-Rough Feature Selection (FRFS) incorporated by Richard Jenson and subsequently different classification techniques in WEKA 3.7.9 version have been applied here for the analysis of this educational dataset [13,20].

2.2   Feature Selection

Firstly, fuzzy rough feature selection method has been applied to remove irrelevant and redundant attributes in the dataset. Feature selector consists of two components: an Attribute Evaluator and a Search Method. FuzzyRoughSubsetEval is selected as Attribute Evaluator and Hill Climber (forwards) as the search method. Default values are considered here for various options under FRFS configuration.

Initially, there are 15 attributes in the datasets as given below.

Attributes: 15
1. Duration_ICT_access 2. UPS_support   3. Fee_ICT_usage 4. Dos_Dont
5. Access_Social_Networking 6. Support_Teaching_Faculties
7. Online_library_resources 8. Social_network_resources   9. email_resources
10. Submit_work_assignment   11. Lecture_notes_slides 12. e-contents_course
13. e-journals_subscription   14. ICT_learning
15. Assessment_ICT

After the execution of the feature reduction method, 3 attributes are eliminated from the dataset and the following result got display as given below:
Method: Fuzzy rough feature selection
Evaluation mode: evaluate on all training data
Search Method: Hill Climber (forwards): {1, 2, 5, 6, 7, 8, 9, 11, 12, 13, 14} => 1.0
Attribute Subset Evaluator (supervised, Class (nominal) :   Assessment_ICT
Dataset consistency: 0.9808306709265175
Selected attributes: 1,2,5,6,7,8,9,11,12,13,14 : 11+1

Table 1. Evaluation Parameters Values after Application of Feature Selection

Evaluation Parameters	QuickRules Fuzzy-Rough rule induction	Fuzzy-Rough NN	VQNN	J48	JRip	FuzzyNN
Correctly Classified Instances	69.0096%	79.5527%	73.4824%	70.607%	74.7604%	79.5527%
Incorrectly Classified Instances	20.7668%	20.4473%	26.5176%	29.393%	25.2396%	20.4473%
Kappa statistic	0.537	0.5781	0.4427	0.3806	0.5135	0.5781
Mean absolute error	0.105	0.0818	0.1186	0.1504	0.1394	0.0818
Root mean squared error	0.3052	0.286	0.2892	0.3065	0.2912	0.286
Relative absolute error	54.6471%	37.5648%	54.489%	69.0816%	64.0194%	37.5648%
Root relative squared error	99.7521%	87.0263%	87.9897%	93.2579%	88.6111%	87.0263%
UnClassified Instances	10.2236%	-	-	-	-	-
Time taken to build model (seconds)	0.53	0	0	0.05	0.16	0

List of Eliminated Attributes

1. Fee_ICT_Usage   2. Dos_Dont 3. Submit_Work_Assignment

Six classifiers as mentioned above are applied here. Various evaluation parameters such as correctly classified instances, incorrectly classified instances, Kappa statistics, etc., are presented with values for the comparative study of the classifiers.

This study has given prime importance to the feature selection as shown in table 1. QuickRules Fuzzy-Rough Rule Induction has least accuracy value among these six classifiers. It is also to be noted that 10-fold cross-validation, as test option, has been applied in all cases to evaluate the classifiers.

Table 2 has shown the values of the various parameters to analyse the degree of accuracy of the applied data mining classifiers. The parameters are TP rate, FP rate, precision, recall, F-Measure, MCC, ROC Area and PRC Area.

The outcome of this study shows that the FuzzyRoughNN and FuzzyNN classifying algorithms have proved to be best with an accuracy of nearly 80%, whereas other have around 75% accuracy.

In terms of with and without feature selection (table not shown), FuzzyNN classifier has shown significant improvement in accuracy i.e. from 77.6358% to 79.5527%. JRip classifier has shown improvement from 72.524% to 74.7604%. VQNN classifier has shown improvement from 72.2045% to 73.4824%. J48 classifier has shown improvement from 69.3291% to 70.607%. Accuracy of FuzzyRoughNN and Quick-Rules Fuzzy-rough rule induction classifiers remain almost the same. Thus, the application of fuzzy-rough feature selection has enhances the performance of all the classifiers to different degree. Considering the evaluation criteria, firstly analysing the values of Kappa Statistics, all classifiers except FuzzyRoughNN have better performance than that of without feature selection. Secondly, the time taken to build the models is equal or better than that of without feature selection except JRip.

Values of Mean absolute error (MAE), Root mean squared error (RMSA), Relative absolute error (RAE) and Root relative squared error (RRSE) of all classifiers except VQNN are lower in the dataset with feature reduction as it is more reliable and robust in compare to the dataset without feature reduction because the errors are comparatively lower, thus enhance the overall performance of the classifier models.

Table 2. Detailed Accuracy of the Classifiers after Feature Selection

Classifiers	TP Rate	FP Rate	Precision	Recall	F-Measure	MCC	ROC Area	PRC Area
QuickRules Fuzzy-rough rule induction	0.769	0.248	0.770	0.769	0.767	0.547	0.748	0.670
FuzzyRough NN	0.760	0.240	0.760	0.760	0.755	0.543	0.785	0.710
VQNN	0.706	0.342	0.647	0.706	0.669	0.403	0.745	0.649
J48	0.735	0.328	0.706	0.735	0.702	0.460	0.801	0.735
JRip	0.748	0.230	0.731	0.748	0.734	0.527	0.774	0.686
FuzzyNN	0.796	0.267	0.795	0.796	0.776	0.593	0.765	0.684

3   Conclusion

The feedback analysis is an important academic activity in Universities. Application of feature selection using fuzzy-rough hybridization module of WEKA has definitely given us more optimum result when various data mining algorithms, as shown in this paper, output positive results of the experiment. FuzzyRoughNN and FuzzyNN classifying algorithms have proved to be best classifiers for the analysis of the dataset in this domain. As this paper has given emphasis on fuzzy sets, rough sets and its hybridization, analysis of various parameters reveals that Fuzzy Rough Feature Selection (FRFS) and subsequently various classification algorithms mostly based on hybridisation have yield better results than that of the conventional methods.

Acknowledgement. We acknowledge the cooperation received from various P.G. departments of The University of Burdwan in conducting this survey among the students and research scholars.

References

[1] Ziarko, W.: Variable precision rough set model. Journal of Computer and System Sciences 46(1), 39–59 (1993)

[2] Cornelis, C., De Cock, M., Radzikowska, A.M.: Vaguely Quantified Rough Sets. In: An, A., Stefanowski, J., Ramanna, S., Butz, C.J., Pedrycz, W., Wang, G. (eds.) RSFDGrC 2007. LNCS (LNAI), vol. 4482, pp. 87–94. Springer, Heidelberg (2007)

[3] Han, J., Kamber, M., Pei, J.: Data mining: concepts and techniques, 3rd edn. Morgan Kaufmann Publisher (2012)

[4] Keller, J.M., Gray, M.R., Givens Jr., J.A.: A fuzzy K-Nearest Neighbor Algorithm. IEEE Transactions on Systems, Man, and Cybernetics 15, 580–586 (1985)

[5] Jensen, R., Shen, Q.: Computational Intelligence and Feature Selection-Rough and Fuzzy Approaches. IEEE PRESS, A John Wiley & Sons, Inc., Publication (2008)

[6] Greco, S., Inuiguchi, M., Slowinski, R.: Fuzzy rough sets and multiple-premise gradual decision rules. International Journal of Approximate Reasoning 41, 179–211 (2005)

[7]   Verbiest, N., Cornelis, C., Jensen, R.: Fuzzy Rough Positive Region based Nearest Neighbour Classification. In: 2012 IEEE International Conference on Fuzzy Systems (FUZZ-IEEE), pp. 1961–1967. IEEE (2012)

[8]   Baker, R.S.J.D., Yacef, K.: The State of Educational Data Mining in 2009: A Review and Future Visions Journal of Educational Data Mining, 1(1) (2009)

[9]   Jensen, R., Cornelis, C.: Fuzzy-rough nearest neighbour classification and prediction. Theoretical Computer Science 412, 5871–5884 (2011)

[10] Jensen, R., Cornelis, C., Shen, Q.: Hybrid Fuzzy-Rough Rule Induction and Feature Selection. In: Proceedings of the 18th International Conference on Fuzzy Systems (FUZZ-IEEE 2009), pp. 1151–1156 (2009)

[11] Jensen, R., Cornelis, C.: Fuzzy-Rough Nearest Neighbour Classification. In: Peters, J.F., Skowron, A., Chan, C.-C., Grzymala-Busse, J.W., Ziarko, W.P. (eds.) Transactions on Rough Sets XIII. LNCS, vol. 6499, pp. 56–72. Springer, Heidelberg (2011)

[12] http://www.cs.waikato.ac.nz/~ml/weka/ (accessed on December 15, 2013)

[13] Jensen, R.: Fuzzy-rough data mining with Weka (2013), http://users.aber.ac.uk/rkj/ (accessed on March 10, 2014)

[14] Auddy, A.: A Formulation of Questionnaire to Study the ICT Utilisation at University Campus. National Journal of Computer Science and Technology 5(1&2) 95–97 (2013) ISSN. 0975-2463

[15] Auddy, A., Mukhopadhyay, S.: Studies on ICT Usage in the Academic Cam-pus Using Educational Data Mining. International Journal of Modern Education and Computer Science 6, 10–20 (2014), doi:10.5815/ijmecs.2014.06.02

[16] WEKA Manual for Version 3-7-2, The University of Waikato (July, 29, 2010)

[17] Witten, I.H., Eibe, F., Hall, M.A.: Data mining: practical machine learning tools and techniques, 3rd edn. Morgan Kaufmann Publishers (2011)

[18] Soman, K.P., Diwakar, S., Ajay, V.: Insight into Data Mining theory and practice. PHI Publications (2006)

[19] Auddy, A., Mukhopadhyay, S.: Data Mining in Higher Education during Recent Years: A Survey. In: Second National Conference on Computing and Systems (NaCCS-2012) Proceedings, Burdwan, March 15-16, pp. 14–19 (2012) ISBN 978-93-80813-18-9

[20] http://users.aber.ac.uk/rkj/ (accessed on December 15, 2013)

[21] Gang, X.: The application of data mining methods, Turku University of Applied Sciences, Bachelor's Thesis (UAS) Degree Program in Information Tec

A Theory on Genesis and Spread of Corruption

Hrushikesha Mohanty

School of Computer and Information Sciences
University of Hyderabad, India
mohanty.hcu@gmail.com

Abstract. Availing a service by an illegal means is usually termed as a corruption. This paper models roles of individuals in genesis of corruption and its spread in a society. Particularly, the roles of individuals, its neighbourhood associations and their social space are studied. Based on these understandings, a theory is proposed to explain genesis and spread of corruption, a society may assume for a given service. The characteristics of an individual include its need, anxiety in availing a service. It also depends on an emergent view on corruption a society projects on its social space.

Keywords: Computational Social Science, Social Distance, Corruption, Vulnerability, micro- and macro-sociolytics.

1 Introduction

Corruption though widely talks of bribing for a service and economic gains, still in current days corruption includes a wider aspects of human actions like *quid pro quo* transactions for cornering more than what deserved, misuses of power for self gain and even misconstrued activities that's legal but unethical. Thus a study on corruption becomes hard, even impalpable unless the nature of individuals and their society are understood [2]. In that sense,here we focus on modelling issues of individuals with respect to a service that's competitive to avail. Also we model emergent fraudulent behaviour of individuals in a society to avail a service. These two make an individual, corruption vulnerable. Corruption vulnerability, when surpasses a threshold value, drives one to commit corruption (say bribe)for availing a service. The paper propounds a theory on need and anxiety to model individual's stakes that push it to commit corruption i.e. making it corruption vulnerable. The contributions this paper includes *i.* modelling micro-sociolytics e.g. *need, anxiety, corruption vulnerability* of individuals. *ii.* modelling macro-sociolytics e.g. *social space. iii.* an approach on understanding corruption genesis and spread. The work can be useful to visualise evolving maps on corruption vulnerability of a society with respect to a proposed service.

2 Review

Corruption in social systems have been studied by economists for two practical purposes, one i. the incentives that allure one to corruption and the other ii.

R. Natarajan et al. (Eds.): ICDCIT 2015, LNCS 8956, pp. 448–451, 2015.

the impacts corruption makes to an economy. Study of corruption is also to encompass social behaviour. Gifts and favours are typically regulated by a norm of reciprocity between parties involved in an exchange. While reciprocity is a cultural etiquette, at times it turns to corruption when purpose in it is doubted. Corruption is not imported always but for most of the times it's originated from within society [3]. Network model is used to predict corruptions (bad events) that may occur next, when given conditions get satisfied [5]. *Game Theoretic Approaches* to model corruption is studied in [6]. Corruption is shown as a game playing by a service provider and a consumer for a win-win situation. *Principal-Agent* model, a basic model is being used by economists and public-administrator for studying corruption in government agencies [8] [6]. The risk on punishment and the gain due to bribing essentially guide to formulate strategies for agents to choose a move in a game towards corruption [1]. *Common Agency* model [7] avoids policing of an agent by granting a flat gain while keeping control on it by enforcing strict laws to ensure restraint.

3   Corruption and Spread

The basic question on why do citizens resort to corruption for availing a service is taken up here for analysis. A person p's tendency towards corruption for a service s is termed as corruption vulnerability cv_p^s. A person p finds self vulnerable to corruption for three reasons and these additive reasons are anxiety $anxt_p^s$, degree of its need nid_p^s for the service s. So. corruption vulnerability of p for the service s is defined as

$$cv_p^s = nid_p^s + anxt_p^s \ ..... \ (1)$$

that results maximum value 1 and the minimum value 0 for addition of two. So, $1 \geqslant cv_p^s \geqslant 0$. Every person has a threshold value on corruption vulnerability i.e. tcv_p^s and the condition to decide to bribe is i.e. $cv_p^s \geq tcv_p^s$. Let's now quantify these two attributes.

Quantifying Need:: nid_p^s specifies how much a person p is in need of service s. The need of a person grows from its habitat modelled by $< K, R, L, Q >$ i.e Knowledge K, resource R and location L and objective Q [4]. And functions $add(p, K) \to q_1$, $add(p, R) \to q_2$ and $add(p, L) \to q_3$ generate objectives for a person p endowed with knowledge K, resource R and location L respectively. Now we define $nid_p^s =$ as one of the three

Case 1:: $\frac{1}{|(q_1)|}$ if $q_1 = q_2 = q_3$ and $s \in q_1$ or q_2 or q_3

Case 2:: $\frac{1}{|(q_1 \cap q_2 \cap q_3)|}$ and $s \in (q_1 \cap q_2 \cap q_3)$

Case 3:: $\frac{1}{|(q_1 \cup q_2 \cup q_3)|}$ and $s \in (q_1 \cup q_2 \cup q_3)$

case 4::   else 0

for not all q_1, q_2, q_3 are empty sets. So, value of $nid_p^s \in (0, 1)$.

Quantifying Anxiety:: Anxiety of a person towards a service is generated from the number of competitors it has for the service. Usually, competitors in one's neighbourhood having the similar habitats create heartburn and anxiety to a person. So, for a person we construct its neighbourhood habitat as combination of habitats of its neighbours. Let this be H_p^n as $\cup H_p^i$ for $i = 1...n$ neighbours of p. Now we quantify anxiety by finding Cos of the angle H_p and H_p^n make. In case of homogeneity of two habitats the angle between them is zero and in vice versa when both are heterogeneous they are at right angle. So, the quantification of anxiety of a person p for service s, we denote as $anxt_p^s$ defined as $Cos(H_p^s, H_p^n) = (1|0| < 1)$ respectively for similarity, dissimilarity and partial similarity between two habitats respectively. Now we see cv_p^s takes value ≥ 0 and ≤ 1 from the least vulnerable for $cv_p^= 0$ to the most vulnerable for value 1. Being vulnerable to corruption, a service consumer decides to bribe when it crosses a threshold value that we need to quantify.

Corruption Threshold:: A metric that quantifies an emergent picture on corruption projected on social space like market place, social media is quantified as

$$\{Pcv_S^s\} \leftarrow cv_p^s * sd_{(p,S)} \quad \forall p \in S.....(2)$$

where $sd_{(p,S)}$ is the social distance between p and social space S. The concept on social distance is detailed in [4]. Fig.1 shows how at a social space a person (p in and q out of a society) views at prevailing corruption with respect to a service. That makes one's threshold corruption value as computed by

$$tcv_p^s = len\{Pcv_S^s\} * Cos(H_p^s, H_S^s)......(3)$$

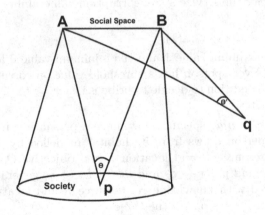

Fig. 1. Social Space

Spread of Corruption: Corruption vulnerability of a person p is redefined by *eq.* 4 due to changes corruption makes to its neighbour q.

$$cv_p^s = cv_p^s + (1 - cv_p^s) * (sd_{(s,q)} - sd'_{(s,q)}).....(4)$$

where $sd_{(s,q)}$ and $sd'_{(s,q)}$ are social distance of q respectively before and after availing the service s; $cv_p^s = 0$ or 1 when $cv_p^s < 0$ *or* > 1 respectively. It may be observed that an observed gain by corruption at neighbourhood encourages the observer while a loss dissuades. *eq.* 4 is to be computed for all neighbours who are observed of committing a corruption. This makes a local view of a person on corruption vulnerability while *eq.* 3 makes a global view on it. If $(cv_p^s > tcv_p^s)$ then a person may decide to bribe for s service. Thus genesis of the corruption is made. Then, if a person commits a corruption and that is made visible to its neighbours then they recompute their respective vulnerability by *eq.* 4. And the change may influence some of them to commit corruption. Thus the chain of making corruption is set in a society.

4 Conclusion

This paper proposes a computational approach to quantify corruption vulnerability of an individual with respect to a service. On providing details of individual habitats [4], the strategy generates maps of corruption spreads for a population with a respect to individual's objectives, habitats and social perception. The proposed model has a basic assumption on a briber behaviour i.e. reflecting its status on corruption to neighbours and society at large. This could be taken as a limitation to the model. However, the problem can be viewed similar to finding probability of detection of an offender in a neighbourhood [5]. Including resolution of this limitation, our aim is to further research on an integrated model (that considers the roles of service owner and disbursing agents, consumers, society and state) in genesis and spread of corruption and to analyse on scenario for deterrence.

References

1. Bayar, G.: Corruption- A Game Theoretical Analysis, Ph.D thesis, Department of Economics, Haziran, sayfa (2003)
2. Kingston, C.: Social Structure, Collective Action, and Corruption: Theory, and Evidence from India, http://ipl.econ.duke.edu/bread/papers/041604_Conference/kingston.pdf
3. Kingston, C.: Social Structure and Cultures of Corruption. Journal of Economic Behavior & Organization 67, 90–102 (2008)
4. Mohanty, H.: Socially Responsive Resource Usage: A Protocol. In: Natarajan, R., Ojo, A. (eds.) ICDCIT 2011. LNCS, vol. 6536, pp. 243–254. Springer, Heidelberg (2011)
5. Baumgartner, K.C., Ferrari, S., Gabrielle Salfati, C.: Bayesian Network Modelling of Offender Behaviour for Criminal profiling. In: Proceedings of the 44th IEEE Conference on Decision and Control, and the European Control Conference, Spain, December 12-15, pp. 2702–2709 (2005)
6. Groenendijk, N.: A principal-agent model of corruption. Crime, Law & Social Change 27, 207–229 (1997)
7. Maier, R.: Explaining Corruption: A Common Agency Approach. In: Discussion paper for the 4th Budapest Summer Workshop for Young Economists, organised by the KTI/IE, June 29-30 (2004)
8. Rose-Ackerman, S.: The economics of corruption. Journal of Public Economics 4, 187–203 (1975)

Social Network Analysis of Different Parameters Derived from Realtime Profile

Paramita Dey[1], Aniket Sinha[1], and Sarbani Roy[2]

[1] Department of Information Technology
Govt. College of Engineering & Ceramic Technology
Kolkata-700010, India
[2] Department of Computer Science & Engineering
Jadavpur University, Kolkata-700032, India
sarbani.roy@cse.jdvu.ac.in

Abstract. The main objective of this work is to study network parameters commonly used to explain social structures. In this paper, we extract data from a real-time Facebook account using Netvizz application, analyze and evaluate network parameters on some widely recognized graph topology using GEPHI software.

Keywords: Social network analysis, facebook, network parameters, Netvizz, Gephi.

1 Introduction

In the last few years, we have witnessed an explosive growth of online social networks (OSNs) that have attracted most attention from all over the world [1]. Facebook, a social network service, has attracted over 1.23 billion monthly active users as of January, 2014 (source: facebook.com). The huge user base of these OSNs provides an open platform for social network analysis including user behavior measurements, social interaction characterization and information propagation studies. However, the huge size of social network graphs hinders researchers from a better understanding of these graphs. So, it can be beneficial, if we extract the useful network parameters of the graphs and use it for further characterization.

2 Social Network Parameters

Some useful network parameters are discussed in this sections.

- The *diameter* of a connected graph G, denoted by $diam(G)$, is the maximum distance between two vertices[2]. The eccentricity of a vertex is the maximum distance from it to any other vertex[3].
- In graph theory and network analysis, *centrality* refers to indicators which identify the most important vertices within a network.
- *Community structure* is denoted as the grouping of nodes in the network such that the grouping demonstrates property of high coupling and low cohesion.

R. Natarajan et al. (Eds.): ICDCIT 2015, LNCS 8956, pp. 452–455, 2015.

- *Clustering Coefficient* [4] is a measure of the degree to which nodes in a graph tend to cluster together.
- The *average path length* is defined as average distance of a graph $G = (V, E)$ of order n.
- On directed graphs, there are two types of degree for a vertex v: the in-degree, i. e. the number of edges beginning at v and the out-degree, i. e. the number of edges ending at v. *Node degree distribution* is one of the most important properties of a graph[5].

3   Graph Visualization Softwares

Netvizz [6] and Gephi [7] are used for data extraction and graph analysis. Both tools are free and open source. Netvizz is a tool that extracts data from different sections of the facebook platform (personal profile, groups, pages) for research purposes. Gephi is open source software for graph and network analysis. It is a tool for people that have to explore and understand graphs.

4   Result

After importing the data tables from Netvizz [6], it forms initial network where each node represents each person and each edge represents the communication between them. Initially it looks like a hairball. Different views of a profile is shown in Figure 1. Networks are formed using Gephi [7]. Force Atlas 2 [8] integrate different techniques such as Barnes Hut simulation, degree-dependent repulsive force, local and global adaptive temperatures. According to Fruchterman-Reingold model [9], continuous network modelling was done depending on Distributing the vertices evenly in the frame, making edge lengths uniform and reflect inherent symmetry.

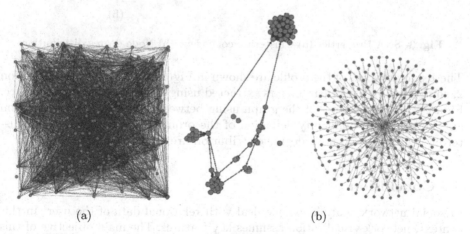

(a)   (b)

Fig. 1. Different views of a profile (a) Hairball (b) Force Atlas 2 and Fruchterman-Reingold model

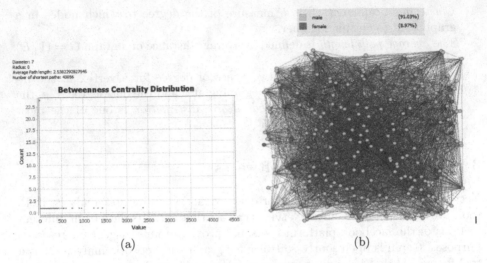

(a)   (b)

Fig. 2. SNA Properties (a) Diameter (b) Male-female community detection

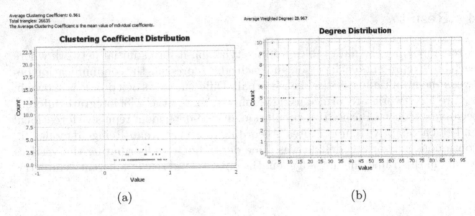

(a)   (b)

Fig. 3. SNA Properties (a) Clustering coefficient (b) Node degree distribution

These two networks of the profile are shown in Figure 1. As discussed in Section 2, some useful network parameters extracted using Gephi [7] are presented here. Figure 2 shows diameter of the graph using betweenness centrality distribution and male-female community detection of the profile under consideration. Clustering coefficient and node degree distribution are shown in Figure 3.

5   Conclusion

In social network analysis, people deal with relational data of the user. In this context, network visualization assumes key features. The main objective of this work is to understand the basic features of the social network, extract and analyzed the important parameters that characterized the social network. As open source tools are used and external module can be added to them, these data can be further characterized.

References

1. Benevenuto, F., Rodrigues, T., Cha, M., Almeida, V.: Characterizing user behavior in online social networks. In: Proceedings of the 9th ACM SIGCOMM Conference on Internet Measurement Conference, ser. IMC 2009, pp. 49–62. ACM (2009)
2. Rodrguez, J., Yebra, J.: Bounding the diameter and the mean distance of a graph from its eigenvalues: Laplacian versus adjacency matrix methods. Discrete Mathematics 196(1-3), 267–275 (1999)
3. Goddard, W., Oellermann, O.: Distance in graphs. In: Dehmer, M. (ed.) Structural Analysis of Complex Networks, pp. 49–72. Birkhüser, Boston (2011)
4. Freeman, L.C.: Centrality in social networks conceptual clarification. Social Networks 1(3), 215–239 (1978-1979)
5. Wang, T., Chen, Y., Zhang, Z., Xu, T., Jin, L., Hui, P., Deng, B., Li, X.: Understanding graph sampling algorithms for social network analysis. In: Proceedings of the 2011 31st International Conference on Distributed Computing Systems Workshops, ser. ICDCSW 2011, pp. 123–128. IEEE Computer Society (2011)
6. Rieder, B.: Studying facebook via data extraction: The netvizz application. In: Proceedings of the 5th Annual ACM Web Science Conference, pp. 346–355. ACM, New York (2013)
7. Bastian, M., Heymann, S., Jacomy, M.: Gephi: An open source software for exploring and manipulating networks. In: Proceedings of International AAAI Conference on Weblogs and Social Media (2009)
8. Jacomy, M., Venturini, T., Heymann, S., Bastian, M.: Forceatlas2, a continuous graph layout algorithm for handy network visualization designed for the gephi software. PLoS ONE 9 (2014)
9. Fruchterman, T.M.J., Reingold, E.M.: Graph drawing by force-directed placement. Softw. Pract. Exper. 21(11), 1129–1164 (1991)

Analysis of Emergency Evacuation of Building Using PEPA

Anil Kumar Singh and Surinder Kaur

Motilal Nehru National Institute of Technology Allahabad,
Computer Science and Engineering Department
Allahabad-211004, India
ak@mnnit.ac.in, rkk.surinder@gmail.com
http://www.mnnit.ac.in

Abstract. Verification and validation is a crucial step of system design. However the verification of evacuation plan during emergency situation in highly crowded areas is often ignored. Analysis of building, urban and mega event plans, performed at the early design phase may reveal the flaws in architectural design such as presence of congestion spots, improper width of stairs or corridor, fewer number of exits etc. and can be removed as early as possible. The paper analyses emergency egress situation of multi-storey building using process algebraic approach PEPA and models- evacuees, building sections, rescuers, the external help and the situation causing evacuation.

Keywords: process, acction, process algebra, PEPA.

1 Introduction

Large buildings and highly crowded places, such as malls, stadiums, public events etc. are inherently prone to risk situations (like fire, stampede, terrorist attacks etc.). But there architecture plans are not verified for the safe evacuation of the persons in case of emergency situations. Simulation is an efficient approach but it is computationally expensive and may leave the scope of some unexplored situations. The mathematical approach for the same considers movement of people in crowd as well as their interaction with both the environment and with other people. It provides better help to evaluate what-if scenarios with reference to specific metrics and criteria. Thus enabling architectural designers and urban planners, in making various design decisions. In the proposed work, the process algebra model for the evacuation of the building is designed and then eclipse plug-in PEPA is used for performing transient state analysis on it.

2 Literature Review

Fruin et al.[1], Kobes et al.[2] analyses human behaviour and its effect on evacuation during emergency situations. Gwynne et al.[3] reviews the methodologies

R. Natarajan et al. (Eds.): ICDCIT 2015, LNCS 8956, pp. 456–459, 2015.

used in current computer simulation of building evacuation. Prof. G. K. Still[4] presented a simulator named Legion. Massink et al.[5] also presented a context dependent analysis of emergency egress model. They considered four processes- evacuees, doors, building sections and request handler for modelling. They compared the results from the two approaches PEPA and Bio-PEPA. They concluded that Bio-PEPA is more suitable for modelling context dependent emergency egress situation. From studies it can be concluded that simulators till date fail in properly simulating the most crucial aspect human behaviour. However stochastic process algebra seems to be a promising approach in this field.

3   Preliminaries

Process Algebra[6] models the objects in the system as processes and the communication between them as activities or action. Performance Evaluation Process Algebra (PEPA)[7,8] is a process algebraic language. The component may either perform activity individually or it may co-operate with other component over set of activities. Each activity is defined as a pair (action, rate). It also has the notion of silent action (Γ) depicting unknown actions. $\top$ represents unspecified activity rate. The syntax of PEPA:

$$\mathbf{P} ::= (\alpha, \mathbf{r}).\mathbf{P} \mid \mathbf{P} + \mathbf{Q} \mid \mathbf{P} \bowtie \mathbf{Q} \mid \mathbf{P}/\mathbf{L} \mid \mathbf{C}$$

where, P,Q are Process, (α, r) is Activity, α is Action corresponding to the activity, r is Rate of the activity, L is Set of action type on which P and Q must co-operate, C is the Constant. The details can be found in referenced papers. PEPA Eclipse plug-in[9,10] is GUI based tool for PEPA, built on the top of the Eclipse[1] technology .

4   Modelling Evacuation of Building

For modelling the evacuation of any building the possible major components are[5]: (i) The persons to be evacuated. (ii) The structural specifications like size, the availability of free space and the space occupancy of various building sections (rooms, corridors, staircase, exit, emergency exit, lobby etc.). (iii) Specification (width, height etc.) of doors, windows, vents and other possible openings of the building. (iv) The intensity of situation. Different emergency situations have different impact on overall evacuation plan and time. (v) Availability of external help. The time required to reach to the spot, the nature of help supplied should also be modelled. (vi) If the building is equipped with smart alarm system, then it should also be modelled. Smart alarm systems guide evacuees to their way out to the exit. However the detailed model may cause the state space explosion. So some level of abstraction may be required.

The presented evacuation model is constructed in the context of a multi-storey building. Each floor of the building except the ground floor has rooms, corridor

---

[1] Eclipse home page, http://www.eclipse.org/

and staircase leading to next floor. Ground floor has lobby and exits. For the proposed building, only persons to be evacuated, building sections:- staircase, lobby, exit., external help(rescuer) and the situation is modelled. To avoid the state space explosion, the model excludes rest of the details.

To model evacuee in any building section considered factors are: its movement to the next building section on its way to exit, its possibility to get hurt, possibility to get stuck waiting for external help to come and possibility to get effected by the situation causing egress.

Process for evacuee in room or corridor is:

$$EvcFloorY = \Gamma.opStairZFX\_FY.EvcStairX + \Gamma.EvcHurtFY + \Gamma.EvcWaitFY + blow\_up.Evc';$$

As the person goes downstairs, it reduces it speed. The process for staircase takes care of the fact by maintaining the information of evacuee's actual floor throughout. Hurt people need help from others (other evacuees or external rescuer) to come out. Otherwise they may get stuck in the building. The process definition is:

$$EvcHurtFX = fX\_got\_u.ResHurtFX + ex\_fX\_got\_u.\Gamma.EvcSaved + ex\_sfX\_got\_u.ExResHurtSFX + \Gamma.EvcHurtFX;$$

Similarly the process for persons who wait for external help are defined. Resuer process is:

$$RescuerX = fX\_got\_u.ResHurtFX + \Gamma.RescuerFX + \Gamma.EvcFloorX;$$

Consideration for modelling External Help are: time required to reach to the building, how they take out evacuee via window or via building exit. Here the assumption is that they enter the building through window.

$$ExRescuer = \Gamma.break\_window.come\_out.\Gamma.ExRescuer + \\ \Gamma.break\_window.get\_in.ex\_fX\_got\_u.\Gamma.out.\Gamma.ExRescuer + \\ \Gamma.break\_window.get\_in.ex\_sfX\_got\_u.ExResHurtSFX;$$

If a place is occupied, it can be freed. If it is free, it can be occupied. Only this should be considered while modelling any building section.

The situation once triggered continuously effect evacuee and/or building sections. Situation that has effect on evacuee interact with evacuee using action blow_up. The other kind of situations has effect on building section such as, dynamic change in building section, fire blocking some portion of building, the presence of smoke reducing the visibility etc. Process definition is similar to the above one but interacting action between building part and situation is *block-Section*. Corresponding changes are made into the building section definition. The action *dirChange* will interact with the evacuee, indicating that the section has been blocked so he should change his direction.

In system equation, the interaction between Evacuee and Building sections, Evacuee and Rescuer, Evacuee and External help, Evacuee and Situation, Building section and Situation are considered. In the corresponding PEPA model of the above mentioned PA model appropriate rate is incorporated with each action. Fluid flow approximation[11] based analysis of the system is conducted. This approach abstracts away the similar type of processes and records only the number of instances of processes in any particular state at any instant of time.

5   Conclusions and Further Scope

PEPA has been proven as promising approach for the analysis of crowd dynamics. Such formal models can provide a good estimate for the evacuation time of any architectural construct. Also they can be helpful for the identification of potential the congestion spots and to determine the external help required for the safe evacuation of the evacuees. The integration of sociological considerations on human behaviour can enhance expressiveness of crowd models. However the study does not takes into account the situation where *bidirectional movement* of crowd takes place. The case study excludes the possibility where evacuee is not familiar to the architectural construct, leading to additional effort and stress on evacuee to find their way out to building. The model for the evacuation of the building can be extended to the evacuation of larger area such as entire city.

References

1. Fruin, J.J.: The causes and prevention of crowd disasters. Engineering for Crowd Safety, 99–108 (1993)
2. Kobes, M., Helsloot, I., de Vries, B., Post, J.G.: Building safety and human behaviour in fire: A literature review. Fire Safety Journal 45, 1–11 (2010)
3. Gwynne, S., Galea, E.R., Owen, M., Lawrence, P.J., Filippidis, L.: A review of the methodologies used in the computer simulation of evacuation from the built environment. Building and Environment 34, 741–749 (1999)
4. Still, G.K.: Crowd dynamics. University of Warwick (2000)
5. Massink, M., Latella, D., Bracciali, A., Harrison, M.D., Hillston, J.: Scalable context-dependent analysis of emergency egress models. Formal Aspects of Computing 24, 267–302 (2012)
6. Hillston, J.: A compositional approach to performance modelling. Cambridge University Press (2005)
7. Gilmore, S., Hillston, J.: The PEPA workbench: a tool to support a process algebra-based approach to performance modelling. In: Haring, G., Kotsis, G. (eds.) TOOLS 1994. LNCS, vol. 794, pp. 353–368. Springer, Heidelberg (1994)
8. Tribastone, M., Duguid, A., Gilmore, S.: The PEPA eclipse plugin. ACM SIG-METRICS Performance Evaluation Review 36, 28–33 (2009)
9. Tribastone, M.: The PEPA plug-in project (QEST), vol. 7(2007)
10. Smith, M.J.: Abstraction and model checking in the pepa plug-in for eclipse. In: 2010 Seventh International Conference on the Quantitative Evaluation of Systems (QEST), pp. 155–156. IEEE (2010)
11. Hillston, J.: Fluid flow approximation of pepa models. In: Second International Conference on the Quantitative Evaluation of Systems (QEST), pp. 33–42. IEEE (2005)

Author Index